DR. M. E. STRIEBY.

Died March 16, 1899.

HENRY WARD BEECHER.

Engraved by F. Halpin, from a Photograph.

MORNING AND EVENING EXERCISES:

SELECTED FROM THE PUBLISHED AND UNPUBLISHED WRITINGS OF THE

REV. HENRY WARD BEECHER.

EDITED BY

LYMAN ABBOTT,

AUTHOR OF "JESUS OF NAZARETH," "OLD TESTAMENT SHADOWS," ETC.

"There is no flower in all the field that owes so much to the sun as I do to Jesus Christ. That love which has redeemed my soul I would fain bear as an atmosphere, 'Speaking the truth in love.'"—H. W. B.

NEW YORK:

HARPER & BROTHERS, PUBLISHERS,

FRANKLIN SQUARE.

1874.

Henry Ward Beecher's congregation is not confined to that which assembles within the walls of Plymouth Church. Alike in the parlors of the wealthy and the cultured, and in the log cabins of the poor and the self-exiled, his words are welcomed—a comfort to those in trouble, a solace to those in sickness, a strength to those in the midst of the battle. To this great congregation, counted by tens of thousands, who have profited by his teaching, though they have rarely or never listened to his voice, this volume is dedicated by

THE EDITOR.

Cornwall Landing, N. Y.

PREFACE.

THIS volume, comprising morning and evening devotional readings for every day in the year, is composed wholly of selections from the published and unpublished writings of Henry Ward Beecher. The work is published with his approval, though the selections were not made by him. In preparing it for the press, however, his thought has never been altered. The reader has Mr. Beecher's thoughts in his own words. The editor's work has consisted almost wholly in the selection of appropriate passages, and in the adaptation to them of Scripture and of poetry.

A definite aim, never consciously departed from, has determined that selection. The book is one simply of devotional readings. Heartily accepting that catholic conception of religion of which Mr. Beecher is the most distinguished modern exponent, I have embraced in this volume a wider range of topics than is usually embraced in devotional literature. Nothing has been inserted for its beauty of expression or for its value as a statement or defense of doctrine; but nothing has been omitted, as inappropriate to such a work, which could help the Christian in his warfare with the world and his daily walk with God. May the reader find in its perusal something of the spiritual strength which I have received from its preparation. L. A.

CORNWALL LANDING, N. Y.

MORNING AND EVENING

DEVOTIONAL EXERCISES:

FROM THE WRITINGS OF THE

REV. HENRY WARD BEECHER.

MORNING AND EVENING EXERCISES.

JANUARY 1: *MORNING.*

Let us search and try our ways, and turn again to the Lord.—*Lam.* iii., 40.

I CAN not bear to go into the coming year just as I came out of the old one. I would fain believe each year to be a mother, and that I am born into the next one, that I may, as it were, with renewed childhood, go forward, endowed with the experience and the strength of the past. I fain would bring something better than that which I do bring to him whom I know I love, and who knows that I love him. I fain would bring a higher thought, a clearer purpose, a character whose essential powers are higher than mine have been. I know that I have felt the grace of God in my heart; but alas! it seems as though God's grace were but as Columbus, that touched the shore here and there, and left the vast continent within almost unexplored—certainly unsubdued and untilled. I am not content when I think of the generosities and magnanimities of which my life should perpetually speak, as a band of music speaks sweet notes, stretching them far out through the air. How is it with you? Are you content with the character which you brought out of the old year, and with which you are setting forward upon the new? Is not this a time for you to review your character, and see what are its elements, how you are shaping it, what you mean by it, and what you have obtained thus far? Is it not a time for you to look into the future? No matter how old you are, it is not too late for you to learn in the school of Christ. And it is a noble ambition with which you should begin the year—not to swell your coffers, not to have more of this world's good, but to begin the year chiefly with the ambition to be more like Christ, and to have the power of God resting upon you, and to know the will of God, and so to live that whosoever meets you shall know that you have been with Christ.

Out of this spirit what blessings will flow! Oh, if you were holier, how much happier would you be! Oh, if you were holier, how would fall down from you straightway those discontents, those cares, those frets, those ill wills, and those thousand torments which so much have snared you, and so much have marred your enjoyment in the days that are past! It is because you are not good that you are not happy. For he that dwells in the secret place of the Almighty, he that lives as in the very presence of Christ, can say, "My Master hath said, I will never leave thee nor forsake thee, so that I can boldly cry, the Lord is my helper, and I will not fear what man shall do unto me."

A friend stands at the door;
  In either tight-closed hand
Hiding rich gifts, three hundred and threescore;
  Waiting to strew them daily o'er the land,
Even as seed the sower.
  Each drop he treads it in, and passes by:
  It can not be made fruitful till it die.

Friend, come thou like a friend,
  And whether bright thy face,
Or dim with clouds we can not comprehend,
  We'll hold our patient hands, each in his place,
And trust thee to the end;
  Knowing thou leadest onward to those spheres
  Where there are neither days, nor months, nor years.

JANUARY 1: *EVENING.*

Redeeming the time, because the days are evil.—*Ephes.* v., 16.

Did you ever sit down and make an inventory of what you do, in order to come to a distinct understanding with reference to your use of time? You probably know all about your possessions. You know every bond, if you have bonds; you know every mortgage, if you have mortgages; you know every dollar that is deposited, if you have deposits of money; you know every piece of property, if you own real estate; you know all your debts and credits. These things you look at both in detail and in the sum. But God has given our chief treasure to us in the use of time; and how many of us know what we do with our time? How many of us have ever taken even a cursory view of one single year, saying, "I am anxious to know, on the whole, how I carried myself with reference to a faithful use of the element of time through January, February, March, April, May, June, July, August, from month to month? What is the habit of my life in this respect? Of the time that is given me, how much of it do I use well; how much do I use indifferently; and how much do I squander?" There is not one man in a hundred that ever thought of these things. We hear the general declaration that we ought to employ our time; men are exhorted to be diligent in business and fervent in spirit; but there are very few who ever sit down to make a deliberate inventory in regard to the element of time, so as to form a correct judgment of their habit of using it. Ought that so to be?

Every hour that fleets so slowly,
Has its task to do or bear;
Luminous the crown, and holy,
If thou set each gem with care.

Hours are golden links, God's token,
Reaching heaven but one by one;
Take them, lest the chain be broken
Ere the pilgrimage be done.

JANUARY 2: MORNING.

And herein do I exercise myself, to have always a conscience void of offense toward God and toward men.—*Acts* xxiv., 16.

How blessed it is to be able, as one is drawing near to his decline, to bear this testimony: "I have a good conscience." And how sad it is that a man's conscience, which begins life like a full-stringed harp, should become like a harp out of which one cord after another has been broken, till at last it is not capable of melody, certainly not of harmony, and is only a remnant of what it once was.

There are some men and some matrons whose age fills me with more respect than any temple. I have stood before great piles of architecture, whose impression so affected me that I trembled as if I had a chill or a fever in my veins; but I have stood before men and women whose greatness, and serenity, and goodness were such that I felt like bowing down in their presence.

I have also stood before men so gaunt, so hard, so selfish, so hackneyed, that I felt that I was in a cave where monsters resorted, and I trembled with horror, as before I had trembled with sympathy and with love.

God grant to you the liberty of a good conscience. And if he does grant it, it must be by your help. You are to form your own conscience, and you are to form the habit of following that conscience implicitly.

JANUARY 2: EVENING.

Fear none of those things which thou shalt suffer: behold, the devil shall cast some of you into prison, that ye may be tried; and ye shall have tribulation ten days: be thou faithful unto death, and I will give thee a crown of life.—*Rev.* ii., 10.

NEED any one be discouraged who has begun to live a Christian life, because so often he has failed and fallen into backsliding? Whatever may have been the arguments of the past, let them be forgotten. Try again. There are thousands of Christians who too soon grow discouraged, saying, "I have proved that I was mistaken. I have proved that the root of the matter was not in me. There is no use; I have tried and failed." There is all the use in the world. No man ever fails until death settles the great conflict. Because you have begun, and then stumbled and lagged, and gone back a little way, do not give up the whole contest. There is encouragement, since we have one that is not ashamed of us in spite of our defections and inferiorities. Why should we not, therefore, gird up our loins and take a fresh hold, with new consecration, on the Christian life? Will not every day's experience give reason and argument for gratitude to such a Lord as this? Is there not in every Christian man's life and experience reason for blessing, for thanks, for gratitude inexpressible to him that has revealed his Son Jesus Christ, the helpful, the loving, the patient, the gentle?

Pilgrim of earth, who art journeying to heaven!
  Heir of eternal life! child of the day!
Cared for, watched over, beloved and forgiven—
  Art thou discouraged because of the way?

Earthliness, coldness, unthankful behavior—
  Ah! thou mayest sorrow, but do not despair;
Even this grief thou mayest bring to thy Savior,
  Cast upon Him e'en this burden and care!

Bring all thy hardness—his power can subdue it;
How full is the promise! the blessing how free!
"Whatsoever ye ask in my name, I will do it.
Abide in my love, and be joyful in me."

JANUARY 3: MORNING.

And whosoever shall give to drink unto one of these little ones a cup of cold water only in the name of a disciple, verily I say unto you, he shall in no wise lose his reward.—*Matt.* x., 42.

WERE cold water as rare and as costly as wine, I believe that it would be counted a luxury beyond all vintage. No wine ever tasted half so good as water does to a thirsty soul; and its rarity would make all men temperance men. But God has made the bounty so universal and abundant that it is without money or price. It throbs under our feet in hidden veins. Every hill has its springs. It gushes out from rocks and seams of mountains. Rivers are full, and lakes; and the clouds go carrying it all around the world; it is distilled in dew, and poured down in rain or snow, beyond all human need, immeasurable and superabundant.

And so, except in rare cases, or under extraordinary circumstances, water is without a market value. The most indispensable article of human life is one that has no price affixed to it, and can have none. What a thing, then, is that for a gift—a thing that is so common that it has no value attached to it. How poor one must be that, looking around, has nothing to give but a cup of cold water! And suppose such a one wishes to do a kindness. He dare not offer it to the great, to the rich, to the strong. It would be an insult. It is needless to convey it to his neighbor or workman. Even the pauper will hardly thank you for it. But a little child may be unable to raise the bucket, and too helpless to manage a pump. It is not his child, nor his neighbor's, but simply a poor little thirsty child. How poor must one be that can find no one to accept the gift but a vagrant child, and that has no gift to offer but a cup of cold water! Surely there is nothing minuter, more nearly insignificant than this. But God says, "If you give a cup of cold water only to a child, in the name of a disciple"—that is, from a genuine sympathy, and with the kindness and the spirit of a disciple—"you shall not lose your reward." There is not any thing so little that it does not carry a blessing if you do it out of a real impulse of Christian kindness.

JANUARY 3: EVENING.

What man is he that liveth, and shall not see death? shall he deliver his soul from the hand of the grave?—*Psa.* lxxxix., 48.

THERE comes a time, my friends, when we can no longer stand in the same relations that we have stood in. Youth fades; the eye grows dim; the ear waxes dull; the foot becomes slower, and the hand less nimble. As, when they take down a tent, one cord slacks after another, and one peg after another is drawn out of the ground, and all are but premonitory symptoms of its collapse and fall, so one and another sign of age, as they come upon us, are but so many testimonies that this material tabernacle is being taken down. If we have gained honors, the time is coming speedily when we must lay them aside; for honors never go to funerals with the men that have worn them. If we have pleasures, the time will come when they will be less remunerative; and they will stop just at the period when most we need them. When age begins to dawn, and our companions have passed away, and we are left solitary and alone; when our health breaks down, and our buoyancy of spirit ceases; when our faces are set toward the grave, and we are marching thither—what can riches do for us? What can all the acclamation of the world do for the man that is dying? It rolls and roars up to his dwelling, where he lies a sufferer, as the thunder of the ocean in the ear of the mariner drowned and cast upon the shore. He hears it not; and if he heard it, it would be but a vain clamor.

But he that has lived for love, purity, duty, heaven, and immortality will be happy under all circumstances. When sickness comes to him, Christ the Comforter comes with it. When sorrows, then the bow of promise comes. And when death itself comes, what is it but the hand of God sent to take him home? Dying is vacation, and joy, and happiness. He only is happy who knows how to be one with Christ, to suffer with him, and to live with him.

Earth's joys are but a dream; its destiny
  Is but decay and death; its faintest form
Sunshine and shadow mixed; its brightest day
  A rainbow braided on the wreaths of storm.

Yet there is blessedness that changeth not;
  A rest with God, a life that can not die;
A better portion and a brighter lot;
  A home with Christ, a heritage on high.

JANUARY 4: MORNING.

O my soul, thou hast said unto the Lord, Thou art my Lord: my goodness extendeth not to thee.—*Psa.* xvi., 2.

If we turn to what we are, if we look to our achievements, if we measure even our hope and aspiration, there is but very little satisfaction, and it is soon worn out. There is not in all the weavings of our fancy, in all the turnings of our thoughts, or in our daily life, enough to gratify us. We need God. He has infinite fullness, greatness, and glory. In him is all purity and goodness, all justice and truth; in him are all things that engage the heart, enwrap the imagination, and fire the soul wit hecstasy. All are born with him and dwell with him; and in his heart is sufficient for all the wants of all the hearts throughout the desolate universe. O Lord our God! when shall we rise to some conception of thee above the things that thou hast made? When shall we see in all these things but mere symbols and interpretations of thy nature, until human life shall be again the book of God to our eye, as it once was to the eyes of prophets and inspired men?

JANUARY 4: EVENING.

He that loveth father or mother more than me is not worthy of me; and he that loveth son or daughter more than me is not worthy of me.—*Matt.* x., 37.

It is hard to lose your children; therefore consecrate them, that they may never be lost. It is hard to see your property dissipated; therefore consecrate it to God, and be content to let God do what seems best to him with his own. It is hard to throw away one's own life; but there is a way of giving one's life to the cause of country, and to the cause of God, such that it is a joy to die and a joy to suffer. But ah! this cometh not forth but by prayer and fasting. This is a higher view, a holier conception of things than men often take. And if we are to go through these trials rejoicing and singing all the way, we must learn to love God and his cause more than houses, or parents, or children, or wife, or husband, or friends, or all these together.

Oh! you do not think, you do not stop to think, what life is, and what it is taking hold of—an infinite God; an eternity of joy; an immortality of glory. Oh! you do not pierce to the meaning of these things. It is but little to suffer, it is but little to struggle, it is but little to be weighed down with a cross, if only it be Christ's cross, in comparison with that eternal weight of glory that shall be revealed in us.

Let us be steadfast, unmovable, always abounding in the work of the Lord, forasmuch as we know that our labor is not vain in the Lord.

JANUARY 5: MORNING.

I am persuaded that neither death, nor life, nor angels, nor principalities, nor powers, nor things present, nor things to come, nor height, nor depth, nor any other creature, shall be able to separate us from the love of God which is in Christ Jesus our Lord.—*Rom.* viii., 38, 39.

It is not that the force of our love to God is so great that nothing can ever root it up—that is not the emphasis of the passage; it is that the love of God to us is so great that none of these things will ever move that procuring cause of good in him. God loves us so that neither law, nor power, nor earthly experience, nor heavenly adjudications, nor any human witnesses, nor any accusing spirits, nor any thing, shall quench, or cause to glow with one diminished ray the intensity of his love. None of these things shall take away that love which led him to give his Son to die for us, and to raise him up to be our everlasting intercessor. It shall be to us like the sun that carries never-ending summer from age to age.

Shall such a God, with such a disposition and such a history, be unwilling to give to his children the help which they need to live and to bear life—to die and to reach heaven? "If God

—and such a God—be for us, who can be against us?" Who is there so wise, or what is there so active and energetic, that it can withstand such a guardianship as this?

JANUARY 5: *EVENING.*

Nevertheless we, according to his promise, look for new heavens and a new earth, wherein dwelleth righteousness.—2 *Peter* iii., 13.

We rejoice that we may have faith when we can not have sight; and that we may have sure confidence in God and in his kingdom, and believe, even against sight, that it is growing and taking possession of the earth, and that it will yet so cleanse it and redeem it that the heavens shall descend, and Christ shall reign again, and the heavens and the earth shall be as one. But, though that far-off time lures our thought and charms our imagination, it is for us to labor in this sin-smitten earth, that groans and travails in pain unto this day. On every side we hear the groaning; but how little in the world is heard, lifted up in the midst of storm and tumult, the holy joys, the rejoicing of God's elect, that in every part of the earth do, day by day, sing his praises. And yet, in the growing storm, the voice of his witnesses still gains in power. Year by year, more there are that join it, and more and more there are voices attuned to the divine melody; and yet one day shall come when the voice of his ransomed people shall outbrave the storms of depravity, and all the harsh, discordant sounds that are now filling the earth, and there shall break forth yet triumphant the music of the sweet Gospel of Christ, and all the earth shall be filled with it. This world, that hath been a choir of sadness and sorrow, groaning and weeping, shall swing round about the throne, full of blessed sounds of gladness, and with music fitting the high estate and majesty of the kingdom of God.

JANUARY 6: *MORNING.*

Wherefore he saith, Awake, thou that sleepest, and arise from the dead, and Christ shall give thee light.—*Ephes.* v., 14.

Those hours when you feel a strange drawing toward that

which is pure, and true, and right, are hours of God's visitation. Your soul is not far from its Maker in such hours. Be grateful for those periods of peculiar yearning away from evil and toward good. Take them. They are open doors to your prison-house. Are there any bad habits, any evil courses to which you have been addicted, about which you have pondered, and of which you have said, "O that I could be set free from them?" Venture; break away from your wicked ways; do not wait till your impulses are stronger; do not wait till the spark becomes a flame; take a little, and go to that toward which it points. It was a star that led the wise men to the place where Jesus lay. When but a single star shines from that which is right, and pure, and true, follow it, and it will lead you to the place where the young child Jesus lies. If you are willing to awake from sleep, and arise from death, God will give you salvation.

For who is God? He is one that will not break the bruised reed, nor quench the smoking flax, till he shall bring forth judgment unto victory; he is one that takes little feelings and ministers to them as gently as you carry a lamp whose flickering flame you do not wish to have blown out; he is one who deals with men so tenderly that if you take these flickering flames which from time to time he sends to inspire in you higher purposes, and lead you on to nobler ends, he will bring forth victory out of them.

JANUARY 6: EVENING.

Oh that I were as in months past, as in the days when God preserved me, * * * * when the Almighty was yet with me, when my children were about me.—*Job* xxix., 2, 5.

The duties of the household we covet when they are no longer possible to us. The love of family, of children, of friends, clustered together in the most sacred relationships—would that we knew how to give them their true value, how to perceive their beauty, and how to take their ministration.

Oh! our cares even are dear to us, though we may not know it when we are in the midst of them. I remember when, with impatient voice, I commanded the children to cease the racket of their sport. Could I not be permitted to read? Must my house be as a bedlam? I would to God that I had children to cry there now. Was your little babe so troublesome that you sometimes wondered that God should make it fretful all night, so that you must needs rise every hour to nurse it and to care for it? and did you begin to talk about your weariness and great pain in taking care of the child? Peradventure God heard you; for he took it to himself. He never begrudges the care of any thing. And then, when you saw the child's little things that were put away in the drawer, how, in the anguish of your soul, you said, "Oh! if it were a thousand times as much pain and care to me, would to God that I might have it back again!"

And so it happens to us, after the words of the poet:

"And she is gone; sweet human love is gone!
'Tis only when they spring to heaven that angels
Reveal themselves to you; they sit all day
Beside you, and lie down at night by you,
Who care not for their presence—muse or sleep:
And all at once they leave you, and you know them!
We are so fooled, so cheated!"

JANUARY 7: MORNING.

And Jacob said unto Joseph, God Almighty appeared unto me at Luz in the land of Canaan, and blessed me.—*Gen.* xlviii., 3.

WHAT other experience is like that of the personal disclosure of God in the soul? We have read of God in books, and believed. We have gazed upon the earth and the sky, and worshiped. We have yielded faith and feeling to inspirations of the sanctuary, and rejoiced withal. But there comes an hour to some, to many, of transfiguration. It may be in grief; it may be in joy; it may be the opening of the door of sickness; it may be in active duty; it may be under the roof or under the sky, where God draws near with such reality, glory, and power that the soul is filled, amazed, transported. All before was nothing; all afterward will be but as a souvenir. That single vision, that one hour, is worth the whole of life, and throws back a light on all that went before. It solves doubts, it glorifies mysteries which no longer seem abysses beneath us, but golden floods above us. It shoots radiant arrows through all doubts and skepticisms, and gives to the soul some such certainty of invisible spiritual truths as one has of his own personal identity. When one has had this hour of divine disclosure, of full and entrancing vision, it can never be retracted, or effaced, or reasoned against, or forgotten. The impression remains, and the soul goes back to it with assurance and trust, from all its fears, and scruples, and intellectual uncertainties. It fulfills the words of the Master, "And he shall give you another Comforter, that he may abide with you forever, even the Spirit of truth, whom the world can not receive because it seeth him not, neither knoweth him, but ye know him; for he dwelleth with you, and shall be in you."

JANUARY 7: EVENING.

O Israel, thou hast destroyed thyself, but in me is thine help.—*Hosea* xiii., 9.

Ask the physician to what he trusts to throw out morbific influences from the human body. What is the stream that carries reparation to the wasted parts, that carries stimulation to the dormant parts, that carries nutrition to the exhausted parts? It is the blood.

And throughout the vast heaven, throughout time and the universe, the blood of the world comes from the heart of God. The mercies of the loving God throb every where—above and below, within and without, endless in circuits, vast in distribution, infinitely potential. It is the heart of God that carries restoration, inspiration, aspiration, and final victory. And as long as God lives, and is what he is, "the Father of mercies, and the God of all comfort," so long this world is not going to rack and ruin. Though men despond, though the work seem to be delayed, though men watch as in the night for the slow coming of the sun of a winter morning, nevertheless, he that has taken his observation, and has based his faith on the character and nature of God, knows that though a thousand years, or cycles of thousands of years may intervene, in the end there shall be a new heaven and a new earth in which shall dwell righteousness. The earth is not forever to groan. There is to come a day when God shall sound the note from the throne where he is, and when, from afar off, catching that key-note and theme, this old earth, so long dismal, and wailing, as it rolls, the sad requiem of sin and death, shall surprise the spheres, and fill all the universe with the chanting song of victory, "Christ hath redeemed us, and reigns in every heart, and over all the earth." The time shall come.

True Tree of Life! of thee I eat and live:
  Who eateth of thy fruit shall never die;
'Tis thine the everlasting health to give,
  The youth and bloom of immortality.

Feeding on thee, all weakness turns to power;
  This sickly soul revives, like earth in spring;
Strength floweth on and in; each buoyant hour,
  This being seems all energy, all wing.

JANUARY 8: *MORNING.*

And unto one he gave five talents, to another two, and to another one; to every man according to his several ability.—*Matt.* xxv., 15.

Men are not unfrequently brought to great suffering by striving to be what others are—by looking at experiences foreign to their nature, and endeavoring to reproduce them. Men think that, if religion is the work of God, it is the same in every body. You might as well say that if flowers are the work of God, flowers are the same every where. In point of fact, they are alike nowhere—they are varied endlessly. And there is nothing truer than that every man's religion is relative to what he is by his religious organization, and to that state to which he has been brought by his education and his relationships in life. All a man can do, healthfully, is to say, "How shall I take this disposition of mine, made up, as it is, of various conflicting elements, and oblige it to conform to the law of God, which is love and benevolence? How shall I do that?" Every man must answer this question for himself.

I think life is like a voyage. Suppose there should start out from your harbor, for the purpose of crossing the ocean, a yacht, a sloop, a schooner, a hermaphrodite brig, a full-rigged brig, a bark, a ship, and a man-of-war. They are all going to make a voyage. Now, then, suppose that the yacht should look at the man-of-war, as she moved down the bay with all her canvas set, and say, "How can I get such sails upon me as that great and noble ship has upon her?" Every man would say, "A yacht must sail like a yacht, a sloop like a sloop, a schooner like a schooner, a brig like a brig, and a ship like a ship. Each vessel must make the voyage with its own hull and sails, and not copy those of any other." Now God has given every man a hull with which to make the voyage of life, and he has rigged every man according to the circumstances in which he has lived; and, to be a Christian, you are not to attempt to make yourself like this man or that man, but to take yourself, whatever you are, and endeavor to serve God, and live in obedience to his laws. The attempt to pattern after other persons will, in ninety-nine cases out of a hundred, only lead to miscarriages, and doubt, and depression of mind.

JANUARY 8: *EVENING.*

After this I beheld, and lo, a great multitude, which no man could number, of all nations, and kindreds, and people, and tongues, stood before the throne, and before the Lamb, clothed with white robes, and palms in their hands; and cried with a loud voice, saying, Salvation to our God which sitteth upon the throne, and unto the Lamb.—*Rev.* vii., 9, 10.

We adore thee, O thou blessed God, thou who art exalted above all ascription; thou that canst not be described, nor enough loved or admired; thou who art in heaven, surrounded by ten thousand times ten thousand congenial spirits, we, too, though far down, are in thy train; we, too, feel this divine impulse; and though with imperfect thought, and with mixed feelings, and with impure hearts, yet claim thee God according to the measure of our power. We rejoice in the blessedness of their victory, nor do we repine that it is not given to us to be conquerors upon earth. Ours is yet the warfare, theirs the rest. We yet are in bodies that require our severest government; we are attempting to bring every thought and feeling into subjection to Jesus Christ's law; we are wrestling with pride that refuses coercion, and watching selfishness that presses like a flood. We are yet endeavoring to contend against principalities, the prince of the power of the air, the spirit that worketh in the children of disobedience; we are laboring in every way of life to perfect the spirit of Christ in us, and it doth not cast any shadows upon us to think that there are some who have finished this work; that they were ours, but now are God's. We are glad for their victory, nor are we discouraged with the battle because they have gone first, but rather we are enheartened, and we are sure that the path which gave them victory is the path that Christ trod and that we shall tread. And we take comfort that there seem to come to us from the very heavens those sweet and nourishing influences which we so much need in life, speaking to us by ten thousand memories.

JANUARY 9: MORNING.

I am the Lord, and there is none else; there is no God besides me: I girded thee, though thou hast not known me.—*Isaiah* xlv., 5.

We are to look upon our life not as some tumultuous whirl in which we have but a chance. We are to understand that this which is to us so much disturbed, and stirred up, and strangely contrary, is appointed of God to be a school; and that men are to be educated in this life by contact with its affairs, and by the discharge of its duties. We are to understand that those things which befall us do not spring from the ground; that our trials and our troubles are not like arrows sent by some adversary; that the restrictions and the difficulties, the burdens borne, the tasks painful to be performed, are not imposed upon us by chance; that there is an overruling Wisdom, a guiding Hand, a purpose of life; and that, though we do not go with our Teacher intelligently, understanding what he means, yet he guides us and conducts us. May we be disposed to accept each day, therefore, as a day appointed of God; and may we search in all our affairs how to approve ourselves before our great Teacher; and may each day educate us in truth, in justice, in honor, in love, in fidelity, in patience, in meekness, in all things that are good. May there be no day in which we are not victorious over some temptation, over some evil; no day in which we are not heroic in some endurance or achievement; no day in which we are not imitators of Christ's divine example.

JANUARY 9: EVENING.

The lines are fallen unto me in pleasant places; yea, I have a goodly heritage.—*Psalm* xvi., 6.

ARE you not happier than you are accustomed to think? Are you not in the midst of more privileges than you are accustomed to reckon? Will it not prove true, by-and-by, that this hour is happier far than you give it credit for being? Are not your friends better than you think they are? Are they not more faultless than in your calendar from day to day they are written down as being? Are not your burdens lighter than your complaining back makes them out to be? Is not the yoke easier? Is it flint under your foot? But is it not flint from the crevices of which flowers are growing? Are there thorns upon the trees? But orange-trees have fruits as well as thorns. Is it a weary thing that you must needs, in your daily toil, go far out from the city to the well to draw your daily water? But is there not a Christ there—yea, even to such a one as the woman of Samaria? Though living in pleasurable sin, and in wrong, was there not waiting for her, even in her daily tasks, a Savior, a Prophet, with the great blessing of instruction? And ought we not, bearing this in mind, to make more of one another; more of our children; more of our parents; more of our brothers and sisters; more of our neighbors; more of the Church; more of the Bible-class; more of the Sabbath-school; more of all works by which we cleanse the morals of men, and raise up the ignorant, and prosper those that are unfortunate? May not life be filled fuller of blessings if only we know how to redeem the time, and appreciate the opportunity to perceive the God that is near us?

Thus often, when we feel alone,
  No help nor comfort near,
'Tis only that our eyes are dim;
Doubting and sad, we see not him
  Who waiteth still to hear.

"The darkness gathers overhead,
  The morn will never come!"

Did we but raise our downcast eyes,
In the wide-flushing eastern skies
Appears the glowing sun.

Open our eyes, O Lord, we pray,
To see our Way, our Guide;
That by the path that here we tread,
We, following on, may still be led
In thy light to abide.

JANUARY 10: *MORNING.*

A little that a righteous man hath is better than the riches of many wicked.—*Psalm* xxxvii., 16.

Let me say a word to those who are in the active pursuit of wealth, and are far advanced toward it. It would be vain, perhaps, to go back upon your path now, and reprobate the means by which you have acquired your wealth. Let that pass. What you have done, you have done. It stands, and will meet you in the day of judgment. That which I am concerned with is your present condition and character. Now I charge you, before God, to be honest with yourselves. What has been the effect, up to this hour, of the process by which you have been obtaining wealth? You can tell, if you will take the trouble to examine into the matter; or, if you can not, your neighbor can. Go and ask him. Enter into bonds that you will not repeat what he tells you. Say to him, "Do you really think that I have been made better or worse by prosperity? Am I more obstinate than I was? Am I uglier than I was? Am I more selfish and arrogant than I was?"

It is a solemn thing for a man that is prospering in life to pass in review not only what have been the ways in which he has acquired his property, but what has been its effect upon him—to say to himself, "I have been getting wealth; what has been the effect of it, thus far, upon my character? What are my purposes now? Am I satisfied with getting, or is the hunger and thirst for wealth in me more imperious than ever before?" Which way is it working with you? So long as a man feels, "I am laboring for wealth as a means of doing good," he may labor with comparative safety; but the moment he has an ambition to be rich he has passed the line of safety—he has crossed the equator into a region where fierce tornadoes sweep over him, all unbidden and unheralded.

JANUARY 10: *EVENING.*

I shall go to him, but he shall not return to me.—2 *Sam.* xii., 23.

Oh, how many of our friends, who have wept upon earth, have long since forgotten to weep. How many that on earth faltered in praise go forth in the grandeur of heavenly joy. How many that lisped by our sides are speaking in the full vocalization of heavenly music. How many who went from us before they spoke at all, might well be our teachers now. We thank thee, O Jesus, that thou art so loved, that thou art embraced by all the myriads of those who have been redeemed by thee in every age. Thou art born up upon the praises of thy blessed sanctified church in heaven. We have those there who are united to us by memory, by love, and by all the ties of earthly relationships. They praise thee, they rejoice in thee, they comfort us when we think of them. We would not call them back; we only desire to hold them in such remembrance that we may follow hard after them, and, in the way where they found victory, find our victory too. We call back none to our arms who are gone forth; we call back none to light our dwellings whose going forth was as the setting sun; we call back no treasures taken to please God, but we only remember that they have gone, and that we shall surely go after them.

JANUARY 11: *MORNING.*

For thus saith the high and lofty One that inhabiteth eternity, whose name is Holy, I dwell in the high and holy place, with him also that is of a contrite and humble spirit, to revive the spirit of the humble, and to revive the heart of the contrite ones.—*Isaiah* lvii., 15.

Thou art pleased, O Father, with the humble and with the contrite, with such as are of a broken spirit; thou art pleased with the first and most imperfect sign of repentance, and forsaking of evil, and yearning for the truth. And we come before thee, not bringing purified gold and silver as offerings, but faint, and hungry, and weary, and often discouraged, and conscious deeply of our own demerit and sinfulness, we come before thee, because thou hast revealed thyself a God of tender mercy, a Savior of sinners. Lift thou upon us the light of thy countenance, for we are in darkness. Send us mercies, for we are weak. Love us, not because we are able to repay thee, but because thou knowest, in the royalty of thy nature, how to love the unworthy, and even the unlovely. Grant, we beseech thee, that to-day we may have developed in us the divine nature, in magnanimity, in generosity, in all tender mercy and kindness.

JANUARY 11: *EVENING.*

But rejoice, inasmuch as ye are partakers of Christ's sufferings; that when his glory shall be revealed, ye may be glad also with exceeding joy.—1 *Peter* iv., 13.

I HAVE heard of men carrying charms or amulets as remedies or protectives against evils or mischief. Here is a charm or amulet which, if you will take it and wear it, will be an exorcism against evil, and against all the annoyances of human life. Think of Christ, and measure your experiences by his; and when you begin to feel that your lot is trying and burdensome, say, instantly, to yourself, "Am I better than my Master? And was not his lot, when he was on the earth, more trying and more burdensome than mine?" In respect to every thing which affects your happiness and comfort in this world—your surroundings, your companionships, your prospects, and your vexations and annoyances—look away to Jesus, and measure your life by his earthly life. Think what he was in his estate here below. Think how much better off you are, for the most part, than he was. Think how many more mercies you enjoy than he enjoyed. Think how much he suffered for us. Think what a legacy he has left us as the fruit of his sufferings.

We transcend him in the abundance of the blessings we receive, and how ashamed ought we to be of that effeminacy which makes us unwilling to suffer the least things with him—yea, *for* him; for remember that when we suffer for Christ we do not merely suffer in our experience on account of our faith in him. Whenever we take any thing which is to us a trial or a burden, and say, "Now for Christ's sake I will bear this," then we are suffering for Christ. And the declaration of Scripture is, that if you suffer for him, you are brought into the most intimate fellowship with him.

JANUARY 12: MORNING.

Neither do men light a candle, and put it under a bushel, but on a candlestick; and it giveth light unto all that are in the house.—*Matt.* v., 15.

You are set on a candlestick to give light to those around you. Do you shine with a true light? Do you show forth the attributes of Christ? Are your life and conduct characterized by benignity, patience, gentleness, love, and the other Christian graces? Do your children see Christ manifested in you? Do you carry yourself in such a way as to lead people to say, "There is such a thing as personal piety; there is a new life created by the power of God in the souls of men?" Is that the effect of your mode of living?

Sometimes the Church think we must have a revival. They think we must go to meeting, and sing, and pray, and strive with God. This is not wrong in its place, but ordinarily the best way to make God's truth efficacious for the conversion of men is to live it before them. The coming up of one bed of crocuses, and the flying of one bluebird or robin, are truer signs of spring than all artificial signs. The way to find out when it is spring is not to look into the almanac, and see what that says, but to look out of doors, and see what the temperature of the air is. And the way to convince worldly people of the reality of piety is to exemplify it in your own lives. The way to preach the Gospel to men is to be filled with its spirit yourself. The way to draw men to Christ is to stand before them radiant with the garments of Christ; it is to put on Christ himself. The place to begin a revival is at home, in your own closet, and in the midst of your own family. Have a revival at morning prayer; have a revival at evening prayer; have a revival in your own experience and relations. This is the way to clothe yourself with Christ; and no man shall do it and not be made instrumental in bringing God to the heart of somebody else.

JANUARY 12: *EVENING.*

How precious also are thy thoughts unto me, O God! how great is the sum of them!—*Psalm* cxxxix., 17.

It is not because we are good, nor easily made good; it is not because we are docile or easily instructible that we have any hope, for we find ourselves coarse, and dull, and worldly, ungenerous, selfish, and proud; at times envious and jealous, and filled with all hatefulness of that which, when it comes to us revealed in the light of higher truths, makes us shrink from ourselves with unutterable loathing, and wonder that God can look with complacency for a moment upon us.

And yet, O God, such is thy love, and such is the patience with which it hath inspired thee, that thou hast not been weary of thy charge. Thou hast borne us up more tenderly than ever did our parents in our infancy, and thy thoughts toward us, how precious and how exceeding great the number of them! The wonder of thy grace, of thy tenderness, and of thy kindness have begun to awaken in us an earnest desire to please thee. But only when we endeavor to please thee do we find how void we are by nature of goodness; only then, when we attempt to reach forth our hand to write thy praise, do we find how rude and untaught our hands are. We stand before thee undressed; we stand empty; with all thy teaching, there is nothing that we should presume to hold up before thee and say, "Be gracious unto us by reason of our excellence." Our whole hope and faith is in the greatness, in the grandeur, in the inexhaustibleness of thy love. In thyself we must needs find our redemption and our sanctification.

JANUARY 13: *MORNING.*

Look not every man on his own things, but every man also on the things of others.—*Phil.* ii., 4.

You have no right to be unconcerned whether men act rightly or wrongly—whether they are good or bad. That spirit which says, "'I will take care of my own self, and let other men take care of themselves,'' is of the devil. The spirit of God is this: "Look not every man on his own things, but every man also on the things of others." That spirit which says of a man's conduct, "Oh, it is his own affair, not mine," is unchristian. It *is* his own affair, but it is *yours* too! In some degree, it is every man's concern how those around about him live. "Am I my brother's keeper?" Yes, you are, to some extent, your brother's keeper. Not by authority, not as a judge, not as an officer, but as a *brother;* not in a spirit of judgment, not under the inspirations of a close-measuring conscience, but in a spirit of sympathy and love. And no man has a right to call himself a Christian who, living among men, finds that the only thing he cares for is himself—that the only things that affect his mind are moral considerations of his own purity and his own enjoyment.

> Lord God, if one without due fear
> Repeat thy ten commandments here,
> And break them then,—not true his love to thee;
> So if one call thee Father, yet
> His brethren own not, or forget,
> Sick is his heart, though sound his words may be.

JANUARY 13: *EVENING.*

Of whom the whole family in heaven and earth is named.—*Ephes.* iii., 15.

How unlike are we one to another, and how exactly alike are we before God! How different in our parentage, how wondrously different in our education, how different in all the parts of our nature, and in all those habits that have been formed upon them—in our views, prejudices, and associations—so different that we scarcely know how to get along with each other, because our pride teaches us to put emphasis on the things in which we differ one from another; but God looks upon us in the things in which we agree. We are all children of the dust; all have common weaknesses; all are alike temptable, stumbling, and falling; all depend upon him in the great needs of our being; all march with one step toward the glorious disenthrallment of the eternal sphere; all are redeemed by Christ's sufferings and righteousness; all wait for the promise of the

Father. How many and how great are the things that band us together, that stamp upon us the name of God, and give us a common brotherhood. God grant that we may feel this high and solemn fellowship, this grandeur and glory of unity. May we be lifted above form, and carried above all mere exponents of truth, and stand in the fellowship of those blessed truths in Christ Jesus. May we learn to love one another, not with mere sentiment, but with truth, and a charity that will show itself in all the phases of life. May we feel that to love is better than to be great, is better than to be refined, is better than to be wise; that love takes precedence of all prophecy, of every kind of knowledge, and of the gift of tongues; that love is higher than hope and faith, and is the very royalty of God.

JANUARY 14: *MORNING.*

Not as though I had already attained, either were already perfect; but I follow after, if that I may apprehend that for which also I am apprehended of Christ Jesus.—*Phil.* iii., 12.

If you suppose that when a man professes Christianity, he is finished, and put into the church, as a marble statue, when it is completed, is put into the exhibiting room to be criticised, you are very much mistaken. When a man begins to live a Christian life, he is very much like the artist's model instead of his statue. It is pretty much all mud and dirt, and it is far from being in the proper form at that. Long labor is necessary to shape the plastic material and bring it to the required proportions. When the model is perfected, the artist hands it to his attendants, who cut it in marble, and at last the statue is completed.

When men go into the Church of Christ, they go as beginners; they go as men that have found out the weakness and sinfulness of their lives, and that ask, "Are there institutions, and ordinances, and means by which a man that is weak and sinful can be supported and helped?" And open flies the door of the sanctuary, and forth sounds the voice of the minister, saying, "Come in hither; here is God's curative Word, and if any man feels weak, here he will find help; if any man feels sinful, here he will find sympathy, and instruction, and influences to release him from sin and build him up in holiness."

From Nature's quarries, deep and dark,
  With gracious aim he hews
The stones, the spiritual stones,
  It pleaseth him to choose.
Hard, rugged, shapeless at the first,
  Yet destined each to shine—
Moulded beneath his patient hand—
  In purity divine.

Lord, chisel, chasten, polish us,
  Each blemish wash away;
Cleanse us with purifying blood,
  In spotless robes array;
And thus, thine image on us stamped,
  Transport us to the shore
Where not a stroke is ever felt,
  For none is needed more.

JANUARY 14: *EVENING.*

Beloved, now are we the sons of God, and it doth not yet appear what we shall be; but we know that, when he shall appear, we shall be like him; for we shall see him as he is.—1 *John* iii., 2.

HERE we know not our own leaves, nor blossoms, nor fruit. This is not our soil; for, as the things that are sown in the winter, to be transplanted when the summer shall come, do not know their own home, nor recognize what they shall be, confined and shut in, so we are but being brought forward, to be turned out into full soil and branching room when God shall give us planting in heaven. It doth not yet appear what we shall be. We know not our glorified faculties. We know not what this sense of right, this conscience that gropes so darkly on earth, and punishes more than it gives reward—what it shall mean when God gives it liberty and sweet fruition. We know not, when the tide of God's nature shall roll divine beneficence through our faltering feeling of benevolence, what that life shall be then. We know not, when all our tastes are quickened; when all that is in our worship and rejoicing therein shall have been purified and lifted up, and we ensphered among influences every one of which, touching with joy and music, rises yet to blessings more and more—we know not what that life shall be in all its amplitude and in all the infinite richness of its details;

but this we know, that it will be enough; that we shall be "satisfied" when we awake in his likeness.

JANUARY 15: *MORNING.*

A good conscience.—1 *Tim.* i., 5.

THERE is a great difference between a conscience enlightened by the average state of the society in which you live, and a conscience enlightened by the absolute truth of God's word. Many men think themselves to be conscientious because they do the things which are required by society, and avoid the things which are forbidden by society. This is very good as far as it goes, but it goes only a little way.

No man can afford to set his chronometer by any thing except the sun. When he has done this he knows the exact time, and can be certain of the correctness of his calculations, and make a safe voyage. And when a man is making a voyage, not across the Atlantic or the Pacific, but across the sea of life, and is steering for the port of eternal happiness or woe, he can not afford to set his conscience by the conscience of every man that he happens to meet; he must hold it up to God's sun, and set it by that. To set it by any thing else than that will be neither safe nor sensible. *Every body does so*—that is no standard for conscience. The question should always be in your own mind, What is God's command? and not, What is my neighbor's opinion? A scriptural conscience will oblige you to assert your religious independence perpetually. It will oblige you to go against fashion, to traverse the very maxims of society, and to oppose yourself to the ways of life of those around about you; but it will be worth all that it will cost you.

JANUARY 15: *EVENING.*

For we are saved by hope; but hope that is seen is not hope; for what a man seeth, why doth he yet hope for?—*Rom.* viii., 24.

YOU can leave your affairs to God when they go well; can you when they go ill? You can rest quietly in God's hands when you are in health; can you when sick? You can trust your family with God when you are comfortable and happy; can you when you are perplexed how to get along, and your children are sick?

But what is a trust in God good for that departs when you need it, and comes again only when you can get along without it? What is a ship good for that is safe in a harbor, but unsafe out on the ocean? What is a sail good for that is sound in a calm, but splits in the first wind? What patience is that which only lasts when there is nothing to bear?—courage, when there is no danger? firmness, when there is no pressure? hope, when every thing is before the eyes?—what are all these worth? But such is the trust which most Christians have in God. It has no virtue in it. It is like a light-house that burns only in daylight, and is extinguished at sundown.

We need a trust that shall take hold upon God with such a large belief of his love and constancy as shall carry us right on over rough as well as over smooth ground; right on through light and darkness; right on through sickness, bereavement, loss, trouble, and long-pressing afflictions. At noon we need not a torch. It is in darkness that one should carry a light.

JANUARY 16: *MORNING.*

And he dreamed, and behold a ladder set up on the earth, and the top of it reached to heaven; and behold the angels of God ascending and descending on it. And, behold, the Lord stood above it.—*Gen.* xxviii., 12, 13.

Shall your ladder, standing on the earth, reach to heaven? or is your ladder, in its whole length, flat along the ground? Stop one moment, and think, you who have started out, or are about starting. By ladder I mean your plans in life. Are they, all of them, lying upon the ground, or, though they begin there, do they really go up, and consciously take hold of the future and of the spiritual? Man must not avoid the world. Every ladder should stand upon the ground. The ground is a very good place to start from, but a very poor place to stop on. The Christian should be a man among men—joined in interest with them, sympathizing in their pursuits, active in daily duties; not above the enterprise, the thoughtfulness, and the proper amount of care that belong to worldly avocations. But woe to him that uses the earth for the earth; whose plans are wholly material, beginning and ending in secularity and materiality; who means by fortune riches, and nothing else; who means by power carnal, temporal power, and nothing else; whose pleasure consists in that which addresses itself to the senses, and in nothing else. Woe be to him who lays out a plan which has nothing in it but this world. At the very time when you plant your ladder on the ground, you must see to it that it is long enough to reach, and that it does reach and rest its top in heaven. This world and the other must be consciously connected in every true man's life, and along every man's ladder should be seen God's good angels; that is, noble sentiments and generous purposes. You are not at liberty to execute a good plan with bad instruments. When you lay the course of your life out before you, and say to yourself that you propose to achieve in your mortal life such and such things, it is not a matter of indifference to you how you achieve them. God's angels must ascend and descend on your ladder, otherwise other and worse angels will.

Do not, however, trust alone to those generous sentiments. Morality is not piety. In the vision of Jacob there was not alone the ladder between the earth and heaven, and the angels ascending and descending, but brightest, and best, and grandest, and behind all the angels, stood God, saying to him, "I am thy father's God." Now high above all a man's plans, high above all his heroic moral resolves, there is to be a living trust in God; and there is to be a soul-connection between ourselves or our business and our God. All our life long we must not be far from him. Piety must quicken morality; then life will be safe, and will be successful.

JANUARY 16: EVENING.

Henceforth I call you not servants; for the servant knoweth not what his lord doeth: but I have called you friends; for all things that I have heard of my Father I have made known unto you.—*John* xv., 15.

We are the children of the New Testament, and not of the Old. Woe be to us if, living in these later days, we find ourselves groping in the imperfections of the Old Testament, in stead of springing up with all the vitality and supereminent manhood which belongs to the New Testament. We are the children of a living Savior. We are a brood over which he stretches his wings. He is our Brother, he is our *elder* Brother, he is our Savior, and our Deliverer, and our everlasting Friend.

We ought to have more than a creed, more than an ordinance. We are not Christians because we keep the Sabbath day, nor because we pray, nor because we read the Bible, nor because we perform duties. They are Christians through whose soul is struck that vitalizing influence by which it can say "Father," and behold God. To be a disciple of the New Testament is to have a living Head. It is to have a vital connection with that Head. It is to be conscious, while all nature speaks of God, and while all the exercises of religion assist indirectly, that the main power of a true religion in the soul is the soul's connection with a living God.

JANUARY 17: *MORNING.*

Now unto him that is able to do exceeding abundantly above all that we ask or think, according to the power that worketh in us, unto him be glory in the Church by Christ Jesus throughout all ages, world without end. Amen.—*Eph.* iii., 20, 21.

NOTICE that this is an ascription to God of the habit and disposition of doing abundantly not only, but *exceeding* abundantly; and not only exceeding abundantly, but *exceeding abundantly more than we ask or think*—more than it is in man to want, or to know that he wants; more than he can compass by that ever-weaving thought that lies behind words; and not only that, but "exceeding abundantly above all that we ask or think, *according to the power that worketh in us.*" When men's thoughts are touched; when men's natures are awakened and inspired; when, in their noblest moments, with their best faculties under the divine influence, they are lifted up as in a transfiguration, and behold all things in their plenitude of beauty, and glory, and truth—then, in those moments when God is working powerfully in them, and teaching them to think by teaching them to feel (and feeling is the truest mother of feeling)—even then it is said that God does exceeding abundantly more than we ask or think. When the soul is on its wings; when it follows the illumination of faith; when it enters into the secret of divine existence; when it takes the noblest conception of its own destiny, and has the truest sense of its own wants; when it is most cleansed from the selfishness of the earth—from its pride, from its vanity—and is in nearest sympathy with those things which make heaven, then will it speak till language shall fail, and then will the words flow on till thoughts fail, and feeling will flow still beyond thought; yet still beyond that, God does for us, not merely up to the measure of our thinking and asking, but exceeding abundantly beyond it. Language can give no farther conception of the amplitude of divine generosity than is conveyed in such words as these.

JANUARY 17: *EVENING.*

The life which I now live in the flesh, I live by the faith of the Son of God, who loved me and gave himself for me.—*Gal.* ii., 20.

Do you live by faith of the Son of God, who loved you and gave himself for you? Is your life for the secular present or for a glorious future? Are all your aims and ambitions centred in this earthly horizon? Are you living for this world—for its gifts and goods, for its friendships and joys, for its ambitions, its power, its pleasures? Are these the whole? Is the world clear and vivid, and is the horizon-line the end of any thing distinct, and all that is beyond nebulous, vague, something yet to be revealed? Or is heaven clear? is God real? is the future the sphere in which your thoughts move?

JANUARY 18: *MORNING.*

I pray not that thou shouldest take them out of the world, but that thou shouldest keep them from the evil.—*John* xvii., 15.

VIRTUES and graces are not wrought out in pews, but in secular employments. You are to follow out the great events of this world. You are to build up society, the household, and property in such a way that, while the outside is being built, the inside will be built also. Is it hard work, and is the remuneration long delayed? Patience and meekness! Is it work among selfish men? Love and beneficence! Is it work that seems to require great outlay, and to promise little income? Disinterestedness! Is it work such that you have to maintain your steadfastness, often and often, by a martyr spirit for the truth? Long-suffering! These are the very schools in which God works out moral qualities in you. No man works out his piety on Sunday and at church. Here is where you get your chart directed and your compass pointed, here is where you get your lesson; but in your daily business God works out your moral qualities. For the way to use this world is to use it so as to work out those qualities, so as to accumulate a store of Christian manliness in us. We are to employ the material agencies by which we are surrounded so that while we are serving the outward life it shall be serving us a great deal more. The man that works right outwardly is the man that is built up inwardly; just as he that teaches children is taught more than he teaches. For I think our children bring us up more than we do them. And all parents that think what their children have done for them must feel that in some sense the father and mother should bow down to the children. If you serve the instrument well, it will serve you well; and no man can serve this life well unless by it he hopes to be served in the life to come.

JANUARY 18: *EVENING.*

Whoso offereth praise glorifieth me.—*Psalm* l., 23.

How shall a man praise God who seems to himself to be in continuous trouble? Look at the history of David, and see how you will do it. I think some of the most wondrous of his Psalms are those that begin in supplication. He says, for instance, "All thy waves and thy billows are gone over me; all mine enemies are upon me; dost thou not care for me?" and then, having exhausted the language of supplication, he breaks out into triumph, and says, "I will praise thee." It seems as though there rose up over the horizon to him the bright star of Christ, and as though the light of it kindled in his soul gladness and peace that he could not refrain from giving expression to. You will find that in some of the psalms the soul begins in a minor key, and by-and-by rises to the major key; and then flies away, and sings as it flies.

Now, if a man is in trouble, let him go to God in his trouble till he gets a sense of the divine loving, pitying, sympathetic nature, and see if there does not spring up in him a spirit of praise. And whenever you feel an impulse to praise, give it wings. Do not lose a chance to praise. It is precious to the soul.

JANUARY 19: *MORNING.*

When he maketh inquisition for blood, he remembereth them: he forgetteth not the cry of the humble.—*Psalm* ix., 12.

Answering does not always stand next door to petition. Prayers, however, are never forgotten when they go up before the faithful One. Long after we have forgotten them, God remembers them. Prayers are seeds; and as air-plants root themselves up in trees, and then grow by reaching down toward the earth, so prayers, methinks, root themselves up in heaven, and then grow down toward us. They sometimes have a long growth before they reach us and blossom, but they do it sooner or later. Of the thousands and thousands of petitions uttered by God's people, some are answered the same day, some the same week, some the same month, and some the same year in which they are uttered; and some are not answered till years pass after their utterance. Blessed be God that it should be so. It indicates that the divine administration is not a meagre administration. "I will, therefore, that men pray every where, lifting up holy hands without wrath and doubting."

JANUARY 19: *EVENING.*

There is but a step between me and death.—1 *Sam.* xx., 3.

Sometimes we long to die, because we are tired of our living; sometimes we are willing to die, as we say, because it will be the end of sin; sometimes we wish to die because the heart calls out with unutterable longing for those who have gone before; sometimes we wish to die because we are filled with a not unnatural nor unheroic fervor, and would fain walk among the called, the sons of God. How many of us feel that heaven is sweet, because at last it will bring the sweetness and summer of love. How many of us mourn over our wants, and weep in contrition day by day because we are so wanting in the spirit of love and of Christ. How many of us wish for death, because at last it will bring us into that which our soul most desires, more than honor, riches, or all that the world can give. Time is short, and but a veil separates you from the world to come. You stand perhaps so near that, if you knew it, by reaching out your hand, as one might say, you could lay it upon the very throne of God.

Father, perfect my trust,
   Strengthen the might of my faith;
Let me feel as I would when I stand
   On the brink of the shore of death—

Feel as I would when my feet
   Are slipping over the brink;
For it may be I'm nearer home,
   Nearer now than I think.

JANUARY 20: MORNING.

But ye shall receive power, after that the Holy Ghost is come upon you.—*Acts* i., 8.

Do you suppose a parent dislikes to see real vigor, and joy, and elasticity, and genius, and attainment, and capacity in his children? Is there any thing that makes a parent happier than to see, so long as it is good, the utmost growth and development in his children? If their powers are not perverted, the more they expand the more satisfaction does the parent derive from them. And does God, who is more than any earthly father, love dry and withered natures, or full and joyful ones, that are pouring out the freshness of their life? Be not a gloomy-eyed, twilight-faced, bat-like Christian, hovering between night and day. Be not a Christian parsimonious of joy, and full of tears and sadness. Do not attempt to be a Christian after the pattern of the ascetic. "The kingdom of God is not meat and drink, but righteousness, and peace, and joy"—righteousness of rectitude and integrity, peace which God gives by the regulation of man's nature, and joy which is the reflection of heaven from the burnished experiences of an enlightened soul.

JANUARY 20 : *EVENING.*

They that are whole need not a physician, but they that are sick. I came, not to call the righteous, but sinners, to repentance.—*Luke* v., 31, 32.

God does not look down on the world, saying, "Men are all sinful; you are doing wrong; stop doing it, and I will look smilingly upon you." God so loved the world when it was lying in wickedness, before it had made any attainment in righteousness, that he gave his Son to die for it. While we were yet enemies to him, God poured out his all-inspiring love upon us, to draw us toward him. As the atmosphere of the globe, sunlit and sun-warmed, is full of influences that give life and health to the plant, so the atmosphere of the soul, permeated by the love of Christ Jesus, is full of influences that vivify and strengthen the higher faculties. That which Christ means by faith in him is that sense of his love, and patience, and goodness which enables a man, though he comes short of what he ought to be and ought to do, to go to the Savior and say, "I know that thou lovest me still." A feeling of certainty of his goodness toward you, no matter how poor you are—that is the faith that Christ wants. That faith which begins little by little to work by love—that is the faith that disenthralls, that is the faith that sanctifies and perfects.

JANUARY 21 : *MORNING.*

I will give him a white stone, and in the stone a new name written, which no man knoweth, saving he that receiveth it.—*Rev.* ii., 17.

In the Orient precious stones were frequently made into signet rings, and, as such, they carried authority, because they suggested the personal identity of the wearer. They were also presents given as tokens of ordinary regard by neighbor to neighbor, or friend to friend; or else they were bestowed as honors. Where a prince or a monarch desired to confer the highest testimony of his appreciation of one that had served him or the kingdom, he gave him a precious stone, with his name cut on it. But a more precious use of these stones was as love-tokens, and in this case they were cut with mystic symbols. As two lovers agree upon names the meaning of which is known only to themselves, or as they speak to each other in endearing terms which belong to them severally, not in baptism, not in common parlance, but by the agreement of the heart, so it was customary to cut in stones names or initials which no one could understand but the one who gave it and the one to whom it was given.

Now these two uses of the precious stones are blended in the figure of the text. God says, "I am the eternal King, and I am the eternal Lover, and to him that is faithful to me, and that overcometh, I will give, as a token of my love and honoring, a white stone." What is meant by a *white stone* I do not know, but I prefer to think that it was an opal, the most human of all stones. The diamond is the more spiritual; there is less of color and more of suggestion in it; but the opal has in it more sympathy, more feeling, more wondrous beauty, more of those moods that belong to the human heart; and of all the stones that are worn to signify human affection, none is to be compared to the opal. And methinks, when God makes this promise of the white stone, it is as if he said, "I will cut your love-name in an opal, and as your King and Lover I will give it to you, and no man shall know the meaning of that name but you yourself."

JANUARY 21: EVENING.

For our light affliction, which is but for a moment, worketh for us a far more exceeding and eternal weight of glory.—2 *Cor.* iv., 17.

If in Kansas the careful husbandman, whose starving cattle have but a faint chance of living the winter through, sees a wisp of straw, a handful of stalks, or a particle of hay being wasted, it sorely grieves him. He is so near to the edge of starvation that he can not afford to have any thing wasted. But go into Illinois and Indiana, where all these things are abundant, and where the herds are their own harvestmen, and tramp down a thousand times more than they eat, and the farmer, when he sees the stack gnawed and scattered around knee-deep, and being wasted, says, "There is no need of my saving such little things; they are mere trifles; I have so much that I do not know what to do with it."

The apostle, arguing according to the same principle, says, "What is a little waste here? The rinds and crumbs of life—a little sorrow; a little loss; a little contempt; a few persecutions, and afflictions, and troubles—what are these in the great circle of God's eternal world? There I am rich and honorable; and what difference does it make if here I am the offscouring of the world?"

If we could only bring this principle home to ourselves, it would act upon us as it did upon the apostle.

Surely yon heaven, where angels see God's face,
Is not so distant as we deem
From this low earth! 'Tis but a little space,
The narrow crossing of a slender stream;
'Tis but a veil, which winds might blow aside:
Yes, these are all that us of earth divide
From the bright dwelling of the glorified—
The land of which I dream!

This life of ours, these lingering years of earth,
Are briefer, swifter than they seem;
A little while, and the great second birth
Of time shall come, the prophet's ancient theme!
Then he, the King, the Judge, at length shall come,
And for this desert, where we sadly roam,
Shall give the kingdom for our endless home—
The land of which I dream!

JANUARY 22: MORNING.

Pray for us: for we trust we have a good conscience, in all things willing to live honestly.—*Hebrews* xiii., 18.

Are you willing to *live* honestly? I do not ask whether you think that honesty is better than dishonesty. I do not ask whether you think it is your duty to be honest, or whether you prefer to be so. For the sake of being honest, are you willing to go slower, and to let that man get ahead of you? Are you willing to live with moderation because you must be honest? Are you willing to lay aside pride and selfishness because you must be honest? Are you willing to be patient and long-suffering because you must be honest? Are you willing to do without wealth, even, because you must be honest? Cast away the miserable precedents of evil men. Take a larger view of what Christian manhood requires of you. Do not measure by the pattern of other men's thoughts and feelings, but listen to the counsels of God. Remember that you are a child of eternity. It will not be long before both the hope and the fear of this world will be like the mists of last year, that have gone down and are forgotten. It can not be long before you and I will have dropped the body, and with it all its feverish frets and vexations, and that part of us that is immortal will stand in the eternal Presence. Oh, in thinking of your life, think of that part which belongs to Christ; think of that part which belongs to God the Father; think of that part which is quickened by the Holy Spirit, and scorn the lower measures of character that you find among beggarly men. Take your conceptions of right, and duty, and Christian manhood from the inspirations of God.

JANUARY 22: EVENING.

For he knoweth our frame; he remembereth that we are dust.—*Psalm* ciii., 14.

THERE is One that knows you altogether. If you do not know how to disentangle the skein of your feelings; if you do not know how to analyze and trace to their source your motives, there is One who knows how to do it perfectly. If you seem to yourself to be put where you meet more difficulties than you know how to get along with, there is One who has been tried in every point as you are, and yet without sin. If you are in a way of temptation, and can find no door of escape, there is One who will make provision for your release, that you may not be overcome.

This amazing, this thorough insight into every part of our life, is accompanied with compassion. Out of this comes the divine mercy. Christ says, "I know you entirely; so why do you try to hide or to cover up any thing that belongs to your being? Do men blame you often? I do not. Do men exonerate you? Oh, my child, I do not. What is imperfection I know, as you can not tell. I have been put into life to suffer the trials that make you sin, in order that I might be your High-priest, your Counselor, your Atoning Friend. Draw near to me, therefore; draw near to me, because I know you so thoroughly. There is no use in your staying away and trying to hide your sin; rather confess it. I have sympathy with you in your imperfection, in your infirmity, and in your sin; and I will forgive you, strengthen you, and ripen, and mature, and perfect you."

JANUARY 23: *MORNING.*

Let brotherly love continue.—*Hebrews* xiii., 1.

THERE can be nothing more a violation of the spirit of the Bible, of the law of God, of the feelings of Christ; nothing more an affront and offense before heaven, than feelings of contempt, bitterness, or hatred toward men. Even indifference and coldness are culpable. Sympathy with mankind is a universal duty. Christ taught us that every man is our neighbor. We are commanded, as we have opportunity, to do good unto all men. There should be an abiding disposition of benevolence, out of which should spring incessant acts of kindness. When the waters of an inexhaustible spring have been conveyed through pipes to your dwelling, it needs only that you should open the vent, and it will gush forth with power and copiousness by its own native force. Even when it is not flowing, it is pressing and urging itself, and longing to flow. Left to itself, night and day it would gush. It must be hindered, it must be stopped, but it needs never to be solicited. There is a well-spring of love which God sinks in the human soul, which throbs without ceasing, and strives to give itself forth. From such a reservoir we need no slow-descending and heavy-rising bucket; we need no forcing-pump, nor instrument of power of any sort. It is its nature to rise up, to go out. The kindness is always there, always ready and waiting. Only opportunity is needed.

JANUARY 23: EVENING.

Take my yoke upon you, and learn of me; for I am meek and lowly in heart: and ye shall find rest unto your souls.—*Matt.* xi., 29.

WHERE can you lay your finger upon a single instance in which Christ acted as though he was proud? And yet you never had a temptation to make you proud that was at all to be compared with the temptations to pride which were brought to bear upon Christ. Where can you lay your finger upon a single instance in which Christ seemed to savor of selfishness? And yet you have never had sudden flaming motives to selfishness that were at all to be compared with those which Christ had. Where can you lay your finger upon a single instance where Christ gave vent to venom, or invective, or ill temper? And yet you have never had provocatives to these things which were at all to be compared with those which Christ had. He was *in all points* tempted like as we are. That is, in all his faculties, in his reason, in his moral sentiments, in his affections, in his passions, in every thing that belongs to a spirit incased in a mortal body, he felt the pressure of temptation, and yet not in one single instance did he sin.

Shall Christ be humble, and his disciples not? Shall he be visited with suggestions of evil from the adversary, and we count ourselves too good to be visited with any such suggestions?

Oh, I am weak; my feeble spirit
   Shrinks from life's task in wild dismay;
Yet not that thou that task wouldst spare it,
   My Father, do I dare to pray.

JANUARY 24: MORNING.

I am the vine, ye are the branches. He that abideth in me, and I in him, the same bringeth forth much fruit; for without me ye can do nothing.—*John* xv., 5.

A PRISONER in a dungeon may have but one small window, and that far up and out of the way of the sun, while for months and months not one single day does the yellow sun send a solitary ray through the poor little window. But at length, in changing its place in the heavens, there comes a day in which, to his surprise and joy, a flash of light springs through and quivers on the wall. It vibrates upon his heart still more tremulously than on the wall. Even this much gives joy. It warms nothing, and lights but little, but it brings back summer to his soul. It tells him that the sun is not dead, but walks the heavens yet. That single ray speaks of fields, of trees, of birds, and of the whole blue heavens! So is it often in life. It is in the power of one blessed thought, in a truly Christian heart, to send light and joy for hours and days. But that is not enough. It is not enough for Christian growth or Christian nourishment that despondency sometimes hopes, and darkness sometimes smiles into light. The whiteness of heavenly robes is the light which they reflect from the face of God. A Christian is to bear much fruit. This he can not, unless he *abides* in summer. For mere relief, even a casual visit of God's grace is potential; but for fruit—much fruit, and ripened fruit—nothing will suffice but the whole summer's sun.

JANUARY 24: EVENING.

I will pour my spirit upon thy seed, and my blessing upon thine offspring; and they shall spring up as among the grass, as willows by the water-courses. —*Isaiah* xliv., 3, 4.

WHAT is the hope of parents in regard to the misconduct of their children? It is to work with them assiduously, and to work in the spirit of love; and, when the results do not follow immediately, to have patience. Is your child fifteen years old? Then there are ten years more for him; hold on for those ten years, and do not be discouraged. "Ah!" you say, "but some are farther along than that." Yes, and in all such cases you must let your patience and your faith in God overmaster the devil's power and the devil's temptations. Say to the foul spirit that seems to possess your children, "I will master you yet by my confidence in God. My children are his, and by as much as they are in peril, by so much I will hold out, and will not give up my faith." The faith of the parent will save the child in hundreds and hundreds of instances where, if the parent's faith should fail, the child would go down and be destroyed. It is the bridge on which the child is to walk over the valley of destruction to the kingdom of glory. Then do not be discouraged about your family. Have faith, and they shall be preserved.

Savior! who thy flock art feeding
  With the shepherd's kindest care,
All the feeble gently leading,
  While the lambs thy bosom share;

Now, these little ones receiving,
  Fold them in thy gracious arm;
There we know, thy word believing,
  Only there secure from harm.

Never, from thy pasture roving,
  Let them be the lion's prey;
Let thy tenderness, so loving,
  Keep them all life's dangerous way.

JANUARY 25: MORNING.

Then saith he to Thomas, Reach hither thy finger, and behold my hands; and reach hither thy hand, and thrust it into my side; and be not faithless, but believing.—*John* xx., 27.

The thought of Christ, and the glory of his helpfulness, and the power of his love, and the endlessness of his grace, may save every man from doubt and despondency; but the moment a man thinks of himself, he finds that he is going down, down, down. The barometer sinks the moment a man begins to think of himself, and rises the moment he begins to think of Christ. Our hope is in him, our help is in him, and our life is in him. In him is no variableness nor shadow of turning. In him is no doubt and no fear, for perfect love casts out fear. And they that know how to forget themselves, they that count themselves to be unworthy sinners, and Christ to be a justifying Savior, have settled the whole question in that one act by which they say, "Lost, undone, and sinful though we are, thou canst love a *sinner;* save me because I am sinful. Take me while sinning to save me from sinning." That ends it, and there is no more room for doubt. "I am persuaded that neither death, nor life, nor angels, nor principalities, nor powers, nor things present, nor things to come, nor height, nor depth, nor any other creature, shall be able to separate us from the love of God which is in Christ Jesus our Lord."—Amen, and amen.

JANUARY 25: EVENING.

Him that overcometh will I make a pillar in the temple of my God, and he shall go no more out.—*Rev.* iii., 12.

If there is any thing in this world that seems to have a solitary time of it, it is a pillar holding up something, and standing still forever. If there is any thing in the world that an active, nervous person—a person full of resources—would rather be excused from taking as a reward, it is being set in a wall of stone, one's self a stone, and standing there to all eternity. Of course it was not meant to strike you in that way. This figure arose from the caryatides. It was customary to carve columns or pillars in the form of slaves—men and women—in some of the earlier temples, as in the Acropolis at Athens. Particularly those columns that stand back upon a wall, and sustain a portico, cornice, or something of that kind, are covered with figures of men holding the load upon their heads. Whatever may be the force and attractiveness of this figure, one thing is certain, namely, that the quality of patient endurance is one which God, by his providence, seeks to develop very largely in the Church. And it is very certain that it is, in the sight of God, among the most noble and eminent of qualities. Persons think, "If I could only do something, then I should feel that I was worth something; but I can not do any thing." They forget that there is a silent work going on in the providence of God in a man's life, and that, though it is not trumpeted abroad, it is more effective than what he did would be if he were producing mere physical results on a far larger scale.

A gentle angel walketh throughout a world of woe,
With messages of mercy to mourning hearts below;
His peaceful smile invites them to love and to confide;
Oh, follow in his footsteps, keep closely by his side.

He will not always answer thy questions and thy fear;
His watchword is, "Be patient, the journey's end is near."
And ever through the toilsome way he tells of joys to come,
And points the pilgrim to his rest, the wand'rer to his home.

JANUARY 26: MORNING.

For riches are not forever: and doth the crown endure to every generation?—*Prov.* xxvii., 24.

When Sheridan had bought him a beautiful place, he invited old Dr. Johnson to go and see it. The stern old cynic went, and looked through the house and the library, and tasted the wine from the cellar, and walked in the garden, and said nothing, till Sheridan asked him, "Well, doctor, what do you think of it?" "Ah!" said he, "these are the things that make death terrible."

There is many a man that has worked all his life to heap up pleasures, and that stands shivering, and shuddering, and saying, "I can not bear to die and leave them all." But die and leave them all you will. No man that has undertaken to make himself happy by seeking any thing in this world has succeeded; no such man can be happy. But he that has lived for love, purity, duty, heaven, and immortality will be happy under all circumstances. When sickness comes to him, Christ the Comforter comes with it. When sorrows come, then the bow of promise comes. And when death itself comes, what is it but the hand of God sent to take him home? Dying is vacation, and joy, and happiness. He only is happy who knows how to be one with Christ, to suffer with him, and to live with him here for that joy and peace that he gives. As the body decays, as its powers fade away, as our earthly honors recede, our heavenly treasures should appear. And remember that out of love come the choicest pearls. And when earthly loves all perish, and are at the grave what shells are whose fish are dead, and that are rolled by the waves out upon the shore, then they that have lived for Christ in his spirit know that their life has just begun. They know that their youth is renewed when the pulse is fading out. We live when we die. Here we are exiles ignominious. Beyond the grave we are crowned kings and priests unto God.

JANUARY 26: *EVENING.*

My God, my God, why hast thou forsaken me?—*Matt.* xxvii., 46.

It oftentimes happens that Christians, when they are tried, and resort in faith to prayer and the Word of God, feel very much cast down because they can get no consolation therefrom. When, in times of distress and temptation, they go to God for help, and his face is hidden from them, and they receive no reply to their prayer, they seem to themselves to be forgotten and forsaken, and that is the hardest of all for them to bear. And yet, when our Savior bowed in Gethsemane, he, too, seemed to himself to be forgotten and forsaken of his Father; and when, after having been carried through the mockery of a trial, he was lifted up upon the cross, his very expiring anguish was this: "My God, my God, why hast thou forsaken me?" In that extremity of our Savior's life God hid his face from him. And shall our Master bear the hiding of God's face, and we his servants be unwilling to bear our part of such experiences?

Savior! our human form once wearing,
  Help, by the memory of that day
When, painfully thy dark cross bearing,
  E'en for a time thy strength gave way.

Beneath a lighter burden sinking,
  Jesus, I cast myself on thee;
Forgive, forgive this useless shrinking
  From trials that I know must be.

JANUARY 27: *MORNING.*

Both riches and honor come of thee, and thou reignest over all; and in thine hand is power and might; and in thine hand it is to make great, and to give strength unto all.—1 *Chron.* xxix., 12.

When a father teaches his boy to swim, he puts him into the water, and stands by him with a hand that is just ready to sustain him if he should begin to sink. The father does not propose to help the boy so long as he can help himself, because his object is to teach him to rely upon the exertion of his own powers; but if he is in danger of sinking, he will catch him.

There is a Father's hand in every man's affairs. When we

are plunged, as it were, into boiling waters, there is a Father that stands by us, as the father stands by his boy in the stream, to help us when we need help. If there is one truth taught in the New Testament more than another, it is that there is a providence that takes care of men when they can not take care of themselves.

"For we have not a high-priest which can not be touched with the feeling of our infirmities; but was in all points tempted like as we are, yet without sin. Let us therefore come boldly unto the throne of grace, that we may obtain mercy, and find grace to help in time of need." Christ feels for every one of us. We are going through life on purpose that we may meet him who is a Guide and a Captain. We are going through life under his convoy. It is not, therefore, a providence of laws that we are subject to. There is a Being, and that Being is a Savior, and that Savior is the Lord Jesus Christ, who is supervising whatever relates to our welfare.

JANUARY 27: EVENING.

But ye are come unto Mount Sion, and unto the city of the living God, the heavenly Jerusalem, and to an innumerable company of angels.—*Heb.* xii., 22.

We are brought "to an innumerable company of angels"—now invisible, nevertheless real. The declaration is not that when we die we shall go where angels live, but that when we come into the new dispensation, by the true spirit of faith, we then come to the "general assembly;" to the "Church of the First-born;" to an "innumerable company of angels." You *have* come to them. Where? It does not matter whether you see them—they see you. It does not matter whether you recognize them, so far as your comfort and use of them is concerned. The mere fact itself stands. You do not see in the summer morning the flight of those birds that fill all the bushes and all the orchard trees; but they are there, and though you do not see their coming, you hear their songs afterward. It does not matter whether you have ministered to you yet those perceptions by which you perceive angelic existence. The fact that we want to bear in mind is that we are environed by them; that we move in their midst. How, where, what the philosophy is, whether it be spiritual philosophy, no man can tell, and they least that think they know most about it. The fact which we prize and lay hold of is this: that angelic ministration is a part, not of the heavenly state, but of the universal condition of men; and that, as soon as we become Christ's, we come not only to the home of the living God, but to the "innumerable company of angels."

Sweet souls around us! watch us still;
  Press nearer to our side;
Into our thoughts, into our prayers,
  With gentle helpings glide.

Let death between us be as naught,
  A dried and vanished stream;
Your joy be the reality,
  Our suffering life the dream.

JANUARY 28: MORNING.

Your garments are moth-eaten.—*James* v., 2.

A MAN may be preserved from crimes and from great vices, and yet have his character moth-eaten. A little tooth, which is almost too small for the microscope, may nevertheless be large enough to cut one thread, and another thread, and another thread; and when you have begun to cut threads, you have begun to make holes; and when you have begun to make holes, the destruction of the garment is at hand. So a character that is moth-eaten, that has begun to be pierced by petty sins and vices, is weakened, and is being prepared for destruction.

Search, therefore, and see whether your garments are moth-eaten. We are told in the Apocalypse to take care of our garments, that no man may take them from us. Beware lest men steal your garments; beware lest the elements consume them; but, most of all, beware lest they become moth-eaten.

Beware of robber passions, of intrusive temptations, of those sympathetic sins which draw men by their better affections to their worst ends. Beware of the wind, of the rain, of the sea, of savage beasts, and of summer and winter in the soul. Beware also of moths, of foibles, of faults, of little, mean, sharp-toothed sins, that cut, and eat, and destroy the garment.

Many a man keeps the fair proportions of manhood in life, and seems to be without crime, or vice, or great fault, who is so pierced, and channeled, and granulated, and eaten by petty faults, that when he is lifted up in the eternal world, like a garment that is moth-eaten, he will fall to pieces and be fit only for eternal burning. "Your garments are moth-eaten." There is in that a declaration as terrible as in that other sentence which God shall pronounce upon those who reject him, and with effrontery of wickedness array themselves on the side of his open enemies. May God keep us from secret sins.

JANUARY 28: EVENING.

Behold, I have refined thee, but not with silver; I have chosen thee in the furnace of affliction.—*Isaiah* xlviii., 10.

THERE are men in God's army suffering what all soldiers suffer, deprivation and hardship on every side; the missiles of the enemy come hurling in, asking no leave. But by life's battle there is being wrought out in them a nobler character, an enfranchised will, a purified courage, a sweeter resignation, an invincible trust in God, and thus they are being prepared to rise superior to their circumstances, and to evince a divinely-kindled manhood. Be not, then, easily discouraged by opposition, nor sit down ignominiously and cry because the way is not made smooth before you. It is this opposition which tests your character and which forms it. Do not count yourself unworthy of suffering with Christ that the divine nature may be developed in you.

This world is a glorious workshop for making MEN. The fire is hot enough to make you a white heat, and the anvil is broad enough to turn you into such shapes as God wants. Be ye men, therefore, and count nothing of experience amiss, whether it be of joy or of sorrow, remembering that all things work together for the good of those that love the Lord. Love him, and so be victorious over life; for he that conquers life shall find death itself conquered, and himself a victor before God and his angels.

Pain's furnace-heat within me quivers,
  God's breath upon the flame doth blow,
And all my heart in anguish shivers,
  And trembles at the fiery glow;
And yet I whisper—as God will,
And in his hottest fire hold still.

He comes, and lays my heart, all heated,
  On the hard anvil, minded so
Into his own fair shape to beat it
  With his great hammer, blow on blow;
And yet I whisper—as God will,
And at his heaviest blows hold still.

JANUARY 29: *MORNING.*

Pray without ceasing.—1 *Thess.* v., 17.

ONE may perceive at a glance how exceedingly wide is the scope of prayer.

It will begin with a supplication for our temporal wants. They are first felt, and felt longest; and, by the greatest number of the world, felt chiefly. Next higher will come petitions for relief from trouble, for remedy, for shelter in danger. In this, too, the soul may exercise its own liberty; there are no metes nor bounds. Then, next, prayer is drawn forth by heart-sorrow. A wounded spirit, a bruised heart, naturally turns for confidence and soothing toward God. Its prayer may be supplication for help, or it may be only recitation for the sake of peace. Next, and far higher, prayer becomes the resource of a heart exercised for its own religious growth. It is the cry for help against temptation. It is the voice of confession. It is a recital of sins committed, and a plaint of sorrow for them. It is the soul's liberty to go to its Father with all its growing pains, its labor and travail in spiritual things. Prayer, also, to one who lives in daily service of God, oftentimes takes the form of simple communion, the spreading out of our life to one who is worthy, whom we love and trust, not for sake of any special advice, nor for sake of special help, but for the heart-rest which there is in the thing itself. For none love confidences so much as they who rarely have them. None love to speak so much, when the mood of speaking comes, as they who are naturally taciturn. None love to lean and recline entirely upon another so much as strong natures that ordinarily do not lean at all. And so the heart that goes shaded and shut, that hides its thoughts and dreads the knowledge of men's eyes, flings itself wide open to the eye of God.

JANUARY 29: EVENING.

Behold, the heaven and the heaven of heavens is the Lord's thy God, the earth also, with all that therein is.—*Deut.* x., 14.

I SEE a mother that, as the twilight falls and the baby sleeps, and because it sleeps out of her arms, goes about gathering from the floor its playthings, and carries them to the closet, and carries away the vestments that have been cast down, and stirring the fire, sweeping up the hearth, winding the clock, and gathering up dispersed books, she hums to herself low melodies as she moves about the room, until the whole place is once again neat, and clean, and in order. Why is it that the room is so precious to her? Is it because there is such beautiful paper on the walls? because there is so goodly a carpet on the floor? because the furniture in the room is so pleasing to the eye? All these are nothing in her estimation except as servants of that little creature of hers—the baby in the cradle. She says, "All these things serve my heart while I rock my child." The whole round globe is but a cradle, and our God rocks it, and regards all things, even the world itself, as so many instruments for the promotion of our welfare. When he makes the tempest, the pestilence, or the storm, when he causes ages in their revolutions to change the world, it is all to serve his own heart through his children—men. When we are walking through this world, we are not walking through long files of laws that have no design; we are walking through a world that has natural laws, which we must both know and observe; yet these must have their master, and Christ is he. And all of these are made to be our servants because we are God's children.

I know I might have seen in every star
  That sheds its light on me,
A lamp of thine, set out to guide from far
  My steps toward home and thee—

Have heard in streams with bending grasses clad,
  Which sparkled through the sod,
The music of the river that makes glad
  The city of our God—

In flowers, plucked but to wither in my hand,
  Or passed with lingering feet,
Have read my Father's promise of a land
  Where flowers are still more sweet.

JANUARY 30: *MORNING.*

Wherefore take unto you the whole armor of God, that ye may be able to withstand in the evil day, and, having done all, to stand.—*Ephes.* vi., 13.

It is magnificent to see a man that is able, when he has done every thing, to stand still and wait. There has been some standing still and waiting that was not so very sublime; but there is a great deal of standing still and waiting that is sublime. If we but had the moral instincts to know it, there is nothing more sublime than the patience, and confidence, and hopefulness of Paul when he was in prison and unfriended, and when he could do nothing but stand and sing those immortal songs, which, being translated to us, have become part and parcel of our legacy.

A mother labors well with her son. She has not failed, since he could understand, to sow good seed, and water the soil in which she sowed them with her own tears, and give the sun of her own heart to pour the seasons upon his. But he has come to that Hell-gate of experience which every man is called to steer through between fifteen and twenty-five, and he swerves, running, apparently, first toward this shore and then toward that; and she stands serene, and says, "I know what I have done. The child is God's. I can no longer reach him. I can only pray for him. But my soul knows that that child shall not be a wreck. He shall come out and be saved." She stands patient and calm; and in the courage, faith, and patience of that mother's heart, waiting for God, there is a moral heroism such as no battle-field ever exhibited.

Oh that we had more of this confidence! Oh that we had more of it in the family, more of it in the Church, and more of it in our dear country! Oh that we believed more firmly that the cause of God could not suffer, and that truth, and justice, and liberty would prevail, though the times were dark, and things looked threatening!

JANUARY 30: *EVENING.*

Let us labor, therefore, to enter into that rest.—*Heb.* iv., 11.

Do not regret it if the eye grows dim. You will see better by-and-by. If the ear is growing heavy, do not be sorry. If your youth is passing, and your beauty is fading, do not mourn. If your hand trembles and your foot is unsteady with age, be not depressed in spirit. With every impediment, with every sign of the taking down of this tabernacle, remember that it is the striking the tent that the march may begin, and that when next you pitch your tabernacle it shall be on the undisturbed shore, and that there, with eyes unwet with tears, through an atmosphere undimmed by clouds, and before a God unveiled and never again to be wrapped in darkness—that there, looking back upon this world of ignorance, and suffering, and trouble, and upon the hardships of the way, you will, with full and discerning reason, lift up your voice and give thanks to God, and say, "There was not one trouble too much; there was not one burden too heavy; there was not one sorrow too piercing." And you will thank God, in that land, for the very things that wring tears from your eyes in this.

Look, then, to that better land, out of all the trouble of the way; sigh for it, pray for it, prepare for it, and enter into it.

Dissolve from these bonds, that detain
  My soul from her portion in thee;
Ah! strike off this adamant chain,
  And make me eternally free.

When that happy era begins,
  When arrayed in thy glories I shine,
Nor grieve any more by my sins
  The bosom on which I recline—

Oh then, never more shall the fears,
  The trials, temptations, and woes,
Which darken this valley of tears,
  Intrude on my blissful repose.

Or, if yet remembered above,
  Remembrance no sadness shall raise;
They will be but new signs of thy love,
  New themes for my wonder and praise.

JANUARY 31 : *MORNING.*

Brethren, if a man be overtaken in a fault, ye which are spiritual, restore such an one in the spirit of meekness; considering thyself, lest thou also be tempted.—*Gal.* vi., 1.

THE man who has a true Christian spirit never takes delight in the faults of others. Does it not give you as exquisite pain to discover faults in those you love as to discover them in yourself? Do you not feel that you would give your own body and blood to save them from ruin? So ought you to feel in respect to all your fellow-men. Their burdens should be your burdens, and their sorrows your sorrows. When a man is actuated by this spirit, how easy it is for him to go to others, and tell them kindly of their faults, and help them to rid themselves of them? Men usually will bear to be told their faults by a man who has this disposition, but never by a person who has it not.

Forget not thou hast often sinned,
And sinful yet must be:
Deal gently with the erring one,
As God has dealt with thee.

JANUARY 31 : *EVENING.*

For we which live are alway delivered unto death for Jesus' sake, that the life also of Jesus might be made manifest in our mortal flesh.—2 *Cor.* iv., 11.

BLESSED are they that are able to see in their troubles such a resurrection of Christ that, in the joy they experience from the realization of the rising of the Sun of Righteousness upon them, they quite forget the troubles themselves.

When once the disciples that watched had been permitted to gaze upon Christ, to clasp his hand, to worship him, where was the memory of their past trouble? What was their thought of the arrest, of the shameful trial, of the crucifixion, and death, and burial? These were all gone from their minds. As, when the morning comes, we are apt to forget the night out of which it came, so, when out of trouble comes new happiness, when out of affliction comes new joy, when out of the crucifixion of the lower passions comes purification, we are apt to forget the process through which this happiness, this joy, this purification came. As there can be no sepulchre which can afford consolation that hath not a Christ ready to be revealed in it, so there can be no sorrow from which we can well be delivered that hath not in it a Christ ready to be revealed.

Often when we are weakest we may be strongest, when we are most cast down we may be nearest the moment of being lifted up, when we are most oppressed we are nearest deliverance, when we are most cut off we are nearest being joined forever and ever to him who is life indeed and joy indeed.

If thus we journey patiently through sadness,
Each grief will make us dearer to our Lord;
But if we flee the cross in search of gladness,
We can not shun his dread avenging sword.
Oh, blessed they who hear the call,
Who take the cross and follow, leaving all!

So help me, Lord, thy holy will to suffer,
And still a learner at thy feet to be;
Give faith and patience when the way is rougher,
And at the end a joyful victory.
Thus grief itself is changed to song
Ofttimes on earth, but evermore ere long.

FEBRUARY 1: *MORNING.*

And now I beseech thee, lady, not as though I wrote a new commandment unto thee, but that which we had from the beginning, that we love one another.—2 *John*, 5.

This world's need is not condemnation, nor denunciation, nor exposition. What it needs is somebody to suffer for it. Inexperience wants experience that is willing to bear with it till it learns. Hardness of heart wants softness of heart to teach it the quality of softness. Stumbling imperfection wants perfection to take it by the hand, and lead it in the right way. We have had thunder enough, and sword enough, and dungeons enough to reform the world a thousand times, if mere justice or mere force would do it; but these are not sufficient. The spirit which Christ manifested when, crowned with thorns, he suffered for others, is what we need. The mother-heart keeps alive in the world this secret of divinity; but kings, judges, magistrates, warriors, fierce with justice, fill the world with the sufferings of punishment. Some quail, some resent, and many grow desperate. Still justice is proclaimed. As if justice itself was any thing but the birth of passions until it is the child of love! As if the rude justice of the earlier developments of society was to be exalted above love, to limit it, define it, subordinate it, and thus a mere leaf and stem arrogate superiority over that blossom and fruit for whose coming they were created. What we want is an atmospheric power of development, like summer on a continent, to inspire growth away from passion and toward love. Love is the mother of all things. Justice and truth will spring from this divine weather in regal beauty and with hitherto unknown sweetness. We need soul-power. We need the power of God. We want God's creative power in Christ Jesus; and that is the power of a pure and great nature to suffer for impure and little natures.

FEBRUARY 1: *EVENING.*

As one whom his mother comforteth, so will I comfort you.—*Isaiah* lxvi., 13.

As a child, unknowing, turns to the bosom that feeds it, so my heart cries out for God. Though I have no clear and distinct conception of the way in which his soul acts upon mine, I am conscious that I am comforted. If in this life we might have no comfort except that which comes from things that we understand perfectly, we should be of all men most miserable.

In the night a child wakes, and, discovering that it is alone, cries out in terror, and the parent goes to it and lifts it up, and brings it to her own couch; and it falls, dreaming, half crying and half smiling, into a sweet slumber by its mother's side. We, at best, like the child in its mother's arms, are not fully awake. We do not know what influences are acting on us, nor much about him that is working in us. All we know is that without God we die, and that when we lift ourselves toward that glorious, and, in this life, uninterpreted and uninterpretable Being, our heart feels the divine power, and rejoices in it. I do not dislike, in its proper place, reason; but reason shall not play despot over the heart.

"So will I comfort you," as when a sobbing child
Seeks sweet heart-comfort on its mother's breast,
By her caresses fond unconsciously beguiled
From memories of pain, soon sinks to rest.

FEBRUARY 2: MORNING.

For as the earth bringeth forth her bud, and as the garden causeth the things that are sown in it to spring forth; so the Lord God will cause righteousness and praise to spring forth before all the nations.—*Isaiah* lxi., 11.

THERE is yet to come, in fuller measure, the down-shining inspiration of God's Spirit, giving sensibility and power to all it touches; and the whole world is not only to come into that state in which men are born in favorable conditions individually, but it is to come into that state in which they shall be confederated into families, with sweeter affections, with truer conceptions of life, and with better ways of developing and manifesting them. And this affection of the household is to be enlarged till family touches family, and neighborhoods are formed. And these neighborhoods are to open and bloom into each other, and are to be but parts of communities. And these communities are to express a finer taste, a sweeter philanthropy, a better, higher, and more noble justice. All the processes of society are to exhibit more of Christ; so that at last the day shall come when in all the earth, like a man without a pain from head to foot, mankind shall be without a sadness, or a sigh, or a sorrow; when the whole globe, in all its parts, shall be filled full of him who filleth all things, who is the head and animating brain of time and the world; and the globe, no longer singing a requiem, no longer singing of things gloomy and sad, clothed with light and inspired with joy, shall go chanting in its rounds, and the heaven and the earth shall sing together. And so the consolation shall come.

FEBRUARY 2: EVENING.

Remember now thy Creator in the days of thy youth, while the evil days come not, nor the years draw nigh, when thou shalt say, I have no pleasure in them.—*Eccles.* xii., 1.

For whatsoever a man soweth, that shall he also reap.—*Gal.* vi., 7.

OLD age is making haste; and there are none of us that can be young long; and many of us have already passed by our youth. Now, in the wisdom of God, the way to be happy in old age is the very way of being happy all our life. It should be borne in mind that in old age it is too late to mend; that then you must inhabit what you have built. Old age has the foundation of its joys and its sorrows laid in youth. You are building at twenty. Are you building for seventy? A man's life is not like the contiguous cells in a bee's honey-comb; it is more like the separate parts of a plant which unfolds out of itself, every part bearing relation to all that antecede. That which you do in youth is the root, and all the after parts, middle age and old age, are the branches and the fruits, whose character the root will determine.

See, link by link the chain is made,
And pearl by pearl the costly braid;
The daily strand of hopes and fears
Weaves up the woof of many years!
And well thy labor shall have sped
If well thou weav'st the daily thread.

FEBRUARY 3: *MORNING.*

We know that we have passed from death unto life, because we love the brethren. He that loveth not his brother abideth in death.—1 *John* iii., 14.

THOSE who are drawn toward God are necessarily drawn toward each other; and therefore we do not need to seek in detail, and with anxious inquiries, to know how we shall be united to the good. Those that are united together in God, and that become sons of God, and heirs of God, and joint heirs with Christ, are in conditions to fit them to be in holy concord and immortal friendship. Blessed hope!

Here is cacophony, here are harsh-sounding discords, here are misunderstandings piled high between men, here are repellencies and antipathies, here are endless disconnections and separations; but if we take hold of this common faith, and with zeal and ardent enthusiasm pursue a life of love and purity, we shall rapidly approach that blessed land where God shall have arranged the conditions, where all discords shall have died out, where nothing that defiles shall enter, and where the noble, the good, and the true, that belong to each other secretly on earth, shall belong to each other openly, and shall be separated no more forever.

Do you love each other? May God not only make your loving more perfect than it now is, but raise it to the higher spheres of your mind. Do you walk together in truth inwardly? Look to this, father and mother. See well to your own connection and union, husband and wife. Take heed, brothers and sisters. Take care, friend and friend, or lover and lover. There may be a gulf between you, and you not know it. Look to God for that divine, that celestial welding, which shall make you goldenly one. And may God grant that at last, with infinite rapture, with transcendent joys expressed, and joys inexpressible and full of glory, we may meet where dangers are ended, and safety with salvation is begun, and begun to be ended never.

FEBRUARY 3: EVENING.

The Lord is good to all; and his tender mercies are over all his works.—*Psalm* cxlv., 9.

God's pity is not as some sweet cordial, poured in dainty drops from a golden phial. It is not like the musical water-drops of some slender rill, murmuring down the dark sides of Mount Sinai. It is wide as the whole scope of heaven. It is abundant as all the air. If one had art to gather up all the golden sunlight that to-day falls wide over all this continent, falling through every silent hour; and all that is dispersed over the whole ocean, flashing from every wave; and all that is poured refulgent over the northern wastes of ice, and along the whole continent of Europe, and the vast outlying Asia and torrid Africa—if one could in anywise gather up this immense and incalculable outflow and treasure that falls down through the bright hours, and runs in liquid ether about the mountains, and fills all the plains, and sends innumerable rays through every secret place, pouring over and filling every flower, shining down the sides of every blade of grass, resting in glorious humility upon the humblest things—on sticks, and stones, and pebbles—on the spider's web, the sparrow's nest, the threshold of the young foxes' hole, where they play and warm themselves —that rests on the prisoner's window, that strikes radiant beams through the slave's tear, that puts gold upon the widow's weeds, that plates and roofs the city with burnished gold, and goes on in its wild abundance up and down the earth, shining every where and always, since the day of primal creation, without faltering, without stint, without waste or diminution; as full, as fresh, as overflowing to-day as if it were the very first day of its outlay—if one might gather up this boundless, endless, infinite treasure, to measure it, then might he tell the height, and depth, and unending glory of the pity of God! The light, and the sun, its source, are God's own figures of the immensity and copiousness of his mercy and compassion.

FEBRUARY 4: *MORNING.*

In all thy ways acknowledge him, and he shall direct thy paths.—*Prov.* iii., 6.

God reveals his will by his providence, and through his administration of events. But there is no such thing as interpreting the will of God unless we have in us the spirit of children. What is the spirit of children? Love—confidence. If a man comes to the interpretation of adverse or of fortunate events in the spirit of pride, or vanity, or selfishness, he will never know their meaning. God locks up his best blessings, but gives to every man a key wherewith to open the lock. Love is that key. Pride could not open the door; vanity could not open it. But if a man has the spirit of filial love; if he says, "My Father knows me, and knows all my circumstances; I love him, and his will is my will;" and if, when events come, he will look at them with a child-like, loving spirit, to him will be given to interpret the revelation of God's will in events. Love is better than philosophy. The intuitions of love are the best guides that are offered to us in this life. If you would know how to read your Father's manuscript, written every day in the letters of events, you must have the spirit of filial love.

FEBRUARY 4: *EVENING.*

Ye are God's husbandry.—1 *Cor.* iii., 9.

Nations and races, spreading abroad through six thousand years, and flowing on endlessly, so that no prophet's eye can discern the end to come; all the broad earth, with its multiplied populations—these are God's husbandry. God is the Great Cultivator. He looks out over his vast estate—the world—as a man looks over his smaller estate. All the agencies of nature are for God. For him the nations are simple instruments of culture. Revolutions, famines, disasters, prosperities—all things that check or push forward the growth of men—are so many implements in his hand by which he tills this great farm of the earth.

The end of the world is the harvest. Sinners are the chaff and the weeds; the righteous are the good seed and the fruit—the one to be swept away, and the other to be garnered up. At last there shall come the winter, when all things shall cease and rest; and the glory of summer shall be in heaven, where all which is vital, and which carries its life, like a seed, in itself, shall be gathered. When this has taken place, and the withered leaves, and the decaying stalk, and all things else which have come to nothing, have fallen to the ground and perished, then shall be the end.

"Ye are God's husbandry." For you he thinks. For you he tills. He is breaking in your disposition. He is preparing the soil of your hearts. He is cultivating you now by ways that make you cry out with pain—for all plowing and harrowing is painful. The seed long sown may not have yet shown its nature. No affliction for the present is joyous, but rather grievous; but afterward it bringeth forth the peaceable fruits of righteousness. "Ye are God's husbandry." Rejoice in it. Let your bosom lie open to his influence as the soil lies open to the sun. Let God do as seemeth him good; and by-and-by, with all your faculties, with every feeling of your nature, you shall, in the great harvest, bless God.

So to God I leave it all;
Whatsoe'er may here befall,
Joy or trial, life or death,
I receive it all in faith,
And this anxious heart of mine
Learns to trust its Guide Divine,
Since it well hath understood
All things work the Christian good.

FEBRUARY 5: MORNING.

And they that are Christ's have crucified the flesh with the affections and lusts.—*Gal.* v., 24.

EVERY man will find his cross in himself, and in the relation of his own mind to the peculiar circumstances in which he is placed. Your own passions will furnish you crosses enough. A great many persons, hearing much about taking up the cross and following Christ, ask themselves, "What is my cross?" In that rebellious tongue, child, which answers back when the parent commands—there is your cross. In that temper, child, which rises up between you and your companions—there is your cross. In that greedy selfishness, my boy—there is your cross. In that lust, that fiery passion, my young friend—there is your cross. In that hungry avarice, man of business, that is making you a miser—there is your cross. In that consuming thirst for glory, in that indomitable ambition, in that inordinate self-seeking, public man—there is your cross. Every man's cross is the subjugation of that nature which God has put into him. Your cross lies in bringing your thoughts, and feelings, and acts into conformity with a Christian life.

Let a man take his conscience, and go forth with an enlightened conception of what is right, and true, and manly, and spiritual, and pure, and say, "I will crucify on this faculty every thing that opposes itself to the will of God," and he will carry a Calvary with him every day.

FEBRUARY 5: EVENING.

For ye have need of patience, that, after ye have done the will of God, ye might receive the promise.—*Heb.* x., 36.

Do not be discouraged because you are not perfect. It does not follow that you are not going on to know the Lord. If you are perfect, oh, tell me how to become so. Once in a while I come into the experience of a bright and sweet conception of the divine nature; and if I were not called to come down from the top of the mountain, I could see my Christ in transfiguration, and there be a constant possessor of pure Christian affections. But how to take the hurly-burly of life, and never lose my undying, unshrinking love to God—how to take the conflict of worldly affairs, and never vary in my steadfast and disinterested love toward my fellow-men, I can not find out. If any man has found that out, I thank God for him—only I would that he should tell us the secret of it, that we might know it too. But if you are discouraged because all your praying, and trying, and striving has availed but very little, I say to you, "Cast not away, therefore, your confidence, which hath great recompense of reward. For ye have need of patience, that, after ye have done the will of God, ye might receive the promise." You are nearer than when you believed to this state, and attainment, and fruition of grace.

FEBRUARY 6: *MORNING.*

And the child grew, and waxed strong in spirit, filled with wisdom; and the grace of God was upon him.—*Luke* ii., 40.

Even Christ was made perfect through sufferings, in order that he might be the Captain of our salvation. He went through the same gradations in his development which we are obliged to go through in our development, in obedience to that law of growth to which every one in mortal flesh is subject. He went through the same experiences which all men are obliged to go through to be followers of him. And so it was with the apostles, whose lives stand out like fruits upon the bough, redolent, and full of tempting beauty. Paul was not heard from till half a score of years after the other apostles were known; and if you look at those things in his writings which stand out in such exquisite condensation, you will find that twenty verses are crystallized into one verse. And as regards those graces which are enjoined upon us as if they were such easy things to attain—why, there is a lifetime put into a single word. Now when we read the Bible, or when we read biographies, or when we look at living men, we should remember that we are not to compare our experiences with the experiences of great men. We should remember that we are yet children; that we are at school; and that we must grow, if we would attain those virtues which we admire in others. And our motto should be, "Grow in grace, and in the knowledge of our Lord and Savior Jesus Christ."

FEBRUARY 6: EVENING.

No chastening for the present seemeth to be joyous, but grievous.—*Hebrews* xii., 11.

SOME seem to think that a man, to be a Christian, ought to be able not to suffer when suffering comes; but the ache of suffering is a part of its medicine. You might as well say that manliness requires that a man should drink bitter draughts, and call them sweet, as to say that Christianity requires that a man should bear suffering, and say that it is not suffering. It requires no such thing. It does not even require that we should illumine suffering so that for the present it shall seem joyous. The Christian, when his companion is taken from him, is not required to say, "I am so wonderfully strengthened that I have no suffering." A mother is not called upon, when she has given up her child to God, to say, "I suffer none." You are to suffer. No afflictions for the present are joyous, but grievous; nevertheless, *afterward* they yield the peaceable fruit of righteousness unto them that are exercised thereby.

Dear Savior, full of grief I find no rest;
Let me but weep my tears upon thy breast.
 Though deeper still my sorrow,
Still I shall be bless'd
 If thou dost comfort me.

FEBRUARY 7: MORNING.

But God, who is rich in mercy, for his great love wherewith he loved us, even when we were dead in sins, hath quickened us together with Christ (by grace ye are saved).—*Ephes.* ii., 4, 5.

No man can, unaided, go through the battle of life, fight his way to heaven's gate, and there present his ticket to Christ, saying, "I have done my part—I have won the victory; it is your part to reward me." If Christ is not to help a man till after he has gone through this earthly struggle, one may as well give it up, for he can not hope to get through it without help. If there is not a Savior that will take me by the hand and co-operate with me before I get through life, then there is no Savior at all. If Christ is a spectator in this conflict, and not a sympathizing actor with me, and by my side, then he is not a Savior in my case.

I do not thank a doctor that comes to me to congratulate me after I get well. I want a doctor that will help me to get well when I fall sick. The real Christ of the New Testament is a being whose nature—not whose office—whose *nature* leads him to have compassion on the weak, the sinful, and the helpless. He offers to help all men, however sinful; not when they have got rid of sin, but when they are in it, that they may get rid of it. It is Christ's work in the soul, to help you against sin, and out of sin. He takes the soul, in all its wickedness, that by the brooding of his heart he may heal it.

FEBRUARY 7: EVENING.

Cast not away, therefore, your confidence, which hath great recompense of reward.—*Hebrews* x., 35.

THERE are many who say, "If I should ever be a Christian, I tell you I shall not be such a Christian as some that I see." Yes, that is the way you feel now. A hundred men have been in just the same delusion that you are in. You have the impression that, when you begin to live a Christian life, you will show men and angels what it is to have zeal and faith; but you will be just like any other poor sinner that is converted by God's grace and brought into his kingdom. You will find that "it is not of him that willeth, nor of him that runneth." You will find that, though you set your will against habits, habits will beset you. Your pride, your selfishness, your vanity, your avarice, your worldly-mindedness—all these, twisted and gnarled in the old soil where they have grown, you will find it difficult to bring into subjection to the laws of Christ; and, crestfallen, you will come to your pastor and say, "I always thought that, if ever I became a Christian, I should live so as to be a pattern to every body; but I have tried it six months, and have not succeeded very well; and I am sorry I joined the Church, for I do not think I am a Christian." Oh, do not cast away your confidence. You are not a saint, very likely; but you may be a Christian, nevertheless. Why, you did not know any thing about a Christian life. You did not know what it was to have a depraved heart, to be reconstructed, and to be fashioned by the power of God's grace acting through your own judgment and will. When a man takes hold of himself to refashion himself in righteousness, he will find that he can not do it in a day, in a month, or in a year, and that he needs patience. And when, at the end, he dies, he will still say, "My work is but just begun."

FEBRUARY 8: *MORNING.*

The Lord did not set his love upon you, nor choose you, because ye were more in number than any other people; for ye were the fewest of all people. But because the Lord loved you, and because he would keep the oath which he had sworn unto your fathers, hath the Lord brought you out with a mighty hand, and redeemed you out of the house of bondmen, from tho hand of Pharaoh, king of Egypt.—*Deut.* vii., 7, 8.

God's love does not depend upon our character, but upon his own. I do not mean to affirm that it makes no difference whether a man has a good or a bad character. I do not mean to affirm that there do not spring up between the Divine nature and ourselves, by reason of our relations to that nature, certain deeper and more wonderful affections. But I do mean to affirm this—that there is a great overshadowing love of God to us, that stands, not on account of our character, but on account of his. God's love for us is not affirmed to exist because God perceived a spark kindled in us gradually flaming forth, and reaching up toward him. It is not affirmed to exist because our hearts, feebly beating, seemed to knock at the door of his heart, rousing, by their very spent and weak sounds, the compassion of the hospitable Divinity.

Do the roots, and grass, and early flowers break forth from winter, and send messengers for the sun to come back? or does the sun, come from its far voyaging, long to overhang the sleeping-places of flowers until they feel his presence, and, drawn by his warm hands, wake and come forth into a warmth and a light that waited above them while they were dead, and that would have bathed them yet, and all summer long, though they had still lain torpid?

FEBRUARY 8: *EVENING.*

All Scripture * * * is profitable for doctrine, for reproof, for correction, for instruction in righteousness; that the man of God may be perfect, thoroughly furnished unto all good works.—2 *Tim.* iii., 16, 17.

The Bible is God's chart for you to steer by, to keep you from the bottom of the sea, and to show you where the harbor is, and how to reach it without running on rocks or bars.

If you have been reading it to gratify curiosity; or to see if you could not catch a Universalist; or to find a knife with which to cut up a Unitarian; or for the purpose of setting up or taking down a bishop; or to establish or overthrow any sect—if you have been reading it so, then stop. It is God's medicine-book. You are sick. You are mortally struck through with disease. There is no human remedy for your trouble. But here is God's medicine-book. If you read it for life, for growth in righteousness, then blessed is your reading; but if you read it for disputation and dialectical ingenuities, it is no more to you than Bacon's "Novum Organum" would be.

It is the book of life—of everlasting life; so take heed how you read it. You can not live without it. You die forever unless you have it to teach you what are your relations to God and eternity. May God guide you away from all cunning appearances of truth set to deceive men, and make you love the real truth! Above all other things, may God make you honest in interpreting it, and applying it to your daily life and disposition!

Who has this Book, and reads it not,
   Doth God himself despise;
Who reads, but understandeth not,
   His soul in darkness lies.
Who understands, but savors not,
   He finds no rest in trouble;
Who savors, but obeyeth not,
   He hath his judgment double.
Who reads this Book—who understands—
   Doth savor and obey,
His soul shall stand at God's right hand
   In the great judgment day.

FEBRUARY 9: MORNING.

And besides this, giving all diligence, add to your faith virtue; and to virtue, knowledge; and to knowledge, temperance; and to temperance, patience; and to patience, godliness; and to godliness, brotherly kindness; and to brotherly kindness, charity.—*2 Peter* i., 5-7.

TRUE religion carries health and strength into the soul. It regulates all things; it subordinates all things to their just positions; it withdraws from men no faculty; it ties up no power; it extinguishes no instinct; it imprisons no part of the mind; it directs and regulates. Religion is only another word for the right use of a man's whole self, instead of a wrong use of himself. It puts men into connection with God; it brings them into harmonious relations to their fellow-men; it gives them direction for the achievement of duty; it opens to them the coming world, and inspires them with ardent desires for it; it makes them love whatever is good, and abhor whatever is bad; it inspires reverence, obedience, and love toward God and toward our superiors among men; it inculcates justice, mercy, and benevolence toward our fellow-men; it endues us with courage, with patience, with contentment; it commands industry, frugality, and hospitality; it enjoins honesty, truthfulness, uprightness, simplicity, and integrity. And that men, in their ignorance and weakness, may feel the importance of virtue and of the truest piety, Christ reveals the immortality of man's nature, the glory of the heavenly state, the sympathy of God with the struggles of human life, and, above all, sets before men, in a perfect pattern, the example of the life of Christ, who was tempted in all points like as we are in this earthly strife, and yet without sin, teaching us both by precept and by his victorious career.

FEBRUARY 9: EVENING.

And ye have forgotten the exhortation which speaketh unto you as unto children, My son, despise not thou the chastening of the Lord, nor faint when thou art rebuked of him.—*Heb.* xii., 5.

WHAT beautiful figures the Bible employs! On a summer day, in the afternoon, as the sun begins to roll toward the west, and shed that charming after-light which it is so delightful to behold, some parent calls his children into the room, and tells them his story. They with eager expectation gather about him, and he, full of gentleness, recounts to them his own history, and tells them what they may expect under such and such circumstances. What a beautiful scene that is! Poets love it, sentimentalists love it; every one that has a parental feeling admires it. And that exquisite passage of human experience God catches, and idealizes, and makes the symbol of a true conception of him, especially in our troubles. "Ye have forgotten the exhortation which speaketh unto you as unto children, My son"—when any body is in trouble, God says to him by that trouble, My son—"My son, despise not thou the chastening of the Lord, nor faint when thou art rebuked of him; for whom the Lord loveth he chasteneth, and scourgeth every son whom he receiveth. If ye endure chastening, God dealeth with you as with sons."

There is the word of the Lord. When your trouble is real and painful, and you carry it to God, and ask for its removal, if it abides with you, you are apt to think, "It must be that God is punishing me for my sins, and that he is hiding his face from me." "No," says the voice of God; "so far from it, I am dealing with you tenderly; I am your parent; I love you, and the trouble that I permit to remain with you is one of the evidences of the affection which I cherish toward you." And if you endure it, he deals with you as with sons.

FEBRUARY 10: *MORNING.*

And I will give unto thee the keys of the kingdom of heaven: and whatsoever thou shalt bind on earth shall be bound in heaven; and whatsoever thou shalt loose on earth shall be loosed in heaven.—*Matt.* xvi., 19.

Every one that has the mind and will of Christ, and abides in his Spirit, stands in the relation to those below him of the holder of the keys. Woe be to him that in time of famine has bread, and lets men starve because he will not part with it! Woe be to him that in time of plague has medicine, and lets men die untended! Double woe be to him that has been enlightened of God, and lets men perish because he will not take, by the authority of God, the light that he has received and carry it to them. Are there not within the touch of the hem of your garment; are there not in your business places; are there not in your daily travels; are there not in the thoroughfares of the city, scores and hundreds into whose darkened minds the light of God's truth never pierced, to whom you never came with a lantern? Here you stand unconcerned—you whose soul is luminous, you that by the power of the Holy Ghost have been ordained to be a teacher, a leader, and a dispenser of spiritual things—and men are wasting and dying in darkness all round about you! God has given you the keys, and he will hold you to a responsibility for the right use of them.

FEBRUARY 10: *EVENING.*

I am with thee to save thee, and to deliver thee, saith the Lord.—*Jeremiah* xv., 20.

Every heart knows its own bitterness. There is often a delicacy in grief. Though sometimes it is clamorous and vocal, oftener it is silent. But there is a process quietly going on, though it may not be apparent, by which those who seem to be separated in the present shall in the future be gathered together by sorrow. Those that weep apart on earth shall joy together in heaven. Those who in their sorrows are cast out from the sympathies of their fellow-men shall be gathered into the fellowship and sympathy of the heavenly host. This separation and disintegration are only apparent. Really, it is a preparation for fellowship in the world to come.

Your salvation is nearer than when you believed. You are not far from that host that waits for you. It can not be long before your sorrows shall end and your eternal joy shall begin. Then be patient. Is the storm fierce? Yet it is almost past, and the time of the singing of birds is at hand.

Cometh sunshine after rain,
After morning joy again;
After heavy, bitter grief,
Dawneth surely sweet relief;
Who in God his hope hath placed
Shall not life in pain outwaste,
Fullest joy he yet shall taste.

FEBRUARY 11: MORNING.

But many that are first shall be last, and the last shall be first.—*Matthew* xix., 30.

THERE are many of the plants of our northern summer which come up quickly, which *rush* to their flowering periods, and do exceedingly well; but they are coarse and rank. And there are many seeds that I plant by the side of them every spring which in the first summer only grow a few leaves high. There is not sun enough in our hemisphere, nor heat enough in the bosom of my soil, to make them do what it is in them to do. But if I take them and put them in some sheltered hot-house, and give them the continuous growth of autumn and winter, and then again, when June begins to burn in the next summer, put them out once more, they gather strength by this second planting, and lift up their arms, and spread out the abundance of their blossoms, and are the pride and glory of the spring. The plants that grew quickest the year before are now called weeds by their side. I doubt not that there is many a man who rushes up to a rank growth in the soil of this world, and of whom men, seeing him, say, "That is a great man;" but there are many starveling, poor, feeble, and effectless creatures in this world who will be carried safely on and up, and rooted in a better clime; and then, lifting up their whole nature, they will come out into that glorious summer of fervent love in heaven, where they will be more majestic, more transcendently beautiful in blossoms, and more exquisitely sweet in fruit, than those who so far surpass them here.

Do not despise men that are less than you are. Do not undervalue men because they are not of much account in this world. A man may not be able to make money, and yet he may be rich. A man may not have the power to generate thoughts here, but by-and-by he will. Birds do not sing the moment they are out of their shell. They must have a season in which to learn to sing. And men do not unfold their true natures, or sing their best songs, many of them, in this world. There is another world beyond; and there is no man that has appearances so much against him in this world that you can afford to despise him, to feel contempt for him, or to regard him as worthless. That term *worthless*, applied to unaccomplishing weakness in this world, is pagan.

FEBRUARY 11: *EVENING.*

And these shall go away into everlasting punishment, but the righteous into life eternal.—*Matt.* xxv., 46.

Sometimes, in dark caves, men have gone to the edge of unspeaking precipices, and, wondering what was the depth, have cast down fragments of rock, and listened for the report of their fall, that they might judge how deep that blackness was; and listening!—still listening!—no sound returns! no sullen plash, no clinking stroke as of rock against rock—nothing but silence, utter silence! And so I stand upon the precipice of life. I sound the depths of the other world with curious inquiries. But from it comes no echo, and no answer to my questions. No analogies can grapple and bring up from the depths of the darkness of the lost world the probable truths. No philosophy has line and plummet long enough to sound the depths. There remains for us only the few authoritative and solemn words of God. These declare that the bliss of the righteous is everlasting; and with equal directness and simplicity they declare that the doom of the wicked is everlasting.

The incorrigibly wicked, the deliberately impenitent, have nothing to hope in the future, if they set aside the light and the glory that shines in the face of Jesus Christ. And therefore it is that I make haste, with an inconceivable ardor, to persuade you to be reconciled to your God. I hold up before you that God who loves the sinners and abhors sin; who loves goodness with infinite fervor, and breathes it upon those who put their trust in him; who makes all the elements his ministering servants; who sends years, and weeks, and days, and hours, all radiant with benefaction, and, if we would but hear their voice, all pleading the goodness of God as an argument of repentance and of obedience.

But remember that it is this God who declares that he will at last by no means clear the guilty.

FEBRUARY 12: MORNING.

Then shall the dust return to the earth as it was, and the spirit shall return unto God who gave it.—*Eccles.* xii., 7.

I NEVER saw a man that did not believe in the immortality of love when following the body of a loved one to the grave. I have seen men under other circumstances that did not believe in it; but I never saw a man that, when he stood looking upon the form of one that he really loved stretched out for burial, did not revolt from saying, "It has all come to that—the hours of sweet companionship; the wondrous interlacings of tropical souls; the joys, the hopes, the trusts, the unutterable yearnings, there they all lie." No man can stand and look in a coffin, upon the body of a fellow-creature, and remember the flaming intelligence, the blossoming love, the whole range of divine faculties that animated that cold clay, and say, "These have all collapsed and gone." No person can witness the last sad ceremonials which are performed over the remains of a human being—the sealing down of the unopenable lid; the following of the rumbling procession to the place of burial; the letting down of the dust into dust; the falling of the earth upon the hollow coffin, and the placing of the green sod over the grave—no person can witness these things, and then turn away and say, "I have buried my wife; I have buried my child; I have buried my sister, my brother, my love."

God forbid that we should bury any thing. There is no earth that can touch my companion. There is no earth that can touch my child. I would fight my little breath and strength away before I would permit any clod to touch them. The jewel is not in the ground. The jewel has dropped out of the casket, and I have buried the casket, not the jewel.

FEBRUARY 12: EVENING.

Thy will be done.—*Matt.* vi., 10.

THE true God, the Christian's God, the God that faith takes hold of, fills the heaven, fills the earth, fills time, fills providence, fills nature, fills the Christian's soul, and is with him by day and by night, in his rising up and his sitting down; and he can say, "Whom have I in heaven but thee? There is none upon earth that I desire beside thee. My flesh and my heart fail; but God is the strength of my heart, and my portion forever." Have you any such God? Can you trust him? Can you worship him? Can you look in the face of Jesus Christ to-day, and say, "Thy will be done?" At that enchantment burdens roll off, cares fly away, darkness lifts, the earth is transformed, events have a new significance, and those experiences that have seemed before to us to be so many persecutions, now begin to letter themselves and form sentences; and every letter and every sentence begins to be a literature interpreting the goodness, the mercy, and the glory of God to us.

I worship thee, sweet will of God,
And all thy ways adore;
And every day I live, I seem
To love thee more and more.

I have no cares, oh blessed will!
For all my cares are thine;
I live in triumph, Lord, for thou
Hast made thy triumphs mine.

And when it seems no chance or change
From grief can set me free,
Hope finds its strength in helplessness,
And, trusting, waits on thee.

FEBRUARY 13: *MORNING.*

The Lord is good, a stronghold in the day of trouble; and he knoweth them that trust in him.—*Nahum* i., 7.

Is not Christ kinder than the heavens? and yet do they not open their bosom, and give us water to drink, and shed down upon us the light of the sun by day, and the light of stars by night? Is not Christ better than the earth? and yet out of its bosom does it not yield us all things which we need for the nourishment of the body? Is not God better than times and seasons, that move ignorantly in vast circuits? and yet do not times and seasons clothe us, and nourish us, and minister unto us? Is the great sentient One—the ever-living, the vast and ocean-hearted God—the eternal Jehovah—is he less pitiful than the heavens, the sun, the stars, the earth, or the seasons?

Oh! there is nothing but God in the universe. All these other things are but his feeble ministers and recipients, in the heavens and on the earth. In the growing leaf, in the blossom, in all fruits, in the streams, in the things that come to us on every side from the vast treasure-houses of Nature, we have but so many means by which God speaks to us. His voice comes to us, night and day, saying to us, "Ye are mine, and I am yours. My everlasting strength is underneath you. Trust me and love me, and I will bear you up, and you shall be saved."

FEBRUARY 13: *EVENING.*

It is enough; now, O Lord, take away my life, for I am not better than my fathers.—1 *Kings* xix., 4.

There are times, I suppose, in which the most zealous would, if it were God's will, be glad to die—to retire from the battle of life—because they think it will make no difference whether they live or die. They have such a consciousness of imperfection, of inferiority, of unfitness in themselves, that they feel that it could scarcely be worse, and that it might be much better, if they were out of the world, and their places were filled by others.

What is a drop of water of itself? What can be more harmless? What is weaker? What is less potent for any effect? It is mist, invisible. It rises through the imperceptible paths of the air, and hangs unseen in the heavens, till the cold strikes it, and it congeals into clouds, and falls in the form of rain, perhaps on the mountain's top, and is sucked up by the greedy earth. Still sinking through the earth, it reaches the line of the rocks, from whose sides it oozes out and trickles down, when, finding other drops as weak as itself, they unite their forces; and the sum of the weakness of all these drops goes to make the rill, which flows on, making music as it flows, until it meets counter streams. These, combined, form the river; the river forms the estuary; and the estuary the ocean itself. And now, when God has marshaled the sum of the weakness of myriad drops together, they lift the mightiest ship as if it were but a feather, and play with the winds as if they were mere instruments of sport. And yet that very drop, which a man could bear upon the end of his finger, is there, and has its part and lot in the might of the whole vast, unbounded sea.

We in our singleness, in our individuality, in our own selves, are weaker than a drop of water, and more unstable; but as gathered together in the great ocean of life, as kept together by the mighty currents which God's providences make, we attain, working together with him, under the inspiration of his Spirit, to a might that makes life not ignoble, but sublime.

FEBRUARY 14: *MORNING.*

Who art thou, Lord?—*Acts* ix., 5.

It is a wholesome question for every man to put to himself, not What is Jesus Christ? but What is *my* Christ? We are conscious that we have different Christs—that is, that Christ appears differently to different ones. We are familiar with yearning after each other's experiences. "Oh!" says one, "that I could have such a joyous view as such a Christian has! Oh! that I had such a comfort in my hope as I perceive in another!" which, being interpreted, amounts to this: that different people have very different Christs. As you bring your own life to the fashioning of your Christ, in some respects he is meagre. He is yet "a man of sorrows and acquainted with grief" to some of you. He is to many of you only a conscience, sworded and armed. To still more of you he is but a problem, an argument, an abstract statement. To many of you God is a power —and a physical power at that—engineering in the heavens; while to many others he is a power domineering on the earth. So different men frame their Gods—their Christ-Gods—differently. But oh! there is no framing, and no following up, that is so unworthy of a man as that which is lean, and meagre, and poor—as that in which pity is less even than in man, or as that in which the commercial element is stronger than in man. Where I see God conditioned, and his mercies limited, and put upon one and another ground, it being said, "If you do so and so, God will do so and so: our God is thus and so;" when I see men piece and patch their notion of God, and circumscribe the effluence and infinite spontaneity of divine love, and the overflowing divinity of Jesus—when I see these things, it seems to me that men hold up here a rush-light, there a wax torch, there a candle, and yonder a smoking pine knot, and call them Gods, each worshiping his own light, while the sun itself, out of doors, blazes all through the hemisphere, and should rebuke the meanness and poverty of the conception which men have of light.

FEBRUARY 14: *EVENING.*

Which hope we have as an anchor of the soul, both sure and steadfast.—*Heb.* vi., 19.

An anchor is not for fair weather. It is for refuge in time of extremity.

Our life requires many ways of using God. We are to use him as bread in the familiarity of our every-day life. We are to use him as we use water, for he is the bread and water of life. We are to use him as we do our garments, for we are commanded to put on the Lord Jesus Christ. There are many purposes which God serves, and which in various passages he opens and sets before us in his Word. In this particular passage there is a use of God for extremities, just as an anchor is used for extremities. It lies on the bows of the ship, quite useless through days, and weeks, and months it may be. It is only relied upon when the winter wind sings in the air with threat of danger, and when there is darkness on the sea in the night. There are also extremities of life when the soul can hold by nothing else but some such hope as this in God. Times when, storm-tossed, it can only say, "I anchor upon God."

Though waves and storms go o'er my head,
  Though strength, and health, and friends be gone;
Though joys be withered all, and dead,
  And every comfort be withdrawn—
On this my steadfast soul relies,
Jesus, thy mercy never dies.

Fixed on this ground will I remain,
  Though my heart fail and flesh decay;
This anchor shall my soul sustain
  When earth's foundations melt away;
Mercy's full power I then shall prove,
Loved with an everlasting love.

FEBRUARY 15: *MORNING.*

The young man saith unto him, All these things have I kept from my youth up: what lack I yet?—*Matt.* xix., 20.

Because you are good-natured, because you are gentle, because all the offices of your mind are performed with mildness, because you have the testimony in your heart that you wish well to every thing, it does not follow either that you are a Christian, or that you are near becoming one. On the contrary, the presumptions are that a mere well-wisher is far from true religion, far from the kingdom of God, far from health, and far from safety. For religion is a system of the most positive character. It is a system which can not be embraced, a life which can not be prosecuted without great plenary, generic volitions, and without an unintermitted series of specific choices or wills.

The first demand which is made of every man is, "My son, give me thine heart." Renounce the life of self-indulgence and of selfishness. Turn away from a conception of life which makes it right for you to use all the powers of your body, and all the powers of your soul, for the production of effects for your own pleasure, seeking your own good either in your person, or distributively in your family, or more distributively in your neighborhood; forsake that life of either direct or indirect selfishness, and be born again into a new life in which the prime and chiefest feeling is love, and the allegiance which love bears. "Love the Lord thy God with all thy heart, and with all thy soul, and with all thy strength, and with all thy mind, and thy neighbor as thyself."

FEBRUARY 15: *EVENING.*

But as it is written, Eye hath not seen, nor ear heard, neither have entered into the heart of man the things which God hath prepared for them that love him. But God hath revealed them unto us by his Spirit.—1 *Cor.* ii., 9, 10.

The life of every Christian on earth hath much in it that is mysterious, for it is aiming at an awful grandeur which has never yet been unveiled. God carries in his bosom the full ideal. We know it not. We go moaning after music. We rudely grope for beauty. We are sick men leaning on a staff, and walking slowly for convalescence. We do not know the things toward which we are tending; but God knows them. There are few that suppose their moanings or yearnings mean any thing; but God interprets them. The apostle says, "The Spirit helpeth our infirmities, for we know not what we should pray for as we ought; but the Spirit itself maketh intercession for us with groanings which can not be uttered."

We see, then, the meaning of those strange longings and aspirations which so many have. They are the foreworkings in us of that which is to appear in the heavenly estate. They are not a mere vagrant restlessness. They are the yearning of the soul for itself. They are the home-sickness of the heart for its future home. They are the attempt of the child to say "Father." We see, too, the meaning of those glimpses and visions which so many have. John says, "It doth not yet appear what we shall be." We are the sons of God, we know; but what that means we do not know.

FEBRUARY 16: *MORNING.*

For there stood by me this night the angel of God, whose I am, and whom I serve, saying, Fear not, Paul; thou must be brought before Cæsar; and lo, God hath given thee all them that sail with thee.—*Acts* xxvii., 23, 24.

WE are all of us, like Paul, voyagers. Sometimes the voyage is calm and prosperous; sometimes it is stormy and disastrous. Every sort of fate attends the various navigation of all that spread their sails upon this voyage of life.

The circle to which a man is united by his heart's affections may be said to be the ship in which he sails. Those that are in the ship are tossed with us, and we are tossed with them. The same sea is under us all. The wind that wrecks them strands us. We can not untie the cords that are plied around us. And as we are all voyaging together on the sea of life, so we are in little groups enshipped together; and the promise is the same to all that can stand in Christian faith by God's angel with love and desire. He will not say to them that prosperity shall be theirs, but he will say to them, as he did to Paul, "Lo, God hath given thee all that sail with thee." Do you ask for any more? Christian parents, if God would fulfill that promise to you, could you not say to him to-day, "Lord, it is enough. I accept it as the satisfaction of my life. Give me all that sail with me in my ship, that I may bring them, after the voyage is over, to thee?" Will not that suffice?

And ye that are teaching in schools, during the week or upon the Sabbath day, is it ever a thought with you how to bring those that sail with you, all of them, safely through? God has given them to you. You are to them as a parent, and it is yours to guide them in the way in which they should go. Are there hours in which you think you hear the angel of God saying to you, "Though thou must stand before Cæsar, yet, lo, I have given thee all that sail with thee?" Blessed promise! sweet assurance! holy hope! There is nothing better that man could imagine in all the gifts and experiences of life.

FEBRUARY 16: EVENING.

In the time of their trouble, when they cried unto thee, thou heardest them from heaven.—*Neh.* ix., 27.

During the summer, on Western rivers, as you are riding or even wading across the ford, you may see, lying a little below you, great flat-bottomed boats used for ferrying. During the summer, while waters are low, and men can cross without help and without danger, these craft lie moored to the shore, with nothing to do. But when heavy rains have swollen the river, and the ford is drowned out so that no man may dare to venture it, then travelers are glad to see the clumsy boat swung round, and, by cords and poles, forced across the swift-running waters for the convenience of those who must pass over.

All our emergencies are like streams. So long as we can cross them without help we use the ford. But when our affairs are beyond our own skill or strength, God sends round his promises, which had lain along the shore tied up and disused, to bear us over the black, swollen waters. And blessed is he who is willing and able to venture across real troubles upon God's stanch promises.

FEBRUARY 17: MORNING.

I call heaven and earth to record this day against you, that I have set before you life and death, blessing and cursing: therefore choose life, that both thou and thy seed may live.—*Deut.* xxx., 19.

He that would enter into the kingdom of God must enter by one of those throes that are like birth-throes. The soul cries out as the child in birth cries, and enters into the new life, not only as one feeble, as one just born, but in pain and tribulation.

No man can begin a religious life except by putting forth such conscious volitions and purposes as reach to the very bottom of the soul. Every step farther in that Christian life is a step in which our hearts are to rise from lower stages and gradations to higher; for we are to follow Christ. No man can literally follow him as the apostles and primitive disciples did. We can only let our actions follow his actions, and from day to day be, according to the measure of our power, and in our special spheres, what he was in the greatness of his power, and according to the sphere and office which he performed on earth. But it is the daily life in which a man is obliged to put forth energy, consideration, and positiveness peculiarly. For there is not an hour in which you are not called to choose between selfishness and benevolence; there is not an hour in which you are not called to choose between the higher and the lower; there is not an hour in which all the best notes of the soul do not sound, and in which all the heavenly influences do not appeal to the higher elements of the soul.

FEBRUARY 17: EVENING.

Wherefore God also hath highly exalted him, and given him a name which is above every name.—*Phil.* ii., 9.

In respect to every one of those qualities which go to make names that are dear to the heart, the Lord Jesus Christ is infinitely above all others. All the love and authority which there is in *father*, even in the most eminent instances, and in ideal instances, is so dark, compared with that special element in the Lord Jesus Christ, that it could scarcely appear by its side. Christ is more in those very qualities which make a father dear to his children, or a neighbor noble to his neighbors, than any or all fathers or neighbors. He is infinite in those things. All those indescribable and tender graces which make *mother* the queenly name in all the earth, Christ has in such abundance and perfectness, that a mother's heart by the side of his would be like a taper at midday. All that which the child yearns for while a child, and remembers with home-sickness afterward, when grown up; all those qualities that make men look back for their paradise to their childhood, and make them feel, too often, that life is a wilderness, and their early homes the place of love, and joy, and sweet fruition, are not so dominant in father and mother as they are in Jesus. He is more fatherly than fathers, and more motherly than mothers. He is more tender in love than any lover ever knew how to be. Language is exhausted in the Bible to signify the inflections of divine tenderness. No love-letter that ever was written, or could be written, could compare with what can be gathered out of the Old and New Testaments, describing the inflections of divine love toward men. There is no such literature known as that which shines and glows in the word of God, to express love in all its infinite inflections.

FEBRUARY 18: *MORNING.*

And Jesus answered and said unto her, Martha, Martha, thou art careful and troubled about many things.—*Luke* x., 41.

More than half that we suffer through fear of troubles is that which we are made to suffer by magnifying them. You suffer ten times as much in thinking about having your tooth drawn as you do in having it drawn. The surgeon's knife does not give half as much pain as the patient suffers in thinking about having the operation performed. We take our troubles, and turn them over, and look at them; we imagine what form they will assume; we make an inventory of them; we muster them, and call the roll, and put them in order, and march them first this way and then that; we annoy ourselves with them as much as possible. Men are infernally ingenious in tormenting themselves with troubles which ninety-nine times in a hundred have no existence except in their imagination.

That we should have a revelation of the life to come by the Lord Jesus Christ; that by the power of the Holy Ghost the love of the Savior should be set home to our souls; that we should be made to know that we are unspeakably dear to God; that we should be brought to realize that our journey through this world is short, and that we are only pilgrims and strangers seeking another and a better home; that a vision of the heavenly glory should be vouchsafed to us—that all these things should be opened up to our minds, and that we, after all, should measure our troubles, not by their relation to the eternal realm, but simply by their effects upon our earthly estate—is that manly? is it apostolic? is it Christ-like? Is it not, rather, base and ignoble? Are we not to turn from all these low considerations of trouble, and take that higher and nobler view of it which has reference to our future existence?

We must learn of Christ how to bear trouble. We must bear it as he bore it, "who, for the joy that was set before him, endured the cross, despising the shame, and is set down at the right hand of the throne of God."

FEBRUARY 18: *EVENING.*

We are the children of God; and if children, then heirs; heirs of God, and joint heirs with Christ.—*Rom.* viii., 16, 17.

We are "heirs of God, and joint heirs with Christ," according to the declaration of the apostle. All that there is of beauty, and richness, and sweetness, and grandeur, and authority in Christ is not simply something to which we are permitted to look, but it is ours. We have the same right in it that a child has in the dignity and elevation of his father. If the father comes to honor, and is of universal repute, the child feels stronger, and richer, and happier. The father's name is the child's glory, as the child's prosperity is the father's joy. All that God has is mine. All that he is is mine. I am what I am by the grace of God. I do not stand in my own being. The sum of my richness is not what I have, but what I am to inherit. In the ineffable love of Christ, in the glory, and beauty, and grandeur of his nature, and in his elevation of character, I have a part and a lot. He is my Father, he is my Brother, he is my Friend, he is my Companion, and shall be forever and forever. He shall lead me by the hand here, and he shall lead me by the hand through the valley of the shadow of death. And I shall fear no evil. I shall meet the mysterious foes that people darkness and space, and say, "The Captain of my salvation is victorious over all adversaries." I shall not fear to face the life to come. I know in whom I have trusted; and what I have committed to his charge he will keep, for he is a faithful Savior. I know that my sins rise up, but he knows them better than I do. I know my inferiority; but did ever bird sit on the nest that it might brood the egg into life, and then wait patiently for the callow bird to fly and sing, feeding it the while, that it had not borrowed something to teach me what God is, who sits with infinite patience, brooding men till they are brought up out of imperfection into perfection, and are able to fly through the realms of power, and grace, and glory? I am imperfect enough, but not I, but Christ that dwelleth in me, gives hope.

FEBRUARY 19: *MORNING.*

Lo, I am with you alway, even unto the end of the world.—*Matt.* xxviii., 20.

How seldom do I find men who have a living Christ. They have a New Testament Christ, a doctrinal Christ, a letter Christ, a sepulchre Christ, a Christ of sacrifice. Some people, when talking about Christ, never say Christ, but always say "cross." They are always talking about "the glories of the *cross*," and "the salvation of the *cross*." Some people seem to think that the cross is Christ. Many people talk about Christ with the idea of his being the Son of Man in his Father's glory, and their Christ is future. Some men have a historical Christ, and others have a prophetic Christ; but very few have a Christ that is fulfilling to them the promise, "I will come unto you, and make my abode with you." Very few have a Christ that is with them at midnight and at noonday, at morning and at evening; in temptation, in sin, in repentance; that is never far off; that is a present help in time of trouble; that is breathing the effulgence of the divine nature upon them, to rescue them, to cleanse them, to pardon them, and to carry them in the bosom of his providence, from strength to strength, until they shall stand in Zion before God.

FEBRUARY 19: *EVENING.*

I am the living bread which came down from heaven: if any man eat of this bread he shall live forever: and the bread that I will give is my flesh, which I will give for the life of the world.—*John* vi., 51.

You have fed upon this undiminishing loaf, you have been supplied by it often and often, but as yet you have seen only the wagons that Joseph sent from Egypt to bring his father down, and the provisions for the way. You have not seen the royal palace, you have not seen the store-houses. There were yet to be many years of famine, and the son sent the father provision for the way, but no more than that. But when he received him, he gave him the fattest land of the whole of well-watered Egypt. You have had provisions sent you sufficient for the way, but your God dwells in a plenitude of joy of which as yet you have no conception. Though you may have sometimes felt that more joy would break the connection between spirit and body, and though you may have sometimes said, "Hold thy hand, O God! it is enough," still it doth not yet appear what your experiences and satisfactions are to be. Have you been comforted in sorrow? You know nothing of comfort as yet. Have you been strengthened in weakness? You know nothing of strength as yet. Have you had light poured upon you in the midst of surrounding darkness? You know nothing of light as yet. Wait till the twilight of God has fallen on your rising head; wait till time has brought the orb of your life into the full sunrising of heaven, and then, when you shall see Him as he is, and enter in to dwell for evermore, you shall begin to find that he is "living bread," fed upon by more myriads than human language can number—that he is the undiminishing loaf of heaven and earth—the "bread of life"—the joy, the satisfaction, the strength of all God's people.

Sweet to look inward, and attend
The whispers of his love;
Sweet to look upward to the place
Where Jesus pleads above;

Sweet on his faithfulness to rest,
Whose love can never end;
Sweet on his covenant of grace
For all things to depend;

Sweet in the confidence of faith,
To trust his firm decrees;
Sweet to lie passive in his hands,
And know no will but his.

If such the sweetness of the streams,
What must the fountain be,
Where saints and angels draw their bliss
Immediately from thee?

FEBRUARY 20: *MORNING.*

Now there was leaning on Jesus' bosom one of his disciples whom Jesus loved.—*John* xiii., 23.

If there be any thing that is striking in the history of Christ's intercourse with his disciples, it is the fact that he formed individual attachments for them. He loved all his disciples, but he loved them with a varying amount of affection. He manifested more love toward some than toward others; and he did it to teach us what the mind of God is, how it moves, and how it carries itself. He bestowed upon them all as much love as they could hold, and a great deal more than they could appreciate. And yet there was this individual love. That which belonged to one was not given to another. Each had his own personal relations to the Lord Jesus Christ. And it may be said in respect to the whole of them that Christ called them by their names, and manifested personal familiarity with them, and addressed himself to their thought and character as they were developed.

Now this is just exactly that which we need in this world. Every heart wants a personal interest in God. Every man wants to feel that he is beloved of God, as an individual, separated from every other individual. And I believe there is no truth more deep or more sacred than the truth that God, looking abroad over the sphere of his government, does behold men in their individuality. We are taught that the particularity of God's knowledge is such that the very hairs of our head are all numbered; and if our hairs, which are the least sensitive, the most unconscious—if our very hairs have been sorted and singled out, do you suppose that the elements of our character, the affiliations of our lives, the tides and throes of our vital existence are not known and individually perceived by God?

FEBRUARY 20: *EVENING.*

The Lord gave, and the Lord hath taken away; blessed be the name of the Lord.—*Job* i., 21.

AH! what are we, that we should set ourselves against any dealing that it may please our blessed Father to visit upon us? Suppose our expectations *are* all unrealized; suppose our life *does* seem well-nigh to be obliterated, like the track of a caravan on the desert; suppose our cherished hopes *are* all crumbled and shriveled, like paper in the flame, and destroyed—what then? Has God taken from you those whom you love? Has he taken the lamp out of your house? Has he taken the delight out of your days? Has he taken the satisfaction out of your years? What then? Are you too good to suffer? Have you a warrant which would clear you from the experience which has belonged to all men that have lived since the first birth on earth, and which will belong to all men that will live hereafter. Christ was a man of sorrows, and was continually acquainted with grief—he was the great Sufferer; and can you stand and look upon him, and say, "I do not deserve to suffer; I ought not thus to be grieved and disappointed?"

FEBRUARY 21: *MORNING.*

For God is my witness, whom I serve with my spirit in the Gospel of his Son, that without ceasing I make mention of you always in my prayers.—*Romans* i., 9.

WHAT one that has ever prayed has not come upon occasions of praying for others, and fluttered on the threshold of petition; not doubting altogether whether God would hear our prayers for ourselves, but wondering whether he would hear prayers for others uttered by us. He is more likely to hear your prayers for others than he is to hear your prayers for yourselves, a great deal.

Does my boy ask me for food? If he asks for food for himself, I am, to be sure, willing to give it to him; but if he comes to me and says, "Father, there is a poor, shivering, hungry boy on the sidewalk—may I carry some food out to him?" though I might have denied him the loaf for himself, when he asks liberty to carry it to an unknown stranger that is suffering, I say, "Go! go! carry it to him;" and I give him double that he asks for. If my son asks a thing for himself, I may not think it best that he should be indulged; but if he asks a thing for his companion in royal friendship, I will be twice as likely to grant his request.

And so, when we ask God for mercies for others, do not you suppose he feels the same emotion which we feel under like circumstances? We are conscious that we grant things asked for others more readily than things asked for self. And it is so with God to a far greater degree than with us. Do you suppose that when a mother prays for her child God does not feel more than he does when she prays for herself?

FEBRUARY 21: *EVENING.*

This night thy soul shall be required of thee.—*Luke* xii., 20.

If God should call you this night, are you prepared to make your final account? Are you prepared to leave things in this world just as they are, with no more done? Are you prepared to leave things undone as they are? Is there no justice that you owe? Have you filled up the measure of bounty? Is there no reparation to be made any where, and no restoration? Is there nothing to be repented of? Is there no half-fulfilled duty of love? Are there no words to be recalled? Is there no quarrel to be reconciled? Is there no cleansing of the heart of vile thoughts, of wrong dispositions, or of base passions and appetites? Are you clean as one that emerges from the stream bathed and purified? Would your soul rise up out of your body unsullied if to-night God should call it? Are you prepared to meet your Judge, who is of purer eyes than to behold iniquity? Is there no taint, no sully, no selfishness, no cruelty of pride, no self-indulgence, no frivolity of vanity, no waste of conscience, no death-poison? How is it with you? If God should call your soul to-night, are you prepared to meet him? Is it not just as our Savior represented it in the parable? Are not men living in a vain show, not a hand-breadth from death, though they seem to themselves to be far from it and secure?

My God, I know not when I die,
  What is the moment or the hour,
How soon the clay may broken lie,
  How quickly pass away the flower;
Then may thy child preparèd be,
  Through time to meet eternity.

FEBRUARY 22: MORNING.

And every man that striveth for the mastery is temperate in all things. Now they do it to obtain a corruptible crown; but we an incorruptible.—1 *Cor.* ix., 25.

THE principle of self-denial and of self-control not only is not impossible to human nature, but is one of the commonest, one of the most universal principles in exercise. When the Christian religion introduces self-denial, symbolizing it by the cross, it does not introduce a new principle, it does not introduce a difficult one. In saying that no man is worthy to be a disciple of Christ unless he take up his cross, and deny himself, and follow the Savior, Jesus is only saying in regard to himself and to the world eternal what this world says in regard to every man that follows it. There is no trade that does not say to every applicant that comes to it, "If you will take up your cross and follow me, you shall have my remuneration." There is no profession that does not say to every applicant, "If you will take up your cross and follow me, I will reward you." There is no pleasure, there is no ambition, there is no course that men pursue, from the lowest to the highest, in the horizon of secular things, that does not say to every man, "Unless you take up your cross and follow me, you shall have none of me." Now the Lord Jesus Christ, standing like the angel in the Apocalypse, with eternity for a background, clothed in garments white as snow, as no fuller on earth could white them, and calling us to honor, and glory, and immortality, says only in behalf of these higher things what the whole world says of its poor, groveling, and miserable things—"Take up your cross and follow me." Lust says so: why should not love say so? Wealth that perishes says so, and earthly glory that fades like the laurel wreath says so: why should not the crown of fine gold that never grows dim say so? And if men will hear it from the world, oh! why will they not hear it from God, and Christ, and eternity?

FEBRUARY 22: *EVENING.*

For we know that, if our earthly house of this tabernacle were dissolved, we have a building of God, a house not made with hands, eternal in the heavens. —2 *Cor.* v., 1.

The child that is at school in the beginning of the term jealously prepares his little bows and arrows, and traps and springs, and riddles and puzzles, and what not. Then they are choice treasures to him, and he mourns if any thing befalls them. But when the last days of the term come, how generous he is in distributing them. He tosses them to one and another of his companions, saying, "Here! you may have them if you want them; I do not want them any more." He is glad to get rid of them. The things that a month or two ago he guarded sedulously in his treasure-chamber now have no value to him, for the hunger of father and mother is on him. He says to himself, "Day after to-morrow I am off;" and he can not eat, nor sleep, nor play, such is the excitement which he feels at the prospect of going home so soon.

What home-sickness is to the child away at school, that to the soul is heaven-sickness, which sets us free from the ten thousand joys and sorrows of this world, if we really *are* heaven-sick.

If one can get such a conception of his own nature as to make him impervious to trouble; if one can attain to a view of Christ that is able to lift him above trouble; if one can arrive at such a sense of the nearness and efficacy of the spiritual world that this world shall seem poor, and low, and mean in the comparison, is not that a noble way to render ourselves superior to earthly things, whose tendency is to annoy us, and fret us, and make us unhappy in our present life?

FEBRUARY 23: MORNING.

And he said unto me, My grace is sufficient for thee: for my strength is made perfect in weakness. Most gladly, therefore, will I rather glory in my infirmities, that the power of Christ may rest upon me.—2 *Cor.* xii., 9.

It is every Christian's duty to have a victory either *over* his trials, or *in* them. And this last is the better of the two, and far the more glorious; for it is a higher exhibition of Christian manliness to be able to bear trouble than to get rid of it. To be able to endure is more manly than to have nothing to endure. Who could not be a Christian if every time any thing touched him to hurt him, prayer was like a shield struck right between the weapon and the sensitive skin, so that he could always avoid pain? But if trouble really wrings the nerve and muscle of a man, and then a heroism is vouchsafed to him, such that he can afford to have it continued, there is awakened in him a manhood which is transcendently higher than that which would be awakened if the trouble were removed in answer to his prayer.

And this is the promise of the Savior to the apostle, and, by analogy, to every one that bears trouble: either that it shall be removed, or that grace shall be given with which to bear it. God says, "My grace shall be sufficient for you. Take trouble and bear it, and I will sustain you under it."

FEBRUARY 23: EVENING.

And Jacob said unto Pharaoh, The days of the years of my pilgrimage are a hundred and thirty years; few and evil have the days of the years of my life been, and have not attained unto the days of the years of the life of my fathers in the days of their pilgrimage.—*Genesis* xlvii., 9.

Let me say a word of comfort to those whose way of life is becoming very hard because they are coming into the infirmities of age. You step three times to make the same space that you used to make with two strides. You multiply your supports, and then walk tottering. You have laid bare your head like the frostbitten field in autumn. You carry white furrows upon your brows. When you think of youth at all, you must needs remember, "I have had all the heyday of youth, and I never can call it back again; I have had the prime years of life, and those that are left must, in the nature of things, be with growing infirmities, with multiplying pains and circumscriptions. How sad it is.

Look forward. Hark! hark! I hear within the beating of this heart another heart. The faint pulsations of this mortal current carry within them, as it were, that other pulsation, that never, never shall be faint nor cease. For as long as my God lives, I shall live; and as long as he garners and holds the spirits of the just, and of the noble, and the true in heaven, I shall be among them. The sun shall go out, and the stars shall forget to shine, and the seasons cease upon the earth, and all things shall be whelmed in universal ruin; but "the ransomed of the Lord shall return and come to Zion with songs and everlasting joy upon their heads." That land is not far away, and you all are coming nearer to it. You *have* come to it—to its precincts and its heralds. You have come within sight of it and within sound of it.

Swift to its close ebbs out life's little day;
Earth's joys grow dim, its glories pass away;
Change and decay on all around I see;
O thou who changest not, abide with me.

Hold thou thy cross before my closing eyes;
Shine through the gloom, and point me to the skies;
Heaven's morning breaks, and earth's vain shadows flee;
In life, in death, O Lord, abide with me.

FEBRUARY 24: MORNING.

Hereby perceive we the love of God, because he laid down his life for us: and we ought to lay down our lives for the brethren.—1 *John* iii., 16.

WHY should any man suppose himself to be too good to do what Christ did. He did not feel that he was misspending his life when he carried his power in subservience for the benefit of mankind. It is declared of him, "He went about doing good."

To do good was the habit of his life. All the power that was in his soul, all the outgushing of his spirit, was not for himself. He said, "I seek not my own will:" "my meat is to do the will of him that sent me." As bread, and meat, and nourishing fluids re-supply the waste of muscle and bone in a man's body, and fill up the measure of his physical strength, so doing the will of God toward God and toward man filled up the measure of Christ's inward strength, and re-supplied the waste of his life. It was his joy and his blessedness to carry himself as he did. Because he was a better thinker than others, he did not arrogate to himself authority over them. Because he had a deeper heart than others, he did not separate himself from them. Because he had in him all the stores of science, and philosophy, and spiritual insight, he did not call men vulgar, and proudly shun them. He continually laid down his life before he died for men. He was the *Way*, literally, and men seemed to walk on him. He put his life, as it were, under their feet, and carried them. Now, why should we think it hard to do that which Christ cheerfully and gladly did for us? Shall the disciple be greater than his master, and the servant greater than his lord?

FEBRUARY 24: *EVENING.*

After this I looked, and behold, a door was opened in heaven.—*Rev.* iv., 1.

Blessed be his name, Christ is the Door of death. You know that gate which is spoken of in the Apocalypse—that gate more resplendent than ever cunning wit carved among men—the gate of pearl—one great pearl. It is called the gate of heaven, because it is the gate of death. And yet men go wandering on the road, and wondering what the experience may be, and what the gate of issuing is. The opening of the pearly gate—that is dying. Going out into life—that is dying. Finding Christ, and being found of him in the moment when, the body dropping its veil from before the eye, and the spiritual sense opening, we can take hold of the great realities, and the only realities above us—that is dying. Christ is the Door out of life. As he has been the Door of faith and love in life, so he is the Door of exit. The coming of the Son of Man for his own is death. When men are death-struck, they are death-called; and when men are death-called, they are God-called; and when they are God-called, they are Christ-found. As we have had Christ in life, we are to have him in dying. Through him we shall die valiantly. He is the Door to men. He is the blessed Door of reception; and he shall stand for all those that have put their faith in him, for all those that have trusted him, in that great invisible world, when, utter strangers, we shall find ourselves well known—nay, shall know even as we are known. There we shall find ourselves; there we shall find our children; there we shall find our most honored companions; there we shall find our best love; there we shall find our soul's life; there, with God, we shall rest from temptation, from unmanly defection; and our every aspiration shall be fulfilled, and our joy shall be completed in over-measure forever and ever.

Thou art the Way; by thee alone
  From sin and death we flee;
And he who would the Father seek,
  Must seek him, Lord, by thee.

Thou art the Life; the rending tomb
  Proclaims thy conquering arm;
And those who put their trust in thee,
  Nor death nor hell shall harm.

FEBRUARY 25: *MORNING.*

Seek that ye may excel to the edifying of the Church.—1 *Cor.* xiv., 12.

MEN are too ambitious, it is said. No; they are not ambitious enough. They are ambitious in wrong ways, and proud of the wrong things. If a man takes his ambition from divine conceptions, he can not have too much of it; and if a man's pride is divinely filled, it can never be too strong or too high. If it be God, truth, justice, love, purity, fidelity; if it be all the things which go to make soul-riches, that a man is ambitious for, and that he is proud over, then the more pride and ambition he has the better. But the trouble is that men are ambitious and proud with reference to foolish things. It is because men have such a mean pride, that pride is mean in history and in literature. If men were proud of things high and noble, then pride would be redemptive; but as it is, men are proud of things that appeal to the passions, and that lead to selfishness, and sordidness, and cruelty. And our ambition is low. Men ought to be made saints by their ambition, whereas, in point of fact, its tendency, in the main, is to make them any thing but saints.

FEBRUARY 25: EVENING.

Weeping may endure for a night, but joy cometh in the morning.—*Psalm* xxx., 5.

Trouble comes to us all, not to make us sad, but to make us sober; not to make us sorry, but to make us wise; not to make us despondent, but by its darkness to refresh us, as the night refreshes the day; not to impoverish us, but to enrich us, as the plow enriches the field—to multiply our joy, as the seed is multiplied a hundred-fold by planting. Our conception of life is not divine, and our thought of garden-making is not inspired. Our earthly flowers are quickly planted, and they quickly bloom, and then they are gone; while God would plant those flowers which, by transplantation, shall live forever.

Nay, ask not back your blossoms,
To the palm-tree said the Nile;
Let me keep them, said the river,
With its sweet and sunny smile.

And the palm gave up its blossoms
To its friend so wise and old,
And saw them all, unsighing,
Float down the river's gold.

The amber-tresses vanished,
And the dear spring-fragrance fled;
But the welcome fruit in clusters
Came richly up instead.

'Tis thus we gain by losing,
And win by failure here;
We doff the gleaming tinsel
The golden crown to wear.

Then let the blossoms perish,
And let the fragrance go;
All the surer and the larger
Is the harvest we shall know.

All the sweeter and the louder
Our song of harvest-home,
When earth's ripe autumn smileth,
And the reaping-day has come.

FEBRUARY 26: MORNING.

But by the grace of God I am what I am: and his grace which was bestowed upon me was not in vain; but I labored more abundantly than they all; yet not I, but the grace of God which was with me.—1 *Cor.* xv., 10.

A GREAT many persons try to serve God softly. The devil puts excuses into their mouths like these: "I ought not to meddle with sacred things. I ought not to put on airs in religion, or give people reason to suppose that I do." And under these guises they do but little, and very soon wither, and go back to their old state. Now, no matter how wicked you have been, make haste to redeem the hours that God gives you, when you are converted, wherewith to serve him with energy and faithfulness. Have you been a swearing man? Your lips must not be dumb now in the praise of God, whom you have been blaspheming all your life. Have you, in all the ports of the world, known all iniquity? Then, wherever you go now, you are, to be sure, to "eschew evil;" but are you not going to be a witness for good? Ten thousand men have known you to be a wicked man; and is there to be no signal by which they shall know that you have abandoned sin and left the dominion of Satan? It is bad enough for a man to hang out a piratical flag; but when he has heartily repented, and come back to allegiance, and is engaged in lawful commerce, shall he be ashamed to hoist the flag of his own country and carry it? And are you ashamed of the colors of him who is your salvation? Are you ashamed to speak for Christ—to wrestle with men, and plead with them in his behalf? Ought you not, in all places and in all company, freely, boldly, and manfully to say, "Christ is my Master? Once the devil was, and all men know it: now Christ is, and I mean that all men shall know it, by the grace of God."

FEBRUARY 26: EVENING.

While we look not at the things which are seen, but at the things which are not seen: for the things which are seen are temporal, but the things which are not seen are eternal.—2 *Cor.* iv., 18.

YOU do not know what is in an organ till the stops are drawn. Nobody knows what he is till love draws some stops, till infancy draws other stops, and till trials draw still other stops of his being. Many men never know what are the depths of their nature till their children reveal them. Idolaters that worship at the altar of the cradle, when they find that the sweet singer and prattler of the evening has gone from them for evermore, stand, at first, stunned and amazed. And as, with rest, reason comes back, and realization of their loss; and as, day in and day out, no little one clambers at the knee, or frolics about the room, or makes music with its voice, they say, "All I have—all my industry; all my wealth; my name; my place—would I give if God would but return to me my child." And what is that but saying that the whole world, being measured in the scale of love, even from a greater to a lesser nature, shrinks and becomes insignificant? When you have a realization of what parental affection is, you feel that there is more in the heart-beat of one little child than in all the pulsations of business throughout the world. In such hours we realize that those things which we have regarded as most visionary are really substantial, and those which we have regarded as really substantial are in truth visionary.

FEBRUARY 27: MORNING.

And account that the long-suffering of our Lord is salvation; even as our beloved brother Paul also according to the wisdom given unto him hath written unto you.—2 *Peter* iii., 15.

A GREAT many persons are perpetually despondent because they feel that they are so unworthy before God. They have a vague sense of being very sinful, of being weak, of being worthless, of being powerful to do wrong, and feeble to do right. Such persons need the assurance that God takes us up, and looks upon us with tenderness, and undertakes to nourish us, and train us, and educate us here with reference to the whole of that which we are to be when we stand on Zion and before God.

In our earthly education we are like a painter's canvas. The artist has an inspiration to-day, and begins to lay in the picture. The canvas is blurred to every body's eyes but his own;

he knows what he means to bring out. On the second and third days there is not much apparent advancement in the picture to the superficial observer, but the painter knows that he is working it up to his own interior idea. And by-and-by, when the picture is perfected, it represents that which he saw from the very beginning.

And where we are spoken of as being presented before the throne without spot or wrinkle, I think I see the trace of the same thing. God is, in this life, training us, educating us. He bears with us, and loves us, and cherishes us. Rude and unlovely as we are, God is producing in us the divine likeness. He is painting on, and is bringing us nearer and nearer to that likeness; and by-and-by, when we are perfected, and we lift up our glorified face before the throne and admiring angels, we shall stand representing that which he saw from the very beginning. Our imperfections God does not love, our sin he does not love, our rudeness he does not love; but he waits patiently for the time when we shall have advanced beyond these, and become that which he is making of us.

FEBRUARY 27: EVENING.

And there was Mary Magdalene, and the other Mary, sitting over against the sepulchre.—*Matt.* xxvii., 61.

How strangely stupid is grief. It neither learns nor knows, nor wishes to learn or know. When the sorrowing sisters sat over against the door of Christ's sepulchre, did they see the two thousand years that have passed triumphing away? Did they see any thing but this: "Our Christ is gone." Your Christ and my Christ came from their loss; myriad mourning hearts have had resurrection in the midst of *their* grief; and yet the sorrowing watchers looked at the seed-form of this result, and saw nothing. What they regarded as the end of life was the very preparation for coronation; for Christ was silent that he might live again in tenfold power. They saw it not. They mourned, and wept, and went away, and came again, drawn by their hearts to the sepulchre. Still it was a sepulchre, unprophetic, voiceless, lustreless.

So with us. Every man sits over against the sepulchre in his garden, in the first instance, and says, "This woe is irremediable. I see no benefit in it. I will take no comfort from it." And yet, right in our deepest and worst mishaps, often and often our Christ is lying, waiting for resurrection. Where our death seems to be, there our Savior is. Where the end of hope is, there is the brightest beginning of fruition. Where the darkness is thickest, there the bright beaming light that never is to set is about to emerge.

When the whole experience is consummated, then we find that a garden is not disfigured by a sepulchre. Our joys are made better if there be a sorrow in the midst of them, and our sorrows are made bright by the joys that God has planted around about them. The flowers may not be pleasing to us, they may not be such as we are fond of plucking, but they are heart-flowers. Love, hope, faith, joy, peace—these are flowers which are planted around about every grave that is sunk in a Christian heart. For the present it is not "joyous, but grievous; nevertheless, afterward it yieldeth the peaceable fruit of righteousness."

'Twas by a path of sorrows drear
  Christ entered into rest;
And shall I look for roses here,
  Or think that earth is bless'd?
    Heaven's whitest lilies blow
    From earth's sharp crown of woe:
Who here his cross can meekly bear,
Shall wear the kingly purple there.

And yet, dear Lord, this shrinking heart
  Still trembles as of yore;
Come, Cross beloved, nor e'er depart
  Till I have learned thy lore!
    Here, scorned with him I love,
    Here, crowned with him above;
Here to the cross with Jesus pressed,
There comforted with him, and bless'd.

FEBRUARY 28: *MORNING.*

Then when lust hath conceived, it bringeth forth sin; and sin, when it is finished, bringeth forth death.—*James* i., 15.

How great is the terribleness of wickedness. How it eats like a canker. How it corrupts the manliness of man. How it blinds eyes that otherwise would see. How it deafens men's ears to the truth which otherwise they would hear. How it imperils a man in his very fibre; in the very elements of his manhood. Is there any joy that goes with wickedness which can compensate for these terrible damages which it inflicts upon men? Is there any thing in this life, any thing in the life to come, that can be a compensation for that sure condemnation which shall overtake monstrous wickedness? It is a terrible thing to be a sinner. It is a terrible thing to be a sinner in a man's passions and appetites. It is a terrible thing to have been confederated in sin, and to have been webbed up in it, and to have been changed inwardly, until the light that was in the man has become darkness. God puts conscience in a man as a kind of signal, guiding light, by which he may keep in right courses; but when that light is darkness, how great is that darkness! It is a terrible thing to be a sinner, in all its moods, in all its degrees. The least sin is a yeast and leaven of condemnation; and how much more these mighty sins, these ocean-like sins, of vast, unfathomable capacities.

FEBRUARY 28: *EVENING.*

Lo, the winter is past, the rain is over and gone; the flowers appear on the earth; the time of the singing of birds is come, and the voice of the turtle is heard in our land; the fig-tree putteth forth her green figs, and the vines with the tender grape give a good smell. Arise, my love, my fair one, and come away.—*Solomon's Song* ii., 11–13.

Scripture has no passages that are mere ornaments. Unlike all other literature, Scripture never merely decorates. If there is a figure, it is always for some errand of moral meaning. There is no poetry for mere æsthetical pleasure. There is always profit withal.

Nature, then, teaches that to every season of trouble and overthrow there comes resurrection. In the deepest January of the year there is a nerve that runs forward to June. Life is never extinguished. That which seems to be death reaches forward and touches that which is vital.

The year breaks cloudily, with many slips and many retrocessions. To-day open, to-morrow shut. Birds too early tempted are driven away by bleak winds. And yet spring, once come upon the earth, is never banished again until it has reaped a victory. All checks, and haltings, and struggles, and storms can not alter the inevitable year. So is it in human affairs. There are cold and dark December days. But be patient; they too have a June waiting for them.

It is hard to go down into the winter of trouble. It is hard to find one's self beset with all the difficulties that oftentimes attend the household. But when a family has through trouble and affliction found the way to God; when through trials and sufferings a family has come to the knowledge of an ever-present Savior, who is afflicted in all our afflictions, who bears our sins, and who carries our sorrows, to that family, though it be in its darkest January days, has come the time of the singing of birds. It is not so much matter that you should be lifted out of your want, as that you should have peace and joy in the Holy Ghost.

FEBRUARY 29: *MORNING.*

But lay up for yourselves treasures in heaven, where neither moth nor rust doth corrupt, and where thieves do not break through nor steal.—*Matt.* vi., 20.

No man can become bankrupt whose wealth consists, not in things of this world, but in moral qualities. A good candle will give light in a silver candlestick as well as in a golden one. And if you are rich and good, your riches may make your goodness more glorious; but if you were to become poor, your goodness would not be put out by your poverty. If a man has a noble nature, he can not lose it by being placed in adverse circumstances. The greatest men that were ever on earth walked with a clouted shoe and patched raiment. The best men that ever lived ground between their teeth the poorest wheat, the coarsest bread. Of the men that bless the world, you will find that there are more that live in hovels than there are that live in palaces. If a man is really great, that which makes him great is imperishable, no matter what his circumstances in life may be. Such men are not usually set around about with wealth; but if it pleased God that they should be, you may be sure of one thing—that when you brushed the wealth away, you would not take any of their greatness from them. On the contrary, if a man is righteous and godly, if a man's life consists in soul-treasure, no matter what may befall him, his nature can not be touched; it will ever shine on. If he is deprived of his worldly surroundings, it is all the more affecting and influential.

FEBRUARY 29: EVENING.

Out of the depths have I cried unto thee, O Lord.—*Psalm* cxxx., 1.

THERE are emergencies of religious experience in which the soul can do nothing but simply abandon itself, and lay hold on God. I suppose that every person who has a work of grace that is deeply rooted in him remembers hours and days in which there was nothing that his soul could rest upon. There is just this one thing: helplessness the most utter hanging upon the neck of strength the most august; a sense of the most profound unworthiness standing before the most profound worth, and purity, and excellence. As the stars that rise in the morning over against the light never rise so brightly nor last so long as the stars of the evening that rise from darkness, and that grow bright by darkness, so out of our spiritual experiences, though there rise up bright conceptions of God, there are none that compare for one single moment with those thoughts of God when the soul feels prostrate in the dust with its own sinfulness. There is majesty in the thought of mercy, and wonder in the graciousness of God, when we feel that we are sinful. In these wonderful hours, when, touched of the Divine finger, we are pervaded with a sense of our unworthiness, there is but one thing for us to do, to hope in Jesus Christ, and hope simply, or else despair. Not that you understand how he atones and pardons; not that you can see what is the relation of Christ to you. There is no philosophy about it; there is nothing but this simple instinct of hope; we clasp, we hold on to Christ, and say, "Thou art my anchor; thou art my safeguard and my surety." It is a feeling, not a thought.

Trembling before thine awful throne,
O Lord! in dust my sins I own:
Justice and Mercy for my life
Contend!—oh smile, and heal the strife!

The Savior smiles! Upon my soul
New tides of hope tumultuous roll;
His voice proclaims my pardon found,
Seraphic transport wings the sound!

Earth has a joy unknown in heaven—
The new-born peace of sin forgiven!
Tears of such pure and deep delight,
Ye angels! never dimmed your sight.

MARCH 1: *MORNING.*

The integrity of the upright shall guide them.—*Prov.* xi., 3.

Some persons are said to stand in their own light. Are there not some of you who have *apparently* stood in your own light? Are there not men whom you have known from their youth up, who were not over-scrupulous in business affairs, who became millionaires, and rose to eminence and power, and now stand high and are prospered? And do you say, "If I could have got over some prejudices that I had, so as not to have been so afraid of departing a little from the line of rectitude, I might have been better off than I am now; but I stood in my own light in my youth, and have been struggling against the current ever since?" But have you not maintained your conscience, your love of truth, your aspirations after a higher and better life? "Yes, I have those still. But then I have no funds, I have no homestead; I have nothing before me." Nothing before you! You have the kingdom of God Almighty before you. You have all glory before you. If you have saved truth, and conscience, and love, and faith, do not envy any body. The wealth of the world will pass away very soon, but what bankruptcy can come over the exchequer of God? And you are heirs of God. You did not stand in your own light when you refused to yield to temptation.

MARCH 1: *EVENING.*

He that loseth his life for my sake shall find it.—*Matt.* x., 39.

Are you sorrowing in family matters? Are you conscious that you are bound with bonds and cords from which you could only release yourself by rending what are called the decencies and proprieties of life? Are you bearing the yoke, and suffering for a parent, a brother, a sister, an orphan, some helpless or dependent one? You who are yielding your opportunities, and joys, and life for another, patiently, are carrying the cross of Christ. Yes, and it is Christ in you that is inspiring you to do that, and saying to you, "Child, a little while longer lose your life. Do not be afraid to be lavish of it. Pour it out. Do not be economical. Lose it, lose it, and you shall save it unto life eternal."

Who are they that I see triumphing in the heavenly host? They that lived in ceiled houses? They that walked the earth with crowns upon their heads? They that knew no sorrow? No. "These are they which came out of great tribulation, and have washed their robes and made them white in the blood of the Lamb;" they that cried from under the altar, "How long, O Lord, how long?"—these are they that stand highest in the kingdom of God. Heaven is just before you. And you that seem to have a long and weary path of suffering will soon be done with your period of trial, and will rise to honor and glory in Christ Jesus.

'Tis but a *little* while—the way is dreary,
  The night is dark, but we are nearing land;
Oh for the rest of heaven, for we are weary,
  And long to mingle with the deathless band!

A little while, and we shall dwell forever
  Within our bright, our everlasting home;
Where time, or space, or death no more can sever
  Our grief-wrung hearts, and pain can never come.

MARCH 2: MORNING.

Let thy saints rejoice in goodness.—2 *Chron.* vi., 41.

I RECOLLECT, when I was young, hearing a great many exhortations to men who were not Christians, on the ground that if they became such they would be exceedingly happy; and I remember distinctly my impression that a Christian was always happy; that only Christians were happy; and that if I became a Christian I should know it, just as I know when I go out of darkness into light, or out of shadow into sunshine. I thought there would be a palpable and distinct change of sensation, and that, so long as I remained faithful as a Christian, I should experience uninterrupted and transcendent joy.

It is true that the Word of God declares joy to be one of the *fruits of the Spirit.* Peace and joy in the Holy Ghost are a part of the kingdom of God in us. And yet I think that if any man sets out to find joy it will be fictitious. It certainly will not be that joy which the Word of God contemplates, and which is unconscious; which comes, as it were, unawares; which comes, not in the form of exhilaration and ecstasy, but in those milder forms which constitute satisfaction rather than intense pleasure.

The effect of the whole of religious living is to produce joyfulness. If, however, you single that out, and hold it up as the special thing after which you seek, you will come short of it, or you will only get a spurious kind of joy; but if you make it your highest end and aim to live for the glory of God and for the welfare of men, and seek your own soul's highest manhood in seeking these things, you will be happy.

MARCH 2: EVENING.

The wise shall inherit glory.—*Prov.* iii., 35.

I ESTEEM it to be one of the blessings of revelation that it does not make known to us a vast, cold, fixed, immovable heaven; that it presents to us a heaven which draws near to us in those aspects which we particularly need. If we are overtasked, heaven comes to us as a place of rest. If we are impatient of our narrow, circumscribed spheres of labor, heaven comes to us as a sphere of unbounded opportunity. If our circumstances are such that we have no resources for pleasure, heaven comes to us as a land of true delight. If we are tired of this world as the abode of imperfect human nature, heaven draws near and presents itself to us as the home of just men made perfect. If we find all human creatures to be weak and fallible, heaven reveals to us God and all the glory of the Godhead. Whatever our want may be, whether of joy, or sorrow, or hope, or aspiration, over against that want heaven bends down, and is easily moulded by our imagination. Heaven is made up of divine and glorious qualities.

MARCH 3: MORNING.

The Lord descended in the cloud and stood with him here, and proclaimed the name of the Lord. And the Lord passed by before him, and proclaimed, The Lord, the Lord God, merciful and gracious, long-suffering, and abundant in goodness and truth, keeping mercy for thousands, forgiving iniquity, and transgression, and sin, and that will by no means clear the guilty; visiting the iniquity of the fathers upon the children, and upon the children's children unto the third and to the fourth generation. And Moses made haste, and bowed his head toward the earth, and worshiped.—*Exod.* xxxiv., 5-8.

GLORIOUS as this passage begins, it comes forth in the end, I think, with undiminished glory; and all the grandeur of that which is merciful and lovely in God is equaled by the grandeur of that indignation with which he looks upon things that are unmerciful and unlovely. There is a necessary repugnance in real goodness to all that is not good.

The judicial forms which the declarations on this point take in the Bible flow naturally from the moral qualities of things. When it is said in the New Testament that God is a consuming fire, I feel that it is not inconsistent with this declaration to couple with it those declarations in which God is represented as having all the gentleness of a kind nurse, and all the tenderness of a loving mother. These two traits, as applied to the divine character, to me seem perfectly accordant.

You feel that there is nothing sweeter than the love and tenderness which a mother manifests toward her infant. It is sweeter to her than the perfume of the choicest flowers can be to any one; and yet, touch that child with harm, touch that child with injury, and see how, in a moment, that which was summer in the mother's heart before is now changed to fierce storms. And you are glad of it. God meant that it should be so, for the child's defense. See how benign and beauteous is Justice when unobstructed and uninterrupted; but see how grand Justice becomes when it hews its path if blocked up.

MARCH 3: EVENING.

O Lord, how long shall I cry, and thou wilt not hear! even cry out unto thee of violence, and thou wilt not save!—*Hab.* i., 2.

How long must men suffer? Just as long as God sees that

as scholars they need to suffer. The period of their suffering is measured by their need. If a little does all that is necessary to be done, then that little is enough, and if not, then more is required. And if much and continuous suffering for a whole lifetime is needful, then a whole life of suffering is only just enough. For do you forget that this whole life, compared to the life to come, is not so big as the little village school-house where you learned your letters is, compared to the great globe itself? And what matters it if we suffer much and long here? Your manhood, your future existence, your immortality—these are of far more value than the sensations of your earthly state.

God be thanked that this law of suffering is applied to us by an infinitely wiser rule than we could administer or conceive if it were explained to us. God administers suffering, saying to every one of us, "When you have suffered a while." "How long, Lord? O Lord, how long?"—to that no answer ever came. As long as it is necessary, and, as a general rule, as long as suffering is irksome, and you say, "I can not bear it," so long you need it. When you have had suffering till you can say, "If it please God I can carry it all my life," then, if ever, God can release you from it.

O thou! so weary of thy self-denials,
 And so impatient of thy little cross,
Is it so hard to bear thy daily trials,
 To count all earthly things a gainful loss?

What if thou *always* suffer tribulation,
 And if thy Christian warfare never cease,
The gaining of the quiet habitation
 Shall gather thee to everlasting peace.

MARCH 4: *MORNING.*

Which of you by taking thought can add one cubit unto his stature.—*Matt.* vi., 27.

WHY take anxious thought for the things of to-morrow? Suppose you think ever so much, will it make your case any better? Can you change to-morrow? Can you render inoperative the law of cause and effect? Can you by solicitous forelooking throw light into the shadow? Can you dissipate the lurking, or the supposed lurking evils by a consideration of them? It is an impossible thing.

You are master of yourself to-day; but God gives you supremacy for only one day at a time. To-morrow is not your kingdom. Of to-morrow you have no sceptre till to-morrow is to-day. No man owns any thing until it has been converted into to-day. As fast as time is ours it is brought to us, and then we administer over it. I never saw a man that could not get through a single day. That is a space that almost any body can stride over. Almost every body says, "I could get through to-day if I had reason to believe that to-morrow—" Oh! to-morrow does not exist to you. If you can bear your burden to-day, if you can carry your cross to-day, if you can endure your pain to-day, if you can suffer the shame of to-day, if you can put down the fear of to-day, if you can find philosophy of contentment to-day, you will get along well enough. Take what comes to you to-day.

MARCH 4: EVENING.

And he humbled thee, and suffered thee to hunger, and fed thee with manna, which thou knewest not, neither did thy fathers know; that he might make thee know that man doth not live by bread only, but by every word that proceedeth out of the mouth of the Lord doth man live.—*Deut.* viii., 3.

Trouble takes off the varnish that overlays the raw material of things, and lets us see them just as they are. It recalls us from idols, from vain plans, from sins, and from backslidings. Assaulted, as we constantly are, by the temptations of the world, we are often unconsciously drawn, little by little, away from God, until at last some trouble comes upon us, and opens our eyes to our true condition. God, by trouble, brings us to repentance; and repentance opens the closed gate, and gives us all the sweetness of a garden of fruits and flowers. Blessed are they that know how to find heaven without leaving the earth. Blessed are they the door of whose closet, when they shut it, shuts out the world. And where men, by business or pleasure, or any worldly attraction, have been led to abandon the closet, blessed are they if they bethink themselves and seek God again in that secret place, and again feel as if they were in the garden of Paradise, where rare and beautiful vines are lifted up, and sweet flowers exhale delightful fragrance around. One can afford to bear all the troubles and afflictions that are put upon us in this world if by them he is taught how to pray and commune with his God.

MARCH 5: *MORNING.*

For your heavenly Father knoweth that ye have need of all these things.— *Matt.* vi., 32.

THAT sentence hangs in the heavens like a bell, to me; and every time I take hold of it, it is like a sexton's taking hold of the old church-bell. If I pull it, it rings; and I hear it every time—"Your heavenly Father knoweth that ye have need of all these things." Nobody else knows as God knows. He knows hundreds of things that nobody else can know. He knows many things that nobody else ought to know. He knows many experiences that you will not tell, and many that you do not understand. Naked and open are you before him with whom you have to do. There is no sorrow so deep, there is no darkness so profound, there is no complication of circumstances so entangling, but that you may say, "There is nothing that affects me which my heavenly Father does not know."

MARCH 5: *EVENING.*

If any man offend not in word, the same is a perfect man, and able also to bridle the whole body.—*James* iii., 2.

THERE are a great many persons who examine themselves for motives—which is right; but how many persons examine themselves in the matter of speech? Do you know what your habits are about talking? Do you talk a great deal too much? Do you say a great many things heedlessly? Do you indulge a great deal in outswelling words of pride? Are your words like sparks of fire, or are they like drops of oil? Do you make life sweet with your tongue wherever you go, or is your tongue like the tongue of a serpent, carrying terror whenever your mouth opens and it comes forth? How often do you think of your speech? Do you know any thing about it? I venture to say that every person in your neighborhood knows more about it than you do. The exaggerations, the overcolorings, the misrepresentations, the lies which escape us when we are speaking about ourselves, about our children, about our families, about our property, about our neighbors, about every thing that we have to do with—what must be their influence upon the world? Still, how few there are that know any thing about the use of their tongue. "Who is a wise man and endued with knowledge among you? Let him show out of a good conversation his works with meekness of wisdom."

MARCH 6: *MORNING.*

For I reckon that the sufferings of this present time are not worthy to be compared with the glory which shall be revealed in us.—*Romans* viii., 18.

Dr. Payson said, when he lay dying, "If Christians could only understand the glory that there is in being children of God, I think they would go about the streets shouting, 'I am a child of God! I am a child of God!'" And I think that if the glory that awaits you in the future; if the love that is treasured up for you in heaven; if all the companionship that there longs for your coming, that it may be more joyful than now—I think that if these things could be revealed to you, if the rind of this world could be stripped off, and you could see the blessedness of the fruit of a hope in Christ Jesus, you would, in the midst of tears, and bereavements, and heart-achings, and yokes, and burdens, and pressures, and spear-points, and sword-thrusts, and sharp nettlings, and the piercing of thorns, say, "I am a Christian; I am a child of God; and I count these things as nothing, that I may win the glory that awaits me beyond this world."

Be of good cheer. The time of your tarrying here below is short. "In the world ye shall have tribulation; but be of good cheer: I have overcome the world."

Time's glory fades; its beauty now
  Has ceased to lure or blind:
Each gay enchantment here below
  Has lost its power to bind.

Then welcome toil, and care, and pains,
  And welcome sorrow too!
All toil is rest, all grief is gain,
  With such a prize in view.

Come, crown and throne ; come, robe and palm ;
 Burst forth, glad stream of peace ;
Come, holy city of the Lamb ;
 Rise, Sun of Righteousness.

MARCH 6: EVENING.

I have showed you all things, how that so laboring ye ought to support the weak, and to remember the words of the Lord Jesus, how he said, It is more blessed to give than to receive.—*Acts* xx., 35.

It is more blessed to do for others than to have others do for you. It is more blessed to bestow good upon others than to have others bestow good upon you. It is more blessed to teach than to be taught. The great law of happiness is the law of outgoing, and not the law of incoming.

But the world does not believe a word of it. Neither does the Church, for the most part. Although Christians, when under examination, indorse that text, they do not live it. The great operating principle in the world and throughout human society still is, that a man is to be happy in proportion as he gets and has. And so human life whirls round and round with its vortex, sucking in as much as possible. And human life is full of disappointment, full of echoes of sorrow and trouble. It is the few only that have accepted this philosophy of the Savior, and found out that men are to be happy in proportion as they are able to give from themselves to others.

MARCH 7: MORNING.

Hereby we know that he abideth in us, by the spirit which he hath given us.—1 *John* iii., 24.

When once we have attained a clear sense of God in his personality, the next higher development of the mind is to give it diffusion, so that the heavens begin to declare the glory of a God, and the earth to show his handiwork to us, and we see him in the morning and evening, in every season, in the tree, and grass, and brook, and rock, and flower, in the brute creation, and in all the developments of human society. Every where, and always, there is this sense of God universally present, until at last we come to that stage of blessed development in which we are no longer dependent upon times and seasons, or upon places of worship, as at the beginning we were. All days are Sunday, all hours are hours of worship, and all places are temples to us. But this is the later stage of development. As the result of culture and habit, and the use of spiritual influences, we come into a state in which, day and night, we are never without a sense of our Father's presence. We live under the same roof with him. He fulfills to us the promise, "I will come in and abide with you."

> Not a brief glance I beg, a passing word,
> But as thou dwell'st with thy disciples, Lord,
> Familiar, condescending, patient, free,
> Come, not to sojourn, but to abide with me.

MARCH 7: EVENING.

Now is our salvation nearer than when we believed.—*Romans* xiii., 11.

Christian brethren, we are advancing nearer and nearer, every year, to the consummation of our life-work. We are coming, every year, nearer and nearer to that final disclosure, when God shall reveal to us what we are. I have sometimes fancied what would be the cause of most surprise and joy in the other life. In some hours, when higher moral feelings predominate, it seems to me that the first thing that will fill the heart of men will be the vision of God—the vision of the Redeemer. In other hours, when craving affections are strongest, it seems to me that whatever may be the glory of the presence of God, the first things the heart will recognize will be its lost ones. At other times, when high and heroic purposes of life are in the ascendency, it seems to me that the sanctified spirits of the noble men that have dwelt upon the earth—the great assembly of the just made perfect—will first astonish and rejoice the heart. But I think, after all, that scarcely less than before God himself, we shall stand in utter surprise and wonder before ourselves when what we are is brought out; when what life has made us begins to be disclosed; when, standing in the divine presence, the soul seems, even in that comparison, so noble and so full of glory that it is able to say, "I am satisfied." The glory that is to be ours doth not yet appear, but there are glimpses of it.

MARCH 8: *MORNING.*

Behold that which I have seen: it is good and comely for one to eat and to drink, and to enjoy the good of all his labor that he taketh under the sun all the days of his life, which God giveth him; for it is his portion.—*Eccles.* v., 18.

YOU can commit a great many mistakes, but none greater than that of supposing that a man's life is to consist of the abundance of the things which he possesses. You may have wealth, you may have honor, you may have respect among men—but mark, these are the lower, the transient, the incidental things. They are what your clothes are as compared with your body, and what your body is compared with your soul. They are servile, instrumental things. But if you wish to live, you must have food. Every faculty in your moral nature requires food. Your yearnings and aspirations must be fed. And where, this side of Paradise, this side of the tree of life, this side of God Almighty, can you get the food which these faculties, and yearnings, and aspirations need? There, oh my soul! must thou come, or hunger on. Woe, *woe* is their lot whose whole life is unvaried hunger. Bread enough in my father's house, and to spare, and I perish with hunger!—that is the testimony of thrice ten thousand lives every day.

Christian brother, you have learned not to despise the world. You have learned that feeding the soul with God does not dispossess one of any of the things that it is desirable he should have, but enhances their value to him. It is your duty, therefore, to bear such a witness that those about you shall see that loving God, and feeding the soul at God, makes you, in all relations of life, more appetizing. It is your duty to show the world that the way to have pleasure is to take things by the highest, because that carries the whole scale with it. When you take things by the highest you take them in harmonies, and when you take them by the lowest you take them in monochords. He that eats the divine bread is capable of enjoying other things in the proportion in which he feeds on that bread. We are capable of enjoying the things of this world just in the proportion in which our higher appetite is satisfied. Bear that testimony to the world.

Now God be praised, and God alone!
  The Source of joy thou art;
Thy love no stint or bound hath known,
  But loves a happy heart,
And sends full many a bright-clear day
To cheer us on our mortal way,
  Bids many a cloud depart.

So grant me, then, in weal and woe,
  Joyful and true to be;
And when life's lamp is burning low,
  And death at hand I see,
Then let this joy pierce through its pain,
And turn my very death to gain
  Of endless joys with thee.

MARCH 8: EVENING.

Thou wilt show me the path of life: in thy presence is fullness of joy; at thy right hand there are pleasures for evermore.—*Psalm* xvi., 11.

When the tide has been coming in, I have often seen how it chafed and fretted, running into some narrow-mouthed bay, filling it, swirling round, and lapping up on the shores, till by-and-by, still flowing on, it filled the bay full, the tide had spent itself, there ran a smoothing ripple all over the surface, and the whole bay at last was at rest. So the soul, while yet it is being filled, is disturbed by ripples and eddies; but by-and-by, when it shall have been filled full of the power and presence of God, it will be satisfied, and will be perfectly at peace, and will be full of joy; and singing forever and forever shall be its sweet employment in heaven. Sorrow and sighing shall flee away, and the old dark, mourning world we shall remember as children in manhood remember the moment's shower of their youth that broke up their pleasure-party. All the sufferings that we have experienced while getting our education will, when we shall once have come to our perfect manhood in Christ Jesus, seem to us only as dreams. And the price that we shall have paid will seem as nothing, and less than nothing, in comparison with the exceeding glory of that which eye hath not seen, nor ear heard, nor the heart of man conceived.

You are nearer home than you think. A step more, and you shall rest; or, if far away, you are under a safe convoy. Press forward. Let nothing discourage you. Though your attainments may be small, and though your sins may be many, remember that you are Christ's, not because you are good, but because you are to be developed into goodness by him. Trust him; follow him; that by-and-by you may live with him.

MARCH 9: MORNING.

As thy days, so shall thy strength be.—*Deut.* xxxiii., 25.

"It is needless," says the Savior, "that you should be bearing troubles; that you should be worrying over long plans ahead; that you should be wearing yourselves out with cares; that you should be subjected to all the suffering of possible evils in days to come. The true scheme of life, the highest wisdom in living, the hope of immortality, ought to dispossess the low and beggarly way in which men live. No man should allow himself to live from day to day under all that accumulation of care and burden which the future foretokens; and especially all the evils and mischiefs which fear and the morbid conditions of the mind forebode. No man has a right to import all these into a single day.

Each single and particular day is marked out by the providence of God, so to speak, that it may cut off the past and all its mischiefs, and that it may intercept and prevent all the possible mischiefs of the future. The question is, Have you grace given you to-day to lift the burdens of to-day? Have you grace given you to-day to be content with the condition of to-day?

I do not mean to be understood as saying that we do not need to lay our plans far ahead. For forelooking is not burdensome. But to look forward or back in such a way as to bring unhappiness—that is disallowed. You have no right to do it. In each particular day you are to concentrate, and burden yourself with, only the troubles which belong to that day—that is, the troubles which spring from the circumstances of that day.

MARCH 9: EVENING.

To be spiritually minded is life and peace.—*Rom.* viii., 6.

Do you believe in the Holy Ghost? Do you believe that God's sun actually comes into contact with the lily, and pours it full, warms it, and changes it? Do you believe that the Holy Ghost shines down into the souls of men that open themselves to its influence? I do. I believe it is the intrinsic nature of God, shining into the soul that receives it, to bring to it light, and warmth, and hope, and cheer, and comfort unspeakable.

As it is the nature of some things to be bitter and the nature of other things to be sweet, so it is the nature of God's spirit to bring to souls that peace which is called one of the "fruits of the Spirit." As some persons, by their very presence, soothe, sweeten, and cheer you, and make you feel better and more hopeful, so God, by his indwelling, fills the soul with peace—that peace "which passeth all understanding;" not the peace of indolence, not a supine peace, but that peace which means the harmony of every faculty raised to the highest point of normal excitement. Perfect harmony—that is the peace which God brings to us when he comes into our souls. Oh, how full of hope and comfort is this view!

MARCH 10: *MORNING.*

Christ is become of no effect unto you, whosoever of you are justified by the law; ye are fallen from grace.—*Gal.* v., 4.

WHILE you are in bondage under the law, there is no faith in Christ. Christ is left with nothing to do except to help you to obey and reward you for obedience. But to you as sinners, and because you are sinners—weak, stumbling every day, and full of infirmities—he is left without an office. You can not, when under the bondage of conscience, come to him, because you are so sinful; but you are perpetually hoping to come to him when you are less sinful. You hope to break your chain, and then ask him for liberty; to get well, and then go to your physician!

Conscience is the salvation of morals. It is the every-day armor of practical life. But when it is pushed out of its place, and made to assume the place and office of the Lord Jesus Christ, I am indignant, and say, None but Jesus can heal the sinful soul. It is the blood of Christ that cleanses from sin; it is the love of Christ that gives us some peace even before we are cleansed; and the man who judges himself by the absolute law of right places himself beyond the reach of liberty—he is a bond slave.

MARCH 10: *EVENING.*

That I might know * * * the fellowship of his sufferings.—*Phil.* iii., 10.

I HAVE great sympathy with those that have been active and energetic, and that by age or sickness, or for some other reason, are laid aside from usefulness. It always seemed very piteous to me—that song which has gone out of fashion more than it ought to, of the knight who was in captivity in a tower, and saw his own brethren sweeping past the castle, not knowing that he was there, and shouted out of the window to them, but all in vain. He saw them, with pomp, and banners, and glory, pass by him and go out of sight; and there he lay helpless in the castle. It epitomizes many a stalwart man that has been active and great in his sphere, but that is now removed from that sphere, and is obliged to stand still and see the great procession of the world thunder past him, he himself neither being called for, nor missed, nor heard, nor felt. And there is a strong natural temptation, under such circumstances, for a man to give way to sourness and complaining, or to say, "I have nothing more to do in this world." Nevertheless, if a man maintains himself with sweet-mindedness and serenity; if he leans his head back on the bosom of God's providence, and says, "If this is the service that God wants of me—to be large-minded, rich-thoughted, and pure-hearted in this position, and to be patient, and to wait—then this is what I want to be and want to do," he manifests a higher type of character than he would if he with power wrought out great results in things that were easy and natural to him. And you may be sure, when God raises up such a character, that he also points spectators to it as a witness, and that there is some one that sees it or feels it.

All things, O Lord, I yield
  But one—to work for thee;
To that my craving spirit clings—
  The only life for me.

Master, this sloth for me is death;
  And yet thou chain'st my hands.
Leave me not thus to waste my breath;
  Loose thou—oh loose my bands!

May I not take thy bread of life,
  And give to souls that need?
Thou know'st I love both thee and thine—
  Thy lambs may I not feed?

"Son—heir of all things—trust!
  My son, thou'rt wearied—rest!
While waiting, grow thou rich in grace."
  Yes, Lord; thou knowest best.

MARCH 11: *MORNING.*

He that overcometh, the same shall be clothed in white raiment; and I will not blot out his name out of the Book of Life, but I will confess his name before my Father and before his angels.—*Rev.* iii., 5.

If I were to summon from the abodes of the blessed those who, being your witnesses, sympathize with you in your troubles, they would say, "We stood hesitating and doubting, as you stand hesitating and doubting, but, inspired by the divine Spirit, we sprang forward to our labor, and overcame all obstacles; and as we, by the grace of God, overcame, so shall you overcome if you have faith and patience, hope and trust." There is not one evil in life which can stand the aggressive spirit of a heart that is touched with divine love. He who calls God his father, heaven his home, all pure and noble intelligences his companions, this world a wilderness, and himself a pilgrim seeking his Father's house, can not be stopped by any fear of shipwreck or disaster from prosecuting his journey. Our Father's house awaits our coming. Its honors and dear delights are ours. And not one thing withstands us that we may not overcome. We are surrounded by God's providences, by his heavenly angels, by all the saints that have been perfected by earthly experience, so that there are more for us than there are against us.

Fret not, poor soul, while doubt and fear
    Disturb thy breast;
The pitying angels, who can see
How vain thy wild regret must be,
    Say, Trust and rest.

MARCH 11: *EVENING.*

The righteous hath hope in his death.—*Prov.* xiv., 32.

Long before winter would let me plant out of doors, I planted under glass, and depended upon artificial heat, and waited for the time when I might remove my early plants; and, as soon as I dared, I set them in the open air in some sheltered nook where the frost should not touch them. But now, in these June days, I have taken them into the broad, exposed garden, and put them where they are to stand and blossom, and they did not weep when I put them there.

Now God has raised us under glass, and nurtured us there, that we might bear transplanting into another and better sphere; and when he comes, and takes us, and plants us out in his open garden, is that the time for us to cry? Beloved, ye are the sons of God; and when the bell strikes, and the angel, hearing the sweet sound, flies swiftly to call you to your sonship and coronation, is that the time for tears? Beloved, it doth not yet appear what ye are to be; and yet are ye so pure, and noble, and true that men can not bear your going from them? And are you lost because all the fragmentary developments of your being are taken into that higher sphere where they are more, not less?

MARCH 12: *MORNING.*

The thief cometh not but for to steal, and to kill, and to destroy: I am come that they might have life, and that they might have it more abundantly.—*John* x., 10.

Are we set to teach God's truth to the young that it shall please them, or shall we take these divinest truths—truths of love, of victory, of hope, of faith, of manhood, of immortality and glory, of triumph over sorrow, and death, and the grave—and so teach them to our children that their prevailing impression respecting them is that, next to being damned, it is miserable to be a Christian? A great many feel that they would rather be born again than be lost forever; but that is all. What a testimony that is to our understanding of the spirit of the Bible—that singing book; that healthy book; that book which has not a morbid spot in it from beginning to end; that book which is full of choirs, full of angel voices, full of inspiration, full of nobleness and grandeur all the way through—what a testimony it is to our understanding of the spirit of that book that we make it a battle-field, whereon we tramp down flowers and harvests in our rude controversies sect with sect. There is a fountain of healing, they tell me, at Gettysburg. Blood-soaked it has been. There is many a Gettysburg where there are theological wounds and bitter tears. But there is also the healing fountain of the Word of God. And I say that it is a correlative duty to please men so as to instruct them, and to instruct men so as to please them, if possible. Not that you are always to avoid tasks, and yokes, and crosses; but the predominant tendency, the genius of inspiration, should be to make instruction pleasant—to make truth seem as pleasant to men as it really is.

For the love of God is broader
Than the measures of man's mind,
And the heart of the Eternal
Is most wonderfully kind.

But we make his love too narrow
By false limits of our own,
And we magnify his strictness
With a zeal he will not own.

MARCH 12: *EVENING.*

But God will redeem my soul from the power of the grave: for he shall receive me.—*Psalm* xlix., 15.

I ASK no other evidence of immortality than that which I have when I see how needful it is that I should be planted again, and have an opportunity to try life over under new circumstances. Oh! if this life were all that I could have, I should weep, it seems to me, from the present hour to the very end, unless I could say, as the ancients did, "Let us eat and drink, for to-morrow we die." I should be in a state of wanton, merry despair on the one side, or of tearful, sad despair on the other side. I must live again. I must make the experiment of life once more. I have made poor work here, but I have met with just success enough to feel that if I had a better chance I could do something. I am like a man that takes the first canvas to paint a picture. He does not know what he will do. He lays in forms in all sorts of ways without coming to any satisfactory result. At last he says, "I can not make any thing of that picture; but I have a conception. Bring me a fresh canvas, and

I will try again, when I think I shall have better success." I have long been trying to paint a true life, and have only partially succeeded; but if God Almighty will give me another canvas, I think I can paint better. And he will. He that brought forth from the dead our Lord and Savior Jesus Christ, will bring me forth.

MARCH 13: *MORNING.*

Lord, I believe; help thou mine unbelief.—*Mark* ix., 24.

It is the right of those who are not possessed of strong feelings of any kind to pray with simplicity, and without any such strength of expression as others have. Prayer, being the offering of your thoughts and feelings to God, should always have a relation to the nature that employs it. There is such a thing as growth in prayer. There is a provision in prayer of instruction from good to better. But the first quality of Christian liberty is the right of every man to lisp if he can not speak; to speak in broken numbers if he is not fluent; to pray in small circuits if he can not pray in large. There is no set form of Christian experience in prayer. One is to bring to his Father just that mind that has been given to him. And as some receive ten, and others only two talents, each may bring according to what he hath, and not according to what he hath not.

True prayer is communion; it is converse; it is a sacred intercourse between the heart of God and our hearts. And if we attempt to pray other men's prayers, unless they happen to fit our case, we shall be as bad off as David was in Saul's armor. He could not wear it. His sling was better for him than the king's whole armor.

I can not pray; yet, Lord, thou know'st
The pain it is to me,
To have my vainly struggling thoughts
Thus torn away from thee.

Yet thou art oft most present, Lord
In weak, distracted prayer;
A sinner out of heart with self
Most often finds thee there.

Prayer was not meant for luxury
Of selfish pastime sweet;
It is the prostrate creature's place
At his Creator's feet.

MARCH 13: *EVENING.*

For the Lord is good; his mercy is everlasting; and his truth endureth to all generations.—*Psalm* c., 5.

God's mercies are fresh with everlasting youth. The stars never wear out: they are just as good to-day as when Abraham saw them directing the Oriental people by night. The sun is not weary from the number of years: there are no wrinkles on its brow. The urns of God are replenished by outpouring, and they increase their fullness by that which they yield. And God's promises are of the nature of his laws. The heaven and earth shall pass away, but not one jot or tittle of God's word shall change or pass away. For thousands of years men have found his promises to be staffs on their journey; armor for defense; sword and spear for battle. Not one promise has ever been unfulfilled. Though these promises of God are almost without number, prodigal, luxuriant, they have never been broken, and the word of the Lord standeth sure to this hour. There is not a witness in God's universe to-day that can testify that he has leaned on a promise of God, and that God forgot to be gracious to him. Of all the martyrs, of all the heroes, of all the men that have suffered for moral principle in this world, not one shall ever be found that can stand before God and say, "Thou didst forget." There is no such faithfulness, there is no such promptness, there is no such punctuality any where else as there is in the bosom of the Almighty.

MARCH 14: *MORNING.*

Unto him that loved us and washed us from our sins in his own blood * * * to him be glory and dominion forever and ever. Amen.—*Rev.* i., 5, 6.

Our conception of Christ is such that we are perpetually in trepidation before him. We are afraid to go to him. We are afraid to confess our sins to him. We are afraid to trust his grace again. We think the stores of his patience are exhausted. We have not known, we have not considered the infinity that there is in love. If love in us is so strong, if love in us is so full of self-denial, and patience, and gentleness; if love in us carries summer through our winter, and the tropics through our whole life, is our name higher in that regard than the name of Christ? Have you pity? Find me pity that stands out among men remarkable, and I will place by the side of it the pity of Christ, and say, "Here is a name which is above every name in that." Show me mercy—that mercy which suffers rather than make suffering—and over against the most saintly and notable instance that you can find, I will lift up a name that is above every other name in that. Show me a love that longs to die rather than that another should die—yea, that is willing to live through tribulation and sorrow to do good to those that are beloved—and over against this rare and wondrous love I will lift up a name of love that is above every name—the name of Jesus, that rebukes our want of faith, and our want of an elevated conception in fashioning him to ourselves.

MARCH 14: *EVENING.*

Examine yourselves, whether ye be in the faith; prove your own selves. Know ye not your own selves, how that Jesus Christ is in you, except ye be reprobates?—2 *Cor.* xiii., 5.

Prayer and the reading of the Word of God are indispensable prerequisites of self-examination. Not because there is any charm about prayer, not because any mysterious influence steals out from this book, but because they bring men into commerce with those things which are necessary as the foundation on which to establish the knowledge of ourselves.

Another thing that is very important is the resolution that you will call things which you detect in yourself by their true English names. If a man tells that which is contrary to the truth, let him not say, "I equivocate:" let him say, "I *lie*." If a man has departed from rectitude in his dealings with another, let him not say, "I took advantage," which is a roundabout, long sentence: let him say, "I *cheated*." That is a very direct word. It springs straight to the conscience, as the arrow flies whizzing from the bow.

Again, it seems to me that we should not come with vain

self-confidence to this work of searching ourselves. We ought to feel that it is a most deceitful and difficult work. When we enter upon it, it is as if we were going upon quicksands, and we are liable to be swallowed up in vanity and ignorance. Let us evermore have a heart that lifts itself up before God, and says, as the ancient servant said, "Search thou me." In other words, come to a deliberate judgment of your own case, and then lift it up into God's presence, and say, "Lord, I have said this of myself."

And if you think this is a process that is hard, that is awful to go through with in this life, what will it be in the day of judgment, when the secrets of every heart shall be revealed and proclaimed abroad—when the light of God's clear-seeing eye shall illumine every part of your life, and you shall see yourself as you are? It is better to know now, and to correct, than to know then with hopeless condemnation.

May God help us all to desire to know ourselves, and then to examine and try our own hearts and our own lives.

MARCH 15: *MORNING.*

The kingdom of God cometh not with observation.—*Luke* xvii., 20.

God is building up a kingdom that is invisible; a kingdom that can not be discerned by the outward man; a spiritual kingdom of holy thoughts, of pure feelings, of faith, of hope, of righteousness. This kingdom advances little by little, some here and some there, all over the world. It is carried forward by a million different causes. God administers it himself, and he means that it shall be perfected. He is determined that the whole world shall be filled with his glory. This kingdom progresses very slowly. It meets with great opposition—so great that sometimes you can not tell whether it is going backward or forward. But God, who is building this great kingdom, sees that though, on account of its magnitude, it is advancing slowly, yet it is advancing surely. You can not build a great house so quickly as you can a small one, nor a city as quickly as you can a house. If God was going to build his kingdom in one family, he might do it quickly; but as he is to do it in all the families of every country, the work is so vast that it can not be done in a day, nor in a year, nor in rolling ages. It takes time to build things that are to be so well built and so glorious as God's kingdom will be when it is completed.

MARCH 15: *EVENING.*

He which soweth bountifully shall reap also bountifully.—2 *Cor.* ix., 6.

WE lay up treasure in heaven in the case of every one whom we send thither by our labors of love and Christian fidelity. A word of yours fitly spoken may have saved some soul. Your fidelity may have brought scores out of ignorance, and you will not fail to reap your reward. You may sow seed in the Sabbath-school, and your class may be scattered, and you may never hear their names again in this world, and, coming to old age yourself, and dying, they may be the very ones that shall greet you, and give you a choral entrance into the heavenly city. Of all the treasures laid up in heaven, none, perhaps, will fill us with more wondrous surprise than those treasures of consciences purified, hearts lifted up, and souls redeemed by our instrumentality.

MARCH 16: *MORNING.*

What doth hinder me to be baptized?—*Acts* viii., 36.

MY watch stops. Something is broken in it. I take it to the watch-maker, and he puts in a new mainspring. I do not know any thing about it except that he does it. And when it is repaired he lays it aside. Presently I go for my watch, and ask him if it is done. "Oh yes!" he says, "but I do not know as it is going;" and he takes it, and, finding that it does not go, he winds it up. And then it does not go, perhaps; but he gives it a little turning shake, and it commences ticking and keeping time.

I know many persons who have a mainspring in them, and have been wound up, for that matter, but who have not been shaken yet! And there they are. If somebody would only take them up, and whirl them round a few times, and say to them, "You are Christians; tick! *tick!*" they would commence keeping time, and go on keeping time. I have known persons that spent months and months not only making no progress, but losing ground, just for want of knowledge of the fact that the office of the Lord Jesus Christ was to take people *in order that they might be good;* and that it was his nature, after he had taken them, to be patient with them, and help them, and encourage them, and bring all the power of his being to bear upon them to save them.

MARCH 16: *EVENING.*

I thank thee, O Father, Lord of heaven and earth, because thou hast hid these things from the wise and prudent, and hast revealed them unto babes. —*Matt.* xi., 25.

WHAT are those things that men can not find out by their wisdom or their prudence, but that the simplicity of the child steers it into? What is it that men find only when they come to that condition in which they are obliged to act with the simple trust of a little child? "Come unto me, all ye that labor and are heavy laden, and I will give you rest."

Oh, it is God and rest in the soul. The whole world is on a race, and if you ask them, "What are you after?" they will tell you, "We are after satisfaction—soul-rest." Now watch them, and you will find that the strong ones and the wise ones are lagging in the rear, and that the weak ones, the little ones, and the ignorant ones—the children—are leading off the race. And when it comes to rest in the soul, babes find it quicker than their fathers.

MARCH 17: *MORNING.*

Thy testimonies are very sure; holiness becometh thine house, O Lord, forever.—*Psa.* xciii., 5.

THE promises of God's Word are often powerless because we are afraid to venture upon using them. There is many a man that would be afraid to trust himself upon a single plank stretched across a deep chasm, though others had walked over on it often without accident. There is many a promise of God that is strong enough to carry men across the abyss of this life, but they do not dare to try it. Many, like Peter, venture from the ship to walk to Christ, but give way to fear the moment their feet touch the water; and many do not dare even to leave the ship. Many men are so timid that, if they chanced to be on a wrecked vessel, where others are escaping to the shore by a line, though they saw one after another saved, they would stand shivering, and would not dare to attempt to follow for fear of the waves. In an emergency, the promises of God are to many men what weapons of defense are to a man who does not know how to use them when he finds that he must fight for his life. There is a sword, with which he might protect himself, but he says, "How shall I wield it?" There are many implements that he might employ, but he says, "My hand is unskilled in the use of them." There are many promises from which we might derive much benefit, but which do us no good because we are afraid to rely upon them.

MARCH 17: EVENING.

Wives, submit yourselves unto your own husbands, as it is fit in the Lord. Husbands, love your wives, and be not bitter against them.—*Col.* iii., 18, 19.

Are you living with each other, husbands and wives, in the truest spirit of love, and in the largest sense of wedding? Are you one? or are you forever and for evermore two? Are you living to help each other or to annoy each other? Are you living in the true excusatory spirit which always accompanies real conjugal love? Do you look upon each other, with all your faults and failings, as the heirs of God? In your hearts, made luminous by faith, do you see heaven blossoming in the face of your companions, and behold that which is to be, but which has not yet been disclosed from the rubbish of imperfect human experience? Do you find yourselves moved to patience, to gentleness, and to holy forbearance? Are you every day twining around each other like two honeysuckles? Do the blossoms of your love send fragrance through all the dwelling, and through every wedded day? Is there nothing to be done by you? Is there no change to be made in your life?

We talk about revivals in the Church. Oh for a revival that shall make husbands and wives love each other, or that shall make those that do love each other more tolerant and patient toward one another! Oh for a revival that shall lead husband and wife to take hold of hands for their children's sake, and say, "Beloved, let us sanctify ourselves."

Oh happy house! where man and wife in heart,
  In faith, and hope are one,
That neither life nor death can ever part
  The holy union here begun;
Where both are sharing one salvation,
  And live before thee, Lord, always,
In gladness or in tribulation,
  In happy or in evil days.

MARCH 18: *MORNING.*

That ye may grow thereby.—1 *Peter* ii., 2.

WOE to that man who finds the brightest experiences of his Christian life in the very beginning of it! for, although there are joys that will be fondly remembered forever, there ought to be fruits of substantial victories in later life that shall quite eclipse in depth and power any early experiences. Are you living so that neither sickness nor health, neither adversity nor prosperity, can reach up to touch your settled peace? Is your life hid with Christ in God? And are you growing in these directions? If not, what is the matter? Is it some secret sin? Is it some bitterness—some revenge—some cherished selfishness—some neglect? Are you living in the full light of God's countenance, and in the enjoyment of perfect peace in Jesus Christ? If not, why should the children of the King go mourning all the day? Is it not time to examine and ascertain why? For the time is drawing near in which the greatness of the way will have been passed, and all our battles will have been fought, and we shall approach the celestial city, and him who dwells therein; and then, in that hour of royal meeting, to have been in conflict, and to have gained victories through suffering, will be more to us than to have empires, or treasures uncountable in our hand. Remember him who bought you with his own blood. Remember him who waits for you in heaven.

Think of those who have gone before and are victorious to-day, and lift up holy hands of fresh consecration. Begin again, and fight boldly unto the end of life.

MARCH 18: EVENING.

I am the door: by me, if any man enter in, he shall be saved, and shall go in and out, and find pasture.—*John* x., 9.

ALL day long the father strives in the office, in the store, in the shop, in the street, along the wharves, wherever his labor calls him; and the whole day has been full of care and wrangling. The head is hot, and the hand is weary, and the pulse is feverish; and as the day draws on, the busy man prepares at last for home.

If he is wise, he will leave his care behind him. Let the dead bury their dead. Leave your calculations at the desk. Leave your anxieties in your store. Never take them into the street, nor bring them home.

The man draws near his dwelling. The door opens to his touch. The children hear it. The elder ones run. The young prattler, mother-borne, gets there first—quicker than the nimblest. Now, how his heart rejoices! He looks around with a sense of grateful rest, and thanks God that the sound of that shutting door was the last echo of the thunder of care and trouble. That is outside, and he is at home with her that he loves best, and with those that are dearest to him. That door opened to let him in to love, and peace, and joy; it shut to keep out the turbulence of the quarrelsome world and the influence of grinding business.

My dear friends, there is a friendship in the Lord Jesus Christ which may be to us what the door of the household is to the most care-bestridden and bested of men. What the home, with all its sweet affection, is to the troubled heart, that the Savior is to those who know how to make use of him—not the Savior didactically taught or controversially preached, but the Savior discerned by a living and personal faith. There is such intercourse and welcome behind him as there is behind the shutting door. There is that in him which shall make every man, in the midst of the most tried and bestormed life, rest upon his bosom.

Oh! if men could but find the Door; if they could but know what peace there is in Christ Jesus for them, I am sure they would not go so friendless, and harassed, and distressed.

In thee my heart, O Jesus! finds repose;
  Thou bringest rest to all that weary are.
Until that Dayspring from on high arose,
  I wandered through a night without a star;
      My feet had gone astray
      Upon a lonely way:
Each guide I followed failed me in my need,
Each staff I leaned on proved a broken reed.

MARCH 19: *MORNING.*

But God said unto him, Thou fool, this night thy soul shall be required of thee: then whose shall those things be which thou hast provided.—*Luke* xii., 20.

I SEE men that attract to themselves the eyes of all the crowd. They have gathered around themselves that which seems to consummate their felicity upon earth. They are at the climax of exhilaration and enjoyment. "Oh happy man!" men cry out. No returning echo comes, "Happy man;" but muffled, almost silent, comes back from the heavens, "Fool! fool!"

Mother, if that child in thine arms is God's child, and if through that child, as through a lens, thou art looking at immortality and glory, blessed be thou of women; but if this child of thine is only a mortal child, an idol indeed, and in it thou seest only this world—oh fool!

Young man, with health and strength, with ambition and opportunity, if these take hold upon glory and immortality, oh, wise art thou; but if they stop this side of that, oh, fool art thou. It is a sad thing to have a price put into a man's hands to get wisdom, and to squander it. Oh, it is a sad thing to be built for God, and end only with the dust which shall cover you. It is a sad thing for one to be brought up under the sound of the Gospel; to know his own necessities; to hear the truth of God sounding in his conscience; to be touched in his heart again and again—it is a sad thing for a man to see all the truth that gleams through the horizon of the Gospel, and, after all, to die as the fool dieth. "So is every one that layeth up treasure for himself, and is not rich toward God."

Made for thyself, O God!
Made for thy love, thy service, thy delight;
Made to show forth thy wisdom, grace, and might;
Made for thy praise, whom veiled archangels laud.
Oh, strange and glorious thought, that we may be
A joy to thee!

Yet the heart turns away
From this grand destiny of bliss, and deems
'Twas made for its poor self, for passing dreams;
Chasing illusions, melting day by day,
Till *for ourselves* we read on this world's best,
"This is not our rest."

MARCH 19: *EVENING.*

The Lord of peace himself give you peace.—2 *Thess.* iii., 16.

WE are born into God's kingdom little children. We have to go through a process of development and education in religious things, as little children in this natural life are obliged to go through successive stages of education and development.

The peace which comes from Christian life does not come with the alphabet. That is not the point at which to look for it. It belongs to Christian experience, but it belongs to a later stage. It is one of the signs of ripeness, but not of blossoming. That peace which passes all understanding is the highest and the most secret stage of experience. Once reached, and the soul is in the land of Beulah; and from the delectable mountain henceforth it will look over upon the celestial city; and at the hush of evening it will hear, or will think it hears, those voices of the blest which rise in endless warbles over the city of God, and of which, I sometimes think, all sweet earthly sounds are only the echoes, or, as it were, wandering and lost sounds which have dropped down through the tumult of this lower sphere, confusedly, and yet have not quite lost their sweetness.

MARCH 20: *MORNING.*

A bruised reed shall he not break, and the smoking flax shall he not quench. —*Isaiah* xlii., 3.

How tenderly God speaks when he describes the way in

which he deals with those who come to him. "The bruised reed I will not break."

Did you ever see reeds or canes growing, that shoot up twenty or thirty feet, and are not thicker than your finger in the whole growth? Even if they are strong and whole, they can not stand unless they are in some way supported by their fellows. But suppose the field is cut through, and, as the reaper passes, he strikes one that is left upon its edge, and its stem is shivered. There it stands, tall and tremulous, but now wounded, so that a breath will cause it to fall to the ground. God says, I will deal so gently with you that the bruised reed shall not break, that such tremulous weakness shall not fall.

"The smoking flax I will not quench." Did you ever watch the flame when it was first applied to the wick, and you could scarcely tell whether you were deceived by your eye, or there was really a light there, and the slightest stirring, the breath that you breathed, would blow it out? It is very hard to make a lamp begin to burn. Now, says God, I will deal with those who come to me for help with such gentleness that the smoking flax shall not be quenched. If your soul to-day has one aspiration, if there is one spark of that glorious flame leaping up toward God, there is the promise of that blessed Spirit that shall take that heart of yours, like a lamp just lit, and God will carry it so carefully and gently that it shall not go out until the whole is enkindled with light.

How soft the words my Savior speaks!
How kind the promises he makes!
A bruised reed he never breaks,
Nor will he quench the smoking flax.

MARCH 20: EVENING.

Thou, O God, hast prepared of thy goodness for the poor.—*Psalm* lxviii., 10.

SEE to it that the less your earthly sky seems clear and bright, the nearer and the surer is your access to the heavenly land. Have a firm hold upon God. Seek his kingdom and its righteousness.

If you are distressed about your worldly estate, do not give up courage, though no prospect opens to-morrow, or next day, or next week. If the Lord wants you to be poor, very poor, are you willing to be poor? If he can glorify himself in your poverty, are you willing? If you say to me, "It is very hard," I admit it. I sympathize with any man who has to go through that struggle. But if you say, "It is not possible," I deny it. It *is* possible. A thousand have vanquished the world in this respect, and a thousand more will do it. And if a man is called to suffer anxiety about his worldly estate, let him remember that here is a place where he can, by calm, sweet confidence and trust in God, bear a testimony to the power of divine grace that not a hundred sermons could make so fruitful in good upon the minds of those that look on.

MARCH 21: *MORNING.*

Behold the fig-tree, and all the trees; when they now shoot forth, ye see and know of your own selves that summer is now nigh at hand. So likewise ye, when ye see these things come to pass, know ye that the kingdom of God is nigh at hand.—*Luke* xxi., 29-31.

Since the sun has begun to come back, who can stop the growing day? Who now can make the hours dark that the sun is making light? It lingers longer in the west, and comes up earlier in the east, and the day is growing. Let the north blow out its puffs of ice as much as it will, let the snow come as much as it will, they can not keep the summer off. It is coming. It is advancing through the air. I hear the birds coming. I smell the flowers, blooming. From far southern latitudes the sun is advancing. The summer will be here before long.

And so, he that is the Sun of Righteousness is bringing in the summer-day of redemption; and all men's belief, and wickedness, and foaming passions may set themselves against it, but it comes through the air. It comes through the ages. It comes by the mighty power of the omnipotent God. And no man shall stop it. The day will yet come when it shall be triumphant over all. Woe be to those that are not on the Lord's side when he comes in the day of his power to execute final justice and judgment.

MARCH 21: *EVENING.*

So likewise ye, when ye shall have done all those things which are commanded you, say, We are unprofitable servants: we have done that which was our duty to do."—*Luke* xvii., 10.

LET us avoid conceit, even though we may have done a great deal. I do not believe any body with a generous nature ever did any good, that the first effect on himself was not to make him feel, "How little I have done, and how poor is what I do!"

When I think of what a work it is to build up a human soul, and what an opportunity God's kind grace has given me for doing it; when I think what a God I have had, and what a Savior I have had, and what advantages have been vouchsafed to me, I feel ashamed and humbled to think that I have done so little in the Lord's vineyard, and have done it so poorly. My opportunities have been vast, and my performances, compared with what I should have done, have been very meagre and poor. And I think mine is not a singular experience. Do you not feel the same way? Do you ever, in the spirit of the Lord Jesus Christ, do any thing that you do not feel, "It is not as good as I wish it were?"

MARCH 22: *MORNING.*

Let the wicked forsake his way, and the unrighteous man his thoughts: and let him return unto the Lord, and he will have mercy upon him; and to our God, for he will abundantly pardon.—*Isa.* lv., 7.

WHAT does God mean when he says he will "abundantly pardon?" Remember that it is God who speaks, infinite in power, infinite in mercy, infinite in love, infinite in empire and in being. When God says that if a man will come back, and forsake his evil thoughts and his wicked ways, he will forgive him, and "abundantly" have mercy on him, what does he mean? What is God's abundance? Who can tell what that clearance, that utter wiping out of sin is, which God promises?

There is no such lover as God. There is no such magnanimity as there is in God's nature. There is no such friend as God. There is no such harbor or refuge as his bosom. If you have done wrong, go to your earthly friend if you will, but go to God by all means. He is loving, he is gentle, he is full of pity. "Like as a father pitieth his children, so the Lord pitieth them that fear him. For he knoweth our frame; he remembereth that we are but dust."

MARCH 22: EVENING.

If we live in the Spirit, let us also walk in the Spirit.—*Gal.* v., 25.

In the country I can take a mirror, and sit in the house, and hold it in such a position as to bring in the adjacent trees: not the trees, but an image of them, which is like the trees to me.

If you are not yourself Christ, your mind may be a mirror by which his image shall be reflected on the minds of the children that you teach, so as to give them a better conception of him than they could get from the Bible itself. For, if you are Christians, you are epistles of God; you are letters in which men read his power, and wisdom, and grace.

For your own children's sake, parents; for your scholars' sake, teachers in the Sabbath-school, in the Bible-class, and in the week-day school; for the sake of those with whom you are brought in contact amid the affairs of life, men of business, become like Christ in your disposition and in your life. Let no man in your presence go down from darkness to death without having the Savior not only taught to him in words, but imaged before him in conduct. So live, and men shall see your good works, and glorify our Father which is in heaven.

Let me wear the white robes here,
Even on earth, my Father dear;
Holding fast thy hand, and so
Through the world unspotted go.

Perfume every fold with love,
Hinting heaven where'er I rove,
As an Indian vessel's sails
Whisper of her costly bales.

Thus appareled, I shall be
As a signal set for thee,
That the wretched, poor, and weak
May the same fair garments seek.

MARCH 23: MORNING.

For I say unto you, That except your righteousness shall exceed the righteousness of the scribes and Pharisees, ye shall in no case enter into the kingdom of heaven.—*Matt.* v., 20.

MANY persons confound the means with the end in moral things, who never do so in ordinary things. They have great scrupulosity of conscience about the use of means; but the absence of higher qualities of manliness, the violation of them, the total sacrifice of them—these things give them little pain. About all the things that relate to religion as educating means they are very scrupulous; but when it comes to those qualities for which these are merely the schoolmasters—unmistakable truth, transparent sincerity, faith in God, courage, and simplicity, and unselfishness, and meekness—when it comes to these, they have no scruples. The idea of striking the Bible gives them great horror, but the idea of striking a man, that is God's temple, has little or no effect upon them. And yet, when the round earth shall burn, the Bibles will burn too. But when the round earth shall burn, not one living soul will burn. All the wide world is but the tool of God for the development of the one fruit, man. Man is the fruit which God means by the husbandry of time—by all the institutions of the world. And what kind of piety is that which stickles for a Sunday, and does not care for a generation or a race? What kind of piety is that which stands tremulous with superstitious fear for Church regulations, for religious ceremonies, and for days, but without concern lets world-currents flow deep as the currents of the Dead Sea over generations and races?

MARCH 23: EVENING.

Then said Jesus, Father, forgive them; for they know not what they do.—*Luke* xxiii., 34.

WHILE yet we were enemies, Christ died for us. Did you ever attempt to imagine what must have been the state of mind that Christ was in when he looked upon those who were not repentant, who were his enemies still, and who were so vagrant as to reject his life-long services, as to cause his passion, and as to work out his death? Did you ever attempt to imagine what must have been that state of mind by which, after having toiled for them, and borne with them, and taught them, he could, in the act of dying, pray for them, saying, "They know not what they do?" Do you get any idea of what the divine feeling is toward a wicked, hating, and hateful being, which manifests itself in dying for him as the means of his restoration? If I say that I will forgive a man when he repents, and not before, I do not know what to do with the example of Christ. He did not wait till I repented. He did not wait till I was good. I should not have been good had it not been for his forerunning grace. It was Christ that waked me up and made me sensitive to that which was wrong. It was Christ's influence on my mind that brought my conscience to feel how hateful my life was toward him. And when I began to feel that I had passed from death to life, I was distinctly conscious that I came to it by the forerunning grace of the Lord God. He saved me while I was an enemy, proud, selfish, and unlovely; and that always comes back to me as a rule of duty.

MARCH 24: MORNING.

But seek ye first the kingdom of God and his righteousness, and all these things shall be added unto you.—*Matt.* vi., 33.

I do not say that discussions on abstract philosophical questions have not certain benefits; but I do say that, though these sharp questions are good to whet a man's faculties, yet, if he rests upon the simple faith of love in Christ Jesus—if it is merely by the hunger of his soul that he is guided to be made whole or better—he can lead a very good Christian life, even though his faculties are not whet. It is not necessary that he should solve the questions relating to the nature of God or of the divine government. He may let them alone.

The precept is, "Seek first the kingdom of God and its"—what did the Savior say? "Seek first the kingdom of God and its"—catechism? No, that was not it. "Seek first the kingdom of God and its"—confession of faith? No, that was not it. "Seek first the kingdom of God and its"—doctrine? No, that was not it. What was it? "Seek first the kingdom of God and its *righteousness*." Let practice and experience precede philosophy. After you have got these, then co-ordinate them, and make your own philosophy. First, true life; afterward the theory of that life.

MARCH 24: EVENING.

Her ways are ways of pleasantness, and all her paths are peace.—*Prov.* iii., 17.

RELIGION, regarded as a theory of a perfect state, is right in pronouncing itself a *way of pleasantness* and a *path of peace.* If a man could but walk perfectly in the way of religion, he would be perfectly happy. The way *is* pleasant, and all the paths *are* peace; and yet along that pleasant way there are groans and sorrows innumerable; and along that way of peace there is struggle, turmoil, combat, and confusion. But the divine plan and intent, the ultimate state, is a state of supreme blessedness. The nature of man is one which, when brought fully up to its divine ideal, will produce constant happiness.

But man is not born into an ideal state—into a perfect state, even. On the contrary, he is born farther from his nature than any other creature on earth. Nothing is so far from perfection when it starts as man. There is nothing so far from the perfection of even his physical powers as man. Born as a babe, what is a man that neither sees nor hears; that distinguishes nothing; that knows nothing? And yet that child is a son of God, and is destined yet, through evolution and education, and sanctifying grace or inspiration, to rise and be but little lower than the angels. But oh, how long the journey from the cradle to the crown.

MARCH 25: MORNING.

The wind bloweth where it listeth, and thou hearest the sound thereof, but canst not tell whence it cometh and whither it goeth: so is every one that is born of the Spirit.—*John* iii., 8.

COME, oh south wind! bring vapor from the sea and warmth

from the equator; bring birds and grass, spring and summer. Come, oh breath of heaven! spread wide abroad over all the continent. Come to the great and come to the little; come to the poor and come to the rich; come to the sick man through his lattice; come to all, bringing—no man can measure what, for abundance. No man can tell whence it cometh or whither it goeth. It wanders up and down the hills, and through all the valleys, and makes itself known from the benefits it brings; yet no man can see the viewless course of the air. So it is with the spirit of beneficence—the true Christ-like spirit in the human soul. It comes, we know not whence; it goes, we can not tell how or where. It is universal; it is endless; it is bountiful as the summer, and blessed as God.

MARCH 25: EVENING.

All things are yours.—1 *Cor.* iii., 21.

If you were to come up and steal some of my flowers next summer, I should not miss them. I have so many that you might take a wheelbarrow load, and I should have enough the next morning. I can conceive, however, that a seamstress, up in an attic, might have a little tea-rose, the only thing she had which savored of taste; and I can conceive how desolate she might feel if the rats had gnawed it and destroyed it, or if some one had stolen it. But you can not trouble me so. You can not make me poor by taking my flowers, I have such an abundance.

If a man has nothing but what grows in this life, you can make him poor and unhappy; but if a man believes in God, and believes in heaven, and believes in the joy that awaits him there, how are you going to bankrupt him? How are you going to overthrow so lordly a spirit as his who has heard God say, "Thou art my son?" Son of God—yes, prince; heir with Christ to all things—forever and forever heir. How is any sudden trouble to run in upon him? In the full consciousness of his estate; in the joy and dignity of his relationship, how shall any man harm him?

MARCH 26: MORNING.

For the love of money is the root of all evil: which while some coveted after, they have erred from the faith, and pierced themselves through with many sorrows.—1 *Tim.* vi., 10.

The love of money has corrupted, in its time, every faculty, and every relation in which a man stands connected with his fellows. It has divided families, it has parted friendships, it has corrupted purity. The love of money, often, is stronger than the love of kindred. See children utterly rent asunder and quarreling over a will! See how natural affection is extinguished! how it extinguishes natural affections! What crimes or vices were ever known that it has not led men to. What is there of selfishness, or pride, or vanity, or deceit—what is there in wickedness, in meanness, in treachery, that money has not been accessory to.

Not only will they who *will* be rich sacrifice every thing, but they will not hesitate to *do* every thing that is required—only, as men that *will* be rich require impunity, it must be safe. And so comes the long, detestable roll of mining, subterranean conduct; the secrecy of wickedness; collusions, plottings, unwhispered things, or things only whispered; that long train of webbing conduct which makes men insincere, pretentious hypocrites, whited sepulchres that are fair without, but that inwardly are full of death and dead men's bones. How many there are who have violated every commandment of God, and almost every law of men, in their way toward badly-gotten gains, and yet who have so far had respect for the opinions of their fellows, and so far desired to stand well among men, that they have concealed it all. And they carry themselves, a swollen, bloated mass of iniquity, under fair colors and fair exteriors. They that *will* be rich at any rate and at all hazards, are the ones of whom the apostle speaks when he says that they shall "fall into temptation and a snare, and into many foolish and hurtful lusts."

MARCH 26: EVENING.

For we that are in this tabernacle do groan, being burdened: not for that we would be unclothed, but clothed upon, that mortality might be swallowed up of life.—2 *Cor.* v., 4.

Life is but a handbreadth. Each year is not so much as the bead that the beauty wears about her neck. Pearl though it be, or iron, it soon passes away. The places that know you will soon know you no more forever. The cares that made you fret yesterday are already below the horizon. The troubles that make you anxious to-day will not be troubles when you meet them. But what if they were? A cloud no bigger than a man's hand is swelling and filling the whole heaven. What then? To-day its bolts may smite you; but to-morrow you will be in heaven. Your children have died and gone home; but what of that? Soon you will follow them. Your friends have gone on before; but what of that? You will soon be with them. Your life is full of troubles and mischiefs; but what of that? Those mischiefs and troubles are nearly over—nearer than you think. The glorious future is almost yours.

O Grave! thy hand crowns as no monarch can. Knighted are we, not by the touch of the sword of any soldier, or king, or prince. Trouble it is that lays its sword on men's shoulders, and says, "Rise up, Sir Knight!" There are things in this life that give men great victories all the way through; but oh! the victory of one moment in the future is worth more than all those earthly victories. One look into heaven pays better than the whole experience of a life of joy here.

O Death! there are who look to thee
  But as the minister of grace,
And who thy dark approach can see
  With smiles, for they have won the race.

There are to whom thy call would come,
  As to the exile's weary heart
Would be the summons to his home—
  That home from which he wept to part.

The good, the bless'd! to thee they trust
  To crown them with the immortal wreath,
And fearless of the dreams of dust,
  As conquerors welcome thee, O Death!

MARCH 27: MORNING.

For even hereunto were ye called: because Christ also suffered for us, leaving us an example, that ye should follow his steps.—1 *Peter* ii., 21.

Oftentimes a man must follow the word of truth when it seems as though it would lead him into destruction. Often Christ comes walking to the disciples on the stormy sea and in the night, and it is necessary that there should be some power of faith, some cogent influence, that shall make a Christian man willing to follow rectitude, duty, honor, truth, no matter where they seem to lead. And therefore it is that God has put all the bows, all the coruscations of his word, around about the issues and ends of essential truth, honor, duty, and rectitude, and that he says to us, "If you would save your life, lose it; do not be afraid." You are oftentimes brought into trials when it seems as though every thing would be wrecked, and the world says, "Prudence;" Experience says, "Draw back;" Policy says, "Change a little;" and Expediency says, "Commute, compromise." But the Word of God, that stands sure and steadfast, and is yea and amen, says, "He that will lose his life for a right principle shall save it." And in the end, when you come to count the wrecks along the shore, you will find that those men who would save their lives by losing their principles are the men that have lost their lives; while those men who brave the storm—those men who followed the superior light that shone in their hearts—those men who said, "Come what will, there is but one way for me, and that is the way that God has marked out"—are the men that have saved themselves.

MARCH 27: EVENING.

Come unto me, all ye that labor and are heavy laden, and I will give you rest.—*Matt.* xi., 28.

Men look upon repentance and humiliation before God very much as they do upon a voyage from the tropics to the North Pole. At every league, as they advance toward the Arctic region, they leave more and more behind them verdure, and fruit, and warmth, and civilization, and find themselves more and more in the midst of sterility, barrenness, ice, and barbarism. So men repent toward the frigid zones. They think that to go toward God is dreary and desolate. It is not. The sinner lives in ice; but if by any means he becomes fired with a conception of a better clime, and takes ship and sails toward the torrid zone, at every league he is surprised by the new forms of vegetation which surround him. And with what satisfaction does he compare the delightful home that he has found with the miserable one that he has left behind.

Consider what is the thought of divine parentage; consider what are all the ways by which God has sought to impress upon the human race the fullness of his love. What figure is there that bears the conception of a power, an honor, an ease, a glory, an achievement, a victory, which God has not taken and set in the sanctuary, to light up in man's mind the divinity of that love which he manifested by the gift of his own beloved Son—a love which is more than motherhood, or fatherhood, or brotherhood, or sisterhood, or friendship, or love of lovers. Sitting central in the immensity of that love, he says, "Come unto me, all ye that labor and are heavy laden, and I will give you rest." It is the invitation of infinite power to infinite weakness, of infinite purity to infinite sinfulness, of infinite riches to utter and abject poverty. "O Israel, thou hast destroyed thyself; but in me is thine help."

MARCH 28: *MORNING.*

I have learned, in whatsoever state I am, therewith to be content.—*Philippians* iv., 11.

WHAT man did you ever see that could stand up and say, "I have learned, in whatever state I am, and in all places, to be content? Put me where you please, and I will make it paradise. Give me my children, and I am happy. Take them all away, and I have that still which will make me happy. Give me friends, and I am happy. Nothing is so dear to me as to be loved, and know that men approve what I am doing and what I am saying. But take them all away, and leave me the consciousness that I am right with God, and that I am right on all the great fundamental truths, and I am happy. Give me the multitude or give me the wilderness, I have one experience for the one, and I have another for the other; and in both places I have learned to control myself, and I am perfectly happy. Oh! give me the abounding experience which belongs to royalty and the realm of the heart in its best estate. Let all heaven seem to be in perspective in the experiences of true loving upon earth, and of course I could be content in that. Take them all away, and let me feel that the deepest feelings of my life have never been touched; let me feel that the depths have been unsounded in me, and I can be contented yet."

Can you say that? Did you ever know any body that could? I should like to have known one man that could; and that man's name was Paul. It was easy and familiar with him.

MARCH 28: *EVENING.*

For whom the Lord loveth he chasteneth, and scourgeth every son whom he receiveth.—*Heb.* xii., 6.

God both chastens and scourges men, and all because he loves them. Wonderful love that is, and yet it is just your love. You have not a child whose body is worth more to you than his mind. No child of yours ever told a lie under circumstances of great baseness—that was bad in itself, and for a purpose that was worse than the lie—no child of yours ever did that when you did not feel rising against him an utter indignation, not because you hated the child, but because you loved him. All your identification with the child plead for punishment. You said, "It is my child; and he is not worthy of me; and he *shall* be worthy of me." And you chastised him, not once, but repeatedly. Oh, how heartily does a man lay on the strokes who loves his child, and wants him to be noble, pure, manly, and fit to wear a crown, though he may never touch it till he gets to heaven. And Christ says that his sympathy with us is not the sympathy of an effervescent feeling, merely going with us when we have a momentary joy or a momentary throb of pain. He sympathizes with the whole of our being, and means that his whole administration, and the administration of our sorrows as well, shall make our manhood larger.

MARCH 29: *MORNING.*

And whatsoever ye do, do it heartily as to the Lord, and not unto men.—*Col.* iii., 23.

Be obedient and faithful; and, as Christ took upon him the form of a man, though he was mighty God, and humbled himself, and became obedient unto death—the worst kind of death that was conceivable among men—so, if you are Christ's, and are put in situations in life where your duty requires you to humble yourself, and you rejoice in such opportunities to serve your Lord and Master, there is the secret offering that you bring to him.

If, child, you have parents who should have been your exemplars, but who have misled you step by step, honor them. For Christ's sake honor them, though it may not be possible for you to honor them for their own sake. If, scholar, you are in a class, and under teachers, and in circumstances such that you are continually vexed and tried, be a Christian in all sweetness, and faithfulness, and fidelity, for Christ's sake. Be sweet tempered and faithful, for Christ's sake; if for no other reason. He will know it and appreciate it.

To every body who is tempted to go according to the world, and not according to grace, there is this motive which never fails, that whatever you do for Christ falls into his heart, and is reckoned there, and makes him happier, and brings back, as it were, the reflection of his thought and feeling, his spirit, in greater abundance to you.

MARCH 29: *EVENING.*

For both he that sanctifieth and they who are sanctified are all of one; for which cause he is not ashamed to call them brethren.—*Heb.* ii., 11.

I take it that there is no Christian who has not such fluctuations of experience as lead at times almost to be unwilling to lift up his face before Christ. We go to Christ sometimes with the same shamefacedness with which we as children went to our parents, when we were conscious that our conduct was such as made them ashamed of us. At such times the child can not look the parent in the face, and turns its eyes away, and is scarlet with blushes. Every Christian has times not only of despondency, but of sober and just conviction that he has humbled himself—not in the noble sense of *humility;* that he has dishonored himself; and that he has brought scandal or dishonor upon the name of his Master. And in these hours one goes to Christ with the feeling that Christ must be ashamed too. As long as the spirit of a man accuses itself only of generic transgression, so long he can in some way find alleviation. But when we have been thrown into the gulf of iniquitous pride; when by vanity we have been snared; when by the feelings we have been led on from wickedness to wickedness; when we have been in the exercise of the malign passions; when the experience is fresh, and conviction comes as by a divine revelation, and we are pierced with thoughts of our own guiltiness before God, then we can scarcely lift up our head before God, and are overwhelmed with the thought that Christ must needs be ashamed of us. And yet, it is of just such that Christ says he is not ashamed. He is not ashamed to call even them brethren.

MARCH 30: *MORNING.*

Unto you, therefore, which believe, he is precious.—1 *Pet.* ii., 7.

Christ is said to be precious to those that "believe"—to those, in other words, whose minds have been so opened that they can perceive what really is in the Savior. To those who have the full vision, and intimate knowledge, and confiding belief in the qualities and in the conduct of the Savior, he becomes precious. And this is no imagination. For, although the conceptions which we may form may prove by-and-by to have been in a thousand respects disproportionate and erring, there will always be the fact that they erred on the side of deficiency.

We can not suppose that we have the truest idea of God—certainly not. "Now we see," says the apostle, "through a glass darkly; but then face to face: now I know in part"—in mere fragments, in bits, having, as it were, the ends of knowledge—"but then shall I know even as also I am known." And all the mistakes that we commit, or are liable to commit, in the knowledge of God, as represented to us in the Lord Jesus Christ, are mistakes of undervaluation. He is infinitely more beautiful than our most extravagant imagination ever paints. He is infinitely more tender and more wise than we ever conceived. He is transcendently nobler than we ever dreamed, doing things with a generosity, with a lordly courtesy, with a supereminent delicacy, with a beauty, with a care for us, and with a harmonizing influence far transcending not only any experience, but any poetic imagination which is wrought out from experience, and carried much beyond it. To those who believe, to those who have had the sacred vision to behold him, Christ is precious.

MARCH 30: *EVENING.*

But Zion said, The Lord hath forsaken me, and my Lord hath forgotten me. —*Isa.* xlix., 14.

Oh how many have felt that God had forsaken them. How many have mourned and felt that the heavens over them were brass, and that the earth was as the ashes of the burnt wilderness. Now hear the answer: "Can a woman forget her sucking child, that she should not have compassion on the son of her womb? Yea, they may forget; yet will I not forget thee. Behold, I have graven thee upon the palms of my hands; thy walls are continually before me." What is it in the journey, what is it in the bivouac, what is it on the field where the wounded are weltering in their blood, that one last looks upon? There in the hand is the little daguerreotype of the wife and children. The last gaze is on that. And the Lord says, "Your portrait is graven on my hands. I carry it on my palms, ever before me. I never lift up my hands to the stars that I do not see it. I never stretch out my hands to fulfill the decrees of Omnipotence, that that picture does not fall upon my eyes." Think what language this is to come from the lips of the crowned head of the universe. Think what comfort and cheer there is in it.

MARCH 31: *MORNING.*

Blessed are the pure in heart, for they shall see God.—*Matt.* v., 8.

Blessed are they that need no argument; and blessed are they whose memories take them back to the glowing hours of experience, in which they have seen the transfigured Christ; in which to them the heavens have been opened; in which to them the angels of God not only have descended upon the ladder, but have brought the divine and sacred presence with them. Many a couch of poverty has been more gorgeous than a prince's couch; many a hut and hovel has been scarcely less resplendent to the eye of angels than the very battlements of heaven. Many that the world has not known; who had no tongue to speak, but only a heart to love and to trust—many such ones have had the very firmament of God lifted above them, all radiant. There is this truth of the Spirit of God that works in the heart of men directly and in overpowering measure. Blessed be God, it is a living truth, and there are witnesses of it yet.

MARCH 31: *EVENING.*

For he hath said, I will never leave thee nor forsake thee.—*Heb.* xiii., 5.

God is your father and your mother. Do you say, "Nobody cares for my soul?" The outstretched arms of him that suffered are about you. There is a Christ who believes in men, thinks for men, longs for men, and strives for men. And there is no man that has gone so far wrong but that, if he will, he may be clean, may be strong, and may be saved. Oh ye weary, why are you weary when others rest? Oh ye sick, why do you suffer when others are healed? Oh starving and hungering, there is bread enough. Oh dying, there is life for you. Oh desponding and despairing, look up and rejoice. A great light has arisen to those that sit in the region and shadow of death. Come to Christ, who loves you, who is drawing you, and who has said to each one of you, "I will never leave thee nor forsake thee."

APRIL 1: MORNING.

We then that are strong ought to bear the infirmities of the weak, and not to please ourselves.—*Rom.* xv., 1.

When a man has acquired money and education, he makes it his business to render himself happy. He surrounds himself with an estate, and fills his mansion, stores it with comforts and luxuries, that he may not be mixed up with the noisy affairs of life, but get out of the way, and have his nest beyond the reach of the storm, and there lie in his little round silky abode, at ease with himself. But, says the apostle, ye that are strong—ye that are men of genius and might intellectually—you have no right to do any such thing. You ought to bear the infirmities of the weak. All human trouble ought to roll itself on to the broadest shoulders, and not to rest on the weak and feeble shoulders. If there is to be any patience, it is to be on the part of men that are the best men. If there is to be any forbearance, it is to be on the part of those men who are the most deserving, and not the least deserving. Rich men are to bear the infirmities of the poor. Wise men are to bear the mistakes of the ignorant. Strong men are to bear with the feeble. Cultured people are to bear with the rude and vulgar. If a rough and coarse man meets an ecstatically fine man, the man that is highest up is to be the servant of the man that is lowest down. You say that it is against nature. Very likely, but it is not against grace. He that will be first must be the servant.

Must I my brother keep,
 And share his pains and toil,
And weep with those that weep,
 And smile with those that smile;
And act to each a brother's part,
And feel his sorrows in my heart?

Must I his burden bear
 As though it were my own,
And do as I would care
 Should to myself be done;
And faithful to his interests prove,
And as myself my neighbor love?

Oh, make me as thou art,
 Thy Spirit, Lord, bestow—
The kind and gentle heart,
 That feels another's woe;
That thus I may be like my Head,
And in my Savior's footsteps tread.

APRIL 1: EVENING.

Wait on the Lord: be of good courage, and he shall strengthen thine heart: wait, I say, on the Lord.—*Psalm* xxvii., 14.

SOMETIMES I have gone with a check to the bank, and the teller has looked at it and at me, and after seeing who I was, and that the check was genuine, has said, "What will you take it in?" meaning, "Will you have it in gold, or silver, or bills? And if in bills, of what denomination shall they be?" Sometimes, in answering my prayers, God has, as it were, said to me, "What will you take it in? Will you take it in the thing, and nothing else, or will you take it in that which the thing was expected to give you—namely, such a spiritual insight or joy as you could not have from specific answers?" I think some men—not all—can rise to a state of mind in which the conception of God's entire control of things is such that there is always peacefulness in the way in which they speak; not so much from a sense of special answers to petitions as from a sense that God governs and overrules all things well.

APRIL 2: MORNING.

For, brethren, ye have been called unto liberty; only use not liberty for an occasion to the flesh, but by love serve one another.—*Gal.* v., 13.

GOD summons you; and he summons you, not as a master summons his slave, but as a father summons his child. That voice which sounded on Calvary, having gone up to heaven, comes inflected back in tones of cheer, and love, and hope, and gladness, and calls you; and Christ—ever-living, not now on earth a man of sorrows, acquainted with grief, but in heaven a Prince and a Savior--says, "My son, give me thine heart;" and this being given, he says, "Now enter into all the royalty of my possession and domain. Thou, as my child, art also heir with me to an eternal inheritance. Thou art to be a king and a priest before God."

Yes, when you are called to be a Christian, you are called unto liberty. You are not called as convicts to do penal service in a spiritual penitentiary. You are called, rather, to the freedom, the largeness, the sweetness, and the manliness of a nobler character than ever dawned on the imagination of heathen poet. To be a true man according to the ideal of the New Testament is to have a heart full of faith and confidence in God, and to have all that liberty which love begets in a child that dares to look his father in the face, and call him by the most familiar names.

He who in Christ believeth
  Is wise, is wise;
He who this Christ receiveth
  Alone is wise.

He who this wisdom winneth
  Is free, is free;
He in whose heart it reigneth
  Alone is free.

He who this freedom graspeth
  Is strong, is strong;
He who this freedom claspeth
  Alone is strong.

APRIL 2: EVENING.

And it came to pass, while he blessed them, he was parted from them, and carried up into heaven.—*Luke* xxiv., 51.

When we are almost worn out and discouraged, there sometimes comes a glancing thought of Christ's patience with us and of his sympathy for us. We are not thinking whether he is or is not divine. All we have is a consciousness that there is the ideal of Christ brought near to us, bearing us up, and lending us his strength. It may go, almost in the moment that gave it birth, but it is real.

I have sometimes seen parents, in playing with their children, go from without to the window, or behind the leaves of a bower —the children not knowing of their presence—just opening a space large enough to show the eye or the brow, and perhaps speaking a name, and then, as soon as the children caught a glance of them, disappear; and the children, with laughter and glee, would pursue them. There is a piquancy in such sportiveness not only to the child's affection, but to his curiosity.

Now it seems to me that there are such effects produced by these momentary outlooks of Christ upon us. Where we have been in great grief, where the days have been sodden and heavy, where the current of life seems to have turned to mud, which has no flow in it, and we are bemired—then often there comes to us out of heaven a sense of Christ's love and life-giving power, and of Christ saying to us, "Because I live, ye shall live also. If ye suffer with me, ye shall reign with me." The thing itself may last only a moment, but the sweetness lasts for years.

APRIL 3: MORNING.

Gentle; showing all meekness unto all men.—*Tit.* iii., 2.

I THINK the thirteenth chapter of 1st Corinthians is the most perfect description of a gentleman that ever was written or thought of. It is Paul's representation of love. If you will substitute *politeness* for *love*, you will see that this is so. Not that I would reduce love to politeness; but while that chapter, as it stands, is the most glorious chant that ever was chimed out of the belfry of inspiration, it has a peculiar significance in this connection if we say *politeness* instead of *love.*

"Politeness suffereth long and is kind; politeness envieth not; politeness vaunteth not itself, is not puffed up, doth not behave itself unseemly, seeketh not her own, is not easily provoked, thinketh no evil"—and so to the end of the chapter.

The beginning of good manners, the beginning of politeness, is the inspiration of a true, pure, generous, loving heart. This every man ought to have. And where a man has this, it will overflow, and show itself in his countenance, in his manners, in his dress, in every thing about him.

APRIL 3: EVENING.

For God sent not his Son into the world to condemn the world, but that the world through him might be saved.—*John* iii., 17.

IN looking up into the heavenly land, the sense of Christ to me seems as real as the last earthly experience through which I have gone. Sometimes it is an ever-changing presentation which I have, full-orbed, and advanced to the very height of transcendent glory. At other times Christ seems to me most companionable, and I fancy that I walk with him, just as his disciples walked with him when he was on the earth, and talk with him. At times I see him to be potential in mercy. At other times I see him encouraging and most sweetly winning. But I think the aspect of Christ which predominates is that in which he shows himself a Savior; in which he is seen to be saving men—saving them from danger, saving them from temptation, saving them from sin, saving them from those snares which sin brings upon them, saving them from those pitfalls into which transgressions plunge them, and out of which it is so hard for them to climb.

The view of Christ as saving his people—as working in them, working for them, working by the great round of providence, working by his special manifestations, and working in them *to will and to do*—the aspect of Christ as one having a saving nature, and that spirit in which he says, "I came not to condemn the world," in which he calls men to him, and which he manifested in laying down his life that he might save the world—this aspect of Christ is the most precious to me, for my own sake, and for the sake of my fellow-men.

APRIL 4: MORNING.

Look unto me, and be ye saved, all the ends of the earth.—*Isa.* xlv., 22.

ALL piety should have a certain degree of self-examination; but there be many persons that are taught, or that incline without teaching, to have an excessive habit of self-consciousness—self-culture as it is called. Every man must know something about himself, but it is very easy for him to know too much. It is very easy for a man to make his own experience the spool about which to wind the whole thread of life. And, under such circumstances, what is a man's piety but a spiritually baptized self-consciousness? How can the heart lift itself in transport? What is there that a man can see who only looks in and down? And, above all, how can a man that is all the time thinking of his own moods and states, or of his own victories and defeats—how can a man that moves about his own self with a perpetual iteration—how can such a man abandon himself generously to a thought of God which shall make his whole soul go out toward him in ecstasy? Praising is not compatible with that style of piety.

I thought upon my sins, and I was sad;
  My soul was troubled sore and filled with pain;
But then I thought on Jesus, and was glad;
  My heavy grief was turned to joy again.

I saw that I was lost—far gone astray;
  No hope of safe return there seemed to be;
But then I heard that Jesus was the way—
  A new and living way prepared for me.

Then in that way, so free, so safe, so sure,
  Sprinkled all o'er with reconciling blood,
Will I abide, and never wander more,
  Walking along in fellowship with God.

APRIL 4: EVENING.

But the God of all grace, who hath called us unto his eternal glory by Christ Jesus, after that ye have suffered a while, make you perfect, stablish, strengthen, settle you.—1 *Peter* v., 10.

Did you ever see a sculptor make a statuette or statue? He begins with dirt, you know. He has a few rude sticks for a frame, and then he puts on the clay. When it is tempered aright he roughs out the general form. Then he begins to scrape off the plaster. Then he works for symmetry, and lines, and grace, and proportions. Then he works for resemblances. And at last, as the work is becoming consummated, he puts on the finest touches. And all the way through it is dirt. Yet, as the sculptor goes on working thus with this lifeless material, to bring out at last the finest lines and lineaments, that the model, when completed, may be transmuted into the glowing marble, or bronze, or silver, or gold, as the case may be—so God is dealing with us; so he is building us up: he is taking off and putting on, that after a while, when the work is completed, we may be transmuted into higher forms, and be as pillars in the temple of our God, and become men in Christ Jesus, glowing with all the light of blessedness and immortality.

Now, to those that are in the midst of trial, to those that are in the crucible, walking through the fire, there is this consolation: your troubles and trials are watched of God, and you are beloved of him; and, though you may be tried with great temptations to wickedness, yet, if you are "steadfast in the faith," he will not forget you, nor give you up, nor suffer you to be tempted more than you are able to bear, but with every temptation will open a door of escape.

APRIL 5: MORNING.

Whom having not seen, ye love; in whom, though now ye see him not, yet believing, ye rejoice with joy unspeakable and full of glory.—1 *Peter* i., 8.

"CAN every man be joyful?" Yes, every man. "Can all men alike be joyful?" No. There will be gradations in joy, as in every other Christian grace; but every man, in his own measure, may be joyful, and every man may strive to increase in joyfulness. If you refuse it; if you thrust it from you; if you make up your mind that you can not attain it before you begin to seek it; if you say, "It is a grace that belongs to saintship, and not to ordinary Christian experience," then there will be no participation in it for you. But if you feel that it does belong to ordinary Christian experience, that it is a radiant circle which God puts about the soul as its crown, and that you have a right to your crown, as every other man has a right to his; if you seek for it as a thing to be desired, then it shall be yours. You that are called of God, you that have a hope in Jesus Christ, have not only a duty, but a right of joy. It is a part of that treasure which God has given you. And you should be increasingly joyful. The older you grow, and the nearer you come to the kingdom of heaven, the more your heart should shine, and the more your tongue should bear witness to the goodness of him that has redeemed you.

Why walk in darkness? Our true light yet shineth:
It is not night, but day:
All healing and all peace his light enshrineth—
Why shun his loving ray?

Are night and shadows better, truer, dearer
Than day, and joy, and love?
Do tremblings and misgivings bring us nearer
To the great God of love?

Light of the World, undimming and unsetting,
Oh shine each mist away;
Banish the fear, the falsehood, and the fretting—
Be our unchanging day.

APRIL 5: EVENING.

But who am I, and what is my people, that we should be able to offer so willingly after this sort? for all things come of thee, and of thine own have we given thee.—1 *Chron.* xxix., 14.

A LITTLE child brought me, one day, some flowers. He evidently did not know much about flowers. He said he picked them by the wayside. Some were savory, and some were not so savory; but as he handed them to me he said, "They are the best I could find." He showed that he would have been glad to give me better ones, though he had only a vague idea of what "better" was in my case. There was just the beginning of generosity in the child manifesting itself through taste; and his feeling was, "I wish they had been better flowers."

Now you never carried flowers to one that you loved without feeling that better flowers were deserved by that one. You never did any thing for one who was dear to you without feeling that the service was far less than you fain would have had it. And no man ever suffered for the Lord Jesus Christ, or served him with any worthiness at all, without saying, "I have not done so well as I would like to do." There is such superiority, such gentleness, such sweetness, such sympathy, such patience, such faithfulness of love in Christ, that one is ashamed of the best service he can render him, it is so far beneath his desert. In serving the Lord Jesus Christ, the more you suffer, and the more you deny yourself, the greater is the evidence which you give of love for him.

APRIL 6: MORNING.

But of him are ye in Christ Jesus, who of God is made unto us wisdom, and righteousness, and sanctification, and redemption.—1 *Cor.* i., 30.

WHAT is it that makes a person a Christian? A very little, with infinite consequences. It takes but very little to make a man a Christian, although the consequences of that little are infinite. Just as soon as a person has any conception of Jesus Christ as the Master and the Model of the life of true benevolence, and purity, and truth which he prescribes for us—just as soon as a person has the simplest conception of the life that Christ lives and that he commands men to live, and then can truly say, "I am willing to begin that life; I am willing to go to school to my master Jesus; I am willing to learn; and I covenant with him to do his will as fast as it is revealed to me; I covenant with him to be a good scholar, to learn, and, as fast as I learn, to practice every thing which he commands me to do, as in the New Testament it is spread out in the four Gospels, showing what the Christian life is as he lived it and commends it to others"—just as soon as a man can say, "Though I shall understand this very imperfectly, and shall come short a great many times, and shall fail here and there, yet I am willing to begin, and I am willing, as far as life, and breath, and strength are given me, to attempt to be a pupil, a scholar, a disciple of the Lord Jesus Christ," just so soon he begins to be a Christian.

APRIL 6: EVENING.

To him that overcometh will I give to eat of the hidden manna.—*Revelation* ii., 17.

CHRISTIANS are in great conflict and peril, and, in consequence of the strifes and dangers of Christian life, they need something more than they can minister to themselves. They need food that is better than the daily bread for which we are taught to pray; and the promise is that, if they are faithful in their Christian life, God will give them this other food that they need. "I will give to every man that is a true soldier," says Christ, "to every man that holds the faith of Christ, and that means to maintain a godly and pure life—to every such man, whatever may be his trials, his perils, and his inducements, if he will only overcome his temptations, I will give a hidden support. I will feed him inwardly. As the Israelite had visible manna, so he shall have manna that is invisible, hidden, mystic."

I would to God that in some adequate way the experience of this truth might be gathered out of that army of suffering ones that the world has seen, and framed into a history, and poured forth upon men, that the world might know how God does do exceeding abundantly more than we ask or think for those that are willing for Christ's sake to cut off the right hand, or pluck out the right eye, or forego any temptation or any inducement of pleasure.

When first before his mercy-seat
Thou didst to him thy all commit,
He gave the warrant from that hour
To trust his wisdom, love, and power.

Did ever trouble yet befall,
And he refuse to hear thy call?
And has he not his promise pass'd
That thou shalt overcome at last?

He who has helped me hitherto
Will help me all my journey through.
And give me daily cause to raise
New trophies to his endless praise.

APRIL 7: MORNING.

What must I do to be saved?—*Acts* xvi., 30.

THE thought can not be entertained for a moment that you will be lost. The question is this: How shall I be saved? God says the difficulties are so many that you must wake up. The work of securing your salvation is a real business. Not by dreaming, not by sweet sentimentalities, not by going into a congregation and chanting hymns that bless God, and weeping at prayers that touch the fountains of susceptibility, and thinking airy thoughts of the past and rosy thoughts of the future—not by these things can you be saved. You must begin at the foundation of your character if you would make it what it should be. Let the wicked man forsake wickedness; let the corrupt man forsake corruption; let men take hold of themselves as they would take hold of an old mansion that they wished to renovate. If it is rotten in the sills, replace the sills; if it is infested with vermin, cleanse out the vermin; if it is filled with dirt, remove the dirt; if the walls are pestilential, scrub the walls and replaster them. Or, if there is no other way, destroy the building, and begin it anew. Be born again, as it were. Count all the years of your past life as if they were nothing at all. Turn round and say, "The day in which I begin to try to live for God is my birthday."

Oh blessed promise, oh wondrous economy of grace, by which a man, after having lived forty or fifty years in sin, can start again, God saying to him, "I will cancel the past; you may begin again as if you never had stumbled and done wrong."

APRIL 7: EVENING.

Thou wilt cast all their sins into the depths of the sea.—*Micah* vii., 19.

GOD gave you the thought of becoming a Christian; the impulse to try to become one; the first slight yearning warmth of soul which you experienced. He is beforehand with you; and he will not wait till you have achieved before he will achieve for you, by you, and in you. He is doing exceeding abundantly more for you than you can ask or think.

To the guidance of that good God let every soul commit itself. Feeble in knowledge; ignorant of the way in which we are walking, and of many things that hinder our progress; blinded as to moral truth; knowing less about those things which we most need to know than we think we do; constantly subject to oscillation and variation; proud and selfish; frequently cruel to each other, and more cruel to ourselves; deceiving others, and striving to deceive God; full of bitterness; of the earth, earthy—oh, what shall we do with such natures as ours if there be no sweetening influence, no divine Leader, no spiritual Instructor?

To that dear Spirit of all light, and all knowledge, and all comfort, I commit you. Put your heart in the summer of divine love, and remember that "all things work together for good to them that love God."

APRIL 8: MORNING.

Lo! these are parts of his ways; but how little a portion is heard of him? —*Job* xxvi., 14.

SEE how endless is God's expression of the infinity of taste. What a marvelous variety is displayed in the vapors, that are renewed every single day. The heavens are God's dome. We wonder at the variety of scenes which Michael Angelo painted in the dome of St. Peter's at Rome; but what is that compared with the variety which we behold in the dome of the heavens, where every day God paints frescoes, and rubs them out, that he may paint again the next day, and never twice alike. Look at the infinite variety which God has displayed in field-pictures—in flowers. There is no conceivable color or form which has not been employed in order that the fullness and creativeness of the divine mind in the line of beauty might be manifested. And if taste, which is an outskirt faculty, is worth such illustration and illumination, what will be the endless variations of creative forms which shall greet our gaze when God lets us look on the interior book, wherein he expresses himself in the height, and depth, and length, and breadth of the delicacies of love? We do not see them now, because, having eyes, we see not; but the endless expressions of divine love, and the effects produced by it, exist, though we do not see them. They are yet to be seen by us when we shall have become educated, and our eyes shall have become refined.

APRIL 8: EVENING.

And it was so, when the days of their feasting were gone about, that Job sent and sanctified them, and rose up early in the morning, and offered burnt-offerings according to the number of them all: for Job said, It may be that my sons have sinned, and cursed God in their hearts. Thus did Job continually. —*Job* i., 5.

Oh! woe, woe is on your child if you can not pray for it. I would rather live in widowhood and childless forever, than to have children and not be able to pray for them. If you can not pray for your children, they will be beggars unless you get somebody to pray for them. For every child there should be laid up treasures of prayer, whose almoner is God, and whose providences shall run through all its years. You are living under an administration, as it were, built on purpose for just such offices of love, just such a laying up of prayers.

Oh, Christian parents, do not forget to pray, and pray much. It is a good way to lay up treasure. And do not let your faith forsake you. Do not, because it seems as though your child was going to ruin, think that God has not heard, and is not going to answer, your prayers in his behalf. Do not forget to trust God. You do not know the future. There are more ways than you dream of, in the economy of God, for bringing souls to heaven. I do not believe one disappointed parent will stand before God and say, "I took thee at thy word, and laid up treasures for my children, praying for them day and night, and now where are they?—they are not here!" God will answer your prayers. Do not stint them, and then do not doubt that they will be answered.

> Yes, pray for whom thou lovest; thou mayest vainly, idly seek
> The fervid words of tenderness by feeble words to speak;
> Go kneel before thy Father's throne, and meekly, humbly there,
> Ask blessing for the loved one in the silent hour of prayer.
>
> Yes, pray for whom thou lovest; if uncounted wealth were thine—
> The treasures of the boundless deep, the riches of the mine—
> Thou could'st not to thy cherished friends a gift so dear impart,
> As the earnest benediction of a deeply loving heart.

APRIL 9: MORNING.

Have faith in God.—*Mark* xi., 22.

You must not compare your own peculiarities with your neighbors', and say, "Their constitutional tendencies are such that they can easily restrain their faculties from working in wrong directions, and they ought to do it; but I am so organized that I can not do it, and it is of no use for me to try. By faith and patience you can do it. There is release for you from your evil inclinations if you will but employ the powers which God has given you with which to overcome them. The crooked can be made straight. As a crooked piece of timber can be made straight though its nature can not be changed, so a man's faults can be corrected though his natural disposition can not be rooted out.

APRIL 9: EVENING.

For by grace are ye saved through faith; and that not of yourselves: it is the gift of God.—*Eph.* ii., 8.

Are there no dangerous elements in your disposition? Are there no savage beasts in the menagerie of your soul, which, if they should break away from the restraints that bind them, would pounce upon and lacerate whatever came in their way? Have you never experienced the feeling of hatred? Have there never been lurid moments in which revenges sprang like fires of hell from your soul?

There are to-day, sailing under the flag of pirates, men whose original elements of disposition were as good as mine or yours. There are men engaged in almost every description of crime to-day whose early tendencies were as good as yours, and who had as favorable a chance as you had of making upright, respectable citizens. Now, why are they in their situation, and you in yours? It is because there has been a sovereign providence, a grace of God, which, for wise and mysterious reasons not revealed to us, has led us in the way in which we have walked, and left them in the way in which they have walked.

APRIL 10: *MORNING.*

Now is come salvation, and strength, and the kingdom of our God, and the power of his Christ.—*Rev.* xii., 10.

THERE is nothing that can enter into the conception of man which is so sweet and glorious as the conduct and nature of God, when viewed in the light of the higher ranges of human experience. I never bless God so much as when I think that he came into the world to search for me and save me; and this fact never comes to me as a living reality that I do not long to stand, with all the intelligences of the universe, and say, "Thou art worthy to take the book, and to open the seals thereof, and to receive power, and riches, and wisdom, and strength, and honor, and glory, and blessing." I can worship such a one. A throne I can not worship. A soul I can worship; a head I can not; a hand I can not; a sceptre I can not; but a heart I can. Before a heart I can bow down, and feel that in bowing down I am forever and forever lifted up.

> Since I have learned thy love, my summer, Lord, thou art—
> Summer to me, and day, and life-springs in my heart.
> Thy blood blots out my sin; thy love casts out my fear;
> Heaven is no longer far, since thou, its Sun, art near.

APRIL 10: EVENING.

Faith which worketh by love.—*Gal.* v., 6.

THAT power of the mind by which we bring definitely and clearly before us invisible truths, whether they be truths of quality, truths of person, or truths of place, that power which enables us to see what the senses can not see, is one mode or form of faith; but that is not its full form. *Faith that works by love* is the faith that saves the soul and sanctifies the life. The largest and best way of receiving the Lord Jesus Christ by faith is to take him in such a sense that our souls go out to him in the form of love. It is such a presentation of the Lord Jesus Christ, through the imagination, to our minds, as draws forth toward him the soul's enthusiasm and secret life. It is the personal allegiance of love to Christ. A perception of his grandeur of nature, of his beauty, of his sympathy with us, of his supreme excellence in every part—such a perception that we clasp him with our feelings, that we put our souls wholly under his influence—that is receiving Christ by the heart.

Both mine arms are clasped around thee,
And my head is on thy breast;
For my weary soul has found thee
Such a *perfect, perfect* rest.
Dearest Savior,
Now I know that I am bless'd.

APRIL 11: MORNING.

For ye are all the children of God by faith in Christ Jesus.—*Gal.* iii., 26.

SUPPOSE that I think of friends who are at my house, but whom I have not yet seen. I am conscious that they are benevolent, and kind, and sympathetic, and that they love me. And yet, if one of them comes into my presence, and in conversation his thoughts and feelings flow and overflow, and I see the actual expression of his affection, it produces in me a far different state of mind from what it did when I merely believed that it existed. For now, in the last case, where I see the person, and feel the power of his affection, there is an *appropriating faith*, as old theologians called it.

Now to think of Christ in a merely general way produces comparatively little effect; but there is such a thing as having such a sense of Christ's presence as answers very nearly to the actual physical presence of a friend who makes demonstrations of affection toward us. What we are striving after, or should strive after, is this *appropriating faith*—this consciousness of Christ's presence and love.

APRIL 11: *EVENING.*

And there shall be no more curse: but the throne of God and of the Lamb shall be in it; and his servants shall serve him; and they shall see his face. —*Rev.* xxii., 3, 4.

DEATH will be a revelation. You do not know how many relatives you have till you are in heaven. Oh! when those that are around you, and that you meet from day to day with little pleasure, meet you again, and they have thrown off the cerements of the body; when you see that in them which is good, and in conditions in which counterpoising evil is taken away; when the whole evolutions of their glorious nature are disclosed, you will not know them. It will be as when one looks upon the banks in January, and says, "How dreary are these banks;" and then in June looks upon the same landscape, and says, "It is not the thing that I looked at before." It is winter here, and we are frostbitten or ice-clad. It will be summer there, and we shall be in fragrant leaf and glorious blossom. And when you reach heaven, you will never be lonesome or restrained. Here the necessities of earth, and the proprieties of life, and the laws and conditions of our lower nature partition and divide us, and we belong to each other more than we do to all the world. But in heaven all that will be gone. Every soul there will belong to every soul; every heart to every heart; every love to every love. We shall be God's, and he shall be ours. I will be his Father, and he shall be my son.

Let us not fail to reach that place. Let us take the royal road to love, that shall bring us home to happiness, to manhood, and to immortality.

APRIL 12: *MORNING.*

But the path of the just is as the shining light, that shineth more and more unto the perfect day.—*Prov.* iv., 18.

It is the doctrine of the blessedness of the Spirit of God that men should be inspired to a higher degree of activity than they could have in their own normal and natural conditions.

Never be afraid of going too far so long as you are under the dominion and influence of sweet affections. Under malign influences you may be inspired into fanaticism; but love never went too fast nor too far; zeal for men never burned too brightly. The zeal of self-sacrifice; the earnest endeavor to do good; faith in the solution of all those great questions of character that fill the world in regard to human nature—these things you may cultivate without the least fear that you will detract from the glory of God's Spirit.

Go forward, then, from day to day, and you will find—the most adventurous man will find—that before him, and shining brighter and brighter unto the perfect day, is the light and the blessing of the Spirit of God.

APRIL 12: *EVENING.*

How shall we escape if we neglect so great a salvation?—*Heb.* ii., 3.

For you, to whom the Gospel is preached; for you, upon whose cradle rested the dew of grace, and whose earliest years were made acquainted with the sacred name of Jesus; the children of pious parents; reared within sound of the sanctuary; never beyond the sound of a Sabbath bell; surrounded and hedged in by ten thousand influences of religion persuading the understanding, importunate upon the conscience—for such as you, if Christ be rejected, there is no salvation. For those who never heard him; to whom no sweet sound of the Gospel ever came; whose week was one long, rolling surge, unbroken by the tranquil shore of any Sabbath, and who, in this darkness and neglect, yet always groped upward, endeavoring to live a life better than their times, yearning and longing to know a better way—may we not hope, in the inscrutable mystery of divine wisdom, that there was some mode of applying to such the benefit of the death of Christ? that the vision rose at last upon their eye, cleansed from the films of flesh? and that, among the myriad voices of heaven, there are some from the heathen world who, though on earth they could give no name to that after which their souls yearned and searched, no sooner beheld the divine glory of the Savior than they cried out, "This is he for whom we have waited?" Yes, I firmly believe that it is by the power of Christ that every man is saved who shall touch the shore of heaven; but I am not authorized to say that God can not, in the sovereignty of his love, conduct men who are in darkness to that salvation which we reject, and give them a reflected light, at least, of that glory which shines full on us.

But for all those who have been clearly taught, who have been moved by their wicked passions deliberately to set aside him of whom the prophets spake, whom the apostles more clearly taught, whom the Holy Spirit, by the divine power, now makes known to the world through the Gospel—for them, if they reject their Lord and Savior Jesus Christ, there remaineth no more sacrifice for sin. If they deliberately neglect, set aside, or reject the Savior, he will as deliberately, in the end, reject them.

Death comes down with equal footstep
  To the hall and hut;
Think you death will stand a-knocking
  Where the door is shut?
Jesus waiteth, waiteth, waiteth,
  But thy door is fast;
Grieved, at length away he turneth—
  Death breaks in at last.

Then 'tis thine to stand entreating
  Christ to let thee in;
At the door of heaven beating,
  Wailing for thy sin.
Nay, alas! thou foolish virgin,
  Hast thou then forgot?
Jesus waited long to know thee,
  Now he knows thee not.

APRIL 13: *MORNING.*

Not slothful in business, fervent in spirit, serving the Lord.—*Rom.* xii., 11.

WORK is not God's curse. Work is God's medicine. If it

had not been for work when Adam and Eve were cast out of Paradise, they would have died of their misery. Work comforted them. Every day ought to have enough work to occupy a man wholesomely. Every day has conflicts enough to fill up a man's whole time. If a man is trying to carry himself according to the spirit of true love, he has enough to occupy him every day. If a man is attempting to subordinate all his passions, he has work enough for every day. If a man is endeavoring to fulfill all the duties of life, he has enough to attend to every single day, without troubling himself about the duties of to-morrow. Every day has occupations of usefulness enough to keep a man busy all the while. A man's secular industry, his spiritual conflicts, and his life of benevolence are ample contents with which to grace and fill up every day as it comes.

APRIL 13: *EVENING.*

Be of good courage, and he shall strengthen your heart, all ye that hope in the Lord.—*Psalm* xxxi., 24.

Oh, army of unknown saints—ye that go silently on missions of kindness among the poor; mothers that die deaths daily for your children, or your sister's children, or orphan children; teachers whose lives are worn patiently and obscurely out, that you may build up other lives; those that succor the friendless and the helpless, and care not for yourselves; the great army of heroes that by faith and hope stand at the bottom of society, doing your duty and asking no reward—daylight is dawning. On your heads it shall shine first. Lift them up. Your salvation is nearer than when you believed. Count not any tear shed, or any pain borne, or any groan uttered, as thrown away. Look not upon any yearning or any sigh as lost. God sits above. He sees all things and knows all things. No heart ever identified itself with a thing that was good, or loved any truth, or followed any course of justice and duty, whose name was not registered on high. When the great day of your uplifting shall come, you shall shine as stars.

It is but a day that we are to live here. It is but a shadow that we are making on the earth. We are passing away. We have no abiding city here. Our city is there. Live for that. Live for Christ, and so live for yourselves.

APRIL 14: *MORNING.*

God is a spirit; and they that worship him must worship him in spirit and in truth.—*John* iv., 24.

We ought to confine our utterances of praise to God to those times when our hearts *make* us praise him. Not only that, but we ought to be governed by the same rule in regard to all other feelings. To go to God with a cold heart, and tell him that we burn with love to him, is simply an insult. To say that we put our whole trust in him, when we know that we do not put a bit of trust in him; to express the utmost confidence in him, and yet hold back and shrink from him with fear—these things are exceedingly offensive, and not the less so because they are formulated. Let one prepare his mind by reflecting upon the grace and mercy of God; let him go through a process by which the imagination and the feelings are sanctified; let him endeavor, as much as possible, to bring himself consciously into the divine presence; let him rid his soul of all lower associations by meditation, and singing, and reading the Scriptures; and then, by-and-by, when the fervor comes, let him pray just what he means, and just what he feels, and stop when the feeling ceases. Such praying would be much more profitable to the subject of it, and much more worthy of God.

APRIL 14: *EVENING.*

O the depth of the riches both of the wisdom and knowledge of God! how unsearchable are his judgments, and his ways past finding out.—*Rom.* xi., 33.

The love of God in Christ Jesus; the greatness, the grandeur, and the glory of the heart that, hating iniquity with an intense hatred, can love the doer of it, and that, abhorring sin with an infinite abhorrence, can give itself to save the sinner—these are past finding out. The marvel of meekness, and sweetness, and love in the God of infinite purity and justice—this it is that is past finding out.

If God cared for the misconduct of men no more than we do for the fiery strifes of an ant-hill, there would be no foundation for such a conception of divine gentleness and divine goodness.

There are some who seem to think that God, when he created men and placed them in the world, set on foot an experiment; that he does not care what they do, but that he is satisfied to let them act as they choose, and see what they will come to. Let them have such an idea of God! I will have none of it! God is the righteous judge of all the earth. He is the eternal author and lover of equity.

"Unto the wicked God saith, What hast thou to do to declare my statutes, or that thou shouldest take my covenant in thy mouth? *Thou thoughtest that I was altogether such an one as thyself;* but I will reprove thee, and set them in order before thine eyes. Now consider this, ye that forget God, lest I tear you in pieces, and there be none to deliver."

God comes, and who shall stand before his fear?
Who bide his presence when he draweth near?
My soul, my soul, prepare
To kneel before him there!

How can I bear thy fearful anger, Lord?
I, that so often have transgressed thy word?
But put my sins away,
And spare me in that day!

Yea, I have sinned, as no man sinned beside:
With more than human guilt my soul is dyed;
But spare, and save me here,
Before that day appear!

APRIL 15: *MORNING.*

Wherefore receive ye one another as Christ also received us, to the glory of God.—*Rom.* xv., 7.

CAN any one who has drunk deeply of the spirit of the Master refuse to accept the injunction of the apostle, "We that are strong ought to bear the infirmities of the weak?" It is as if a strong swimmer should turn back and lend a helping hand to buoy up and lift across the flood one that was weaker or less able to swim than himself. We have no right to disregard, much less to hinder, the welfare of any human being. Have I a right to go tramp, tramp, tramp, according to the law of my physical strength, among little children? If I am where they are, I am bound so to walk as not to tread upon or injure them. A man is bound to hold his knowledge, his conscience, his affections, his pleasures, his privileges, his influence, subject to this great law, "Christ died for men, and I must live for men, and restrain my power, and forego my rights, even for their sake. There is nothing on earth that ought to be so sacred to me. Myself should not be more sacred to myself than is that human being for whom Christ died." But how we love to lash with our tongue men that do not believe as we do! We love to specify different gradations and classifications of men, and indulge in contemptuous remarks concerning them. And yet there is not a man born on whom God does not look every day, and say, "I died for him." There is not a human being who has not stamped on him the image and superscription of the dying God. What right have I to impugn him, or treat him with contempt? What right have I to walk over him in my liberty, real or fancied? What right have I to tyrannize by my superiority over any man for whom Christ died?

APRIL 15: *EVENING.*

To him that overcometh will I give to eat of the tree of life, which is in the midst of the paradise of God.—*Rev.* ii., 7.

THANK God, when I go home to heaven, I shall leave behind many things that will be of no use to me there. When an engine is taken from one boat and placed in another, it is not necessary that the fastenings should go with it. The screws, and clamps, and feeding-pumps that belong to that particular ship from which it is taken may be left behind. The screws, and clamps, and feeding-pumps that have been necessary to keep my mind in this body, and to patch and mend which has given me so much trouble, I shall leave in the grave. But my supremest reason, my divinest sentiments of religion, my affections, my loves, my tastes—these God, the blessed Pilot, shall carry safely through the grave and its darkness; and I shall be planted again in heaven, where snows never fall, where frosts never come; and I shall bring out leaf, and blossom, and fruit; and then, with leaf, and blossom, and fruit, I will present myself to the throne of God, saying, "Thou hast given me life, and life again, and life forever: to thee, and to thee only, be praise, and honor, and glory evermore."

APRIL 16: MORNING.

My voice shalt thou hear in the morning, O Lord; in the morning will I direct my prayer unto thee, and will look up.—*Psalm* v., 3.

Mine eyes prevent the night watches, that I might meditate in thy word. —*Psalm* cxix., 148.

A MAN may read one verse of the Bible, and it shall be the rudder of his mind from morning till night; or a man may read a whole chapter, or a page, and get nothing at all from it. And so with prayer. That man has prayed whose soul has been in the conscious presence of God, though he may have uttered only a sentence, or a word, or though he may not have uttered a word; and a man may address God for hours without lifting his soul up into the presence of God, and not pray. Prayer is what we need more and more, in proportion as men are less and less accustomed to pray. In times of revival, when the air is full of sympathy, and when every body speaks it to you, then you multiply seasons of prayer. But when you are overwhelmed with cares, and your affairs require you to rise early and sit up late, and your temptations augment, and you are thrown out on the wild sea of secular pursuits, then, under the pretence of excessive business, you grow remiss in the duty of prayer. Now that is the time, above all others, when you need to be faithful in this duty. Usually men pray least when they most need prayer, and most when they least need it.

No man is so busy that he can not read the Word of God daily, and no man is so busy that he can not daily stop to bathe himself in the heavenly atmosphere. If a man has not time for these things, then he has not time to eat. Prayer and the Word of God are as the bread of life and as the water of life. The soul must day by day be fed on these, or go hungry.

A moment from this outward life,
Its service, self-denial, strife,
  I joyfully retreat;
My soul, through intercourse with thee,
Strengthened, refreshed, and calmed shall be,
  Its scenes again to meet.

APRIL 16: EVENING.

Then shall we know if we follow on to know the Lord.—*Hosea* vi., 3.

SPEAKING of the whole round of men's experience in this estate, the apostle says, "As long as you live in this world you will see the brightest truths and the clearest outlines as through a glass darkly." But does that put what you do know to shame? No; it is real knowledge as much as any. It is fragmentary, but it is the beginning of knowledge. It is only a part. It is seen, not too much, but too dimly. And when you die and go to heaven, let no man say "your earthly knowledge has all perished." No; we shall trace again the lines which here we traced but feebly. There will glow the everlasting light; and all the impressions which here were but seminal, there will be in full blossom and fruit. All those truths which we saw, and saw in the twilight—shall we not see them yet more gloriously, because the twilight is swallowed up in everlasting day? We shall not have occasion to despise our earthly thoughts and yearnings, and knowledges and longings, but we shall improve them, and with them and beyond them go on forever and forever with the Lord.

How blessed it is to begin such a life upon earth. How poor are they who are without God and without hope in this world. They are the richest men who are laying up the brightest, the clearest, and the most helpful and noble conceptions of God. That way lies manhood. That way lies joy. That way lies everlasting blessedness.

APRIL 17: MORNING.

The lame take the prey.—*Isaiah* xxxiii., 23.

SUPPOSE that twenty of you are making a pilgrimage across the continent on foot. You travel twenty miles a day. Some of you are so full of vigor that you can make circuits, and chase the hare, and run down the bird in addition to walking your twenty miles. That distance is nothing to you. The next five walk their twenty miles in comparative ease, without any special difficulty, but they have no strength to spare. The next five get along pretty well, but the journey tells upon them. They find it hard to keep their courage up, and are glad enough to have night come so that they can rest. The last five are tired when they begin, and are tired all the way, and love to sit down and rest often, and they linger behind the others, and it is long after the camp is pitched, and the fires are lighted, that one by one they straggle in. But they all get in. There is a great deal of difference between them. Some make the journey easily, some do it less easily, some do it with difficulty, and some with still more difficulty; but they are all pilgrims and travelers, and they all advance over the route.

Now, in going to heaven, some make the journey more easily than others. Owing to the circumstances of life, there are very many differences in this respect. But, although it is desirable to be a joyful Christian, it is not of so much importance that you should be joyful as that you should be true, conscientious, earnest. Rejoice in the Lord. But do not *aim* at rejoicing. Have a cheerful, hopeful, joyful courage if you may, but aim at no motive lower than God's favor. Aim at the truth. Aim at Christian benevolence. Aim at building up a holy manhood that shall be higher than that which belongs to the world around you. Then, doubtless, you will find more and more that the fruit of the Spirit in you is joy and peace.

APRIL 17: *EVENING.*

For as the rain cometh down, and the snow from heaven, and returneth not thither, but watereth the earth, and maketh it bring forth and bud, that it may give seed to the sower, and bread to the eater: so shall my word be that goeth forth out of my mouth: it shall not return unto me void, but it shall accomplish that which I please, and it shall prosper in the thing whereto I sent it.—*Isaiah* lv., 10, 11.

All the stripes and persecutions that men have borne for the sake of goodness; all the sympathy that they have treasured up in their hearts for their fellow-men; all the blood that they have poured out for the cause of truth and righteousness—all this has been garnered and placed to their account, not in the books of men—God has taken care of it; and he declares, for the encouragement of his fainting children, that as the rain and the snow shall not return without accomplishing that whereto it is sent, so not the slightest thing put forth for goodness, and usefulness, and purity shall perish. Though it disappear, though it be hidden, it is that it may do its office-work.

Do not work when you are in the sunshine alone. Do not count only those things useful the effects of which you can see. The results of usefulness are often covered up. It is well that it is so, for man's pride and vanity easily get drunk on the wine of success. From those, therefore, that do the most is hidden much that they do. It is not best that they should know it all. But God knows it; and there comes a registering day, a reaping day, an exhibition day, a day of welcoming and gratulation, when good men go home to heaven to be surprised with the harvest of which they only sowed the seed—the much that has come from the little.

> Say not "'Twas all in vain"—
> The patience, and the pity, and the word
> In warning breathed 'mid passion's hurricane,
> Unheeded here—but God that whisper heard,
> The tender grief o'er strangers' sorrow shed,
> The sacrifice that won no human praise.
> In faith upon the waters cast thy bread,
> For "thou shalt find it after many days."

APRIL 18: *MORNING.*

As they went to tell his disciples, behold, Jesus met them, saying, All hail! And they came and held him by his feet, and worshiped him. Then said Jesus unto them, Be not afraid!—*Matt.* xxviii., 9, 10.

All hail! Be not afraid. These may almost be called the voices of the grave. Within the hour of his coming forth doubtless the disciples had met him. The cool of the rock was yet upon his brow. The sadness of death was yet scarcely cleansed from his eye. He came from death and the grave, saying, "All hail! Be not afraid!"

His was the inspiration of the other world coming through, as a narrow passage, the grave—the rock-grave. He spake in the spirit of the land from which he had come; and to every one that has heard of Jesus, from that day to this, that voice still rings out. His salutation to each one is, "All hail!" and to every one his greeting is, "Be not afraid." Very God, our Judge yet to be, holding the destiny of every man in his hands, the sovereign Lord and Monarch, yet he meets every one who goes to him, how poor soever he may be, how sinful, how neglected, how outcast; and his greeting is, "All hail to thee!" And to every one who looks up, and is conscious of his greatness, still his greeting is, "Be not afraid." The grave is but the shutting of the angel-hand that keeps the treasure, and conveys it safely to the other side. As they who sail over the seas go down into the vessel, and are hid, so the grave is but the resting-place of the dead for a little time—not decay; not loss; not final separation in darkness. No; instructed by these words, the voice should sound out to every one of us that comes to the grave-side, "All hail!" and as we look again, "Be not afraid."

APRIL 18: *EVENING.*

How often would I have gathered thy children together, even as a hen gathereth her chickens under her wings, and ye would not.—*Matt.* xxiii., 37.

Do not be afraid to confess your sin, and, above all, do not be afraid to confess your sin to Jesus. If you are afraid of God—though you should not be—then turn to Jesus. It is easy for sorrow to confess to love.

When the stern father overtakes the child that is in fault, and anger is on his brow, anger also is in the heart of the child; and the intense firmness of the father kindles an intense obstinacy in the child. He will not bend, nor break, nor confess. But when the sun goes down, and the pain is over, and the obdurate child is gathered to the household in the evening, and twilight comes with all its softening influences, and he is alone with his mother, who wipes the tears that she can not keep from her eyes, and loves him, and puts her arm fondly about him, and only looks at him, and utters no word of reproach, oh! how does the generous child, with a turbulent tide of feeling, burst out into tears, and say, "Mother, I *did* do it—I *did* do it!" And what the father failed to extract, the mother's look has brought.

If for justice' sake, if for fear of the law, you will not confess your sin and forsake it, look unto the love of Jesus, the tenderness of Jesus. And if you would make it easy, oh! turn to the bosom of Christ; let him put his arm about you, and let him look upon you with those sorrowing eyes. "How often would I have gathered you as a hen gathereth her chickens under her wings, but ye would not."

APRIL 19: *MORNING.*

Being filled with the fruits of righteousness, which are by Jesus Christ, unto the glory and praise of God.—*Phil.* i., 11.

I AM a citizen on the Fourth of July; but I am no more a citizen then than I am on the fifth, or on the sixth, though I make a great deal more ado about it. And a man is Christ's, not because he feels so very much lifted up, but because his reason, his judgment, and his heart have agreed together to accept the commandments of Christ, and the person of Christ, as their chief, and because he is determined, by the help of God, to live in this mind all the days of his life. It is that act of the will, that choice, which gives men the evidence that they are Christians, and makes them Christians.

Some days you read the Bible, and like it—so do I; some days you read the Bible, and do not see any thing in it—so do I. Some days you enjoy prayer—so do I; some days you do not—nor do I. With every body it is just so. And so it will be until people are balanced so exactly that there is no rising too high or falling too low—so it will be, in other words, to the end of the world. It is not safe for persons to judge whether they are Christians or not by watching their transient moods.

APRIL 19: *EVENING.*

Then were the disciples glad when they saw the Lord.—*John* xx., 20.

To those who are mourning the hiding of Christ's face; to those who are conscious that, by reason of unbelief or doubt, Christ is much hidden from them, I would say, Remember that he disappeared from among his disciples only for a few hours, and then reappeared never to be separated from them. He left them for their good. He restored himself to them that that good might be consummated in them. If you have once had a saving knowledge of the Savior, and have lost it, it may be renewed. For, as when two that are really knit together in affection have had some misunderstanding, and have gone apart, both hearts are empty, and both are hungry for reconciliation, so it is between the soul and the Savior—only with this difference, that as he is the greater, and the truer, and the nobler One, he yearns for us more than we know how to yearn for him. And as he stood gathering and mustering again the disciple band after his resurrection, so he stands now, saying to every wandering, darkening soul that has lost its hold on him, "I am he; I am the way."

APRIL 20: MORNING.

For me to live is Christ.—*Phil.* i., 21.

We are very apt, in the regularity of teaching, to carry forward our faith of Christ to the dying hour, and to think of a Christ that can rise upon us in that mortal strife with healing in his beams. We are not apt to have Christ with us every day in its vicissitudes and disappointments; we are not apt to take Christ into the checks, and frets, and hindrances, and misdirections of this world, into our bereavements and misfortunes. We are apt to regard Christ as remote from us, and to put him forward to the time of our final dismission from this world.

He who has learned how to die in his passions every day; how to die in his pride from hour to hour; he who has Christ in each particular thwarting and event of life; he who knows how, from the varied experiences of life, to bring forth day by day a Christian character, need not fear the grand and final experience of earth to which he is coming. There is no death to those who know how to die beforehand. Those who lay themselves upon Christ, and take the experiences of every-day life in the faith of Christ; those who see the will of God in every thing that abounds, whether wounding or healing—they have nothing left at the end of life except peace, translation, and the beginning of immortality.

APRIL 20: EVENING.

Oh, love the Lord, all ye his saints.—*Psalm* xxxi., 23.

Christ comes to every man and demands of him love. He presents himself in every aspect in which a greater mind can be presented to a lower; he presents himself as the Son of God, the Savior of the world, your personal friend, and your elder brother; he embodies in himself every tender relationship of which we can conceive; and he asks, he claims as his right, that you should love him.

If love were a sealed fountain, if you had never learned to love, you would be less to blame for neglecting to love Christ. But among the things taught earliest is love; among the things most experienced in life is love; and among the things remembered latest is love. When the child comes into life, almost the first thing he does is to send out his heart in trust, and confidence, and love; and though the objects of his primal affection are limited and imperfect, they are sufficient to excite in him the dormant spark of love. But when it is the infinite Creator; when it is the glorious God; when it is he that has laid down his own life for you; when it is he, rather, that has taken it up again, and lives to intercede for you; when it is he that sends you day by day fresh glories, and that night after night surrounds you with mercies; when it is he that through all the periods of your life watches over you with most tender solicitude and scrupulous fidelity; when it is he that outvies all other affections, and showers his own upon you more copiously than clouds ever rained drops or seasons ever gave forth fruit; when it is he that comes to you, and says, "My son, give me thine heart," what will you do with this Jesus that yearns for your love? Will you not love him?

Oh, see how Jesus trusts himself
  Unto our childish love!
As though, by his free ways with us,
  Our earnestness to prove.

His sacred name a common word
  On earth he loves to hear;
There is no majesty in him
  Which love may not come near.

APRIL 21: *MORNING.*

Happy are ye, for the spirit of glory and of God resteth upon you.—1 *Peter* iv., 14.

Before any daisy or violet, before any blossom is seen in the field, the sun lies with its bosom to the ground, crying to the flower, and saying, "Why tarriest thou so long?" And day after day the sun comes, and pours its maternal warmth upon the earth, and coaxes the plant to grow and bloom. And when days and weeks have passed, the root obeys the call, and sends out its germ, from which comes the flower. And it was the sun that brooded it into life. Had it not been for the sun's warmth and light, the flower could never have come to itself.

So the eternal Spirit of God rests on the human soul, warming it, quickening it, calling it, and saying, "Oh, my son, where art thou?" And it is this divine sympathy and brooding influence that at last brings men to God, and leads them to say, "Am I not sinful?" and to yearn for something higher, and purer, and holier. It was God's work. He long ago was *working in you, to will and to do of his own good pleasure.*

APRIL 21: *EVENING.*

He that is slow to anger is better than the mighty; and he that ruleth his spirit than he that taketh a city.—*Prov.* xvi., 32.

Do not tell me that confession is all a degrading thing. Do not tell me that it is all a painful thing. It is painful as long as you strive against it; it is rendered painful by many of the lacerations of expiation; but, after all, through confession of sin and renunciation, we come to an atmosphere in which we breathe the very breath of heaven itself. No one who has done wrong can feel so happy as he who has come out of it, and has not covered it up, but has forsaken it, and confessed it, and risen beyond it. That is the royal way.

Some of the highest and most noble experiences that men have in this world are those that they have when they have overcome a wrong, clearly, avowedly, and are conscious in their whole being that they stand beyond it; when they have confessed it to God and forsaken it; when they have gained a victory over their own disposition. A victory within us is ten thousand times more glorious than any victory than can be outside of us. A man that subdues himself is better than a man that subdues empires to himself.

It is glorious to be conscious
  Of a glorious power within,
Stronger than the rallying forces
  Of a charged and marshaled sin.

APRIL 22: MORNING.

Therefore let us not sleep, as do others; but let us watch and be sober.—1 *Thess.* v., 6.

THIS is a military figure. Although watching may be a domestic figure, ordinarily it is military. A tower, a castle, a fort, is not content with simply the strength of its walls and its various defenses. Sentinels are placed all around about it, and they walk both night and day, and look out on every side to descry any approaching danger, that the soldiers within may put themselves at once in a condition to receive attack.

Still more are a moving army watchful, whether upon the march or in the camp. They throw out advanced guards. The picket line is established by night and by day. Men are set apart to watch on purpose that no enemy may take them unawares; that they may constantly be prepared for whatever incursion the chances of war may bring upon them.

Now we are making a campaign through life. We are upon an enemy's ground; we are surrounded, or liable to be surrounded, with adversaries who will rush in upon us, and take us captives at unawares. We are commanded, therefore, to do as soldiers do, whether in fort or in camp—to be always vigilant, always prepared.

APRIL 22: EVENING.

But when he saw the wind boisterous, he was afraid; and beginning to sink, he cried, saying, Lord, save me. And immediately Jesus stretched forth his hand, and caught him, and said unto him, O thou of little faith, wherefore didst thou doubt?—*Matt.* xiv., 30, 31.

MANY persons are discouraged on account of their feebleness of will-power. Nevertheless, their souls must be saved. They must go to heaven with the sailing apparatus which God has given them. And when the last keel has touched the heavenly shore, although the first and swiftest, that outran all the others, may be the best, and the next one may be the next best, and the next one may be the next best, yet the clumsiest old scow, that moved slowly and had to be steered bunglingly, if at last it does touch the shore, shall be welcome. You will say, "Lord Jesus, I am here, and that is all." And he will say to you, "I had an errand to be performed by some one who should cross the stormy deep in just such a structure as this. That patience and persevering faith which you have manifested I wanted worked out. You have accomplished the task which was set apart for you. It was the very thing that I appointed you for. Others have beaten you in speed, but there is no other that shall take your crown."

Persevere, and work manfully, with weakness and temptation, in darkness and light, and you will reach your heavenly Father soon. No father on earth was ever so lenient with the faults of his child who wanted to do right, as God is with your faults if you want to do right, and will try to do right. In a little time you will know that this is so.

APRIL 23: MORNING.

Now he that hath wrought for us the self-same thing is God, who also hath given unto us the earnest of the Spirit.—2 *Cor.* v., 5.

One simple breath of perfume indicates the blossom, the blossom indicates the cluster, the cluster the fruit, and the fruit the vintage; and so, in the experiences of the soul, a single note of love, that means companionship, means glory in the heavenly state. Here is a yearning of the soul. What means this yearning? What child, who had never known father or mother, ever wept from home-sickness? What child who has known father and mother, if separated from them in a far distant land, has not shed some tears of longing for home? And what are his tears but an earnest of the joy that awaits him when he returns to the bosom of his parents and the companionship of his brothers and sisters?

And what mean these hungerings of the soul? They mean something in the world to come. They are fore-tokens and fore-gleams. They are earnests of the promised possession. True Christian experiences in this life not only indicate that we are in a Christian state, but are God's tokens that we are coming to a perfection of those experiences in the future life.

They are so many earnests or first payments of that which we are to have paid wholly to us when we stand in Zion and before God.

What must it be to dwell above,
  At God's right hand, where Jesus reigns,
Since the sweet earnest of his love
  O'erwhelms us on these dreary plains.
No heart can think, no tongue explain,
What bliss it is with Christ to reign.

APRIL 23: EVENING.

Blessed be God, even the Father of our Lord Jesus Christ, the Father of mercies, and the God of all comfort: who comforteth us in all our tribulation, that we may be able to comfort them which are in any trouble, by the comfort wherewith we ourselves are comforted of God.—2 *Cor.* i., 3, 4.

God sometimes puts a man in such a position in life that he is at peace with himself and out of joint with the outward world; and that is a very solemn situation to be in. A man who is thus placed is ordained to be a preacher of consolation to all the world about him, and woe be to every such man who betrays his trust! In proportion as a man is harmoniously organized within, and is placed in outward circumstances where he has to pass through struggles which develop in him a rich experience, God says to him, "Let your struggles in those circumstances be an example and an encouragement to others. Strive for their sake. Be to them something of what Christ has been to you, and what he is to all the world." If a man takes this equipment within—the harmonious organization with which he has been endowed—and makes it a means of gratifying his selfishness, and sits down for his own pure delight, he has betrayed his trust most grievously. God requires very much of those who have no struggle of their own to wage.

APRIL 24: MORNING.

Enter not into the path of the wicked, and go not in the way of evil men. Avoid it, pass not by it, turn from it and pass away.—*Prov.* iv., 14, 15.

It is said, in one of the old "Lives of the Saints," that the devil found a young man at a theatre, and took possession of him; and the saint rebuked him, and said, "Why do you take one of the Lord's children?" and the devil said, "What business has one of the Lord's children on my ground?" It is thus in temptation. Men tempt the devil. They send a message to him, inviting him to come and take them.

There are men who live so near to cheating that, though they do not mean to cheat, circumstances can not bend them without pushing them over. There are many men who are like an apple-tree, whose trunk and roots, and two thirds of the branches are in the garden, and one third of whose branches are outside of the garden wall. So there are many men whose trunk and roots are on the side of honesty and uprightness, but who are living so near the garden wall that they throw their boughs clear over into the highway where iniquities tramp and are free.

It is never safe for a man to run so near to the line of right and wrong that, if he should lose a wheel, he would go over. You should keep so far from the precipice that, if your wagon breaks down, there is room enough between you and the precipice; otherwise you can not be safe.

APRIL 24: EVENING.

Confirming the souls of the disciples, and exhorting them to continue in the faith, and that we must through much tribulation enter into the kingdom of God.—*Acts* xiv., 22.

ETERNAL measurements magnify some things and reduce others. Suppose, in God's providence, you are reduced to poverty, and compelled to exchange your comfortable dwelling for more humble quarters? Does an Arab cry because his tent is pitched here this morning and taken away to-morrow morning? Can God's providence make you poorer than when you came into the world? You have got along somehow thus far, and do you not suppose that you can get along somehow to the end? There are only two things to go through in this life—a door to get in at and a door to get out at, and I think you can go through these. When a man is born nothing can prevent his dying, and dying is the best thing that can happen to a Christian. You are on the way to it; and every batter, every blow, every care, every trouble, every fear, every disappointment—these are but just so many conspiring winds in your sail. They waft you quickly over life's tempestuous sea. They are so many things that make it easier to leave the world; that chasten your affections; that deepen your piety; that cool the fever of your selfish desires; that throw the light of ineffable and eternal glory upon the worthlessness of earth's possessions. We need to rise from our low and sordid estimates of this world, and judge of times, and events, and experiences by the other sphere.

Our life is not in all these brief possessions;
Our home is not in any pleasant spot:
Pilgrims and strangers we must journey onward,
Contented with the portion of our lot.

These earthly walls must shortly be dismantled;
These earthly tents be struck by angel hands;
But to be built upon a sure foundation,
There, where our Father's mansion ever stands.

There shall we meet, parent and child, and dearer
That earthly love which makes half heaven of home;
There shall we find our treasures all awaiting,
Where change, and death, and parting never come.

APRIL 25: MORNING.

If thou wilt enter into life, keep the commandments.—*Matt.* xix., 17.

Nothing will convict a man of his sinfulness sooner than the attempt to practice the teachings of Christ. Many persons seem to think that there is to be a projected conversion; a spiritual phantasmagoria, if I may say so. They seem to expect that there is to be brought before them, by the power of God's Spirit, something equivalent to Calvary, with its three crosses, and the Savior hanging on the sacred middle one. They seem to be looking for some mysterious disclosure which shall answer to the very crucifixion of Christ. They are waiting to behold the wondrous spectacle, whereas they should at once endeavor to obey God's law. The first step in that direction will show you how far you are from obedience. Try to love, try to pray, try to practice the Christian virtues, and do it from hour to hour, and you will not be long in finding out how selfish you are, how proud you are, how unsympathetic you are in spiritual things, how closely allied you are to worldly things.

APRIL 25: EVENING.

For the Lord your God is gracious and merciful, and will not turn away his face from you, if ye return unto him.—2 *Chron.* xxx., 9.

THE reconciliation of a man's soul with Christ is, I will not say one of the easiest, but one of the simplest things in life.

Have you ever had a quarrel with your father and mother? You have, unless you have been an exceedingly good boy. Do not you recollect how you did some wrong that you did not want your parents to know; and how you feared that they would find it out; and how you looked to see if they knew it, after the servant had threatened to tell them, and thought they did when they did not; how all this time you shrank from them; and how, by-and-by, they expressed a confidence in you which showed that they did not know it; and how an impulse came over you to make a clean breast of the matter, and you went to your mother and burst into tears, and told her yourself, and put your head in her lap, and cried; and how you felt better; and how, the first thing you knew, her hand was on your hair, and she said, "Well, my child, I am sorry you did wrong; but you have done right now in coming to me and telling me. I do not believe you will do it any more. Look up, and kiss me;" and how she put her arms about you, and drew you to her? Was it not the sweetest and best way, when you had done wrong, to go and tell your mother, and get her blessing? If you do not know, I do, how good it was, when I had done wrong, to be reconciled, so that I could go on again with a light heart, singing like a bird.

Now the Lord Jesus Christ is dearer than any mother, sweeter than any parent, more tender than any lover, better than any friend. Most gracious and helpful is your God. Go to him. On your way you may stop and tell your minister or friend; but go straight to God and say, "Father, I have done wrong; take me and help me."

APRIL 26: MORNING.

My soul shall be joyful in the Lord: it shall rejoice in his salvation.—*Psalm* xxxv., 9.

A CHRISTIAN life is not one of burdensomeness, but one of cheerfulness and gladness. It is not one of drudgery, but one of friendship and love. No man presents a type of Christianity who lives simply by force of duty. If there is no love in you; if there are no bubbles that reflect heaven before they break; if there is no singing joy; if there is no cheerfulness; if there is no spontaneousness; if there is no automatic life, then, although you may be a Christian, you are a Christian in the same sense in which a chicken is a bird when it is just breaking the shell, when it can not run, nor fly, nor do any thing except peep. You are like an unfledged robin in the nest. And how different is the robin that is grown, and that can mount up and make circles through the air in its flight! The peculiarity of Christian life in its characteristic elements is that it has so taken God to be its Father, and Christ to be its elder brother and Savior, and the service of God in all purity and nobleness to be its delight, that it becomes spontaneous. It is joyful living; not drudgery, nor even duty.

APRIL 26: EVENING.

Oh that men would praise the Lord for his goodness, and for his wonderful works to the children of men!—*Psalm* cvii., 8.

THE history of man's life, in respect to the gifts of God that come to him through his physical endowments, is, in the main, a history of independence by reason of favor received without scruple from God's royal bounty, expressed in head, in hand, in foot, in throbbing heart, in sensitive nerve, in strong bone, in living muscle. All the sinews that God has put together to create the most noble thing made under the heaven—we take them all as a gift of course. We arrogate to ourselves personal beauty if we are handsome, personal strength if we are powerful, personal skill if we have the hand to execute. We take all these sovereign gifts of God not with thanksgiving, not as if they brought us nearer to him in sweeter obedience, not as benefits received, but to separate us from God and our service to him. Is it not so? Look all around about you and say, is it not so? Is there a man that is not obliged to acknowledge, "I have been ungrateful even in the mere matter of my bodily life; my life has been marked by ingratitude to God; I have never rendered thanks for the many favors received."

The hosts of heaven proclaim thee wise and just,
  And every flower that blooms beside our ways,
Each tiny worm that creeps along the dust,
  Or murmuring forest-bough, declares thy praise.
Alas! that man, for whom these all were made—
  Himself his Maker's master-piece—that he
  So slow to praise and gratitude should be,
So apt to rest in what must pass and fade.

APRIL 27: MORNING.

But as many as received him, to them gave he power to become the sons of God, even to them that believe on his name.—*John* i., 12.

It is no time for Christian men to disown the ideal of human character set forth by Jesus Christ. The hope of the world lies in its *ideals.* He is the worst of all iconoclasts who vulgarizes, or obscures and hides the world's *ideals.*

It is not for us to deify common moralities, good as they are, and indispensable to human life. But they are only the root-leaves. When the long-shining summer sun has drawn up from among them the slender flowering stem, opened its fragrant blossom, and evolved its precious fruit, is it for us to take sides with the dirt-spattered seminal leaves, and to hesitate and waver in mind whether they are not, after all, good enough?

There was never so much as now a time when men who have seen that true light, and who have tasted of the power of the invisible world, should hold up the reality, the beauty, and the immense superiority of the true Christian character, as the product of God's Spirit working upon the human soul, over all barren attainments and results of man's volition, acting unaided within the realm of sensuous natural law.

APRIL 27: EVENING.

Neither is there salvation in any other; for there is none other name under heaven given among men whereby we must be saved.—*Acts* iv., 12.

There is nothing so piteous as the weakness of men, and their trouble and suffering under sin. Life is full of it. Life sometimes seems to me like a boiling caldron, and men like bubbles that come to the surface and burst at every moment. Still they rise and perish, and still the caldron boils. And at times I have the darkest thoughts as to such a world as this, seemingly so abandoned. If I lost faith that the heart of the world was love, and that it was still driven by the energizing and recreating power of God, I should lose faith in every thing. I should hardly want to live; or, if I did, I should want to shield my eyes from the suffering that is in the world. And the truth that Christ who was in the flesh now lives, advanced at the right hand of God, clothed with power, and having a sympathetic heart; that he is still laboring to save men; that those who have sinned against him have no other friend who is so near to them, who is doing so much for them, and who is willing to do so much for them—this truth is extremely precious to me. I thank God that Jesus Christ is at work in the world, that he has pity for men, that he is going forth still, by his Spirit, to seek them and to save them. It is my growing consolation. It is my only hope for myself and for others.

APRIL 28: MORNING.

Flesh and blood can not inherit the kingdom of God.—1 *Cor.* xv., 50.

There is immortality beyond this veil. There is a soul that can not die. What hast thou done for that soul? Oh moral man, thou art to live in the presence of God! Where is thy title, and where are thy tastes? Thou art to speak another language than that of men upon earth. Speak now some sentences of the heavenly tongue. Thou art to be brighter than the stars if thy destiny be fulfilled; but where are the signs and tokens of it? Your bones do not inherit immortality.

Flesh and blood shall not inherit the kingdom of God. Holy thoughts and the power of thinking them, heavenly aspirations and the power of realizing them—it is these things that belong to God's kingdom. It is these that can not die, and that the world can not touch.

Let love die here; let my name perish here; let my house pass to another; let my children wither as leaves upon a bough that has been plucked off; let my life be as him who dwelleth in a desert overblown with choking sands, if in that moment, when I stand in heaven, God shall say to me, "Enter; thou art welcome." In that one hour I shall reap more than compensation for all. But, though my house be builded of gold and silver, and my head crowned with chaplets of roses, and all sweet delights wait on my feet, and my life be one long-rolling symphony of joy, that one word, "Depart! I know you not," will overmaster and storm out of the memory the whole of this joy. "What shall it profit a man if he gain the whole world and lose his own soul?"

> In having all things and not thee, what have I?
> Not having thee, what have my labors got?
> Let me enjoy but thee, what further crave I?
> And, having thee alone, what have I not?
> I wish not sea nor land, nor would I be
> Possessed of heaven, heaven unpossessed of thee.

APRIL 28: EVENING.

Jesus answered and said unto him, Verily, verily, I say unto thee, except a man be born again, he can not see the kingdom of God.—*John* iii., 3.

CHRISTIAN experience is a spiritual experience produced in the soul by the direct action of the Holy Spirit of God upon the faculties of the soul. It is a new life. It is not reformation simply, nor a more perfect obedience to rules or principles, but a new sphere, new influences and new experiences, and a new and transcendently nobler class of emotions, aspirations, and powers. This dispensation of the Spirit began at Jerusalem at the day of Pentecost. Thenceforth the apostles are scarcely to be recognized as the same men. Then followed those extraordinary experiences of gifts and miracles under the effusion of the Spirit. An evolution had taken place. A new race had developed. The human soul had found its way into the realm whither lower natural law was unable to bring it, but where there were great spiritual natural laws waiting to stimulate, fertilize, and mature it.

From this hour the ideal of character changed. The higher rules the lower. What man could do under lower influences no longer sufficed. All common virtues, moralities, endeavors, benevolences, must be measured by the new standard. Henceforth he is Christian whose soul is intersphered with Christ's soul. It is faith, or life by the power of the invisible, that saves. It is faith that works by love, and purifies the soul, that redeems.

APRIL 29: MORNING.

The servant of the Lord must not strive, but be gentle unto all men, apt to teach, patient, in meekness instructing those that oppose themselves.—2 *Tim.* ii., 24, 25.

When I see men that are crushed to the ground by their own vices and dissipations, and people say "Can these men live?" I always think, "Yes, if any body is willing to suffer for them, they can live." If there are those who love the soul of a man who is weighed down by his own sins so that they can give their life for him—not in the sense of laying it down, but better, in the sense of going to him, and identifying themselves with him in such a way that he knows he has friends who will stick forever with him, and pity him, and rebuke and pain him if need be, and be his better self to him, and give him the benefit of their reason when his reason is clouded, and lift him up when he stumbles, and bring him back when he wanders out of the way—if there are those who are willing thus to suffer for such a man, he may be plucked out of the gates of hell, and out of the jaws of destruction. No man need be lost if there are those who will do for him what Christ did for all of us. A mother will do it for a child; and a father, if he is not too proud, will often be found to do it for a son. But multitudes are not saved because there is nobody to take their place, and suffer for them and with them.

There is a great harvest-field, and the labor is terrific, but the laborers are few.

APRIL 29: EVENING.

But straightway Jesus spake unto them, saying, Be of good cheer; it is I; be not afraid.—*Matt.* xiv., 27.

Although we fain would see the Savior coming with a smile, he chooses to come often with frowns. Blessed be his name, that frowns and smiles alike mean love with him. Just as, in the great cycle of the year, frost and dew are the same thing, and come with a like merciful errand, though with a different function—both of them serving the fruitfulness of nature, and being a part of God's ministration of mercy—so is the divine presence in the midst of great sorrows. Though dark, though acerb, though filling us with pain, sorrows carry in them the Savior. We may may not know it, but he knows it.

Is your hold upon the promises so feeble that you are tempest-tossed, and fear mightily, at times, utter wreck? And do you wonder, turning your eye upon what seems to you empty space, that Christ should suffer his little ones to be so beset and so tried? Remember that he comes to us in various guises—not alone as a radiant Savior and a God of power, but as a man of sorrows. He comes in sorrows, and in strifes, and in temptations.

My God once mixed a harsh cup for me to drink it,
And it was full of acrid bitterness intensest.
The black and nauseating draught did make me shrink from it,
And cry, "Oh thou, who every draft alike dispensest,
This cup of anguish sore, bid me not to quaff of it,
Or pour away the dregs and the deadliest half of it!"
But still the cup he held; and seeing he ordained it,
One glance at him—it turned to sweetness as I drained it.

APRIL 30: MORNING.

But the greatest of these is charity.—1 *Cor.* xiii., 13.

Without love, every other grace and every other attainment is void.

Love is the one interpreter between God and man.

Love is the one facile harmonizer of the internal discords of the human soul. It induces an atmosphere in us in which all feelings find their summer, and so their ripeness. Around no other one centre of the human soul will all the faculties gather in submission and in obedience, but they will around love. It has power to control rage and anger, and subdue them. It breaks self-will and obstinacy. It persuades pride. It stimulates imagination, and enriches it. It gives energy to all the moral sentiments; ennobles them; sweetens them; gives them more power. While it fires each individual power with intense fervor, it mingles the different manifestations of power, like flames, in a harmonious fellowship. Love it is—not conscience—that is God's regent in the human soul, because it can govern the soul as nothing else can.

And love is the only experience which keeps the soul always in a relation of sympathy and of harmony with one's fellows, and so it is the truest principle of society.

APRIL 30: EVENING.

The secret things belong unto the Lord our God: but those things which are revealed belong unto us and to our children forever, that we may do all the works of this law.—*Deut.* xxix., 29.

VERY little of detail is taught in the Bible in respect to the future. It is clearly and triumphantly taught that men live on after leaving this mortal state, that the good are transcendently happy, and that their happiness springs from the presence and influence of the Redeemer. Beyond this nothing is clearly to be found out. The wicked, too, go on in life, and are supremely miserable. But this generic truth comprehends all. The specific experiences are not revealed. The fancy materials with which the Tuscan, Roman, and mediæval imagination depicted the sufferings of the lost are gross and impious presumptions, and are to be utterly rejected. The portraitures of heaven which fond imaginations are never weary of drawing, less mischievous, are not less purely fictitious.

Our business on earth is to get to heaven, and not to trouble ourselves with our probable experiences there. If, in reference to even our earthly state, the Master forbade us to worry about what we shall eat, or what we shall drink, and wherewithal we shall be clothed, how much more would he reprobate the folly of anxious forethought as to our condition in the heavenly life. If "sufficient unto the day is the evil thereof," much more sufficient unto this world are the troublous questions thereof.

The bride eyes not her garments,
  But her dear bridegroom's face;
I will not gaze at glory,
  But on my King of Grace—
Not at the crown he giveth,
  But on his piercèd hand:
The Lamb is all the glory
  Of Immanuel's land.

MAY 1: *MORNING.*

And he said, So is the kingdom of God, as if a man should cast seed into the ground; and should sleep, and rise night and day, and the seed should spring and grow up, he knoweth not how.—*Mark* iv., 26, 27.

Men suppose that when they are converted, or born again, they can, by reading or prayer, inherit all the graces ready made. When they want hope, or faith, or love, or any of the various moral powers, they suppose that they can obtain them by fasting for them, and reading for them, and praying for them, and they seek them in that way; whereas, when God produces these graces, he produces them through the actual experience of daily life. A woman prays for patience, and God sends her a servant, that she may have an opportunity to exercise it. A mother prays for faith, and God takes away her highest delight. Her heart's love and her soul's joy are deluged, and she says, "God has ransacked me, and left me nothing." And God says, "It is that I might give you the necessity for faith, and the opportunity of exercising it, that I have done this." When God works out perseverance in men, he puts them in circumstances where they require perseverance. When God means to make a man's back strong, he puts a pack on it, and the man learns to bear it. A strong back was the thing he wanted, but he did not want to get it in just the way that God pleased to have him.

Suppose a boy says to his father, "I want my arm to be as strong as Samson's." The father says, "It shall be so," and binds him out to a blacksmith. The boy did not like the hard work that he was obliged to perform; but a strong arm was what he wanted, and in order to have it he was obliged to take the means necessary to obtain it. If a man wishes to have an athlete's muscle, he must go through an athlete's training in a gymnasium. He must practice temperate habits, and take severe exercise, and at last his object will be attained.

So it is in respect to the Christian graces. God takes the minds of men, and places them in ten thousand relations of life, which are so many departments of his primary school—this world. He takes men and puts them into this or that department, according to their aptitudes, and assigns them their appropriate lessons. Little by little they unfold, and by-and-by they attain to perfection in each of the Christian graces.

Teach thou our weak and wandering hearts
  Aright to read thy way—
That thou with loving hand dost trace
  Our history every day.

Then every thorny crown of care,
  Worn well in patience now,
Shall grow a glorious diadem
  Upon the faithful brow.

MAY 1: EVENING.

Of myself I will not glory; but in mine infirmities.—2 *Cor.* xii., 5.

WHILE Fort Moultrie was held by seventy men through more than seventy days, when nobody threatened to take it, and nobody wanted to take it, nothing was said about the bravery of these men; but when trouble came, and the illustrious seventy threw themselves into Sumter, and then, looking into the eyes of the black-mouthed cannon that surrounded them on every side, stood up and held their own against the three thousand that threatened to take them, and against the whole state that was bent on their overthrow, the whole nation rose up and said, "That is brave! that is noble!"

Now when a man stands in the midst of prosperity, and nothing interferes with him, what chance is there for him to display Christian courage or manliness? But when trouble comes, and he is exposed to assaults from every direction, then there is a chance for him to display these qualities; and if he says, "I will stand my ground and endure to the end," every body admires his heroism.

The endurance of troubles that have been brought upon us is a more clear illustration of God's work, and so is a more significant token of his power, and honor, and glory, than the mere alleviation and taking away of trouble. The fewer instruments or means a man has, the more illustrious is that genius by which he brings about great results. The more you are limited, humbled, reduced, if you are yet able to bear the trouble that is put upon you, the more apparent is it to mankind that there is God in you.

MAY 2: MORNING.

Learn of me.—*Matt.* xi., 29.

CHRIST did not demand the full type of Christian experience as a condition of acceptance. He set the ideal before men; and then he accepted, or promised to accept, every one who would sincerely strive after that ideal, no matter at what point he stood, from the highest endowment of genius down to the very child himself. Every man who, looking toward this ideal of purity, and peace, and divinity in his soul, says, "I will follow after it;" every man who, pointing toward this ideal, says, "I accept this life, and I will try to realize it"—every such man, no matter how slowly he advances, no matter how imperfectly he lives, has the sympathy of Christ. Of all strivers in that direction, he says, "They shall be mine." He calls them his *scholars*. And those who go to school, or are willing to go to school to Christ, to learn by what steps they may be good; those who are willing to go to this university of experience; those who are seeking for this graduating power of Christianity, however limited may be their attainments, their knowledge, their victories, are pupils. If a man has gone into that school sincerely to learn, and is willing to practice what he learns, he is accepted of God.

MAY 2: EVENING.

He hath said in his heart, I shall not be moved; for I shall never be in adversity.—*Psalm* x., 6.

THE experience of every fresh mourner is, "I knew that Death was in the world, but I never thought that my beloved could die." Every one that comes to the grave says, coming, "I never thought that I should bury my heart here." Though from the beginning of the world it hath been so; though the ocean itself would be overflowed if the drops of sorrow, unexpected, that have flowed should be gathered together and rolled into its deep places; though the life of man, without an exception, has been taken away in the midst of his expectations, and dashed with sorrow, yet no man learns the lesson taught by these facts, and every man lays out his paradise afresh, and runs the furrow of execution around about it, and marks out its alleys and beds, and plants flowers and fruits, and cultures them with a love that sees no change and expects no sorrow.

A plow is coming from the far end of a long field, and a daisy stands nodding, and full of dew-dimples. That furrow is sure to strike the daisy. It casts its shadow as gayly, and exhales its gentle breath as freely, and stands as simple, and radiant, and expectant as ever; and yet that crushing furrow, which is turning and turning others in its course, is drawing near, and in a moment it whirls the heedless flower with sudden reversal under the sod.

And as is the daisy, with no power of thought, so are ten thousand thinking, sentient flowers of life, blossoming in places of peril, and yet thinking that no furrow of disaster is running in toward them—that no iron plow of trouble is about to overturn them. Sometimes it dimly dawns upon us, when we see other men's mischiefs and wrongs, that we are in the same category with them, and that perhaps the storms which have overtaken them will overtake us also. But it is only for a moment, for we are artful to cover the ear, and not listen to the voice that warns us of our danger.

MAY 3: MORNING.

For we walk by faith, not by sight.—2 *Cor.* v., 7.

It is that which is invisible that enables us to control the circumstances and conditions which belong to us in this life, and to go through it unscathed, unharmed, and with great courage. We grow rich, and strong, and joyful just in proportion as our treasures consist of noble thoughts, of holy feelings, of wrestlings with God in communion. Blessed are they, then, who can say as said the apostle, "We walk by faith, not by sight." And yet how few there are of such. God, through his Word, is constantly proclaiming, "I will never leave you nor forsake you; and yet men on every hand are crying out, "Lord, why hast thou left me and forsaken me?" They live by sight; and when the natural has failed them, all has failed them. Do you live by faith in God, by the promises of the Savior, by the influences of the Holy Spirit? If you do, you are blessed indeed. He that can live by the invisible, as revealed by the Word of God, is prepared for whatever may await him in this world, whether it be weal or woe.

> What though mortal powers may falter?
> Earthly plans and prospects fail?
> With a heaven-born hope which entereth
> E'en to that within the veil,
> All is light, all is light!
>
> What though all my future pathway
> Be from mortal sight concealed?
> With the love of Jesus glowing,
> As it lies to faith revealed,
> All is light, all is light!

MAY 3: EVENING.

In this was manifested the love of God toward us, because that God sent his only begotten Son into the world that we might live through him.—1 *John* iv., 9.

THE grandest deeds in this world are the loving condescensions of great natures to the help of weak ones. No crown so becomes a king as the service of low and suffering natures by those that are high and happy. The magnanimity of love, the patience of love, the endless gifts of all fruitful love—these are fitter to reveal the grandeur of God than thrones, and orbs, and the whole stellar universe. That he built the world, that he sustained it—this gives us a thought of God by the outside. That he suffered for it, that he gave his life for it—this shows us God within. Now we see the heart and feel the disposition.

MAY 4: *MORNING.*

That ye may be blameless and harmless, the sons of God without rebuke in the midst of a crooked and perverse nation, among whom ye shine as lights in the world.—*Phil.* ii., 15.

It is not hard for a man to die for Christ, nor for his faith, nor for his party. It is ten thousand times harder to live right than to die right. It is not difficult for a man to give his life up through the chamber of death. But to give your life while you hold it—yes, and to *use* it so that it is a perpetual benefaction all through—that is hard, and that is the special Christian duty. To live in such a way that, as from the stars by night and from the sun by day, light and guidance are issuing, so from you shall proceed an influence that comforts, cheers, instructs, and alleviates the troubles and sufferings of life—this is a true following of the Lord Jesus Christ.

MAY 4: *EVENING.*

For I am with thee, saith the Lord, to save thee. For I will restore health unto thee, and I will heal thee of thy wounds, saith the Lord.—*Jer.* xxx., 11, 17.

It is not because God is indifferent to moral qualities that he loves sinners. His love is medicinal. His life is a world-nursing life. He cleanses whom he loves that he may love yet more. God's nature is infinitely healing and cleansing. They that are brought in contact with the divine heart feel it by the growth that instantly begins in them. And his being is so capacious that all the want of all sinful creatures, through endless ages, neither exhausts nor wearies him. Ten thousand armies might bathe in the ocean, and neither sully its purity nor exhaust its cleansing power. But the ocean is but a cup by the side of God's heart. Realms and orbs may bathe and rise into purity. No words will ever hint or dimly paint the height, and depth, and length, and breadth of the love of Christ. It is love that pours, endless and spontaneous, just as sunlight does —simply because God is love. By the side of Christ, a mother's love, that on earth shines high above all other, as a star above night-candles, is in comparison like those glimmering, expiring stars when the sun shines them into radiant eclipse. In the bosom of such a God there is salvation for every one that will trust him. As the mother takes the new-born babe, that can do nothing but cry, and folds it in her bosom, there to find its food, its warmth, its raiment, its every thing, so God takes needy souls, that can only cry out, "God be merciful to me, a sinner," and wraps them up in the bosom of his love, there to find their food, their raiment, their all.

I ask if thou canst love me still, O God?
They say thou canst not love so weak a thing—
One that was angered by a Father's rod,
One that hath wayward and rebellious been,
Unstable, thankless, prone to every sin.
Thou knowest all—yet whither shall I go
To leave my sins, and with them leave my woe,
Except to thee, who only help canst bring,
And bid me live thy pardoning love to sing?
I come; my sinful thoughts have vexed me long;
And I am weak, but thou, my God, art strong.
I lay my head upon thy loving heart,
I hide beneath the shelter of thy wing,
And, helpless, to my Father's love I cling.

MAY 5: MORNING.

But unto you that fear my name shall the Sun of Righteousness arise with healing in his wings.—*Mal.* iv., 2.

When, after a long, frigid, barren winter, the spring comes and loves the earth a little while, how wondrous is the change that takes place. When the month of May comes, and sits upon the North as a bird upon her nest, there come forth from under its feathers sounds of new life. The forest echoes with the voices of joyous songsters; the roots start; the grass grows; the air smells sweet; all things are full of richness and beauty. Just so it is when spring comes to the soul; when the heart is touched with the fructifying power of love. How instantly, under such circumstances, does there grow up beauty, and fitness, and satisfaction. When it is human heart that touches human heart, what a wondrous spring it brings—what flowers and promises of fruit; but oh! when it is the heart of God that brings spring to our hearts; when it is the heart of God that sets every root, and every bud, and every leaf in us a-growing, how wondrous is the beauty that is evoked—how wondrous is the promise of fruit that is held out! And when we have once loved Christ with all our heart and soul, and mind and strength, and are able to say, "To do thy will is my meat and my drink," we have achieved the victory; we have overcome all adversaries; we have found the way that is cast up, on which the ransomed of the Lord are to return and walk, with songs, and everlasting joy upon their heads.

Ice lay upon my heart—
  Ice-fetters still and strong,
When the living spring gushed forth
  And filled my soul with song.

That Summer shall not fade;
  That Sun it setteth never;
The fountain in my heart
  Springs full and fresh forever.

MAY 5: EVENING.

Thy gentleness hath made me great.—2 *Sam.* xxii., 36.

God's forgiveness is unspeakably generous, and, if I may so say, unspeakably more fine, delicate, and full of strange gentleness than ours. I believe the more we come to know the disposition of Almighty God, the more we shall find in it, in magnitude and power, those traits which we call, among men, rare in their excellence. And when God undertakes for us, if we have thrown ourselves upon his mercy, and we have really meant to be his, and are really striving to be his, I believe that his feeling toward us transcends that of the tenderest love, of the most generous parentage, of the most romantic friendship in men; that he is not less than men in these emotions of friendship and of generosity in it, but transcendently more; that in him they spread over a broader ground, and take on a more wondrous experience. And instead of being likely to overestimate the volume of the divine goodness and mercy toward those who fear him, we are always under the mark. We always think less of God, and more meanly of the divine nature than we ought to do.

To every one who does not mean to sin, though he oft falls by temptation into it; to every one who is seeking, from day to day, as in the sight of God, to live a truly Christian life—to all such there are held out, in the New Testament, the most encouraging views of God's mercy, gentleness, and forbearance. They wait on us always and every where.

MAY 6: MORNING.

In those days, and in that time, saith the Lord, the iniquity of Israel shall be sought for, and there shall be none; and the sins of Judah, and they shall not be found; for I will pardon them whom I reserve.—*Jer.* l., 20.

I RECOLLECT, when a lad, and while attending a classical institute in the vicinity of Mount Pleasant, sitting on an elevation of that mountain, and watching a storm as it came up the valley. The heavens were filled with blackness, and the earth was shaken by the voice of thunder. It seemed as though that fair landscape was utterly changed, and its beauty gone never to return. But the storm swept on, and passed out of the valley; and if I had sat in the same place on the following day, and said, "Where is that terrible storm, with all its terrible blackness?" the grass would have said, "Part of it is in me;" and the daisy would have said, "Part of it is in me;" and the rose would have said, "Part of it is in me;" and the fruits and flowers, and every thing that grows out of the ground would have said, "Part of that storm is incandescent in me." And if you ask what becomes of the sins that we commit after we become Christians, I reply that God, by the power of his love, transforms them into sovereign blessings, and mercies, and graces. That is what becomes of them.

It is God's nature not to punish—though there is justice and punishment for the incorrigibly sinful—but to forgive. And where there is in a soul any sprouting upward, any yearning and growing toward the bright ideal of truth and right, God's nature is not avenging, but remedial, healing, fostering. It is to the human heart what sunshine is to the plant, warming and stimulating it. It is the nature of God not only to hold men to account for sins persisted in, but to cleanse away from the book of his remembrance sins forgiven. And by his grace it is that we are saved.

MAY 6: EVENING.

Father, if thou be willing, remove this cup from me; nevertheless, not my will, but thine be done.—*Luke* xxii., 42.

It is one thing to say "Thy will be done" theoretically, and another thing to say it practically. How many of you dare to-night to go to the cradle where sleeps your child that you adore, and that is dearer to you than the apple of your eye, and lay your hand on its head, and say to God, "Thy will be done, not mine?" The child is consecrated. It is offered as a sacrifice. God may take you at your word. Draw back the hand, and recall the sentence, unless you mean what you say. What do you love most in this world? Is there one thing that you love more than any other? Do you dare to go, in the darkness of this night, into the presence of God, and, taking that love, hold it up before him, and say, "Thy will be done, and not mine?" If there is any one, any purpose, any pleasure, any ambition, any thing that you do not dare to take into the presence of God, saying, "Thy will be done, and not mine," then God says to you, "You are not worthy of me."

If thou shouldst call me to resign
What most I prize, it ne'er was mine;
I only yield thee what was thine—
"Thy will be done!"

Renew my will from day to day—
Blend it with thine, and take away
All that now makes it hard to say
"Thy will be done!"

MAY 7: MORNING.

Then shalt thou delight thyself in the Lord.—*Isa.* lviii., 14.

All that part of our life which is exercised through the six days of the week, and taxed by strife, is to have rest on Sunday. Our strife of soul and strife of body, our working thoughts and our working members, are all of them to have that rest which comes from no longer working. This is the lower form of its benefit. We are, on that day, by giving this rest to the lower nature, to give enjoyment and inspiration, and a chance for development to that part of our nature which is usually overborne during the week by secular affairs, and which ought to have some special time to itself for culture and development. The object of Sunday is to say to that in men which is secular and animal, "Rest;" and to that which is intellectual, and moral, and social, "Grow." Nevertheless, the general effect of the Sabbath-day is not to be burdensome. It is not to be a restricted day. It is not to be a day of seclusion. It is not to be a day in which a man is to afflict his soul. It is to be a day whose impression on the whole, whose average and general effect, shall be such on every man that he shall feel that it is a delight, that it is honorable, and that it is memorable.

And we fondly pause to look
Where, in some daily-handled book,
Approval's well-known tokens stand,
Traced by some dear and thoughtful hand.

Even so there shines one day in seven
Bright with the special mark of Heaven,
That we with love and praise may dwell
On him who loveth us so well.

MAY 7: EVENING.

Forgetting those things which are behind, and reaching forth unto those things which are before, I press toward the mark for the prize of the high calling of God in Christ Jesus.—*Phil.* iii., 13, 14.

Do not be deceived by the descriptions that are sometimes given of wisdom's ways. They are ways of pleasantness, and they are paths of peace. But do not think that to be a Christian is to walk in a sphere of morality only slightly advanced beyond that in which you have been walking in past days. A true Christian is one that takes the character of Christ, the law of God, as his model, and attempts to conform his disposition thereto, whatever that disposition may be. The conflict may be a long one. In some persons it is a conflict which has a series of progressive victories. To-day it is a victory in one point, and to-morrow it is a victory in another point. It is always *attaining;* so that, with the apostle, the true Christian can say, "Not as though I had already attained;" I have not subdued every faculty and every sentiment; I have not brought all my powers to love spontaneously and intensely the thing which is just, and true, and pure, and right, and noble, and best;

I have not yet become such a Christian that I feed upon the bread of heaven; but, "forgetting those things which are behind, I press toward the mark for the prize of the high calling of God in Christ Jesus." This is a true Christian life.

MAY 8: MORNING.

Fear not; for they that be with us are more than they that be with them. —*2 Kings* vi., 16.

GREAT are the forces that are ready to pull you down; but if you did but know it, greater are they that are for you than are they that are against you. God has made the course of nature and of human society such that righteousness profits in the end better than wickedness. Give your heart to God. Love him. Then, living in the daily commerce of thought with God, and in the commerce of your fellow-men, animated by the spirit of love, ere long habits will be formed, and those habits will become armors of offense and defense; and at last, some years having passed, it will be more easy for you to be true, and just, and honest, and upright, and faithful, than not to be. Their opposites will become discords—moral discords. And when once you are established, and every bone is hardened, and every muscle is knit firmly, in this better way, then, whether you are rich or poor, life will have been saved. You can not lose happiness, you that are at peace with God and at peace with your fellow-men, as you can not have happiness if you are in opposition to God and your fellow-men.

MAY 8: EVENING.

The heart knoweth his own bitterness.—*Prov.* xiv., 10.

THE sorrows that are the most difficult to bear are sorrows that are smothered, and that burn smouldering slowly within. And there is no place like the closet for such sorrows. Sometimes, when I read the sad stories in the papers, I wish I could never hear of any more suffering. I look out on the world, and I marvel at God's patience. I think none but a God could endure it. It wears me out, it almost discourages me, to see how much of sorrow and suffering there is in the world. And when

I look upon all the suffering of men, I say, "Oh that they had a refuge for their suffering. Oh that prayer meant to them what it means to me. Oh that they, like me, had a place where they could cast off their burden, and find courage and strength of soul, and, above all, get calmness, and serenity, and heart-rest."

MAY 9: MORNING.

Grow in grace and in the knowledge of our Lord and Savior Jesus Christ.—2 *Peter* iii., 18.

To increase in the knowledge of God is distinctly commanded, not in this passage alone, but in very many. The progress of the mind in the knowledge of scientific truth depends very much upon the exercise of the senses upon matter, but the growth of knowledge in moral truth depends upon the exercise of moral feelings. While sense is the source of physical or scientific knowledge, disposition is the source of the knowledge of moral truth. Growth in the knowledge of a divine Being unites both of these. That is to say, there is a revelation of God in the natural world, and there is also a revelation of God in society and in the social nature of man. But as the Lord Jesus Christ is a representation of divine nature in its moral aspects chiefly, rather than in its forensic or executive elements, it is to be learned by moral growth in ourselves more than in any other way. Hence the text is, "*Grow in grace,*" as if it were in that way only that you could grow "in the knowledge of our Lord and Savior Jesus Christ." Grace is the schoolmaster of knowledge.

MAY 9: EVENING.

But whoso looketh into the perfect law of liberty, and continueth therein, he being not a forgetful hearer, but a doer of the work, this man shall be blessed in his deed.—*James* i., 25.

Do not shrink back when you find, in the providence of God, that cares, and fears, and troubles are upon you; when you find yourself environed by those daily struggles which are incident to your social organization. Mother, whose household is heavier than you can bear, whose children are a burden that you can not carry — who in sickness, in nervous weakness, in despondency and discouragement, are trying to live faithful to your husband, faithful to your children, faithful to your name and to yourself —does it seem to you every day as though the spirit of life would be crushed out of you? You want to do right, but you say, "The cloud is evermore over me, and life is a burden; and if it were not for my children I would not care to live." How many are there—oh, sad commentary on life!—who say, "If it were not for one and another I would be willing to die?" Right in the midst of life, in the midst of youth, and in the plenitude of years, how many there are whose fears, and cares, and sorrows, and rasping experiences are such that they would die if they could.

Are you willing to take those cares and those fears which God has put upon you as a yoke and as a burden, and to stand in them, and go to Christ and say, "Lord Jesus, I accept all these. Thou hast said, 'Come to me through cares and through burdens,' and I have come; and I shall die if there is not some help sent to me." Ah! the dark closet, how often does it prove to be the gate of heaven.

Grant me the grace,
Whilst Martha's busy offices demand
My lesser care, to cast my better thoughts
Down at thy feet—to sit with Mary there,
And listen to thy words of truth and love.
Teach me, with mind unruffled and serene,
To meet the hourly incidents of life,
And let the tones of gentle patience lend
Their soft sweet music to my lightest word.
Oh! may I bear in mind that from the roots
Of withered and neglected duties spring
The rankest sin-weeds which infest the heart;
That wisdom infinite has placed me here
To work thy will, watched o'er by angels' eyes,
Cherished and cared for, not alone by those
Whom thou hast given to tread life's path with me.
But with a love beyond all human ken,
By thee, on whom my hopes of heaven depend,
My Lord, my God, my Savior, and my Friend.

MAY 10: MORNING.

Unto thee, O Lord, do I lift up my soul. For thou, Lord, art good, and ready to forgive, and plenteous in mercy unto all them that call upon thee.—*Psalm* lxxxvi., 4, 5.

Men ask, "Why is it that we have a right to go to the Lord Jesus Christ and ask him for blessings?" The reason is, that "it is more blessed to give than to receive." He said it out of his own experience. And it is a thousand times more blessed for God to give than for man; for we give with a spark in our natures, and he gives with a whole sun in his nature. What must be the impulse of generosity in the bosom of God, who measures himself by infinities, and who, by searching, can never be found out.

When, therefore, there are troubles that spring out of infelicities of disposition, and unregulated thoughts, and fancies, and feelings that defy our volition, and elude our watchfulness, and are turning against us with a kind of Bedouin-Arab fight, firing when they retreat as well as when they advance, we have a right to go to the Lord Jesus Christ and say, "Thou hast given thine own life a pledge of love; art thou not willing to give the help I need, that is so much less?" On this foundation confidence may be built up.

MAY 10: EVENING.

He that overcometh shall not be hurt of the second death.—*Rev.* ii., 11.

A man says, "I have certain passions, and inbred sins, and dispositions that I know I can not overcome." You can not overcome them as long as you pamper them. You can not as long as you excuse them. Just as long as you hide behind them, and shelter yourself from those vivific influences by which alone the soul can rise to its higher life and to its supernal nature, you can not do these things. You can not do them so long as you hold yourself aloof. No man overcomes difficulties by cowardice.

But there is no passion, and there are no lusts, and there is no stature of pride, and there is no frivolity of vanity, and there is no wide, diffusive selfishness, which can not be overcome by the grace of God, if once a man will enter the warfare; but it is to be a warfare, and it is to be begun. It will never come to a man as a completed victory, but it will come to him, if he be victor at all, when he has earned it at the point of his spear and by the edge of his sword.

MAY 11: *MORNING.*

With good will doing service, as to the Lord, and not to men: knowing that whatsoever good thing any man doeth, the same shall he receive of the Lord. —*Ephes.* vi., 7, 8.

We are said to be followers of Christ. We follow him in his glory and exaltation. But there were other periods of Christ's life besides days of exaltation and glory; there were other periods of Christ's life besides the day of transfiguration and the day of resurrection. There was a time when he had not a place to lay his head. Where are the disciples of Christ without a place to lay their head? He had not where to go for food. Where are the disciples of Christ who hunger? He was the pensioner of women. Where are the men who are ridden by the stress of poverty? Where are those that want to volunteer in the ranks of Christ, and that are willing to serve him in any position, if he will only receive them at all?

At one time, when the boys were flocking into an Indiana regiment, there came a lad, who was scarce fifteen years of age, to have his name put down. He strove, in all the companies, and by various devices, to get accepted; and at last he says, "Let me go as a drummer." No, they had their full complement of drummers. "Let me go as something." "You can not do any thing." "Yes, I can; when the men fight I can carry water to the wounded soldiers." And he went to carry water to the wounded. Ah! that was the right spirit. He could not fight nor perform music, but he could carry water to the wounded. How many of us are saying, "Lord, put me to the lowest work if thou wilt, only take me into thy service."

Since service is the highest lot,
  And all are in one Body bound,
In all the world the place is not
  Which may not with this bliss be crowned.

The poorest may enrich this feast;
 Not one lives only to receive,
But renders through the hands of Christ
 Richer returns than man can give.

The little child, in trustful glee,
 With love and gladness brimming o'er,
Many a cup of ministry
 May for the weary veteran pour.

MAY 11: *EVENING.*

But we all, with open face beholding as in a glass the glory of the Lord, are changed into the same image from glory to glory, even as by the Spirit of the Lord.—2 *Cor.* iii., 18.

WE are all planted here. We are working out from our material conditions as a seed works out from under the soil. We are just beginning with the very tips, as it were, of our faculties to come up into the pure sunlight. But all that we have of experience in this world is still obscure, sub-mundane, subterranean; and we shall learn, really and fully, when we see him as he is, and are like him. With the utmost of certainties, we still are surrounded by uncertainties. Knowledge is rude and imperfect here. We are voyagers exploring new seas, and edging along new coasts and continents. Life is something sublime, and something grander than men think, who only grind and eat their daily bread, and know no difference between themselves and the beasts that perish. We are beginners. We are little children, and petitioners for liberty to come to our manhood, surrounded by more invisible things than there are things visible, and under mightier influences supernal than are the influences actual and physical, and are holding on our way to that other state of being. Man is more than man knows. Life is grander than it shows itself to be. Every man that stands and looks back from the other life to see what was the importance of this, and to measure it by its results there, will be filled with amazement that he should have lived so blind, and so unknowing, in the midst of so grand an arrangement of divine Providence.

Grafted in thee, by grace alone
 In growth I daily rise,
And, springing up from thee, the Vine,
 My top shall reach the skies.

MAY 12: MORNING.

The kingdom of heaven is like unto leaven which a woman took, and hid in three measures of meal, till the whole was leavened.—*Matt.* xiii., 33.

It is said that there must be a distinction between Christians and the world. If there is to be a distinction, it should be in this: that he is more generous; that he is more just. The distinction is to be one of a higher purity, a sweeter love, a nobler manhood; and if you have not that, you have no right to put a distinction between yourself and another man on the ground that you belong to a Church and he does not. External badges of distinction are worse than useless. They are deceptive. They are mischievous. There ought to be a difference between men of the world and Christian men. And yet, when the training of Christian families and the training of Christian institutions has so affected law and public sentiment that men, by outside active experience, are reared up externally to a high Christian propriety and morality, then ordinary men and Christian men will not have any marked external difference. Certainly there will be no discrimination against the Christian life as though it were a less free or a less liberal life. "The earth is the Lord's, and the fullness thereof." Whatever any man on earth who is not a Christian has a right to do innocently and purely, that, for a higher reason, the Christian man has a right to do, because he stands nearer to God than any body else. A Christian has a right to all innocent pleasure, to all industry, to all generous rivalry, and to all modest ambition. A Christian is an actor in the world that now is in a larger and nobler way than any other one can be. Looking at him externally only, you would hardly know that there was any difference between him and an ordinary good citizen. The difference, however, is very great, assuming that he is not merely a professed Christian, but a real one. The difference is in that which does not appear. It is in that which lies behind conduct. It is in the *hidden* life.

MAY 12: *EVENING.*

Therefore are they before the throne of God, and serve him day and night in his temple; and he that sitteth on the throne shall dwell among them. They shall hunger no more, neither thirst any more; neither shall the sun light on them, nor any heat. For the Lamb, which is in the midst of the throne, shall feed them, and shall lead them unto living fountains of waters; and God shall wipe away all tears from their eyes.—*Rev.* vii., 15–17.

No man can guard himself against suffering in a world that is sin-smitten and shrouded with troubles; in a world where God educates men by trials and afflictions; in a world where there is an endless funeral march, and where sorrow beats the drum to which all men in the procession keep step. In such a world men must suffer, and suffer to the end.

But oh, the cleansing of suffering! God grant that we may have the cleansing, and not the baptism alone. God grant that there may be such a cleansing that by-and-by, in some future world, another revelator shall stand and see you and yours shouting in the throng of ineffable glory, and, being asked "Who are these, and whence came they?" shall say of them and you, "These are they which came out of great tribulation, and have washed their robes, and made them white in the blood of the Lamb."

Through sorrow and through loss, by toil and prayer,
Saints won the starry crowns which now they wear,
And, by the bitter ministry of pain,
Grievous and harsh, but oh! not sent in vain,
Found their eternal gain.

If it be ours, like them, to suffer loss,
Give grace, as unto them, to bear our cross,
Till, victors over each besetting sin,
We, too, thy perfect peace shall enter in,
And crowns of glory win.

MAY 13: *MORNING.*

If thou canst believe, all things are possible to him that believeth.—*Mark* ix., 23.

In this day, when there is so much done to uproot our confidence in Christ, when so many are departing from the faith and falling into a lower form of belief, it is transcendently important that those who *know* that their Redeemer liveth, and know it by the sense of joy and peace which he has created in their souls, should speak of God's work in them. And it is pre-eminently desirable that the power of this hidden life should be made to stand over against the cold, disorganizing, dividing skepticisms which are now coming in upon the world.

If you want more influence and power, you must enter more into the hidden life of Christ. It is only so that you can have converting power, and achieve success in your efforts to rescue the souls of men. You can not carry men any farther along than you have gone in your own experience.

MAY 13: *EVENING.*

Yet a little while, and the world seeth me no more; but ye see me.—*John* xiv., 19.

THIS is our faith and our hope: Jesus is risen, and is our Savior—our personal Savior. He loves us more than we love ourselves. He understands us better than a mother understands the babe that she nourishes. He knows all our ailments. He knows our sins and every suggestion of the devil, and he will shield us. So long as that voice sounds from the heavens, "Because I live ye shall live also," so long we have presage and assurance of final victory. We take up our cross and follow our Savior. What is the cross since Christ left it? No longer a burden, but rather a staff and a stay to us. No longer is there death in it, but life eternal; no longer wounding, and shame, and disgrace, but honor, and influence, and glory, and immortality.

To them the cross, with all its shame,
With all its grace, is given;
Their name—an everlasting name;
Their joy—the joy of heaven.

To them the cross is life and health,
Though shame and death to him;
His people's hope, his people's wealth,
Their everlasting theme.

MAY 14: *MORNING.*

Only let your conversation be as it becometh the gospel of Christ.—*Philippians* i., 27.

There are some persons who are naturally slow of feeling; persons in whom caution is strong; persons in whom reason predominates over feeling. If such persons will determine to obey the laws of the Savior, to imitate his disposition, to carry his spirit, to work out in life just what he worked out in his life, two results will follow. First, Christian character follows; and, second, it is a fact, that if you perform the actions that spring from a certain feeling, the feeling itself will come by-and-by. You can develop conduct from feeling, and you can also develop feeling from conduct. The man who begins to imitate Christ reverently, child-likely, and continuously, will by-and-by begin to feel that he has the emotion of love as well as the fruit of love. The fruit is more important, the emotion being latent in the first instance, developing itself only as a motive pressing him to right thought, right feeling, and right conduct. By a patient continuance in well-doing the emotion will grow, so that by-and-by the man who had only emotional life and conduct will begin to feel that while he is feeling as a Christian, he should also begin to live as a Christian.

Sometimes the light surprises a Christian as he sings. Sometimes a man who has long been living in the performance of Christian duty begins to have intuitions, revelations, as it were, of his higher nature. And this is the safer way.

MAY 14: *EVENING.*

And the peace of God, which passeth all understanding, shall keep your hearts and minds through Jesus Christ.—*Phil.* iv., 7.

Do you remember what, in his last interview with his disciples, in that prolonged love-feast which preceded his crucifixion, when the cloud was on him, when the great eclipse began to show itself, and the shadow was falling, and he was uttering his last words to them, and preparing them with all zeal to be scattered like sheep without a shepherd—do you remember what in that hour was the state of mind of Christ? He says, "My peace I give unto you." In that hour of tempest, and darkness, and coming anguish, while there was agitation every where else, in the heart of Christ there was peace — peace enough not only for his own wants, but for the wants of his dear disciples. And when you think of Christ as a man of sorrows and acquainted with grief, think also that he gave an exemplification of the power of the soul to overcome these things.

Who shall hush the weary spirit's chiding?
  Who the aching void within shall fill?
Who shall whisper of a peace abiding,
  And each surging billow calmly still?

Only he whose wounded heart was broken
  With the bitter cross and thorny crown;
Whose dear love glad words of joy had spoken,
  Who his life for us laid meekly down.

Blessed Healer! all our burdens lighten;
  Give us peace, thine own sweet peace, we pray;
Keep us near thee till the morn shall brighten,
  And all mists and shadows flee away.

MAY 15: *MORNING.*

Quench not the Spirit.—1 *Thess.* v., 19.

It may be asked, "How shall we secure the divine help?" We are responsible, though God is working with us, for right thinking, for right willing, and for right and wise action. We have no right to despise customs, nor those normal processes by which experience has taught society best to develop itself, nor natural laws, nor any of that vast economy by which God, through his providence, is stimulating development in the natural, the social, and the moral world. "How, then, are you going to secure the divine help to stimulate us to judge right, to think right, and to do right?" By living in right dispositions; by keeping in all those moral channels through which divine purity flows, if it comes at all to you; by seeking rational ends; by being in the current of providence; by cultivating sensibility to high and pure moral impressions. In all these ways.

In all the relations of life maintain equity, and purity, and integrity, and then keep your moral sentiments and your nature so open to righteousness, to purity, to aspiration, to love, to faith, to joy, to the very Spirit of God, that you shall receive easily the ingress of God's Spirit as it flows abroad and fills the whole universe.

MAY 15: *EVENING.*

And Enoch walked with God.—*Gen.* v., 24.

God makes himself, by the power of the Holy Ghost, a guest, and he abides in the souls of those who know how to accept him. There is such a thing as communion with Christ, as one speaketh to a friend, face to face. There is a banqueting-house where he sits down with those who are his disciples. He is with them in their solitary hours. In the solitude of Western forests I have lifted psalms and hymns to God, and have had communion with him such as I never had in the sanctuary. There is many a man on the lonely watch at sea; there is many a solitary watcher on the land; there is many a one in the recesses of business; there is many a one in the toil, and fatigue, and vexation of the week-day, or in the broad calm of the Sabbath, that has this soul-communion with Christ. It is the banquet of love. What words can describe it? It is ineffable. It is full of glory—at times, of inexpressible glory.

All those glancing thoughts; all that sense of yearning; all that lifting up of every thing in the soul that is unanalyzed and undefinable; all that rising up of the spiritual nature under the strong drawings of God's very presence; all that peace which passeth understanding, and which God knows how to rain down into the soul when he comes near, and puts his arms about you, and takes you into his very bosom, so that you can look up and say, in that rapturous moment, "Whom have I in heaven but thee? and there is none upon earth that I desire beside thee"—these are parts of the hidden life. And they are indeed poor followers of Christ who have never had those joyful experiences which proceed from the hidden life. That is a poor road for a man to travel in which he can not find a sunny spot in winter, or a shady spot in summer, where he may sit down and eat his food. That must be a savage country in which there are no resting-places. The soul's resting-places in this world are many. Yea, it must needs be that there are many, when even a pile of stones is a pillar good enough for a child of God, sleeping thereon, to see angels ascending and descending between him and heaven.

MAY 16: *MORNING.*

I will sing with the spirit, and I will sing with the understanding also.— 1 *Cor.* xiv., 15.

A Church who do not sing have hard sledding. Sleigh-riding in winter, and no bells—think of it! A Church who do not sing are like a spring without any birds, or like a garden without any flowers. Give me a singing Church. And in a Church where the Spirit of the Lord is, singing must break out, it seems to me.

Not only in the church, in the household there ought to be a great deal more singing than there is. I do not believe there ever was a singing family that quarreled much. It is very hard to break away from a good song into a round quarrel; and if two people that have quarreled could be set over against each other, so that they could not get at each other, and made to take a hymn-book and sing, I think that by the time they had sung five verses they would feel pleasantly toward one another.

Then, in private experience, there is a great deal of power in singing to control one's thoughts; to withdraw one from an overestimate of this world; to comfort one's self in sorrow; to cheer one's self in perplexity; to make one's self patient and long-suffering in adversity. If one only had a hundred or a thousand hymns in his memory, and with every changing mood he was accustomed to hum to himself some sweet descant of experience, he would not easily be made unhappy, and he would not wander from the path of rectitude. For singing is the golden bow and arrow with which Satan would be smitten through and through, and temptations would be disarmed.

MAY 16: *EVENING.*

O Lord, how manifold are thy works! in wisdom hast thou made them all: the earth is full of thy riches.—*Psalm* civ., 24.

I have in my house a little sheet of paper on which there is a faint, pale, and not particularly skillful representation of a hyacinth. It is not half as beautiful as many other pictures I have, but I regard it as the most exquisite of them all. My mother painted it; and I never see it that I do not think that her hand rested on it, and that her thought was concerned in its execution.

Now, suppose you had such a conception of God that you never saw a flower, a tree, a cloud, or any natural object, that you did not instantly think, "My Father made it," what a natural world would this become to you. How beautiful would the earth seem to you. How would you find that nature was a revelation of God, speaking as plainly as his written Word. And if you are alone, in solitude, without company, desolate in your circumstances, it is because you have not that inner sense of the divine love and care which it is your privilege to have, and which you ought to have.

Why comes this fragrance on the summer breeze,
  The blended tribute of ten thousand flowers,
To me, a frequent wanderer 'mid the trees
  That form these gay, yet solitary bowers?
One answer is around, beneath, above—
The echo of the voice—that God is love!

Why bursts such melody from tree and bush,
  The overflowing of each songster's heart,
So filling mine that it can scarcely hush
  A while to listen, but would take its part?
'Tis but one song I hear where'er I rove,
Though countless be the notes—that God is love!

MAY 17: MORNING.

And why take ye thought for raiment? Consider the lilies of the field, how they grow; they toil not, neither do they spin.—*Matt.* vi., 28.

THIS is the season of the year when, if ever, one must needs have his senses attracted. The peach-trees are holding up their silent lessons in pink; the cherry-trees and the pear-trees are holding up their silent lessons in white; the apple-trees are holding up their silent lessons in both colors; all the grass is full of germinant flowers; the grass is lifting up its hands, and clapping them for joy. The common birds are here—the several sparrows, the robins, the bluebirds, and the goldfinches, or yellow-birds. Even in the city you can not but see the amazing bounty of God; and if you will step out toward the suburbs of the town—and you can, if you will but rise early enough, without any prejudice to your ordinary work or to your health—you will gain some idea of the boundlessness and profusion of that bounty, as exhibited by the flowers in the country. And whenever you see flowers, understand that there is a meaning in them, and remember that Christ has said, with reference to them, "Consider." You have no right to pass by the smallest, the tiniest, the most inconspicuous flower, and say, "Oh, it is a little common flower." A common flower? It is God-opened, and God-built, and Christ has said respecting it, "Consider." Yes, there is a meaning in flowers. It is a precious meaning—one that you need, and one that will kindle up your life, and make your soul glow with radiance. Take it, and profit by it.

Beautiful are the heralds
  That stand at Nature's door,
Crying, "Oh traveler, enter in,
  And taste the Master's store!"
One or the other always crying—
  In the voice of the summer hours,
In the thunder of the winter storm,
  Or the song of the fresh spring flowers.

Only, before thou enterest in,
  Upon the threshold fall,
And pay the tribute of thy praise
  "To him who gives thee all."
But they who never bent the knee
  Will smile at this my story,
For, though they enter the temple gates,
  They know not the inner glory.

MAY 17: EVENING.

Having your conversation honest among the Gentiles; that whence they speak against you as evil-doers, they may, by your good works, which they shall behold, glorify God in the day of visitation.—1 *Peter* ii., 12.

No real conception of Christ is reproduced before men that they do not long to have the same thing in themselves. And out of this yearning comes aspiration, out of aspiration comes intuition, out of intuition comes realization, and out of realization come conversion and sanctification, so that no man preaches so much and so effectually as the man that does not speak a word, but whose whole life is one revelation of the higher forms of Christian development.

Oh mother! because you are in the household, it does not follow that you are not also in the pulpit. There are these open pulpits; there are these domestic pulpits. The candle that is lit for your table in the cottage, and gives its light there first, shines out of the window also, and throws its rays far down the road, and the weary traveler sees them, and plucks up courage, and says, "There is succor at last!" and follows the light, and finds your house, and is rescued. And while you are giving yourself to your children in sweetness and love, and prayer and trust, a light shines down the road to those that have lost their way, and many a soul may be brought, by your example, home to Jesus.

Do not be discouraged because you have not an ampler sphere of testimony. Live, love, trust, and wait, and, ere long, forever and forever triumph and rejoice.

MAY 18: *MORNING.*

Be not high-minded.—*Rom.* xi., 20.

Man's natural strength is right in his way when he is out of joint with God, and he is putting between himself and the thing needed the strength of an arrogant reason. That self-reliance which is so necessary to him in secular things is a hindrance to him in spiritual things. That independent purpose and determination by which a man is carried forward through his outward life, when it comes to the inward and spiritual life, is the very thing that is an obstacle to his success; and this is the reason why we do not find God's yoke easy or his burden light. When we come into the service of the Lord Jesus Christ, we do not find that that service gives us the deep satisfaction we expected it would. We can not see the reason; but God knows the reason. He understands that no person can come into a state of perfect rest until he comes into a state of implicit trust; until all his purposes, and thoughts, and feelings are so yielded to God that at every hour of the day he can say, "Thy will be done," and can roll his burden upon God. Our burdens are easy when they are upon God; and our burdens are upon God when he is in us, and when he fulfills the promise that he will come and abide with us, and we are conscious that our soul moves in harmony with his.

MAY 18: *EVENING.*

Draw nigh to God, and he will draw nigh to you. Cleanse your hands, ye sinners, and purify your hearts, ye double-minded.—*James* iv., 8.

It is possible to hold the world and its vast occupations so subordinate that all things earthly shall seem like shadows. But how shall we come into that state of mind by which we shall be able to do this? Not by mere wishing. Some come into it more easily than others; but even those that come into it most easily can do it only by making it a definite object of attainment that is ever present to their mind, and laboring for it, and helping themselves by daily pondering the Word of God, and by prayer. He that prays has wings. He ascends to the tops of mountains that are inaccessible to his feet; he goes out of this world, and becomes a citizen of another; he converts sense into spirit; he walks without a path for his feet, and is as a bird of God that flies through the trackless air whithersoever it will. In our atmosphere, the higher we go the less we can breathe; but in the atmosphere of prayer, the higher you go the better you can breathe. And when, by prayer, and by pondering the Word of God, a man comes to that state in which he is able to measure earthly things by heavenly things, the visible by the invisible, then life itself turns round and helps him. If he attempts to do it without the use of means of grace, life resists him; but if he attempts to do it by communion with God and obedience to the divine will, he will find that his occupations day by day will minister to that end.

Lord, what a change within us one short hour
Spent in thy presence will avail to make;
What heavy burdens from our bosoms take;
What parched grounds refresh, as with a shower;
We kneel, and all around us seems to lower;
We rise, and all the distant and the near
Stand forth in sunny outline, bright and clear;
We kneel, how weak! we rise, how full of power!

Why are we ever overborne with care?
  Why should we ever weak or heartless be,
Anxious or troubled, when with us is prayer,
  And joy, and strength, and courage are with thee?

MAY 19: *MORNING.*

Oh, how great is thy goodness, which thou hast laid up for them that fear thee.—*Psalm* xxxi., 19.

It seems to me we have testimony in the workings of the providence of God in the experiences of our daily life that God's love is still shed upon us, although we may be unconscious of it. I recollect to have read the case of a man in a city of Southern Europe who spent his life in getting property, and became unpopular among his fellow-citizens on account of what seemed to them his miserly spirit. When his will was read after his death, it stated that he had been poor, and had suffered from a lack of water; that he had seen the poor of the city also suffering from a lack of water, and that he had devoted his life to the accumulation of means sufficient to build an aqueduct to bring water to the city, so that forever afterward the poor should be supplied with it. It turned out that the man whom the poor had cursed till his death had been laboring to provide water for the refreshment of themselves and their children. Oh, how God has been building an aqueduct to bring the water of life to us, he not interpreting his acts, and we not understanding them!

MAY 19: *EVENING.*

Glorious things are spoken of thee, O city of God.—*Psalm* lxxxvii., 3.

We are glad that above the storm, and above the sound of earthly troubles, there abides the land of sacred peace. Thither have flown some that sang by our side. There are some whom we folded and taught to speak with earthly language. There rest many who taught our hearts to love. There are the chief desired ones, and we are glad for their escape. Nor is the world altogether poorer for their going. They are with us yet, with more power than when they were bodily present.

When we rise to our better selves, and by faith can discern the invisible, we are not separated from them. In our holiest thoughts and in our purest affections we are more theirs than ever we were in the infirmities of the common earthly life. They are not taken from us. They are but a step before us. It is their voice which we hear crying out perpetually from the invisible city, Come, come. And we are coming. We are coming toward them, and toward thee that hath made them lovely, Lord Jesus. By faith of thee, by the strong drawing of thy love, by the gracious light and inspiration of the Holy Spirit, we are coming to that higher and better life. Would that our steps were faster. Would that we might begin to fly. Yet we are grateful that our face is set thither; that the light strikes upon our countenance; that we behold thee sometimes, and see the city itself afar off, as pilgrims behold the glimmering city which they have not nearly reached; that we are in sympathy with them; and that there are many hours in which we can stand in Zion and before God, with the spirits of just men made perfect, and enter into sympathy with all their rejoicings and thoughts.

MAY 20: *MORNING.*

This sickness is not unto death, but for the glory of God, that the Son of God might be glorified thereby.—*John* xi., 4.

There are those that by sickness are prematurely laid aside from usefulness; that are bedridden, and that feel that, in being denied the opportunity of engaging in the active duties of life, they have lost life itself. But it will be found that it is not the sunflower, garish and possessed of power to lift itself up, that is most esteemed, but the hidden flower that blossoms in the shadow of the hedge, that in every adversity is fragrant still. Christ will do as you do that never wear the sunflower, but often the violet. God will take the humble ones, and make them into that precious knot which he will wear on his very heart.

If God has called you to an inactive sphere, he has called you there that, by holy thought and affection, you may wreathe for him offerings of silent love, and hope, and desire, which are more precious in his sight than any outward activities can be.

Thus saith the Lord, "Thy days of health are over,"
  And, like the mist, my vigor fled away,
Till but a feeble shadow was remaining—
  A fragile form fast hastening to decay.
Then sighs of sorrow in my soul would rise,
Then rushing tears would overflow my eyes;
But I beheld *thee*, O my Lord and God,
Beneath the cross lay down the shepherd's rod:
Is this thy will, good Lord? The strife is o'er;
    Thy servant weeps no more.

MAY 20: EVENING.

Your life is hid with Christ in God.—*Col.* iii., 3.

Every person of richness of soul feels that the dearest part of his life—that which seems to him the finest, the noblest, the deepest—never is fully and fairly exposed. If you think a moment, you are conscious that all those subtlest sentiments, those rarest feelings which, when they manifest themselves in you with power, and give you some sentiment of divinity, are the strains of the soul which you can not speak—which you certainly do not. Thus our feelings toward each other, the feelings that parents have toward their children, orb up and swell the soul, but are unutterable. There is more in one look that the eye gives than in what the tongue utters in a lifetime.

But this hidden life is more strikingly illustrated in the course of all refined affections. Of all feelings, there is none of which men need be so little ashamed as of true love, and none which so much puts on all the appearances of shame; for love is born behind blushing defenses. And after it has won its victories, and subdued to itself the whole of life, it then more than ever has in it the necessity of hiding itself; for love, like the blood in the human body, though it be the cause of all the life that appears, is itself hidden within the veins, and never seen.

When the apostle, therefore, speaks of the Christian life as a hidden one, it is neither a paradox nor a mystery, although at first it may strike one as being so. Interpreted by the analogy of the soul's best habits, it is only declaring the Christian's hope to be the secret and spring of all the rest of his life. That which is the strongest in him, that which is the truest to his divine nature, that which he considers the best part of him—in short, that which he will call his real life, is hidden. "Your life is hid with Christ in God."

MAY 21: *MORNING.*

Fear hath torment.—1 *John* iv., 18.

"Fear hath torment." It is a tormentor. It haunts men night and day. Great fears may come seldom; but the poison emery, the dust of fear, comes in, as it were, at every crevice, and settles down upon every fair thing in life. There are innumerable petty fears; there are ten thousand little hauntings. How full is life of fear which takes away from men the enjoyment of their prosperity! Fear stands by the cradle and threatens the mother; and all her love and thankfulness can not make her happy while fear scowls and threatens. The spectre of fear hovers between lovers, and they dread and suffer. It shoots like a meteor along the twilight meditations of evening; it hides the sun at noonday with clouds; it threatens health with sickness, and sickness with death, and death with numberless terrors. Cares are the offspring of fear. They sting like noxious insects in tropical nights. Fear discourages poverty; it takes ease away from riches; it is the persecutor of ambition; it is the parasite of conscience. Fear perpetually exaggerates. It is always changing, and coming up in new forms, and always dread forms. It is full of illusions. All the way through it is undermining the joys and hopes of life. And all this, too, in the realm where Christ has been revealed. Go from house to house, and mark down how large a play there is of fear; how much of motive is fear; how largely men work for fear of more suffering than they choose to have. And see how men are restrained by fear, standing in the place of conscience. See how fear is like broken glass, every particle of which cuts the foot that treads on it. How is fear the destroyer of men's peace, perpetually rasping them and beating them? One would think that the name of the God who governs this world was Fear.

Right over against the gloomy face of Fear stands the Lord Jesus Christ, and the words of ineffable cheer, "Our Lord Jesus

Christ himself, and God, even our Father, which hath loved us, and hath given us everlasting consolation and good hope through grace, comfort your hearts." That is just what hearts that are sick want—*comfort;* and they have it in Christ Jesus and in the fatherhood of God, and nowhere else, in such measure or with such pertinency of application.

MAY 21: EVENING.

Ye are Christ's.—1 *Cor.* iii., 23.

Are you endeavoring to live so as to overcome every known sin? Do you desire, above all things, to obey the Lord Jesus Christ? Is it your purpose to continue in this mind as long as you live? If so, you have a right to look up to Jesus, and say, "Thou art mine." This very foretaste of Christian joy, this very yearning for more, are evidences that Christ is calling to you. What you need to do is not to stop any more to think about yourself, but to go right forward in the Christian life in your household, in your daily business, wherever you are. Whether you are laboring for other people as you have opportunity, or whatever you are doing, take the sphere in which God's providence has cast your lot, and go right forward, and say, "I am Christ's little child. He has redeemed my soul, and I am blessed in his love. I rejoice, therefore, in the Lord." Appropriate that which comes to you. Take it to yourself, and believe it to be true.

MAY 22: MORNING.

Old things are passed away; behold, all things are become new.—2 *Cor.* v., 17.

Every Christian ought to have his day of Pentecost. In other words, he ought to come (and the sooner the better) into a Christian manhood. He ought to come to a higher sense of the love of God to his soul in Jesus Christ. He ought to have a more enthusiastic, passionate, clinging, and fiery love of Christ—one that shall lift him above pain, and temptation, and circumstances in which before he has wavered and oscillated, into a higher region of Christian experience in which Christ becomes to him all in all. This is the privilege of the Christian life. There is an experience of the love of Christ which goes far beyond the ordinary experience of Christians, and yet it is open to us all. There is an experience of the Lord Jesus Christ's presence and living power in the soul that will make you so different from what you are by nature that you will not know yourselves; and it will be true to you, in your feelings, that *old things are passed away, and all things are become new.* This enthusiasm of love and faith is so intense and deep, and so all-controlling, that, in comparison with it, every thing which has gone before seems as nothing.

MAY 22: EVENING.

And our hope of you is steadfast.—2 *Cor.* i., 7.

When you are like Christ, you will bear all the scourgings, and temptations, and inconveniences of life with patience and gladness. Then, in accordance with the divine injunction, you will count it all joy when you fall into divers temptations; and you can say, with the apostle, "I take pleasure in infirmities, in reproaches, in necessities, in persecutions, in distresses, for Christ's sake." When you have arrived at this state, you will have arrived at the climax of human experience. We are to go beyond the stoic, who bears troubles without complaint from a mere sense of duty. We are to come into such a state that we shall be able, through divine grace, to take pleasure in our allotments in life, whatever they may be, as a part of God's will toward us; so that, standing in the midst of things that make other men weep, we can look upon them rejoicingly. To do these things is to suffer with Christ; and we have the promise that if we so suffer with him, we shall be especially united to him in his glory in the world to come.

Through cross to crown; though through thy spirit's life
Trials untold assail with giant strength,
Good cheer, good cheer! Soon ends the bitter strife,
And thou shalt reign in peace with Christ at length.

Through death to life; and through this vale of tears,
And through this thistle-field of life, ascend
To the great supper in that world, whose years
Of bliss unfading, cloudless, know no end.

MAY 23: MORNING.

Whatsoever things were written aforetime were written for our learning, that we, through patience and comfort of the Scriptures, might have hope.— *Rom.* xv., 4.

THE New Testament is a book of joy. There is not in the world a book which is pervaded with such a spirit of exhilaration. Nowhere does it pour forth a melancholy strain. Often pathetic, it is never gloomy. Full of sorrows, it is full of victory over sorrow. In all the round of literature, there is not another book that can cast such cheer and inspire such hope. Yet it eschews humor, and foregoes wit. It is intensely earnest, and yet full of quiet. It is profoundly solemn, and yet there is not a strain of morbid feeling in it.

Some books have recognized the wretchedness of man's condition on earth, and, in some sense, have produced exhilaration; it has been rather by amusing their readers. They have turned life into a comedy. Not so the Christian Scriptures. They never jest; they never ridicule; they never deal in any wise in comic scenes. They disdain, in short, all those methods by which other writings have inspired cheer; and yet, by a method of their own, they produce in all who accept them a reasonable sympathy, elevation of mind, high hope, and cheerful resignation.

Other writers gild the nature of man with the light of an indiscriminating benevolence. They tell us, in substance, that wickedness is not so wicked as we think; that we put too much emphasis on conduct, and attach too much importance to events; that we must look upon men more as if they were clouds coming and going in the sky, or like leaves which flutter, without self-help, as the wind determines. But the New Testament unfolds the nature of man in the darkest colors. It paints no paradise of innocent sufferers. It sweeps a circle around a guilty race, lost in trespasses and sins, and so given over to them that all strength for recovery is gone; and Death, universal and final, towers and glooms over the race like a black storm that will soon burst forth, unless some kind wind arises to bear it back, and sweep it out of the hemisphere.

Strange as it is in statement, it is while dealing with such a scene that the New Testament writers suffuse their compositions with a transcendent joy. Not once, nor twice, but always, and all the way through, they flash with radiant hope and joy—hope and joy in the divine nature as revealed to the apostles; in the God of all grace, the Christ of infinite suffering love, and in the helpful, life-giving influences of the Holy Spirit.

MAY 23: EVENING.

For the good that I would, I do not; but the evil which I would not, that I do.—*Rom.* vii., 19.

CONSCIENCE, instructed in the Word of God, and then vitalized by the imagination, points men to a way so high that few succeed in climbing to it; and if they reach it at all, it is to limp and shuffle with such ungracious steps that conscience, in angry disgust, hurls them down again. Conscience has an eye like the eagle, and, alas! its talons too. And it is this very fact that the sensitive growth of moral feeling is far beyond the growth of our practice that makes it impossible for any man to find peace under the adjudications of conscience.

The conscience becoming more sensitive and more critical at every step of moral improvement, at length the soul is so staggered and appalled by the growth of conscience, and by the impossibility of being at peace with God on the ground of obedience to the law, that there must come a time in which the soul shall despair, and give up, and look to God for help as from a free love, not as from justice; as a grace, not as a due; as a gift, not as a desert. There must come a time when you will put yourself in the arms of God, and say, from the depths of your experience, "I have tried to dress myself, and to cleanse myself, and to make myself fit for thy taking, for I could not endure the idea of putting myself into the hands of so sublime and pure a Being in so wretched a state; and I have put on every thing, and thrown off every thing, and made such wretched work, that, at last, poor, and miserable, and ragged, I come to thee; and if I am taken at all, I must be taken as a sinner." The sooner a man comes to that experience the better, for come to it he must, or revolve in misery. No man will have peace till he learns that Christ sympathizes with men because they are sinful, and longs to heal them. God's heart is medicinal. Christ's nature carries a remedial sympathy. He is soul-physician, and comes to us, accepts us, and abides by us, not because we are well, but that he may make us well.

Mine is a day of fear and strife,
A needy soul, a needy life,
A needy world, a needy age;
Yet, in my perilous pilgrimage,
I cast my soul on thee,
Mighty to save e'en me,
Jesus, thou Son of God.

To thee I come—ah! only thou
Canst wipe the sweat from off this brow;
Thou, only thou, canst make me whole,
And soothe the fever of my soul;
I cast my soul on thee,
Mighty to save e'en me,
Jesus, thou Son of God.

MAY 24: MORNING.

Be careful for nothing.—*Phil.* iv., 6.

As little children will frolic, and play, and talk to themselves, and sing, and be happy, if every time they look up they can see their mother's form or shadow, or hear her voice, so we, in God's greater household, are to have such a consciousness of our Father's presence as shall make us happy, cheerful, contented in our sports and duties. We are dear to God. He will not forget us, nor cease to take care of us. We are so much more precious than many things which he never forgets, that we stultify ourselves if we refuse to be serene, as they are serene. Did you ever know Spring to forget to come? Did you ever know a spring in which the dandelions forgot to mock the sun with their little sparkling faces in the grass? Did you ever know a spring in which the ten thousand vines that creep along the breast of the earth, and send out their little flowers, or in which the grass or the mosses forgot their turn, and time, and function? God never yet lets these things oversleep. He always calls them, and they always come. And he has been calling them, and they have been responding to his call, for six thousand years. "Wherefore, if God so clothe the grass of the field, which to-day is, and to-morrow is cast into the oven, shall he not much more clothe you, oh ye of little faith?"

MAY 24: EVENING.

I will bring the blind by a way that they knew not; I will lead them in paths that they have not known.—*Isaiah* xlii., 16.

THERE is one that sits in heaven and controls the elements of our being, and holds in his hand the threads of our destiny for time and eternity, as I hold in my hand the threads of my child's destiny so far as his education for the pursuits of this world is concerned. What a glorious office-work must that be which he is carrying on for us. Oh, what joy it brings to me to think that I am not a lonely wanderer trying to find my way, but that the vague and inexplicable yearnings which I have, and which I am following, are the drawing-strings thrown out to lead me by one who knows just what my necessities are, and who stands ready to relieve them all. He is my King, my Priest, my Prophet, my all in all, to do whatever I need to have done, in body or soul, for time and for eternity. Blessed be God for the enunciation of so glorious a doctrine. Be thou, Lord Jesus, my head, and let me follow thy beck.

God hath kept me hitherto;
Can he cease, then, to be true?
Why should I just now despair;
Can he weary of his care?
Hence, tormenting terrors, hence!
God shall be my confidence;
Let him lead me as he will,
Oh my soul, and be thou still.

MAY 25: MORNING.

If ye love me, keep my commandments.—*John* xiv., 15.

Do you notice how many times our Savior expresses this thought? It is as if a child should rush passionately to its mother, and throw its little arms around her neck, and hug her, and say convulsively, "Oh mother, I do love you so!" "Well, my dear child, if you do, why are you not a better child?"

How many times is that heard in the family? Our Savior said the same thing. "If ye love me, do not suppose that that is love which goes off into an enthusiasm, an emotion, a paroxysm, a flash of joyous feeling. That is very well; but if you love me, let your feelings take on the shape of life, disposition, conduct." And afterward, how many times was it said by his apostles, in various shapes, that the evidence that we love Christ is that we love the brethren—that we keep the commandments?

Then let such questions as these be used to determine your state in a Christian life: Am I willing to accept Christ's commands? Am I willing, therefore, to find out what they are? Am I sincerely, every day, seeking to frame my disposition according to his commands? Am I moulding my life to benevolence, and not to selfishness? Do I imitate Christ's example? Do I practically trust him? Do I trust his daily providence? Do I put my care upon him? Do I every day endeavor, so far as I have light, to act in such a way that if Christ were present with me he would have occasion to know that I was trying to be like him?

MAY 25: *EVENING.*

For Christ also hath once suffered for sins, the just for the unjust, that he might bring us to God.—1 *Peter* iii., 18.

You believe in the Bible, you believe in prayer, you believe in a great many things; but do you believe in Jesus? Do you accept the love of Christ as it is taught, in all its fullness, preciousness, and universal application, as yours, *absolutely* yours, not only without condition, but, I had almost said, against conditions? The particular difficulty which many men feel is that Christ will love them upon a condition; that, if they repent, if they come to him, and if they are in a converted state, then he will love them; whereas the Scripture truth is, that while yet they are afar off, while they are enemies, long before they are converts, Christ loves them; and that this foregoing love of Christ is the very cause of their feeling, and the very reason why they desire any thing more, and why they strive for any thing more.

The love of Christ is not something that is to be dependent upon our performance. It is a love that hangs over us night and day, just as the sun hangs in the atmosphere. Whether men are blind or whether they see, whether they go out of doors or stay and hide themselves in the house, the sun goes on shining in all his fullness. And the love of Christ is immeasurable. It pours abroad for all; and whoever will, let him come and take it freely.

MAY 26: MORNING.

For we also are weak in him, but we shall live with him by the power of God toward you.—2 *Cor.* xiii., 4.

As an encouragement to our perseverance, God is pleased to accept the reed-forms of all right experiences, of all graces and virtues, until we have time to develop them. He does by us as we do by our children. We make allowance for our children's mistakes; we excuse their shortcomings; we do not spare discipline; we rebuke, we exhort, we coerce in various ways. Not because we are angry, but because we see that the inexperience of the child can be treated in that way better than in any other. For the child's good, we surround him with various motives; and God is pleased to deal with us in the same way. He takes us as we are, and says to us, "Here are the bright ideals to which you are to aspire; but you are children, and I will bear with you, and educate you, and accept the best you can give, all the way up, so that by-and-by you shall praise me with understanding and perfectness in heaven."

Do you say, "I do not love God as he deserves to be loved?" Not even the redeemed in heaven love Christ as he deserves to be loved; and do you suppose that God is such a task-master that he will take nothing but that love that even heaven can not give? If you can only bring to God reed-forms and beginnings, then bring those. He will accept them. Bring to God the little feeling that you have, and be content with it, and thank God for what you have, and love him as much as you can, and wait patiently in the use of means, and you will find that feeling grow year by year, and every year toward greater and greater disclosures.

MAY 26: EVENING.

I have blotted out, as a thick cloud, thy transgressions, and, as a cloud, thy sins: return unto me, for I have redeemed thee.—*Isa.* xliv., 22.

Be not discouraged because you are sinful. It is the very office of Christ's love to heal all your sins. Not, then, only when you have overcome them yourself is he prepared to receive you; it is his delight to give you help while in the very bitterness of wrestling with your sins. He is your pilot to lead you out of trouble. No pilot would he be who only then would take my ship when I had gone through the narrows, and could see the city, and was quite free of all danger. Who would need a physician if he might not come to his bedside until after the sickness was healed? what use of school-master if one may not go to school till his education be complete? what hope of salvation if God would give us no help till the whole work of subduing the natural heart were completed? No! Our Savior is one who begins and completes in us the work of grace. He is the author of our faith, and the finisher of it. It is his power that works in us to will and to do of his good pleasure. He comes to you when you are morally dead, and by his touch brings you to life. When you are weak, he inspires you with strength; when you are tempted, he opens the door of escape; when you are vanquished, he appears, that he may lift you up and bind your wounds. Yea, bending under all our burdens, and loaded down with our own sins, behold that Christ of whom it is said, "He was wounded for our transgressions, he was bruised for our iniquities; the chastisement of our peace was upon him, and with his stripes we are healed. All we, like sheep, have gone astray; we have turned every one to his own way, and the Lord hath laid on him the iniquity of us all."

When my sins, in aspect dread,
Meet like waters o'er my head,
Seen in light of God's own face,
Darker for his offered grace;
When I sigh for healing rest,
By a hopeless yoke oppress'd;
When I meet some foe unknown,
Shall I find myself alone?
Hear the Shepherd's voice of old,
Looking on his helpless fold:

"Every feeble sheep I know;
Life eternal I bestow;
None shall pluck them from my hand."
Shall that word of promise stand?
"Heaven and earth shall pass away,
Not my words," so Christ doth say.
In death's grasp "his *truth* shall be
Shield and buckler unto thee."

MAY 27: MORNING.

As the Lord hath called every one, so let him walk.—1 *Cor.* vii., 17.

All men that labor productively and skillfully are real benefactors of the community. And why do not they know it? why do not they feel the honor? why do not men preach it to them? why are they not told that they should not look upon the mere self-side of their avocations? The merchant, the mechanic, the day-laborer, bearing endless benefactions to the community—why do not they regard their labors in a higher light? Why do they not feel that they are contributing to the welfare of their fellow-men as well as to their own welfare, and that so they are following Christ? If they only did their life-work on purpose to follow Christ; if they only did it because it was following Christ; if they only joyed in following him, and if the consciousness of following him was their reward, then they would rise to the dignity of some remote imitation of the Master; whereas they are without the reward, even though they do the same things, if they do them only for selfish, pitiful pelf.

Let every man, then, follow the occupation that God has given him, and understand that in following it he is rendering a service to his fellow-men; let him feel, "I am honored in these appointed channels of God's providence, that I am permitted to give my life for my fellow-men—that is, to *live* it for them."

MAY 27: EVENING.

Charge them that are rich in this world that they be not highminded, nor trust in uncertain riches, but in the living God, who giveth us richly all things to enjoy.—1 *Tim.* vi., 17.

When men come to walk the shadowy way, when the great Tax-gatherer calls all men before him, to one he says, "Give me thy ships." "Oh Death, they are thine," saith the man. To others he says, "Give me thy houses and lands;" and they and their possessions part company without papers. To another he says, "Give me thy funds that thou hast toiled for;" and the man that stood highest in his day and generation is stripped bare, and goes out of the world with no capital for the life to come.

Then comes another man, a man of *dreams*, as he is called. Death says to him, "Yield up thy ships." "I have none." "Yield up thine acres." "I have none." "Yield up thy bonds and funds." "I have none." "Yield up thy thoughts." "Nay, oh Death, my thoughts are mine, and beyond thy power." "Yield up thy affections." "Nay, Death, thou canst not touch my affections. And my hope, my immortality—these are not in thy schedule. That which I am by the grace of God, thou canst not tax or hold. I carry all that with me." The man that is mightiest in this world leaves his might behind him, and the man that is weakest in this world carries his might with him. When we step into that other world where things are measured according to their realities, the man that has the most has the least, and the man that has the least has the most. And so the first shall be last, and the last shall be first.

I love (and have some cause to love) the earth;
She is my Maker's creature, therefore good:
She is my mother, for she gave me birth;
She is my tender nurse: she gives me food.
But what's a creature, Lord, compared with thee?
Or what's my mother, or my nurse, to me?

Without thy presence, earth gives no refection;
Without thy presence, sea affords no treasure;
Without thy presence, air's a rank infection;
Without thy presence, heav'n itself's no pleasure.
If not possessed, if not enjoyed in thee,
What's earth, or sea, or air, or heaven, to me?

MAY 28: *MORNING.*

Lo, children are a heritage of the Lord.—*Psalm* cxxvii., 3.

It is a very solemn and serious matter for you to be intrusted with the care of God's little children. One would think, to see the mating that goes on in society—and it is a beautiful thing in its way—that butterflies were let loose, so light, and gay, and happy are the hearts that sail together and play around each other. One would think, to hear the cheerful congratulations that accompany the putting out of a young life in the family state, that there was no responsibility connected with the event. And when there begin to be "angels unawares" coming into the household, one after another, how joyous it is! The silver cups and little congratulatory notes are plenty. But how few there are who feel that, from the time the door of life opens, and a child is born, God has drawn his hand out from near to his own heart, and lent something of himself to the parent, and said, "Keep it till I come; take this, my own child, and educate it for me, and bring it to heaven, and let its improving and its profiting appear when ye and it stand together in the last day." It is a very solemn thing to have a family, and to have children, of which you are not only the parent, but the guardian and the guide, and in some sense the savior.

MAY 28: *EVENING.*

Who gave himself a ransom for all.—1 *Tim.* ii., 6.

I AM glad to give emphasis and power to the fact that Christ gave his life as much while he was living as while he was dying, and that to give life may mean either to use it or lay it down. It is said that Christ gave, not his life, but *himself*. He gave himself in dying, but he also gave himself in *living*. All his life was a giving. For he lived not for himself. He sought not his own. He did not employ his reason, nor his moral sentiments, nor his active forces, nor his time, nor his power, for himself. And the three years, or nearly three, that preceded his death, were in some respects a far more remarkable gift than was the death itself. He *used* his life for others as really as he laid it down for them. He gave his life while it was in his own keeping, as really as when it was taken away from him. The gift of Christ is the gift in its totality, in all the variations of his experience. Though on some accounts the tragic circumstances of his death lift it up into conspicuity, though by reason of man's fears and man's education there is given to it a sombre importance that belongs to no single act of his life, yet I think, as we become clearer in our moral perceptions, and finer in our nature, we learn, not indeed to disesteem that part of Christ's example, but to go back and give more emphasis to the other part, and to lift up the daily conversations, the daily patience, the daily love, the ten thousand fidelities which belong to so great a life, carried wholly for its benefit upon others, and not at all for his own mere personal convenience or gain.

MAY 29: MORNING.

Let us not be weary in well doing; for in due season we shall reap, if we faint not.—*Gal.* vi., 9.

There are many that seem to themselves to have done little on earth. You do not know what you have done. The bud that is bursting to-day on the tree you could take between your thumb and finger; but let it grow this summer, and then see what that bud is when it bears branches, and those branches bear other branches. And yet these are all contained in that little bud. Now, all the good we do in this world is a bud in the garden of the Lord, which will in the future grow and spread, and yield grateful fragrance, and bear abundant fruit. Because you are working in obscure places, and do not see the results of your labors, do not suppose that your life is thrown away. All the more, if you see no results here, believe that you shall see them in the heavenly land. Have patience, and work on. It is a hard soil that can not be cultivated at all.

Go make thy garden fair as thou canst,
  Thou workest never alone;
Perchance he whose plot is next to thine
  Will see it, and mend his own.

And the next may copy his, sweet heart,
  Till all grows fair and sweet,
And when the Master comes at eve,
  Happy faces his coming will greet.

Then shall thy joy be full, sweet heart,
  In the garden so fair to see,
In the Master's words of praise for all,
  In a look of his own for thee.

MAY 29: EVENING.

They that use this world as not abusing it.—1 *Cor.* vii., 31.

If you stand in affinities one with another, do not break the silver bands in order to be a Christian. Polish them. You say, "I am engaged in weighty affairs; I minister to the times in which I live." If the affairs are right affairs, do not lay those affairs down to be a Christian. You are God's minister in those very things, and I say, Keep them—for Christ's sake, keep them. "But if a man becomes a Christian, must he not suffer?" How suffer? Just as a man who has broken his leg suffers when it is set. But it is a little suffering for the sake of life-long health of limb, just as men who are sick take medicine that they may get well. Do you then say that a man had better be sick all his life rather than go through the pain and penalty of getting well? If you are only a little bit of a Christian—if you have just enough religion to keep a fire burning under your conscience, you will suffer; but if you give yourself to religion—if you accept it—then it is another name for the total education of your moral being and life. If you bring your life and disposition into consonance with those laws of life and character which God has laid down, then ye are come to the "heavenly Jerusalem, and to an innumerable company of angels, to the general assembly and church of the first-born, and to God, the Judge of all, and to the spirits of just men made perfect, and to Jesus, the mediator of the new covenant, and to the blood of sprinkling, that speaketh better things than that of Abel."

MAY 30: MORNING.

The discretion of a man deferreth his anger, and it is his glory to pass over a transgression.—*Prov.* xix., 11.

We must be patient with men who are not patient themselves with us or with their fellow-men. There are a great many men that are, by the heat and momentum of their passions, swept into unconscious cruelty. With all such men we are to be patient. Every man seems to think that he is called to avenge wrong in this world, and one of the subtlest and wickedest of all pleas is, "I did not give him any more than he deserved." Who made you a judge or an executioner to give men what they deserve? "Vengeance is mine; I will repay, saith the Lord;" and you have no right to take upon yourself the prerogatives of God, and punish men, though they are wicked, except in cases where, by unmistakable providences, or by ordinances of men, you are authorized to deal with such cases. When, therefore, men are cruel, and even persecuting, they are not put beyond the bound of your duty. "Be patient toward all men."

Do naught but good; for such the noble strife
  Of virtue is—'gainst wrong to venture love,
And for thy foe devote a brother's life,
  Content to wait the recompense above;
Brave for the truth, to fiercest insult meek,
In mercy strong, in vengeance only weak.

MAY 30: *EVENING.*

We love him because he first loved us.—1 *John* iv., 19.

Men never find Christ, but are always found of him. He goes forth to seek and to save the lost. It is not the outreaching of our thought, the abstraction of our heart, the strong drawing of our sympathy and yearning, that brings him to us. It is the abounding love of his heart that draws us up toward him. His love precedes ours. We kindle our hearts at his. As the sun is up before the sluggard, so the twilight and dawn of his love is upon the hills when we wake; and when we sleep, even, his thoughts burn above us as the stars burn through the night.

This willing, winning, pleading Christ, who wields all the grandeur of justice and all the authority of universal empire with such sweet gentleness that in all the earth there is none like unto him, is your personal friend. He knows you better than your mother knew you. He has called you by name. In your households you are not so familiar to your most cherished friend as you are to the heart of Christ. Not so indelibly is your name recorded in your father's memory, or in the baptismal register of the sanctuary, or in the family Bible, where the tabular leaf for births holds your infant name, as upon the ever-remembering heart of the Lord Jesus Christ.

MAY 31: *MORNING.*

As the Father hath loved me, so have I loved you; continue ye in my love. —*John* xv., 9.

OUR Lord addressed himself to men's love, and he still addresses himself to their love. He offered and offers all, and he demands all. Though calm, our Savior was an intense lover. His own need, everlastingly, is to be intensely loved. *With all the heart, mind, soul, and strength*—that is the heavenly love-formula. A passionate love to Christ was practically the whole creed of the primitive Church. They thought less than we do, by far, of the Bible; for then only the Old Testament was in their hands, and the New was not written. In the primitive Church there had been drawn out no doctrines. They believed the supreme fact that Christ came, died for our sins, rose again, and ascended up on high. The whole of their belief was comprised in this personal fact. It not only was the whole creed of every primitive Christian, but it is still the whole creed of every deeply spiritual Christian. He who knows how to love Christ supremely finds that from that vivid, vitalizing centre spring all precautionary and all formative influences, so that every truly spiritual Christian learns that the operative power in his soul is the personal love which he enthusiastically bears to the Lord Jesus Christ.

MAY 31: *EVENING.*

Behold, the eye of the Lord is upon them that fear him, upon them that hope in his mercy, to deliver their soul from death.—*Psalm* xxxiii., 18, 19.

WHEN your time to die comes, and you are to leave this world, do you suppose the Lord Jesus, who loves you better than you love yourself, has not arranged every thing so that you will be willing to go? You want to feel willing now; but he does not want you to be willing. You want to be willing to leave your children when God wants you to stay with them and take care of them. You have the knowledge, the spirit of fidelity, and the strength which qualify you for that work; and what are these but indications that your duty is to live and take care of them. This equipment is a sign and token that now, to-day, your duties are here; and it is right that at this time you should feel unwilling to die, though one year hence, or one month hence, you may feel, and it may be proper for you to feel willing to die.

When, by-and-by, God leads you step by step down to the trouble which you are thinking of, there will have been wrought such changes, and such preparations will have taken place, that it will not seem like a trouble.

> Thy hand in his, like fondest, happiest child,
> Place thou, nor draw it for a moment thence;
> Walk thou with him, a Father reconciled,
> Till in his own good time he call thee hence.
> Walk with him now, so shall thy way be bright,
> And all thy soul be filled with his most glorious light.

JUNE 1: *MORNING.*

Thy youth is renewed like the eagle's.—*Psalm* ciii., 5.

CHRISTIANITY is, in its very nature, the endowing of a man with royalty of character. It is the making things strong and sweet, and fruitful and beautiful. Beauty and liberty, and life and power, belong to every single element to which a man is called in the Christian life. Christ and the Christian life are the only way in which a man can fulfill his nature; the only way in which a man can rightly develop his reason, and subordinate passion to moral sentiment; the only way in which moral sentiment can come to all its blossoms and to all its beauty. Without religion, a man is like gold which is hidden in a mountain. With it, he is like the gold when it is dug out, and becomes coin, or is made into ten thousand beautiful objects. Without religion, a man is as a seed. With it, he is as the oak which is developed from that seed, or the wine that has been produced from that seed, or the flowers that have sprung from that seed.

If a man, therefore, looks upon the Christian life, and says, "Oh, it is a dreary, cross-bearing, sighing, solitary kind of life!" I say it is not. If he says, "It is not the life for the young eagle or the lion," I say it is just the life for the young eagle, and that "the Lion of the tribe of Judah" is its model. The eagle is the very symbol employed; and God calls us eaglets, to be borne aloft by his power.

JUNE 1: EVENING.

Lord, teach us to pray.—*Luke* xi., 1.

THERE may be many reasons why you do not like to pray. One may be that you are really not a Christian, and can not speak the language of Canaan. Another reason may be that you have not learned to pray in a manner that is adapted to you. It may be that you undertake to employ forms of speech which to you are unbefitting. You remember how David attempted to fight the battle with Goliath in Saul's armor, how he found it too large and too heavy for him, and how he went back and got his simple sling, with which he slew the giant. Many of you make a similar mistake in praying. You try to pray as the minister does, or as some elder or class-leader does, or as some fluent brother does, and you do not succeed. You try to walk in the prayer of another person who has had more experience than you have, and it rattles about as Saul's armor did about David. It is a world too big for you. It does not fit you any where. I do not wonder that you do not want to pray under such circumstances. If, imitating David, who went back to the sling, the simplest of all weapons, you would be content to pray as a little child—if you would go back to lisping, monosyllabic prayers, you would have less difficulty, and would like prayer better.

JUNE 2: MORNING.

They think that they shall be heard for their much speaking.—*Matt.* vi., 7.

SOME persons attempt to bring down blessings by much praying. They bombard the throne of grace, as it were, without any definite object in their mind. They pray without knowing exactly what they are praying for. This is not wise. In my own experience, I have found that when my thoughts have been withdrawn to other things, and, being brought back to God, my mind is not eager to hold converse with him, it is not well to plead with him in measured prayers, as though I were bound to say so much to him every day, and as though he would not be satisfied with any thing less. My father, and mother, and friends never required me to talk with them a given amount. If I came where they were, and did not feel like talking, they bore with my silence. So, when I go to God, if I do not feel like making long prayers, I make short ones. I do it, first, because I have not much to say, and it is not truthful to go on praying when you have nothing to say; and, secondly, because short prayers under such circumstances are positively more beneficial than long ones.

JUNE 2: EVENING.

For thy sake I have borne reproach.—*Psalm* lxix., 7.

THERE are many persons who will bear the cross provided they receive recognition and applause. As long as you can have friends to come in and say, every day, "Your lot is a very hard one; I wonder how you can bear it," you feel that it is worth while to have a cross to bear, for the sake of the sympathy and praise that it brings. But suppose nobody saw you, would you bear it then? Suppose people did not believe it of you when others told it? Nay, suppose they misconstrued it—suppose you found that injurious stories were circulated about you in respect to that work into which you were putting all your strength—suppose you found yourself buffeted and reviled, do you think you would not revile again, and that you would say, "Lord Jesus, only be thou true to me, and I care not what all the world do; I will follow thee, and I will take up my cross, and count my life not dear to me; and I will do it for the sake of those who are outcast and who need me. As thou hast been a Savior to me, so I will be a savior to them?" Nay, can you go night after night to Christ, and say, "Lord, how can I enough thank thee for permitting me to do it? for accounting me worthy, not only to be called by thy name, but to suffer for thy sake?"

Thou must walk on, however men upbraid thee,
With him who trod the wine-press all alone;
Thou may'st not find one human hand to aid thee,
One human soul to comprehend thine own.

JUNE 3: MORNING.

But the wisdom that is from above is first pure, then peaceable, gentle, and easy to be entreated, full of mercy and good fruits, without partiality and without hypocrisy.—*James* iii., 17.

It is only by having patience with men that you can retain any hold upon them. You must not break that sympathetic cord in your soul and theirs by which alone you can convey to them the mercies and blessings of God. The moment a man is outside of your pity and forbearance, that moment he is outside of your diocese. You can not do any thing for a man that you dislike. You can not help him; you can not pray for him; you can not draw him; you can not teach him. If you are to do good to men—if you are to stand between their Savior and them—you must do it by maintaining that patience and gentleness which love inspires. Only so can you help men.

Would you have sympathy for the racked victim of the Inquisition? And ought you not also to have sympathy for the inquisitor? Would you have sympathy for the victim of the guillotine? And ought you not also to have sympathy for the judge that condemned him? There is an eternity of joy or woe for the one as well as for the other; and though you hate the wickedness, you ought to have patience and sympathy with the man. It is easy to have sympathy and patience with those that are wronged or suffering, but it is hard to have sympathy and patience with those that inflict the wrong and cause the suffering. Yet it is only by doing this that you can do them good. And it is a sad thing for a human soul to have such dispositions as disqualify him for touching another soul with recuperative power.

JUNE 3: EVENING.

All thy works shall praise thee, O Lord.—*Psalm* cxlv., 10.

Ye are come not only to the home and city of the living God, and to angels, and to the spirits of just men made perfect, but ye are come to God himself. Ye are brought into the loving presence, and into the living, immediate, and continuous sympathy of God. What is the grandeur of the night, or what is the glory of such an over-canopying day but this, that it is the heaven of my God, and that it brings him nearer to me? What is the grandeur of the field, the pomp of the hill, the glory of the summer, the wealth of the autumn — what are all forms, and all colors, and all forces, and all sounds, and all harmonies therein but this, that they minister, either individually or collectively, the sense of the beauty, the grandeur, and the reality of the presence of God? It is God that makes the stillness of the air so sweet. It is God that makes the tumult of the storm so enjoyable. It is God that makes the night better than the bed to our weary thoughts. It is God that makes the daylight full of splendor and full of glory. It is God that rules the year. Nature would be scarcely worth a puff of the empty wind if it were not that all nature is a temple of which God is the brightness and the glory. And whenever a man becomes a Christian, he comes into such an apprehensive state that he comes right home to God in every thing and every where. Not the Bible alone, but the earth, teaches us of God.

JUNE 4: *MORNING.*

And every one that hath forsaken houses, or brethren, or sisters, or father, or mother, or wife, or children, or lands, for my name's sake, shall receive a hundred-fold, and shall inherit everlasting life.—*Matt.* xix., 29.

If you will go into any jeweler's shop you will find that, where the manufacturing is carried on, what with the leather aprons that the workmen wear, and a perfectly tight floor with a checkered frame of wood over it, the dust and filings of gold that fall are all caught, so that nothing is lost. So admirable are the arrangements of the Assay Office in New York, that not any appreciable amount of the gold that is sent there is lost in any of the processes. It is caught out of the smoke, and out of the acids, and swept up with the dirt, and every thing that goes in comes out again refined and purified. It seems lost in the alembic, and in the corroding acids, and it seems to be passing off in the air through the funnels, but by chemistry it is saved, and at last reproduced. It seems to us as if we were losing. No, we are not. God's laboratory in this world is carefully arranged to save every particle of all that is valuable. Of the things that you think you are losing, not one is lost. God saves them all; heaven keeps them all. And among the surprises of the other life will be, I think, that we shall find that on all that on which we have written "loss" here, angels will have written "gain" there.

JUNE 4: EVENING.

And though the Lord give you the bread of adversity, and the water of affliction, yet shall not thy teachers be removed into a corner any more, but thine eyes shall see thy teachers: and thine ears shall hear a word behind thee, saying, This is the way, walk ye in it.—*Isaiah* xxx., 20, 21.

I BRING to your memory a Savior who is in sympathy and in blessed relations with you. Fall not into that weak and poor way of thinking of the sympathy of Christ as if it were merely showering sunlight on you. God makes his sun to rise on the good and on the evil alike. The sun does not know how to make any difference between things and men. It makes no discriminations. It shines on me, and it shines on every thing else just as much. But when my God looks on me, I hope he makes a difference. I hope, when he administers toward me and the brute, it is not all the same. I want to feel that he is pressing down the bad and lifting up the good in me. And if it hurts, only let me know what the hurt means, and I am willing to bear it. If it is only God, let him take any thing and every thing. Empty my crib; empty my cradle; wring my heart; shut me up; do any thing—Lord God, love me, and then do any thing.

To be loved of God; to be nurtured here; to be disciplined; to be taught; to be prepared for the heavenly estate, and then go home to be present with the Lord forever—that is joy unspeakable, as it shall be full of glory.

Oh Love, who thus hath bound me fast,
 Beneath that gentle yoke of thine—
Love, who hast conquered me at last,
 And rapt away this heart of mine—
Oh Love, I give myself to thee,
Thine ever, only thine to be.

JUNE 5: MORNING.

If thou bring thy gift to the altar, and there rememberest that thy brother hath aught against thee, leave there thy gift before the altar and go thy way; first be reconciled to thy brother, and then come and offer thy gift.—*Matthew* v., 23, 24.

MANY men substitute a certain sort of religious sensibility for religion, instead of evolving a practical religious life, which, day by day, and hour by hour, exerts a powerful constraining and inspiring influence upon them.

How stand the facts in your case? Have you never injured a man, and often and often resolved that you would make reparation, and have you not omitted to make that reparation? Is there no vice in your affairs of which, as often as it comes, you say, "This shall be repaired," and is it not unrepaired to this day? Is there nothing in your method of treating your wife—no hardness, no arrogance, no overbearingness of temper—which you have meant, time after time, to overcome, and have you made one single efficient effort to overcome it? Is there nothing in your treatment of your husband that you know is inconsistent with true and gracious love, and have you followed your convictions of right on this point? Are there not in your relations to your children whole harvest-fields of duties that you have been meaning to perform, but that will be unreaped unless you make haste to perform them? In your relations to your parents, to your brothers, and to your sisters, could you not count up scores of duties that you ought to have performed long ago, but which you have neglected to perform? If you were to make an inventory of the things which you have known to be right, but have not followed, how many they would be.

JUNE 5: EVENING.

I have fought a good fight, I have finished my course, I have kept the faith: henceforth there is laid up for me a crown of righteousness, which the Lord, the righteous judge, shall give me at that day; and not to me only, but unto all them also that love his appearing.—2 *Tim.* iv., 7, 8.

SELF-DENIAL is a universal principle which belongs to every

sphere and part of human life. Without it no man can go through the world. And the only question that we have to settle is this: Will you employ self-denial for the sake of exalting yourself, or will you employ it for the sake of debasing yourself? Will you use it as a staff to lead you higher and higher, or to go down deeper and deeper, murkier and more degraded?

"And every man that striveth for the mastery is temperate in all things. Now they do it to obtain a corruptible crown, but we an incorruptible."

While yet they live, the leaves grow sear upon their brow. Their very footsteps, with which they sound the dance, shake down these withered leaves, and they are discrowned in the very wearing of their crowns. But around about our heads that follow Christ invisible leaves there are; or, if they are visible, men call them thorns—as they should be called, since we follow him that wore them; but as the angels behold them, they are those imperishable flowers—that amaranth which never blossoms to fade or to fail. And our crown shall be bright when the stars have gone, and the sun has forgotten to shine.

JUNE 6: MORNING.

If any man speak, let him speak as the oracles of God; if any man minister, let him do it as of the ability which God giveth, that God in all things may be glorified through Jesus Christ: to whom be praise and dominion forever and ever. Amen—1 *Peter* iv., 11.

A MAN'S life as a Christian ought to be like a farmer's life. It is raining to-day, and the old farmer says, "Well, what of that? I meant to get in my hay to-day, but there is something else that I can do. There is that old hay to be moved into the old barn, and there is that door to be hung on new hinges. I have been waiting for a rainy day to repair this machine. There is the big wagon to be fixed. Besides, I must mend that harness." There is enough work for five wet days; and is he not working on the farm as much while doing these things as though he were getting in his hay? He has a wide range of occupation; and, although his work varies from day to day, and from season to season, it is all husbandry.

Now a Christian ought to live on so broad a scale of experience that if to-day he does not feel like acting in one direction, he will in another. To-day it may be your duty to teach. It may be your duty to-morrow to receive instruction. It is Christian life to-day filled with fervency of prayer. To-morrow it may not be feeling of this type; it may be benevolence, that produces sympathy for others in trouble. The next day it may be some other Christian disposition that will open up in you. It may be the restraint of selfishness. It may be doing a generous deed. There are a thousand things that go to constitute you an agreeable, kind, loving, and loved Christian—one whose light, shining before men, is such that they want it, and seek to kindle their lamps at the same altar where you kindled yours. In that way a man can live so that his life will be spontaneous all the time.

JUNE 6: EVENING.

But we had the sentence of death in ourselves, that we should not trust in ourselves, but in God which raiseth the dead.—2 *Cor.* i., 9.

THERE are times in which we are beaten off from all confidence in men, in which there seems to be no feeling of trustworthiness; times of affliction in which the soul seems obliged to let go of every thing; times of sickness, which are also times of great weakness, in which one has neither courage nor weapon for life's battle. The peculiarity of many of the afflictions of life is that they take man's strength out of him. There is nothing in him left to rise up against trouble.

There is but one thing under such circumstances that affords any consolation. When, by reason of afflictions of any kind, life is paralyzed, and there is no sensibility left, if the soul can lift itself up to feel that there is life in God—that there is a vital connection between itself and the life of Christ; that, though it die, it shall live—the simple thought that Christ lives and so shall I, that is an anchor which sustains the soul in its extremity and emergency of grief.

Steadfast faith and hope unshaken
Animate the trusting breast;
Step by step the journey's taken
Nearer to the land of rest.

All unseen, the Master walketh
  By the toiling servant's side;
Comfortable words he talketh,
  While his hands uphold and guide.

Grief, nor pain, nor any sorrow
  Rends thy heart to him unknown;
He to-day and he to-morrow
  Grace sufficient gives his own.

JUNE 7: MORNING.

Then came also publicans to be baptized, and said unto him, Master, what shall we do? And he said unto them, Exact no more than that which is appointed you.—*Luke* iii., 12, 13.

Our worldly occupations and our religious life are only two names for one thing. They are parts of our life, and never should be separated. Our daily business should be a part of our daily religion, and our daily religion should also be a part of our daily business. We never should antagonize them in our thoughts. The spiritual element is to the practical what the dew, and rain, and sunlight are to the growing field of corn. In the closet we cleanse and inspire the soul, but in our business we use that strength which we have gained by this inspiring and cleansing. Our whole life is a religious life. The experiences of inspiration may be spiritual in the closet, but the real life of every man is that into which he puts his energy, his strength, his vitality, his power. Wherever men are, there they ought to put their power of understanding, their power of sentiment, their power of feeling, their power of planning and execution. That is the thing for a Christian man to do. And the kind of power which he has, and the moral quality of it, depend upon the influence of the interior and invisible life.

JUNE 7: EVENING.

Jesus saith unto him, I am the way, the truth, and the life: no man cometh unto the Father but by me.—*John* xiv., 6.

Oh ye that are so conscientious, and so tremulously afraid of idolatry that you go groping in heathen antiquity with a vague feeling unexpressed for the Father, the great Almighty; ye who long for that God, will you press away the brightest exemplification, the real and literal embodiment of this everlasting Father—Jesus Christ? Praying for light, praying for knowledge, and having it brought to you in the person of Christ Jesus, who loves and lives to love, and reigns, and reigns to love, and by love shall subdue all disobedience, and cleanse all sin, and redeem the world to everlasting rapture and glory through righteousness, will you not take that pre-eminent representation of God—the best that can be given to the human understanding and the human senses; and will you not, with all that are in heaven, and all that yet shall be upon earth, bow the knee, and cry, "Crown him, crown him Lord of all?" Oh that I could show you God as he is represented in Christ Jesus —the self-sacrificing God; the fatherly God; the God who is represented as giving himself rather than let you destroy yourselves; as taking men's sins, and carrying them in his own experience, rather than that men should suffer. That God who is represented in Christ Jesus is the cure of fear and doubt, and is the very anchor of the soul in all its wanderings, and driftings, and storm-drivings.

Conquering Prince and Lord of glory,
  Majesty enthroned in light,
All the heavens are bowed before thee,
  Far beyond them spreads thy might.
Shall I fall not at thy feet,
And my heart with rapture beat,
Now thy glory is displayed,
Thine ere yet the worlds were made?

As I watch thee far ascending
  To the right hand of the throne,
See the host before thee bending,
  Praising thee in sweetest tone,
Shall I not, too, at thy feet
Hear the angels' strain repeat,
And rejoice that heaven doth sing
With the triumph of my King?

JUNE 8: *MORNING.*

And after six days Jesus taketh Peter, James, and John his brother, and bringeth them up into a high mountain apart.—*Matt.* xvii., 1.

Are you fretted with care? Are you troubled with men that are ugly? If you are not, I wish you would put me in your place. Does life chafe you? Are there many buckles in the harness in which you work? and is every one rubbing the skin off?

When August comes, take a trip to the White Mountains. Go up to the top of Mount Washington. Go alone. Ride, as I rode, back for two hours, all alone, on the mountain top, lifted up into the ether. Why, there was nothing to be heard there but the blunt sound of my horse's feet, and that was not to be heard half of the time, for I stopped him. I looked upon the shimmering country, and it seemed no more as if it was populated than a map. I said to myself, "Is there an ocean thundering on the shore? Are there cities lining it? Is there a Portland? Is there a Boston? Is there a New Haven? Is there a New York? Are there wild, crashing, and rolling sounds of business? Are men mad?" I laughed at the idea that any body should be mad at any thing, every thing was so sweet, so pure, so tranquil, so peaceful. Why, I looked upon life, and it seemed to me that I was as far from its noises and troubles as from the fury and strife of ants in their hills. Look at them. Behold their fiery industry. How they fight and rage. And you stand absolutely unconcerned. And so you may stand on the outside of the greater ant-hill of human life, and look with unconcern upon men's trials, and be only as near to heaven as the top of Mount Washington. That is not far up; and yet it is up far enough to so take you out of the smoke and din of worldly affairs as to bring back sanity to your mind, and deliver you from drunken ambition, and swirling passions, and feverish desires, and enable you to look more tranquilly, and with a clearer vision, upon the scene of conflict out of which you have so lately come, to which you are soon going back, and in which you will be again swamped. There are a great many men who, under such circumstances, say, "Oh, I should like to make a tabernacle, and live in the state that I am now in; I should be so calm, so tranquil, and so sweet-minded."

These were but seasons beautiful and rare;
Abide in me, and they shall ever be:
Fulfill at once thy precept and my prayer;
Come and abide in me, and I in thee.

JUNE 8: EVENING.

For if we would judge ourselves, we should not be judged.—1 *Cor.* xi., 31.

WHEN you want to find out how you stand, it is very well for you to make an estimate of your material resources. Go and look at your bank account; see what your stocks are worth; ascertain the amount of your gold, and silver, and bills; examine your tax-list, and acquaint yourself with men's opinions concerning you. These things are all very well. Then, in the hour of prayer, in the conscious presence of God, take an account also of the treasures within you. See how much you have of righteousness, and godliness, and faith, and love, and patience, and meekness, and disinterested goodness. And when you have first measured outside, and then measured inside, you will have the measurement of the cask, and also of the wine which it holds.

JUNE 9: MORNING.

And whatsoever ye do in word or deed, do all in the name of the Lord Jesus, giving thanks to God and the Father by him.—*Col.* iii., 17.

SEEK to live with diverse experiences. Have a broader conception of Christian life than that it consists in merely saying prayers, singing hymns, and talking to men about their souls. These are an important part of Christian duty frequently; but ah! there are a thousand other things that are essential. There is the beauty of holiness as well as the power of holiness. There is the soothing duty as well as the rousing duty. There is instruction as well as exhortation. There is preparation for future duty as well as the execution of present duty. These are all parts of one Christian character. Every man should live so broadly that day by day he will find something to do which he wants to do, and which he does with appetite. Then other duties which are regular, which press themselves upon him, let him do because they are duties. And if he can not do even that, and they are urgent duties, let him do them, whatever the motive may be. So he will rise higher and higher toward the true Christian plane, which is the plane of spontaneity, of involuntary activity, of being and doing from the love of that which is essentially true, and beautiful, and pure, and right, and good.

JUNE 9: EVENING.

But if we hope for that we see not, then do we with patience wait for it.—*Rom.* viii., 25.

Reverie, or castle-building, may be carried to extremes and be unprofitably indulged in, but nevertheless there is in it a glorious element of moral improvement. It is just that that the apostle means when he says, "We are saved by hope." Blessed be the man that, when he can not bear the present, knows how to leap out of it and revel in a bright future.

God's grace upon our troubles develops in us a divine power of faith and hope, or that state of mind which enables us to create, in spite of the real, a satisfying and sustaining ideal. We live by faith. We walk not by sight The true Christian must live, not in the things that he sees, and handles, and knows, but in the things which he believes. In the midst of abounding prosperity, when the visible seems to be all that we need, it is hard for us to live upon the invisible; but when God visits us with adversity, and sweeps away all our visible supports, then we find ourselves obliged to live upon the invisible.

JUNE 10: MORNING.

For he shall give his angels charge over thee, to keep thee in all thy ways. —*Psalm* xci., 11.

There is an angel ministry. Its range, its methods of administration—in short, the diocese and duty thereof—God knows, and man does not. But it has been the testimony of the Bible from the beginning, and the faith of the church universal from the beginning, that there is an angel ministry. It is not a modern doctrine; it is as old as the patriarchs, and older. Angels preluded the Savior, appeared to him in his anguish with comforts, and guarded his sepulchre. They ministered to his apostles. One stood by Paul on the eventful night of tempest and despair. And that time Paul saw him. Often, however, they minister, without a doubt, when they are not seen. God gives his angels charge, it is said, to bear up his chosen ones, lest they dash their foot against a stone. The angels of the Lord encamp around about his people. They are ministering or serving spirits—that is, they are helpful ones, sent to minister to them that are heirs of salvation.

And is there care in heaven? And is there love
In heavenly spirits to these creatures base,
That may compassion of their evils move?
There is; and oh the exceeding grace
Of highest God, that loves his creatures so,
And all his works with mercy doth embrace,
That blessed angels he sends to and fro,
To serve to wicked man, to serve his wicked foe.
They for us fight, they watch, and duly ward,
And their bright squadrons round about us plant,
And all for love, and nothing for reward;
Oh, why should heavenly God to men have such regard!

JUNE 10: *EVENING.*

Thy word was unto me the joy and rejoicing of my heart.—*Jer.* xv., 16.

THERE is that in the Bible which will keep it intact and make it potential as long as there is a heart to feel sorrow or to beat with hope. It is its humanity. It is its courage. It is the might and power of its love. It is the vast sympathy which wraps mankind as the atmosphere wraps the globe. It is its thought and care for men in all their wants. For the poor, the needy, the weak, the helpless, the crying, the sighing, the discouraged, the downtrodden, the unvictorious, the captives, little children, mighty monarchs, peasants, nobles—for all men—there is here a throb and a yearning. There are thousands of blessings held out to them—strength, bread, fruit, water, wine, swords, spears—every thing for humanity—whatever they need in their masterly struggles in this world. This Book is an ark into which men will run, as long as the world stands, for succor and consolation. And who should have made such a Book as this, as a way cast up on which "the ransomed of the Lord shall return, and come to Zion with songs and everlasting joy upon their heads," if it be not God?

JUNE 11: *MORNING.*

The same Lord over all is rich unto all that call upon him.—*Rom.* x., 12.

CHRIST says that in every burdened hour he is your staff; that in every peril he is your rescuer; that in every temptation he is the gate through which you are to escape; that in every sickness he is your physician. Yea, he stands in the portal of the grave itself, and declares that he has power over death. "Because I live, ye shall live also." He takes the very keys of the other life, and opens the door thereof, and stands the universal Savior, and with a voice like that of one born to command, and clothed with *the* supremacy of divine power, he says, "Lo, I am with you alway, even unto the end of the world."

Consider what scope there is in these representations of Christ. All our wants for time and for eternity are made to point toward and centre in him as their everlasting supply. Suppose, then, instead of hunting texts, and attempting to prove by force of logic that he is absolutely God, we should take that other process, which consists in every day attempting to employ him as he is presented to be employed in the New Testament; suppose our life should settle this matter; suppose we should find in our personal experience evidence of his divinity, what would be the effect? If he feeds you, if he quenches your thirst, if he wakes your imagination, if he inspires your sweetest thoughts and feelings, if he sustains you, if he is your vital breath and your strength here and your salvation hereafter, and you acknowledge what he does, and accept him as what he is, then, I ask, can any worship be higher than that which you offer to him? Can you reserve and thing better than you have given to him?

JUNE 11: *EVENING.*

Christ Jesus is our peace.—*Eph.* ii., 14.

INTROVERSIVE and analytic self-examination, by persons who are incompetent to trace, to connect, or to judge of fugitive mental states, is a fertile cause of trouble. Good, innocent, simple-minded persons hear their ministers preach about self-examination, and the duty devolving upon them to study their motives and analyze their characters. It would be a good thing if they could do it; but they can not. And yet they undertake to do it, and direct their minds inward only enough to stop the flow of thought—only enough to perplex and turn back the course of life. Persons often work exceeding great mischief by this pernicious habit of introspection. The fact is, there is little in a man that he had better see. When he looks inside himself he never promotes peace, and never promotes joy. Even when men are competent to examine themselves in this way, they never produce any thing by it except humiliation and suffering. If you wish to have peace, you can get it in no way except by looking at Christ Jesus. No man ever yet got peace by looking at himself, and no man ever will.

JUNE 12: *MORNING.*

Him that is weak in the faith receive ye, but not to doubtful disputations. *Romans* xiv., 1.

A MAN opens a school among the colliers of England—men and women that have lived under ground all their lives, and to whose darkened minds the light of knowledge has never penetrated. Tidings of this school spread abroad, and some traveler says, "I understand that education is making great strides among those colliers, and I will go and see what progress they have made." He goes into the school where men and women are learning to read, and he hears an old man with gray locks that hang down on his shoulders, and with a black finger with which he rubs dirt along the book before him, spell "B—a—k—e—r, baker." After he has heard the old man spell a few such simple words slowly and painfully, he says, "Well, if that is your idea of education, then I am done," and goes out in great disgust. He thought he was going down to see these poor colliers made into philosophers at a touch, and, instead of that, he sees ignorant creatures that have been made to realize their ignorance, and that are willing to creep before they walk, and walk before they run, going over rudimentary lessons, in order that by-and-by they may have some intelligence. A sensible man would rejoice to see these small beginnings of what promise to result in enlightenment in the future.

Now men are colliers when we bring them into the Church. They have been in the grimes and mines of sin. They have been groveling in the earth; and to begin a Christian life is to be conscious of one's imperfection, and sin, and guilt before God. It is to turn round and say, "Who will instruct me in the better way? who will teach me the letters of salvation?" Here is a man beginning with faltering lip to learn the first principles of a Christian life, and what cruelty it is for one to come in and say, "A Church-member! That man is what you call a saint, is he?" No, he is not a saint; he is the rude beginning of that which, when God shall lead him through some years of earthly discipline, and then take him home to himself, shall glow in the light of heaven. Then and there he will be a saint, but only then and there.

JUNE 12: EVENING.

Who is a God like unto thee, that pardoneth iniquity, and passeth by the transgression of the remnant of his heritage? he retaineth not his anger forever, because he delighteth in mercy.—*Micah* vii., 18.

Oh that men had faith to discern what treasure of goodness is in thee, O God; what resources of power are thine; what wondrous helpfulness thou hast; how thou art the all-nursing God as well as the God of judgment; how thou art the pitying God as well as the God of inflexible righteousness; how thou dost teach as well as rebuke; how thou dost bear up in thine arms the trembling and the sinful, as well as carry the iron sceptre for thine adversary. Wondrous art thou; blessed in thy justice, in thy purity, and in thy truth. Thou art thyself the pledge that wickedness shall not dwell forever in thy realm. Sorrow, and sighing, and tears, and sickness shall flee away, and the former things shall be found no more, because thou art strong, and wise, and just—a God of righteousness and of judgment. Who shall abide thy coming, and who shall abide thine administration? Thou art a God of mercy to heal the sinful, to bind up the wounded, to give life to the dead, to do all in all, that we may become the sons of God.

JUNE 13: *MORNING.*

Though I speak with the tongues of men and of angels, and have not charity, I am become as sounding brass or a tinkling cymbal.—1 *Cor.* xiii., 1.

All religion that fails to produce love is imperfect, and so far false. Love to Christ is the one indispensable element. If every thing is gained but this, religion is like the gold setting from which the diamond has dropped out. Love is not only important, but essential. It is so vital that if it be present—this true love—it carries with it all privilege, all promise, and all prerogative. If it be absent, nothing can take its place. There is no equivalent nor substitute for it. All is void if there be not love. Apostolicity is nothing, reverence is nothing, sincerity is nothing, if this element is lacking. A religion which results in true and abiding love, no matter how it expresses itself, no matter how heretical it is, no matter how it is organized, no matter what ordinances are present and what are absent—such a religion is divine; and all that profess it, and have it—grace be upon them. They love the Lord Jesus Christ with incorruptible, undying love. But the human soul that is without personal union with God is sunless and summerless, and can never blossom nor ripen.

JUNE 13: *EVENING.*

The merciful man doeth good to his own soul; but he that is cruel troubleth his own flesh.—*Prov.* xi., 17.

There is apt to grow up in us a conceit in reference to our work. We get on the wrong side of our own labor oftentimes. We think we have given a good deal when we have watched and prayed long and earnestly for others, when we have given time and money, when we have suffered buffet. Our pride or vanity hardly fails to keep a little account of these things. And we rather assume the air of benefactors. We think, "How much have I done!" And sometimes there is the language of complaint: "Why should one who has done so much as I have be treated as I am?" There is a kind of injured innocence that we put on.

Now there never was a person that did any thing worth doing who did not really get more than he gave. This is pre-eminently true where the good which you do is less and less physical, and more and more moral and spiritual; but no man ever rendered discreetly even any bodily service to another that he was not more blessed than that other. No man ever discreetly gave away a dollar that that dollar did not make him happier than it did the recipient. No person ever watched with the sick, sympathized with the sorrowing, or carried burdens and bore cares for other people, who, if he would scrutinize his experience, would not say, "The happiness that it gave me more than repaid me for all my trouble."

JUNE 14: *MORNING.*

I waited patiently for the Lord; and he inclined unto me, and heard my cry.—*Psalm* xl., 1.

If my child asks me for a tuberose, though I plant a bulb immediately, and comply with his request at the earliest possible moment, months necessarily elapse before he gets the flower. So our prayers are not answered at once, not because God would tantalize us, but because the things for which we ask are often so large, and require such a development, that there is of necessity a space between asking and the getting.

I believe that the prayers that my mother uttered over me have never forsaken me, from the time she died to this hour. If convinced of any thing, I am convinced that praying ancestors have been the occasion of my prosperity and usefulness; and I love to think, especially, that my mother prayed for me. I know that she set me apart, in the cradle, for God's uses and purposes. I know that she opened the path to heaven, and made it bright with the sacred feet of faith, as she walked daily up and down between the cradle and the throne of the Eternal Father. I am what I am because God gave me such a mother, and because she sent up so many prayers for me. In heaven they have hung, and they are pouring down showers of blessings on my head all the time; and I believe that they will not be spent to the day when I join her and that sainted host with whom she dwells. I believe that if there is any thing that God will not forget, it is a mother's prayers.

JUNE 14: *EVENING.*

Turn, O backsliding children, saith the Lord; for I am married unto you.—*Jer.* iii., 14.

If any say, "How can purity be pleased with impurity? How can God be pleased with that which he must needs look upon if he becomes companionable with the human soul?" you know, and I know how he can. You know, and I know, that we love, and love dearly, those that not only are full of faults, but that are rude and impure. Woe be to children if it were not possible to love those that are inferior, and poor, and bad. But every mother's heart, every father's heart, has learned the divine lesson, has learned this law by which to interpret the divine nature itself, in this, that we learn to love children, not so much for what they are as for what they are to be. Over and above that mere blind impulse by which we love infants—the mere love of offspring—is companionable love. Every man is conscious in regard to his children, and I trust, also, in a large sphere, in regard to many of his friends, that the love he bears to them is not love of their faults, but love in spite of their faults. We see through fault the coming virtue. We see through blemish the dawning beauty. When, in the orchard and in the gardens, lying far northward, the russet cloak of winter first began to unbuckle, and let out the blossoming buds, and all the trees stood, not yet beautiful, but with a faint color, prophesying the coming of beauty, on the tip of petal and leaf, we, looking upon them, saw nothing but the russet brown, and yet we rejoiced in the coming blossoms by anticipation. And so it is in every household of virtuous and intelligent parentage. So is it, also, in God's greater household. Men are looked upon in all their rudeness, in all their imperfections; but these are the nascent states, the struggling states, the states that are working toward something higher. There is manhood beyond. There is something yet for which the soul is reaching and striving. And these very battles and defeats which it has here are all of them on the way to something higher and better. Men see it in a small way in their own households; God in a larger way in the whole race.

JUNE 15: MORNING.

In the night his song shall be with me.—*Psalm* xlii., 8.

I do not know which is the most beautiful thing to see, a rich man, humble as a child, and using his place with gentleness and humility, not thinking of himself, nor thinking of his own glory, but making himself a benefactor to every body that draws near to him; or to see a man so poor that poverty despises him, and yet not humbled a particle by it; to see a man that has such a sense of the dignity of the Christhood in him that he walks among men with an unblenching face, every inch a man among them. Though he goes with rags, he has that in him for which Christ died; he has that in him which allies him to the Godhead. And why should he hang his head, or be ashamed of his poverty? Christian self-respect and Christian conscious power among the very poor, and Christian humility, and Christian gentleness, and purity, and sweetness among the rich—set these two pictures over against each other, and see which is the handsomer. Put them together, and let them stand there. The one is as handsome as the other.

One of the letter-writers, who have been the true historians of our war, narrates the fact that at Gettysburg, after the terrific cannonading which took place on the third day, when some four hundred cannon answered each other on Cemetery Ridge, there came a sudden lull, as the enemy were about to make a charge; and that the birds, having been scared out of the peach-trees, out of all the fruit and shade trees, by the fearful uproar, came, one by one, gently flying back; and that, during this momentary lull, the sparrows opened their mouths and began to sing again. Right in the midst of blood, right in the midst of ten thousand bleeding corpses, and when the echo had hardly died out of the heavens, these sweet birds were singing.

I think it is just so with troubles, and trials, and temptations in the world. If men that have carried themselves into the shock and into the terrific conflicts of human life have had this power which Paul had, no sooner is there a pause or a moment's peace, than up there spring in them birds that begin to sing again. They never are far from the singing of the birds who have faith, and hope, and love dominant in their souls.

Father, beneath thy sheltering wing
  In sweet security we rest,
And fear no evil earth can bring,
  In life, in death, supremely bless'd.

For life is good, whose tidal flow
  The motions of thy will obeys;
And death is good, that makes us know
  The love divine that all things sways.

JUNE 15: *EVENING.*

Partakers of the inheritance of the saints in light.—*Col.* i., 12.

THE heavenly state is the state of glory, because it is purified to such a degree that every volition and thought of one excites the admiration of others. When you live in that state you will diffuse joy among others by the admirableness of your moral conduct, and you will receive joy from the admirableness of their moral conduct. Having learned the lessons of this mortal state and escaped from its lower thralldoms, having come into the spiritualities of the heavenly realm; having, above all, been touched by the divine life and brought into sympathy with God, you shall rise, with the elect of God, into that blessed land where each one shall be the theme of joy and praise of every other; where detraction, and deception, and jealousy, and bitterness shall be unknown; where every one shall be crystalline, and radiant, and sweet to the utmost extent of the imagination, and where every pulsation of the hearts of those who circle about him who is the centre of that land shall be pulsations of joy.

God grant that, by patient continuance in well-doing, you may seek for glory, and honor, and immortality; that, finding them, God may give you an eternal life therein.

JUNE 16: *MORNING.*

Mighty to save.—*Isaiah* lxiii., 1.

I UNDERSTAND the Lord Jesus Christ to take men, not because when they are converted they are clean, but because they are willing to be taken. He takes them in all their poorness, and leanness, and irregularities, and says, "I am willing to carry you and bear with you through your whole life if I can see that in the end my love and patience will bring you into the enjoyment of the eternal inheritance."

It is that cleansing, forgiving, enduring, remedial love of Christ Jesus that gives a man hope. When wrong rises up in me, I feel that there is something higher than that. When my sins lie in the horizon, I see also in the horizon a Sun that turns all my sins into clouds of glory. It is the faithfulness of Christ, and the wonderful power of Christ's love to redeem men finally from all sin, that gives me hope and comfort. I am encouraged, not because I am good, but because I am in the hand of one who will never leave me nor forsake me.

There is an amplitude, and power, and grandeur, and glory in the love of Christ, in which the poorest man, if he is only conscious of what a Master he has, can stand up and say, "Though I be sinful, I rejoice in the Lord."

JUNE 16: *EVENING.*

Who is among you that feareth the Lord, that obeyeth the voice of his servant, that walketh in darkness, and hath no light? let him trust in the name of the Lord, and stay upon his God.—*Isaiah* l., 10.

A GREAT many persons have said to me, "I can not understand how there should be a special providence of God. I can not reconcile the theory of special providences with my ideas of general law and of God's agency in nature." That is to say, when God lays down an unquestionable command, of the most explicit kind, unless you can go behind that command, and can find out the philosophy of it, you will not accept it at his hands. Simply as a thing commanded by your Father, you will not, with the faith of a child, accept it. If you can spin it on your wheel, and then weave it in your loom, and make it conform to your pattern, you will accept it; but as simply from the hand of God, you will not accept it.

Now I like to reason; I like to search out results from causes; but it is sweet for a man, in the midst of the turmoils and troubles of life, where he can, to rest himself on his faith in

God. It is sweet for a man to be able to say, "I do not care for to-morrow. I do not fear what shall befall me. I will trust in God." To understand the philosophy of a divine command, where I can, affords me satisfaction; but where a command comes from such authority, and with such variety of illustration in nature as this one, I do not care whether I understand the philosophy of it or not. My soul is hungry for it, and I accept it because my God has given it. I trust and rest in God simply because he has said, "You may, and you must." That is ground enough.

JUNE 17: *MORNING.*

Thou shalt in any wise rebuke thy neighbor, and not suffer sin upon him.—*Levit.* xix., 17.

WICKEDNESS which a man can prevent, and which he does not prevent, inculpates him. We are not morally responsible simply for the wickedness which we do, but for the wickedness which we can prevent as well. In an important sense it is true that men are responsible for mischief which they could have hindered. If you put the torch to your neighbor's house, you are guilty in one way; but if another puts the torch to that house, and you go by, and see the flames, and say, "It is not my business; I did not kindle that fire; and, besides, he is an enemy of mine," you are culpable in another. If you are impelled by a feeling of animosity, and you strike a dagger to a rival's breast, of course you are a murderer and an assassin; and if you know that another man is going to do it, and do not interfere and stop him—if you permit the act to go on under your eye without raising your voice or lifting a finger, then you become a party in the crime, and the guilt rests on you. Men bring upon themselves the guilt, either in part or in whole, of whatever evil they can stop and do not stop.

JUNE 17: *EVENING.*

She hath done what she could.—*Mark* xiv., 8.

SOME farms are prairie land, on which there are no trees, but which are covered with a tough sward, to subdue which requires a great deal of culture. Some are so wet that they need much draining. Some have a great many rocks scattered over their surface, so that a vast amount of blasting is necessary. Some are covered with thorns, and brambles, and shrubs, which are to be grubbed out. Some are rich, and some are poor.

Now men are farms, and God is the great husbandman, and he expects they will produce harvests according to their nature.

You are trying to plant for God. God is just and kind in his judgment, and he says that if, according to the powers you have, you are endeavoring to serve him, he will accept what you bring to him, whether it be a rich harvest or but a few flowers. And he will give you remuneration, not according to what you have given him, but according to the greatness of the heart to which you have given.

Master, behold my sheaves!
Full well I know I have more tares than wheat—
Brambles and flowers, dry stalks, and withered leaves;
Wherefore I blush and weep, as at thy feet
I kneel down reverently, and repeat,
"Master, behold my sheaves!"

I know these blossoms, clustering heavily
With evening dew upon their folded leaves,
Can claim no value nor utility,
Therefore shall fragrancy and beauty be
The glory of my sheaves.

So do I gather strength and hope anew;
For well I know thy patient love perceives
Not what I did, but what I strove to do;
And though the full ripe ears be sadly few,
Thou wilt accept my sheaves.

JUNE 18: *MORNING.*

Howbeit Jesus suffered him not, but saith unto him, Go home to thy friends, and tell them how great things the Lord hath done for thee, and hath had compassion on thee.—*Mark* v., 19.

Some of the most precious experiences that ever grew on the boughs of the human soul you have had, but have never uttered. You have never told them even to your companion. Frequently husband and wife are ignorant of each other's richest experiences. We do not talk enough one to another about these things. As we go through life, God is doing exceeding abundantly more for us than we ask or think in every way; and there is great comfort and evangelizing power in his grace, but it lies dead. Neighbors should talk with neighbors, and acquaintances with acquaintances. If you talk with strangers, it should be with deference to their feelings. It should be with a consciousness that you are invading their personality. You should honor them while you speak to them. Your business is to make men feel the sweetness there is in religion; and if you talk of some real experience of your own, you will not be likely to go amiss.

JUNE 18: *EVENING.*

For we have not a high-priest which can not be touched with the feeling of our infirmities, but was in all points tempted like as we are, yet without sin.—*Heb.* iv., 15.

ALL attempts to live a religious life which leave out this living, personal, present sympathy of the Christ-heart with our human heart, will be relatively imperfect. Men's lives will be imperfect enough at any rate, but when they neglect this vital inspiration, it seems scarcely possible to live at all with religious comfort. Our religious joy never springs from the conception of what we are, but of what God is. No man's life, attainments, purposes, or virtues can yield him full peace. It is the conviction that we are loved of God personally, by name and nature, with a full divine insight of our real weakness, wickedness, and inferiority, that brings peace. Nor will this become settled and immovable until men know and feel that God loves them from a nature in himself, from a divine tendency to love the poor and sinful, that he may rescue and heal them. God is called a sun. His heart, always warm, brings summer to the most barren places. He is inexhaustible in goodness, and his patience is beyond all human conception. If he is our friend and lover, if he conducts our life from a fidelity that belongs to his nature, and not from reasons existing in us, then our trust will stand in the majesty and certainty of divine goodness, and not in unworthy moral conditions in ourselves.

JUNE 19: *MORNING.*

Therefore, leaving the principles of the doctrine of Christ, let us go on unto perfection; not laying again the foundation of repentance from dead works, and of faith toward God.—*Heb.* vi., 1.

No man ought to be contending with the same evil propensities all the time. He ought to be continually rising to higher and higher conflicts. To be fighting late in Christian life is a sign that you have not been taught aright, and have not known what was wisdom. And yet how many of us can say that our old conflicts are all ended?

If you go into the house of an old baron, you will see hanging up in the hall the trophies of the victories that he has achieved over wild beasts: here a stag's head; there the hide of a wolf; there the tusk of a boar; and these are evidences of the old baron's valor, the proofs of his conquests.

Now go into the house of your experience. Where is the grinning head of that wolf passion, hung up as a memento of your victory? How many memorials have you of conflicts that you have successfully waged? How many trophies have you of your baronial skill? Are you not hunting the same beasts that you were in early life? Are you not about as proud, and vain, and avaricious as ever? You have varnished your old disposition; you sing hymns over the sepulchre in your soul; but is not that sepulchre filled with bones, and dust, and hideous passions? Is your religion any thing more than a mere getting along as well as you can with passions that have not been tamed? What acchievements have you made in cross-bearing? What rebellious faculties have you crucified that do not need to be crucified again?

Jesu, victor over sin,
Help me now the fight to win.
Thou didst vanquish once, I know,
Him who seeks my overthrow;
So to thee my faith will cleave,
And her hold will never leave,
Till the weary battle's done,
And the final triumph won;
For I, too, through thee may win,
Victor over death and sin.

JUNE 19: *EVENING.*

For it is God which worketh in you both to will and to do of his good pleasure.—*Phil.* ii., 13.

Many Christians, who are but partially enlightened, think that they may have Christian experiences and graces simply for the asking. They think, if they want joy, all they will have to do will be to go to God and say, "Dear Lord, give me joy." Joy can be had, but you can not have it without establishing the causes that produce it. You want to be aspiring, and you go and ask God for aspiration, and think it will be given you without any task on your part. Nay, verily. If you want joy and aspirations, you shall have them, provided you do the things that lead to them. A man goes and asks God to give him patience, and thinks God will teach him, and say, "Be thou patient." No, God will not. But in his home, in his business, in his work, wherever he is, God will give him opportunities to practice patience. And thus he answers our prayers by working in us to will and to do of his own good pleasure.

So it is with every Christian grace. You can not pray meekness into yourselves. There is not a single Christian grace that you can acquire except in accordance with this great law of God, that you are to have what you earn.

JUNE 20: *MORNING.*

He that loveth his brother abideth in the light.—1 *John* ii., 10.

Perhaps one half of the uncertainties of men, and of their anxieties about their personal experience, arise from their seeking religion as a selfish stimulant. They want evidence that their sins are forgiven for the sake of the joy that will spring out of it. They want evidence of Christ's presence with them on account of the delight that it will afford them. They want assurance of adoption, rapture in worship, joy in meetings, stimulus in preaching—they want every thing that will play music on their soul. They are seeking experiences that shall be radiant, and eminent, and full of joy.

If people, instead of seeking joyful experiences for themselves, would seek to make other people's experiences joyful; instead of seeking to get rid of their own burdens, would seek to bear the burdens of others; instead of examining whether they are in the true way, would seek to bring back to the fold of Christ those that have wandered from it—would seek to *do* good rather than to *be* good, they would accomplish both objects. They would find that doing good is the shortest road to being good, and that contributing to the welfare and happiness of others is the shortest road to securing their own welfare and happiness.

JUNE 20: *EVENING.*

Therefore the redeemed of the Lord shall return, and come with singing unto Zion; and everlasting joy shall be upon their head: they shall obtain gladness and joy; and sorrow and mourning shall flee away.—*Isa.* li, 11.

Of all battles, there are none like the unrecorded battles of the soul. Without banners spread or trumpets sounded, with no visible conflict and clash of arms, God and angels know that the fiercest and bitterest strifes of the universe are those which are waged in the secret places of men's souls, where the earthly, sensual, and beastly elements of human nature are in conflict with that which is pure, and sweet, and spiritual in them. These are the battles that God registers, which are going on in men, and which, blessed be God, issue, or may issue in the "peace which passeth all understanding," in that land where love, and conscience, and faith, and hope appear, chanting the song of victory, and wearing upon their heads the laurel wreath, and where selfishness, and pride, and passion are humbled to become the servants of the soul, and no longer to be its despots and masters.

When the combat ends, and slowly
  Clears the smoke from out the skies,
Then, far down the purple distance,
  All the noise of battle dies.
When the last night's solemn shadows
  Settle down on you and me,
May the love that never faileth
  Take our souls eternally.

JUNE 21: MORNING.

Every man shall give as he is able, according to the blessing of the Lord thy God which he hath given thee.—*Deut.* xvi., 17.

You are rich if you have a hundred dollars over and above what you need for the support of life. You are not to measure yourself by a man that is worth a hundred thousand, and say, "He ought to use his riches according to the Word of God: he has enough and to spare. I have only a poor hundred more than I need for my bare necessities, and I can not be expected to part with that." The divine command is, Beware lest ye be rich and lay up treasure to yourselves, and are not rich toward God. If you have a surplus of one thousand dollars, the command is to you; if you have a surplus of ten thousand, it is to you; if you have a surplus of ten hundred thousand, it is not a whit more to you.

Now, my Christian brethren, are you rich toward God in the proportion in which you have been increasing your worldly wealth? Unless your sympathies increase, unless your charities increase, unless your disposition to benefit your fellow-men increases in the proportion in which your riches increase, you can not walk the life you are walking without falling under the condemnation of the teaching of Christ. Your life is one of getting, getting, getting; and there is but one safety-valve to such a life: it is giving, giving, giving.

JUNE 21: EVENING.

Better the day of death than the day of one's birth.—*Eccles.* vii., 1.

When the apple-tree blossoms you laugh, and you do not cry when you pick the apple; but when man blossoms man laughs, and then, when God picks the fruit, he cries. Why, your child is not your child till you have lost him. That which you can put your arms about is that which you can not afford to love. No bird cries when the shell is broken and the birdling comes forth, or when, a little later, it leaves the nest, and wings its way through the air. Only mothers do that when their children, released from earth, fly away to a better world. And yet only they are worthy of immortal love that escape from the clog of this mortal state.

Now let us thank God, not that men die, but that they live. So far as it pleases God to develop and endow them, let us be glad; but when they go to a better realm, let us say, "Thank God they have gone where they shall be perfect; they have blossomed and are bearing fruit." Is not this the Christian way?"

> Death has not slain them; they are freed, not slain.
> It is the gate of life, and not of death
> That they have entered; and the grave in vain
> Has tried to stifle the immortal breath.
>
> All that was death in them is now dissolved,
> For death can only what is death's destroy;
> And when this earth's short ages have revolved,
> The disimprisoned life comes forth with joy.

JUNE 22: MORNING.

And, behold, a woman in the city, which was a sinner, when she knew that Jesus sat at meat in the Pharisee's house, brought an alabaster box of ointment, and stood at his feet behind him weeping, and began to wash his feet with tears, and did wipe them with the hairs of her head, and kissed his feet, and anointed them with the ointment.—*Luke* vii., 37, 38.

LET every man who is going to begin a Christian life pursue the same course that she pursued. Let every man whose ear has been reached by the truth, and whose conscience and heart have been touched by the Spirit of God, reform as she reformed. How was that? Did she—this child of a guilty life—after hearing the Master, go away to the silence of her own chamber, and say, "I will return to virtue?" No. Without asking permission, with the intrusiveness of a heart bent on purity, she mingled herself at once with the train of Christ's disciples; and, all unasked, she pressed through the portals of the proud man's dwelling as Christ her Lord sat at meat; and, while filled with a sense of her own deep need, stood waiting, until at last, surcharged, she broke forth in an anguish of tears. When she came to Christ first, she came to the right one; and going to him, it was to his feet. Come ye to Christ. Come to the *feet* of Christ.

And, oh friend! do as she did; for when she came, she took

the precious ointment, by which she had made herself beautiful for sin—the instrument of her transgression—and consecrated it to holy uses, pouring it upon the feet of the Beloved, worshiping him, and weeping as she worshiped. Bring whatever you have used before in the service of sin, and at the feet of the Beloved bow down yourselves with holy desires, and consecrate your powers, within and without, to the service of Him who loved you, and redeemed you, that he might present you spotless before the throne of his Father and your Father. Come to Jesus.

JUNE 22: EVENING.

For unto you it is given in the behalf of Christ not only to believe on him, but also to suffer for his sake.—*Phil.* i., 29.

I REMEMBER once being called to see a sick girl, who was, perhaps, seventeen or eighteen years of age. A gentleman informed me that she had been sick for twelve months, and that she had become quite disconsolate. Others said, "Go and see her, for if any body ought to be comforted she ought to be. She has the sweetest disposition, and she is the most patient creature imaginable; and you ought to hear her talk. One can hardly tell whether she talks or prays. It is heaven to go into her room." I wanted a little more of the spirit of heaven, so I went to see her. I was engaged in a revival of religion at the time. She said, "I hear of what you are doing, and of what my companions are doing, and I long to go out and labor for Christ; and it seems very strange to me that God keeps me here on this sick-bed." "My dear child," said I, "do you not know that you are preaching Christ to this whole household, and to every one that knows you? Your gentleness, and patience, and Christian example are known and read by them all. You are laboring for Christ more effectually than you could any where else." Her face brightened; she looked up without a word, and doubtless she gave thanks to God, and angels sang more sweetly than before.

Now do you seem to yourself to be useless, and say, "Oh that I was eloquent. Oh that I could wield the pen of a ready writer. Oh that it was given to me to go forth and be an apostle of Christ." It is given to every one of you to be an epistle of Christ, known and read of all men. By your humility, by your truthfulness, by your justice, by all the things that make you like Christ, you become his minister, and you are known and read where you never suspect that you are being known and read. Take care, then, and speak right things of Christ. See to it that the testimony you bear of Christ is such as he would have you bear.

JUNE 23: *MORNING.*

Wherefore, if God so clothe the grass of the field, which to-day is, and to-morrow is cast into the oven, shall he not much more clothe you, O ye of little faith?—*Matt.* vi., 30.

If God takes care of birds and flowers, will he not take care of us? May we not at least have such an assurance of God's watchfulness over us that we can shake hands with care, and say, "I never will know you again?" May we not have such a trust in God that we can bid good-by to anxiety, and say, "I never will again bear your despotic burden?" Was it not for the very purpose of giving us such an assurance and such a trust that Christ gave us the promise of the text? Did he not design that we should rid ourselves of the harassing solicitudes and troubles of life? Did not Christ mean that every day, when we lifted up our eyes, and beheld the flowers and birds, we should recognize a remembrancer, saying to us, "Are ye not much better than they? And if I love them, and care for them, do I not love you, and care for you?"

Did God ever die for birds? Did he ever lay down his life for flowers, for the grass, or for the trees? But for us he did. And, rising, will he forget that for our sakes he himself was forgotten and laid in the sepulchre? By how many direct affirmations, by how many commands, by how many of these glancing and suggestive images is this lesson brought home to us, and yet there is no other thing so little heeded.

The child leans on its parent's breast,
Leaves there its cares, and is at rest;
The bird sits singing by his nest,
And tells aloud
His trust in God, and so is bless'd
'Neath every cloud.

The heart that trusts forever sings,
And feels as light as it had wings;
A well of peace within it springs,
Come good or ill:
Whate'er to-day, to-morrow, brings,
It is his will!

JUNE 23: *EVENING.*

Seek ye out of the book of the Lord, and read: no one of these shall fail, none shall want her mate: for my mouth it hath commanded, and his spirit it hath gathered them.—*Isaiah* xxxiv., 16.

How sweet are thy words unto my taste! yea, sweeter than honey to my mouth.—*Psalm* cxix., 103.

As there are always among violets some that are very much sweeter to us than others, so among texts there are some that are more precious to us than others. When I go to the Bible, it is not once in a hundred times that I read a whole chapter for my own devotions. As one that goes out into the field to rest does not take the first spot that presents itself, but waits till he finds a nook where the mosses, and the flowers, and the shrubs are right, and then sits down and feasts his eyes on the beauties around, so I wander along till I come to a passage which, though I can not tell why, I read over, and over, and over again. One or two verses or sentences perhaps will linger in my head all day, like some sweet passage in a letter, or like some felicitous word spoken by a friend, coming and going all the time. I find often that one single text, taking possession of the mind in the morning, and ringing through it during the whole day, does one more good than the reading of a whole chapter. Frequently some one thing that Christ said fixes itself in my mind, and remains there from morning till night.

JUNE 24: *MORNING.*

Knowledge puffeth up, but charity edifieth.—1 *Cor.* viii., 2.

We are to hold knowledge and to impart it in such a way that it shall edify or build up men in honor, in love, in duty, in rectitude. Our pleasures are subject to the same law. In spite of yourself, you are woven into society. You can not therefore say, "It is nobody's business what I do." What you do is the business of every body who is within the reach of your touch. Yonder oak may say, "It is nobody's business how I grow;" but there is a feeble plant trying to grow under it, and it is that plant's business how the oak grows. In the kingdom of mere conscience it may be nobody's business what you do, but in the kingdom of love it is the business of every one whom you touch what you do. Therefore, in your speaking, in your writing, in your pleasuring, in your social intercourse, in whatever you do, you are to bear in mind that your conduct is to be made subservient to the welfare of your fellow-men. You are not to live for yourself alone, but for others.

Let us do what we can for edification. It will make our lives sweeter and happier. Let us be continually actuated by this thought: How shall I build myself up in a Christian manhood, and how shall I exercise my rights and liberties so that I shall build men up in such a way as to make them better?

JUNE 24: EVENING.

Oh that they were wise, that they understood this, that they would consider their latter end!—*Deut.* xxxii., 29.

How desolate must old age be to the man who has no heaven beyond; who stands trembling with infirmities, declined in ear, and eye, and tongue, his hand palsied, his memory gone, looking back across the dreary stretch of life that he has just passed over, and forward with fear to the life of which he thought so little. How glorious for an old man to stand, as Moses stood, upon the top of the mount, looking across the Jordan into the promised land, and viewing the fair possessions that awaited him Moses died, and did not go over; but the old man shall die, and go over, and shall find it in that day a land rich, beautiful, and glorious.

If you would come into old age with these transcendent hopes, begin the work of preparation early. Live rightly all the way through. Do not think that, if you live as you please now, you can live as you please then. Live now as you want to live in old age. Lay such walls on such foundations and of such materials as will support you; and then, when heart and flesh shall fail, it will only be because God thus breaks open the tenement that he may let out the spirit to enter into that high and serene existence where there shall be everlasting youth, and where everlasting blessedness awaits you.

What are we set on earth for? Say to toil!
  Nor seek to leave thy tending of the vines
  For all the heat o' the sun, till it declines,
And Death's mild curfew shall from work assoil.
God did anoint thee with his odorous oil
  To wrestle, not to reign; and he assigns
  All thy tears, ever like pure crystallines,
Unto thy fellows, working the same soil,
  To wear for amulets. So others shall
Take patience, labor, to their heart and hand,
  From thy hand, and thy heart, and thy brave cheer,
  And God's grace fructify through thee to all.
The least flower with a brimming cup may stand,
  And share its dew-drop with another near.

JUNE 25: MORNING.

The children of Israel brought a willing offering unto the Lord, every man and woman, whose heart made them willing to bring for all manner of work which the Lord had commanded.—*Exod.* xxxv., 29.

Many say, "Oh, I wish I could be useful. I want to work for the cause of God. Tell me what I can do."

First of all, free yourself from the conception that doing good means a suppression of certain of the faculties of your nature. Some of you are very mirthful and humorous, and you say, "How can I give up my mirthfulness and humor?" I should as soon ask a Spitzenberg to quit tasting good as I should ask you to give them up. God, when he gave them to you, meant that you should use them for his sake and for the sake of your fellow-men.

God has given many of you imagination. What is that? It is a candle in a window in a dark night; it is a light-house on a stormy coast; it is a festive song. And do you say that it should be sober and matter-of-fact in religion? It should not. God gave it to you, not that you should use it selfishly, but that you might be a missionary of imagination, and go among men that are unimaginative and literal, and wreathe it about their literalness. Another man says, "I have neither mirthfulness nor imagination." Well, you have courage. Half the people in the world lack this element, and to every man of courage God says, "I ordain you to support the weak." If God has given you power to stand up, it is that you may help those who have not that power. It is your mission, every where you go, to succor those who are discouraged, and teach them how to be strong. Still another has not so much courage as hopefulness, and God has made him a natural comforter of the poor and rich. The poor are always with you, and if you have a hopeful disposition, why are you not carrying comfort to those who are desponding?

Take that in which you are superior to those around you, and understand that God makes you responsible for the ministration of that toward all those with whom you come in contact.

JUNE 25: *EVENING.*

But these are written, that ye might believe that Jesus is the Christ, the Son of God; and that believing ye might have life through his name.—*John* xx., 31.

SHALL I follow Christ through all my life; behold his beauty; twine about him every affection; lean upon him for strength; behold him as my leader, my teacher; feed upon him as my bread, my wine, my water of life; see all things in this world in that light which he declares himself to be—in his strength vanquish sin, draw from him my hope and inspiration, wear his name and love his work, and through my whole life, at his command, twine about him every affection, die in his arms, and awake with eager uprising to find him whom my soul loveth, only to be put away with the announcement that he is not the recipient of worship? Well might I cry out in the anguish of Mary in the garden, "They have taken away my Lord, and I know not where they have laid him."

Christ is the soul's bread—eat, ye that hunger. He is the water of life—drink, ye that thirst. He is the soul's end—aim at him. He is the soul's supreme glory—yield to every outgush of joy, of enthusiasm of worship that springs up in your heart toward him. Those that are in heaven bow down before him, and ascribe "Blessing, and honor, and glory, and power unto him that sitteth upon the throne, and unto the Lamb forever and ever." Let us not fear to do the same.

JUNE 26: MORNING.

Jesus said unto him, Go, wash in the pool of Siloam (which is by interpretation, Sent). He went his way, therefore, and washed, and came back seeing. —*John* ix., 7.

SUPPOSE that one who, being almost starved, and having struggled with starvation through the whole summer, praying, every day, "Give me my daily bread," should, in October, discover that there were esculent, nutritious roots growing abundantly in the edge of a wilderness near by, and should say, "It seems very strange to me that I should have been suffered to want for food, when I prayed, day and night, 'Give me my daily bread,' and when these roots were within my reach, if I had only known where to go for them; why did not God tell me?"—you would smile. Suppose a person should say, "Here I have been shaking with chills and fever for weeks and months, and all the time there has been this Peruvian bark next door, with which I might have cured myself, if I had known that it would cure me; but I did not know it, though I constantly prayed to God to cure me." You would say at once, "No prayer will ever bring you medicine. You must know that it exists, and then apply it in obedience to natural laws, or it will not meet your case."

Is it so morally? Yes; and nothing shows it more plainly than the history of the Church and of good men. A man may live in needless suffering for forty years, praying to God every day, and finding no relief, if God has made provision for his relief in natural law, while he merely prays, and does nothing more. "If any man be a worshiper of God, *and doeth his will*, him he heareth."

JUNE 26: EVENING.

Not that I speak in respect of want: for I have learned, in whatsoever state I am, therewith to be content.—*Phil.* iv., 11.

"I HAVE learned," says the apostle. It took him forty years to learn it, too. And yet how many there are who, though they have been only a few years in the Christian life, are discouraged because they can not put on at once the virtues which were the experience of these forty years of the apostle's life. They think they are not Christians. They measure themselves by certain moral states and attainments that belong to later and riper conditions. Why, a man may be a Christian sowing the seed-corn of experience, just as much as another man who, having sown, is in the harvest-field reaping ripe ears with his sickle. Paul learned contentment. He had a great many trials before he learned it. He learned it first in one point, and then in another. He continued to practice, and was not discouraged or thrown back. All his life long he was growing in that direction, until at last he came to that power in which he lived open-faced at heaven's gate, and the crown of righteousness, which the Lord, the righteous judge, reserved for him, and not for him only, but for all of them also that loved the appearing of the Lord Jesus Christ, flashed evermore in his view. It was his sun by day, and it was his star by night. And this it was that he learned in long years of experience. So do not be discouraged because you do not learn it in a day, or a week, or a year. Your business and privilege is to see that every year you are learning more and more; that your faith is stronger in you; and that, in some respects, you are gaining. This do, and you may be content.

> The seed bursts not to ripened grain in one short summer day,
> The goal is reached by patient steps along the weary way:
> Shall the Christian sink discouraged, and cast his weapons down,
> If the first hour of the conflict brings him not the victor's crown?

JUNE 27: MORNING.

I will greatly rejoice in the Lord, my soul shall be joyful in my God; for he hath clothed me with the garments of salvation, he hath covered me with the robe of righteousness, as a bridegroom decketh himself with ornaments, and as a bride adorneth herself with her jewels.—*Isaiah* lxi., 10.

Is there any thing more beautiful in a lower sphere than the dressing of a bride for her wedding? The tender hands of kind nurse, of loving sisters, and fond mother—how they all wait upon her! How the hours are consecrated to her glory! How her hair is parted and braided with sweet simplicity! How the veil is thrown over her with exquisite grace! What bracelets, what rings, what jewels contribute to decorate her person! It is a great thing to go to the toilet-table of a bride in a wealthy family, and see what the jewel-box contains.

Now God has opened the jewel-box with the contents of which he dresses his bride, the Church: "Blessed are the poor in spirit." "Blessed are they that mourn." "Blessed are the meek." "Blessed are they which do hunger and thirst after righteousness." "Blessed are the merciful." "Blessed are the pure in heart." "Blessed are the peacemakers." "Blessed are they which are persecuted for righteousness' sake." "Blessed are ye when men shall revile you, and persecute you, and shall say all manner of evil against you falsely, for my sake. Rejoice and be exceeding glad, for great is your reward in heaven: for so persecuted they the prophets which were before you."

Who wants to wear jewels? There they are. Put them on.

JUNE 27: EVENING.

The cup which my Father hath given me, shall I not drink it?—*John* xviii., 11.

Does God so comfort you that you are able to bear the yoke and to endure the piercing thorn? And when God enables you to bear it, is your first thought this, "I am now admitted into the sacred church of the sufferers; I am now marked with the cross, as one that bears for others; I am lifted up among my fellow-men, not to be praised, but that I may go about as my Master did, and minister to them the consolations by which I myself have been comforted?" Do not say, "The cup is too large and too bitter." Never! The hand that was pierced for you takes the cup and gives it to you, and Christ loves you too much to give you a cup that you can not drink. Do not say, "The burden is too great; I can not bear it." He that loves you as you do not even yourself love yourself—the Redeemer, "the God of all comfort," "the Father of mercies"—lays every burden on you; and he that lays the burden on will give you strength to bear it. Take up your cross and follow him. Remember the promise: "If we suffer we shall also reign with him."

JUNE 28: MORNING.

Do ye thus requite the Lord?—*Deut.* xxxii., 6.

If a poor child should meet me in the street with a broken and withered flower, I should see the child's heart, not the condition of the flower, and should thank the child, and should feel a strange fragrance, not from the flower itself, but from the thought that he wanted to do me a kindness. But ah! when Christ takes his own heart, broken, wounded, bleeding—his sacrifice and his love—and brings it to us, and makes it a present; when, out of his own misery, out of his own degradation, out of his own suffering, he proposes to lift us up into everlasting bounty and benefit, is there no requital, are there no thanks, is there no gratitude due? When God requires the service of our life and the fullness of our heart, is it an exacting requisition?

JUNE 28: EVENING.

And their eyes were opened, and they knew him; and he vanished out of their sight.—*Luke* xxiv., 31.

Hours of religious peace, hours of spiritual delight, never seem so precious to us, hours of religious duty are never so dear to us, while we have them, and they are, as it were, in their ministration, as when they are gone. In our religious life we continually find fault with our fare. We are dainty about our religious privileges. Or, we are given over to that last folly of conceit: we have set ourselves to take care of our neighbors' faith. So we crush our grapes to extract wine from them, and then we keep the wine until it turns to vinegar on our lips. Our heart's blessings—how many there are! You have innumerable hours that bring to you Christ's choicest thoughts. Ah! when your friends shall be no longer about you, when you shall be a stranger in a distant settlement, or a dweller on the sea, or in a distant land, and heartily homesick—then how like stars will those hours seem to you that now you pick to pieces and complain of because they bring no joy! Those very hours which you reluctantly gave to the Sabbath-day—how you will covet them when you have lost them!

Having squandered with discontent the privileges which we have now, memory will hoard them, every one, like a miser.

Oh that wisdom were given us to know what the blessing of to-day is, and what the blessing of the hour is, that we may not then see what it is, when, like Christ, it vanishes at the moment of its disclosure.

O day! with holy duties thickly blossomed,
And every blossom dropping precious balm;
Sermon and prayer, and sweetly-chanted psalm,
And privy thoughts, to God alone unbosomed—
I would have stayed thee with a fond constraining,
Fain such an antepast of heaven to eke,
And stretch its sweetness through the weary week,
Six days of dearth—to one of bread!—remaining;
But could not clip one pinion of thy flight,
That borrowed, from thy bliss, an unwont fleetness.
So while thy beauty fadeth from my sight,
I must content to win a sacred sweetness
From thy divinest influence, for all
The week's sharp toils and cares that to my hap may fall.

JUNE 29: MORNING.

The fear of the Lord is the beginning of wisdom.—*Psalm* cxi., 10.
Perfect love casteth out fear.—1 *John* iv., 18.

That tender, tremulous fear that we shall not do all that we ought to do, or all that we wish to do, for the honor and the pleasure of those whom we love, and whose life is more to us than our own, is exquisite, elevating, noble; but that fear which drops far below the sentiments, and moral feelings, and affections, and that produces a state of antagonism between a man's lower interests and his higher feelings, is paralyzing, demoralizing, unmanly.

A man that is never afraid to stand up for the right; that is never afraid to say what he thinks ought to be said; that is never afraid to do what he thinks ought to be done; that now is willing, if need be, to stand like Mount Calvary; that now is willing, if need be, to thunder like Mount Sinai; that can follow the dictates of his conscience, and not care for the consequences—such a man is a pattern of true manliness. One of the worst things a man can say, when pursuing a course of wickedness in the midst of evil influences, is, "I don't care;" but the best thing a man can say, when pursuing a course of rectitude in the midst of Christian influences, is, "I don't care." There is an infidel "don't care," which is the devil's net to catch the heedless; and there is a Christian "don't care," which is a cord of God to draw men toward heaven.

JUNE 29: *EVENING.*

Forget not all his benefits.—*Psalm* ciii., 2.

You have friends whom you trust; friends who would not desert you if you were sick or unfortunate in business; who would, to the extent of their power, stand by you in the dark hour; who would never fail to give you good counsel, and to sympathize with you in trouble. But God, the best and most inexpressibly precious Friend, whose life is one prolonged, continuous benefaction to us, is the very one that we trust the least. Though a thousand dark hours have come to us, and God has helped us in every one of them, we have failed to carry along a faithful remembrance of them, so that when the threat is in the heaven, we are just as much alarmed as though it had never been there a thousand times before. When a great sorrow is upon us, we act as though we had never known sorrow before, and had never before been delivered from sorrow. In the midst of our various experiences of life, how we fail to believe that God loves us, that he is faithful to us, and that he will never leave us nor forsake us.

JUNE 30: *MORNING.*

Lay not up for yourselves treasures upon earth.—*Matt.* vi., 19.

This is not a stroke at riches. It is not undervaluing worldly good in its own place. It is substantially saying, "You are not beasts, that are born into life, and live only in this world. You are really children of God. You are to have a life so long, so noble, and so above all that is in the brute creation, that you should live for that other interior and higher life, and not for the lower one. Make the higher life and the nobler development the aim; and make this secondary and secular life the mere instrument by which you attain that."

Here, then, is the grand aim. While the great mass of mankind live through the senses for the senses, and in the present for the present, exclusively, Christ says, "Do you live for the higher, the spiritual, and the eternal life. 'Seek ye first the kingdom of God and his righteousness'—*first* in the order of time, and *first* in intensity—'and all these things shall be added unto you.'"

JUNE 30: *EVENING.*

And God spake unto Noah, saying, Go forth of the ark, thou, and thy wife, and thy sons, and thy sons' wives with thee.—*Gen.* viii., 15, 16.

Oh what joy, what gladness is there in families whose last child is finally converted to Christ! The floods of temptation and sin swell and surge, and threaten the household, and one is rescued from danger, and another, and at last the ark of life is sent to take the last child, and it is saved. Is it not time to bring in the whole of your household? Can you imagine any happiness greater than that of the parent who can say, "Christ has twice given me my children; once for this world, and once for the world to come. Now, happen what may, nothing can befall me or mine, whether poverty or riches, joy or sorrow. Pledges of immortality God has given me in my children?" Sing! sing! break forth into rejoicing! There are seldom places in this world for such triumphs as there are in such experiences—experiences of souls renewed and sins forgiven; in these victories of grace, and, above all, these victories of grace in the family, where God sanctifies the father's and the mother's heart, and brings in, one by one, the children.

Covenant-believing parents, are your children among those who are yearning for Jesus Christ, and hoping and singing? Have you done any thing? Have you thought? Have you prayed? Have you asked before the open heart of God, that sounds out louder than the ocean in your presence, saying, "Whatsoever ye shall ask in prayer, believing, ye shall receive?" Have you asked that your children might be gathered into the kingdom of Christ?

> Oh happy house! whose little ones are given
>   Early to thee in faith and prayer—
> To thee, their Friend, who from the heights of heaven
>   Guards them with more than mother's care.

Oh happy house! where little voices
  Their glad hosannas love to raise;
And childhood's lisping tongue rejoices
  To bring new songs of love and praise.

JULY 1: *MORNING.*

Put away the evil of your doings from before mine eyes; cease to do evil; learn to do well.—*Isa.* i., 16, 17.

What repentance, what reformation is possible in your life? Are you willing to look in upon yourselves? Are you willing to search your hearts down to the bottom? Are you willing to question your motives? Are you willing to go into the dark chambers of your experience? Are you willing to call God to go with you there? Are you willing to open the door of the sanctuary, and let the whole light of the eternal throne blaze upon your secret thoughts and feelings, and say, "O God, interpret to me my nature, my heart, my life, my character, my every thing, that I may bring out whatever is evil in thy sight, and, for the sake of the world, sanctify myself, and be a better man for the year to come?" It is quite in vain to talk about sin in general. Will you search your disposition trait by trait? Will you go all through your business, your pleasures, your affections, every thing that relates to your happiness or well-being, or to your misery and woe, and lay the law of God upon every part of your life with this solemn and earnest purpose?

Let it be so. As the housewife, taking her broom, begins and brushes every web, however gauzy, out of the angles, and clears every thing off from the windows, and sweeps in every corner and nook, and dusts in every alcove, and cleans every part, and gathers the collected dirt, and marches it in a battalion toward the door, and gradually works it through into the hall, and across the hall to the outside door, and at last, with one blow, sweeps it all out, and bids farewell to it, so let your hearts be cleansed. For the sake of God, for the sake of the Church, for the sake of the family, and for the sake of the cause of God in our day, I call upon you to sanctify yourself.

And I would have this soul of mine
  Made clean and pure within—
My Savior's chosen dwelling-place
  Free from all taint of sin.

The work is thine, oh holy Dove!
  I gladly welcome thee;
Come in, bless'd Spirit of the Lord!
  Possess both mine and me.

JULY 1: EVENING.

If ye, then, being evil, know how to give good gifts unto your children, how much more shall your Father which is in heaven give good things to them that ask him?—*Matt.* vii., 11.

SINCE our conceptions of God are made up of the best conceptions and experiences of human life, refined and idealized, and fashioned by the imagination, they will always be under, and never above the reality; so that the mistakes which might be fatal in other measurings are harmless in measuring our God. When you argue from a man to God, you are accustomed to say, "Ah! that is not a fair argument—God is a different being." "No," says Christ; "take whatever is good in man, and argue that God is not only that, but infinitely better. In fashioning your conception of God, make it as resplendent in justice, as august in truth, as noble and pure in love, as radiant and wondrous in pity, and as enduring as you please. Never be afraid that you will overdraw the divine character. God is never better in your thought or imagination than he is in himself. Your descriptions of God will not transcend, but will come short of the reality. When your heart is warmest, noblest, truest, and best, when it flashes out its ideal conceptions of God, that ideal is far more likely to be near the truth than one that is coldly, critically, philosophically deduced from definite premises. For God's nature really outruns the human capacity for reasoning.

JULY 2: MORNING.

With my mouth will I make known thy faithfulness to all generations.—*Psalm* lxxxix., 1.

BEAR the precious name of Jesus with you into every part of your life; and in all the experiences which rise up to you in that blessed name, do not forget to be grateful at the time. Do not forget to have some souvenir and memorial by which you shall connect these various kindnesses of God, and be able, every year, to set up another testimony, and say, "Hitherto hath God helped me." And by-and-by, when sickness comes, may God grant that you may go through all the region of the valley of the shadow of death, saying, "Hitherto hath the Lord helped me." When you come to the brink of the river, do not shrink. As you go out of our sight, and reach the far shore, send back some airy voices to say still, "Hitherto the Lord hath helped me." And when you rise and stand in Zion and before God, God grant that you may be able to say, in the presence of all the holy angels, "Hitherto hath the Lord helped me."

JULY 2: EVENING.

Man goeth to his long home.—*Eccles.* xii., 5.

DEATH is but a going *home.* A child is away at school, and the vacation is near at hand; and you may be sure that the father and mother long to see the child more than the child wants to see father and mother. So, according to the good old custom, the father takes the carriage and wends his way to the school. In the midst of his tasks on the last day, the child is suddenly greeted by the voice and presence of his father; and no sooner are the first salutations exchanged than the father says, "Are your things ready? we go to-morrow." Wine is not so sparkling as the joy in the child's heart. He can neither eat, nor sleep, nor play. The thought that his father has come, and that he is going home to see his mother, and brothers, and sisters, has quite intoxicated him.

By such glorious images as this God is pleased to represent our departure from the present life. The Lord Jesus Christ shall come to our poor old weather-stained school-house in this world, and say to us, "Come home; you are wanted."

Heaven is not a great bleak shore to which you are driven by the storm, and where you are cast among savage inhabitants. Heaven is a blessed place of rest. It is your home. You have friends there, the chiefest among whom is he that loved you, that gave himself for you, that has ever watched over you during your earthly pilgrimage, and that soon, very soon will come for you, as already he has for yours. They are glorious there; and in all their glory, if they could but speak a word to us, would it be such a poor stumbling word as that which they spoke in the hour of death? If they could speak to us from the eternal world, what hope and consolation would they give us!

We wait for thee with certain hope—
 The time will soon be over;
With childish longing we look up,
 Thy glory to discover.
 Oh bliss! to share
 Thy triumph there,
When home, with joy and singing,
The Lord his saints is bringing.

JULY 3: MORNING.

The light of the body is the eye. If, therefore, the eye be single, thy whole body shall be full of light. But if thine eye be evil, thy whole body shall be full of darkness. If, therefore, the light that is in thee be darkness, how great is that darkness!—*Matt.* vi., 22, 23.

THERE is nothing that God ever gives to a man like a clear-eyed, wholesome, sensitive, prophetic, magisterial conscience, which shows him the path, even where men's feet have not walked, interpreting what is right and what is wrong, and keeping him on the side of whatever is good and just, and true and pure, and of good report among men or angels. But, though this is the greatest gift that God ever makes, it is the one that men are most careless about. You may destroy almost every thing else in a man, but so long as you keep that in him you have in him the root of manhood. You may destroy that, and keep every thing else, and the man will be utterly undone. Christ called it *the eye.*

No disaster can befall a man so great as the perversion and destruction of the eye of his soul.

A man may cut away every mast on his ship and yet pursue his voyage. A man may have every thing on deck carried overboard and yet make some headway. A man in the middle of the ocean can afford to lose every thing else better than he can afford to lose the compass in the binnacle. When that is gone he has nothing to steer by. That little instrument is his best friend; it is his guide. And that conscience which God has given you is your compass and guide. You can afford to lose genius, and taste, and reason, and judgment better than that. Keep that as the apple of your eye. Be in love with your conscience, and let your conscience be in love with God. A conscience held in love is the very foundation not only of a spiritual manhood, but of happiness in an earthly manhood.

JULY 3: EVENING.

Worthy is the Lamb that was slain to receive power, and riches, and wisdom, and strength, and honor, and glory, and blessing.—*Rev.* v., 12.

What will be the glorious disclosure of the divine nature in heaven—the lovableness of God, the attractive beauty that there is in him, so disclosed by the Savior? How sweet will be that society to which we shall be admitted when we come among the innumerable throngs that are transformed to the same likeness, and behold what are the endless stores and riches of that God who for thousands of years has borne with this cancerous world, and made his nature the healing of all the nations! How worthy to reign! how worthy in his holiness! And if it be permitted us to stand at last by his grace and power, made like him, who of us will not say, "Thou art worthy to reign?" Ah! the privilege of enjoying sweet intimacy with such a One—glorious, rich, full, and infinite in patience; of being inspired by such a One; of being loved by such a One, and of becoming more and more like such a One. How blessed is that heaven to which we are going! how sweet is that society into which ere long we shall emerge! how joyous is that meeting which awaits those who are like God!

Who would not go
With buoyant steps to gain that blessed portal
Which opens to the land we long to know,
Where shall be satisfied the souls immortal;
Where we shall drop the wearying and the woe
In resting so.

Oh, wondrous land!
Fairer than all our spirit's fairest dreaming:
"Eye hath not seen"—no heart can understand
The things prepared, the cloudless radiance streaming.
How longingly we wait our Lord's command—
His opening hand.

JULY 4: MORNING.

If the Son, therefore, shall make you free, ye shall be free indeed.—*John* viii., 36.

THE men and women that are patriots—who are they? Mothers who are bringing up their children in the nurture and admonition of the Lord—they are writing better Declarations of Independence than ever Thomas Jefferson inscribed. Humble fathers, who are training their children in essential manliness, in self-reliance, in independence, making them ashamed to beg, and proud to rely upon their own resources—they are patriots. They are lovers of our country. The humble schoolmistress, that gathers her summer brood and pours her refined life into the bosom of these rustics—she is a patriot. The school-master, who stands nearer to the work of God in the world, and, in our age, than even the minister himself does—he is the patriot. The editor, that is taking knowledge, and giving to it multiform wings, and setting it flying round and round the world—he is the patriot. Those men who augment the substantial qualities of manhood—the preachers of the Gospel; the humble missionary; the colporteur; the devoted Christian in every neighborhood—those men who are working for the spiritual development of man—they are God's truest patriots.

God speed the right; and from year to year, as this Fourth of July comes round, and the national inspiration swells the heart, God grant there may be an expression that shall be better than the firing of crackers or the discharge of guns. These are well; but may the Fourth of July, in every decade of years, to us and to our children, more and more mean, "We have broken the yoke of Satan, and have trodden under foot the passions and the appetites, and Christ has made us free."

JULY 4: EVENING.

I will very gladly spend and be spent for you.—2 *Cor.* xii., 15.

No man knows what divine power or divine peace is until he is in sympathy with God, so that he can feel that all things are his, because all things are renounced by him. We never have such power over nature or over human life as when we are independent of the one and of the other, and when it is a matter of indifference to us whether we live or die, whether we are honored or despised, whether we work, or sleep and rest from work. To be in such perfect accordance with God as to feel that you are willing to spend and be spent, whether it be in a position high or low, whether it be in honor or disgrace—this is to be in a high sphere. It is to be in an atmosphere without storms. One does not need to *go* to heaven to *feel* heaven. It comes to us in the darkest hours and in the most troublous times. There is a peace which passes all understanding, but it is not in conscious virtue or in conscious strength. It is experienced when the soul is quickened by a divine sympathy with God, which gives a willingness to lay down one's life for the sake of others.

JULY 5: *MORNING.*

O Lord, I know that the way of man is not in himself: it is not in man that walketh to direct his steps.—*Jer.* x., 23.

We are fragmentary in our lives. The work of past generations is hinged upon this, and the work of this generation is hinged upon that of generations to come; and God sits in sublimity of counsel, putting part with part, so that when we see the connected whole, the things that now seem most insignificant will shine out in wonderful beauty and magnificence.

Imagine how Solomon's temple was built, that went up in Jerusalem without sound of the hammer. When the hewer of wood, the carver of stone, and the worker in metal, from the various seclusions where they had wrought, each on his separate part, came together to see what had been made with all the different parts, and saw in the columns, in the cornices, in the decorations, in all the paraphernalia of the wonderful temple the result of their toil, they stood entranced, and wondered that out of things so insignificant in the mountains there should come such glory in Jerusalem.

God has sent some to the cedar forest, some to the stone quarry, some to the dark and dank places of this world, but he is collecting materials which will glow with untold splendor in the temple that he is building for the New Jerusalem. What the issue of life is to be you can not tell now; but you are working for God, and with God, and according to God's plans, and ere long you will be summoned to see the result of all your work. Before that time you can not tell what that result is to be.

Be not discouraged because it is your lot to be in humble circumstances; because your work is insignificant in the eyes of men; because you are called to labor in obscurity. You are laborers together with God if your heart is with him, and if your will is obedient to his will. Be patient till you shall see the meaning of that life, which is a life carried by God, with God, and for God.

No act falls fruitless; none can tell
   How vast its power may be,
Nor what results infolded dwell
   Within it silently.

Work on, despair not, bring thy mite,
   Nor care how small it be;
God is with all that serve the right,
   The holy, true, and free.

JULY 5: EVENING.

For God so loved the world that he gave his only begotten Son, that whosoever believeth in him should not perish, but have everlasting life.—*John* iii., 16.

Do not be afraid to bow before Jesus. Oh that cross!—blessed be God, it is the enfranchisement of theology. It stands up against heaven to say, "God, with his infinite power, is not cruel. God is the sufferer, and not one that makes suffering." The divine nature is not one that oppresses mankind. The testimony of Christ's life, and the mission of Christ's death, and that everlasting love that streams from the cross of Christ is, "God so loved the world." Loved it? No mother ever loved her child half so much. And yet what mother is there that did not, in her small, feeble way, symbolize the whole atonement of Christ? What mother is there that did not bring forth her child with pangs, and strong crying, and tears? What mother is there that did not take the utter helplessness of the little babe for weeks and months, and give her life for it? How she gives up the whole royalty of her rich nature to that little child that can neither speak, nor think, nor know what helps it! And then through what sickness does she watch! And with what labor and pain does she develop the child! And how does she bring it finally to intelligence, and virtue, and manhood, all the way through a living sacrifice of love for the child!

Is not the cradle a Gethsemane? Is not the cradle a Calvary? Is there not hidden in, veiled under these acts and fidelities of the household, a symbol of that everlasting truth, that God is not a tyrant, that God hates cruelty, and that all the suffering and sorrow which we see on earth is only on the way to a coming victory, and gladness, and joy? I beseech of you, turn not away from such a blessed God as that.

JULY 6: MORNING.

Grow up into him in all things, which is the head, even Christ.—*Ephes.* iv., 15.

How long is it since you thought yourself to have entered upon the Christian course? and how far have you traveled in acquisition? If you sent a boy to school, and examined him at the end of two years in mathematics, in the natural sciences, or in any other branch to which he had given his attention, and you found that he had made no more progress than you have in this divine work, would you feel that he was an apt scholar? You are a learner. You are to learn gradually, but you are to learn all the time. Now what progress have you made? Have you made any? Do you think you are really any more humble than you were in the beginning? Do you think your pride is any easier to manage? Do you think it is any more under your control? How is it with your tongue? Do you make it an instrument of anger, of irritating passions, of petty revenges? or is it a golden member, from which flow sentences of instruction and words of love? Is it the harp of a harper full of melody and harmony? What is your thought of your inward life? Do you feel that the graces of Christ Jesus are budding and growing in you? Can you say with thanksgiving and humble gratitude that you are conscious that you are growing in grace, and in the knowledge of the Lord and Savior Jesus Christ? Do you think you are experiencing more of the reality of a

Christian life now than you were when you first embraced Christianity?

There is great danger that persons, when they have gone through the preliminary throes of conviction, and have come into the Church, and have formed a kind of decent and respectable habit from motives of consistency, will lean upon that habit, and will go on to the end of life without any material change. Such ought not to be a Christian's life. It ought, rather, to be like trees that never let a season pass without growth. They are renewed every spring, and nourished through the long summer. And a true Christian is like a tree by the river of waters, whose roots know no drought, and whose leaves shall never wither.

JULY 6: EVENING.

Daniel kneeled upon his knees three times a day, and prayed, and gave thanks before his God.—*Dan.* vi., 10.

SHOULD young people be encouraged to avoid hours and places of prayer, and led to feel that they need only pray when they feel like it? No, very far from it. It is better that there should be set occasions and places, only there must be no feeling of bondage. You must learn to make the hour of prayer and the place of prayer sweet. If the sweetness does not come in one way it must come in another. At any rate, there must be freedom from bondage in the matter. You must not go to God as to a hard yoke or a heavy burden. A yoke that is not easy, or a burden that is not light, is neither acceptable to God nor profitable to you. In by far the greatest number of instances where you set apart time and place for devotions, and regularly observe them, they will soon become attractive. When the habit is once formed, it will become one of the most delightful experiences of your life, and will be a source of amazing comfort to you. It will be like the bath in the morning and at evening, which cools, and cleanses, and exhilarates the body. There should be no day without prayers, and many of them; and if there be set occasions of prayer in the morning, at evening, and even at noonday, as is the case with some, the soul loses no time. The old proverb is, "He that prays well studies well;" and you may say that he who prays well works well, and does every thing well.

JULY 7: MORNING.

But to do good and to communicate, forget not; for with such sacrifices God is well pleased.—*Heb.* xiii., 16.

A HEART to do good will always find opportunities. If there is a willingness and a wish to be kind to the unfortunate and the suffering, God will administer the opportunity; but if there is no such willingness or wish, though ten thousand opportunities passed before you, you would never know it.

Oh you who profess to have been born unto Christ, and who daily call him Lord and Master, did you ever see that book called the New Testament? Have you ever read what Christ, who had not where to lay his head, did for the sake of helping the poor and wretched? Did you ever read that when he came, the high, and rich, and educated did not seek him, but the low, and poor, and ignorant, thieves and harlots, those who were the most wretched; and little children crept up to him, and looked into his eyes, as if they saw in him new hope and succor. Though you have read these things, and though you claim to be disciples of Christ, and to have been born in him, you are saying, "I wish I knew how to be useful." Ah! ask God to give you a heart that wants to do. Then you will have opportunities enough.

JULY 7: EVENING.

He fell asleep.—*Acts* vii., 60.

THE figures by which death is represented in the New Testament are exquisitely beautiful. One is that of *falling asleep in Jesus*. When a little child has played all day long, and becomes tired out, and the twilight has sent it in weariness to its mother's knees, where it thinks it has come for more excitement, then, almost in the midst of its frolicking, and not knowing what influence is creeping over it, it falls back in the mother's arms, and nestles close to the sweetest and softest couch that ever cheek pressed, and, with lengthening breath, sleeps; and she smiles and is glad, and sits humming unheard joy over its head.

So we fall asleep in Jesus. We have played long enough at the games of life, and at last we feel the approach of death. We are tired out, and we lay our head back on the bosom of Christ and quietly fall asleep.

> I shall sleep sound in Jesus,
> Filled with his likeness rise,
> To live and to adore him,
> To see him with these eyes:
> 'Tween me and resurrection
> But Paradise doth stand,
> Then—then for glory dwelling
> In Immanuel's land.

JULY 8: *MORNING.*

Give ear unto my prayer, that goeth not out of feigned lips.—*Psalm* xvii., 1.

I WOULD not tolerate any friendship with myself, and you would not tolerate any friendship with yourselves which was not sincere. It is not consistent with the highest conceptions of God for a man to approach him with ascriptions of adoration and praise, or with confessions of sin, which he does not feel. We are to abound in prayer. We are all the time to be in a spirit of prayer out of which such expressions and ascriptions will be literally true. They will be more intense at some times than at others, but they never should be less than simply true to our own consciousness. I do not say that a man must feel intensely before he utters a word. A man may recognize a thing with a tender consciousness, and not with an intense feeling of its truth, and his expression of it may be acceptable to God; but no man has a right to employ language in prayer which does not represent any thing that exists in him at the time.

JULY 8: *EVENING.*

Wilt thou be made whole?—*John* v., 6.

WHATEVER may be the systems of philosophy under the influence of which you have been brought up, are you not conscious, personally and experimentally, that you are in a low moral state? that there is a want of spirituality in you? that you need the inspiration of the Holy Ghost? Are you not conscious that there is needed in your soul something that shall lift you into a larger manhood? Are you content? Have you nothing to desire in yourself? Do you accomplish your ideals? Have you marked the frame-work of character? and have you filled it up? Are you not leaving out the revealed truths of Christian manhood? Are you, even on the pattern of mere secular manhood, what you would be? Are there no continually-dropping faults? Are there no eating sins? Are there no bondages of pride and selfishness? Are you not subject to evil influences in such a way that you hold up your hands, and cry out, often and often, "Who shall deliver me from the body of this death?"

To such Christ comes, as he came to the poor sick man of the porch, and says, "Though the ordinary means of healing do not avail for thee, wilt thou be made whole?" There is healing in the Lord Jesus Christ for all men, even for those who do not know what they believe; who doubt other people's belief. There is a spiritual point where grace can take hold and heal souls, so that, little by little, from the experimental point, they shall find their way out from the solution of the difficulties which environ them.

Are your trials past the telling?
  Are your sins as crimson dye?
Jesus sees your sad heart swelling
  'Neath accusing Memory.

From your sins he waits to cleanse you—
  You, the slave by Satan bound;
Messages of love he sends you—
  Where can such a Friend be found?

Now! it is the time to try it,
  Test him by his written Word;
Come, for he will ne'er deny it;
  Come to Christ, the risen Lord.

JULY 9: *MORNING.*

Provide things honest in the sight of all men.—*Romans* xii., 17.

How many men there are who say and feel that a man is obliged to go against honesty in many avocations! It is supposed that the doctor has a right to say to the patient, "You are not in danger," if he thinks it will be for the patient's good, and will give him a better chance for success. It is supposed that parents have a right to tell little pet lies to their children because they are not old enough to understand these matters. And so in all avocations it is supposed that there are certain permissive departures from rectitude.

But can a man pursue any avocation in life and be honest? It matters not whether he can or can not. You are bound to be scrupulous, truth-telling, and honest men, if you would save your souls; and if it obliges you to revolutionize business, then you are missionaries for that work. When a man is called by the Lord Jesus Christ, he is not called to bear the cross where it is light, and lay it down where it is heavy. The law requires that you set your conscience by God's Word, and take a straight path right through business, however many obstacles you may meet. Sometimes it will bring you to harm in the beginning, but it will bring you to joy afterward.

JULY 9: EVENING.

I beseech you therefore, brethren, by the mercies of God, that ye present your bodies a living sacrifice, holy, acceptable unto God, which is your reasonable service.—*Rom.* xii., 1.

WHEN you consider what have been the mercies of God, does it not appear a reasonable service? Is it not reasonable that he who has given himself to you should ask you to give yourself in a life of love to him?

Do not tarnish God's inestimable gifts by selfishness. Consecrate your hearts at once to the divine service. Be willing to work, and let others have the praise; be willing to work, and let others reap the fruits of your labor. Be like Christ, who gave his life to save men. Be more noble. Heroically bear your cross. Carry your burden without murmuring. It is only a little while that we shall have to suffer. We are almost down to the river, and it is not half so deep as you think. We are coming to the shore already, and methinks I hear, wafted from the other side, that sweetest song of them that cry ceaselessly, "Come, come." They are crying to you, and they are crying to me, "Come up hither, and wear the bridal robes at the marriage-supper of the Lamb." Every one of us must go sooner or later; by-and-by we shall all be there; and oh, the joy that is laid up for us who serve Christ!

The captive's oar may pause upon the galley,
  The soldier sleep beneath his plumed crest,
And Peace may fold her wings o'er hill and valley,
  But thou, oh Christian, must not take thy rest.

For here we all must suffer, walking lonely
  The path that Jesus once himself hath gone:
Watch thou in patience through the dark hour only—
  This one dark hour—before the eternal dawn.

JULY 10: *MORNING.*

Jesus saith unto him, Rise, take up thy bed, and walk.—*John* v., 8.

MANY persons who are desirous of becoming Christians think they have no right to discharge Christian duties until they have gone through certain appointed steps of conviction. They wish to be Christians, and to feel like Christians, before they live like Christians. Do you say, "If I had been convicted and converted, and was a Christian, I would live like a Christian?" Begin to live like a Christian; that is more important than any preliminary steps you could take. Do you think you would pray if you were a Christian? Pray now. Do you think you would instruct your children if you were a Christian? Instruct them now. The very way to become a Christian is to do Christian duty. Would you praise God if you were a Christian? Praise him now, then. Do you think you would talk to men of salvation if you were a Christian? Talk to men of salvation now. The doing of these things will make you a Christian. Being a Christian is no mysterious thing. If you would feel like a Christian, act like one, live like one. The way to be a Christian is to do as the scholar does, go to studying; as the traveler does, start on the journey; as the workman does, take hold and work; as the farmer does, put in the spade and the plow. The way to be a Christian is to let alone the thing that is wrong, and take hold of the thing that is right.

"Still dost thou wait for feeling?" Dost thou say,
  "Fain would I love and trust, but hope is dead;
I have no faith, and without faith who may
  Rest in the blessing, which is only shed

Upon the faithful? I must stand and wait."
  Not so. The Shepherd does not ask of thee
Faith in thy faith, but only faith in him;
  And this he meant in saying "Come to Me."
In light or darkness seek to do his will,
And leave the work of faith to Jesus still.

JULY 10: *EVENING.*

Increasing in the knowledge of God.—*Col.* i., 10.

There is but one God, unchangeable, infinite in power, and wisdom, and goodness. But, after all, *our conceptions* of God are perpetually changing, and changing according to our own moral growth. As we grow ourselves, with an increasing capacity to think new thoughts and feel new emotions, our conception of God changes, as it ought to change, from year to year, in the direction of nobleness, and attractiveness, and beauty. That God, who shone to you like a star on the horizon in your morning, should have ascended the heights of experience at your midday, and should shine down with the fullness of the sun upon your heads.

I sometimes think it is with our experience as it is with streams in mountain valleys. A thousand little silver rills start, they know not where, and bring up at the bottom of the mountain, and form one flower-banked stream. This stream is fed by a thousand rills; it grows by other additions; and, as it flows on, it grows deeper and broader until it reaches the ocean. And that which is born of drops of experience in the mountain runs down and on, as it were, growing broader and wider by the accumulation of experience-streams, and empties at last into the infinite. We find our thought of God growing and growing until it is developed into the eternal. And so our God ought perpetually to augment, and fill our heaven more and more to the end of life.

JULY 11: *MORNING.*

And Paul, earnestly beholding the council, said, Men and brethren, I have lived in all good conscience before God until this day.—*Acts* xxiii., 1.

You ought to have a conscience so active, so sensitive by daily communion with God, so bathed in the sweet ways and meditations of a Christian life, that you shall be misled and deceived by no example and by no specious reasoning. A man who has a correct watch learns to trust it. After he has thoroughly tried his faithful servant in the pocket, and knows that through months and years it has given him true reports, he places great reliance upon it. He may ask the time of the town clock, but if it gives a different report from that given by his watch he at once says to the clock, "Thou liest." He may ask the time of his friend whom he meets in the street, and he takes the report of his friend's watch till he looks at his own, when, finding that they differ, he says, "Mine must be right, for it never deceives me." Every man should keep an account of celestial time, and, setting his own heart and his own conscience by the beats and throbs of God Almighty's heart, he should take counsel of, and believe in, no other. He should compare himself daily with this standard, and should take no testimony against that. He that has an open face, and looks into the open face of God, shall be a child of light, a child of liberty, and a child of glory.

JULY 11: *EVENING.*

I have compassion on the multitude.—*Matt.* xv., 32.

It is an unspeakable pleasure to know that there is a being who has a heart of exquisite susceptibility, and that he knows you intimately, and what your troubles are, and says, "I sympathize with you; I am touched with the feeling of your infirmities." "Ah! but," you say, "I could get along with the infelicities of life if it were not for this consciousness of wickedness—if it were not for these throes of ignominious guilt. If I was worthy of God I could bear any thing." When we have the greatest sense of our unworthiness and of our sin, it is the hardest to strive toward God. And yet the sympathy of Christ includes our sin. He is sorry for us, and sympathizes with us on account of our sin. Calvary, mountain of blessings, is testimony that God so loved the world that he gave his only begotten Son, that whosoever believeth in him should not perish, but have everlasting life. No trumpet will ever speak as the death of Christ speaks in evidence that our woes and sorrows affect the sympathetic heart of God, and make him sorrow for us. Living, he gave himself for us; dying, he gave himself for us; living again, he lives to intercede for us; and the nearer we can bring it home to our consciousness of guilt that our God is a forgiving God, and loves to forgive us our sins, and to cleanse us from all our unrighteousness, the more nearly shall we come to the feelings of Christ toward those who are sinful.

JULY 12: *MORNING.*

Let your moderation be known unto all men.—*Phil.* iv., 5.

Many persons who are in right courses, and have substantially right views, go beyond all prudence and all bounds of discretion in the use of themselves. I know many women who, in the family and in the school, every day exert themselves a half more than they have any right to. They exhaust themselves by an industry so far beyond their own capital and their own endowment of strength, that they are perpetually held back and hindered. They are hurt in their Christian life by excess.

The same thing is true out of the family and out of the school—in business. Many a man does more work in one day than he has a right to put into three. Many a man works so that he breaks the law of God in almost every single point. Excess of enterprise and industry is a national sin with us.

There are special emergencies in man's life when he has a right to draw on his capital. If there is sickness in the household, and you are the only well one there, it is not a time for you to talk about health. There are certain things that must be done, and you must do them. It is right, in times of great peril, when the ship may be foundered, or in times of battle, or in other emergencies, for men to draw on their resources. But these are exceptional cases. The ordinary law is, that no man has a right to go beyond a certain amount of consumption of his excitability. If he does, there comes a reaction, with all its morbid feelings, its temptations, its suggestions, and its irritableness. You sacrifice a thousand times more graces of the spirit by irritableness, which comes as the result of overexertion and inordinate activity, than you can gain by prayers and reading.

JULY 12: *EVENING.*

To die is gain.—*Phil.* i., 21.

LIVING is death; dying is life. We are not what we appear to be. On this side of the grave we are exiles, on that citizens; on this side orphans, on that children; on this side captives, on that freemen; on this side disguised and unknown, on that disclosed and proclaimed as the sons of God.

If we could break down by our faith the barrier which our senses interpose; if we could but walk the garden road and move through the celestial air, beholding the lustrous beauty, the glorious largeness and liberty, the wonderful purity and joy of those whom God hath called and crowned with immortality, we should lay aside our sorrow and break forth in thanksgiving. Since only days and weeks are between us and those who have gone before; since joy and sorrow alike, and the whole course of earthly experiences are bearing us straight onward to the same abode, ought we not to find consolation and patience, yea, and a sobered gladness, that we are known in heaven by our forerunners? Children are the hands by which we take hold of heaven. By these tendrils we clasp it, and climb thitherward faster as every cord is loosed that bound us here, faster as every heart that we loved draws us upward.

JULY 13: *MORNING.*

Let thy garments be always white.—*Eccles.* ix., 8.

THE materials which make a man's character or his name must be good materials, such as are fit to build a man for the duties of this life and for eternal life, to which this life is but a door or stepping-stone. These materials must not be like the furniture of our shut-up parlors. For, as men have ordinary rooms and ordinary furniture for common use, and elegant rooms and magnificent furniture for special use, so men have certain imaginary and heroic virtues which they keep in the romance-chamber, and in which they like now and then to dress themselves up. But it is those qualities which we use every day, it is those articles with which our living room is furnished, that go to make the impressions of others about us; not what we are under the heat of instruction, under the influence of views brought to bear upon our inflamed imagination, but the things that fall out day by day, and that show the average of our thoughts and feelings. The things we use in ordinary life are the materials which are operative in the production of our character, and which constitute our name.

JULY 13: *EVENING.*

If ye be without chastisement, whereof all are partakers, then are ye bastards and not sons.—*Heb.* xii., 8.

MANY of our troubles are like snow, which, starting snow, becomes rain before it meets the ground; while many others are like snow which falls to the ground snow, but which, though it lies there all winter long, is sure to melt when spring comes. And as the snow-drop becomes the rain-drop, and the rain-drop becomes the juice of fruits and flowers, so our troubles, though they fall cold on the branch, melt and carry sap to the root. There are many troubles that God brings upon his people, or permits them to bring upon themselves, which he does not care to take away from them, and which it is not best for them to have removed. Continued troubles are not, therefore, evidences of God's displeasure. He expressly affirms that, unless you have such troubles, you can not be his sons—he can not be a loving parent to you. "Ye have forgotten the exhortation which speaketh unto you as unto children."

JULY 14: *MORNING.*

Ye are witnesses of these things.—*Luke* xxiv., 48.

MEN who are endeavoring to live Christianly say often, "Let my example speak, and not my lips." Why should not a man *interpret* his example? Why should a man leave it to be inferred in this world that he is living simply by the power of his own will? When the lines are drawn in this world, and there are but two parties—one comprising those that live by the Spirit, and the other those that live by the flesh—why should a man live by the divine Spirit, and yet not give credit to the Spirit by which he lives? Every man who is conscious that his character has been brought under the power of the Spirit of God is bound to let men know that the life which is flowing out from him now is not his own natural life, but one which proceeds from the Spirit of God. He is bound to make a public witness and testimony that the work of morality, of virtue, of spiritual fervor, of higher manhood to which he has been called, and in which he is beginning to live, is a divine work, and not one that springs from a lower form of natural causes only.

JULY 14: *EVENING.*

To the righteous good shall be repaid.—*Prov.* xiii., 21.

THERE are four spiritual elements which should precede and underlie all other experiences—truth, honesty, fidelity, purity. Taking them in their inverse order, by purity is meant the dominance in the soul of the higher affections and sentiments over the lower appetites and passions. It is the term that antagonizes with a life of lust and of salacious desire. By fidelity one means the absolute faithfulness of men to trusts reposed in them—that tendency in a man which makes it sure that he will be faithful in his relations to others, and in all his trusts. By honesty is implied righteous, equitable dealing in all relations between man and man—not what the law requires, but what is, according to a man's best light, right between man and man. By truth is meant the inward love of that which is, and the disposition to use the truth of fact and the truth of relation, just as they are, in all our representations among men. These qualities must exist in controlling strength in every worthy character.

Truthfulness, honesty, fidelity, and purity—these constitute the term righteousness; and a righteous man is a man that is built upon these four great qualities. They will, in spite of all covering, determine a man's reputation. Your course in respect to truth, honesty, fidelity, and purity will determine your character. You can not help it.

JULY 15: *MORNING.*

Charity rejoiceth not in iniquity, but rejoiceth in the truth.—1 *Cor.* xiii., 6.

THE man who has a true Christian spirit never takes delight in the faults of others. It pains him almost as much to see faults in others as to perceive that he has faults himself. Tell me, does it not give you as exquisite pain to discover faults in those you love as to discover them in yourself? Do you not feel that you would give your own body and blood to save them from ruin? So ought you to feel in respect to all your fellow-men. Their burdens should be your burdens, and their sorrows your sorrows. When a man is actuated by this spirit, how easy it is for him to go to others and tell them kindly of their faults, and help them to rid themselves of them. Men usually will bear to be told their faults by a person who has this disposition, but never by a person who has it not.

Send back the wanderer to the Savior's fold—
That were an action worthy of a saint;
But not in malice let the crime be told,
Nor publish to the world the evil taint.

Rebuke the sin, and yet in love rebuke;
Feel as one member in another's pain;
Win back the soul that his fair path forsook,
And mighty and eternal is thy gain.

JULY 15: *EVENING.*

By love serve one another.—*Gal.* v., 13.

THE day is drawing to a close. Through all its hours a slave has been moving about the house; and now, as twilight comes on, hear the slave singing a hymn. And what is it that this angelic choir is singing to? It is a little nothing called a baby. And who is this slave, fit to be an angel in royalty of gifts and in richness of cultivation? It is Mrs. Browning, the poetess, noble in understanding, versed in the lore of ages, deep in nature, full of treasure such as no king, no court, and no palace ever had. She sings. And when the little child is uneasy, she serves it. And when the child tires of the pillow and the cradle, it makes a pillow of her. When she is weary, if the child does not wish to go, she still holds it. When at last it will lie down, she still wakes for fear the child will awake. In every single hour of the night she hears its call. Not a whimper or sound from the child escapes her notice. She is up before the morning star; and, though weary, all day again this slave serves this little baby—this little uncrowned despot of the heart.

Ah! there is no slave out of heaven like a loving woman; and of all loving women, there is no such slave as a mother. How royal, next to God himself, are slaves! But remember what kind they must be. "By love serve one another." That is the coin that buys them. It is love, and it is giving one's self for another's benefit, and to another's life in the fullness of love, that makes true slavery.

JULY 16: *MORNING.*

In the morning sow thy seed, and in the evening withhold not thine hand; for thou knowest not whether shall prosper, either this or that, or whether they both shall be alike good.—*Eccles.* xi., 6.

A MAN can do good in his garden in two days, but he can not in his child's heart. In the lower departments of life you can see the results of your work as you go along, but in the higher realms you can not. The higher you go the slower is your work, and the greater is the patience that is required in waiting for results. The finest, noblest, truest things are those which require a lifetime of patience and work. A man should therefore lay out the work of his life as he does the work of his garden. In his garden he sows different kinds of seeds, and expects that they will produce flowers at different periods of the season—some in March, some in April, some in May, some in July, and some not till August or September, and he waits patiently for those which blossom late. He does not insist that all shall blossom in March, or April, or May, and he understands that those that he waits the longest for are best worth the waiting. Then "let us not be weary in well doing"—that is, in sowing causes of good as seeds—"for in due season"—at the proper time—"we shall reap, if we faint not."

JULY 16: EVENING.

Come, and let us return unto the Lord.—*Hosea* vi., 1.

God is sovereign, and he calls upon men as he pleases. Some he calls amid thunder and storm, some in a calm, some in winter, and some in summer. Some he calls as he calls flowers in spring, and some as he calls flowers in autumn. Our business is not to determine what is the way in which God must call us, nor the way in which we should like to come, but to get up and come to our Father, walking in whatever path our feet find. *Come*—that is the thing—with a deep experience, if you have it; without a deep experience, if you have it not; with a great tumult, if you can not help it; without much tumult, if it please God that it should be so. It is not to come in any particular way, or with any particular experience, but to arise and come to our Father, and say unto him, "Father, I have sinned against heaven and before thee, and am no more worthy to be called thy son; make me as one of thy hired servants."

JULY 17: MORNING.

I have chosen him to be my son, and I will be his father.—1 *Chron.* xxviii., 6.

Men who have lived years and years as Christians ought not to give themselves much anxious thought as to whether they are Christians or not. What if a wife should say to her husband, "My dear, I am exceedingly perplexed, and have been for weeks and months, in trying to find out whether I love you or not," would he not say very quickly, "Well, I know?" I do not mean to say that there are not babes in the Christian life; I do not mean to say that there are not bond-servants of the Lord. I believe many disciples are the Lord's hired men, and work on wages; I believe many are the Lord's stewards and agents. But there are those who are the Lord's children, living at home. Can you say the Lord's Prayer, and appropriate it to yourself? There are but few men that ever say spontaneously, "Our Father."

Where are the blossoming men? Where are those men who

show that summer has broken out of heaven and is resting on their heads? They are the men who are "the light of the world." They are God's dear children, risen out of the lower atmosphere and above the storm. They have left the thunder and the cloud beneath their feet, and are standing on the mountain-top in blessed transfiguration with the Lord.

JULY 17: *EVENING.*

For what shall it profit a man if he shall gain the whole world and lose his own soul?—*Mark* viii., 36.

If you lose heaven, you lose every thing. You can not carry your ships there; death will take them all away from you. You can not carry your reputation and professional skill there; these are local. All your treasures, and things that make you great in the eyes of men, you leave this side. You can carry there nothing but your relations to the Lord Jesus Christ—only your moral character. If you are deceived in that; if, when death comes, it strikes off all physical possessions and secular ranklings; more than that, if, when you come before God, he takes the veil away, and you see that you are bringing up an unsanctified heart, corrupt affections, and that the battle of life has never been fought by you, or that you came out of it with disgraceful defeat, you lose every thing—the life that now is, and the life that is to come.

And then comes this terrific denunciation of Christ: "What shall it profit a man if he shall gain the whole world and lose his own soul?"

JULY 18: *MORNING.*

For our Gospel came not unto you in word only, but also in power, and in the Holy Ghost, and in much assurance; as ye know what manner of men we were among you for your sake.—1 *Thess.* i., 5.

You may put all the skeptical men that ever lived on the face of the earth on one side, and they may plead in my ears; and all the scientists may stand with them, and may marshal all the facts of the universe to disprove the truth of Immanuel—God with us; and yet, let me see my mother walking in a great sorrow, but from the surface of her sorrow reflecting the light of cheer and heavenly hope—patient, sweet, gentle, full of comfort for others—yea, and showing by her life, as well as by her lips, that with the consolation with which she is comforted she is comforting others, and that single instance of suffering is more to me, as an evidence of the truth of Christianity, than all the arguments that the wisest men can possibly bring against it. The sight of piety is absolutely convincing. And to see the soul of a man globe itself up where other men shrink, and show itself to be clothed in great power where other men are very feeble; to see men able to shed tears with their eyes while smiles are on their lips; to see men give up every thing, and stretch out their arms to take in every thing; to see men stand upon the earth, and by faith lift themselves above storms, till the sun of the eternal world rests upon their heads—to see this is to see the preaching of the Gospel. To present such a spectacle is to preach Christ indeed.

Is the cradle empty? That empty cradle is your pulpit, from which you are to preach Christ. That is the place from which to preach Jesus, "a present help" to you "in time of trouble." Are you cut off, as it were, from the hope and from the joy of life? Oh no! oh no! Stand in your lot; and in this bereavement, as from a pulpit, preach that Christ who has promised peace to those that come to him.

In conscious weakness thou shalt hang
  On my almighty arm;
Soon as the thorn inflicts its pang,
  I'll pour my love's rich balm.
Thou plainest in thy deepest woe
  Shalt feel me at thy side,
And, for my praise, to all shalt show
  Thou art well satisfied.

JULY 18: *EVENING.*

No man, when he hath lighted a candle, putteth it in a secret place, neither under a bushel, but on a candlestick, that they which come in may see the light.—*Luke* xi., 33.

When a light-house keeper, on a stormy, dark, tempestuous night, is told to go into his attic and take care of his lantern, why does he receive such instructions? Because the ocean-burdened ship, afar off, is coming upon the coast. He is to do it because wind-driven craft are creeping toward the land, and need the guidance of the light. It is for the sake of the imperiled mariner that he is sent to take care of the lantern. But suppose he should say, "I am told to take care of this light," and should put up the shutters, saying, "The wind is not going to blow this light out." The light is safe, and it illumines the little room in which it burns, but on the sea it is dark. He might just as well let the light go out; for the only object in keeping it is that those on the ocean, who are approaching the shore, may be directed by it.

Christians are God's light-houses, and he says to them, "Shine out for the poor, the ignorant, the neglected, the wretched. Let your light so shine before men that they may see your good works, and glorify your Father which is in heaven."

JULY 19: *MORNING.*

A friend of publicans and sinners.—*Luke* vii., 34.

I PITY men who, overtaken with trouble, and made to feel their need of God, have lifted up their head beseechingly to him, and the answer has been delayed, and they have given way to despair, and come to the conclusion that God will not hear them.

No matter how deep your sin is; no matter how proud and selfish you have been; no matter how sensual, how cruel, how insincere, how skeptical you have been; no matter how mischievous your example has been to other men; no matter if you have ruled with an infidel rule, and destroyed thousands of souls, it is the nature of God, the moment you feel your need of him, and turn to him for mercy, to have mercy on you.

There is no man, therefore, who goes to God, saying, "Help me to be free from sin," but may be perfectly certain that God's whole nature moves toward him, as broad and irresistible as the summer moves from the south toward the north. If you go to God and say, "Make me feel right while I am sinning," he will not. But if you feel the plague of pride, of selfishness, and of being godless in this world, and you want somebody to help you out of your unhappy condition, I do not object to your going to your minister or some friend, but first go to God. He is the best Friend, and Pastor, and Lover that the soul ever had.

JULY 19: *EVENING.*

My son, give me thine heart.—*Prov.* xxiii., 26.

Oh that God should want my soul! I have no doubt that many a woman has said, when asked to be the wife of some great nature, "It can not be." True love is always modest. It is always grateful. It always wonders, "Why am I beloved?" It always says, "How can I repay this love?" And to think that God wants me! To think that this glorious excellence, the plenitude of the beauty, and power, and wisdom of heaven, comes to me—nay, that it comes to me in the manifestation of Jesus Christ; that it comes to me with all the sweetness of attraction, and with all the self-sacrifice and suffering of dying love! And yet God, from whose brow flames beauty, and in whose bosom love proudly sits, says to me, "My son, give me thy heart," and proffers his own. With what quick response should I love him! with what instant apprehension should I go to him! Lord, thee, and thee only, I choose. Now thy enemies are my enemies. If they be in my heart, they are my enemies still; though they be in my household, if they hate thee I will hate them. Do not I hate them that hate thee? O Lord, search me, try me, and see if there be any evil way in me. Thus I have covenanted that I will be thine in time and thine in eternity.

What offering can I make,
Dear Lord, to love like thine?
That thou, the God, didst stoop to take
A human form like mine!
"Give me thy heart, my son:"
Behold my heart—'tis done!
I would love thee as thou lov'st me,
O Jesus most desired!

Thy heart is opened wide,
Its offered love most free,
That heart to heart I may abide,
And hide myself in thee.
Oh, how thy love doth burn,
Till I that love return!
I would love thee as thou lov'st me,
O Jesus most desired!

JULY 20: MORNING.

Search the Scriptures.—*John* v., 39.

PEOPLE read the Bible far less intelligently than they do the dictionary; for, if a man goes to the dictionary, he knows just what he wants to find; if he goes to the Bible, he does not usually know what he wants to find. He has this feeling about it: that all good men love the Bible, and that, if he is going to be good, he must love it; that all Christian men read the Bible, and that, if he is going to be a Christian man, he must read it. But where to read, how to read, how long to read, and how often, and when, he does not know.

You ought to go to the Bible to get certain effects by certain causes. What do you want? Do you want to know something of God's existence? There are truths that will give you light in that direction—seek them. Do you want to be enlightened on the subject of Christ's love? Then seek those texts which treat of that subject. Do you want to shield yourself from temptation? There are passages that put you on your guard, and that address themselves to your reason, and fear, and conscience—go and search them out. You are to make yourselves acquainted with the Word of God, that you may know what its various instrumentalities are in this respect.

JULY 20: EVENING.

But if ye forgive not men their trespasses, neither will your Father forgive your trespasses.—*Matt.* vi., 15.

AN unforgiving spirit puts a man farther from God than any other thing. It is one of those dispositions that provoke even God to retaliation. I think it is often far more criminal before God than that sin over which it domineers. It is a perilous thing for a man to carry in his heart a spirit that refuses to forgive. And when you forgive, let the forgiveness be large, let it be thorough, let it be like that which God, for Christ's sake, has afforded you.

I have known families where the father and daughter had not spoken to each other for months; partners that had some disagreement, and could not meet each other peaceably; men, who were avowed Christians, that would not walk on the same side of the road with each other. Here is the royal lore of divine conduct, of the glorious majesty of mercy, of the wonderful richness of that love which, rolling out of the heart of God as from an inexhaustible fountain, covers down human transgression—all this is before men; and yet, though they bear the sacred name of Christ, they carry within them a cankerous heart of unforgiveness—and that with reference to little, petty, trifling affairs that are hardly worthy of a thought. The very dust of life turns us to such bitterness, often, that we are toward our fellow-men in the same attitude which Satan is in toward us—that of "accusers of the brethren." Oh, how little have we learned of the spirit of Christ! Until we have learned to forgive so thoroughly that the heart, instead of fostering bitterness and animosity, has become a heart that would nurse and that would bless, we can not be said to be true and faithful exemplars of the gospel of our Lord and Savior Jesus Christ.

JULY 21: MORNING.

Forever, O Lord, thy word is settled in heaven.—*Psalm* cxix., 89.

RELIGION does not mean church any more than summer means tree. What is a church but a mere instrument of religion? A church bears the same relation to the kingdom of God that a hot-house bears to summer. A hot-house is a place to keep plants in till the summer is so warm that it will do to put them in the open air, and churches are hiding-places for giving men a chance to grow till the warmth of the world is sufficient to enable them to grow without them. Churches may die, but the Bible does not die. The instruments of religion may perish, but God does not perish. This service, this doctrine, this creed may become unfitted for the uses of the time, but the eternal principles of truth remain. Conscience remains, and throbs in every heart. Purity remains, God-given and God-enlightened. Faith remains, still gazing upward, and beholding what the natural eye can not behold. Love remains in the household, in the neighborhood, and in the nation.

Christ's work on earth is advancing, and filling the world with the glory of God.

JULY 21: EVENING.

And they came to Jericho: and as he went out of Jericho with his disciples and a great number of people, blind Bartimeus, the son of Timeus, sat by the highway side begging.—*Mark* x., 46.

Oh, to be blind! To see no face; to read no book; to behold no field, or tree, or flower; to have no morning and no evening, but unbroken night forever; to see no coming spring, no changes in the purpling bark of yet unleaved trees, no sprouting grass, no coming birds; to see neither father nor mother, neither friend nor companion; and oh! to lose the ineffable bounty of God in little children, that fill the eyes with such delight that one might for hours ask only to wander and gaze upon them; to be among those that see, and you not to see; to be unable to look when one cries "Lo here—lo there!" to almost forget that you do not see, and accept darkness as if it were light; timid steps and groping for manly walking—this is indeed a bitter thing.

There is a spiritual realm, and that man who can not perceive spiritual truth is blind. The heavens declare God's glory, and the firmament showeth his handiwork. The world is full of the evidences of his being and presence. And yet there are many that gaze minutely upon all these letters written upon sky and ground, and never discern the secret of the literature. They admire nature, but never God. They admire the treasures of nature, but never the hand that created them. There are those who see nothing in spiritual life; nothing in their own sinful condition and its misery; nothing in the Christian's life—no joy, no triumph, no argument of courage and hope.

To all such Jesus comes. He passes by whenever his name or word is proclaimed. As along the road from Jericho he passed within sound of the blind man, so by his Spirit and by his truth he passes not far from every one.

Rise. Call for help if you feel that you need it. Call, not once, nor twice, but until your cry is heard. If checked, if hindered, if seemingly drawn away, call again, and put your heart and soul into the supplication. And there shall come to you the voice, the influence of one that says, "Bid him come to me." Go to Jesus, and if he says, "What wilt thou that I should do unto thee?"—and he says it to every needy supplicant—say with him of old, "Lord, that I might receive my sight."

Sad one, in secret bending low,
A dart in thy heart that the world may not know,
Wrestling the favor of God to win—
The seal of pardon for days of sin—
Press on, press on, with thy prayerful cry—
"Jesus of Nazareth passeth by."

JULY 22: MORNING.

And every creature which is in heaven, and on the earth, and under the earth, and such as are in the sea, and all that are in them, heard I saying, Blessing, and honor, and glory, and power, be unto him that sitteth upon the throne, and unto the Lamb forever and ever.—*Rev.* v., 13.

If, when I rise in the last day, and look upon Jesus Christ, I may not cast my crown at his feet, then let me die in ignorance of his name. For he has told me that he is mine, and that I am his. He has said that he dwells in my heart, and has told me to come into his heart. He has called himself by every sweet name. Nature itself is precious to me because I associate it in so many ways with him. There is nothing in the day, or in the night, or in the year, that has not been sanctified and made use of as a love-term for the Lord Jesus Christ. And now may I not love him, so that by love I shall hold on through life, and go through the ford of death? Did he not tell me to cling to him? Did he not tell me to aspire toward him? Did he not open to me every thing in him that was sweet and attractive? And have I not a right to let my heart go out to him in simplicity and trust?

Oh, poor bewildered soul, do not be afraid. There is no rock in the harbor where you are going. Love on, love more; and do not fear that in the last day you will find that you have put the crown on the wrong head. Crown the Lord Jesus Christ—*crown him Lord of all*—for you are safe in worshiping him. Love him, and he will take care of you. Dismiss your jealousies. Dismiss your fears and your distress. Only be sorry that you do not love enough, and that your life does not conform enough to love.

"He that honoreth the Son honoreth the Father also." At no time does the Eternal Father rejoice in us more than when we are giving our life and our being to Jesus Christ our Savior.

JULY 22: EVENING.

For we are laborers together with God.—1 *Cor.* iii., 9.

No crown that any earthly monarch could put on your head, no distinction that could be conferred by writing your name in the book of nobles, would be an honor so great as that which God bestows upon you when he permits you to go down to the poorest beggar's child and labor for its coronation in heaven. And yet we do not esteem it so. The Christ that is in the privilege does not appear until the privilege is taken from us. We take all the external toil, and fail to find the hidden Christ of joy in faithful Christian labor.

When the clouds drop down low, and it is rainy, and chilly, and misty, there is nothing in them but discomfort; but when, the sun having risen, they get off a little distance, every body claps his hands, and calls out and says, "Oh, behold the rainbow!" What is the rainbow? Nothing but that cloud which, when it is passing you, weaves a garment that is disagreeable and hateful to you, but which, when it is removed a little distance from you, with the sun shining on it, is clothed with glory and beauty. Dull duties a little way off may become God's rainbows to men.

Working, O Christ! with thee,
    Working with thee,
Unworthy, sinful, weak
    Although we be,
Our all to thee we give,
For thee alone would live,
And by thy grace achieve,
    Working with thee.

Savior, we weary not,
    Working with thee;
As hard as thine our lot
    Can never be.
Our joy and comfort this—
Thy grace sufficient is;
This changes toil to bliss,
    Working with thee.

JULY 23: MORNING.

This also I saw, that it was from the hand of God.—*Eccles.* ii., 24.

If God were to recount what he has done for us, it would seem as though our life was a golden chain, in which one golden link clasped another, every hour being a link, and every day lengthening the chain. Yet we frequently feel as though our life was a desolate, barren life, because we have not noticed what the benefits of God to us really were; because we have taken no such heed as to be impressed that the Lord was guiding and defending us, and giving us victory. One mercy covers down another like waves of the sea. We do not stop to think that the events which redeem this day, which fill this hour with peace, and which open the future to us, are special divine mercies. Life is full of events of mercy, only men do not heed them. They do not know that God is performing marvels around about them. The unthought-of things are often full of beauty and full of strangeness.

I sometimes think, of a night, that it is a sin to go into the house and leave God's glory flashing abroad in the northern lights, or in the stellar exhibitions in all the broad expanse above, without a witness. What are men's inventions and ingenuities compared with those astonishing developments which every summer's day shows us in the clouds, in the storms, and in frescoes of light and beauty? Every single day there is, in the silence of nature, and in the might of nature, enough to fill the human soul with joy and gratitude. But, while day tells it to day, and night repeats it to night, man sees but little of it.

JULY 23: EVENING.

Wherefore also it is contained in the Scripture, Behold, I lay in Sion a chief corner-stone, elect, precious; and he that believeth on him shall not be confounded.—1 *Peter* ii., 6.

The preciousness of Christ is not merely in his divinity nor in his mediatorship. The familiar experience of Christ, if it were to report itself, would show that the preciousness of the Savior grows upon us by his personal relationship to us. It is what he becomes to us severally, in our various scenes and stages of development in life, which makes him most precious to us.

There are those who have received from the Lord Jesus Christ an inspiration. There has come over their soul a new influence. They are conscious that there is lifted upon them, from him, a light which has widened their horizon, and given them a new conception of the ends of life, and made men of them. There are those who are able to say, from day to day, "If it had not been for my conversion to the love of the Lord Jesus Christ—if it had not been for that which Christ has done for me, I never should have been, and never could have been, what I now am." And he becomes precious because he has indicated to them that which is unspeakably valuable to them—that soul-growth which takes hold upon eternal conditions; which inspires in us not simply intellectual development, but that heroism which gives us higher ideals of life, and breaks us off from being the mere animals which we are to begin with, and teaches us how to be men, and how to revere those who are men like ourselves.

JULY 24: *MORNING.*

Seek and ye shall find.—*Matt.* vii., 7.

It is yours to sing, it is yours to rejoice, it is yours to have ecstatic visions, it is yours to live in a state of mind in which you can never be disturbed. No agitation of the elements, no storm, no thunder above or earthquake beneath, can shake or move those who know how to be built; but you must be willing to be the artificer, and search for the rock, and seek till you find it, and build thereon in Christ Jesus. This blessing is for every man who desires it, but it is by work it is to be obtained. We know that God gives graces; but does he give them without the instrumentality of human exertion? No more than he does harvests; no more than he does education. They that *seek* shall find; to those who *knock* it shall be opened unto them.

JULY 24: EVENING.

Then Samuel took a stone, and set it between Mizpeh and Shen, and called the name of it Eben-ezer, saying, Hitherto hath the Lord helped us.—1 *Sam.* vii., 12.

THE coming on of a great trouble or grief; the hours of anguish, which we may or may not confide to another; those habitual troubles which weigh down life with a perpetual gravitation; and, on the other hand, the rolling away of grief; the glad morning after the night; the dawn of great affections in the soul—which are the best blessings that God ever gives, and are to us what the coming of the morning sun is to the day; the emerging into the light of a new faith; victories over easily besetting sins; the conquest over inbred sins; clearer views; stronger impulses of conscience; a new sense of manhood infused into our souls; a more heroic impulse taking the place of a craven or mere physical habitude of obedience—all these critical inward experiences are worthy of some external recognition. We should specialize them. We should think of them in their individuality and in their sequences; and it would be well for us if we could set up some memorial, and be able to bear witness to one another, saying, "Hitherto the Lord hath helped us."

JULY 25: MORNING.

Brethren, if a man be overtaken in a fault, ye which are spiritual restore such a one in the spirit of meekness; considering thyself, lest thou also be tempted.—*Gal.* vi., 1.

As when a man in a march has stumbled and fallen headlong, they that have not fallen lift him up, and put him on his feet again, so, saith the apostle, if a man be taken in the very fact of sin, those that are good and pure must restore him to their love and confidence and to his own self-respect. "Restore him in the spirit of meekness; considering thyself, lest thou also be tempted." We are not to take hold of a man with that stern spirit which conscience inbreeds, or with an air of authority, and say, "Thou hast done wrong; I judge thee!"

Nor are we to meddle with wrong-doers in a spirit of self-conceit; nor yet with what is harder for proud men to bear — a proud, patronizing, and self-conscious, condescending spirit, as if all the help we gave was but another way of showing our superiority to them. We are to deal with a gentle and sweet meekness, as if we too were weak and fallible. We are to approach them with that high, serene, tranquil spirit which God's Spirit breathes upon the human soul when he inspires it with something of his own infinite gentleness and compassion; and, enwrapping them in the bosom of this goodness, we are to nourish them back to their better life.

Give words, kind words, to those who err;
Remorse much needs a comforter.
Though in temptation's wiles they fall,
Condemn not; we are sinners all.
With the sweet charity of speech,
Give words that heal, and words that teach.

JULY 25: EVENING.

Lord, save us: we perish.—*Matt.* viii., 25.

MAN is not only weak, but guilty. His own conscience condemns him; and God is greater than his conscience. He has need of help in the Mediator, in the Intercessor, in Christ Jesus. And a sense of this need I suppose to be an inseparable part of every true Christian experience. A great many persons, however, undoubtedly take the initial steps of a Christian life, and live more or less Christianly for years before they are brought to this state of feeling. Sometimes men are shut up unto sorrow; sometimes they are shut up unto despondency; sometimes they are shut up unto doubts, and are beset with temptations to unbelief; and some come in one way, and some in another, to the fullness of a Christian life. Just as vessels sailing for New York from the east, the southwest, the south, and all points of the compass, converge, and make the same port, so Christians with widely different experiences all tend to the same spiritual condition.

Whosoever comes, howsoever he comes, Christ will in no wise cast him out. Nevertheless, as the sense of the need, so will be the realization of the divine love which supplies it. Unto whom much is forgiven, the same loveth much.

JULY 26: MORNING.

Of the Rock that begat thee thou art unmindful, and hast forgotten God that formed thee.—*Deut.* xxxii., 18.

THE gifts of God, expressed in the human mind and disposition, seldom form the basis of thought, much less of thanks. We are neither thankful for the casket, nor for the jewels that God has put within the casket. Indeed, the more men have, the less apt are they to be grateful. They become vain of their mental gifts, arrogant, worldly, foolish. We bitterly inveigh against princes who abuse their power in the oppression of their subjects, but there are no princes endowed as royally as those whom God makes eminent by mental gifts. What is the history of the human race in this regard? That the highest are the humblest? That the richest by the gift of God inwardly are the most loving, the most gentle, the most sensitive to divine power? Those whom God has lifted nearest to him stand farthest from him. We are more often apt to be grateful when we receive some temporal gift—when some impending mischief to our prosperity is removed, than with the thought of God's goodness that we bear about in reason, in flashing imagination, in hope, in love, and in every thing that goes to make up the human disposition. The gift of God to us, touched with immortality that, once kindled, burns on forever, radiant past all comparison of star, or sun, or lesser things like these—we carry this from the cradle to the grave, and scarcely think to praise or to love God for his gifts and benefactions.

JULY 26: EVENING.

I shall be satisfied when I awake with thy likeness.—*Psalm* xvii., 15.

WHEN Michael Angelo was employed in decorating the interior of that magnificent structure, the Sistine Chapel, the Pope demanded that the scaffolding should be taken down, so that he could see the glowing colors that with matchless skill were being laid on. Patiently and assiduously did that noble artist labor, bringing out his pictures, wondrous for their beauty and significance, until the work was done. The day before it was done, if you had gone into that chapel, what would you have seen? Posts, planks, ropes, lime, mortar, dirt. But when all was finished the scaffolding was removed. Then, although the floor was yet covered with rubbish and litter, when you looked up, it was as if heaven itself had been opened, and you looked into the courts of God and angels.

The scaffolding is kept around men long after the fresco is commenced to be painted; and wondrous disclosures will be made when God shall take down this scaffolding of the body, and reveal what you have been doing. By sorrow and by joy; by joys which are but bright colors, and by sorrows which are but shadows of bright colors; by prayer; by the influences of the sanctuary; by your pleasures; by your business; by reverses; by successes and failures; by what strengthened your confidence, and by what broke it down; by the things you rejoiced in, and by the things you mourned over—by all these God is working in you. And you are to be perfect, not according to the things that you plan, but according to the divine pattern. Your portrait is being painted, and God, by wondrous strokes and influences, is working you up to his own ideal. God is working to make you like him. And the simple but wondrous declaration is, that when you stand on Zion, and before God, and see what has been done in you, you shall be "satisfied."

JULY 27: MORNING.

Take heed, and beware of covetousness; for a man's life consisteth not in the abundance of the things which he possesseth.—*Luke* xii., 15.

WHAT are houses, and ships, and armies, and kingdoms to him that once has known the name of God? What to him that has heard the joy that sounds evermore above all the loudest or the sweetest sounds upon earth? What to him is any thing that this world can afford who never forgets, by day or by night, that he is a pilgrim, who can not be seduced by any enticement from reaching forward to the true, the pure, the good? Not that he disdains wealth and power, or counts them to be in vain in their spheres, but he remembers that manhood lies above them all. For they that seek that supremely yearn after it, dream of it, and see in it visions of the day, year in and year out; and God and brotherhood are more to them than silver or gold, or sceptre or crown. As men grow toward God, they long more, not only for God, but for the godlike.

> Yes, he is mine; and naught of earthly things—
> Not all the charms of pleasure, wealth, or power,
> The fame of heroes, or the pomp of kings,
> Could tempt me to forego his love an hour.
> Go, worthless world, I cry, with all that's thine;
> Go! I my Savior's am, and he is mine.

JULY 27: EVENING.

Looking unto Jesus.—*Heb.* xii., 2.

THE vague and sad forebodings of Christians as to their final safety are very unreasonable in the light of God's revelation. There are men that hope sometimes, but doubt much more. This arises from an almost exclusive regard to one's own sickness, and an almost utter neglect to look at the fullness, richness, freeness, and inexhaustible bounty of God's love for men. No man can find any reasonable comfort, I think, so long as he is more conscious of his own state than of the amazing grace and power of God. I do not know the man who, if he should look merely at his own disposition, at his past life, at his Christian experience, could find argument for any thing but sadness and dissatisfaction in regard to the past, and fear in regard to the future. It is not in that direction that hope springs up. As long as a man looks in upon himself, he is like one that opens a trap-door and looks down to see the stars. The stars are not to be seen by looking that way. You do not want to look down into a well to see the light, but into the heavens above.

JULY 28: MORNING.

He hath sent me to bind up the brokenhearted, to proclaim liberty to the captives, and the opening of the prison to them that are bound.—*Isaiah* lxi., 1.

A SINFUL man is like the man in the castle whose story amused our youth. His hands are bound; his feet are fettered; thick walls, windows far up, heavy doors, many bolts, and jailors, make his escape impossible. So he only awaits the day of execution. But as he sleeps, some night, a strange dream haunts him of home. He thinks his mother has come to him. Starting up, he sees standing beside him a beauteous form, who says to him, "Make haste. Lift your hands, that I may release them." And she takes off the chains. She has beheld him, and she knows his name, and love has brought her there. It is the castle-keeper's daughter. "Lift up your feet," she says, "that I may set them free." What he could not do for himself, love and mercy are doing for him. "Now follow me silently." The guards are all asleep. The door is opened; he never could have opened it. The passage-ways are threaded; he never could have found his way through them. He feels again the midnight air beginning to lift his damp hair, long matted. He begins to breathe once more the atmosphere of liberty. Can language be found with which, under such circumstances, one would turn to his benefactress, though he had known her but in the hour of his release? Would he not be a monster whose heart did not leap out in thanksgiving at such a time?

You are such prisoners. Jesus is that mercy and that love. He has come down to your dungeon, and unlocked your chains, and inspired you with courage and strength, and opened the door, saying, "I am the way." Follow him; every step will make you stronger. Follow him; every step will take you farther from bondage and nearer to liberty. Follow him; every step will lead you toward your true manhood. Follow him, and soon you shall stand in Zion and before God.

JULY 28: EVENING.

I was strengthened as the hand of the Lord my God was upon me.—*Ezra* vii., 28.

No man who is entering the precincts of a higher life; no man who is drawing near to the twilight of his true manhood; no man who begins to know that he is a son of God, and to hear voices whose meaning he can scarcely discern, and to recognize the call of God, and to respond to that call by beginning to live in obedience to his higher instead of his lower nature—no such man ought to say, "I can be a Christian a little way."

You can be a Christian *all* the way. There is nothing in you, if you have started on the Christian course, so bad that you can not overcome it by the grace of God. It is your privilege to receive power from on high that shall give your will such firmness, and your judgment such directness, and your moral feelings such predominance, that you shall be able to overcome any passion or appetite. Whatever may be your sin, your lust, your vice, it is in your power to correct it. No man should in a cowardly way enter upon a Christian life, saying, "I can do some things, and I can live better than I have been living." You can live *victoriously*. God gives you the power—and he will refresh and invigorate that power in every man's soul—to overcome every snare, every delusion, every passion and appetite, every thing that is wrong in you, and to become perfectly victorious.

JULY 29: MORNING.

He calleth his own sheep by name.—*John* x., 3.

I NEVER see the sun rise in majesty, or go down in glory, that my heart does not go out after God. I thank him that he has taught me in the Bible that it is a symbol of the Father. And yet it is not enough for me. The sun pours its rays alike on every thing, good or bad. It works toward decay as much as toward growth; it ministers to death as much as to life; it labors for the icicle as much as for the violet; it pours its beams on the coffin that goes to its long home, and also through the window where the child sleeps in the cradle, and it does not know the difference.

I want a God that knows me by name as I know my children. I love to think of Christ standing in the garden when Mary addressed him, and could not see him because her eyes were so full of tears. There are a great many that can not see Christ because their eyes are full of tears. She, thinking him to be the gardener, said, "Tell me where thou hast laid him." And he said—what? "Follow me, and I will show you?" No; he said, "Mary." It was life from the dead. That single word told her all. And I think our Father in heaven calls us by name. He knows how to think and speak of us individually. Every one of us stands before him as different from all other beings. You have a right and title in God just as your child has in you. You have a personal relation to him. You may come to him as having a separate interest in him. There is a place for you in his regard as just what you are. He is your own. He made you distinct from every body else, and he meant that you should trust in him for your peculiar wants.

Yes, for me, for me he careth
  With a brother's tender care;
Yes, with me, with me he shareth
  Every burden, every fear.
Yes, o'er me, o'er me he watcheth,
  Ceaseless watcheth, night and day;
Yes, even me, even me he snatcheth
  From the perils of the way.

JULY 29: EVENING.

Although the fig-tree shall not blossom, neither shall fruit be in the vines; the labor of the olive shall fail, and the fields shall yield no meat; the flock shall be cut off from the fold, and there shall be no herd in the stalls: yet I will rejoice in the Lord, I will joy in the God of my salvation.—*Hab.* iii., 17, 18.

THE time to test religion is in the emergencies of life. When every thing is prosperous, when your health is good, when your spirits are fine, when your circumstances are as you would have them, that you are joyful in religion is a thing to be thankful for; but, after all, it is not a test of religion in you. If it were presented as evidence of your piety, men would say, "Why should he not rejoice in the Lord? He has every thing he wants. Take away his property and his family, and then see if he will be such a happy Christian." But if, when a man is unprosperous, he has a religion that will carry him through, that is a religion to be proud of—in the better sense of *pride.* If, when a man is in great affliction, he has a religion that will hold him up; if, when a man is under vehement temptation, he has a religion that is like a coat of mail; if, when a man has lost all that the world clings to, he still has that which is more to him than houses, or lands, or friends, or honor; if, finally, when heart and flesh fail, God is the strength of his salvation, his joy and his triumph, then he has a religion that is worth having. And nobody can well afford to be without the experience of intimate faith and love by which the soul is sustained in temptation, in adversity, and in death itself.

JULY 30: MORNING.

Herein is my Father glorified, that ye bear much fruit; so shall ye be my disciples.—*John* xv., 8.

When people want to make things attractive in farming, they give exhibitions of their products. The women bring their very best butter, moulded into tempting golden lumps; and the men bring the noblest beets, and squashes, and vegetables of every kind, and from the orchards they bring the rarest fruits; and when you go into the room where all these things are displayed, they seem to you attractive and beautiful.

It seems to me that is the way a Christian church ought to represent the Christian life. You ought to pile up your apples, and pears, and peaches, and flowers, and vegetables, to show what is the positive fruit of religion. But many people in Christian life do as farmers would do who should go to a show, and carry—one, pigweed; another, thistles; another, dock; and another, old hard lumps of clay, and should arrange these worthless things along the sides of the room, and mourn over them. What sort of husbandry would that be? Christians are too apt to represent the dark side of religion in their conversation and meetings.

Christ prayed for his disciples, that they might bring forth fruit. He declared to them that in the divine administration, God, as vintner, sought to make the vine bring forth more and more fruit. Bearing fruit, sweet, luscious, and blessed, is the business of the Christian life.

JULY 30: EVENING.

Unto thee will I cry, O Lord, my Rock.—*Psalm* xxviii., 1.

A great mountain lifts itself up, with perpendicular face, over against some quiet valley; and when summer thunders with great storms, the cliff echoes the thunder, and rolls it forth a second time, with majesty increased; and we think that, to be sublime, storms should awaken mountain echoes, and that then cause and effect are worthy of each other. But so, too, an oriole, or a song-sparrow, singing before it, hears its own little song sung back again. A little child, lost and crying in the valley, hears the great cliff weeping just as it weeps; and, in sooth, the mountain repeats whatever is sounded, from the sublimest notes of the tempest to the sweetest bird-whisper or child-weeping; and it is just as easy to do the little as the great, and more beautiful. Now God is our rock, and from his heart is inflected every experience, every feeling of joy or grief that any human soul utters or knows.

JULY 31: *MORNING.*

Keep yourselves in the love of God, looking for the mercy of our Lord Jesus Christ unto eternal life.—*Jude* 21.

It is in the power of no other influence to do so many difficult things, and make them as easy in the doing, as the love of God shed abroad in our hearts. For love equalizes all things. It is the power which makes weakness strong, which takes darkness away from the dark, which gives tenfold radiance to light. It is that which enters all things, goes over or through all obstructions, discovers all things that are hidden. It is that which levels all inequalities of fortune, makes men prosperous in adversity, gives them health though sick, crowns them with victory in defeat, and smooths all rough ways. So that a soul that feels the full breath of love; that feels itself filled, inspired, lifted, and overmastered by, and overblessed with the love even of one on earth, whose love is worthy, is like a region on which the sun rises in spring, bringing all brightness, and warmth, and life—is like the morning that comes after the darkness of the night, when all birds fly and sing, and all flowers open and breathe perfume; when all mists rise up and fade to blue; and when forest, and field, and air, and water, and trees, and grass, and stones are bathed in rosy joy. The rising of Christ upon the soul is very significantly said to be the rising of the sun of righteousness with healing in its beams.

> Thy love, O God! restores me,
> From sighs and tears, to praise;
> And deep my soul adores thee,
> Nor thinks of time or place.
> I ask no more, in good or ill,
> But union with thy holy will.

'Tis that which makes my treasure,
'Tis that which brings my gain;
Converting woe to pleasure,
And reaping joy from pain.
Oh! 'tis enough, whate'er befall,
To know that God is all in all.

JULY 31: EVENING.

Be of the same mind one toward another. Mind not high things, but condescend to men of low estate. Be not wise in your own conceits.—*Rom.* xii., 16.

To be of the same mind one toward another is to have a feeling of community, a feeling of common universal sympathy; and we are expressly forbidden to do what every one, in the proportion in which he is educated, tends to do—to aspire to the exclusive association of those who have risen in the world by reason of the same privileges.

How foolish it would be for a man to judge of trees in the nursery, or in the orchard and garden, as we are wont to judge of men. How foolish, in selecting grapes, to judge of their value by the trellis on which the vines are fastened; by the nature of the timber composing the stakes on which they are supported; by the quality of the bands by which they are tied to the stake, that the wind may not shake them down. Men never select plants and trees with their eye fixed upon their external fastenings and conditions; but when they turn to that most wonderful creation of God, a human being, rare in faculty, illimitable in outreach, complex in intellectual faculties, rich in domestic affections, sublime in moral sentiments, a creature carrying a double nature of matter and of spirit in a double life—an earthly and a heavenly one—him they judge, not by these interior, divine, constituent elements, but by his garb, by his place in life, by the trade which he follows, by the merest transient connections which he forms.

AUGUST 1: MORNING.

I know thy works: behold, I have set before thee an open door, and no man can shut it: for thou hast a little strength, and hast kept my word, and hast not denied my name.—*Rev.* iii., 8.

The Spirit of God sympathizes with the difficulties which lie in our life in the material body. All our physical wants, all our bodily weaknesses and sicknesses, and the infelicities that arise from them—these things men who are in health are very hard and uncharitable about. Many a person disappoints you—does not fulfill your expectation; many a person lets fly casual words which irritate you; but if you knew out of what utter weakness—if you knew out of what a sense of almost deathly feebleness these things often come, methinks it would excite in you, as doubtless it does in God, a spirit of pity and compassion, rather than of blame for their wrong-doing. There needs to be pity for the sinning, although their sins are to be repressed. God has sympathy and compassion for those who have temptations that are preying upon them, and who are weakened by overexertion, or who suffer in body, or who are in discouragement and despondency of mind, so that they are led to do things which are wrong. Society may disregard them, but there is one Heart that never forgets them, nor ceases to compassionate them. There is one summer place for people who are sinning or doing evil things. It is the heart of the divine Spirit.

AUGUST 1: *EVENING.*

For I say, through the grace given unto me, to every man that is among you, not to think of himself more highly than he ought to think; but to think soberly, according as God hath dealt to every man the measure of faith.—*Rom.* xii., 3.

When you measure yourself, you must not measure by what the world thinks of you, nor by a social standard, nor by a commercial standard, nor by an intellectual standard, but by a religious standard. You are to estimate yourself according to the grace of God in your heart, and the fruit of God's Spirit which you manifest in your life. Mercy, kindness, humbleness, meekness, goodness, gentleness, humility, long-suffering, patience, disinterestedness, faith, love—these are the traits you are to sum up when you wish to know what you are. You can not find out what you are by the till, by the coffer, by the ledger, by any book or paper, nor by reputation. You can only find out what you are by the qualities of goodness in you.

Did you ever attempt to measure yourself in this way? How many times in the course of a year do you suppose you judge of yourself strictly and impartially according to your religious worth; not thinking of yourself more highly than you ought to think, but soberly, according as God *has dealt to you the measure of faith?*

AUGUST 2: MORNING.

My brethren, count it all joy when ye fall into divers temptations; knowing this, that the trying of your faith worketh patience. But let patience have her perfect work, that ye may be perfect and entire, wanting nothing.—*James* i., 2–4.

The place for true virtue is where virtue is tempted. The place for courage is where there is danger. The place for manhood is where there is a stress in the other direction. It is where men mingle with men, and are tempted to selfishness, and rise above it, and to pride, and hold it in subjection; it is where men are tempted to be fiery, and bitter, and cruel, and greedy, and aggressive, and they, in the midst of these temptations, strengthen the other tendency, and lift it into vitality—it is there that manhood is developed. That is God's pulpit; it is God's Church; it is where men are formed. No man is formed in a cave; that is the place for bats. No man is formed as an anchorite or ascetic. You are to be living men among living men, overcoming evil tendencies and temptations. It is there that God calls you to be full-orbed men in Christ Jesus.

Hark! 'tis a martial sound—
  To arms, ye saints! to arms!
Your foes are gathering round,
  And peace has lost its charms.
Prepare the helmet, sword, and shield,
The trumpet calls you to the field.

No common foes appear
  To dare you to the fight,
But such as own no fear,
  And glory in their might.
The powers of darkness are at hand;
Resist, or bow to their command.

AUGUST 2: EVENING.

And I say unto you, That many shall come from the east and west, and shall sit down with Abraham, and Isaac, and Jacob in the kingdom of heaven.—*Matt.* viii., 11.

The number of redeemed ones is augmenting still; heaven

has room for all that the earth can ever send thither; there is a place for every one which none other can take. There are garments and palms for every single soul, though it be hoary in years or though it be an infant of days, though it be washed out from immeasurable corruption or though it speed without stain or contamination out of life. For all and every condition there awaits in heaven a robe, a place, and a God; and there, in that eternal summer; there, in those innumerable joys; there, in that great company of the redeemed, whose robes are washed in blood, and made whiter than the snow; there, in ranks, in cities, in nations, in races, and in multitudes without number, they dwell in holy liberties and in blessed experiences. They are monuments of the goodness of God and companions of his glory, full of ineffable joy. Nay, we conceive not, nor have we power to conceive, the joy of those that have gone before, our companions on earth, who are now companioning with God in heaven.

AUGUST 3: *MORNING.*

Wherefore let him that thinketh he standeth take heed lest he fall.—1 *Cor.* x., 12.

A MAN takes a boat, and rows down the harbor, and the tide is with him, and he is swept away from the shore. He is after pleasure, and the tide and wind are with him, and they sweep him on and out. When the sun goes down, how glorious are the heavens, and the reflecting, mirroring ocean. Still out and on he is swept, thoughtless and full of poetic fancies. He is not seeking the night, but the night is seeking him. He is not courting terrific storms, but already the sky is full of clouds that bear the elements of his destruction. It is one thing, with the wind and tide, to sweep out upon the ocean, and it is another thing against the wind and tide, in the night, and in the midst of a terrific storm, to find the shore again; and so, helpless, he goes down to the bottom, with none to hear his faint outcry.

In life, tens of thousands, benighted and bestormed, have sunk beneath the waves of iniquity, and you, knowing it, say, "Yes, they sank, but I shall not sink." But you will, unless, warned, you turn to God, and learn that the ways of integrity are the only safe ways, and that every way of wickedness is full of peril, and leads to certain disaster in the end.

AUGUST 3: EVENING.

Looking for that blessed hope, and the glorious appearing of the great God and our Savior Jesus Christ.—*Titus* ii., 13.

The Christ that delivered us; the Christ that sustained us when our babe dropped away from our arms; the Christ that sustained us when we buried our dead, almost hopeless and crushed; the Christ that sustained us when we were in bankruptcy; the Christ that sustained us when all men were against us, and it seemed as though the full breath of winter was cutting through and through; the Christ that sustained us in the hour of despondency; the Christ that stood by us when all men had deserted us; the Christ that was our friend on the sea and on the land, in the prison-house and on the battle-field; the Christ of the household; my mother's Christ; my father's Christ; my brother's Christ; my sister's Christ; the Christ of the lecture-room and of the prayer-meeting; the Christ of all my life, at last begins to rise before me in my later years. As I die, I do not go toward the barren and the voiceless land; I go toward all that my heart has ever known of joy and of nobility. I am living toward myself, and I shall die toward myself, because "for me to live is Christ, and to die is gain." And so, at last, when I go to that fatherland—the land of my fathers—I shall not be a stranger; nor shall I need to learn the language of that land; nor shall I need to be introduced to him that is the head there, for all my life long I have been learning. And when at last I hear that voice, compared with which all music of earth shall be as a dry and cacophonous sound, saying, "Well done, good and faithful servant," then, in that hour of joy, of full possession, and of blessed presence, I will cast my crown at his feet, and say, "Not unto me, but unto thy name, be the praise of all that I am, and all that I ever shall be."

Dear name! the rock on which I build
  My shield and hiding-place;
My never-failing treasury, filled
  With boundless stores of grace.

Jesus, my Shepherd, Husband, Friend;
  My Prophet, Priest, and King;
My Lord, my Life, my Way, my End,
  Accept the praise I bring.

AUGUST 4: MORNING.

Be courteous.—1 *Peter* iii., 8.

Life is made a great deal pleasanter, intercourse is made a great deal smoother, if men observe the little forms of propriety in life, which may not mean a great deal, but the absence of which is felt. It is very little to say "Good morning," and yet, if every time you meet a friend or a neighbor you look him in the face and say "Good morning, my friend," or "Good evening, my friend," is not the effect which is produced very different from that which is produced if, when you meet a man, you hardly look at him, and pass on? Is there not a difference in his feeling? Is there no difference in yours?

Good manners are not, of course, the same as virtues, but they stand very closely allied to virtues. There seems to be with many an impression that honesty and frankness require a species of gruffness and rudeness. The young—particularly those that are less cultured than they might have been—have the impression that there is a kind of manliness in being rude and blunt. There is not. It is a misfortune for a man to have rude manners, no matter where he is or who he is. A shipmaster on the sea, or a collier in the mine, is all the better if he has courteous manners—and he may have them. It lies with him to possess them. Social harshness has nothing in it that is beneficial. In all things, remember that true politeness, and the source of true good manners, is a Christian, generous sympathy.

AUGUST 4: EVENING.

Harden not your hearts, as in the provocation, in the day of temptation in the wilderness.—*Hebrews* iii., 8.

Blessed are they that have sorrow. Sad are they that are without it. He must be a very good man that has lived in this world and has not had any trouble. Steam-ships do not care whether the wind blows or not, because they have internal motive forces; but we are not steam-ships, and we need troubles as winds to bear us on. We make no voyages without troubles, unless we are very good indeed.

Blessed be God, then, that gives us sorrow upon sorrow, trouble upon trouble, stroke upon stroke. These things are so many knockings at the gate of heaven, saying, "Open, Lord." Let heaven's gate fly open when they fall on you. See to it that they take you to God. Never in sorrow be sorry for any thing which you have done that was right, and pure, and true. Never in sorrow say, "Oh that I had the leeks and onions of Egypt, and were not obliged to eat this food of the desert which I so much loathe." When God is taking you through the wilderness toward the promised land, never look back nor shrink. Bear your trouble, and say, "Strike, God, and strike again, and as often as needful; do any thing to me, and take every thing from me, but let me have thee, and life, and life eternal." Though troubled on every side, be not distressed; though cast down, know how not to be destroyed.

AUGUST 5: *MORNING.*

Brethren, if any of you do err from the truth, and one convert him; let him know, that he which converteth the sinner from the error of his way shall save a soul from death, and shall hide a multitude of sins.—*James* v., 19, 20.

Is there any thing worth living for more than such a mission? It is good for a man to write a book. A book will live, and shall have no sexton; but he himself will soon die and be laid away. A book is an invention by which men live after they are dead so far as this world is concerned. A hymn or song that deserves to live is lifted above persecution. The tyrant or despot can not touch it. But oh! neither book, nor hymn, nor song, nor any product of the human mind, is to be compared with the immortal life itself; and ye that save one soul, and lift it, by the power of your instrumentality, blessed of God, into the sphere of immortality and glory, shall shine as the stars in the firmament. Such achievements will be a source of more joy, when you stand in Zion and before God, than all the treasures of the world. For when death comes, not your ships, not your store-houses, not your piles of gold, not your reputation among your fellow-citizens, not even the joys of the future state, if you could rise and see them in the light of eternity, would you value in comparison with the satisfaction of having been permitted to save one soul.

Go forth to life, oh child of earth,
Still mindful of thy heavenly birth;
Thou art not here for ease or sin,
But manhood's noble crown to win.

Then forth to life, oh child of earth!
Be worthy of thy heavenly birth.
For noble service thou art here;
Thy brothers help, thy God revere.

AUGUST 5: *EVENING.*

I will not fail thee nor forsake thee.—*Joshua* i., 5.

If you are endeavoring for yourself, and against social entanglements, to rise to a true Christian life, remember that you need, and that you shall have the help of God. It is a lonely way that the repentant sinner walks, yet there are stars behind the clouds for him. It is a most solitary path that he who has done wrong, and means to do right, has to tread; but remember, as you tread it in all the pain of solitude, that if you could but see you would behold the form of another walking by your side. There is one that says to you in the hour of your discouragement, "I will never leave thee nor forsake thee." That faithful Chief, that loving Christ, that Shepherd who seeks the lost sheep, and, if they can not walk, bears them in his arms; he that redeemed your soul with his own precious blood, and seeks to lift you from a lower to a higher plane—from ignominy, dishonor, disgrace, and death, to the joy of his ownership—he will never leave you nor forsake you.

If God is calling you to-night, listen to him; if God is drawing you to him to-night, do not hold back. Oh, generous and loving nature, snared in the wrong, but now repenting toward the right, let nothing draw you back. It is life if you go forward, and death if you go back. The call will never come again as it has come. Forsake father, and mother, and brother, and sister; give up all friendship, and each pleasure, and every prospect. One single moment in the forefront of that all-rewarding heaven, where Christ, in the glory of his Father's kingdom, and God's angels shall meet you, will more than repay you for that which you suffer here.

AUGUST 6: MORNING.

And that every tongue should confess that Jesus Christ is Lord, to the glory of God the Father.—*Phil.* ii., 11.

THERE are many hearts that turn toward the Lord Jesus Christ with an enthusiasm of love, with a clasping of affection, with an entire allegiance, with a hope, a yearning, a desire, that carries with it every thing which their heart has to give; and they have been so educated that if you say to them, "Do you think he is divine?" they can not say that they believe him to be so; but their heart is making him divine all the time: and the loving worship of Jesus as divine is a true worship. By the heart, man believes unto salvation; and there is many a man who may err in his speculative ideas, but whose heart makes correction for all his mistakes, if it is really and truly, with all its power and enthusiasm, fixed on the Savior, and loves him.

Are not all your best feelings consciously excited in you by the thought of Christ, by the presence of Christ, and by the truth as it is in Christ? And although you see manifold inconsistencies and imperfections in yourself, and live far below your ideal, are you not conscious that about that name your best experiences, the very best things your soul knows, cluster every day? Then you need not be afraid to put the name on that Being. You need not be afraid to crown him. Your heart has crowned him already. You have made him your Chief, your Leader, your Guide. You have ascribed to him, not by thought, but by affection, every thing that constitutes allegiance to divinity. Your heart is worshiping him.

AUGUST 6: EVENING.

And he spake a parable unto them to this end, that men ought always to pray, and not to faint.—*Luke* xviii., 1.

MANY men seem to shrink from prayer as though it were a matter of doubt whether *they* could pray. They would pray, but they do not feel that they are worthy to. Who ever was? There never was a worthy prayer. Never did a man receive a gift of God that was deserved. Never was there a divine gift that was not a mercy. And yet men are held aloof from prayer by the false notion that God's mercies are hindered by their unworthiness, as though he had not declared himself to be one that gives beyond their asking and beyond their thought. He will not measure you and give you less than you expected. He does not determine from your character and desert what he shall give. He expressly declares that, and he tells us to act in the same manner. "He maketh his sun to rise on the evil and on the good, and sendeth rain on the just and on the unjust." These testify to his love. Alas! that he should need such witnesses as these. When men no longer witness for him, the clouds and the daily recurring sun are his witnesses.

God, then, does not limit himself by the desert of those to whom he gives mercies, but takes his patterns from the largeness and generosity of his own nature. He pleases himself by giving.

When the great organ sounds, it does not sound according to the size of your ear, but according to the size of its own pipes. Its harmony does not depend upon your ability to appreciate it, but upon the vastness and complexity of its own stops. So our God sits in heaven with infinite resources and power, and does, not according to our thought, but exceeding abundantly more than we can ask or think.

"God hath spoken once; twice have I heard this—that power belongeth unto God. Also unto thee, O Lord, belongeth mercy; for thou renderest to every man according to his work."

O Lord, how happy should we be
If we could cast our care on thee,
  If we from self could rest,
And feel at heart that one above,
In perfect wisdom, perfect love,
  Is working for the best:

Could we but kneel and cast our load,
E'en while we pray, upon our God,
  Then rise with lightened cheer,
Sure that the Father, who is nigh
To still the famished raven's cry,
  Will hear in that we fear.

AUGUST 7: MORNING.

But when ye pray, use not vain repetitions, as the heathen do.—*Matt.* vi., 7.

A MAN has been running without an observation for days and nights; he is whelmed in darkness; he fears he is going on to a dangerous shore, and he is in great distress. But by-and-by the wind shifts, and the clouds which have so long covered the heavens begin to break, and the man runs and gets his instrument, and a cloud lifts for a single instant, and out shines a familiar star, and he catches a glimpse of it, and down shuts the cloud again. "Ah!" he says, "shut, if you want to; I've got all I want." He has borrowed from the underlying sky, from the regular movements of the divine clock-work, what he needs for his reckoning, and it did not take him more than a minute. And he says, "Now I know just where we are." Was not that minute's work as good as if he had been an hour about it?

Now a man that prays, and that, praying, feels the heart of God—a man that prays, and that, praying, feels that his soul, like a quick bird that darts from the forest shade into the sunlight, is, by thought or feeling, lifted into the presence of God, into the influences of the eternal world, into the heavenly state, has got an impulse, and has obtained the desired object. Being sorry because one can not pray long, when a short prayer answers every purpose, is absurd. Prayer is not to be measured by the yard. It is a thing of quality, not a thing of quantity. That prayer which gives you the hope of God, and the love of God, and the aspiration of purity, and a heavenly spirit all day long, is the best prayer for you; and that prayer which is long and multitudinous, without giving you any such things, is no prayer at all.

AUGUST 7: EVENING.

And when they had platted a crown of thorns, they put it upon his head, and a reed in his right hand: and they bowed the knee before him, and mocked him, saying, Hail, King of the Jews!—*Matt.* xxvii., 29.

JESUS CHRIST was the greatest of all his contemporaries—King of the world, of time, and of eternity, because he was the crowned Sufferer. Other kings there were, but he was the greatest. Other crowns flashed splendor from stones beyond price, but no stone ever yet was to be valued with these spines of thorns for glorious beauty. What is a stone, a diamond, an emerald, an opal, but mere cold, physical beauty? But every thorn in that crown is a symbol of divine love. Every thorn stood in a drop of blood, as every sorrow stood deep in the heart of the Savior. And the great anguish, the shame, the indignity, the abandonment, the injustice, and that other unknown anguish which a God may feel, but a man may not understand—all these were accepted in gentleness, in quietness, without repelling, without protest, without exclamation, without surprise, without anger, without even regret. He was to teach the world a new life. He was to teach the heart a new ideal of character. He was to teach a new power in the administration of justice. A divine lesson was needed—that love is the essence of divinity; that love, suffering for another, is the highest form of love; that that love, when administered, carries with it every thing that there is of purity and justice; and not only that love is the fulfilling of the law, but that God himself is love.

The crown of thorns is the world's crown of redemption. The power of suffering love, which has already wrought such changes in the world, is to work on with nobler disclosures and in wider spheres; it is to teach men how to resist evil; how to overcome sin; how to raise the wicked and degraded; how to reform the race; how, in short, to create a new heaven and a new earth, in which is to dwell righteousness.

> Where, then, is glory to be found?
> Here, here, upon this shameful tree,
> Where heaven's King, a victim found,
> Is made a sacrifice for me.
> For love is highest excellence,
> The source of all the joys above;
> 'Tis stronger than omnipotence,
> And Jesus' richest crown is love.

AUGUST 8: MORNING.

He that dwelleth in love dwelleth in God.—1 *John* iv., 16.

A MAN by mere prayer does not come near heaven, by mere psalm-singing does not come near the throne of God, but by every single heart-beat of true love takes one broad wing-beat of flight toward God himself. And when he comes near to that state in which, morning, and noon, and night, he abides in the spirit of true love, he is not far from heaven and the throne of God.

How is it with you? Since you made a profession of religion, is your life more full of the fruits of love? Have you a more comprehensive benevolence toward all mankind? Every year do you less and less regard the service of loving men as a task, and do you more and more accept it with cheerfulness? Do you find that the currents of your thought and feeling are setting outward instead of inward? Are you beginning to learn that you are not to sweep the circuit of life, and draw its treasures in to you, to bless you and gratify you; but that, like Christ, you are, so far as in you lies, to disseminate blessings, forgetting your own comforts, and living for others in such a way that you shall have a special care for all with whom you have to do, whether parent or child, employer or employed, brother or sister, husband or wife, teacher or scholar, companion or friend? Are you more full of the sweetness of a true Christian love? In this direction you must measure, to know whether you are growing in grace and in the knowledge of our Lord and Savior Jesus Christ.

Prayer is the dew of faith,
  Its rain-drop, night and day,
That guards its vital power from death
  When cherished hopes decay,
And keeps it, 'mid this changeful scene,
A bright, perennial evergreen.

Good works, of faith the fruit,
  Should ripen year by year,
Of health and soundness at the root
  An evidence sincere;
Dear Savior, grant thy blessing free,
And make our faith no barren tree.

AUGUST 8: EVENING.

First the blade, then the ear, after that the full corn in the ear.—*Mark* iv., 28.

Christian experience is a growth, and when things grow they grow in their own order. Though you may accelerate growth, you can not anticipate the after products before the intermediate steps have been taken. Men desire to be like Paul in the culmination of his experiences, but they do not want to be like him in those detached steps by which he came to those experiences. Many men would like to know what the student knows, but they would not like to undergo the process of mental application that the student underwent in obtaining his knowledge. Many men want to be deep, but they do not want God to dig the well; they want to be strong, but do not want God to put them to those tasks that shall make them strong. God gives men the necessary material; he also puts them through the drill by which these things are wrought out. Do not forget that, though in God's house there are many things, yet there is an order that belongs to those things, and that order can not be changed.

AUGUST 9: *MORNING.*

Our sufficiency is of God.—2 *Cor.* iii., 5.

WHAT is more beautiful than the morning-glory in the morning, which, as if nature loved it, and decked it with her fairest jewels, is adorned on every line and lineament with exquisite pearls? When the sun glances on it, what leaf is more beautiful, what vine is more graceful, what blossom is finer in texture and form than those of this flower? But, ere ten o'clock has come, it has all collapsed, its pearls have exhaled, its form has shriveled up, and its glory has passed away.

What are our best productions of the mind but morning-glories, that, ere they are fashioned, are gone, and gone forever? We can build houses, and they will stand; but when we build structures of thought, of grace, of love, of purity, how fragile and transitory they are! How quickly are our highest virtues broken down and taken away!

Our comfort lies in this—that he who began a good work in us will continue it to the day of its perfectness in Christ Jesus. We derive satisfaction, not from any confidence which we have in ourselves, but from the confidence which we have that our God, who has loved us, and redeemed us by the blood of his only Son, having undertaken to educate us and perfect us, will complete the task.

AUGUST 9: *EVENING.*

For our light affliction, which is but for a moment, worketh for us a far more exceeding and eternal weight of glory.—2 *Cor.* iv., 17.

In distinction from the quick-made and quick-perishing glories of earth, the apostle speaks of the glory of the other life as one that is past all measuring, past all ordinary experience, and past all thought. It is exceeding and eternal. We rise into a normal condition in which we shall abide for evermore; in which every part of our nature shall be so high, so full, so perfect, that it shall make its impression of completeness in excellence and beauty upon every one that is present or that shall come near. God himself shall look on you and say, "How beautiful!" You that cower down, and shrink, and hide yourselves from the shining eye of God with a consciousness of imperfection, God shall yet take you, and look upon you; and his face shall light up with admiration, because you shall be so beautiful, so perfect, so illustrious in excellence. We are not wasting, we are not wearing, but we are going on and up toward a land where God means to glorify himself by our glory; and we are to stand there to illustrate to eternal ages the height, and depth, and length, and breadth of love, and wisdom, and eminent glory, by the admirableness of the glory to which we ourselves shall have attained.

AUGUST 10: *MORNING.*

Take, therefore, no thought for the morrow; for the morrow shall take thought for the things of itself. Sufficient unto the day is the evil thereof.—*Matt.* vi., 34.

To-morrow you have no business with. You steal if you touch to-morrow. It is God's. Every day has in it enough to keep every man occupied without concerning himself with the things which lie beyond.

When the pilot is steering on the Ohio River, he looks at the headlands miles beyond him, in order to know where he is; for he has been accustomed to judge of the twisting and tortuous channel by certain of these headlands. And so a man may take headlands far down in the future to steer by, in order that he may be better enabled to run his keel in the channel that he is now in. By foresight we enable ourselves to get along better to-day, and by so much we have a right to look into the future. But all the foresight of a given day is only to be such as shall better fit us for the duties of that day. And when a man has got through with the waking hours of any single day, he has got through with his duty up to that point of time. Duties will begin again to-morrow, but all duties lapse and end with each sphere of active time given to man. You have enough work to occupy all your time to-day. Blessed be the man whose work drives him. Something must drive men; if it is wholesome industry, they have no time for a thousand torments and temptations which they would otherwise have. Let him be thankful who has, every day, enough legitimate work to keep him busy.

AUGUST 10: *EVENING.*

Repent ye, therefore, and be converted, that your sins may be blotted out.—*Acts* iii., 19.

MANY persons think they are not Christians because they can not say that they have had any overmastering conviction of sin. Have you ever had such a conviction of sin as led you to be discontented with your daily life? Have you ever experienced so much dissatisfaction with yourself that you felt that your life must be reformed? Have you ever had such a sense of sin that you felt that God must help you, and that it was a case which was beyond mere human power? Have you ever had such a sense of sin that you felt, "If I might, I would begin to-day to live a different life?" Have you ever had such a sense of sin that you made it a part of your daily business to correct the faults and to resist the temptations to which you were subject? Have you ever had such a sense of sin that it seemed hateful to you to do wrong, even when you were doing it—more hateful than at any other time? Have you ever had such a sense of the repellency of sin that you earnestly longed to live a pure, noble, Christian, devout, devoted life? Have you ever had those impulses? Why have you not obeyed them, then? You are like a child that wants to read a book, but will not learn his letters because he does not want to touch a book till he can read it all. You must learn your letters before you can read.

AUGUST 11: *MORNING.*

So then every one of us shall give account of himself to God.—*Romans* xiv., 12.

WHAT this account is, and under what circumstances it will be given, we know not. It is not the way of revelation to teach details. We are so unspiritualized that we could not understand them. The fact is merely stated, and left. When the great day of reckoning comes, then for all we have received; for each talent that has been given us; for every faculty of our being; for each opportunity that we have enjoyed; for all that, being offered us, we have taken and improved to our good, or rejected with harm to ourselves; for the influences that we have set in motion; for the influences that have been exerted upon us; for the formation of our character; for our habits; for every thing that has contributed to make us rational and responsible beings—for all these things we are to give account to God.

What should be the effect of such a truth as this? Will you not make it a monitor to dwell in your conscience? When you are perplexed and influenced by conflicting motives, will you not let it come to lead you in the right way, by whispering in your soul, "Thou, God, seest me, and I shall give account of myself to thee?" How many struggles would have come to a happy issue if this great, this awful truth had been brought to bear upon your thoughts and feelings.

AUGUST 11: *EVENING.*

And they shall call his name Emmanuel, which being interpreted is, God with us.—*Matt.* i., 23.

THERE is nothing like the consciousness of Immanuel for men

that are fighting the battle of life. Give me, of all mottoes, "Immanuel—God with us." Oh that I might write it on my child's cradle, "Immanuel—God with us." Oh that I might write it over the threshold of my child's entrance into wedded life, "Immanuel—God with us." Oh that I might write upon all the garments that my child wears the same motto, "Immanuel—God with us." Oh that I might write it on every single book and task, "God with us." Oh that it might be inscribed on every fear and sorrow, "God with us." I would see gleaming in the first light of the morning those words, "God with us." At evening, when the sun goes in glory to his rest, I would have borne back to my eyes upon its last rays the same words, "God with us." And in the silence of the night I would still have running through my mind the thought of "God with us." Always and every where I would have for my motto, "Immanuel! Immanuel! Immanuel!" If God be for us, who can be against us? What power, what joy, what inspiration to nobleness comes with this consideration when it has become familiarized and domiciled!

Sweeter sounds than music knows
  Charm me in Immanuel's name;
All her hopes my spirit owes
  To his birth, and cross, and shame.

When he came the angels sung,
  "Glory be to God on high!"
Lord, unloose my stammering tongue;
  Who should louder sing than I?"

AUGUST 12: *MORNING.*

For we are members one of another.—*Eph.* iv., 25.

In Christ we are a family. All men who love Christ belong to that family. They may not mean it; they may not know it; they may not belong to any Christian organization, yet they belong to that family. Outward organizations may be necessary for educational purposes, but not for spiritual union. The moment a man's heart touches the heart of Christ in living faith, he becomes, whether he knows it or not, the brother of every other in heaven or on earth who has come into the same relationship with Christ. Whoever is united to Christ is brother or sister to every body else who is united to him. But, above all, we are of one father; we take of his nature; we are the objects of his love; we are redeemed by his sacrifices, by his death. God's union with men is not a shadow, is not a figure, is not a dream; it is the statement of a fact as literal as any law in nature. The union of sunlight with vegetables is not more real than the interfusion and union of God's soul with the soul of men.

AUGUST 12: *EVENING.*

The kingdom of heaven is like to a grain of mustard seed, which a man took and sowed in his field: which, indeed, is the least of all seeds, but when it is grown is the greatest among herbs.—*Matt.* xiii., 31, 32.

When a man begins to be a Christian, he is like a seed that has just come up with two small, tender leaves. If you plant the seed of an apple, it does not come up a tree covered with fruit. You never saw an orchard, each tree of which, when it first came up, did not consist of two baby leaves. From these small beginnings came in after years the orchard. A Christian does not come up a full-grown Christian. He comes up with but two leaves at most, and sometimes with only one. The kingdom of God in man at first is so small that it is like a grain of mustard seed, the smallest of all seeds. But the moment a man has had the first feelings consequent upon conversion, the moment he has begun to say, "I accept God's will as the rule of my life, and I intend to live according to the counsels of Christ," that moment he is a Christian. But he has only begun. A new birth is not a new life, but only the beginning of it. There is yet a great deal to do in the man, in his family, in business, in his relations to society. He must enter upon the work of settling all his affairs according to a new law—the law of love.

Sower divine,
Sow the good seed in me,
Seed for eternity.
'Tis a rough, barren soil,
Yet, by thy care and toil,
Make it a fruitful field,
A hundred fold to yield.
Sower divine
Sow deep this heart of mine.

AUGUST 13: *MORNING.*

And he said unto another, Follow me. But he said, Lord, suffer me first to go and bury my father. Jesus said unto him, Let the dead bury their dead; but go thou and preach the kingdom of God.—*Luke* ix., 59, 60.

WHEN Christ was on earth, a great many persons that came to him were going to be his disciples after a preparation. One says, "I will follow thee, but suffer me first—" "Stop!" says the Savior; "I do not want you unless you will follow me at once." These suffer-me-first folk are not the ones to follow Christ. If you have any secular preparation to make, you are not the one to follow Christ. When he was on earth, and people came to him, what he demanded of them was this: "Follow me now." And that is what he demands of every person to-day. If any say, "Lord, we do not understand the doctrine yet," he says, "Then follow me for that reason, and I will teach you." "Lord, we do not feel that our hearts are sufficiently subdued." "Follow me, and they will become subdued." "But, Lord, we do not know that we shall hold out." "You certainly will not if you do not begin; follow me just as you are." You must either follow Christ or go away from him. You must either accept him or renounce him. If you are conscious of being sinful, and have a burdened conscience and a heavy heart, and need consolation and salvation, I beseech you to follow Christ unhesitatingly, unquestioningly; and he will reveal, hour by hour and day by day, what your duty is, and all that is needful for you to know.

AUGUST 13: *EVENING.*

For we are made partakers of Christ, if we hold the beginning of our confidence steadfast unto the end.—*Heb.* iii., 14.

I KNOW churches that would shiver if I were to go into their lecture-room, and were to say, "If a man is united to the Lord Jesus Christ by faith, and is his disciple, it is not only his privilege and right, but it is his *duty* to know it." They would say that it was a most audacious assumption for a man to even think that he was in Christ. Ministers of the Gospel often teach people that it is a fatal thing to cherish such a belief, and attempt to keep them in a state of uncertainty under the false impression that such uncertainty is beneficial. But I do not believe in uncertainty. It is not a thing that is recommended in the Bible. Hope, confidence, positiveness, is characteristic of a true Christian, as set forth in the word of God. The undying conviction that Christ loves you and that you love him; the allegiance of the whole soul to the banner of the Lord and Savior, and the knowing that you are fighting under it—this I believe to be indispensable to any great growth in grace. And as to uncertainty in these matters being a benefit, it is no more a benefit than it is to be ignorant as to which side you are on in any other great question of moral and spiritual truth. It is a positive damage.

A great many men *may* be Christians, and yet be in great doubt about their experimental evidences; but a man *ought not* to be in doubt, and does not *need* to be in doubt on this subject. The nature of Christian experience, the nature of the truth, and the disclosures of God in men's conversion and sanctification, do not require that they should be in any uncertainty in the matter.

AUGUST 14: *MORNING.*

Set your affection on things above, not on things on the earth.—*Col.* iii., 2.

HEAVEN answers with us the same purpose that the tuning-fork does with the musician. Our affections, the whole orchestra of them, are apt to get below the concert-pitch, and we take heaven to tune our hearts by. In this way, instead of making the heavenly state a romance-ground, we are every day framing it by the imagination, and ascribing to it all our higher, and nobler, and finer ideals, and then taking this state and bringing it down to measure our daily life by. And so, instead of taking us away from the duties of life, it brings us back to them with renewed strength, with better moral discriminations, with more patience, more gentleness, and more hope. We thus set our affections on heaven without taking them away from the world.

A man deposits in the bank a thousand dollars, and draws on it, and keeps depositing, and keeps drawing. And we deposit what we are in heaven, and then draw on that. We first invest our whole life, and then take back from it for use here, and then lay back what we take; and thus, repeatedly using it on earth, and remitting it again to heaven, we maintain a kind of heavenly temper while performing our earthly labor.

AUGUST 14: *EVENING.*

For I know whom I have believed, and am persuaded that he is able to keep that which I have committed unto him against that day.—2 *Tim.* i., 12.

If I were starting from Europe, and a friend should come to me and say, "My only child, my daughter, is going to America, and she is all alone on the ship—will you take charge of her during the voyage?" I should be sensibly touched by his confidence. And, aside from my attachment to the child (if I had known her and loved her) and my regard for her parents, do you suppose I would suffer my oversight of her to intermit, though I might be in need of rest and sleep, and though I might be sick and require attention myself? Would I not, night and day, carry that charge on my mind, to see that her wants were all supplied, and that no accident befell her? And could I live if, by any fault of mine, she walked too near the perilous edge, and fell overboard, and was whelmed in the tide and lost? How could I ever look my friend in the face again?

Now, when God has put his children in the arms of the Lord Jesus Christ, that he may carry them across this perilous voyage of life, and land them safe in heaven, and when Christ has promised to present them pure and spotless before the throne, do you suppose he, under whose feet is all power, will fail to fulfill his promise, and to perform what he has undertaken? If there were nothing but ourselves, we might fear; but as long as we have the amplitude, the fidelity, the tenderness, and the love of Christ, we have that which is more than a match for all our sin. Doubt yourself as much as you will, but do not doubt Christ.

AUGUST 15: *MORNING.*

For ye know the grace of our Lord Jesus Christ, that, though he was rich, yet for your sakes he became poor, that ye through his poverty might be rich. —2 *Cor.* viii., 9.

There are some men who complain of their condition in this world. They do not know why other men should have been born so much better off than they were. You will hear them say that they were born under circumstances of great deprivation, that their early advantages were extremely few, that their parentage was very humble, and that they had no such start in life as other men have; and, if they do not find fault with Providence, they certainly come very near to doing so, in their spirit and disposition. But is there any reason why you should have been born under better circumstances than your Master was? He had no father. His mother, without a city, without a house, with only a stable for her shelter, was almost an absolute outcast. From that low point he began his life. Was there ever a man that was born lower than our Savior was born? It pleased him, the Prince, the Crown of Glory in heaven, to humble himself, and take upon himself the form of a servant; and, being found in fashion as a man, he humbled himself unto death, even the ignominious death of the cross.

A great many men, whatever may have been their experience in life, are accustomed to complain of the usage they have received in the world. They fill the ears of those who have the misfortune to be their friends with lamentations respecting their own troubles. But is there any man whose lot will at all compare with the lot which the Lord Jesus Christ endured when on earth? Can any man measure his experience in life by the experience which the Savior had in this world, and say, "I am worse off than my Redeemer was?" Are you more of a man of sorrow than he was? Are you better acquainted with grief than he was?

AUGUST 15: *EVENING.*

Who, for the joy that was set before him, endured the cross, despising the shame.—*Heb.* xii., 2.

I know that Christ is predicted as a man of sorrows, and acquainted with grief; yet it is the very wonder and mystery of his being that, through every sorrow, his heart sent such a flame of love and joy that affliction became the fuel of gladness. Do we not know that there are, in our own houses, children who, for their father's sake, will bear suffering and not shed a tear? and are they more than Christ? Are there not parents and companions that will carry troubles vehement for the sake of those round about them, and make them so luminous that none shall see them? And is it not woman's peculiar office to walk a martyr, and yet wear a face of joy, and hope, and radiancy, so much does her affection overcome and quite subdue material suffering and lower forms of disappointment? How many men carry a world of trouble for the sake of their country and their fellow-men, and yet stand prophets of peace and joy themselves! How many confessors and martyrs have borne inexpressible torments for the sake of truth, singing while the flame itself was scorching their flesh, their soul beating down the nerve and overcoming the body, and making them triumphant over physical and mental suffering by the power of higher feelings, which quite adumbrated and put out the lower ones! And must we conceive of Christ as one who crouched under suffering? Was he the only one that did not know how to make clouds carry colors? Was he one who bore suffering with weakness? Was he one that was overcome and cast down by suffering? No; the glory of Christ was this, that he accepted his mission with such cheerfulness, and gladness, and enthusiasm; that he did the will of God with such alacrity; that, though he was pre-eminently and above all that ever lived a man of suffering, yet he counted it a joy to suffer—that he was an overmastering sufferer.

AUGUST 16: *MORNING.*

Or despisest thou the riches of his goodness, and forbearance, and long-suffering; not knowing that the goodness of God leadeth thee to repentance?—*Rom.* ii., 4.

HAS your thankfulness to God been in any proportion to benefits received? Has thankfulness accompanied every day's benefaction, and measured the mercies that you have received? Has it ever been a common experience—thankfulness, lively and quick? Has it acted to promote obedience, to make you sensitive to God's feelings and wishes? The child of unnumbered kindnesses, the object of unnumbered mercies, covered all over with memorials of God's tender thought and kind consideration, have the mercies of God, that have been from the heavens poured out copious as the light; that have streamed through all the avenues of life abundant as the floods of the ocean—these mercies of God, that have watched you from youth up to this hour, that have poured abundant every day through all the channels of your life—have they ever brought forth in you a profound sense of recognition? Have they ever made you yearn to requite God for his goodness, and led you to consider the obedience and the honor which are due to him from you?

Oh wonderful, oh passing thought,
 The love that God hath had for thee,
Spending on thee no less a sum
 Than the undivided Trinity.

Father, and Son, and Holy Ghost,
 Exhausted for a thing like this;
The world's whole government disposed
 For one ungrateful creature's bliss!

What hast thou done for God, my soul?
 Look o'er thy misspent years and see;
Cry from thy worse than nothingness,
 Cry for his mercy upon thee.

AUGUST 16: *EVENING.*

O thou afflicted, tossed with tempest, and not comforted, behold, I will lay thy stones with fair colors, and lay thy foundations with sapphires. And I will make thy windows of agates, and thy gates of carbuncles, and all thy borders of pleasant stones.—*Isaiah* liv., 11, 12.

If you have built your character on truth, justice, purity, and piety, you need not be afraid. Give yourself liberty. Do not ponder nor turn back. Do not fritter away your life by those unprofitable introversions and analytical processes of mind by which you attempt to detect the nature of your thoughts and feelings. Be sure of one thing—that a round, robust, moral manhood is safe. Trust it. Give it power. Let it run. No man that is doing wickedly ought to be other than anxious;

but any man that is conscious that he has a judgment that is directed toward virtue, and piety, and God, and the welfare of his fellow-men, need not be watching himself. The only man that is free, the only man that may do what he wants to, is the man who wants to do only what is good. He stands strong. He is full of joy now, and is full of anticipations of joy in days to come, and of certainties of joy when the sun and moon shall have passed away.

Blessed are they that have trusted in the Lord. They shall stand firmer than the mountains. Far above the disturbing influences that annoy the feeble, the weak, the guilty, and the fear-driven, they bathe their head in the upper sky. On them rest earliest, and latest, and longest the benignest rays of the sun. Afar off they are seen in all colors and all forms of beauty. They shall be as Mount Zion, which God loveth.

AUGUST 17: *MORNING.*

Stand fast, therefore, in the liberty wherewith Christ hath made us free, and be not entangled again with the yoke of bondage.—*Gal.* v., 1.

THE ways of religion are ways of pleasantness. They are not grievous. You are called to come out into the clear air of perfect freedom and unspeakable delight, that you may be—what? Servants of Jesus Christ? No; not servants any more, but friends; and not friends only, but sons; and not sons only, but heirs—"heirs of God and joint heirs with Christ." The fuller, the freer, the stronger, the richer your manhood is, the more you glorify God. And if, at last, when you come up to the judgment seat, you stand condemned, remember there can be no such excuse rendered there as "I would have been a Christian, but it seemed a hard service—a bondage." It is not a hard service, and there is no bondage in it. Ah! it will be the condemnation of that hour, that God's service was liberty, that God's way was easy. His yoke is easy and his burden is light. If the worst thing, the very symbol of bondage and burden, is turned to joy, what will be the higher experiences?

AUGUST 17: EVENING.

And it came to pass that the beggar died, and was carried by the angels into Abraham's bosom; the rich man also died and was buried.—*Luke* xvi., 22.

THE one dwelt in magnitude of earthly fame. He touched the springs of material power. His life was full of praise and glory, but they were of a lower kind. And when he died out of his earthly estate, he rose into that land where they do not take copper for gold, nor lead for silver. There he is nothing, although he was every thing here.

And that man whom he disdained to look at; that man whom he despised; that man who thought much, and loved to do good, but who was poor and of no repute, is every thing there. There went up heavenward a radiant procession, amidst an outburst of song, heralding the approach of some bold conqueror, crownless and sceptreless. It was the resurrected spirit of this servant of God. He lived at the bottom here, but there he lives in eternal fame.

Thou that art doing noble things and asking no praise; thou that art living to do good because it is sweet to do good, and be like Christ, and bear his cross, and walk with him in sorrow, go up; thy Christ waits for thee. And come down, thou hoary head of power, that on earth art despoiling God's fair creation as food for thy lowest appetites, and living in selfishness for thyself alone; there is no road between thee and God that does not break short on the gulf between earth and heaven. The last shall be first, and the first shall be last.

AUGUST 18: MORNING.

Thou therefore endure hardness as a good soldier of Jesus Christ.—*2 Timothy* ii., 3.

IT has pleased God to call his disciples soldiers, and we are of the army of the Lord Jesus Christ. Is there any thing very brave or very good in being filled with Christian sentiments and emotions in days of tranquillity and peace? When God's people come under fire, that, after all, is the time to test them. Any body can run down hill, but it is not every body that can take a load and walk up hill. Any body can be satisfied when he has his own way, but it is not every body that knows how to give up his way to God's will. Any body can trust God when he has in his hands every thing that he wants, and more; but it is not every body who, when God is taking out of his hands continually, can still say, "Though he slay me, yet will I trust in him." When God builds up your way, of course you can walk on it; but when he tears up your foundations, and puts you in a rugged path, where at every step you are liable to stumble, if then you can walk, blessed are ye.

AUGUST 18: *EVENING.*

Wherefore henceforth know we no man after the flesh; yea, though we have known Christ after the flesh, yet now henceforth know we him no more. —2 *Cor.* v., 16.

HAVE you ever stood in Dresden to watch that matchless picture of Raphael's *Madonna di San Sisto?* Engravings of it are all through the world, but no engraving has ever reproduced the mother's face. The infant Christ that she holds is far more nearly represented than the mother. In her face there is a mist. It is wonder, love, adoration, awe—all these mingled, as if she held in her hands her babe, and yet it was God.

That picture does not mean to me what it does to the Roman Church; but it is full of meaning to me, because I believe that every mother should love the God that is in her child, and that every mother's heart should be watching to discern and see that in the child which is more than flesh and blood—something that takes hold of immortality and glory. And as our children grow up around us, we are to seek in them, and perpetually, not that which is like the flesh in us, not that which affiliates them and us to this earthly mechanical condition, but that which is of God, that which is to live after the body dies; and we should strive to lift up our heart's affections into that higher sphere, so that, whatever we love, we shall have put it above blast and above frost—so that we shall have put it where death itself can only glorify it, can never destroy it. An unsanctified affection is always an imperfect one.

AUGUST 19: *MORNING.*

The Lord is very pitiful, and of tender mercy.—*James* v., 11.

God is not indifferent to the task and tax which one undertakes when, with so many obstacles to contend against, he endeavors to live a life of obedience. God looks upon it as a thing most difficult. He knows it is a thing hard in itself; he knows, too, that the majority of men are weak, so that it is extremely difficult for them to do right things and avoid wrong things. God does not stand like a burning furnace of rage and wrath to consume a sinner because he sins. He pities the sinner. He sympathizes with the poor and the feeble. He is indeed more lenient toward the sinner than toward any other creature in the universe. Though he sees that his sin is sin; though he sees how devastating its tendencies are; though he sees how full it is of pain, how it may go on breeding pain forever and forever; though he has all knowledge of what is the exceeding sinfulness of sin, there is no being that looks upon it with more pity, more compassion, more sympathetic helpfulness than God.

AUGUST 19: *EVENING.*

Behold, the rod of Aaron for the house of Levi was budded, and brought forth buds, and bloomed blossoms, and yielded almonds.—*Numb.* xvii., 8.

God gives every body, I think, a cross when he enters upon a Christian life. When it comes into his hands, what is it? It is the rude oak, four-square, full of splinters and slivers, and rudely tacked together. And, after forty years, I see some men carrying their cross just as rude as it was at first. Others, I perceive, begin to wind around about it faith, and hope, and patience, and after a time, like Aaron's rod, it blossoms all over; and at last their cross has been so covered with holy affections that it does not seem any more to be a cross. They carry it so easily, and are so much more strengthened than burdened by it, that men almost forget that it is a cross by the triumph with which they carry it. Carry *your* cross in such a way that there shall be victory in it; and let every tear, as it drops from your eye, glance also, as the light strikes through it, with the consolations of the Holy Ghost.

Through the cross comes the crown; when the cares of this life,
Like giants in strength, may to crush thee combine,
Never mind, never mind; after sorrow's sad strife
Shall the peace and the crown of salvation be thine.

AUGUST 20: MORNING.

Who art thou that judgest another man's servant? to his own master he standeth or falleth.—*Rom.* xiv., 4.

EACH of us must appear before the judgment seat of God, and give an account of himself. Every man has a right, therefore, to demand liberty of conscience and judgment. Let each, then, respect the liberty of the conscience and judgment of every other. Men may seem bad because they do not think as you do, and yet they may be better than you on that account. They may be worse than you, but that is their business and their Maker's. Your business is to take care of yourself. We are not to be indifferent to other men's thoughts and feelings, but we are to exercise no authority over their judgments, and to pronounce no condemnation against them because they follow their own consciences. To their own Master they stand or fall. We all stand in our own individuality. Let us help and not hinder each other. Indulge in prejudices, bitterness, and railing toward none. Let this doctrine have that benign influence which it was designed to have in the teachings of God's Word, holding us more strictly to duty, more tolerant toward others, and exacting only toward ourselves.

How camest thou on the judgment seat,
Sweet heart? Who set thee there?
'Tis a lonely and lofty seat for thee,
And well might fill thee with care.

Ah! the judgment seat was not for thee,
The servants were not thine,
And the eyes which adjudge the praise and the blame
See farther than thine or mine.

AUGUST 20: EVENING.

Pray one for another.—*James* v., 16.

WHEN your brother offends or does wrong, pray for him. Do not report his fault. Rejoice not in iniquity. If we prayed more we should blame less; we should be far more tolerant; we should not suspect so much; we should not carry stories so much; we should not do wrong so much.

There is nothing that makes a man so charitable as that which he himself has suffered. Do you see men who have great faults of temper, and who are almost intolerable? If you have had faults of temper, you ought to know how to bear with these men. If there is any thing that you do not like in your neighbor, look and see if you have not the same thing in yourself in some form or other. Is there something that makes the company of a certain person distasteful to you? See if the same thing, in some mode of development, has not found a place in you. Look into your hearts, and learn to be charitable toward those who sin. It may be that you sin in the sight of God a hundred times more than those whom you blame. Often, when we are blaming men, our blame is more sinful before God than their transgression.

By confessing our faults one to another, and praying for one another, we learn humility on the one side, and on the other side that large charity which covers transgression and hides a multitude of sins.

AUGUST 21: MORNING.

The great day of the Lord is near: it is near and hasteth greatly, even the voice of the day of the Lord.—*Zeph.* i., 14.

We are moving away, and faster as every cord is loosed that binds us to earth, faster as every heart that we loved draws us upward. Let us rejoice. And as in autumn the very earth prepares for death, as if it were its bridal, and all the sober colors of the summer take higher hues, and trees, and shrubs, and vines go forth to their rest wearing their most gorgeous apparel, as ending their career more brightly than they began it, so let our spirits cast off sombre thoughts and sable melancholy, and clothe themselves with all the radiancy of faith, with every hue of heavenly joy.

"Blessed are the dead which die in the Lord."

AUGUST 21: *EVENING.*

Whose are the fathers, and of whom as concerning the flesh Christ came, who is over all, God blessed forever. Amen.—*Rom.* ix., 5.

In heaven are our parents, revered and beloved; there our earthly companions; there our brothers and sisters, who went away before we could go, having finished their tasks and been called thither; there those children whom with frowns of grief we forbade to Christ when they heard his voice saying "Come unto me." Mightier was their love and his than ours; and, though it broke our hearts, they went, and we live to give thanks, and we visit them again in faith, and behold their royalty, and feel that we are not worthy now to touch their shoe's latchet. There are many who wrought with us early, and bore the burden and heat of the day, and did not despise the day of small things. They rest from their labors; their works do follow them, and they are to-day blessed.

Yet, when we look through all those who are martyrs, and confessors, and apostles, and holy ministers, and saints, and our children, and those who are dear to us as our own soul, still, rising above them all, and nobler, and drawing us with stronger love, stands the Pierced One, saying to us from out the heavens, "Peace be unto you"—still to our eye reaching out the hands that were wounded for us, but are mighty against all wounds. Thou, Jesus, art our soul's joy and delight. Whom have we in heaven but thee? There is none upon earth that we desire beside thee.

Thou art my all—to thee I flee;
  Take me, oh take me to thy keeping;
Make me thy vine, thy husbandry;
  Be thine the seed-time, thine the reaping.

Oh, there is naught in yon bright sky
  Worthy this worthless heart to own;
On earth there's naught; friends, creatures fly;
  I pant, my God, for thee alone.

AUGUST 22: *MORNING.*

Let every man abide in the same calling wherein he was called.—1 *Cor.* vii., 20.

Commercial sagacity, creative industry, financial ability—

these are only so many ways by which one may bring his gifts to bear upon the great ends of life, and serve God. Some men, who are capable mechanics, capable artists, capable business men, wish to do good, and they say, "Do you not think I had better preach?" I think you had. Every man ought to preach. If you are a banker, behind the counter is your pulpit, and you can preach sermons there which no man in any other situation can. By practicing Christian integrity in a business where others take permissions of selfishness, you can preach more effectually than in any other way. The Pentecostal day was marvelous because every man heard the language in which he was born, and understood it perfectly. When you do a scrupulously honorable thing, where you could do the other thing without blame of men, and do it in such a way that men know you are acting from principle, you preach in a language that money-brokers can understand better than any other in the world. I might preach the doctrine of Christ to them week in and week out, and not come so near to their conscience as you could by one honest act done from the force of Christian principle, where you might have done the other thing with impunity. So you had better stay and preach the Gospel where your business is.

AUGUST 22: EVENING.

I have sworn by myself, the word is gone out of my mouth in righteousness, and shall not return, that unto me every knee shall bow, every tongue shall swear.—*Isa.* xlv., 23.

When men make a chain, they make the links separately, and join the second to the first, the third to the second, and so on till the chain is completed.

We are links of that chain which God is making. Here is a man who undertakes a good work in this world, and carries it forward a certain distance, and then dies. But that work does not stop. Another man takes it up where he left it, and carries it forward still farther, and then he dies; and so this one, and that one, and others who follow them, are links of an endless chain that shall reach to the very heaven. One set of men, not knowing what they do, bring down the work of God's kingdom to a given point, others bring it down still farther, and it goes on, stretching out and stretching out, until it is consummated. We are to rest upon the fact that God is carrying on his work in this world; that he never forgets that work; that it is ever going forward, though we may not see it advance, and even though it may seem to be receding. Christ's kingdom goes forward from age to age, though we may not discern the steps by which it is going forward. God's Word abides, and it predicts that the time shall come when the knowledge of the Lord shall fill the earth as the waters fill the sea; and that time is coming.

AUGUST 23: *MORNING.*

Beloved, let us love one another, for love is of God; and every one that loveth is born of God, and knoweth God. He that loveth nct, knoweth not God; for God is love.—1 *John* iv., 7, 8.

LOVE is the river of life in this world. Think not that ye know it who stand at the little tinkling rill—the first small fountain. Not until you have gone through the rocky gorges, and not lost the stream; not until you have stood at the mountain passes of trouble and conflict; not until you have gone through the meadow, and the stream has widened and deepened until fleets could ride on its bosom; not until, beyond the meadow, you have come to the unfathomable ocean, and poured your treasures into its depths—not until then can you know what love is. When two souls come together, each seeking to magnify the other; each, in a subordinate sense, worshiping the other; each helping the other; the two flying together so that each wing-beat of the one helps each wing-beat of the other—when two souls come together thus, they are lovers. They who unitedly move themselves away from grossness and from earth, toward the throne crystalline and the pavement golden, are indeed true lovers.

Father and mother, do you love each other so? Brother and sister, have you Christian love? Newly come and newly found, is this your ideal of love? Is it some faint, hazy, but beauteous dream? Is it some romance of imagined excellence? True love carries self-denial, labor-pain for another. True love pivots on honor and respect—both self-respect and respect for another.

True love thinks; true love feels; true love strives; true love pleases; true love improves; true love creates in the soul of the one loved a higher life. And so, beginning in this world, and loving little and low, men rise up through intermediate stages until they touch the higher flights. Old age often sees the flame burned out, but the coals that remain are warmer than all the flames were. There is no loving like that which experience has taught, when that experience is ministered by the instruction, and wisdom, and purification of the Holy Ghost.

Gracious Love, why art thou hidden so on earth,
That scarce a heart now knows the truth of thy exalted birth?
In God himself there lies thy spring,
Whence in grace dost flow
To make all creatures, every thing,
Work man's true good below.

Loveliest love, why art thou now so all-concealed,
We can not taste thy sweetness, nor see thy power revealed?
Yet thou the bitter world canst fill
With honey sweet and pure;
The sorest pain thy touch can still,
The heaviest sorrow cure.

AUGUST 23: *EVENING.*

Strive to enter in at the strait gate.—*Luke* xiii., 24.

If there ever was a mild and calm teacher, it was Christ; and yet, when one asked him, "Are there few that be saved?" he said, "Strive to enter in at the strait gate; for many, I say unto you, will seek to enter in, and shall not be able." The gate was built for entering; it was designed expressly for that purpose; and God desires that men shall enter, and has made arrangements for all to enter, and yet he saw reasons that led him to say calmly and affectionately, but plainly, "Strive—*agonize* to enter in." One word from the lips of Christ should be more potent than all the reasonings of philosophy; and seeing danger, he declared that the circumstances in which men lived were such that we should agonize—that is to say, put forth every effort to enter eternal life. When Christ speaks thus, I know there is peril about; that there is danger which may well demand our attention, and call forth our utmost skill and exertion. No man is in so much danger as he who thinks there is no danger.

AUGUST 24: MORNING.

They that be whole need not a physician, but they that are sick.—*Matthew* ix., 12.

THE moment that any one loses sympathy with a fellow-man, that moment he has fallen from the grace of the Lord Jesus Christ. The fact that a man is a gambler does not take him from the category of my brethren. Has he not a soul? Is there not coming to him a dying hour? Is not that very man who is hardened in transgression a child whom the mother consecrated in her prayers, and are there not mercies waiting for him in heaven? Who am I, then, that I should set him aside from human sympathy because he is wicked? It is true I deem it my duty to labor with him and show him the truth, but it should be done, not in hatred, but in love. Is there a man that reels in drunkenness who is so bad that you can say, "I can not afford to associate with that man?" And yet it was to such an one that Christ came with such ineffable care, and tenderness, and kindness, that since his day it has been for his followers to understand that there is no man so low that a person with Christ's love in his heart can not go down to him. In some respects, as men grow worse, our sympathy for them should grow stronger. To whom does the doctor run but to those who are desperately sick? Slight sicknesses may suffer delay, but dangerous ones must have speed and quick remedy.

AUGUST 24: EVENING.

Where is he that is born King of the Jews? for we have seen his star in the east, and are come to worship him.—*Matt.* ii., 2.

DID you ever reflect that there is not, in the whole New Testament, one caution or guard against our overtrusting and over exalting Christ? If I may put my being on him; if I may feel that he has suffered for my sins, that he has borne my sorrows, and that my life is grafted into him; and if I may pour out every thing in me of thought, and zeal, and worship toward him, then blessed be God for him; but if it is wicked for me to do these things, then I can not thank God for him. God should not have added to the misery of our condition by giving us such a being, and then making it wicked for us to worship him.

But I am not afraid to worship Christ. I will trust myself to worship him. I will trust those dearest to me to worship him. In the arms of Christ's love nothing shall hurt you. Love on, trust on, worship on. Let go your most ardent devotions toward him. There is no divine jealousy. The anxieties that afflict the sons of earth in their ideas of God never exist in heaven. Christ is the soul's bread—eat ye that hunger. He is the water of life—drink ye that thirst. He is the soul's end—live for him. He is the soul's supreme glory—yield to every outgush of joy and enthusiasm of worship that springs up in your heart toward him. Those that are in heaven bow down before him, and ascribe blessing, and honor, and glory, and power to him that sitteth upon the throne, and to the Lamb, forever and ever. Let us not, then, fear to worship.

O Jesus, King unspeakable!
Victor, whose triumph none can tell,
Whose goodness is ineffable—
    Alone to be desired—

The heavenly choirs thy name, Lord, greet,
And evermore thy praise repeat;
Thou fillest heaven with joy complete,
    Making our peace with God.

We follow thee with praises there,
With hymn, and vow, and suppliant prayer;
In thy celestial home to share,
    Grant us, O Lord, with thee.

AUGUST 25: MORNING.

The pillar of the cloud departed not from them by day, to lead them in the way; neither the pillar of fire by night, to show them light, and the way wherein they should go.—*Neh.* ix., 19.

God in Christ Jesus comes down to this world, and says, "You are all in mortal conflict. You have all sinned, and are sinning. You do not know the way by which you can get back. But I have found it." What is the way? "*I*, your loving God—*I*, your atoning Savior, am the way. Love me, and let me walk with you all the time, and I will see that you have a perpetual consciousness of such a power as will give victory to the soul." That is the philosophy of salvation through the Lord Jesus Christ—a great soul come down to take care of little souls; a great heart beating its warm blood into our little pinched hearts, that do not know how to get blood enough for themselves; a great nature, with the experience of ages, and with the infinite love of the effulging God, that comes down and says to every poor creature, "My arms are open. Come. Can not you walk? Let me take you up by my own strength, and I will carry you. Love me, and let me love you, and I will save you."

This is Christ loving the human soul. It is this sympathy with men, and this willingness to suffer for them, and bear their burdens, and carry their sins, that cleanses a man's soul. It is the impact on him of God's nature, it is the opening of the soul of God, so that the divine influence flows right in on him, it is this that gives my upper nature strength, and hope, and elasticity, and victory.

AUGUST 25: *EVENING.*

And when he had taken the book, the four beasts and four and twenty elders fell down before the Lamb, having every one of them harps, and golden vials full of odors, which are the prayers of saints.—*Rev.* v., 8.

WHAT a heavenly wonder must be the Book of Prayer that lies before God! For groans are interpreted there. Mute joys gain tongue before God. Unutterable desires, that go silently up from the heart, burst forth into divine pleadings when, touched by the Spirit, their imprisoned nature comes forth. Could thoughts or aspirations be made visible, could they assume a form that befitted their nature, what an endless procession would be seen going toward the throne of God day and night! Consider the wrestlings of all the wretched, the cry of orphans, the ceaseless pleadings of the bereaved, and of those fearing bereavement; the prayer of trust betrayed, of hope darkened, of home deserted, of joy quenched; the prayers of faithful men from dungeons and prison-houses; the prayers of slaves who found man, law, and the Church twined around and set against them, and had no way left to look but upward toward God! The hearts of men by myriads have been pressed by the world as grapes are trodden in a wine-press, and have given forth a heavenly wine. Beds of long, lingering sickness have learned such thoughts of resignation, and such patient trust and joy, that the heavenly book is bright with the footprints of their prayers. The very silence of sickness is often more full of richest thought than all the books of earth have ever been.

The influences which brood upon the soul in such a covert as the closet are not like the coarse stimulants of earthly thought. It is no fierce rivalry, no conflict for victory, no hope of praise or hunger of fame, such as throw lurid light upon the mind. The soul rises to its highest nature, and meets the influence that rests upon it from above. What is the depth of calmness, what is the vision of faith, what is the rapture, the ecstasy of love, the closet knows more grandly than any other place of human experience.

AUGUST 26: *MORNING.*

I will cure them, and will reveal unto them the abundance of peace and truth.—*Jer.* xxxiii., 6.

THERE are many who have been led to put their trust in God by great misfortunes. There are instances where it seems as though God meant to shut men up to himself. He drives them from one step to another; he cuts them off from one refuge after another; he takes away from them one idol after another; he brings them to such a state that their soul, from its own mere necessity, must stay itself on him; and then, when they come into that final experience, they exclaim, "Why did I not know it before? I was wandering here and there, seeking rest where it could not be found. I was miserable, because I did not seek happiness in the right direction. The things by which I meant to make life bright and cheerful left life dismal and troublous. When I lost these things, and seemed to have lost every thing, I found God—I found rest, peace, and satisfaction."

It is a brave thing to ride over the waves of the ocean, but it is a braver thing to ride over the troubles of life. It is a brave thing to have wings like an eagle's, but the eagle shall be weary in its flight before they shall be who mount on the wings of faith, soaring above the trials of this world. For such there is a great peace—a peace which is represented as flowing like a river, inexhaustible, deep, abundant—a peace that refines and purifies the soul, that makes life noble here, and that is a prophecy of nobility in the life to come.

AUGUST 26: EVENING.

I am the Lord that healeth thee.—*Exod.* xv., 26.

DISCIPLESHIP is pupilship, and qualification is need of help and willingness to receive it. Are you blind? do you want to see? Are you deaf? do you want to hear? Are you sick? do you want to be healed? Are you, in short, sinful in every faculty and part, and are you contented with your state, or do you desire that God should cleanse you? If you desire to be cleansed, then you have the condition for salvation. You have a Savior whose delight it is to heal the sick and cure the wounded, and you are sick and you are wounded. You should be Christ's, and all that you require to make yourself his is that you should have faith that he will take such as you, and should cast yourself upon him. The provisions of mercy in the Lord Jesus Christ are not for men who are entirely delivered from sin. Is sin your daily curse and distress? Are you willing to be rescued from it by providence and grace in the Lord Jesus Christ? Remember that the evidence of piety does not consist in your sinfulness, but in your wish to be redeemed from sin.

AUGUST 27: MORNING.

Herein is love, not that we loved God, but that he loved us, and sent his Son to be the propitiation for our sins.—1 *John* iv., 10.

MEN mount up into flashes of glorious realization when it seems as if God then began to love them, because they then first become sensitive to his love. When a man has passed through religious changes from darkness to light—when he has put off his worldly character and taken on the character of Christ—when, coming out of despondency, the compassionate Savior rises before him, then he says, "Christ has begun to love me." His impression is that the divine love for him began when the burden which had weighed down his soul was rolled off.

Just as if a blind man, who had never seen the heavens, nor the earth, nor the sweet faces of those that loved him, should have a surgical operation performed upon his eyes, so that he could see objects around him, and should think to himself, on going out of doors, "Oh, how things are blossoming! The earth is beginning to be beautiful. Mountains and hills are springing up in every direction. The forms of loving friends are being raised up to greet my gaze. And the sun has just begun to shine forth from the heavens." But have not these things existed since the flood and since the creation, although the man's eyes have not before been in a condition to enable him to see them?

AUGUST 27: EVENING.

Rest in the Lord, and wait patiently for him.—*Psalm* xxxvii., 7.

When you have nothing to do, and there is nothing to produce anxiety, it is easy to wait—for it is laziness, and all men are apt by nature to be lazy. But when there is any thing that you have set your heart upon, it is very hard to wait, especially if the thing does not come as soon as you expect it to. Waiting is easy when it is sinful, and hard when it is a duty. The Bible is full both of instances of patient waiting, and of exhortations and explanations respecting the duty and benefit of waiting—of waiting, not because you can not help yourself; of waiting, not because you can not do any thing else, but of waiting in the sense of waiting on God; of waiting, because you believe that God governs in this world; that he will bring to pass, in his own time, righteousness, justice, and truth, and that, therefore, you can afford to wait as long as he will have you. That is the ground of true Christian waiting.

We are very much hindered in our Christian duty of patient waiting by the habit of looking at things in their minute parts, each particular day, without considering that every thing that happens in this world is part of a great plan of God that runs through all time, culminating in eternity, and that we are to regard daily events as only elements of greater events that require long periods for their consummation.

Pray on, then. Trust in God. I beseech of you, have faith, not in man, but in him that loved you, that redeemed you with his precious blood, that sitteth on high, and that doeth all things well.

What can these anxious cares avail,
  These never-ceasing moans and sighs?
What can it help us to bewail
  Each painful moment as it flies?
Our cross and trials do but press
The heavier for our bitterness.

Only thy restless heart keep still,
  And wait in cheerful hope; content
To take whate'er his gracious will,
  His all-discerning love hath sent.
Doubt not our inmost wants are known
To him who chose us for his own.

AUGUST 28: *MORNING.*

Let all those that seek thee rejoice and be glad in thee.—*Psalm* lxx., 4.

I CAN scarcely conceive it possible that the soul of a man should be in intimate relations with the divine soul without having a desire to praise God excited in him. How is it with us? How many dull, drudging days do we have? How many days unillumined by one single wish to utter thanks or gladness? How many selfish days of duty? How many days of fear? How many days of secret uneasiness? How few days do we find in which we experience a spirit of praise, except those rare days of health in nerve and pleasure in external condition? Now and then, with many persons, there is a salient day, a kind of pinnacle, on which they are joyful, and feel like praising God. But a true Christian experience would find, during some part of every day, the soul in a condition to love and praise God. To be in a praising state, one must be in a most unselfish condition of mind; he must live relatively humble as before God; he must be sensitive to his obligations to God; he must have a faith that shall enable him to see God in the events which are transpiring about him. The desire to praise God presupposes a large experience. For one to have this desire is almost the same as to be a rich and ripe Christian.

AUGUST 28: *EVENING.*

It is good that a man should both hope and quietly wait for the salvation of the Lord.—*Lam.* iii., 26.

It oftentimes is the case, with minds not organized for endurance, that the reaction caused by strong feeling is such as almost to carry them into insanity. There are multitudes of Christian persons that go for consolation and instruction to their pastors because, as they say, they can not have feeling enough, but whose difficulty is that they have had too much feeling. They get drunk on religious excitement, and then, when they wake from their exhilaration, and find themselves relaxed and in an awful state of feeling, they go to the minister to know how it is that God has forsaken them and the devil has taken them captive. It is not so. They have been gourmands of feeling, and they are having a slight experience of what the Bible means when it says that we can not see God and live. Having had an excess of feeling which has consumed their strength, they have come into a corresponding excess in the opposite direction, and they think that they are being tempted of the devil. It is only because they have been burning ten wicks where they should have burned but one, that the devil seems to be tempting them. Their present darkness bears the same relation to the intense light in which they have been indulging that heaviness and sleepiness at the end of the day bear to the activity of noonday. Nature is praying for a chance to go to sleep. Their feelings are all crying out against such a squandering of their forces; and much of what is called being abandoned of God, and the hiding of God's face, is nothing but God putting his merciful hand on faculties that have been overtaxed, and saying, "Hush! go to sleep."

AUGUST 29: *MORNING.*

Fight the good fight of faith.—1 *Tim.* vi., 12.

If you mean to live for immortality, it will not do for you to live by half measures. You must give your whole soul to the great and sublime end of living with God forever and forever. You must rank every thing as relative to that end. It is worth every man's endeavor, and it must have every man's endeavor.

If self-denial, therefore, in you is earnest, if it is bold, if it is almost unthinking; if you go into the work of religion, the work of right living, the work of manhood, as a warrior goes into battle, then it becomes easy. Then the conflict which the apostle likens to that physical warfare in which the excitement and wild exhilaration are such that the soldier does not feel his wounds, nor notice his fatigue, nor mind his circumstances—that conflict becomes easy. That which we know to be the case in the lower life in this respect, is still more so in the higher life, where a man gives himself to it wholly, with all his heart, and mind, and soul, and strength. A man who means to live religiously, and puts his whole power into it, lives easily, and no other man can live easily.

AUGUST 29: EVENING.

When he came to himself, he said, How many hired servants of my father's have bread enough and to spare, and I perish with hunger!—*Luke* xv., 17.

WHEN the prodigal first came to himself, he thought of his father and his fatherland, and determined to go back and confess his wrong. And he made up his story. "I will go to my father," he said, "and acknowledge my fault, and ask him to forgive me and take me again, and let me be his servant." He started; but he was not permitted to go clear back before he was welcomed. The father saw him afar off, and had compassion on him, and ran to meet him. Although the father was the one that was injured, although the father was right and the son was all wrong, it was the father that went and made the concession, as it were. When the son began his confession, the father cut it in two, and called for the robe, and the sandals, and the ring, and the feast. And there was blessedness in that man's heart. He had risen into manhood; he had come to himself; his father had found him; and he was indeed blessed.

Return, return thee to thine only rest,
    Lone pilgrim of the world,
    Far erring from the fold—
By the dark night and risen storms distressed;

List, weary lamb, the Shepherd's anxious voice,
And once again within his arms rejoice.

Return, return, thy fair white fleece is soiled,
And by sharp briers rent—
Thy little strength is spent;
Yet he will pity thee, thou torn and spoiled.
There, thou art cradled on his tender breast;
Now never more, sweet lamb, forsake that rest.

AUGUST 30: *MORNING.*

Prepare ye the way of the Lord.—*Matt.* iii., 3.

I know thy works, and thy labor, and thy patience.—*Rev.* ii., 2.

WAITING when you should work is just as bad as would be audacious interference in things above our reach. Every man must do what he can, and men are much more in danger of doing too little than too much. Indolence is more frequent than irreverence. No shipmaster interferes upon God's prerogatives when he takes care of his ship in a storm. No farmer feels that he is encroaching upon God's sovereignty when he cultivates the crops for which he prays. He asks for daily bread, and then earns it. No manufacturer or business man feels that he is trespassing upon God's prerogative when he looks after his own business. They believe in God's blessing, but they always say, "If a man would receive God's blessings, he must prepare a soil for them to blossom on."

So it is in spiritual things. We are to work in reliance upon means, and then wait for God's blessing. And waiting for God to do for us what we can do for ourselves, although it may bear the name of religion, is really nothing but infidelity. Waiting for God implies first doing faithfully all that in you lies, and then waiting patiently for the result. No man waits for God that does not first prepare the way of the Lord. Every man is, as far as he can, to take the blessings which he needs, and when he has gone as far as his experience, or light, or teaching enables him to go, then he is to be patiently expectant.

AUGUST 30: *EVENING.*

If any man be in Christ he is a new creature.—2 *Cor.* v., 17.

A NEW creature in Christ Jesus is the apostolic definition of being a Christian. It is the endeavor to substitute for the worldly character a divine and spiritual one. The kingdom of God is to be within us. The evidences of it are to be hope, and joy, and faith, and love, and fidelity. And the aim of the true Christian life is not so much to keep its ordinances, or to believe in this or that disclosure of technical truth: it is larger manhood, patterned on Christ Jesus. It is to make yourself nobler, purer, sweeter, truer, more faithful, more heroic, and more worthy to look God in the face and say, "I am thy son." We are exhorted to live worthy of the vocation with which we are called, and that vocation is sonship in Christ Jesus. We are to live so that we shall feel worthy to say, "God is my Father, and I am his son."

AUGUST 31: *MORNING.*

Oh come, let us worship and bow down: let us kneel before the Lord our maker.—*Psalm* xcv., 6.

WHEN a man, standing before a magnificent work of art, or some wonderful phenomenon of nature—some rugged mountain, some thunderous fall like that of Niagara, or some beautiful landscape—finds his taste so awakened that he loses command of himself, and breaks forth into an ecstasy of admiration, his sensations are transcendent.

But when we stand, not before unspeaking canvas, or inert mountains, or senseless water, but in the presence of some hero —some man that has stood among men nobler than the noblest, and truer than the truest, and has carried the fate of a nation in his hand without betraying it—some Kossuth or some Garibaldi—then how do we tremble in transports of delight! It is a joyful intoxication. It is an ecstasy.

What, then, ought our feelings to be when we stand, not before a man, but before the everlasting God—that Being who created the innumerable orbs of which this earth is but a specimen; whose ways generations and ages have sought in vain to find out; of whose love all the affections of father, and mother, and husband, and wife, and child, and brother, and sister, and friend, and lover are but faint intimations, and of whose attributes the divine qualities of men are but the slightest hints? And when he comes as our Maker and Preserver, and the Author of the eternal bliss prepared for us, how blessed ought to be the prerogative and privilege of making him the object of our highest worship.

Oh can it be that Power divine,
  Whose throne is light's unbounded blaze,
While countless worlds and angels join
  To swell the glorious song of praise,

Will deign to lend a favoring ear
  When I, poor sinful mortal, pray?
Yes, boundless goodness! he will hear,
  Nor cast the meanest wretch away.

Then let me serve thee all my days,
  And may my zeal with years increase;
For pleasant, Lord, are all thy ways,
  And all thy paths are paths of peace.

AUGUST 31: *EVENING.*

If any man will come after me, let him deny himself, and take up his cross daily, and follow me.—*Luke* ix., 23.

Our self-denials lie just where our duties do. If it is difficult for you to speak, overcome that difficulty, and in that way you will practice self-denial. If it is hard for you to be benevolent, correct your avarice, and make it give away the things that you would hoard, and thus you will practice self-denial. Are you proud? Then practice self-denial by being humble. Are you envious? Then the way for you to be self-denying is to cultivate generosity in your consideration of other men's condition as compared with your own.

Now and then we get, through some little event which comes under our notice, such as the performance of a generous deed, a conception that reveals to us for a moment the carriage of our life with respect to self-denial. But how many of us keep such an accurate account of our daily conduct that we know our tendencies in this regard—that we know whether we are living all the time to make men serve us, to secure prosperity for ourselves, to make every thing work in our favor, or whether, while we are diligent and exact in business, and considerate of our own interests, our desire and aim are perpetually to work for the benefit of others?

SEPTEMBER 1: MORNING.

And the Lord your God, he shall expel them from before you, and drive them from out of your sight; and ye shall possess their land, as the Lord your God hath promised unto you.—*Josh.* xxiii., 5.

We are in many respects like the Israelites. We have a promised land, into which we are brought by our hopes in Christ. Our promised land is just like Palestine. Its mountains and passes are filled with unsubdued inhabitants. They are all about us. We, too, are watched. Often incursions are suddenly made against us, and we are carried into captivity or are humbled in battle. Often, too, the hand of the Lord is lifted up in our behalf, and the battle goes against the inhabitants of the land, and we beat them down, and we drive them back, so that they have no more dominion over us for a time. We are full of conflicts. Yet we maintain our ground, and hold ourselves only by vigilance, as in the presence of a continually watching enemy. This great warfare goes on with all true Christians, and goes on just in proportion as they are truly Christian; just in proportion as their standard of Christian life is high; just in proportion as they are determined to bring every thought and feeling into subjection to the Lord Jesus Christ; just in proportion to the comprehensiveness and richness of that which they mean by being Christians in their life and disposition.

SEPTEMBER 1: EVENING.

Be patient, therefore, brethren, unto the coming of the Lord. Behold, the husbandman waiteth for the precious fruit of the earth, and hath long patience for it, until he receive the early and latter rain. Be ye also patient; stablish your hearts; for the coming of the Lord draweth nigh.—*James* v., 7, 8.

I had a bed of asters last summer that reached clear across my garden in the country. Oh, how gayly they bloomed! They were planted late, and they came up late. On the sides were yet fresh blossoming flowers, while the tops had gone to seed. Early frosts came, and I found one day that that long line of radiant beauty was seared, and I said, "Ah! the season is too much for them; they have perished;" and I bade them farewell. I disliked to go and look at the bed. It seemed almost like a grave-yard of flowers. But four or five weeks ago one of my men called my attention to the fact that along the whole line of that bed there were asters coming up in the greatest abundance; and I looked, and behold, for every plant that I thought the winter had destroyed there were fifty plants that it had planted. What did those frosts and surly winds do? They caught my flowers, they slew them, they cast them on the ground, they trod with snowy feet upon them, and they said, leaving their work, "That is an end of you." And the next spring there were, for every root, fifty witnesses to rise up and say, "By death we live."

And as it is in the floral tribe, so it is in God's kingdom. By death came everlasting life. By crucifixion and the sepulchre came the throne and the palace of the eternal God. By overthrow came victory. Do not be afraid to suffer. Do not be afraid to be overthrown. A man cast down rises stronger than ever he was before. It is by being cast down and not destroyed; it is by being shaken to pieces, and having vitality in every piece, that men become men of might, and that one becomes a host; whereas men that yield to the appearance of things, and go with the world, have their quick blossoming, their momentary prosperity, and then their end, which is an end forever.

Thou wearest not the crown,
  Nor the best course canst tell;
God sitteth on the throne,
  And guideth all things well:
Trust him to govern, then,
  No king can rule like him.
How wilt thou wonder, when
  Thine eyes no more are dim,
To see these paths which vex thee,
  How wise they were and meet;
The works which now perplex thee,
  How beautiful, complete!

SEPTEMBER 2: MORNING.

If any of you lack wisdom, let him ask of God, that giveth to all men liberally, and upbraideth not; and it shall be given him.—*James* i., 5, 6.

THE oftener you go to God for help, the more welcome you

are. When a man comes to you for counsel concerning things that are important as affecting his welfare, it not only does not impoverish you to give him the benefit of your knowledge and wisdom, but you are gratified at his consulting you, and you take pleasure in lending yourself to him to that extent. I can not conceive of a man who, having a store of discreet knowledge, should be unwilling to use it for the succor of his fellow-men. If ducats were as plenty with me as thoughts, I should be most happy to lend to every body.

Now, when we go to God, we ask him to do things that please him. It is more blessed for him to give to you and to help you than not to do it. And when a man is in trouble, and goes to God, and says, "I have done all I can. I do not know what to do more. I am willing to suffer or to be relieved. Thy will be done," I believe that then God hears and answers prayer, even though the trouble be of a secular nature. I do not believe that in doing it he violates natural laws. I believe, on the contrary, that he controls natural laws, and makes them perform errands of mercy. I should feel almost as though I were an orphan if that doctrine were taken out of the world.

SEPTEMBER 2: EVENING.

Thy word is a lamp unto my feet, and a light unto my path.—*Psalm* cxix., 105.

If one has a Bible of his own—and every one should have; if one has a Bible that he reads to the exclusion of every other one—and every person should have a Bible that he is as used to as he is to his father's garden or door-yard, so that he can readily put his hand on any chapter or verse in it—if one has such a Bible, he may register any significant event by marking certain texts or passages. In that way he will form the habit of selecting passages of Scripture which are adapted to the various exigencies of this life. And how beautiful it is! If you keep a kind of register, so that the text refers to and is associated with the event, your Bible becomes a memorial. You are setting up, all the way through it, stones of remembrance, as it were. You are providing a record for your old age. By-and-by, when you take down your Bible, and put on your glasses, and look back upon your past life, not only will it be the Word of God, but you will find how the Word of God fed you in the wilderness, strengthened you in sickness, and comforted you in circumstances of discouragement. How many things a man can record on the fly-leaves of his Bible which will afford him pleasure and profit in after life! How precious that Bible will become to him when he has woven it into his experience as a kind of epitomizing of his life!

SEPTEMBER 3: MORNING.

This is the day which the Lord hath made; we will rejoice and be glad in it.—*Psalm* cxviii., 24.

I HAVE noticed that the slender brook which carries the mill is more musical on Sunday than on any other day, because the mill stands still, and the brook, having nothing to do with its water, gurgles over the rocks, and flounders over the dam, and makes a thousand times more merry noise than on any other day. But Monday comes, and the gates are hoisted, and the mill runs, and the brook is not so musical, but the mill is more so. The mill did nothing on Sunday, and the brook is doing more on Monday than it did on Sunday. It played on Sunday, but it works on Monday. And Christians, as it were, play in the spirit, and have a holy jollity on Sunday; it is a holiday for them. Nor would I undervalue their experience or joy. But they are not so busy when they sing, and pray, and rejoice in the sanctuary as when, by the power of some moral emotion, they are combating temptation, and resisting pride, and overcoming selfishness, and building again the kingdoms of this world with the holy stones of the New Jerusalem. Then, when piety *costs;* then, when it means bearing, heroism, and achievement; not when it seeks joy, but when it seeks battle—then men are nearest to God and most like Christ. When a man stands upon the deck, and at the bench, and by the forge, and in the furrow, and in the colliery, then, if ever, if he has a life to live of true piety, is the time; and there, at the post of duty, is the place.

Thou art a day of mirth;
And where the week-days trail on ground,
Thy flight is higher, as thy birth.
Oh let me take thee at the bound,

Groping with thee from seven to seven,
 Till that we both, being tossed from earth,
 Fly hand-in-hand to heaven.

SEPTEMBER 3: *EVENING.*

To Jesus, the Mediator of the new covenant, and to the blood of sprinkling, that speaketh better things than that of Abel.—*Heb.* xii., 24.

THE dearest place, to the imagination of the Jew, that there was on earth was old Jerusalem, hoary and grand. And yet ye are come to a higher Jerusalem than that, says the apostle. "Ye are not come to the sound of a trumpet and the voice of words, which voice they that heard entreated that the word should not be spoken to them any more. Ye are come unto Mount Zion, and unto the city of the living God, the heavenly Jerusalem, and to an innumerable company of angels, to the general assembly and church of the first-born, which are written in heaven, and to God the Judge of all, and to the spirits of just men made perfect." Ye are not come to that sight which was so terrible that even Moses said, "I exceedingly fear and quake;" but ye are come "to Jesus, the Mediator of the new covenant, and to the blood of sprinkling, that speaketh better things than that of Abel." Not ye are coming, but ye are *come.* It is in the present. It is a part of the privilege which belongs to the early ministration of your faith. Ye *have* come. The very fact that you spiritually are leaning on Christ Jesus gives you advent and access. Every true disciple affiliated with Christ belongs to this great household. Do not fear, therefore, to accept Christ, for it gives you all that you had before, and a thousand times more. It advances you out of the twilight, and out of the storm-clad horizon of your past faith, into the glorious illumination of a more spiritual worship, where all forms of fear and ghastly motives of terror cease, and where companionship, and divine guidance, and infinite blessings await you.

SEPTEMBER 4: *MORNING.*

Unto me, who am less than the least of all saints, is this grace given.—*Eph.* iii., 8.

THE humility of the Bible is not the exaggerated sense of

man's wretched imperfection. No man is humble who is looking down. Humility is the sense of such ineffable excellence, that when a man's aspiration looks up, and he compares what he is with what he would be, he is humble. It is a state of appreciation in a man of excellence, and an ideal of an excellence beyond, sitting in judgment on his relative position, that makes humility. Humility is a head-up quality, not a dragging, miserable, mean feeling. Many men have mortified pride, and call that humility. Many men have the blues, and call them humility. Many men palm off all the wretched and reactionary feelings of their nature, and call them humility. Humility is one of the noblest and one of the most resplendent of all the experiences of the soul. When every part of a man's nature is sensitive and apprehensive, and when the sense of character and of being is so radiant and large that the man feels his own relative imperfection, compared with that which he now perceives to be possible, then it is that humility is born. It is the child of aspiration.

SEPTEMBER 4: EVENING.

Confess your faults one to another.—*James* v., 16.

As long as you make your faults a bulwark to stand behind and fight me, so long I am your enemy and you are my foe. But if we could only understand how imperfect we are; if our hearts were only filled with a true humility; if we felt every day of our lives that God had a hard task to get along with us, it would make us far more gentle and amiable. It is not the offense, but the *defense* of the offense, that makes it hard for us to bear with one another. A man may say to me, "You are a vile sinner;" he may rain his words on me like blows; but if he comes back when his passion has gone down, with tears in his eyes, and says, "Oh! forgive me; I did not mean it," it is all gone, quicker than a flash of lightning. I love him all the more. The fault is not hard to bear. It is the defending the fault, it is the refusing to make up under fault, that rankles, and makes us ugly in return. Where there is one ugly man, there are generally two.

How wise, then, is James's command, "Confess your faults one to another."

SEPTEMBER 5: MORNING.

Wherefore lift up the hands which hang down, and the feeble knees.—*Heb.* xii., 12.

OUGHT there not to be in us such a likeness of Christ that we shall have toward sinful men the same spirit that he has? Those who have not the spirit of Christ are none of his; and, in some degree, ought we not to have that spirit of mercifulness, and hopefulness, and gentleness, by which he drew imperfect and evil men to him? If we are Christ's, ought not his Spirit to be reproduced in our conduct and our lives? I beseech of you, look upon your children, and sorrow for them as Christ sorrows for you. Look upon the scholars in your class, and feel for their want as Christ feels for your want. Are there those in your families whose imperfection is your daily annoyance? But is not their misery more than your annoyance? Do you rail at them? are you bitter against them? and is there no heart in you to feel toward their imperfection as Christ feels toward yours? Are you met by wicked men in the world, and are you tempted to give railing for railing, and revenge for wrong? Remember Christ, who meets sin and wrong with patience and gentle restoration, and do you meet it in the same way. Carry yourself, as much as in you lies, in the spirit, not merely of peace, but of recuperative love, and God shall give you many out of your house, many out of your Church, and many out of your community. Blessed are they that lead souls from their sins. They shall shine as stars in the firmament forever and ever.

SEPTEMBER 5: EVENING.

They should seek the Lord, if haply they might feel after him, and find him, though he be not far from every one of us.—*Acts* xvii., 27.

I READ an account of a man who, traveling at night, not long ago, in the midst of a snow-storm, and seeking a house, but concluding that he should not be able to reach it, turned over his sleigh, and wrapped himself in his buffalo robe, and waited till morning, when he found that his sleigh was turned up against the door-yard fence of the very house that he was seeking.

Now, hundreds of Christians are sleeping in God's door-yard, and do not know it. They have fulfilled every condition of the Gospel, and nothing is wanting but that they should look up and say, "Why, there is the very house that I was looking for!"

If you are conscious of your own want and imperfection, and if you are satisfied that it is the purpose of your life to fulfill the law of God, then you are in that state in which the Lord Jesus Christ takes men, and all you have to do to be happy is to feel, "Christ is my Savior, and I am saved, not because I am perfect, but through his redeeming love." God is near to many men that are unconscious of his presence. The perfume of divine love is around about many men that do not perceive it. You are like men who have no sense of smell. You are in the garden of the Lord, and you call it a wilderness. But wake, oh soul, out of despondency! If you are—as you know you are—sinful, and you long for something better, take hold of the hand of Christ, and go toward it. He will hold fast to your hand, and will lead you to the end; and then you will be saved, not because you are perfect, but because he has swept you into that charmed and blessed sphere where the flesh and the world shall drag us down no more, but where our enfranchised manhood shall lift itself up in ineffable glory, crystalline purity, and perfect symmetry. May God bring us all there.

I know thou art not far,
My God, from me; yon star
Speaks of thy nearness, and its rays
Fall on me like thy touch. Oh raise
These eyes of mine
To see thy face, even thine,
My Father and my God!

Thou wilt be nearer yet,
And one day I shall get
The fuller vision of thy face,
In all its perfect light and grace,
When I shall see thee as thou art,
And in thy kingdom bear my part,
My blessed King and God!

SEPTEMBER 6: MORNING.

But my God shall supply all your need according to his riches in glory by Christ Jesus.—*Phil.* iv., 19.

When I think how I love my children; when I think how

my heart clasps those that are dear to me, as a fragrant vine clasps the branches of the tree upon which it grows; when I think how I could almost let go my own life for their sake; and then, when I think that I do not know how to love, that God is the only true lover, that by the amazing wealth of the tides that flow from his heart he is giving to me the little affection that I am capable of experiencing, I feel as a daisy must if the sun, addressing it, should say, "Oh, sweet daisy, the light which I shed I mean for thee!" The daisy, seeing the whole hemisphere of light, the whole day, says to itself, "What shall I do with such a flood of light? Oh, who ever had such loving as the sun gives to me! I have no room for it all." And the sun sweeps on, filling the heavens and the earth, and comes again, and continues pouring forth its light, and does not stop because the daisy can not hold it all. And so God pours out the tides of his love, not according to the cup-like, acorn proportions of my soul, not according to my ability to receive, but according to his infinite resources and his endless power to give.

Will you doubt such a one? Are you afraid to venture, with him to stand by you and help you? Behold, in your path stand the fullness, and mercy, and helpfulness of your God! God knows every tear that you shed; he sees your silent thoughts and feelings; he knows every part of your life. No rude attritions, no yearnings unsatisfied, no griefs of love, no aspirations unfulfilled—none of these things are hidden from God. He is the Father revealed in Jesus Christ as the Lover, and he says, "Because I am working in you to will and to do of my good pleasure, be of good cheer, take courage, and work out your own salvation."

God grant that we may hear the voice, feel the inspiration, and win the victory!

SEPTEMBER 6: *EVENING.*

If ye loved me, ye would rejoice, because I said I go unto the Father.—*John* xiv., 28.

Oh, mother, my heart breaks with your heart when your cradle is empty; but shall I call back the child? Nay; sooner pluck a star out of heaven than call back that child to this wintry blast. Shall I call back your young, and dear, and blooming friend? Nay; you are left in some bitterness for a time, but make not a man out of angel again. Let him rejoice. In all our outlook, dying is triumphing. Not any bower of roses is so festooned in June. Not where the jessamine and honeysuckle twine, and lovers sit, is there so fair a sight, so sweet a prospect, as where a soul in its early years is flying away out of life and out of time through the gate of death—the rosy gate of death; the royal gate of death; the golden gate of death; the pearly gate of death. It is guilt and fear that blacken dying. Hope and love make it sweeter than being born. And so the day of death is better than the day of birth; and it is better to go to the house of mourning than to the house of feasting. It is really so to those who know it and put it to proof.

SEPTEMBER 7: MORNING.

But their eyes were holden that they should not know him.—*Luke* xxiv., 16.

Not long ago there was a researcher of art in Italy who, reading in some book that there was a portrait of Dante painted by Giotto, was led to suspect that he had found where it had been placed. There was an apartment used as an outhouse for the storage of wood, hay, and the like. He sought and obtained permission to examine it. Clearing out the rubbish, and experimenting upon the whitewashed wall, he soon detected the signs of the long-hidden portrait. Little by little, with loving skill, he opened up the sad, thoughtful, stern face of the old Tuscan poet.

Sometimes it seems to me that thus the very sanctuary of God has been filled with wood, hay, and stubble, and the divine lineaments of Christ have been swept over and covered by human plastering, and I am seized with an invincible desire to draw forth from its hiding-place and reveal to men the glory of God as it shines in the face of Christ Jesus. It matters little to me what school of theology rises or falls, so only that Christ may rise and appear in all his Father's glory, full-orbed, upon the darkness of this world.

SEPTEMBER 7: EVENING.

Jesus heard that they had cast him out; and when he had found him, he said unto him, Dost thou believe on the Son of God? He answered and said, Who is he, Lord, that I might believe on him? And Jesus said unto him, Thou hast both seen him, and it is he that talketh with thee. And he said, Lord, I believe. And he worshiped him.—*John* ix., 35-38.

NEVER has a man undertaken one step in the right direction, and begun to suffer for it, that Christ did not look after him. You may not see him; he may not be visible to you just yet; but he is on your track. He will find you. Do not murmur, do not repine that you have taken one step. Do not be sorry that you have begun to see. Do not be afraid of being cast out. No matter if your Church does disown you; the Lord Jesus Christ is mightier than any church. No matter if your neighbors do desert you; the Lord Jesus Christ is more to you than all the men in any community could be. No matter if your parents forswear you; the Lord Jesus Christ is better to you than parents. No matter if your own selves seem to sink in solitariness and in darkness; the Lord Jesus Christ is yours, and he offers not simply to continue his past mercies to you, but to take you by the hand and lead you on to higher and nobler experiences. Trust him now, that you may know him more fully hereafter.

SEPTEMBER 8: MORNING.

And to know the love of Christ, which passeth knowledge.—*Eph.* iii., 19.

ALL the hints and tokens in our possession respecting the intercourse of Christ with his disciples show that it was rich beyond all conception in the element of love. And to a nature such as his, what must have been men who could not at all repay the love that he bestowed upon them? He gave them as much as they could take, but oh, how much more was there to give! And how little could they receive! To say that Christ filled their hearts is like saying that the River Amazon fills the shells along the banks of the river. But how much does it take of the Amazon to fill those shells? Besides that, what volumes roll out into the ocean? Christ filled those little disciple-cups, and the great flood of his love seemed undiminished by a drop, and moved on and on. And in the realities of love he was alone, as he was alone in the realities of imagination, of reason, and of all that which was most dear to him. There were none that could talk with him, or understand him when he talked. He was obliged to say to his disciples, "I have yet many things to say unto you, but ye can not bear them now."

SEPTEMBER 8: *EVENING.*

And though I bestow all my goods to feed the poor, and though I give my body to be burned, and have not charity, it profiteth me nothing.—1 *Cor.* xiii., 3.

Have you the disposition of love? Do your father and mother say of you, "This child, that used to be so wayward and ill-tempered, is now well-behaved and gentle?" Do your brothers and sisters now say of you, "Since my brother joined the Church he is changed in disposition. Before he was disobliging and selfish, but now he is kind and generous, and manifests a loving spirit?" Do your tenants say, "I should have known that he had become a Christian by the way he collects his rents?" Do your business associates and your neighbors say, "How much more fair and just he is in his dealings than he used to be?" Is your nature, that once was as hard as a granite rock, now soft and mossy on the surface, so that vegetation might almost grow upon it? It is your *life* that is to determine whether you have the spirit of Christ; and if you have not the spirit of Christ you are none of his. Though you have passed through hell and heaven; though you have been attended by angels in long processions every day since you heard of God; though you have the gift of prophecy, and understand all knowledge; though you have all faith, so that you could remove mountains, if you have not love, these things profit you nothing.

Holiest Love, how we forget thy very name,
So that thy heavenly nature on earth wins only blame!
While lip-religion fills the land,
Nay, worldly talk is heard,
Till Christian souls in peril stand
To lose the living Word.

God-fearing Love, why do thy foes, alas, prevail?
For many boast the Christian name, yet at thy service quail:
They bear naught, shun naught, love their pelf,
Fast not, and run no race,
Nor pray, nor rest, nor die to self,
Yet trust they shall find grace.

SEPTEMBER 9: MORNING.

In honor preferring one another.—*Rom.* xii., 10.

He that is the most tolerant, the most patient, the most charitable, the most gentle, and that finds himself able to love the most, and to see the most in each person to admire and to thank God for—that man, I think, stands highest in the kingdom of heaven. Yea, he that sees these things not only, but in honor prefers men; who feels that other men are better than he, perhaps, in these respects, when they are not; he that is willing to serve his fellow-men for the sake of that which is in them; he that has that illustrious nobility that shone in Paul, when he said, "Some, indeed, preach Christ even of envy and strife, not sincerely, supposing to add affliction to my bonds." "What then? notwithstanding, every way, whether in pretense or in truth, Christ is preached, and I therein do rejoice;" he that is willing to suffer for others, and to bear others' faults, if by such means he can develop the divine element in them—that is the man that stands nearest to the heart of God. Such men are the true benefactors of the world.

It is not the trumpeters that fight the battles, though you would think so to hear them. And it will not be the men that make the loudest proclamations, or that utter them with the most eloquent lips, that shall stand highest in the world that is to come.

SEPTEMBER 9: EVENING.

Speaking to yourselves in psalms, and hymns, and spiritual songs.—*Ephes.* v., 19.

As I grow older, there is an increasing love for those hymns that "seem," in the language of another hymn, "to throw their arms about the neck of Christ and plead." I have, more and more, a sense of the soul's need of God, and somehow the old-fashioned hymns, that plead on their knees, as it were, meet my wants better than the newer hymns. Those are beautiful and useful, but I find myself guided back to the more childlike and utter abandonment of the soul before God; and it seems to me there is no person who has been a Christian who has not, first or last, walked in the footsteps of these hymns of prostration, and yearning, and pleading. The experience may not come in a concentrated form; it may not come so that one can take it out, and look at it intellectually, and pronounce it to be just this or that; but humiliation before God, in view of one's sin and of one's consciousness of the sufficiency of Christ, and an irresistible yearning for Christ's help, love, and forgiveness—these have been, in a greater or less degree, the experience of every man that has the right to call himself a Christian.

SEPTEMBER 10: *MORNING.*

That Christ may dwell in your hearts by faith.—*Eph.* iii., 17.

THE reception of Christ by the heart is by an actual experience—by such a co-operation of the reason with the imagination that we are able to bring the invisible person near to us, and so bountifully reproduce him, and so beautifully set him forth, that he becomes to us the "chiefest among ten thousand," and the "one altogether lovely," so that every sweet thing in us goes out to him as every dewdrop in the sunshine evaporates and goes up toward the sun. This is receiving Christ by faith. It is not the rejecting of the senses; it is the non-using of them rather. It is not the despising of the reason; it is an auxiliary use of the reason. But it is the manly way of taking hold of the Lord Jesus Christ by the enthusiasm of love, and making him the supreme object of our desire and of our allegiance. This is receiving Christ by faith; and if we continue so to receive him, then he dwells in our hearts by faith—that is, by heart-sanctifying love.

There can be no Christianity to the man who does not personally take Christ by faith. There is no substitute for this personal experience, and there can be no system of Christianity which does not provide for this personal experience toward the Lord Jesus Christ.

SEPTEMBER 10: *EVENING.*

The disciple is not above his master, nor the servant above his lord.—*Matthew* x., 24.

There is victory for each true Christian heart over its troubles. He whose crown of thorns is now more illustrious and radiant than precious stones could make a crown, says to every one of his disciples that have thorns piercing them, "My grace shall be sufficient for you." Is the disciple better than the Master? Would you, if you could, reach forth your hand and take back one single sorrow, gloomy then, but gorgeous now, that made Christ to you what he is? Is it not the power of Jesus in heaven, and to all eternity will it not be his glory, that he was the Sufferer, and that he bore suffering in such a way that he vanquished suffering? And is he not the Lord over all by reason of that? Now you are his followers; and will you follow Christ, and will you desire to be worthy of his leadership, and yet slink away from suffering? Do not seek it; but if it comes, remember that no sorrow comes but with his knowledge. If he does not draw the golden bow that sends the silver arrow to your heart, he knows it is sent, and sees it fall. You are never in trouble that he does not know it. Trouble brings you nearer to the heart of God than prayers or hymns. Sorrows bring us closer to God than joys; but sorrows, to be of use, must be borne, as Christ's were, victoriously, carrying with them to the heart intimations and sacred prophecies of hope, not only that we shall not be overborne by them, but that by them we shall be strengthened, and ennobled, and enlarged.

It was no path of flowers, through this dark world of ours,
   Beloved of the Father, thou didst tread:
And shall we, in dismay, shrink from the narrow way
   When clouds and darkness are around it spread?

O thou, who art our life, be with us through the strife;
   Was not thy head by earth's fierce tempest bowed?
Raise thou our eyes above, to see a Father's love
   Beam, like the bow of promise, through the cloud.

SEPTEMBER 11: *MORNING.*

The wrath of the Lamb.—*Rev.* vi., 16.

Nothing seems to me so terrible as that part of Revelation

where Christ is presented as the Lion of the tribe of Judah at the same time that he is the Lamb of God—where he is interchangeably likened to the lamb, the most gentle and innocent thing on earth, and the lion, the most savage and ferocious beast of the field. What must be the terribleness of meeting such a God, whose love, that has fallen upon us, we have deliberately rejected and set aside, shutting our hearts against it, and refusing to be softened by it! What must be the terribleness of meeting such a God, to whom we have deliberately said, "I will not have thee to reign over me!" Do not marvel that Christ says that those who despise and reject the love of God shall rise to everlasting shame and contempt.

Beware how you treat the love of God. By as much as it is glorious to be loved, and, being loved, to be lifted up into all purity, by so much will it be terrible if you are loved unfructified and unsaved.

God calling yet, and I not yet arising,
So long his faithful, loving voice despising,
So falsely his unwearied care repaying;
He calls me still, and still I am delaying.

SEPTEMBER 11: *EVENING.*

To speak evil of no man, to be no brawlers, but gentle, showing all meekness unto all men.—*Titus* iii., 2.

When I think of the way in which people, and even Christian people, talk of each other, there is nothing that seems to me more horrible. There may be an innocent conversation—badinage, or something of that kind; but I mean the low, the worse than unkind way in which we are accustomed to look at others, and pick flaws in their character, and criticise their disposition, judging them in the lowest possible court of the mind. There is no remedy for this like praying for one another. If it is your habit to pray to God concerning your neighbors; to think of their wickedness as that of immortal creatures; to consider that they are journeying toward heaven like yourself, and that their faults are impediments in their way to be removed, and transgressions to be forgiven, and for the forgiveness of which you have plead with God—if you are in the habit, in other words, of dissecting those persons' history in the light of

God's countenance, and striving to obtain God's forgiveness in their behalf, then, in the solemnity of such circumstances, you will sympathize with them and refrain from speaking of them in a damaging way. The habit of taking each other before God in prayer, familiarly and by name, is eminently beneficial. It will cleanse you. It will sweeten your disposition. It will take away from you every particle of the raven, that loves to feed on carrion.

SEPTEMBER 12: *MORNING.*

The fruit of the Spirit is love.—*Gal.* v., 22.

HE who has entered into the true spirit of love, and lives in it, and speaks of it, and sings in it, and works in it, is a Christian; but he who works, and sings, and speaks, and lives in any other spirit except that of love, is not a Christian. He has not reached the typical character which belongs to Christ's disciples. And just in proportion as this spirit grows in a man, he is growing in Christ. He is the truest Christian who is becoming the sweetest, the mildest, the easiest to be entreated, the gentlest. He who is overcoming the obliquities of his natural temper; he who is working out, one after another, every part and element of his nature, so that he lives habitually in a Christ-like disposition, in a spirit of love, is the one that is growing in grace.

SEPTEMBER 12: *EVENING.*

Blessed are they that do his commandments, that they may have right to the tree of life, and may enter in through the gates into the city.—*Rev.* xxii., 14.

WE are all sailing across the sea of life in different vessels. Some of them leak, some of them are slow, some of them are very fine and stately, some of them have cruel captains, and some of them have good captains; but when once we get our feet on the shore of the New Jerusalem, we shall not care what took us over there, nor what our fear was on the way.

See to it, then, that you reach the heavenly city; see to it that God is your God; see to it that you have a child's right. Of all the trumpets that you can lift up at the heavenly gate, there is but one that will let you in. Blow the trumpet, if you will, of your own good deeds, and there is not an angel in all the heaven that will know the sound. Speak through your pride, or through your vanity, and you will fail to summon a messenger to the heavenly gate. But blow the trumpet of love, and its first lisping sound will quickly roll back the bolt, nad lift the latch, and open the heavenly gate, and you shall come in with a child's welcome, and find your Father's house, and your heart's delight. Learn this love, and rise to this home, through Jesus Christ our Redeemer.

SEPTEMBER 13: *MORNING.*

Praise ye the Lord: for it is good to sing praises unto our God; for it is pleasant; and praise is comely.—*Psalm* cxlvii., 1.

Oh that we could reason less about our troubles, and sing and praise more! There are thousands of things that we wear as shackles which we might use as instruments with music in them, if we only knew how. Those men that ponder, and meditate, and weigh the affairs of life, and study the mysterious developments of God's providence, and marvel why they should be burdened, and thwarted, and hampered, how different and how much more joyful would be their life if, instead of forever indulging in self-revolving and inward thinking, they would take their experiences, day by day, and lift them up, and praise God for them. We can sing our cares away easier than we can reason them away. Sing in the morning. The birds are the earliest to sing, and birds are more without care than any thing else that I know of. Sing at evening. Singing is the last thing that robins do. When they have done their daily work; when they have flown their last flight, and picked up their last morsel of food, and cleansed their bill on the napkin of a bough, then, on a topmost twig, they sing one song of praise. I know they sleep sweeter for it. They dream music; for sometimes, in the night, they break forth in singing, and stop suddenly after the first note, startled by their own voice. Oh that we might sing evening and morning, and let song touch song all the way through.

The lark is in the sky, and his morning note is pouring:
He hath a wing to fly, so he's soaring, Christian, soaring;

His nest is on the ground, but only in the night,
For he loves the matin-sound, and the highest heaven's height.
Hark, Christian! hark! at heaven's door he sings,
And be thou like the lark, with thy soaring spirit-wings.

SEPTEMBER 13: *EVENING.*

Know ye not that your bodies are members of Christ?—1 *Cor.* vi., 15.

NOTHING is more certain than that ill health develops in some religiousness of the most enthusiastic kind, and in others torments of doubt and dread. No mere moral remedies can ever reach such cases. Bodily health will bring soul-health under such circumstances, and nothing else will. Long and wasting sickness; exquisite suffering; bereavements and losses; great exhaustion from continuous pressure of cares, from too great labors, from watching with the sick; long, severe, and exhausting study—in short, any cause which sucks the brain dry, and leaves it supersensitive, will be apt to induce a whole train of morbid moral symptoms, the only remedy for which is a restoration of health.

I know men that are beset with temptations of the devil and all manner of spiritual troubles, who, if I could send them to California by the overland route, would soon override the devil; and, the moment their physical health was restored, they would find that all their spiritual troubles had vanished. I do not wish you to understand, however, that all spiritual difficulties come from this quarter; this is only one class of them. Air, sunlight, recreation, wholesome food, sound sleep and enough of it, and exercise, will gradually reinstate the minds of those who have become prematurely exhausted and weakened. Then, and not till then, the conscience will begin with regular beat to swing its pendulum, and the mind and the soul will keep time with it.

SEPTEMBER 14: *MORNING.*

Thou compassest my path.—*Psalm* cxxxix., 3.

HE that can look up into the heaven at midday, and dwell long, and yet return his thoughts whence they came, without once having felt that God was there—I pity him. He that can look into the darkness of the night, and come back again to the light of his own countenance, and not have found God there—I pity him. He that can sit down upon a bank on which the sun shines in the spring, and watch the roots, and young insects, and all that nature is doing there, and not have one single thought of God—I pity him. He that can hear the sounds of the night, the voices of the sea, or feel the stillness; he that can look upon the face of a friend; he that can witness a marriage feast, or stand in the marble presence of death; he that can go any where, and not have the shadow of the eternal throne cast upon him—I pity him. He that has to hunt for his God, and shuts his God up in a closet, and keeps a lock and key on him, and goes there to find him—I pity him. My God is every where.

SEPTEMBER 14: *EVENING.*

And when he would not be persuaded, we ceased, saying, The will of the Lord be done.—*Acts* xxi., 14.

When our Savior went with the apostles to Emmaus, he made as though he would go farther, but they entreated him to abide with them, and he then turned aside and spent the hours with them there. So God's providence often looks as though it would go on; if you don't want it to go on, stop it. Love oftentimes says "No," in order that it may be made to say "Yes." In the dealing of God with you through the events of life, beware lest you submit too easily; beware that you are not too forward with resignation; beware that you do not give up your will too soon. It is a great thing to give up one's will, when it *must* be given up, nobly and thoroughly, but it is a great thing not to give it up until you are really compelled to do it.

But, on the other hand, remember that no energy is blessed, no enterprise is divine, which does not carry in it, latent, the spirit of resignation and submission. In the day of battle, fight as though you were a lion; in the day of defeat, yield. Persevere in your endeavor to the very last; but the moment the event has transpired which settles the question, accept the will of God, and yield to it.

When obstacles and trials seem
  Like prison walls to be,
I do the little I can do,
  And leave the rest to thee.

And when it seems no chance or change
  From grief can set me free,
Hope finds its strength in helplessness,
  And gayly waits on thee.

Ill that he blesses is our good,
  And unbless'd good is ill;
And all is right that seems most wrong
  If it be his sweet will.

SEPTEMBER 15: *MORNING.*

Thou shalt love the Lord thy God with all thy heart, and with all thy soul, and with all thy strength, and with all thy mind, and thy neighbor as thyself.—*Luke* x., 27.

THIS love is to comprehend every part of the mind, and all the time. The expression *love* is equivalent to our idea of dominance. It does not mean that we are to be thinking about God all the time. Nobody thinks of any one thing all the time, nor can. To do that would be insanity. Not the mother, nor the lover, newest and least expert, does it. It is contrary to our organization; for the mind is not a monochord; it is a complex instrument, and must alternate its states and experiences. What is meant is simply this: That the whole soul in free play, whatever part of itself it exerts, must be active in the spirit of benevolence—of love toward God, and of a true well-wishing toward men; that a strong predominant love to God and man shall so pervade the soul that there can not be, in all the action of the mind, one feeling that will go contrary to that spirit. The reason must be a reason acting in the spirit of love; the conscience must be a conscience acting in the atmosphere of love; the taste must be a taste acting in the atmosphere and spirit of love—love to God and love to man. The appetites and passions, and every other faculty of the mind, in all their power, or variety, or versatility, may act, but they will act as steeds that feel the one rein, which goes back to the hands of the one driver, whose name is Love. This it is to be under the perfect law of love.

SEPTEMBER 15: EVENING.

A good name is better than precious ointment; and the day of death than the day of one's birth.—*Eccles.* vii., 1.

Dying is like the folding of the flower. It is a gentle wind dying away. It is a tide flowing out to the depths beyond. It is a taper going out. It is a spark extinguished. It is a silent bird at twilight shooting through the sky, half rosy-lit, to its nest. It is, therefore, not the fact itself, it must be the associations, that make death terrible to men. Living is far more terrible in reality than dying. It is life that forges sins; that multiplies evils; that foments pride; that inflames vanity; that excites the passions; that feeds the appetites; that founds and builds habits; that establishes character, and, binding up the separate straws of action into one sheaf, hands it into the future, saying, "As ye have sowed, so shall ye reap." Yet life, which is the mischief-maker, is not at all feared. Death, that does no harm, and is only the revealer of life's work, *is* feared.

SEPTEMBER 16: MORNING.

The hand of our God is upon all them for good that seek him.—*Ezra* viii., 22.

There are critical experiences which befall every household, and they ought to become a part of the calendar of that household. The birth of a child; the death of a child; the marriage-hour of a child; the point at which a child is received into the visible body of the Lord Jesus Christ; times of bankruptcy; times of recovery from poverty; times of sickness; times of returning health—these are eminently significant. It is not enough to think of them as among the rubbish of mere secular happenings. They go back. They have vital bearings. They make us worse. They make us better. They lift us up. They crush us down. They are at work on our immortality. In heaven the threads of being will be traced all the way down to experiences here upon earth. As these things occur, it is wise for us to heed them, to study them, to set them apart from the ordinary flow of events, and to say in respect to them, "The Lord hath done this;" or "The hand of the Lord is in this."

SEPTEMBER 16: EVENING.

For a fire is kindled in mine anger, and shall burn unto the lowest hell, and shall consume the earth with her increase, and set on fire the foundations of the mountains.—*Deut.* xxxii., 22.

When I think that God sits—oh how long!—seeing every day, as the great revolving wheel of human life turns before him, all the operations that take place in the thicket; all the operations that take place in the open field; all that is done under crowns and under democracies; all that happens in dungeons; all that transpires in the streets of commerce—when I think that he is cognizant of all the revolutions and scenes of blood which are carrying sorrow to so many of the helpless and innocent throughout the earth, and of all the other evils by which men every where are afflicted—when I think that he sees and knows these things, and when I at the same time remember that he is the infinite and omnipotent God of the universe, I do not wonder when I read that his anger burns to the lowest hell; I only wonder that that anger is held back so long. It is God's great patience which calls forth my warmest admiration. It is that trait of his which, more than any other, excites my wonder; and I would crown him with everlasting chaplets of undying flowers, saying, "Thou, that art long-suffering and infinite in patience, shalt reign, God eternal."

He undertook our souls' salvation,
Our sad condition moved him so;
And came to us, from pure compassion,
To raise us from our depths of woe.
Oh wonderful, surpassing love,
Which brought him to us from above.

O Lord, of goodness so amazing
Not one is worthy—no, not one;
We stand in shame and wonder gazing
At the great things which thou hast done.
Thy crowning grace and precious blood
Have reconciled us with our God.

SEPTEMBER 17: MORNING.

Know ye that the Lord he is God; it is he that hath made us, and not we ourselves; we are his people, and the sheep of his pasture.—*Psalm* c., 3.

There are many that are born to misfortune, trial, and

trouble. They carry organized suffering with them. But that, for the most part, is not our lot. We are born so that our whole life is strong and our body vigorous with various pleasure. The separate elements that go to constitute this gift of our organization are marvelous if we consider them in detail. If the eye could keep a journal of all the pleasure that it has brought to us; if it could make a representation of what it is capable of yet bringing; if the gift that God has conferred upon us in the eye could be adequately described, no tongue could measure our obligations. If the ear could give its amount of pleasures issued; if all our senses—if the whole of our body could rise up and bear witness to God's goodness in its organization, what a history, what a complex series of service would be exhibited from God to us! What is the habit of our mind? Do the gifts of God, that come to us through the body day by day, inspire us with a profound sense of obligation, of thanksgiving to God? On the contrary, is not life, and health, and strength more frequently a reason of indifference? The poor hump-backed cripple often thanks God; whereas the man whose free blood beats without pain, the man that carries his body so as scarcely to know that there is more than an animal nature in it, uses it for variety, for pleasure, for pride, for worldliness—rarely for devotion.

SEPTEMBER 17: EVENING.

Verily, verily, I say unto you, The servant is not greater than his lord; neither he that is sent greater than he that sent him.—*John* xiii., 16.

As Christ was, so are all that are to be his. He did not walk a bright morning star all the way through the days of his life. He was not permitted to shine. He dawned on the world, went into eclipse, and emerged again from the grave. Death had woven his wreath and imposed upon his head its coronal. It was by suffering, by humiliation, by death, that he rose beyond the power of them all, and became a Prince, a Savior, and a Captain of salvation to those that follow after him.

Into such a world as this come all his true disciples, and they come hearing him declare, "The servant is not above his lord." If they have called the Master Beelzebub, will they call you any thing better? If they pursued him; if he was plied by temptations; if he was buffeted; if he was subjected to various trials; if he was called to go through his Gethsemane, and at last to bear his Calvary, will the disciples come into the world to bear nothing—no cross, no trial, no trouble? Shall we go unbaptized with affliction through to the. end, when Christ set the example of suffering, and said, "Take up your cross and follow me?"

Thou knowest, not alone as God, all-knowing;
  As man, our mortal weakness thou hast proved;
On earth, with purest sympathies o'erflowing,
  O Savior, thou hast wept, and thou hast loved!
And love and sorrow still to thee may come,
And find a hiding-place, a rest, a home.

Therefore I come, thy gentle call obeying,
  And lay my sins and sorrows at thy feet,
On everlasting strength my weakness staying,
  Clothed in thy robe of righteousness complete;
Then rising and refreshed, I leave thy throne,
And follow on to know as I am known.

SEPTEMBER 18: *MORNING.*

Even the Spirit of truth, whom the world can not receive, because it seeth him not, neither knoweth him; but ye know him; for he dwelleth with you, and shall be in you.—*John* xiv., 17.

Experimental religion is not a delusion. I *know*, and ten thousand witnesses join me in the affirmation, that there is a distinctive experience of feeling and thought belonging to a Christian nature which results directly from the communion of our minds with God's mind. There is a state in which Christ seems a real Being; in which he seems inexpressibly beautiful in all his attributes; in which he presents himself, not merely as your Creator in the beginning, and your Judge in the end, but intermediately, and all the way through, your Lover, your Brother, your Friend, whose friendship was sealed in blood—your Redeemer, who comes to you bringing with him from the eternal world all that there is in the Infinite of self-denying love; in which his true nature is so distinctly portrayed before you that you involuntarily exclaim, "This is my Lord and my God!" and in which you have the feeling, "My Christ is the universal providential Governor; all things are given to him in heaven and upon earth; the issues of my life are in his hands; he loves me; I am utterly his; all that concerns me is of his ordering; he will save me in life, and when I die he will receive me to dwell with him eternally in the heavens."

SEPTEMBER 18: *EVENING.*

And he arose, and rebuked the wind, and said unto the sea, Peace, be still. And the wind ceased, and there was a great calm.—*Mark* iv., 39.

Be heroic in your faith. If storms and darkness come, remember that there is a Christ in every ship that sails the Lake of Gennesaret. We have a Christ in our ship; and when he seems to be asleep, and fears begin to rise, speak to him, and he will take command not only of the ship, but of the troubled sea, and of the angry waves, and there shall be a calm. Living or dying, let us be the Lord's. It is base to ask permission to live by forfeiting the principles which alone dignify human life and human nature. It is glorious to live and fight the battles of the Lord, and win trophies of grace by overcoming the adversaries of our King; and when, at last, you who suffer with your Lord shall rise through the periods of time to stand in his presence in heaven, he will crown you with victory there. And the memory of all that you have suffered, what will it be but as the drops of a storm when you look at it in reverse, and see but a rainbow. Our troubles, with the heavenly light shining upon them, will be bright and joyous.

SEPTEMBER 19: *MORNING.*

Finally, brethren, whatsoever things are true, whatsoever things are honest, whatsoever things are just, whatsoever things are pure, whatsoever things are lovely, whatsoever things are of good report; if there be any virtue, and if there be any praise, think of these things.—*Phil.* iv., 8.

How many persons are there who are beautiful in temper? How many Christians are there who, under provocation, blossom into beauty—that is, who have meekness? How many persons are there who, in the midst of their gains, are humble—that is to say, have such a sense of that which lies before them that they are not puffed up; that they do not behave themselves unseemly; that they do not think of themselves more highly than they ought to think? How many persons are there whose good nature is any thing more than the mere product of good health, so that when they are unwell they are cross, and when they are well they are good-natured? How many persons are there in whom there is any thing like disinterested benevolence; who really like to do good, and who act benevolently without stopping to ask whether it is for their interest or not—who do not depend upon the poor crutch of self-interest to hold them up to their benevolence? How many persons are there who sow not expecting to reap again? How many persons are there who do kind and beneficent things from the love of doing them? How is it with you? Has your Christian character strength enough to go alone? Is it pure gold? Are you in God's earthly choir, or does your life add discord to the sweet sounds of Christian experience in life? Can you say with the apostle, "Our conversation"—that is, our citizenship, our life—"our conversation is," not shall be, "*is* in heaven."

SEPTEMBER 19: *EVENING.*

If so be that we suffer with him, that we may be also glorified together.—*Rom.* viii., 17.

THIS world is a place for apprenticeship. It is a shop in which the ore is taken and put into the furnace, and melted, and taken out, and put on the anvil, and hammered. It is fire and hammer, fire and hammer all the way through. This world is a magnificent place in which to forge instruments for future use, but it is a wretched place for any thing else. If you look to find in it perfection in institutions, in laws, in dispositions, in characters, in any thing, you will be disappointed. It is a place for beginning and carrying forward a work that is to be carried forward by suffering. "Whosoever doth not bear his cross and come after me can not be my disciple." Men are trying to take up the cross and follow Christ, and yet are murmuring because the cross brings sorrow and suffering. Do you think that you can be a child of Christ and evade sorrow and suffering? You must suffer with the Master if you are to reign with him.

Suffering is essential to human growth and human education. Think it not strange, then, when you come to your Calvary.

Oh that my faithless soul, one great hour only,
  Would comprehend the Christian's perfect life,
Despised with Jesus, sorrowful and lonely,
  Yet calmly looking upward in its strife!

For poverty and self-renunciation,
  The tutor yielded back a thousand-fold;
In the calm stillness of regeneration
  Cometh a joy we never knew of old.

SEPTEMBER 20: *MORNING.*

Whether therefore ye eat, or drink, or whatsoever ye do, do all to the glory of God.—1 *Cor.* x., 31.

You need not go out of your house, or shop, or profession to do good. Where you are, and in what you are doing, you are to do good. If you are a Christian, and suppose that you can do good only as you can get away from your home and house, you have a very false conception of what doing good is. You need not envy persons who have the privilege of going out of doors. That privilege may be withheld from you because God thinks he can glorify himself by your staying at home. Let no one believe that he is far from the gate of heaven who has the opportunities of the household. It is the best place in the world; and I do not think that any woman, mother or sister, who spends her life at home ministering to the wants of the loved ones there, has any occasion to envy those who sit upon thrones and occupy positions of influence. It is a sublime sphere. To provide for the family; to prepare their clothes; to watch over the little ones; to perform the duties which belong to domestic life, and to do it patiently and humbly, for the sake of Christ and in the spirit of benevolence, is glorious.

SEPTEMBER 20: *EVENING.*

And he, bearing his cross, went forth.—*John* xix., 17.

Every true cross-bearer learns to carry his cross as if it were an ornament rather than a burden, and finds, after a time, that it carries him. It gives more strength to him than he gives to it.

Yet how many persons there are who scarcely attempt to carry the cross! It is thrown on them, and they sink down under it. And that they, when Christ comes to them to comfort them, should not be comforted—that years should pass over their heads, and they should still be crushed and overborne, is strange and culpable. What is there in this world that is worthy of such a sacrifice of manhood, especially in those who are called by such a Savior, and such a luminous example, and have round about them so many stimulating influences? Shall grief be forever a tyrant? Shall sorrow forever usurp the attributes of the Almighty, and stand domineering over men as if the name of God were Sorrow? I marvel that there are not more victories. I marvel that there is not more glorying over the cross. I marvel that there are not more songs of victory sung; for there is no joy greater than that of grief overcome.

How shalt thou bear the cross, that now
  So dread a weight appears?
Keep quietly to God, and think
  Upon the eternal years.

Bear gently, suffer like a child,
  Nor be ashamed of tears;
Kiss the sweet cross, and in thy heart
  Sing of the eternal years.

SEPTEMBER 21: MORNING.

I in them, and thou in me, that they may be made perfect in one.—*John* xvii., 23.

Every where in the New Testament this one element stands forth—the personal identification of the human heart with the Lord Jesus Christ.

The forms of expression are as many and as rich as are the forms which vegetable life takes on in the tropics. All the occupations of life yield whatever they have in them which touches the heart, in phrases and figures, to bring out this idea. All the habits of higher love; all the analogies of sustentation of life in the body; all civic, economic, juridical, domestic traits—these are borrowed to expand and enforce this idea, the supremacy of allegiance and of love toward the Lord Jesus Christ.

He is light, bread, water, wine, meat; he is the vine, we being the branches; he is the householder, the lawgiver, the shepherd, the father, the friend, the lover; he is judge and leader; he is God over all, blessed forever. Whatever there is in day or in night that is sweet, and soothing, and nourishing to domestic love, is sanctified by being transferred to a higher function and use in the illustration of this noble experience of the soul of each individual man with its head, Jesus Christ. This heart-allegiance to the Lord Jesus Christ is to you the highest, the only true Christianity.

SEPTEMBER 21: EVENING.

Because thou hast kept the word of my patience, I also will keep thee from the hour of temptation which shall come upon all the world.—*Rev.* iii., 10.

Resolutions should not be hastily cast aside because they have been broken. If a man should start to carry water to wounded soldiers from a spring afar off, and if, owing to the inequalities of the road, he should spill the water on one side and on the other till one half of it was gone, what would you think of him if he should say, "I have spilt and spilt till it is half gone, and I won't have any of it," and then throw it down in a moment of vexation? It would be very natural for a passionate man, but how foolish and how inhuman it would be! When he was just within hearing of feeble voices of men that cried for water, would it be any reason for throwing away what he had because it was less than he intended to bring?

There are many persons who form resolutions and break them, and renew them and break them again and again, and at last say in vexation, "I will have no more of them; it is of no use for me to resolve." A resolution which takes in the whole of a right life, though it be broken once, twice, thrice, or a hundred times, is still to be clung to, and renewed till the end.

SEPTEMBER 22: MORNING.

I am a companion of all them that fear thee, and of them that keep thy precepts.—*Psalm* cxix., 63.

One may travel all over the world and never be out of reach of his relations. If you go to every part of our own land, there are Christians there, and they are your brethren. If you go under other skies, there are Christians there, and they are your brethren. You will find Christians on every continent. Yea, if you go into other religions than your own, you will find Christians there. If you go from the Protestant family into the Catholic Church, you will find Christians there. Wherever you see individuals whom Christ has loved, and that are accepted of him, instantly you feel a brotherhood toward them.

And the moment that feeling comes to any one, how from the presence of it all selfish feelings and all worldly resistances die away! There is in the consciousness of union with Christ an established fellowship one with another, and there is in it an element that dissolves prejudices and takes away those repellences that separate men.

Men that love Christ can not be far from me. If a man loves prayer, and loves Christ, and loves the Church, he and I must have a language that will make us brothers. It is a blessed thing to feel that you have, through the Lord Jesus Christ, kindred the world over, and that there is a principle of love and faith that is stronger even than blood-love and family connection.

SEPTEMBER 22: *EVENING.*

But Jesus answered and said, Ye know not what ye ask. Are ye able to drink of the cup that I shall drink of, and to be baptized with the baptism that I am baptized with?—*Matt.* xx., 22.

It is possible for men to be educated into a love of God. It is possible for men to be educated into faith of the divine presence. It is possible for men to be educated into that peace which passeth all understanding. It is possible for men to be educated into the power of rising above sorrow, so that they count it all joy when they fall into divers temptations and trials. These things are before men, and they can have them if they will pay the price at which they are held. But men are coming to God as the mother of Zebedee's children came to Christ, when she asked that her two sons might sit, the one on his right hand and the other on his left in his kingdom. And God is saying perpetually in his providence, "Are you able to drink of the cup that I shall drink of, and be baptized with the baptism that I am baptized with?" If you can, then the crown may be yours.

Lord, we know that we must ever
 Take our cross, and follow thee
All along the narrow pathway,
 If we would thy glory see.
Then, oh help us each to bear it,
 By thine own hard life of shame;
Let us suffer well and meekly,
 Let us glorify thy name.

SEPTEMBER 23: MORNING.

For thus saith the Lord unto the house of Israel, Seek ye me, and ye shall live.—*Amos* v., 4.

MEN suppose that when we are born again by the Spirit of God, we are brought into a perfected state—a state so much more eminent than that out of which we came, that it may be called a *miraculous translation;* and that, instead of anticipating sin, and weakness, and imperfection in himself, the Christian ought to expect never to do any thing wrong.

A child means to be educated; and that purpose is not to be invalidated by the fact that his mother keeps him at home very often to do house-work, or that she permits him to go a visiting or playing, or that he plays truant and forgets his books, and looks after flies, and butterflies, and what not, and is full of whims and caprices—full of spirit to-day, and all deliquescence to-morrow—full of all manner of infirmities. He is a scholar, and is getting his education, notwithstanding all these hindrances. So a Christian is Christ's scholar, and is in Christ's school, and his heart is set on education, and his purpose is to learn; but oh, with what lingerings, with what accidents, with what diversions to the right and to the left! And yet, taking it year by year, his eye is on the one object which he has set out to attain, and he means that more than any thing else, and is following on after it.

SEPTEMBER 23: EVENING.

God, my Maker, who giveth songs in the night.—*Job* xxxv., 10.

How many there are who have gone through the fires of affliction and trouble, and come out of them unscorched, saying, "Jesus has been faithful to his promise. I have suffered, but no more than was for my good. He has comforted and sustained me, and I am as happy now as a sweet little child in the arms of its mother."

Oh, bear witness. These are precious things that you are concealing. Wear those jewels. Let men see what it is to be comforted in the midst of trials and troubles.

I know how I feel myself. I am constantly called to funerals. Some mourn for whom I am sorry. Their rain is turned to ice. Grief is beautiful, as in winter ice-clad trees are beautiful when the sun shines upon them; but it is dangerous. Ice breaks many a branch; and so I see a great many persons bowed down and crushed by their afflictions. But now and then I meet one that sings in affliction, and then I thank God for my own sake, as well as for his. There is no such sweet singing as a song in the night. You recollect the story of the woman who, when her only child died, in rapture looked up, as with the face of an angel, and said, "I give you joy, my darling." That single sentence has gone with me years and years down through my life, quickening and comforting me.

SEPTEMBER 24: *MORNING.*

I will make all my goodness pass before thee.—*Exod.* xxxiii., 19.

WHEN Moses said, "God, show me thy glory," God refused to show him his glory in the sense in which he thought of it—that is, with the scenic outflash of all creation, revealing angels trooping about the throne, and exhibiting all the manifestations of divine power. Moses thought to see wonderful visions, but God said, "I will show you my *goodness.*" It is as if God rebuked the false notion which Moses had, and, pointing to his goodness, said, "This is my glory."

What is God's goodness? "The Lord, the Lord God, merciful and gracious, long-suffering, and abundant in goodness and truth, keeping mercy for thousands, forgiving iniquity, and transgression, and sin." Although he brought up the end by saying, "And that will by no means clear the guilty," you see there was but one clause of that, while all the other branches and twigs of the sentence were of mercy and goodness.

If God was permitted to be good to you all the time, he never would be any thing else. He is severe only when you need severity. It is not for the sake of gratifying any desire to inflict pain that he administers chastisement, but to fulfill the declaration, "Whom the Lord loveth he chasteneth, and scourgeth every son whom he receiveth."

SEPTEMBER 24: EVENING.

Ye are not under the law, but under grace.—*Rom.* vi., 14.

THE moment a man rises into that higher state in which his life is suffused by love, and God pours his life down upon the soul, he does not think of law any more, or transgression any more; he no more thinks about whether he is perfect or not. This last stage of Christian experience in this world is one in which we are so swallowed up in the consciousness of God's goodness, and nearness, and sweetness, and love, that we do not think much about ourselves. Our life is in Christ. We are not all the time ferreting out transgressions, or looking at this or that wrong that we have done. If we fell into sin, we should be sinking down into that lower state where conscience would catch us, and then we should have condemnation. But so long as we are living in this state of liberty and higher development, though we are not perfect (no man is perfect; God meant man to be man in this world; and no man is perfect so long as there is any thing to be added in his development); yet, so far as the law is concerned, it is dead to those who live by love. There it is, away down below, to catch them if they fall; but if they keep up where they are it will not touch them.

SEPTEMBER 25: MORNING.

And the city had no need of the sun, neither of the moon, to shine in it; for the glory of God did lighten it, and the Lamb is the light thereof.—*Rev.* xxi., 23.

To us here the glory of God shines as the sun shines in a cloudy day. Now it is hidden altogether; now a procession of clouds pass over it, and there comes through them a fitful checkered light; and now it is disclosed to full view. But there is a place where the glory of God shall be an uninterrupted stream, which shall be so clear, so apparent, that we shall live in the presence of it—that is to say, when we stand so as to see God as he is, there will not be a single thought nor a single emotion that shall not fill the soul with rapture; there will not be a single emotion nor a single thought that shall not touch the soul as the hand of the musician touches the chord of the instrument; there will not be a single thought nor a single emotion that shall not vibrate with admiring joy, for God is the centre of glory, and he acts on a pattern of grandeur in moral attributes such that to stand in his presence and see him is to be ceaselessly agitated and affected by the wonder of such a Being. We shall see him as he is, the God of glory, and our eye will be so strengthened that we can behold him and not die.

SEPTEMBER 25: EVENING.

Abide in me, and I in you.—*John* xv., 4.

THERE are some who have found the King's palace, though they only walk before it, and do not see his royal presence. Some there are who sit in the garden, and have glimpses as he passes to and fro within. Some there are who stand upon the threshold and behold his comely presence, and yet do not go in. Some there are who stand within, and yet as servants. Some there are who are admitted to his presence, and hear him say, Henceforth I call you not servants, but friends. And some there are who abide with him, and he knoweth them. Thrice blessed are they. Oh that we were of their number! Oh that we were within, and always within, and always hearing thee, and seeing thee, and loving thee, and rejoicing in thee, and rejoiced over! for what can hurt those who are surrounded by thine arms? What can pierce them, or reach to disturb their settled peace? All the earth might weep, but they are lifted in thy divine strength above sorrow. Yea, in sorrow is sweetness to them. They learn to suffer with rejoicings. How precious are the revelations of thyself to those who have the secret of God!

SEPTEMBER 26: MORNING.

Till we all come in the unity of the faith, and of the knowledge of the Son of God, unto a perfect man, unto the measure of the stature of the fullness of Christ.—*Ephes.* iv., 13.

A TRUE religion never is in the way of any thing which a man ought to desire. It undertakes to give a man more, in every way, than in his ignorance he could have had. It teaches him restraint in one place only to enable him to reach forth to larger liberty in another. It undertakes to give a man the whole of himself. When a man would rob himself by taking undue liberties with one part, leaving all the other parts unoccupied, religion teaches him a higher and a better use of all his powers. It undertakes to give a man the most that can be harmoniously educed from every faculty of his nature, and therefore refuses to let him overtax some, and underuse other parts of his being. Its very end is to give men salvation in the life to come, by making them better men in the life that now is. It seeks to make a man happier; it seeks to give him liberty, and power, and superior quality in every faculty of his nature. When, therefore, men enter upon a Christian life in this large and generous method, God declares that such a course, while it secures, ultimately, the high ends of eternal salvation, shall also secure secular good. "Godliness is profitable unto all things, having promise of the life that now is, and of that which is to come." Religion shall bless a man both in this life and in the life that is hereafter.

SEPTEMBER 26: EVENING.

He shall sit as a refiner and purifier of silver.—*Mal.* iii., 3.

TROUBLE, anxiety, forelooking, foreboding, anguish, bereavement, disappointed affection—these are only so many tools which God is employing by which to polish, and make fair and comely the qualities of your soul; and by-and-by, out of this shop-work, out of this tribulation, you shall rise fair as the sun, glorious forever, and shining as the stars in the firmament of God.

Take courage, then. Do not look down and within. Wait for the hour of transfiguration. As from a mountain-top behold your hope, like Christ, whiter than snow; and in that royal moment look up and take your measure and conception of life from this highest and most radiant point, and then rejoice.

Soon pride will have done its battle. Soon selfishness will have run out. Soon all disturbing passions will have lost their power. More and more time itself helps you to bring all the royal attributes of your soul into fullness and harmony, and soon death shall put the crown on your head, and then you shall be as beautiful as God—he being Father, and you children, and heaven the glorious land of beauty.

SEPTEMBER 27: MORNING.

And he arose, and came to his father. But when he was yet a great way off, his father saw him, and had compassion, and ran, and fell on his neck, and kissed him.—*Luke* xv., 20.

To those who have gone wrong, and who would retrace their steps, I would say, Your hope is in God more than in men. There is one Heart that is never weary of bearing with you. There is one Heart that will never cease to have compassion upon you so long as you are in the land of mercy and hope, until you have passed that line beyond which there can be no compassion. There is one Heart that is filled with generous kindness toward every man who wants to repent. Whatever may be your transgression, whatever may be the obstacles that stand in the way of your reformation, whatever sympathy you may lack from the world, God is on your side, and will help you. Are there wistful hours when, out of the entanglements of evil, which, little by little, like rust and mildew, have collected upon you, there are lookings away and longings for something better? The voice of God is calling you. The sound of your Father's voice is in your heart. Those very yearnings that you have are inspired of God, and they are meant to bring you out of your transgression. Heed them; understand whence they come; trust them, and trust God. Then that which you can not do in your own strength, and which men are not wise enough nor strong enough to help you to do, God will help you to do. Remember that he is on your side, and that he would rather heal than punish you. He does not desire that any man should die, but rather that all should turn and live.

SEPTEMBER 27: EVENING.

Wherefore I say unto thee, Her sins, which are many, are forgiven; for she loved much: but to whom little is forgiven, the same loveth little.—*Luke* vii., 47.

I THINK I have learned more of the nature of my Master from my bad than from my good. We learn both ways. But it is the sense of God's *graciousness* that impresses me. When I am penetrated with a conviction of my unworthiness; when my sins look like mountains to me; when my heart sinks within me, and there comes over the mountain, dawning bright as the morning-star, the thought of Christ's full mercy and endless patience; when I have a sense of the great goodness of God as it is revealed, in urgent contrast with my own sense of inferiority—then it is that my conception of God is more glorious to me than any other experience. Out of all my deficiencies, out of my ten thousand blemishes, there rises up the view of a gentle God. He not only grants me forgiveness, but fills me with zeal and holy purpose. God grant that this view may be stronger and stronger till I go home, to return love for love; till I stand in Zion and see God. Then temptation shall die forever from the light of his countenance; then, when once I am there, there shall be no more selfishness, no more temptation, and no more fear, but perfect love, which casts both out.

My sins, my sins, my Savior,
They take such hold on me,
I am not able to look up,
Save only, Christ, to thee:
In thee is all forgiveness,
In thee abundant grace,
My shadow and my sunshine
The brightness of thy face.

Therefore my songs, my Savior,
E'en in this time of woe,
Shall tell of all thy goodness
To sinful man below—
Thy goodness and thy favor,
Whose presence from above
Rejoice those hearts, my Savior,
That live in thee and love.

SEPTEMBER 28: MORNING.

Be not overcome of evil, but overcome evil with good.—*Rom.* xii., 21.

A TRUE Christian manhood has in it the elements of positive, overt power of goodness rather than the negative condition of the avoidance of evil. Christianity does not disdain fear, nor conscience, nor circumspection, nor watchfulness against evil. It enforces these things heartily and often; but they are incidental. It relies mainly upon the direct energy of a man's faculties in things that are good. It seeks not to repress life and keep down growth because abundance of being is more difficult to restrain. Rather, it urges men to seek right things with such force, and with such persistence, that no strength shall be left for wrong ones. We are to overcome evil by doing good and by being good. There is not in Scripture any ground for that miserable heresy which teaches that vigorous, fruitful, enterprising being should be restrained because there is some danger that so much of it may lead to overaction. That heresy belongs to the weakness of men; it has no characteristic element of the strength of God.

SEPTEMBER 28: EVENING.

If they have persecuted me, they will also persecute you; if they have kept my saying, they will keep yours also.—*John* xv., 20.

Do not be discouraged because any part of a Christian life seems to you so hard. It is God that worketh in you. Is the yoke very heavy? He will carry it for you. Is the burden crushing? He will raise it up. Is the way dark? Christ is the way, and he will lead you in it.

And it is but a little time that you will have the trial. Do not give up because you have begun a Christian life and found unexpected obstacles. Remember how the Master went step by step in his experience clear to the garden, when it seemed as though his troubles had so thickened upon him, as though he had been overtaken by such a weight of grief that he must needs go back. But what did he do? He cried out in his anguish, "O my Father, if it be possible, let this cup pass from me." The next moment one would have expected to hear him say, "I can not drink it." But no: he said, "Nevertheless, not as I will, but as thou wilt." And he triumphed in that moment.

If your cup seems too bitter, if your burden seems too heavy, be sure that it is the wounded hand that is holding the cup, and that it is he who carried the cross that is carrying the burden. Oh, dear Jesus, thy love is greater to us than ours is to each other.

The way seems long, dear Leader, and my feet
Are weary, pressing oft these thorns; 'twere sweet,
Methinks, to rest; this heavy cross remove;
Thou surely needst not thus my love to prove.
"Rest not, weak heart, nor lay thy burden down:
For earth's short rest, wouldst lose thy heavenly crown?"

Onward, dear Jesus: safely by thee led,
"Faint, yet pursuing," still the path I'll tread;
Gird me with strength, then e'er my prayer shall be,
"Father, e'en so it seemeth good to thee."
"And as thy days thy strength shall ever be,
While heaven's eternal glory waiteth thee."

SEPTEMBER 29: MORNING.

Follow me, and I will make you fishers of men.—*Matt.* iv., 19.

Our obligations to Christ for our own salvation, and the possession of Christ's spirit of sympathy and love—these are the grounds on which men ought to labor for the salvation of their fellow-men. Though parents, teachers, and ministers are expected to labor on account of professional reasons, the root of the obligation is not that we are parents, or teachers, or ministers, but that we are *Christians.*

It may be that some have better adaptations and better opportunities than others. That may be a reason why some should do more than others, but it is not a reason why some should not do any thing. Every man has some power, and is under obligation to the Master to exert it. If you have ten talents, you are responsible for ten; if you have five, you are responsible for five; and cursed be the man that, having but one, wraps it in a napkin, and digs a hole and buries it. If a professional man can do more than you, it does not justify you in not doing the little that you can do. The obligation is not professional, but moral. To live days, and months, and years without personal solicitude and personal effort for some individual soul is a sign so bad as to invalidate the evidence of piety. You must have somebody to love, and watch over, and sympathize with. Every single heart should have its part in this great, common, universal, individual, and personal duty of acting upon others for their religious growth, as God acted on you for yours.

Men die in darkness at your side,
   Without a hope to cheer the tomb;
Take up the torch and wave it wide,
   The torch that lights time's thickest gloom.

Toil on, faint not, keep watch, and pray;
   Be wise the erring soul to win;
Go forth into the world's highway,
   Compel the wanderer to come in.

SEPTEMBER 29: EVENING.

For in that he himself hath suffered, being tempted, he is able to succor them that are tempted.—*Heb.* ii., 18.

There is no possible experience that is not easily, familiarly known in the presence of God in Christ Jesus. Every man who has been subject to the temptations which belong to deceit and dishonesty; who has felt the fiery thrusts of the passions; who has experienced the envies and jealousies which come in the attritions of society, or who has had great hopes turned to disappointment—every such man can go to Jesus and say, "Lord, thou hast not sinned; but these feelings that are tried in me to the uttermost have been tried in thee;" and the response from heaven would be, "In that I have been tempted, I am able to succor those who are tempted." There is succor for every man who is tempted, no matter how low he may be. There are men who stand in the shadow of perdition; men who say they are tempted of the devil; men who, from the very beginning, count themselves unworthy of hope; and yet no temptation befalls a man that is so low, or so gross, or so brutal, that he can not carry it into the presence of Christ and say, "O thou Tempted in All Points as I Am, help me;" for that is his name—*Tempted in All Points as I Am.*

Nothing is so exquisite in you, nothing so multitudinous,

nothing so venomous and painful in the way of moral temptations, that it has not had some part in the experience of Christ, so that it is interpreted to him perfectly. And every sigh, every groan, every aspiration, every thought, that will not even look up, but that, looking down, despairs—God knows them all, and knows them quick, for they bound, as it were, against his heart, bringing up suggestions of trials experienced in his own person.

SEPTEMBER 30: *MORNING.*

Praying always, with all prayer and supplication in the Spirit.—*Eph.* vi., 18.

WHOEVER draws near to God in the spirit of sincere, winning, loving, filial conversation, worships. This is prayer, this is communion, whatever may be the mode. Some pray by the lips of another; some pray by their own lips; some pray in silence, without uttered thoughts; some pray at stated seasons; some pray only in circumstances that inspire peculiar feeling; some pray by written forms, and some without them. The range is large. The liberty is absolute. That which your experience teaches you to be best you have a right to. But one thing is to be common—we are to pray; we are to *abound* in prayer.

The want of devotion makes every effort at Christian life a burden. With devoutness, with the fiery elevations which come from devotions, with the realization of the great spiritual realm above us and around about us, a thousand things become easy. The heart that loves God and goes to him in prayer finds things to be light which others find to be heavy. Duties are no longer duties, but they become volitions, and men do automatically what aforetime they did, if at all, imperfectly, by force. There can be no eminent development of Christian life without this. It is the breath of the soul.

SEPTEMBER 30: *EVENING.*

The chiefest among ten thousand.—*Sol. Song* v., 10.

IN each quality which makes the dearest names in human life, Christ so excels that he is infinitely above all others. We are not accustomed to weave into his name all those sweet, familiar attributes which we see in the household, or which we meet in a circle of friends; and yet, in respect to every one of those qualities which go to make names that are dear to the heart, the Lord Jesus Christ is infinitely above them, infinitely superior to them in every thing. Christ is infinitely more in those very qualities which make a father dear to his children, or a neighbor noble to his neighbors, than any or all fathers or neighbors. All those indescribable and tender graces which make *mother* the queenly name in all the earth, Christ has in such abundance and perfectness, that a mother's heart by the side of his would be like a taper at midday. All that which the child yearns for while a child, and remembers with home-sickness afterward; all those qualities that make men look back for their Paradise to their childhood, and make them feel, too often, that life is a wilderness, and their early homes the place of love, and joy, and sweet fruition, are not so dominant in father and mother as they are in Jesus. His name is above every name. He is more fatherly than fathers, and more motherly than mothers. He is more tender in love than any lover. Language is exhausted in the Bible to signify the inflections of divine tenderness.

OCTOBER 1: *MORNING.*

Thrust in thy sickle, and reap: for the time is come for thee to reap; for the harvest of the earth is ripe.—*Rev.* xiv., 15.

October is the opal month of the year. It is the month of glory, of ripeness. I love to think that when the summer, with all its fullness of innate beauty, has gone through its course, and is about to die, it knows how to break out with more gorgeous beauty, and die with more glory on its head than it had in its positive freshness and vernal beauty. And so it should be with Christians. They should be bright and beautiful through all their youthful life, and gorgeous as they grow old and are about to step into the kingdom of God's glory. Let us begin again, in this picture month, in this month of the revelation of God's glory in the outward world about us, to pray and work, with the hope that we shall rise by-and-by into that resplendent land from whence we shall go out no more forever.

OCTOBER 1: EVENING.

What are these which are arrayed in white robes? and whence came they? —*Rev.* vii., 13.

THOUGH, when you look upon that rejoicing throng, you see no face that you ever knew, that is your father. On earth he was an old man, bowed down and wrinkled with many a disaster. You remember how he appeared then. Now look into that sainted face, and you shall find no wrinkle. Every sign of the remembered weakness is gone, and gone forever. That is a child of affliction, whose woes on earth were a marvel. She seemed to have been set apart for suffering, as a rock on an ocean coast seems to be a mark toward which the waves are aimed. But look now at the fair celestial beauty of her countenance. Hear her sweet flowing song. There is not one note nor indication of all that she suffered here below.

Then suffer on. Be patient. Ask God to bless your trouble. Be more anxious for manhood than for happiness. When in trouble, be more anxious that God should bless that trouble than that he should take it away, and seek that it may prepare you, not so much for pleasanter places in this life as for those higher seats, and the saintly ceremonies and joys of Paradise.

OCTOBER 2: MORNING.

But let all those that put their trust in thee rejoice: let them ever shout for joy, because thou defendest them: let them also that love thy name be joyful in thee.—*Psalm* v., 11.

THERE is a testimony of joy which we owe to the Savior, to ourselves, and to our fellow-men. The sweetness, the power, and the frequency of that joy which God sheds abroad in the converted soul ought to be made known.

I am touched to think how little joy there is in the world. I am touched by the mute supplication of universal experience for some joy. The very wildness with which men rush after pleasure, the very remorselessness with which they seek first one thing and then another, is a silent testimony to the desert condition of their heart. Men know that there is such a thing as joy; they long for it; they seek it; they strive after it; but alas! the experience of men is that there is comparatively little joy in this world.

When, therefore, one says, "Christ has blessed my soul, and brought me into a sweet knowledge of himself, and at times I have joy unspeakable and full of glory," the knowledge thus conveyed that there is such a joyful state is most powerful to bring men into the Christian life, as it has been in the cases of multitudes in the past. And it is the duty of every man that is a joyful Christian to bear witness to the good that he has received at the hand of God. It is his duty to go into all his neighborhood, and, with suitable words and with proper discretion, to bear testimony to the joy-producing power of faith in the Lord Jesus Christ.

OCTOBER 2: EVENING.

Wash me thoroughly from mine iniquity, and cleanse me from my sin.—*Psalm* li., 2.

WILL you not say, "I am willing to-night to forswear the evil tendencies of my passions and appetites, and, by the grace of God, I am determined to do it?" Have you been covetous? Will you not to-night in your chamber, in the presence of God, make a solemn vow that you will break the idol of covetousness, and put in its place the God who made you? Will you not say, "I mean to live for imperishable riches, and not for earthly wealth?" Have you been a man of fiery temper? Is it not time to make a resolution of reformation in this regard, and to seal it in the presence of God? Is there no habit that you will yield up? Is there no evil tendency that you will break away from? Is there no sin that you have been rolling as a sweet morsel under your tongue which you will abandon? Christ says, "If you give a cup of cold water in my name, you shall not lose your reward." Here is encouragement for you. You can not do the least good without receiving a remuneration therefor. Seek, then, to turn away from that which is evil, and cleave to that which is good, and go on advancing from strength to strength till you stand in Zion and before God.

OCTOBER 3: MORNING.

Casting all your care upon him.—1 *Peter* v., 7.

Lay your burdens upon God, and he will take care of all your mistakes not only, but of all your wisdoms and of your successes. His nature is beneficent, and Christ says, "The very hairs of your head are all numbered." He says that not a sparrow falls to the ground without the Father's notice. He has called himself my Father, and he has told me to call him Father—and I will. He has told me that every thing is naked and open before him. He has told me that he is bringing me up through trouble and suffering for eternal life and immortal glory, and I believe it. All that is generous and manly in me, and all that in me which has aspiration for dignity and honor, makes me believe that I am being conducted through this great and strange world by an all-guiding Father for the sake of making me worthy to be his son in the kingdom of his glory. And I will have the benefit of that belief. I will bring my Father into each particular day, and say, "The providence of this day is thine. Manage it as thou wilt. I do not seek to pry behind the philosophy and find out how it is. Sufficient is it that I may cry and thou wilt hear. It is enough that I may cast my burden on thee, and that thou wilt take care of me." It is enough that the voices of thousands of witnesses in every age have risen up and said, "We have cast our burdens and cares on the Lord, and he has sustained us."

OCTOBER 3: EVENING.

Oh wretched man that I am! who shall deliver me from the body of this death?—*Rom.* vii., 24.

Oh children of faithful parents! Oh men who for years have lived to violate your own convictions! Oh ye that have submitted to the bondage of this world, and felt all the time that it was an ignominious bondage!—are there none of you that, out of the prison-house, hold up your hands and cry for deliverance? Are there none who are in bondage to unworthy habits? none that shake their chains and say, "Who will deliver us from this bondage?" none who look back upon the time that is spent and past? none to whom sad feelings come sighing, as in autumn, when the leaves fall and the wind sighs through the fields and the forests? Is there no autumnal feeling breathing over your soul to-night, and awaking yearnings and longings?

Let discordant creeds alone. Do not mind the quarrels of churches. Listen to your own inward want. Hear your own heart. Believe the testimony of your own conscience. Give heed to your own reason. Yea, hearken to the voice of the Savior passing by.

Come to Jesus! Are you lonely?
Solace sweet he will afford;
Lean on Jesus—Jesus only:
Come, and find a loving Lord.

He is waiting—will you have him
Pleading at your heart in vain?
He is willing—oh believe him!
He may never call again.

Come, oh come this day, and try it—
Jesus' words are proved and true;
Take his gift; you can not buy it—
He hath waited long for you.

OCTOBER 4: MORNING.

Wash ye: make you clean.—*Isaiah* i., 16.

There is nothing that is wrong in the human soul that can not be put right. And you have the power to put it right, provided you are clothed with the Spirit from above; provided you take into your hands the implements that come from the armory of God. There is power in the Lord Jesus Christ for a perfect victory over the flesh, the appetites, and the passions, and to bring you into the supremest triumph of the spiritual life.

Let no man, then, coddle his faults and say, "I was made as I am, and it is not possible for me to be an eminent Christian." That is another question—how far it is possible for you to be an *eminent* Christian, in the sense of experiencing original thoughts and feelings, and bearing into the world a new tide of ideas; but in so far as the rectification of your own nature is concerned, God has given you power to govern yourself. Hard as it may be to transplant the tree of your soul, difficult as it is to sever the roots that hold it down, the Master says "there is power to do it." However many faults you may have, that branch their roots out in every direction, and difficult as it is to transplant them by the ordinary instrumentalities, nevertheless faith in the soul will give you power to pluck them up by the roots and cast them from you, or transplant them to better soil, where they will grow to a better purpose.

OCTOBER 4: EVENING.

He that eateth me, even he shall live by me.—*John* vi., 57.

Our inarticulate yearnings, the longings which come we know not whence, and point we know not whither, until by the Holy Spirit we were enlightened; the prayers uttered through us by the Spirit; the groanings for us which can not be uttered—all these teach us of God's work and of his wonderful way toward men. What we are we know not. If we look forth into the boiling tumult of human life to behold what man is, measured by time, how poor a thing is he! But there is something more to man than that which is revealed here. This is but the first summer, and not the blossom-bearing summer. There is another life; there is a higher realm; there are other developments. God has reserved him for a higher sphere, and all the outgoings toward him of the divine nature interpret him to be of a stature worthy to be called a son of God. It is in the fact that we carry the germ of immortality, and that we are to rise far above the power of sublunary things, and stand redeemed from every trace and taint of sin and weakness—it is in this that we have joy, and it is in this that we glory. It is the beyond that we long for; it is the right to be ourselves in all the largeness of a true and royal nature; it is that we may become like unto God; it is the hope of that blessed society in heaven which makes life tolerable; and we rejoice that we are not left dimly to guess, that our pulse is not left to beat feebly with expectation. Christ has spoken it, and the words have come to our ears and to our hearts, and we believe it—"Because I live, ye shall live also."

OCTOBER 5: MORNING.

Take ye heed, watch and pray.—*Mark* xiii., 33.

PRAYER is to be joined with vigilance. When fleets near the coast at night they give and receive signals. It is not enough that light-houses warn them of danger, so they throw up rockets as signals, to be answered by other signals from the land. I think these signals are much like our prayers and the answers to them which we receive. God has set light-houses all through the Bible; but we want something more than these, so he permits us to throw up rockets of desire, and he signals back to us.

Therefore watch and pray; watch as those who are talking with God; watch as those who have felt the affinity of God's soul with theirs, and are living as in the presence of the Invisible One. Then watching will become easy, and then it will become potent.

The time is short; the days make haste. Watch, for it will be but a few days before you will put your foot upon the shore of the eternal world, when you will see the height and depth, the length and breadth of that treasure which awaits you there, and when all the tears, and the strifes, and the watchings of earth will seem to you as the meanest price to pay for such endless dignity and glory.

OCTOBER 5: EVENING.

But thou, O man of God, flee these things, and follow after righteousness, godliness, faith, love, patience, meekness.—1 *Tim.* vi., 11.

GOD will never receive us upon any invoice sent from this world. Every man is to be reappraised, unpacked, examined, mostly thrown away; and that which is least esteemed here will be measured and judged as the best and the highest, so that the last shall be first, and the first shall be last. The ten thousand who go without a procession to the grave, whom no man knows to have died, and no man misses, have their procession on the other side, and armies in triumph shout them home; while men who are followed to the grave by a long procession, who are buried with much state, and who fill the world for a time with the sound of their fall, are received on the other side silently and without procession; and happy is it for them if they do not rise to shame and everlasting contempt.

Your honors here may serve you for a time, as it were for an hour, but they will be of no use to you beyond this world. Nobody will have heard a word of your honors in the other life. Your glory, your shame, your ambitions, and all the treasures for which you push hard and sacrifice much, will be like wreaths of smoke; for these things, which you mostly seek, and for which you spend your life, only tarry with you while you are on this side of the flood.

Only, then, that which happens to a man's inward nature, that which goes to form his habits, and so becomes his character—only that goes forth. The intellect and its habits; the affections and their habits; the moral sentiments and their habits—these, and only these, will go forth. "For we brought nothing into this world, and it is certain we can carry nothing out."

OCTOBER 6: MORNING.

Be patient toward all men.—1 *Thess.* v., 14.

Men's conduct may be wicked; it may be against moral character; it may be such that your whole moral sense revolts against it; but you are to remember that behind the wickedness there is a human heart; a susceptible throbbing nature; a spark of the divine Being; an immortal spirit. You can not hate wickedness too much, but you are never to hate wickedness so much as to forget that the actor and the doer is a suffering creature before God, destined in his providence to judgment and eternity. And you are to remember what of God and what of immortality is in every living man.

Consider, also, that it is by this very patience on God's part that we ourselves are saved. Do you suppose that any man on this earth, judged by our moral sense, is as bad to us as we, judged by God's moral sense, are to him? Do not you suppose that if God takes his pure truth, and by it measures truth in us, we seem ten thousand times falser to him than the basest man on earth seems to us? Do not you suppose that if God judges us in the matter of kindness by his own generosity of love, he sees us farther down on the scale than it is possible for us to see any man on the scale below us? Yet God bears with us. And if you refuse to bear with men because they are so vile, what if God dealt with you in the same way? You would be instantly burned up with the divine indignation. Not one of us could endure.

Breathe thoughts of pity o'er a brother's fall,
  But dwell not with stern anger on his fault:
The grace of God alone holds thee, holds all;
  Were that withdrawn, thou too would'st swerve and halt.

OCTOBER 6: *EVENING.*

But let every man take heed how he buildeth.—1 *Cor.* iii., 10.

WE are all of us architects, or, rather, we are laborers together with God as the great Architect. We are building up the soul into character. The building which we construct is, to be sure, not visible, for it is the soul. It is not formless, however, because it is invisible, but real and substantial—only with a finer substance than the senses can perceive. And a wondrous pile it is of many parts and eternal uses. Like Solomon's Temple, it goes up without sound of hammer or toil. No solid granite, no glistening marble, but thoughts, feelings, purposes are its materials. Out of these thin and evanescent things we are building a structure that shall outlive the mountains, the globe, and time itself. Day by day the courses go up, tier upon tier, story above story. A thousand ready workmen are our feelings and faculties, building, building, forever building. Only when we sleep is there cessation. At all other times the noiseless work goes on. Foundations are laid, materials are coming in of every kind from every quarter. And so year by year we build. Oh that we could stand afar off and see what we build! But no, the soul is built in silence; invisible, it yet abides like adamantine.

Oh glorious process! See the proud
  Grow lowly, gentle, meek;
See floods of unaccustomed tears
  Gush down the hardened cheek.
Perchance the hammer's heavy stroke
  O'erthrew some idol fond;

Perchance the chisel rent in twain
 Some precious, tender bond.

Ye looked on one, a well-wrought stone,
 A saint of God matured;
What chiselings that heart had felt!
 What chastening strokes endured!
But marked ye not that last soft touch—
 What perfect grace it gave,
Ere Jesus bore his servant home
 Across the darksome grave?—

Home to the place his grace designed
 That chosen soul to fill,
In the bright temple of the saved,
 Upon his holy hill—
Home to the noiselessness, the peace
 Of those sweet shrines above,
Whose stones shall never be displaced—
 Set in redeeming love.

OCTOBER 7: MORNING.

Love is the fulfilling of the law.—*Rom.* xiii., 10.

CHRISTIAN love is that condition of the soul in which it takes hold of every thing with a spirit of sympathy, and kindness, and yearning. It is that spirit which makes the soul hunger for the happiness of others. It is that development of the heart which makes us Godlike.

Christian love, then, is to be the disposition. It is not to be the sweetmeat and confection; it is to be the bread. It is not to be a disposition which, once in a great while, going to the cabinet where it is kept, you shall take out of the casket, allowing it to shine and emit all its precious rays. It is to be a disposition that is to be worn as your eyes are worn, to be possessed as your heart is possessed. It is to be, not an occasional experience, but an orbed disposition that, though it changes by revolving, never leaves its orbit. This love is to be to the soul what summer is to the earth—not a passing gleam, but an abiding state, which broods in the air, penetrates the soil, and draws forth and nourishes all the growths of earth or air.

OCTOBER 7: EVENING.

He careth for you.—1 *Peter* v., 7.

BLESSED be God that he has a care for us all, and that he is, for his own love's sake, doing for us what the mother does for her unconscious babe. In the bosom of God we are having an experience, the meaning of which the day of revelation will show us when we shall stand in heaven. Then we shall see that we have not shed a tear too many; that we have not borne a stripe that was too severe; that we have not had a blow that was not needed.

Are there any that are discouraged, and that are on the point of giving up? Gird up your loins and try once more. Do you sometimes think that no one was ever placed in such a situation as yours? The living God is by your side, and he will not leave you nor forsake you. Having made a profession of religion, and fearing that you are not children of God, are you sometimes almost ready to renounce your stand, and go into the world and do as you list? Oh, throw not away the hope that is in you. There is great reward in it. Are you sometimes led almost to doubt whether there is any reality in religion at all? Seize again with holy faith upon the eternal verities of God's word. Hold fast to your hope with courage, and God will bring you through.

OCTOBER 8: *MORNING.*

Forasmuch as ye are manifestly declared to be the epistle of Christ ministered by us, written not with ink, but with the Spirit of the living God; not in tables of stone, but in fleshly tables of the heart.—2 *Cor.* iii., 3.

You are the Bible which worldly men read. Men think more of what the Bible teaches from you than from the word of the text; and your conduct, whatever it may be, they are apt to ascribe, in the main, to religion. The Church is God's interpreter and commentator of the Bible.

What a position, then, does a Christian man occupy! See how you stand related to those that God makes the first objects of your care—your children. You can not help exerting an influence for good or for evil over them. During the first twelve or fifteen years of a child's life, father and mother are like God to it. The things you do are the model after which your children pattern. You are, by your words, your deeds, and the flow of your conduct, the interpretation of the Bible in your own houses. Your whole life is a silent teaching and preaching to those around you. How important it is, then, that you should be clothed with Christ for their sakes, who are dearer to you than your own life, as well as for the sake of all others in the world who look to you for an example. We are to be clothed with Christ, and to stand in his place teaching worldly men what is right by our lives. If, instead of that, they are led to see that they are better without religion than we are with it, how disastrous will be our influence upon them and upon the cause of truth!

In your own family, in the circle of your business, where your motives are scrutinized, wherever you go, is your influence that of a true Christian, and your conduct such that men recognize in you the spirit of Christ?

OCTOBER 8: EVENING.

I will not let thee go except thou bless me.—*Gen.* xxxii., 26.

There is many a man with whom this mysterious messenger of God wrestles; and if he be in earnest; if he will not let God's Spirit go except he bless him; if he feels that his life is in the struggle, and he will be blessed of God, there is no man so wicked but that he may become pure, and his flesh return to him again like the flesh of a little child.

If there are any who feel as though others might improve and turn back, but as though it were too late for them; as though they had gone too far; as though they had become too old; as though their habits had become too fixed—as far as your own will is concerned, it may be true that you would never be able of yourself to turn to God. But there is a provision in God's bounty by which, by his grace and by his power, you may be cleansed, you may be set free from evil thoughts and imaginations, and your passions may be restrained. A new heart God can give you, and from thence shall issue life, and life eternal.

Come, O thou Traveler unknown,
Whom still I hold, but can not see,
My company before is gone,
And I am left alone with thee:
With thee all night I mean to stay,
And wrestle till the break of day.

Yield to me now, for I am weak,
 But confident in self-despair;
Speak to my heart, in blessings speak;
 Be conquered by my instant prayer—
Speak, or thou never hence shalt move,
And tell me if thy name be Love.

My prayer hath power with God; the grace
 Unspeakable I now receive;
Through faith I see thee face to face—
 I see thee face to face, and live:
In vain I have not wept and strove;
Thy nature and thy name is Love.

OCTOBER 9: *MORNING.*

If thou, Lord, shouldest mark iniquities, O Lord, who shall stand? But there is forgiveness with thee, that thou mayest be feared.—*Psalm* cxxx., 3, 4.

When one comes under the conscious influence of the divine Spirit, the soul lifts itself up with unwonted clearness, faith, joy, trust, effluence, and liberty. What a bird was when it lay in its little round nest, an egg, compared with what it is when it sings in the dewy morning near heaven's gate, such is the soul by nature compared with what it is in the joy of sweet and loving intercourse with God through Jesus Christ our Lord. It is a life which comes to some by flashes. It is a life which comes to some by blessed dreams. There is a kind of spiritual haze which seems to befall some men, as there is an Indian summer which befalls the year; but there is also a true life. It is possible for the human soul to live in abundance, and freedom, and blessedness, so that it shall be forever at rest and at peace. Does it not sing? Yes. Is it perfect? No, no. There is no perfection without full growth. Does it keep the law? It may, or it may not. Yet the grace of God is so abounding, and the nature of divine love such, that when once the whole of a man's life is directed upward toward the bosom of God, minor discords are not noted. The soul's life with God is like the child's life with the mother. She pours over the child such a flood of love that, though its life is not perfect, though its whole being is imperfect, yet through sympathy, and kindness, and forgiveness, she accepts it. So the soul rises into such a communion with God that though, in its relations to time and space, it may be subject to a thousand imperfections and discords, yet those imperfections and discords are overlooked and excused by God's great love.

OCTOBER 9: EVENING.

There is a sore evil which I have seen under the sun, namely, riches kept for the owners thereof to their hurt.—*Eccles.* v., 13.

Many men think they have ravaged the world; but the world has ravaged them. Many men think they have led honor captive; but they have dishonored and disgraced their essential manhood. Many men think they have built a great Babylon; but God beholds how, after all, they are as beasts, on whom feathers or hair doth grow, and has sent them to browse as beasts upon the very ground. It is a base thing for a man to be put into God's workshop, which was set up on purpose to make men, and come out on the other side without a single attribute of manhood.

Ah, such wastes as there are! For a man to walk through cities and towns, and see what becomes of manhood, is enough to turn his head into a fountain of tears. It is enough to see the wastes of antiquity—the battered statues; the toppled-down columns; the fractured walls; the ruins of the Parthenon. It is a sad experience, mingling both pain and gladness. But of all the destructions that have gone on in this world, and that are now going on every day in the great cities, which are grinding and crushing out manhood, the destruction of men is the saddest. Men are as clusters in the vine-vat, and the feet of temptation tread them down as the vintner's feet tread the clusters, and blood flows out as wine. And yet this is a world that was made on purpose to make men better; to grind them to shape; to sharpen them; to temper them. Woe be to the man that is burned, or that is crushed, and that comes out worthless, and goes into the rubbish-heap of the universe!

OCTOBER 10: MORNING.

He that hath my commandments, and keepeth them, he it is that loveth me; and he that loveth me shall be loved of my Father, and I will love him, and will manifest myself to him.—*John* xiv., 21.

Many think that they are generous because when an object

of charity is presented to them they respond to it liberally. It is not so. You must carry the spirit of generosity with you all the time, or else you are not generous. Many think themselves to be good because they are susceptible of being made to feel good. It is not, however, being able to feel good, but knowing how to reduce good feeling to a practical form in every-day life, that makes a man good. Many think that they are Christians because, when Christ is set before them, crowned with glory, their soul rises up and says, "Thou art my Lord and my Savior." They forget him the moment the door is between them and the speaker, and their conscience ought then to say to them, "Are you a Christian, you that care for Christ only when he is held up before your mind so as to excite in you pleasurable feelings —you that never think of him except when your thoughts are directed to him by some external influence, and that never carry him into your life?"

On the other hand, there are hundreds that spend their whole time in endeavoring to please God by following the things that are right, and just, and true; who, because they hardly ever mount up into the ecstatic feelings that others experience, ask, doubtingly, "Am I a Christian?" Yes, they are ten times as much Christians as they would be if they had these feelings without the practical life of holiness which they are living. If you can not have both the feelings and the life, take the life. Rather than high feelings, that are like strong winds and freshets, and that come with rending and exhaustion, choose low-toned feelings, that are like the gentle and wide-spreading dew, and that carry nourishment, and tend to fruit-bearing.

OCTOBER 10: *EVENING.*

He that spared not his own Son, but delivered him up for us all, how shall he not with him also freely give us all things?—*Rom.* viii., 32.

WHAT must be the value of any thing desired when the price you are willing to pay for it is one of your children! What personal pain in watching, in care, in patience, are not parents willing to undergo for the sake of their children, rather than that those children shall be given up to any trouble? What abundant trouble does the eager parent take upon himself to shield the child? What ease, what prospects in life has the parent gladly given up for the sake of the well-being of his child? How easily would one sacrifice his property—the whole of it, if need be—rather than that his beloved child should suffer! How many a one would say, as David said, "Would to God I had died for thee, O Absalom, my son, my son!" The tenderness of the record may be rare, but the experience is common. When, then, an emergency comes in which a parent consents to give up even a child, what an unspeakable testimony is that to the strength of his feeling! There is no other thing in human life that can measure feeling like such an instance as this.

Now that is the image which God sends to kindle in our heart and imagination some faint conception of what was the power, the depth, the omnipotence of his feeling of love toward the whole race of men. Consider what must be the heart of God, in whom there exists such a feeling of desire and love that it puts into a subordinate place his love for his own darling Son! What must be that emotion which rises higher than our love for our own offspring! And transferring that idea to God, considering what is the might and majesty of every feeling in God over the slender experience of the human heart, considering what is the wonder of increase in every emotion in God when compared with the corresponding emotions in us, what must have been the length, and breadth, and height, and depth of the love of God to human souls! This is that which the apostle holds up before us in the question, "He that spared not his own Son, but delivered him up for us all, how shall he not with him also freely give us all things?"

O love of God, how deep and great!
Far deeper than man's deepest hate;
Self-fed, self-kindled like the light,
Changeless, eternal, infinite.

We read thee best in him who came
To bear for us the cross of shame;
Sent by the Father from on high
Our life to live, our death to die.

O love of God, our shield and stay
Through all the perils of our way;
Eternal love! in thee we rest,
Forever safe, forever bless'd.

OCTOBER 11: *MORNING.*

And the Spirit and the bride say, Come. And let him that heareth say, Come. And let him that is athirst come. And whosoever will, let him take the water of life freely.—*Rev.* xxii., 17.

Ye that feel the motions of sin, ye that yet throb with intemperate passions, here is that Savior who had to do with such as you, and will have pity on you. Ye that stumble in darkness, here is that light of the world which shines without quenching and without mutable ray. Ye that are burdened beyond what ye know to bear; ye who carry the dead in your very heart, and may not tell your anguish; ye that suffer an inward crucifixion as enduring as life itself; ye that may not sleep for the voice within that cries like a child, and can find none to trust; ye that sit in the dust out of which you thought you would rake gold, and in which you find only dross; ye that are as one that eats and is not fed, and drinks and is not quenched in thirst; all ye that in various ways of life are hampered, and troubled, and vexed, behold the Deliverer, your Christ and my Christ, who came and gave himself for us, and lives now to give himself daily for us again. Come all who know sin and want relief; all who know sorrow and want consolation; all who know what bondage is and want a Deliverer, come and take Christ to be the bread of your life and the strength of your life.

OCTOBER 11: *EVENING.*

In his love and in his pity he redeemed them.—*Isaiah* lxiii., 9.

For those who have done wrong to any degree, there is yet a place in God's heart. For those who have sought to break away from wrong and met with the poorest success, there is a place of mercy and pity with God. For those who have tried to reform—not once, but twice, and thrice, and many times, and broken solemn resolutions and obligations—there is divine leniency. For those who have given God occasion to draw his sword of judgment and smite them asunder, there is hope of salvation if only they are willing to be subdued and led by the infinitude of divine goodness. If they love sin and mean to sin, there is no grace for them; but if, sinning, their heart abhors sin, and if, in their better moments, they abjure it, and, like the apostle, they cry out, "Who shall deliver me from the body of this death?" there is grace for them. For all those who will repent, there is room for repentance, and help for repentance, and succor during reformation.

OCTOBER 12: *MORNING.*

And they sang together by course in praising and giving thanks unto the Lord; because he is good, for his mercy endureth forever toward Israel. And all the people shouted with a great shout, when they praised the Lord, because the foundation of the house of the Lord was laid.—*Ezra* iii., 11.

Blessed be God for hymns! Hymns are songs of the soul. And any man that wants to chord any state of mind can do so if he is familiar with the hymn-book, for the hymns that it contains are representations of real experiences in others, and we find that representations of experiences which came from a reality in others are apt to touch a corresponding reality in us. As for myself, I count the singing of hymns as being among the most eminent ways in which the soul can be brought into the conscious presence of Christ at its own sweet will. The shepherds heard the angels singing in the sky. Soon, however, the angels left them, and they heard them no more. But we have a sky in which the angels sing, and we can hear them when we choose. The songs of saints are angel-voices to us.

OCTOBER 12: *EVENING.*

He hath given us of his Spirit.—1 *John* iv., 13.

Every man must be a worker with God for his own salvation; but no unaided intelligence, no power of the soul exerted merely by yourself, will be sufficient for you. Unless God by the Holy Ghost works in you, you will come short of that very vivific influence which is the peculiar test and characteristic of the Christian. But God's spirit is loving and gentle, persuasive and universal. It is distilled upon you as the dews of the night upon the blossoms. It overhangs the earth as the sun overhangs this continent. God knocks at the doors of your heart, of your conscience, and of your understanding; thrice ten thousand times you have resisted him; you have turned away. Open now your heart; for, although you can not, without the Spirit of God, be a Christian, yet you can not turn your heart toward God with even the sigh of a wish but instantly the Spirit of God is with you. "The bruised reed will he not break, and the smoking flax will he not quench, until he brings forth judgment unto victory."

In the silent midnight watches,
  List thy bosom-door;
How it knocketh, knocketh, knocketh,
  Knocketh evermore!
Say not 'tis thy pulse's beating—
  'Tis thy heart of sin;
'Tis thy Savior stands entreating,
  "Rise and let me in."

OCTOBER 13: *MORNING.*

Every branch in me that beareth not fruit he taketh away; and every branch that beareth fruit, he purgeth it, that it may bring forth more fruit.—*John* xv., 2.

Blessed are they that fly so high that no fowler can snare them, and no archer can strike them. Blessed are they whose life is in the soul. And when they part from this world, and rise to the other, how glorious will be the entrance there to those who have been forged on the anvil of affliction and well shaped—who have been tried as gold in the fire—whose sins have been washed away! Sorrows that cleanse us; disappointments that make us heavenly minded—blessed are these.

When trees grow so that their branches are mostly on one side, we never restore branches to the deficient side by cutting the opposite side. We cut the most barren side, and there nature, in seeking to restore what we cut, drives out new buds and branches. The gardener knows that where he puts the knife there will follow the fruit of the tree. And blessed are they whom the heavenly husbandman prunes, that they may bring forth more fruit, if, when he cuts, there is a bud behind the knife; but woe to them who, being cut, have no bud to grow, and are more disbranched and barren for being pruned.

God grant that we may so live that when we die, whatever we leave behind, we may carry more with us, going forth with affluence of soul, clothed with holy affection, full of divine sentiments, possessing a character that fits us to be children of God, and companions of his holy angels and saints in heaven. May we enter there with joy upon our heads, to reign forever and forever.

OCTOBER 13: *EVENING.*

And he went in to tarry with them.—*Luke* xxiv., 29.

THERE is a state of the soul in which it has attained such a transcendent perception of the divine Being that it not only sees God by voluntary thought, but sees him every where involuntarily. Every thing in nature and society suggests the sense of God. All things reflect him; they are symbols of him. Every voice has something of the divine voice. Every form of glory brings something of the divine to the mind. Every thing that is great or little draws the soul toward, and not away from the divine Being, till one can say, "He fills the heavens, he fills the earth, he fills the body, he fills the soul, and my life is hid in his life. My life is but a taper; his life is the sun; and what taper can be seen while the sun is abroad in the day?" There have been souls in which the calm, the peace, did pass all understanding, and into which God did come, and abide, and sup, as Christ promised that he would. There have been souls conscious that they carried Christ with them day and night. They have lived in such a state that he dwelt in them. It may be overclouded, just as our life is by the period of sleep; but as, though we have lost our life in sleep, we wake up again, so, though this state may be overclouded by care and duty, and may for a moment intermit, it returns. And these persons abide in it, identified with God, living in the very highest realm of spiritual feeling and spiritual intuition, upon the borders of the heavenly land.

OCTOBER 14: *MORNING.*

Wherefore God also hath highly exalted him, and given him a name which is above every name.—*Phil.* ii., 9.

WHAT barns are to mansions, that this world is to heaven. What animals are to men, that men are to the superior beings of the heavenly world. When we have carried these suggestions from the realm of experience up to the line of the invisible and imagined, we shall find that the name of Christ is superior to them. There are declarations in the Word of God that that name, which has risen above every name here, rises there again. For there are beings that rise not only higher than men in wisdom, power, goodness, delightfulness, and companionableness, but there is a gradation among them. There are dominions, and thrones, and powers, and principalities in long succession. As we find long successions of natures among men, and below them still longer successions all the way down through creation, so we have intimations in the Word of God that this succession is continued, and goes up; and we are told that over all these Christ rises—not by arbitrary ranking, not by force, but by the intrinsic grandeur of his nature—by the essential grace and beauty of his disposition. And because he is "chief among ten thousand" and "altogether lovely;" because he is Alpha and Omega, the first and the last, the beginning and the ending, the bright and morning star, he sits upon the throne coequal with the Eternal.

And yet the name of Christ is a hidden name. Yet it is a name undisclosed. Far above every thing that is named upon earth, and far above every thing that is named in heaven, which is at all understood, his name still goes on. And not until we are there—nor then, until ages have rolled around and given us an experience—shall we know what is the height, and the depth, and the length, and the breadth, and what the universal glory of that name which is above every name.

OCTOBER 14: *EVENING.*

Hold fast that which is good.—1 *Thess.* v., 21.

Make resolutions, even if you break them. Make them—only make them wisely, with a strong will and with practical wisdom. Try them on every day. Do not forget them. If you do, renew them. And even if, when renewed and tried, they are much abused and much neglected, cling to them. It is better to have an imperfectly-kept resolution than to drift toward damnation without hindrance or let. Hold fast to ideals of good and to purposes of amendment. It is better to have a good purpose, even though you may not fulfill it to your satisfaction. Do not be discouraged though the way seems long, and perfection seems to delay in coming.

Through much tribulation we must enter into the kingdom of heaven; but when once we are there the battle will die away, and the darkness will be like a retreating storm, and it will be easier to do good than evil. We fight our way here, but when we enter the gate of our home above, and know as we are known, we shall find that this very conflict has been for our education, and has prepared us for the fruition of the everlasting abode of the blessed.

OCTOBER 15: *MORNING.*

For in this we groan, earnestly desiring to be clothed upon with our house which is from heaven.—2 *Cor.* v., 2.

All along the way of life we have premonitions of a coming future. Our very struggles, our sorrows and yearnings, are so many indications of that coming state. The tears that men shed, if they be of ungodly sorrow, are of no moral moment, but jewels every one, if they are symbols of unrest which the inward life experiences by reason of the imperfection of the outward life. In this state we groan, being burdened, not that we would be unclothed, but clothed upon. We groan not so much because we are discontented with the allotments of God's providence here, but because he has given us a conception of things hereafter so much better that our aspirations rise above the present with longing for the future. It is not so much discontent as aspiration. There is high meaning in these yearnings of the soul. The summer is passing; the autumn is coming; birds are gathering—they meditate a far-distant flight. And shall the soul have no sense of migration? There come to God's children hours of transfiguration in which the heavens are opened, the ground is suffused with glory, and Christ, our Head and Savior, shines out royally before us. And these momentary glances into the invisible world are the most precious part of a man's life.

OCTOBER 15: *EVENING.*

To him that overcometh will I give to eat of the hidden manna.—*Rev.* ii., 17.

THERE are some natures that only tempests can bring out. I recollect being strongly impressed on reading the account of an old castle in Germany with two towers that stood up mighty and far apart, between which an old baron stretched large wires, thus making a huge æolian harp. There were the wires suspended, and the summer breezes played through them, but there was no vibration. Common winds, not having power enough to move them, split, and went through them without a whistle. But when there came along great tempest-winds, and the heaven was black, and the air resounded, then these winds, with giant touch, swept through the wires, which began to ring, and roar, and pour out sublime melodies.

So God stretches the chords in the human soul, which ordinary influences do not vibrate; but now and then great tempests sweep through them, and men are conscious that tones are produced in them which could not have been produced except by some such storm-handling.

A man may lose all things, in the common acceptation of the term, and yet be exceedingly happy and blessed of God. A man may be stripped of property, may be bereft of friends, may lose his health, may have the way of usefulness blocked up to him, and yet he may experience a happiness that is indescribable if he only has left this thought: "Heaven can not be touched. On earth I am like a vessel borne down before a tempest, and swept hither and thither; but there is a rest that remaineth: God keeps it for me, and ere long I shall reach it. I am sure that I am a better and happier man by reason of the things which I have been made to suffer, since they have rendered my soul susceptible to the mysterious touches of God's hand." The man that is willing to stand wherever, in the providence of God, his lot may be cast, and that stands victoriously, God will feed, not outwardly alone, but inwardly.

Then sorrow, touched by thee, grows bright
  With more than rapture's ray,
As darkness shows us worlds of light
  We could not see by day.

OCTOBER 16: MORNING.

Neither is there any creature that is not manifest in his sight: but all things are naked and opened unto the eyes of him with whom we have to do. —*Heb.* iv., 13.

Blessed be God, there is not one single wicked thing in you which has sprung up since you began a Christian life that has surprised God in the least. Persons sometimes think, "Ah! if that friend knew this, he would not love me. I would not have it come to his ears for any thing. He took me to be high and noble, but if he found this out he would cast me off." Now there is nothing for God to find out about you. When he took you, he took you knowing the uttermost. He took you as a mother takes her child. She thanks God for it, though she knows it will be vain, and proud, and selfish, and possess all the evils of temper that belong to the race from which it comes. It is hers, and, in spite of its faults, she loves it with unspeakable love. And God clasps every soul that he once takes, and takes it for good or for evil.

OCTOBER 16: EVENING.

I thank my God always on your behalf, for the grace of God which is given you by Jesus Christ.—1 *Cor.* i., 4.

Let us open a Christian picture-gallery, and take all men who have been martyrs; all men who, for the sake of maintaining truth, have left home and country, and lived in mountains and caves; all who have exiled themselves, and wasted their lives in dungeons and hospitals; all who have stood patiently in their lot, and suffered, and died, and gained their victory, and gone to glory. I look upon the portraits of these and say, "That grace which has carried every one of them through can carry me through." That grace which made a saint out of so tumultuous a nature as Peter; that grace which could take such a nature as John's, who invoked fire on the heads of the villagers because they would not receive Christ, and make it so sweet; that grace which transformed the most fiery temper, and took away the desire of vengeance from men, can subdue the hardness and obduracy of our hearts. Oh! to see men who have been much tried get through safely; to stand by men who feared death, and see them go into the river to find that all fear is taken away from them; to question them as they go deeper and deeper, and hear them say, "I fear no evil;" to hear the rustle of vague sounds, as of heavenly music, from that exceeding throng on the other side that bear them victoriously home—this gives comfort. Can any one witness the departure of a man from this life, and his victory over death, without feeling more fortitude, more faith, more courage for his own battle?

OCTOBER 17: *MORNING.*

And he departed, and began to publish in Decapolis how great things Jesus had done for him.—*Mark* v., 20.

WE do not bear witness to Christ's work in us half so much as we ought. Every day and every where he is with us. It is by the grace of God that we are what we are in all that is good. He is not far from any of us. He is near to comfort you, and to inspire you with courage, and to press you forward in the Christian life. At home you are still with the Lord. He follows you out from home into your business. Where care and temptation are, there is rescue. Where suffering and sorrow are, there is comfort. Where darkness comes, there comes illumination. Where discouragement comes, there come instruction and hope. Your life is enveloped in a perpetual atmosphere of divine guardianship. And how much of all this wondrous experience of the dealing of God with your soul are you using for other people's instruction, to incite and encourage them?

When you go home to glory in the other land, and in music chant God's goodness to you, nothing will seem more wonderful to you than your own experience, except the mercy of God that delivered you by reason of it; and shall you delay until that glorious hour all recognition of this living work of God in your soul?

OCTOBER 17: *EVENING.*

The gentleness of Christ.—2 *Cor.* x., 1.

WITH a conception before your mind of what God is in his moral aptitudes and discriminations, as well as what he is in his infinity, omnipotence, omniscience, and omnipresence, consider what tax he has had on his patience and his forbearance, and what his gentleness must be in the light of human provocations.

The life of every individual is a long period of moral delinquency. No one who has not had the experience of a parent can have any adequate conception of the patience and gentleness exercised even by a mother in rearing her child, from the cradle to the door of the world, when, at twenty-one years of age, he goes forth from her care. It is only after-experience that can give the child a true idea of how much the mother bore with him, and how much kindness, love, forbearance, generosity, delicacy, and gentleness she showed toward him during his passage from infancy to manhood. True mothers are God's miniatures in this world, and we see portrayed in them, on a small scale, the very traits and delineations of that character which makes God the eternal Father of sinful men.

Lord, what am I, that with unceasing care
Thou didst seek after me? that thou didst wait,
Wet with unhealthy dews, before my gate,
And pass the gloomy nights of winter there?
Oh, strange delusion, that I did not greet
Thy blessed approach! and oh, to heaven how lost,
If my ingratitude's unkindly frost
Has chilled the bleeding wounds upon thy feet!
How oft my guardian angel gently cried,
"Soul, from thy casement look, and thou shalt see
How he persists to knock and wait for thee;"
And oh! how often to that voice of sorrow,
"To-morrow we will open," I replied;
And when to-morrow came, I answered still "To-morrow."

OCTOBER 18: *MORNING.*

If a man say I love God, and hateth his brother, he is a liar; for he that loveth not his brother whom he hath seen, how can he love God whom he hath not seen?—1 *John* iv., 20.

There are not two sets of duties and two classes of feelings required of men—one a lower, and called virtue, and the other a higher, and called piety. Piety and virtue are just the same at root and in moral quality. Love is one and the same whether you apply it to men or to God. Truth is one and the same whether you apply it to your fellow, to an archangel, or to him who is the King of both. Piety is the taking of man's reason, and moral sentiments, and affections, and exercising them toward God. Virtue is the taking these same faculties and exercising them toward men. It is more noble to love God than to love a man; but, after all, the feeling is the same. We should therefore maintain this unity. Piety is not a substitute for virtue. If a man does not love, honor, and obey his fellowmen, he will not love, honor, nor obey his God; and if a man has the qualities which make him a good Christian, he has the qualities which will make him a good husband, a good citizen, and a good neighbor.

OCTOBER 18: *EVENING.*

He that loveth his life shall lose it; and he that hateth his life in this world shall keep it unto life eternal.—*John* xii., 25.

I STOOD in the public burning-place at Oxford, where the old reformers were burned, and with inexpressible feelings I went back in thought and history to their time; but I have seen cases of martyrs that were burned at the stake which were much more piteous than these. I have seen many a woman who, because she would not betray fealty, and because she could not yield love, was day and night burned at the stake of an intemperate husband, bound to him, suffering more than he suffered, covering his shame, hiding his faults, repairing his mistakes, studying his welfare, pouring out her life for his worthless life. Oh martyrs of to-day, be not discouraged. You are following in the steps of the great Victor, who by defeat was victorious. Remember that Christ gained his victory by patient waiting in suffering. Remember what, by his servant, he said, "No chastening for the present seemeth to be joyous, but grievous; nevertheless, afterward it yieldeth the peaceable fruit of righteousness unto them which are exercised thereby."

OCTOBER 19: *MORNING.*

Be ye angry, and sin not; let not the sun go down upon your wrath.—*Ephes.* iv., 26.

NOBODY is at liberty to carry himself in an irritable, an ill-tempered, a waspish mood. That is sinful always and every where. It is without justification. Where we meet with things that are mean, we should *feel* that they are mean; where we meet with things that are dishonorable, we should *feel* that they are dishonorable. Do not hesitate to give expression to your hatred of things which are essentially untrue, essentially base, essentially mean, but let not the sun go down on your wrath. Be angry when there is a just cause for it, but get over it speedily.

When brought into the presence and under the temptation of evil, men are to rouse up the power of indignation that God has planted in them, and they are to clothe the higher moral nature with such resentment as shall change the temptation from a solicitation into a loathing. The command is that we shall strike dead whatever is low, and vile, and mean with the energy of a certain divine hatred. This is not merely a permission, it is not a doubtful power; it is a part of your Christian duty, it is a religious excellence.

OCTOBER 19: *EVENING.*

Behold how he loved him.—*John* xi., 36.

I FIND many persons that speak of loving Christ, but it is only now and then that I meet those who seem to be penetrated deeply with a consciousness of Christ's love to them, of its boundlessness, its wealth, its fineness, its exceeding delicacy, its transcendency in every line and lineament of possible conception. Once in a while people have this view break upon them in meeting, or in some sick-hour which leaves the mind not only not obscured, but more acute, or in some revival moment. That is a blessed visitation which brings to the soul a realization of the capacity of God to love imperfect beings with infinite love, and which enables a man to adapt this truth to his shame-hours, his sorrow-hours, his love-hours, and his selfish hours, and to find all the time that there is in the revelation of the love of God in Christ Jesus all-sufficient food for the soul. It is, indeed, almost to have the gate of heaven opened to you. The treasure is inexhaustible.

Immortal love, forever full,
  Forever flowing free,
Forever shared, forever whole,
  A never-ebbing sea.

OCTOBER 20: *MORNING.*

He, being dead, yet speaketh.—*Heb.* xi., 4.

When the sun disappears below the horizon he is not down. The heavens glow for a full hour after his departure. And when a great and good man sets, the west is luminous long after he is out of sight. A room in which flowers have been is sweet long after the flowers have been taken away; they leave a fragrance behind. And a godly man, who lives unselfishly, and disinterestedly, and seeks the good of other men, can not die out of this world. When he goes hence he leaves behind much of himself. There have been many men who left behind them that which hundreds of years have not worn out. The earth has Socrates and Plato to this day. The world is richer yet by Moses and the old prophets than by the wisest statesmen. We are indebted to the past. We stand in the greatness of ages that are gone rather than in that of our own. But of how many of *us* shall it be said that, being dead, we yet speak?

OCTOBER 20: *EVENING.*

For which cause we faint not; but though our outward man perish, yet the inward man is renewed day by day.—2 *Cor.* iv., 16.

What am I but rude granite? God found me lying in the hedge, and by troubles he drilled and blasted me out, by troubles he lifted me up, and now with constant clink of chisel and mallet he is fashioning me. God's chisel works inside and not outside, and the things that he chips off are the very things that we do not want to have chipped off. That is the reason why the blows he inflicts on us are so painful. God wants to make us patient, and cheerful, and happy, and good; he wants to make us rich in the inward part; he wants to make us superior to the body; he wants to prepare us for a state of eternal blessedness, and the means which he employs in doing this are the troubles of this world. We look at them merely in their relation to our condition in the present, and, not understanding their relation to our condition in the future, regard them as misfortunes. But Christ says, "Do not grieve over these things.

They are for your benefit. I love you, and that is the reason why I punish you. It is a punishment, not of vengeance, but of love, that I call you to bear. It is because I love you that I afflict you and develop your higher nature. I would fain work out in you a character worthy of you and of your God; therefore do not faint."

OCTOBER 21: MORNING.

That which we have seen and heard declare we unto you, that ye also may have fellowship with us: and truly our fellowship is with the Father, and with his Son Jesus Christ.—1 *John* i., 3.

Why is it so difficult, in talking with people, to lead them to throw aside their doubts and accept Christ as their Savior? Because our efficiency in Christian work depends very much upon the state of our own soul. A man whose Christ is near and dear to him, and who has a glowing experience, and pours it out into the souls of others, will help them faster and farther than almost any one else. The most fruitful days that I have had have been those in which I had something to tell the inquirer about Christ that I myself had felt. I have had the best success when I had a heart filled with love, and zeal, and enthusiasm, which, flowing out in tides, would catch the hearts of those with whom I was laboring, and carry them along. And I have seen many persons converted.

Have you never, after a cloud has long cast its dark shadow on a field, seen the shadow slowly move away, and leave the field exposed to the full light of the sun? I have seen the shadow move off from the souls of persons in the same way, and leave them exposed to the light of the Sun of Righteousness.

OCTOBER 21: EVENING.

Preach the word; be instant in season, out of season; reprove, rebuke, exhort with all long-suffering and doctrine.—2 *Tim.* iv., 2.

Although winter is not the time for sowing seed, every gardener who has a glass house will tell you that there are some seeds to be put in in the winter time. Although spring is the general time for putting in seed, every farmer will tell you that he sows some kinds of seed in June and July, and other kinds in September and October.

It is just so in moral husbandry. And what is meant by being "instant in season and out of season" is working at the appointed times and by the usual methods, and then working intermediately whenever you get a chance, and, if need be, by methods differing from those ordinarily adopted.

Of the seeds that I sowed last spring on the side-hill, where there was a strong wind, some did not go into the little furrows that I had made, but were blown to other places, where they sprang up; and I have noticed that some of the stockiest, strongest, and best plants are those that were chance-sown.

Now that which is true of the garden is true in respect to religious work. Some things that are done without prescribed form are more profitable than things that are done in a formal way. Work out of season is oftentimes as much blessed of God as things done in season.

OCTOBER 22: MORNING.

This is the victory that overcometh the world, even our faith.—1 *John* v., 4.

It is hard to turn a life that is misdirected into right channels; it is hard to change wrong feeling to right feeling; but it can be done. And the victory will pay for the struggle. Not those victories which come easiest are most sweet to us.

When we draw near to that other and better city whose bright domes flash God's eternal light, and over whose battlements come sweet voices to us to-day, saying, "Come, come," one single look, one waft of its perfume, one echo of its joy, will repay us for every tear, for every sorrow, and for every discouragement.

Then gird up your loins. Take a new lease of life. Form a higher purpose for the future. Have more courage—not courage which comes from a consciousness of your own strength, but that courage which comes from the certainty that "it is God which worketh in you both to will and to do of his good pleasure." O children of the living God, my Father's children, my brothers and sisters, heirs with me to an eternal inheritance, let us take hold of hands with a new covenant, with new sweetness of love and joy, and begin to live for the heavenly land.

OCTOBER 22: EVENING.

O the hope of Israel, the Savior thereof in time of trouble.—*Jer.* xiv., 8.

SURROUNDED by cares, afflicted by various experiences, borne down with bereavements, harassed by troubles, harnessed to business that will not let you go, you wilt, you grieve, you faint, you stumble, you fall down, you are biased and swayed, and you come to live by the very stress of your physical life—by sight and not by faith. And that which you need above all other things is such an entire subjection of your inward nature to the will of God and to the welfare of mankind, that you will rejoice in suffering, and count it all joy when you fall into divers temptations. Do you say it is unnatural? Yes, it is unnatural. It is of grace, and not of nature. But it is of the interior life, in which there is victory over ease, over trouble, over temptation. And when you are tempted to look by the natural eye, and to judge things merely by secular wisdom, you need to turn to the cross of Christ, and understand the foolishness of that cross, and know that, after all, it is the very power of God.

OCTOBER 23: MORNING.

A word spoken in due season, how good is it!—*Prov.* xv., 23.

A SINGLE word spoken, you know not what it falls upon. You know not on what soul it rests. In some moods, words fall off from us, and are of no account. But there are other moods in which a word of hope, a word of cheer, a word of sympathy, is as balm. It changes the sequence of thought, and the whole order and direction of the mind. A single word is often like a switch on a railroad, which, although it is a point almost too fine to be seen, yet is sufficient, when turned, to change the course of the train from one track to another, and perhaps from one road to another. Single words have often switched men off from bad courses, or off from good ones, as the case may be. Many a man, by a simple action which was born of virtue, and which passed by him unconsciously, has determined the fate of those who were looking up to him. A good man stands in the community as a tree stands on a lawn in summer, full of blossoms, of which it is unconscious, but which every one who goes past the lawn sees, and blesses the tree for. The sweet odor of the apple-tree is wafted in every direction, and myriads are participators of its life and efflorescence, or of its after-fruit. And so a great nature stands forth in bud, and in blossom, and in after-maturation, and there go out from him in every direction influences for instruction, confirmation, inspiration. A thousand things which the man never thought to do, he does. More are the things which you do, not meaning to do them, than are the things which you do, intending to do them.

OCTOBER 23: EVENING.

For as the sufferings of Christ abound in us, so our consolation also aboundeth by Christ.—2 Cor. i., 5.

SUFFERING is sometimes an infirmity, sometimes a misfortune, and sometimes a sin; but, whichever it is, there is in it an argument of patience. Christ suffered too. Arm yourselves, therefore. Hear him saying, "In the world ye shall have tribulation; but be of good cheer: I have overcome the world." "In that he himself hath suffered, being tempted, he is able to succor them that are tempted." Is it sickness of body? Is it disappointment of outward support? Is it the overthrow of all your worldly expectations? Is it the bitter thrust of the child's disobedience? Is it bankruptcy of heart at the loss of one much beloved? Is it trouble occasioned by your own pride? Is it the irritableness of your passion? Is it some surprising sin that leaped out like a lion from ambush, and took you down? Is it backsliding along the soiled and slimy way of the passions? Is it any duty so great that you dare not assail it? What is the trouble or trial that you have? Is it greater than those troubles and trials that overshadowed Jesus? Is it possible for the fibre of your little soul, however much it may be tried, to suffer in any direction as Jesus Christ's great sounding soul suffered in that same direction? He has declared, Because I have been a sufferer, right where you are, and was triumphant, I have power to give triumph to you.

Come boldly, then, to this suffering Savior. Make his sufferings the argument of your consolation, and rejoice in this that you are strong, because great is he that hath undertaken for you.

OCTOBER 24: MORNING.

He maketh both the deaf to hear and the dumb to speak.—*Mark* vii., 37.

HAVE you no testimony to give? If God should call you back again to start in life, would you live your life over again just as you have? Were there no fundamental mistakes? Are there no passions whose mastery you would disallow, and whose blight you have felt? Is there no experience that would corroborate the testimony of God's word, that righteousness is prosperity, and that the higher the scale of motives which man brings to bear upon business, the better is it even for business, even setting aside its moral influence upon character? Is a man to go through life working out these great moral problems, and thus come to results which are of vital importance to the young, then to be dumb, and never bear witness? Would Isaiah have done right, when God's Spirit inspired him with great truths, if he had refused to utter them? Does not God, all your life, inspire you with truths of which you are bound to be a witness? Men sometimes declare, "I am a Christian, but I have nothing to say;" and yet the most momentous problems of moral being have been wrought out in your history. You have lived a life that is more wonderful than was the original circumnavigation of the globe. Captain Cook's voyages are mere child's play compared with the voyage that every adult man has made. The experiences which you have known, interpreted in the light of God's truth, are of momentous importance. And will you be dumb?

Ah! never can I praise enough
  The mercy thou hast shown;
When days were dark and storms were rough,
  Thou mad'st thy kindness known.

Ah! though I lived a thousand years,
  And spake with thousand tongues,
I could not tell with words nor tears
  What praise to thee belongs.

OCTOBER 24: EVENING.

When he giveth quietness, who then can make trouble?—*Job* xxxiv., 29.

CHRIST alone slept on the sea when every thing else raged, and, awakening, he quieted the turbulent elements. When men were bestormed, he was the only one who could say, "Peace I give you—my peace." So, in the midst of the sorrows and troubles of life, those who bear the spirit of the Master, and see fit to be his companions, though they seem to be left almost alone, are, after all, the only ones who are rich and strong; for as the sources of the stream are in the mountain, where there is no drought, so the consolations of the soul are with God, the eternal friend, the everlasting companion.

If, then, you have been discouraged, gird up your loins again. If you think you are forgotten; if you feel that you are neglected; if you are conscious of being cast out as a stranger in a strange land; if you seem to yourselves to have toiled thanklessly, do not look on the dark side of your experience. Remember that you are not alone as long as you have faith in Christ. You have father and mother, and brother and sister, variously grouped in one, under the arch of divine love; and the love of God in Christ Jesus is enough to fill you with peace, and satisfy the yearnings and desires of your souls. Then look to Christ.

OCTOBER 25: MORNING.

Ye that love the Lord, hate evil.—*Psalm* xcvii., 10.

GOD made the earth full of soft and tender things, and just as full of hard and rugged things; and both are good in their places. Can any thing be gentler and sweeter than the million glad things that are opening their eyes in the grass to-day? or harder than the rocks and roots that they grow among? The blossoms of orchards and gardens, how delicate and tender! the wood that holds them, how hard and tough! The clouds that fill the summer days, and move without footsteps in the air, are yet full of bolts that rend oaks and make the earth to tremble.

And, in like manner, God has clothed the human mind with all sweet and gentle tastes, with all yearning and climbing affections, with all relishes; but the soul is clothed also with a power of wrath the most terrible, and for the most beneficent uses. There is given to good men almost a sublime indignation, a high and godlike hatred of evil, the exercise of which, under appropriate circumstances, is an act of the highest virtue and of the sublimest piety.

OCTOBER 25: EVENING.

Bear ye one another's burdens, and so fulfill the law of Christ.—*Gal.* vi., 2.

WE must have the spirit of Christ or we are none of his. Do men offend against you? Do your children try you? Do those around about you vex you? And does it never seem to you as though *you* were trying your God? Does it never seem to you as though you were offending against Christ? He bears with you, and so you are to bear with those that, to the extremest point, wring your spirit and try your life. Are there those about you who need succor and help? Have you done some things for them? We oftentimes think we have done our duty when we have spoken a word of warning, or have taken a step to render them assistance. If they come to us twice or thrice, we become discouraged with our work, and give it up. But how long has God borne with us? With what generousness and love does he carry us, our sins, and our sorrows? And can we not bear and forbear with our fellow-men? Are you a teacher? Are you not guilty of impatience and severity? Is it not easier for you to condemn than to inspire; to punish than to heal? Are you in relations of life where men serve you? Have you the spirit of Christ toward them? or are you irritable, exacting, impatient, making every one take the consequence of his own sin, and saying, "I told you how it would be, and now you must carry your own burden." Christ taught us to bear one another's burdens.

OCTOBER 26: MORNING.

Our Father which art in heaven.—*Matt.* vi., 9.

WHAT a history has there been to this Lord's Prayer, if it

could be gathered up from all the hearts and homes that have felt its benign influence since it fell coined from the lips of the Savior! It has been breathed from the budding lips of children and from the withered lips of the old; it has gone up from dungeons, from mansions, and from palaces. The exile, the prisoner, the rover, the sick, have found it a ready aid to their sorrows. How many sweet scenes has this prayer witnessed! how many mothers teaching it to their children! how many households gathered together hushed in worship by this simple formula! Oh, what is the Lord's Prayer to us, who were the children of Christian parents! It comes to us bearing not alone its divine meanings, but clothed with the associations of our early days. We see again the village. We hear the Sabbath proclaimed by the far-sounding bell. Father and mother are more sacred to-day. The air is clearer, and earth more wondrously beautiful. Silence is on the fields. The world seems to be worshiping God. In those hours of memory we uttered with inattentive lips these golden sentences; but, though they meant little to us then, how much more do they bring with them of precious recollections from those strange, fantastic days of childhood! And never do we hear the opening words, "Our Father which art in heaven," that we do not glance back to our earthly father and our early home, and we enter the heavenly presence taught by the love and reverence of the earthly.

OCTOBER 26: EVENING.

Israel doth not know, my people doth not consider.—*Isaiah* i., 3.

We are too selfish to know God. We do not ourselves know enough love to talk in the language of heaven; and that which we have is too often so allied to things lower and baser, that it is adulterated love. We can not understand our God because we are so far from him, and so unlike him. Yet that does not destroy us; for, as we care for our children long before they know us, as we care for them when sickness takes away their reason and judgment, so God, looking upon the distemperature of our souls, and seeing all the misery that it threatens, is still patient with us, and his heart is our nursery. There are we tended and cared for. Oh that we but knew it! Oh that we but knew the royalty that is around us. With what meanings would his providence every day speak to us if our eye was only cleansed from all films, and our hearts from selfishness; if we could at times know how he watches over us in sickness; if in the darkness of our delirium we could understand that he is not far from us—not far from any one of us; not far from the most sinful; not far from the guiltiest and wickedest. If we but knew these things, what hope of recovery would come to us! What joy of salvation! It is thy gentleness that shall save us, O Lord Jesus! it is not the might nor the power of our own will; for the more sternly we stand up, the more brittle are we, and the more easily are we snapped before the breeze. It is thy love, it is thy patience, it is that power working in us —that holy and blessed Spirit of light and comfort. By thy mercy, by thy goodness, by thy gentleness we shall be saved.

Men spurned God's grace; their lips blasphemed
The love that made itself their slave:
They grieved that blessed Comforter,
And turned against him what he gave.

No voice God's wondrous silence breaks,
No hand put forth his anger tells;
But he, the Omnipotent and Dread,
On high in humblest patience dwells.

And still the Father keeps himself,
In patient and forbearing love,
To be his creature's heritage
In that undying life above.

OCTOBER 27: MORNING.

We know not what we should pray for as we ought.—*Rom.* viii., 26.

I GO to God and say, "I am very poor, I am very ignorant, I am very sinful, I am utterly unworthy to speak to thee; but let me, O God, speak right on, and do thou sort out what I say, and put it in its proper relations. Let me relieve my mind." And I speak on; and sometimes it is petition, sometimes it is revery, sometimes it is soliloquy. I do not give myself any trouble about my prayer. God hears me, and he sorts what I say, and gives it its right name. I never think of husbanding all that my ground raises from my sowing. I winnow my grain; and God winnows my prayers, and lets the chaff fly, and saves the wheat.

Why give yourself any trouble about whether the things for which you pray are best? If it comforts you to pray about them, then pray about them; otherwise do not. Put yourself under the direction of God's spirit, and follow its leadings. And as respects all questions which are to turn on human judgment, my own habit is to pray for things just as I want them to be, and then say, "Now, if there is any thing better, please do that." I make up a case the best way I can, and then say, "If God sees any thing better, let him please to do it."

A capitalist, writing a letter of instruction to his agent in Marseilles, says, "I have a million dollars' worth of property in France, and the state of the empire is such, politically, that I think you had better dispose of it so and so; but you are on the ground, and I have perfect confidence in your judgment, and if you see reasons why these directions should not be followed, depart from them, and do as you think best."

OCTOBER 27: EVENING.

In all places where I record my name I will come unto thee, and I will bless thee.—*Exod.* xx., 24.

Some of the brightest insights come to Christians suddenly, in unexpected places, without any volitional preparation. Some of the most amazing joys break forth in hours not set apart for joy. As many of the Lord's days prove dull days, so many days that are not Lord's days prove bright days. For, though God meets us in the church, and meets us at the altar, he does not confine himself to the church nor to the altar. The road is his; the mountain still is his; the valley yet is his; the river-course, the edge of the sea, and the broad ocean are his; and God, who is every where, whose bounties are innumerable, who flashes forth his glory from the great temple above, filling the earthly temples, and filling the dwellings, and the fields, and all places —God is to be sought where you need him. He is to be found wherever the soul is ready to receive him. In some tender moment, amidst cares, and toils, and sorrows, often there starts up the thought of the divine presence with such majesty and beauty as a thousand Sabbaths could not shadow forth in the ordinary experience of Christians. Christ may be found at the well, if you come there to draw. Christ may be found at the receipt of custom, where Matthew found him. Christ may be found behind the bier, where the widow found him. Christ may be found on the sea, where the disciples found him when they were fishing. He is moving with world-filling presence every where.

OCTOBER 28: MORNING.

By me if any man enter in, he shall be saved.—*John* x., 9.

I HAVE sometimes thought that a doubter might well be compared to one lost in a blinding snow-storm. If any of you have had experience on our Western prairies, you know that here in this thickly-settled and forest-clad country there is no match for the storms that take place there in winter. On the open prairie, one starts upon his journey, every landmark clear and the way familiar. Little by little, as the hours pass on, a haze creeps down the horizon. The sun is gone, with a pale and watery farewell. Snow in scattered flakes begins to descend, and gradually increases. The road is soon whitened and obliterated. There are no fences, and nothing by which he can direct his course. He begins to be uncertain of the direction, and is alarmed. And with alarm comes exertion, which makes his case worse and worse. His course is devious and circuitous. He wanders round and round. His own very track is covered almost as soon as made. Often and often he is in the same place. He is moving in circuits, though he thinks himself to be going forward. He grows chilly and numb. Drowsiness steals over him. He thinks he will rest, though he knows that rest will be his death. He thinks he must sit down; yet he will not. And just as the struggle seems about to be decided against him, he discerns a light. It is faint and somewhat distant, but it is enough. With faint resolution he follows it. And he stumbles at last, headlong as it were, upon the door of the cottage which dimly appeared through the descending snow, and his very violence bursts it open; unable to sustain himself, he sinks down as one dead. And he is safe. The storm is behind him, and he has found rescue. Not by his own strength, not by his own wisdom, but simply by the protection which has come to him, he is saved.

So there are men that have wandered in this world from church to church, from theory to theory, from doctrine to doctrine, from belief to belief, from belief to unbelief, and from unbelief to restless yearning, saying at last, "Who will show us any good?" Round and round they wander, over their own paths undiscerned, until at last, well-nigh discouraged, they give up. But for all this, there comes the opening, at last, of a door through which streams the light of Christ Jesus. There comes an hour to many a doubting wanderer when Christ is presented to him so beauteous, so real, that he clasps him. And as one will not give up a dream that he has dreamed, so sweet was it to him, but frames it into a picture and cherishes it in his memory, so men looking upon Christ, and doubting whether he be a reality or a vision, hold on to the brightness, the joy, and the living power of Christ Jesus, and thus are cured of all doubt.

OCTOBER 28: *EVENING.*

For other foundation can no man lay than that is laid, which is Jesus Christ. . . . If any man's work abide which he hath built thereupon, he shall receive a reward. If any man's work shall be burned, he shall suffer loss: but he himself shall be saved; yet so as by fire.—1 *Cor.* iii., 11, 14, 15.

A NOBLE life, begun early and completed wisely, looks to me like a fair building which taste erects. The left hand is taste, and the right hand wealth. Although, when the house is being built, men do not see exactly what is meant, beholding dirt thrown out, the materials scattered around, and the workmen's chips and shavings, the mortar and the lime surrounding, and the scaffold hiding it, yet, when the building is completed, the scaffolding taken down, the soil and dirt removed, and the household are moved in, and the lights burn in the windows, and there is music in every room, and love consecrates every hall and passage, how beautiful then is that accomplished building! Such is the life of a good man. A bad man, whose life is a failure in all its moral purposes—what is that? It is like the burnt district in Charleston—the saddest sight I ever saw in my life. I walked up and down its streets, and took a lesson which, if I were to live a thousand years, I should never forget. It was a city of my own land. I loved it as I love my own. The fire had devoured it. There stood the stacks of chimneys, gaunt against the avenging sky; and there stood the tottering walls; and there huge heaps of noisome materials, where reptiles resorted; weeds grew rankly, and the dried stalks of last year's weeds grimly stood thick all around. Street after street was marked with emptiness and desolation. Such seems to me to be the life of many a man, all the ways of whose life are cumbered with the wrecks of the past, and all of whose plans at last shall perish as with an eternal fire and desolation.

In the elder days of art,
Builders wrought with greatest care
Each minute and unseen part;
For the gods see every where.

Let us do our work as well,
Both the unseen and the seen—
Make the house where God may dwell
Beautiful, entire, and clean—

Else our lives are incomplete,
Standing in these walls of Time
Broken stairways, where the feet
Stumble as they seek to climb.

OCTOBER 29: *MORNING.*

For what man knoweth the things of a man, save the spirit of man which is in him? even so the things of God knoweth no man, but the Spirit of God.—1 *Cor.* ii., 11.

THE soul has greater power than the body. The interpretation of the senses is not to be compared to the interpretation of the moral consciousness. And when God comes to the soul, he does not come through the eye, nor the ear, nor any sense; he comes through the soul's gate; he comes through that inward way which is plain to those who know it, and inexplicable and mysterious to those who do not; he comes fulfilling what he has declared, that he would manifest himself to his people, not to the world. What this process is, no one can tell. No one can explain the philosophy of it. When you wish to sound the understanding, there is a line and plummet with which you can touch the bottom. When you wish to sound the various senses, you can reach them. It is only when you come to the heart that you find places too deep for measuring. It is in the heart that the elements of eternity and infinity are found. No man has ever fathomed the heart's experiences. Poets have striven in vain to describe the emotions of the soul when it blossoms in all the ecstasies of love. And if this is so when one human soul touches another, how much less can it be understood or expounded when God touches our heart and kindles his affection on the altar of our affections! All we can say of it is, that it is the secret of God; but once having known it and felt it, no man doubts it again.

OCTOBER 29: EVENING.

Christ is all and in all.—*Colos.* iii., 11.

Consider what Christ is, and especially what he is to *you*. Consider what it is to have one who is in himself the sum of all those excellences which, in their separate and scattered elements, you so much admire and desire to see among men. I not only think of God along that line of analogy which is derived from human nature and human character, but I love to think that there is in him a perfection of these things which I see and admire in their simple forms in men. My God is, above all other things, Poet. I, that admire Shakspeare, and Milton, and Chaucer, love to think that these were shoots thrown out, and that the great Singer is my God. I follow the footsteps of men that have walked in the way of beauty—the carvers, and painters, and builders, and makers of music—all the children of art; and I say, when we stand with God, we shall find him to be the great Architect, the great Builder, the great Moulder of beauty, the great Painter. He lets us see from day to day something of the frescoes which he has painted in the heaven that is above our head with a prodigality that is amazing. And I love to think of God as the sum of all these excellences. Wiser is he than the wisest statesman that attracts admiration; more eloquent than the finest speaker; more lordly than the bravest warrior; more kingly than the highest potentate; more glorious than the most beauteous spirit that ever walked upon the earth. All that you see in the faculties of men orb themselves up and form in him infinite attributes. And there is a wealth in him, such that when you stand in his presence alone, it will be as if you stood in the midst of the whole universe of poets, and artists, and orators, and noble natures, God himself being all of them, and the fountain from which all of them draw their supplies.

OCTOBER 30: *MORNING.*

Whereupon, O king Agrippa, I was not disobedient unto the heavenly vision. —*Acts* xxvi., 19.

No men in this world are more worthy of being called noble than those who keep their soul sensitive to every revelation of right and duty, and who are accustomed to follow every intuition and disclosure of right and duty with instant obedience and performance. How is it with you? Are you conscious that you have put doing right under all circumstances higher than every thing else? Is that life which you are living, as a member of the Church and as an avowed follower of the Savior, a life which has come to this point of prompt obedience to duty? Are you conscious that, at the moment you perceive the right, you perform it? Have you come to this settled conclusion: "I will never fail to follow that which is revealed to me as right, whether in little things or in great things, whether in words or deeds; whatever I see to be right, no matter what company I may be in, no matter what interest I may sacrifice, no matter what risks I may run, I will follow?" Has this radical idea of instantly following that which is right leavened your religion? Is there this determination in you: "I will follow my moral convictions in my interests, in my pleasures, in my sympathies, in the customs of society; I will follow, not the thing which my business will allow, but what seems to me right; if I fail to do this, I shall be guilty in the sight of my own conscience and before God?"

OCTOBER 30: *EVENING.*

Because I live, ye shall live also.—*John* xiv., 19.

That is the end of trouble. Now sorrow is crowned with hope. Now the gate is thrown open. Now the angel sits upon the stone. Now the emergent Christ walks forth light and glorious as the sun in the heavens. Now the lost is found. Now all the stars hang like gems, and jewels, and treasures for us. Now, since Christ says that out of all these experiences he shall bring forth life, even as his own life was brought forth out of the tomb, what is there that we need trouble ourselves about?

Christian brethren, do you know how to be glad, and to make others glad in the midst of your trouble? Do you know how to stand in the midst of your losses and disappointments so that men shall say, "After all, it is not troublesome to be afflicted?" Do you know how to be peaceful in the midst of deepest bereavements? Do you know how to seek Christ in the very tomb? Do you know how to employ the tomb as the astronomer employs the lens, which in the darkness reveals to him vast depths and infinite stretches of created things in the space beyond? Do you know how to look through the grave and see what there is on the other side—the glory and power of God? Blessed are they to whom Christ hath revealed the meaning of grief.

By thy command, where'er I stray,
Sorrow attends me all my way,
A never-failing friend;
And if my sufferings may augment
Thy praise, behold me well content—
Let Sorrow still attend.

It costs me no regret that she
Who followed Christ should follow me;
And though, where'er she goes,
Thorns spring spontaneous at her feet,
I love her, and extract a sweet
From all my bitter woes.

OCTOBER 31: *MORNING.*

If any man be a worshiper of God and doeth his will, him he heareth.—*John* ix., 31.

It has been held by some that there is an efficacy in prayer such that we have a right to go to God without the use of means. Accounts are given of men who have built orphan asylums, hospitals, and other benevolent institutions, and professed to do it through the power of prayer, without any kind of prevision, or provision, or consideration of the application of means to ends. The lesson taught in such books, if there is any lesson taught in them, is that prayer is, in and of itself, a sufficient instrumentality for all the wants and needs of men, so that if we only have faith and come to God in prayer, whatever we desire he will provide for us. Now I can not doubt the power of prayer, nor can I doubt that direct and pertinent answers are received to the faithful supplications of God's people; but I do not believe that there is any such power in prayer as this. We are to pray, but prayer is to accompany and supplement the exercise of our own natural powers. God did not give us an understanding for nothing. He did not intend that we should lay it aside and not use it. It is to be employed according to its law. We are to exert ourselves in things that are right, and pray for help. Then, when human wisdom comes short, we may expect that God will supplement it with his better wisdom; and so far as by ignorance, or even by the limitations of sin, we are rendered inadequate for the emergencies in which we are placed, we may look for the interposition of God by his providence in our behalf.

OCTOBER 31: *EVENING.*

Wherefore, seeing we also are compassed about with so great a cloud of witnesses, let us lay aside every weight, and the sin which doth so easily beset us, and let us run with patience the race that is set before us.—*Heb.* xii., 1.

Although we may see ourselves before a vulgar age, in an uneducated community, and among men that lack appreciation, yet let us remember that these are not the only spectators of our acts. There are airy hosts, blessed spectators, and sympathetic lookers-on that see, and know, and appreciate our thoughts, and feelings, and acts. If we can bring ourselves to realize this, it will lift us above the necessity of vulgar praise, and above any depression that we may feel for the want of appreciation and praise from men. It is the great tribunal, airy and invisible, before whom we live more really than before visible and fleshly men. We perceive, then, that by-and-by, if men live with patient continuance in well-doing, they shall have honor and glory. You only sow the seed here. You do not reap the remuneration here, but you live with, and toward, and among an invisible host that understands the law of excellence; that understands how much more valuable are the higher traits and magnanimities than the lower; that understands how much more noble and admirable are the things which the soul does than the things which the mind does, and how much more noble and admirable are the things which the mind does than the things which the body does. All, therefore, which is hidden in obscurity in this world is reserved for disclosure in the world to come.

A crowd of witnesses around
  Hold thee in full survey;
Forget the steps already trod,
  And onward urge thy way.

'Tis God's all-animating voice
  That calls thee from on high;
'Tis his own hand presents the prize
  To thine aspiring eye.

NOVEMBER 1: *MORNING.*

Verily I say unto you, Wheresoever this gospel shall be preached in the whole world, there shall also this, that this woman hath done, be told for a memorial of her.—*Matt.* xxvi., 13.

As the wax taper burns in the temple by night, unconscious both of its own substance and of the light which it emits, so there be many persons who, in their humility, count themselves to be doing nothing in life, but who are diffusing the divinest influences in every direction. Fidelity, disinterestedness in love, pure peacefulness, love of God, and faith in invisible things, can not exist in a man without having their effect upon his fellowmen. It is impossible that one should stand up in the midst of a community and simply be good, and not diffuse the influence of that goodness on every side.

And the reach is incalculable. I have heard persons say that they seemed to themselves to be doing nothing in life. No man and no woman who is faithfully following the Lord Jesus Christ can be said to be doing nothing. It is not the eloquent tongue that speaks the most. It is not the heroic action which men sound forth that is, after all, the most potential in the affairs of men. The symmetrical example of holy souls has a voice which sounds out further, and reaches forth a hand that is felt further than more positive and more declarative influences.

NOVEMBER 1: *EVENING.*

Shouldest not thou also have had compassion on thy fellow-servant, even as I had pity on thee?—*Matt.* xviii., 33.

SUPPOSE God should treat us as we treat men, what would become of any one of us? If he were strict to mark and to judge, to condemn and to punish, who of us could stand for one single moment? We are the very men that are set forth in the parable of the unmerciful servant. Is it not so? Are we not described in that parable? Are there not dangerous pitfalls that any of us may plunge into at an unguarded moment? You may not be liable, perhaps, to temptations of violence, but then you may be liable to temptations of avarice. You may not be liable to temptations of dishonesty, but you may be liable to temptations of social hilarity. You may not be liable to drunkenness, but you may be liable to lewdness. You may not be tempted by any of the passions, but you may be tempted by that hard-hearted selfishness which makes the heart like the desert of Sahara—sand, sand, sand, without a green thing in it. Who is there that can rise up before God and say, "I have a right to condemn, for I have never sinned?" When God says, "I have found a ransom for sinners," who shall turn himself with bitter and vindictive fury upon transgressors?

NOVEMBER 2: *MORNING.*

Ye are complete in him.—*Colos.* ii., 10.

THE word of the Lord comes to us in our bondage to the animal appetites, in our bondage to opinions, in our bondage to carnal and secular pursuits, where we are all moping, and groping, and looking down, and we are called to a higher life. We are called to more freedom in reason, to more freedom in moral sense, to more freedom in affection, to a wider, purer, finer, nobler way of living. There is not one feeling in ten in your nature that you use. But God calls you to the whole of yourself.

And the way to come to one's whole self is through a true Christian experience. A man who knows how to be a better husband, a better father, a better friend, and a better neighbor, is happier for it. A man who is called to a Christian life, and responds to the call, does business easier and more naturally. Whatever a man does, he can do better if he does it as a Christian does it than if he does it as a man of the world does it. There is nothing that so helps a man in the discharge of the ordinary duties of life as harmonizing his whole self with the divine conception.

In being called to a Christian life, then, we are called, not to circumscription nor to gloom, but to largeness, and power, and symmetry, and fineness, and fullness—in short, to *beauty*. Every man who becomes a Christian ought to seem more radiant than ever before. And he will, if he is living in a full understanding of his privilege, and up to his privilege, or any where near it. For it does not require perfection to be handsome. A moss-rose bud is handsome before it blossoms.

NOVEMBER 2: EVENING.

For ye shall go out with joy, and be led forth with peace.—*Isaiah* lv., 12.

God can give grace to endure poverty, to thrive under hardships, to bear up under grief, and to pluck fruit from thorns, and flowers from weeds. But so, also, can God fill the heart of his people with a spirit that shall overflow and sanctify all business, all commerce, all learning, all art. The channels that are now filled with passions are to be emptied of them and filled with something better.

We are not to seek to know how to enter the kingdom of heaven in sackcloth. We are not to eat in the wilderness locusts and wild honey. We are to sit at the King's table because we are the King's sons. And the time is coming when men will be able, as it were, to sit at king's tables on earth, and bear honors, and be better for it, more sovereign in love, more mighty in purity and in truth, and more effectual in doing good to others. Joy, not sorrow, should be the key-note of our Christian experience. Sorrow is the medicine by which we come to it. I believe that, when the time of ripeness comes, it will be found that beauty and power are the only appropriate garments of piety. They have been stolen by the passions and the appetites, but they are to be worn in their fullest glory only by the highest sentiments that are in man.

NOVEMBER 3: *MORNING.*

Let us, therefore, come boldly unto the throne of grace, that we may obtain mercy, and find grace to help in time of need.—*Heb.* iv., 16.

"LET us, therefore," on account of these two things—first, God's sympathy; and, second, God's perfect knowledge of all our wickednesses—"come boldly to the throne of grace"—and why? "That we may obtain mercy, and find grace to help in time of need." We go not to exonerate ourselves, not to plead our righteousness; we go boldly, saying, "Thou knowest that I am sinful, but thou sentest thy Son to atone for sins; I am sick, but thou hast the medicine for souls that are sick; I am wicked, but thou art he that delightest to forgive wickedness." We are to go boldly to God's throne, because he is so full of mercies for our want; so full of goodness for our wickedness; so full of forgiveness for our sins. And God's knowledge of what we are, and all we do, instead of being an argument for fear, is an argument for confidence.

In every pang that rends the heart,
The Man of Sorrows had a part;
He sympathizes with our grief,
And to the sufferer sends relief.

With boldness, therefore, at the throne,
Let us make all our sorrows known,
And ask the aids of heavenly power
To help us in the evil hour.

NOVEMBER 3: *EVENING.*

Thus saith the Lord, Israel is my son, even my first-born.—*Exod.* iv., 22.

I NEVER like to hear people speak of a religious or Christian life by its negatives—by its limitations, and restraints, and necessary pains and self-denials; for, although at times there are struggles, and though there may be a proper mention of them, yet no man can consider what are the elements of a true faith, what are the promises and inspirations of God, without perceiving that those shadows are alternative, occasional, exceptional states, and that the New Testament designs the Christian man to be a child of light and joy. He is set free. He is adopted into the household of God. He is a friend, no longer a servant. He is an heir expectant, but is not, like many heirs, waiting until the bequeathed estate comes to him; for he has the earnest of it sent before, as it were, to support him on the road to it.

NOVEMBER 4: MORNING.

Not with eye-service, as men-pleasers; but as the servants of Christ, doing the will of God from the heart.—*Eph.* vi., 6.

I THINK it is affecting to see with what tenderness God has taken care of those that no one else cares for. How he goes down to the poor, and the ignorant, and the enslaved! How he goes down to those that can find no motive whatsoever for right living in the ordinary flow of their experience, or the ordinary action of their faculties, and says to them, "Serve, obey, be faithful, be industrious, be Christian-minded, if not for the sake of your Master, then for my sake!" It pleases God to stand behind every single duty that has in it no conceivable motive addressed to any of the normal human faculties, and say, "Consecrate that duty to me; and, though you do not serve any body else in it, serve me in it." He puts exceeding great and precious promises on lower places of life in this way, and makes things attractive that otherwise would be unattractive; for, once let us know that we are serving onewhom we love, and one who loves us, and love vanquishes difficulty. There are no obstacles too great for love to overcome. Is there any thing we can not do joyfully for Christ?

NOVEMBER 4: EVENING.

Behold, I stand at the door and knock.—*Rev.* iii., 20.

As one who returns to his dwelling in the night, after a journey, and, finding it locked, knocks at the accustomed door of entrance in the front, and, getting no answer, goes to the door in the rear, then to the side door, if there be one, and then to every other door, in order, if possible, to get into his house, so Christ, who longs to enter into the soul, goes to every door in succession, and knocks, and listens for an invitation to come in, and leaves not one chamber in the soul-house unsought, or one door untried! He knocks at the door of Reason; at the door of Fear; at the door of Hope; at the door of Imagination and Taste; of Benevolence and Love; of Conscience; of Memory and Gratitude. He does not neglect a single one.

Beginning at the upper and the noblest, where he ought to come in as a King of Glory, through gates of triumph, he comes round and down to the last and lowest, and retreats wistfully and reluctantly, returning often, morning, noon, and night, continually seeking entrance with marvelous patience, accepting no refusal, repulsed by no indifference to his presence, and no neglect of his message.

If he be admitted, joy unspeakable is in the house, and shall be henceforth. The dreary dwelling is filled with light from the brightness of his countenance, and every chamber is perfumed from the fragrance of his garments. Peace and hope, love and joy, abide in the house, for Christ himself takes up his abode therein. But if, after his long knocking at the door and patient waiting for entrance, his solicitation be refused or neglected, by-and-by there shall come a time when you who have denied him shall be denied of him; for, when you shall knock at the gate of heaven for admittance into the mansions which he has prepared from the foundation of the world, he will say unto you, as you said unto him, Depart! But that dreadful day has not yet come, and he still stands at the door, his locks wet with the dews of the morning, and waits to be invited into the chamber of your soul. Hear his voice once more, and yield to its gentle persuasion—"Behold, I stand at the door and knock; if any man hear my voice, and open the door, I will come in to him, and will sup with him, and he with me."

NOVEMBER 5: MORNING.

And I give unto them eternal life; and they shall never perish, neither shall any man pluck them out of my hand.—*John* x., 28.

You, dear Christian friends, who have just united yourselves with God's people, have entered a service the most blessed that can happen to the human heart in this world. Do not be discouraged because you find difficulties. You are not saints. But you have entered upon a service in which your Master is gentler than your parents could be—a benignant Savior, a magnanimous Savior, an ever-present Savior, who is not ashamed of you, and will not be, whatever you do or wherever you go. Oh! if any where the snare entangles your feet; if the net is thrown over you; if you do wrong, and fall utterly prostrate, remember, in your deepest penitence and anguish of sorrow, to hear the voice saying still, "My child, I am not ashamed of you." If you can not look in the face of man, look up into the face of God. There is more mercy there than there is in all the world besides.

Never forget that you are the children of divine love. It is love that bore you. It is love that has brought you to these moods of penitence and these drawings toward a better life. It is love that will take care of you, even to the end—love better than the father's, better than the mother's, better than all earthly love.

O gracious Shepherd, bind us
  With cords of love to thee,
And evermore remind us
  How mercy set us free.

We are of our salvation
  Assured through thy love;
Yet oh, on each occasion,
  How faithless do we prove!

But thou wilt not forsake us,
  Though we are oft to blame;
Oh let thy love then make us
  Hold fast thy faith and name.

NOVEMBER 5: EVENING.

He giveth grace unto the lowly.—*Prov.* iii., 34.

The blossoms are not always on the tops of the trees. They are sometimes on the branches that are down near the ground. I have seen aunts, maiden sisters, plain sewing-women, those who were lowest in poverty, who stood with such erect, sweet, pure heavenly-mindedness, that it was worth one's while to look at them, to renew his own faith in himself. Sometimes I have heard these same people say that it was a mystery to them that God should have debarred them from the usefulness that they longed for; that they should have been made obscure; that they should have no tongue for speaking. Do you suppose that when a honeysuckle blossoms, and its fragrance goes abroad, it has any idea how far it goes? It leaves the blossom, and the stem and vine know no more about it. It is wafted by the wind—it is sent through all the neighborhood, and the blossom does not know how it sheds its sweetness every where. It is unconscious. Do you suppose a candle in an eminent place knows how much light it sends out, or how many see it? Do you suppose a star knows what is said about it? It, too, is unconscious. And it is the unconsciousness of a symmetrical Christian life and character that is its very richness and power.

NOVEMBER 6: MORNING.

Who shall lay any thing to the charge of God's elect? It is God that justifieth. Who is he that condemneth? It is Christ that died, yea rather, that is risen again, who is even at the right hand of God, who also maketh intercession for us.—*Rom.* viii., 33, 34.

What is a man's power? He has power to resolve. And what is the power of resolution? It is the power of a bubble, which reflects for one instant the glory of heaven, and then is broken and gone. Our resolutions are good for a second, and then they are forgotten. What are men's throes and struggles against inward passions and outward temptations? They are as nothing. We are swept before the evil influences which come upon us in this world as chaff before the summer's storm. We are routed and driven as miserable, cowardly militia before courageous soldiers.

When a man looks at his own state, and thinks whether he shall be able to prevail and stand in Zion and before God, it is not at all wonderful that his courage fails him. But why should he think of himself? Why should he measure his chances of everlasting life merely by the slender forces that he can address to the work of salvation? Have you no God? Have you no Savior? Was it not for you that Calvary became memorable? Was there one thought, was there one feeling, did one drop of blood fall to the ground on that blessed mount in which you had no right, nor part, nor lot? The treasure of Calvary is the birthright of every child who has come into life since the death of Christ; and all that was then manifested by God in word, or thought, or act, was but a feeble expression of the unspeakable love that was behind it all. All that he did was for you.

NOVEMBER 6: EVENING.

For now we see through a glass, darkly; but then face to face: now I know in part; but then shall I know even as also I am known.—1 *Cor.* xiii., 12.

You and I, Christian brethren, are coming—and that, too, very fast—to that hour when we shall behold, with wondrous disclosure, the glory and the beauty of him who, when once seen, shall never be lost again; for it is said, "We shall go no more out." It is not long that you have to bear your cross. It is a short way, not to Calvary, but to the New Jerusalem, in which is no Calvary, but the Savior rather, who sanctified it. Heaven is waiting for you, and God is waiting for you. And when once death shall give that touch, from you shall dissolve all opacity of time and matter, and you shall behold him who, when once seen, shall shine upon you forever and forever with healing in his beams—an unsetting Sun in the heavenly land; him whom John beheld in glory, and of whom he declared that he was the light of the heavenly land.

Hold on, then, with patience; bear, suffer, if you must, but irradiate your care and your suffering with the joy and the expectancy of this near hour when you shall stand in Zion and before God.

Soon—and forever
  Our union shall be
Made perfect, our glorious
  Redeemer, in thee,
When the sins and the sorrows
  Of time shall be o'er—
Its pangs and its partings
  Remembered no more;
When life can not fail,
  And when death can not sever,
Christians with Christ shall be
  Soon—and forever.

NOVEMBER 7: MORNING.

Watch ye and pray, lest ye enter into temptation.—*Mark* xiv., 38.

Let others set their watch where they need it, and you set yours where you need it. Each man's watchfulness should be according to his temperament and constitution. And this is not all. Every man should know what are the circumstances, the times, and the seasons in which he is liable to sin. There are a great many who neglect to watch until the proper time and seasons for watching have passed away. Suppose your fault is of your tongue. Suppose your temper takes that as a means of giving itself air and explosion. With one man it is when he rises in the morning, and before breakfast, that he is peculiarly nervous and susceptible. It is then that he is irritable, and things do not look right. It is then that his tongue, as it were, snaps, and throws off sparks of fire. With another man it is at evening, when he is jaded and wearied with the care and labor of the day. He has emptied himself of nervous excitement, and left only excitability, and then is the time when he is liable to break down in various ways.

Men must set their watch at the time when the enemy is accustomed to come. Indians usually make their attack at three or four o'clock in the morning, when men sleep soundest; and that is the time to watch against Indians. There is no use of doing it at ten o'clock in the morning. They do not come then. If it be when you are sick that you are most subject to malign passions, then that is the time when you must set your watch; or if it be when you are well that the tide of blood swells too feverishly in you, then that is the time when you must set your watch. If, at one time of the day more than another, experience has shown that you are liable to be tempted, then in that part of the day you must be on your guard.

NOVEMBER 7: EVENING.

Remember, therefore, from whence thou art fallen, and repent, and do the first works.—*Rev.* ii., 5.

If you have ever lived a religious life, and if you are, in a feeble manner, trying to eke out your old hope, let the past go, and seek at once the loving heart of the Savior. To-night, without for a moment dishonoring Christ's patience and goodness, say, "Let the dead bury their dead; let the past suffice for the past; now, Lord, for the future, for thee, and for life eternal, I will live, with thy help." Begin like a little child again, right where you stand. Throw away all excuses; throw away all pride; throw away all vanity; throw away all shame; throw every thing away that stands between you and your soul's highest good. There is nothing worthy of a man but to obey God, and to let the fullness of the divine blessing fill his heart as he obeys.

NOVEMBER 8: *MORNING.*

The glorious liberty of the children of God.—*Rom.* viii., 21.

When a man has risen to that state of love and hopefulness which breeds in him all divine sympathies and all human sympathies; when he has all diligent continuance in well-doing; when he has drilled himself so that he is gentle, and sweet-minded, and humble, and soft-voiced, and gracious, and charitable in consideration of other men's thoughts, and full of peacefulness, and full of that disposition which bears cordial to other men; when by the summer of love he is ripened into these things till he performs all kind offices without thinking—then he has risen to the state of spontaneity in Christian life. If you meet such a man, and ask him, "Do you do your duty?" he will say, "Duties? I do not know that I have any duties." When persons have come thoroughly into this stage, all holy exercises, all Christian graces, all activities and labors, all sufferings and trials, become first joyful, then spontaneous, and finally habitual. We pass into that state which we call the *state of liberty*, the *state of adoption*, of which the Scripture speaks. We are the children of God, and live at home, and are never afraid to see our Father's face, and are always glad to hear his voice. We dwell in his presence, and there is nobody that we love so much as we do him. We are children, and live at home, and have liberty.

NOVEMBER 8: EVENING.

An inheritance incorruptible, and undefiled, and that fadeth not away, reserved in heaven for you.—1 *Peter* i., 4.

MANY do not know where to get bread for to-morrow; but bread from heaven, reached down by angel hands, waits for them to come and pluck it. They are on their way to that land where want shall be no more known, except as a faint background of memory on which to portray, in various colors, their joy and ecstasy. They have treasures laid up in heaven, and God waits to bless them with the unexpected disclosure of their possessions. Thousands of men in this world live in sumptuous houses who are good men. Thousands of men are rich in this world's goods who are richer in the things of the kingdom of God. But how blessed shall be the waking of the poor, who have suffered want, and neglect, and abuse here, when they come to the full possession of those higher treasures which shall not be taken from them! There remaineth a rest for the people of God. The treasures of the soul are never stolen, or worn out, or wasted, or abated; they are sure, they are unspeakably great in the beginning, and they augment forever and forever.

Jerusalem the glorious, the glory of the elect!
Oh dear and future vision, that eager hearts expect,
Even now by faith I see thee; even here thy walls discern;
To thee my thoughts are kindled, and strive, and pant, and yearn.

Oh sweet and blessed country, shall I ever see thy face?
Oh sweet and blessed country, shall I ever win thy grace?
Exult, oh dust and ashes, the Lord shall be thy part;
His only, his forever thou shalt be, and thou art.

NOVEMBER 9: MORNING.

He that saith he abideth in him, ought himself also so to walk even as he walked.—1 *John* ii., 6.

THERE should be no cause for doubt that you are a Christian. A man is bound to live toward his country so that there shall be no mistake about his patriotism. If he lives so that his patriotism is suspected, he is guilty. "You are bound to live toward God so that in some way men shall *see* that you are his children." The apostle declared of Christians, "Ye are our epistles, read and known of all men." Many men attempt, partly through ignorance, partly by reason of carelessness, and partly on account of too low an estimate of the sacredness of their religious obligations, to serve God with their right hand and Mammon with their left; and men see it, and they doubt such half-hearted Christians. And that is not the worst of it—they doubt God, they doubt Christ, they doubt the reality of religion. No man, therefore, has a right to allow any mistake to exist in the matter of his Christian character.

You need to examine yourself thoroughly to settle these questions: "Where is my allegiance? Am I with God and for God supremely? Does my desire to live in conformity with his will control all my other desires, or am I with the world, and is my allegiance rendered to that?"

NOVEMBER 9: EVENING.

Now our Lord Jesus Christ himself, and God, even our Father, which hath loved us, and hath given us everlasting consolation and good hope through grace, comfort your hearts, and stablish you in every good word and work.—2 *Thess.* ii., 16, 17.

THIS passage is a revelation of God's disposition. "Now our Lord Jesus Christ himself." That is much, but there is more—"and God." And then, as if that word *God* would not be fruitful in our imagination—"even our Father." That draws him very near. And as if the word *Father*, as applied to a Being who has such an immense family—the universe—were not enough, the apostle still qualifies it—"which hath loved us." And as if that declaration would require still farther opening, he adds, "and hath given us everlasting consolation and good hope through grace;" breaking away the misty horizon, and giving us to see the whole sweep and strength of the coming life. But, as that is something afar off, the apostle seems to go back again, and show that not alone this future glory, but something nearer and more personal, is given. "Now our Lord Jesus Christ himself, and God, even our Father, which hath loved us, and hath given us everlasting consolation and good hope through grace, comfort your hearts, and stablish you in every good word and work."

If a man is comforted in his very heart, and if he is established in every "word" and in every "work," what more can he have? What more can a man ask than a revelation which brings the Lord Jesus Christ near to him as his personal Friend, and God as his Father, with the promise in his hand of immortality and glory; hope through grace being brought in to comfort him in the very source of his feelings, his heart, and to give him that comfort not as a mere luxury, but in such a way that it shall establish him in the whole of his life—in all that he speaks, all that he purposes, and all that he does?

NOVEMBER 10: *MORNING.*

A prudent man foreseeth the evil, and hideth himself.—*Prov.* xxii., 3.

You might just as well attempt to let the spark fall upon the powder, and then take care of the powder, as to let temptation fall upon the passions, thinking that then you can bind them. Beforehand or never! No repentance does you any good that does not prepare you by watchfulness to resist temptation. Very little is done, if one sins through the passions, by simply praying, and asking to be forgiven. That is well in its way; but as a preventive, unless it inspires a man to inquire how he felt, and what was the way in which the enemy approached, and prepares him for the approach again, no repentance is of any practical use. Passions are snares; and the way to extract a man's self from snares is not to be caught in them. Passions are lions in ambush; and the way to deliver one's self from the lions is to take another path, and go where they are not. Passions are dangerous, like pitfalls, like precipices. It is not safe to get near them. You are safe if you give them a wide berth. You do not know that you are safe if you do not. And who is he that has not passions? They are the overmastering part in many natures. They swell as the tides swell. They burn as the fires burn. They sweep as storms and winds sweep. No man can perform his duty to himself—certainly not to his God—who does not understand that the battle of the passions is one which must be watched. It is a battle in which watchfulness is wisdom.

NOVEMBER 10: *EVENING.*

My soul waiteth for the Lord more than they that watch for the morning: I say, more than they that watch for the morning.—*Psalm* cxxx., 6.

How many persons are there who, when they have done the best they can do for their children, are able to stand over their incomplete work and say, "I wait upon God?" When your child, breaking away from restraint, moves off upon the rough waters, you stand upon the shore watching the skiff as it recedes; and, after it has disappeared from your view, you wait till it reappears, and the storm-driven child, repentant, seeks safety by your side. There are many parents whose children have gone astray, and who can not see them coming back for the tears they shed; and how many under such circumstances can say, "My soul waiteth for the Lord more than they that watch for the morning?"

You know what the figure is. It is of a sentinel who at night walks backward and forward, and, tired and faint, longs for relief and rest, and watches anxiously for the morning, as sentinel parents watch for the day when there shall be a dawn of hope upon their children. Or is it of the watcher of a fevered patient, who wearily passes the night in the sick-room, and watches, as star after star arises above the horizon, for the morning star to appear, often going to the window that he may catch the first glimpse of the dawn of day? When weary with watching, and yearning to see the coming day, you look toward the east, just as the darkness begins to break away, nothing is more beautiful than the gray, pearly dawn. The coming day for our offspring is waited for more anxiously than morning to the watcher, the sentinel, or the stormed mariner.

As those that watch for the day,
  And know that the day will rise,
Though the weary hours delay,
  As they pass under midnight skies;
Though the Sun of Righteousness
  Only Faith's eye can see,
Because thou hast promised to bless,
  Lord Jesus, I wait for thee.

NOVEMBER 11: MORNING.

Now thanks be unto God, which always causeth us to triumph in Christ, and maketh manifest the savor of his knowledge by us in every place.—*2 Corinth.* ii., 14.

Give me the men, and I will write a Commentary on the Bible that will not need any explanation, for most Commentaries are more troublesome than the Bible which they are designed to explain. I will put them, not in the sanctuary on the Sabbath, but at home, in the street, in their neighborhood, in all the intricacies of business—every where; and no matter where they may be, they shall be a savor of Christ, sweet as the odor of blossoms. They shall be garden-men that have some flowers for every month, and that are always fragrant and redolent of blossom and fruit. Give me a hundred such men, and I will defy the infidel world. I will take and bind them into a living volume, and with them I will make the world believe. After a long age of religious corruption, and hollow-heartedness, and outside observance, and filling the empty air with empty words, and neglecting the weightier matters of the law, there comes a man like Luther—all the corruptions of the Church are forgotten, and men, looking on him, say, "There is truth in religion after all." One Luther is enough to qualify a hundred years' growth of infidels and hypocrites. Now give me a hundred men—not men who are glowing while they sing and heavenly while they pray, though I would have them so, but men that are, morning, and noon, and night, born of God, and that so carry the savor of Christ that men coming into their presence say "There is a Christian here," as men passing a vintage say "There are grapes here" —give me a hundred such men, and I will make the world believe. I do not ask to be shown the grape-vine in the woods in June before I will believe it is there. I know that there are grapes near when the air is full of their odor; and the question under such circumstances always is, "Where is the vine?" and never "What is it that I smell?" You are to be a savor of love, and peace, and gentleness, and gratitude, and thanksgiving, so that wherever you go the essence of the truth that is in you shall go out to men.

NOVEMBER 11: EVENING.

The lot is cast into the lap, but the whole disposing thereof is of the Lord. —*Prov.* xvi., 33.

ONE person says, "If I had known, I never would have taken that journey. My child never was well afterward. And I might have known. I was cautioned by my neighbors."

Another says, "I ought not to have had that physician. If I had taken the other doctor, I think I might have had my child with me now."

Another says, "The child dropped off between two o'clock and four, just when I was asleep, though I slept but ten minutes. It was wrong for me to go to sleep at all. If I had been awake, and if I had stimulated the child just at the time when it began to run down, it probably would have rallied. But when I awoke it was too late, and the child died. If I could only—" *If, if, if!* These *ifs* are dragon's teeth to most men.

Now, did not you do all that you could? Did not you do the best that you knew how? Did not your heart prompt you to do every thing in your power? Did not you bring all that God gave you to that hour? Even if you made a mistake, are we not permitted to make mistakes? All men make mistakes. If we were omniscient and omnipotent, it would have been different. But we are finite, peccable creatures. You did the best you could. Why not, therefore, shut up that chapter of experience, and let it go? Why mourn and carry heavy griefs on account of the troubles of the past? It is not wise.

NOVEMBER 12: MORNING.

Continuing instant in prayer.—*Rom.* xii., 12.

PRAYER is to be not merely the ascription of praise to God, not merely the recognition of the greater truths of theology and of the moral realm, but the offering of our minds to God in their greatness and in their littleness—in all that relates to them. It is communion; it is commerce of thought and commerce of feeling; it is a child coming home to the father's feet, and standing there to speak, as a child has a right to speak to a father, of great things and of little things, of all things. And the moment you take this more comprehensive view of prayer, that very moment you perceive that one need not say, with set purpose, "Our Father," but that every glancing thought becomes an act of prayer. For prayer is intercourse. It is sunning some thought or feeling in the light of God's face. It is a recognition of the presence of God. It is the habit of moving one's thoughts toward God. It is making every thing you do, under all circumstances, suggest God more or less, and carry you easily where he is. Prayer that does this is the highest prayer.

NOVEMBER 12: EVENING.

And not only so, but we glory in tribulations also; knowing that tribulation worketh patience; and patience, experience; and experience, hope; and hope maketh not ashamed; because the love of God is shed abroad in our hearts by the Holy Ghost which is given unto us.—*Rom.* v., 3–5.

In the sultry insect-breeding days of summer, how insects abound! Every tree is a harbor for stinging pests. Wherever you sit, they swarm around and annoy you, and destroy your peace and comfort. By-and-by there come those vast floods of clouds that bring tornadoes, and that are thunder-voiced; and up through the valleys, and over the hills and mountains, sweep drenching and cleansing rains. And when the storm has ceased, and the clouds are gone, and you sit under the dripping tree, not a fly, not a gnat, not a pestilent insect is to be seen. The winds and rains have driven them all away.

Has it never been so with those ten thousand little pests of pride, and vanity, and envying, and jealousy, and unlawful desire, that for days have teased and fretted you, and kept you busy with conscience, and taste, and affection, and all the higher faculties, until God sent upon you some great searching sorrow, some overwhelming trouble? There was that babe, that lived in your heart; and God laid heart and babe together in the grave. He subverted your household. He brought on you such torrents of suffering that it seemed as though the foundations of the great deep were broken up. And in those hours he graciously sustained you, and lifted you up toward himself, so that, although you suffered unutterable affliction, you felt that it had cleansed you from jealousies, envies, vanity, pride —the whole swarm of venomous and stinging insects that had beset you. It is a blessed thing to have such hours of vision, and such fruits of them.

For all the warnings that have come
  From mortal agony or death;
For even that bitterest storm of life
  Which drove me on the rock of faith;

For even that fearful strife, where sin
  Was conquered and subdued at length,
Temptations met and overcome
  Whereby my soul has gathered strength;

For all the past I thank thee, God;
  And for the future trust in thee,
Whate'er of trial or blessing yet,
  Asked or unasked, thou hast for me.

NOVEMBER 13: *MORNING.*

Ye can not serve God and mammon.—*Matt.* vi., 24.

EVERY one knows by his own experience that there are some states of mind which preclude others. A man can not be mirthful and angry at the same time. The mind is apparently made with antagonistic passions, and if one is in ascendency, its opposite is in depression, always. No man can be saturated with pride, and have any discernment of those spiritual truths which turn on humility. No man can be filled with sensuous passions from day to day, and yet know any thing about the truths of disinterestedness, and pure, true, spiritual friendship. No man can live from day to day in the spirit of self-indulgence, and yet have any conception of what Christ meant when he said, "Take up the cross and follow me." No man can live in a spirit of grasping selfishness, and yet have any conception of affluent benevolence. If you are living in the indulgence of the lower passions of your nature, it is impossible for you to see any truths except those which are colored by those passions. No mechanical obstruction could be more effectual than this moral obstruction. In the very nature of things, where lower passions fill the mind, the soul is blind to higher moral elements. In the very nature of the case, the service of mammon precludes the service of God.

NOVEMBER 13: EVENING.

Why are ye so fearful? How is it that ye have no faith?—*Mark* iv., 40.

There are a great many persons whose conscience is educated to watch over them, so that it becomes the torment of their life. They are always afraid they will make a mistake. They are forever on the doubtful edge of fear and hope. They are never able to say, "I know that my Redeemer liveth." And even if they have moments of triumph, they are like flowers that are exposed to an uneven temperature. If they have plants of righteousness, they are like early vegetables that have no settled summer. They lose all the seed sown in early periods.

Now, if there is any meaning in the promises of Scripture, God's mercy is comprehensive. Of all the conditions of human experience, he knows the end from the beginning. He undertakes to convey you safely through life, who put your trust in him.

When you take passage for England in a ship, the shipmaster does not merely undertake to carry you so long as the water is smooth and you are within sight of the shore—he undertakes to carry you by day and by night, through calms and through storms, until he lands you on the other side. This he *undertakes* to do; but he may fail to do it through human weakness. But God has made his Word stancher than any ship, and if you put your feet on that, you are in a bark which no tempest shall whelm or shipwreck. No matter what temptations may betide you, it is able to bear you safely through them. Wherever you may be, so long as you have the Word of God for your support, you need have no fear. Whatever may be your changes, nothing changes God, and his promises give you a right to feel that you will be taken care of, and that to the end.

NOVEMBER 14: MORNING.

Declare his glory among the heathen, his wonders among all people.—*Psalm* xcvi., 3.

Much of the want of faith in the promises of Christ comes from a neglect on the part of Christians to bear witness to the fulfillment of those promises in their own experience. You have been in emergencies when it seemed as though an earthquake were shaking your foundations from under you, and you caught hold of some of the promises of God, and they held you up and comforted you, and you have never borne witness to their sustaining power in the prayer-meetings, at the conference-meetings, or elsewhere. There are hundreds of men whose life God has made significant and memorable, and they have never uttered a word about it to those around them. Many and many a time God has brought you out of great trouble, when you have made no mention of his mercy and goodness to any one. God's promises are not enough talked of. If all the blessings that men are conscious of having had, in fulfillment of God's promises, should receive tongue, this city would be like the New Jerusalem for shoutings and praises. Too many witnesses of God's goodness in his promises are silent witnesses.

NOVEMBER 14: *EVENING.*

The fear of the Lord is to hate evil.—*Prov.* viii., 13.

It is unregulated anger that is wicked. But anger toward evil, because it is evil, is right. Anger that works with God and toward God, because it is inspired by God, is right. But be careful that you do not indulge in passion, and call that indignation. Be careful that you do not indulge in cruel anger, and excuse yourself by saying, "The Bible tells me to be angry." See to it that your force-giving feelings are subordinate to your moral sentiments, and that they work toward that which God works toward. Love that which God loves, and hate that which he hates. If you are going to walk with Christ you must have the spirit of Christ, and he loves no man can tell how much. You must walk in the spirit of this love. But God abhors iniquity. It is said that his anger burns to the lowest hell. We can not interpret this mystic sentence. We can not know what is the fierceness of the indignation of the soul of God when it flames out against meanness and untruth, and injustice and wickedness. If you love the Lord you must partake of this spirit. You must have some of these divine elements of love and hate, though you can not have the full measure of either. They are apparently discordant, but they are perfectly consistent one with the other, and you must reconcile them in the harmony of a Christian life.

NOVEMBER 15: *MORNING.*

Watch thou in all things.—2 *Tim.* iv., 5.

Do you say that vigilance and watching are painful? In one sense they are a crown of thorns; but as the crown of thorns which Christ wore carried in them the salvation of the world, so these are floral wreaths to those who understand them. If it be love of God, if it be love of Christ, if it be the soul's hunger for heaven, that actuate us, it is not hard to be vigilant. For a man who does not want to be vigilant it is hard; but for a man who has enough of manhood in him to recognize his immortality, and to feel drawn upward; for a man who feels that there are waiting for him crowns of glory and the companionship of God, the Judge of all, and of Christ, the Savior of all—for such a man it is not hard. And if it is hard for any of you, remember that all our vigilance is the vigilance of God-watched children.

We only wait, as sinners, till the glad birthday
  Shall crown us kings before our Father's throne:
As princely exiles here, we struggle, toil, and pray,
  With eyes by watching very weary grown.

NOVEMBER 15: *EVENING.*

Being made perfect, he became the author of eternal salvation unto all them that obey him.—*Heb.* v., 9.

We are not of this world, as the flowers are that spring up, and perish, and are known no more. Rising higher than all things which thou hast made, we are destined for thy kingdom above. For us is a life beyond. We are planted here; transplanted there; growing that we may grow better hereafter; prepared for our fruit; for all that endless expansion and glory of being which the eye hath not seen, which the ear hath not heard, and which it hath not entered into the heart of man to conceive. And yet how great is the way through which we are passing toward our own selves! We behold our manhood in the royalty of Christ. Thou, oh Jesus, wert the only perfect man that the earth has ever seen, and though thou art God thou art man. In thee we behold the stature of the perfectness of manhood. To that we aspire. Through passions, through temptations, through defilements, through darkness, through weakness, through mortal hinderances, we are pressing toward it. We have not reached it yet. We see it afar off. It goes down. As the lights sink when the ship is storm-tossed, so, often, our guiding star is lost. The light by which we steer is gone. And yet it comes again, and through storm and through night we press forward that we may reach this mark; that we may come to this prize; that we may inherit our high calling.

NOVEMBER 16: *MORNING.*

In every thing, by prayer and supplication, with thanksgiving, let your requests be known unto God.—*Phil.* iv., 6.

THERE is not a thing that touches you in any way, or concerns your welfare, that you may not make mention of to God. Go to him with all your needs, with all your fears, with all your hopes, with all your memories, and with all your mistakes. If you are disposed to dwell on one theme, do it; if not, do not feel that you must. There is liberty for you, because you are God's child, to go often, and to speak much or little; and if you can not speak at all, sit in silence. You are called unto liberty; and the liberty of prayer, the joy of prayer, the strength of prayer, and the hope of prayer are yours; and if the prayer to which you have been accustomed has brought no hope, no strength, no joy, no liberty to you, try the other kind. You have prayed too long; you have prayed too much; you have prayed in the wrong way, it may be. Begin now to pray of things that are real to you, and you will find blessings to flow in upon you. And if you can pray but little in words, remember that aspiration is prayer, that interjection is prayer. Prayers are like single words in the sentence of the day, and the smallest word is a *word.*

NOVEMBER 16: *EVENING.*

Be not a terror unto me: thou art my hope in the day of evil.—*Jer.* xvii., 17.

When you are disappointed or vexed, or hedged in or thwarted, when you are seemingly abandoned, remember, son of God, heir of heaven, that you are being prepared for the higher life. You need courage, patience, perseverance, and that is the way to develop them. You need faith, and you never will have it unless you are brought to circumstances in which you are compelled to act by the invisible rather than by the visible. You need those Christian graces of which the Bible speaks and of which the pulpit preaches; and practical life, with its various vicissitudes, is God's school in which you are to acquire these things.

Do not be discouraged, then, nor cast down. When you are bestead, remember that God is dealing with you as a good school-master. Though he be a severe one, you will thank him for his severity by-and-by. When God is dealing with you in the cradle and in the crib, in the chest and in the till, in ambitions and in strifes, do not accuse him. Do not cry out, "Why hast thou forsaken me?" Remember that to those who are exercised thereby God shows his love and his fatherhood. Bow yourselves meekly to the chastisements of God, and study, not how you can get away from trouble, but how you can rise above trouble by being made better by it.

NOVEMBER 17: *MORNING.*

All thy garments smell of myrrh, and aloes, and cassia, out of the ivory palaces, whereby they have made thee glad.—*Psalm* xlv., 8.

He who is a good man at home is a good man abroad. No man can carry the sun in a dark lantern. A man whose heart is really radiant can not help showing it every where—in the car, on the stage-coach, on the prairies, in the distant mine, or on the sea.

I go into my garden and collect a handful of fragrant leaves and blossoms—this leaf of geranium, and that leaf of sweet-scented verbena; this blossom of mignonnette, and that blossom from yonder bush—and carrying them in my hand, in a thoughtful mood, at last I put them heedlessly in my pocket. I go into my house, and instantly the little prattler comes running about me and says, "What have you got?" "I have got nothing," I say. Presently my friends come around me, saying, "You have a perfume about you." I can not keep the secret. It will out. These fragrant leaves and blossoms that I carry concealed from view send out fragrance so that every body knows that I have some sweet-smelling substance about me.

A man who has really trained his heart in friendship and enriched his affections, so that he is generous and noble, can not keep it secret. The fragrance of it will diffuse itself, whether he wants to have it or not. It will go wherever he goes, and make itself manifest.

NOVEMBER 17: *EVENING.*

The impotent man answered him, Sir, I have no man, when the water is troubled, to put me into the pool: but while I am coming, another steppeth down before me.—*John* v., 7.

Does God say, "Repent of your sins, and forsake them all, and come to me, and then I will help you?" I am not prepared to say that that would not be worthy of everlasting thanksgiving in heaven, but I will say that if God will not take a man till he has repented of his sins, and rid himself of them, there will not be one in heaven to know whether it will be a cause for gratitude or not; for, although we need God's help under every possible circumstances, the time when we need it most is when we are trying to break away from wickedness. When one is doing wrong, and trying to do right, is the time when he needs the most encouragement. The time when the child needs the most leniency is when it is doing wrong, and is under the parent's discipline. And when men need God most is when, conscious of their wickedness and ill desert, they are striving to become better. For God to say, "Reform thyself, cleanse thyself, purify thyself, and then come hither, and thou shalt find a place reserved for thee"—that might be something; but every soul penetrated with a sense of want and wickedness would fall down and say, "O God, there is no help for me in my misery and wretchedness if thou dost not come and uphold me." Like the man that waited for the troubling of the pool, if asked, "Wilt thou be made whole?" he would say, "I have no man, when the water is troubled, to put me into the pool; but while I am coming, another steppeth down before me." There must be a Savior that shall say to him, as Jesus said to that man, "Rise; take up thy bed and walk."

NOVEMBER 18: *MORNING.*

Having loved his own which were in the world, he loved them unto the end. —*John* xiii., 1.

WHO can conceive what the love of Christ must be? It is only when you take a mother's or a father's love, and add to that the love of another mother or father, and go on augmenting its volume till you have given it infinite proportions, and then call it Christ, your Lord and your God, and then think of what he did on earth—how he came to dwell with you, to teach you, to bear your sins, to die for you, and to lift himself up through death and the grave, triumphant, that he might never forget you, and how, with a faithfulness that puts to shame all your earthly faithfulness, he waits, and yearns, and loves—it is only when a man gets such a conception of Christ as that, one thus full of overflowing love and all its ministrations, that he begins to take courage and say, "I shall grow; I am imperfect; I fall into mistakes every day; but he that loves me has such amplitude of love that he will keep me from going utterly astray; I am weak, and every day I find myself stumbling, and doing wrong through pride, and vanity, and selfishness; but my schoolmaster is patient, and is waiting for me. He punishes me, and I am glad of it; he makes me suffer, and I am glad of it; but by his patience and love he will bring me through, and I shall triumph at last."

"Himself hath done it" all! Oh how those words
Should hush to silence every murmuring thought!
Himself hath done it—he who loves me best,
He who my soul with his own blood hath bought.

"Himself hath done it!" Can it then be aught
Than full of wisdom, full of tenderest love?
Not *one* unheeded sorrow will he send
To teach this wandering heart no more to rove.

And when, in his eternal presence bless'd,
  I at his feet my crown immortal cast,
I'll gladly own, with all his ransomed saints,
  "Himself hath done it" all, from first to last.

NOVEMBER 18: *EVENING.*

But go ye and learn what that meaneth, I will have mercy, and not sacrifice: for I am not come to call the righteous, but sinners to repentance.—*Matthew* ix., 13.

ARE you willing to take upon yourself, through sympathy, something of the suffering of those about you? Unless you are, you are not of Christ. "I will have mercy, and not sacrifice." That is a very solemn enunciation. Sacrifice is worship. You may pray devout prayers, you may sing sweet hymns with rapture, you may rejoice in all the peacefulness of the Sabbath well observed, you may be a religious man, and yet you may not have mercy; men may perish about you, and you be indifferent; works of beneficence may be going on under your eye, and you have no part or lot in them. It is possible for a man to be a religious man and not a Christian. To be a Christian, a man must have that spirit which led Christ to give himself to be a ransom for the world, and he must carry his life so as to be a perpetual benefaction to others. To be Christ-like in these regards is to be a Christian.

NOVEMBER 19: *MORNING.*

The beauty of holiness.—2 *Chron.* xx., 21.

I BELIEVE it is possible for men to be in this world harmonious, brave, noble, and beautiful. It costs some trouble, but it is worth all it costs a thousand times over. And we are called to it. When men tell me that this life is to be poor in order that the other one may be rich, I deny it. It is not so. If we are only willing to be rich and beautiful in the right place, in the right way, and in the right elements, then this life calls for riches and beauty.

We are not true enough Christians to make folks want to be like us. We do not live high enough. We are not beautiful enough. But Christ says to every one of us, "Plant. Let all sweet graces come up in you. Let them blossom. Let there be something for every month of the year. Let the twining vines and the trees hang low with fruit. Let the whole garden be filled with fragrance and beauty, that men, seeing your good things — your blossoms and fruit — shall glorify your Father which is in heaven." That is the way we ought to live, but alas! alas! it is not the way many of us do live.

NOVEMBER 19: *EVENING.*

Bring forth, therefore, fruits meet for repentance.—*Matt.* iii., 8.

Upon the trunk of a huge tree, where a branch has been broken off by the wind, decay sets in. Little by little the infection makes its way inward, and the worms help on the work of destruction. At length the husbandman, looking at the falling fragments, says, "That should be attended to; unless it is, the weather will soon destroy the tree." But other business wiles him, and he forgets it till he makes the circuit of his orchard the next spring, when he says, "There! I meant to attend to that, and it slipped my mind; but I will do it now." But, as before, other business draws his attention from it, and before another spring comes round, in the midst of a violent storm the tree falls to the ground, when he says, "There! I have lost my tree because I did not attend to it."

Are there no branches broken off from you? Are there no spots on your character where infection has commenced the work of destruction? Can you not look back upon duties that touch the marrow of manhood, that take hold on time and stretch forward to eternity, but that you have neglected? How many times has God said to you, "It is time for thee to adjust thy accounts and cleanse thy ways?" Many a time in the watches of the night you have thought of your improper life; and many a time in the tranquillity of a Sabbath morning you have thought of your childhood, and your mother and father have seemed to be with you again, and often when you have been thinking of these things a tear has fallen from your eye which nobody but God could interpret. You have looked at your state sentimentally, but have you taken steps toward reformation? Have you solidified volition? If so, where are the proofs that you have changed? Where is the conduct that betokens change in you? Where are the "fruits meet for repentance?"

NOVEMBER 20: MORNING.

If any man have not the Spirit of Christ, he is none of his.—*Rom.* viii., 9.

No man has attained to such a state that he has a right to call himself a Christian until he begins to see, and others begin to see, that there is in him, in his life, in his disposition, and in his conduct, such a resemblance to Christ that when men see him they think of the Savior. We are to take the traits manifested by the Lord Jesus Christ, and in the spirit of these traits we are to fashion our own characters. Then we are to stand before men, known as Christians, not because we are in the Church, not because we are observant of the customs of the Church, but because, wherever we go, we exemplify the spirit of Christ. We are called to the putting on of a state of heart and disposition which shall make us, in our sphere and according to the measure of our might, like our dear Master, Jesus Christ.

How sweet a thing, then, it is to be permitted to be a Christian! If Christianity is a reality to our thought, if we are satisfied that there is nothing better for us in this life or in the life to come than to be imbued with the spirit of Christ, and if we are conscious of becoming more and more like him, then how sweet a thing it is to attempt to be a Christian! Some persons seem to think that becoming a Christian is like walking into unexplored caves that have small entrances, that are very dark and very damp, and that are divided into dismal, gloomy apartments filled with all manner of things that are disagreéable. But to become a Christian is to go up toward the centre of all glory; it is to become like Christ himself.

NOVEMBER 20: EVENING.

There remaineth, therefore, a rest to the people of God.—*Heb.* iv., 9.

Far beyond our knowledge and reach, and in contrast with all that we deal with in this life, there is that most glorious rest remaining. Almost nothing remains in this world. Nations do not remain; they have been ground up again and again. Cities do not; they have been overturned till their very sites are questionable. The most triumphant monuments of art have been crumbled and wasted. Things that once were centres of the world's admiration and worship are gone. Who can tell where Minerva is, that took the sun first and took the sun last on the Acropolis? Who knows where Phidian Jove is, that men thought it unfortunate to die without seeing? Who can tell what became of it or who destroyed it? Who can tell where the stateliest temples are? The pomp of those days in which these things existed is gone, and only rude fragments and heaps of stone remain to tell the story of their greatness. Castles are wasted. Even the mountains are gradually wearing away. The earth itself seems to be changing, changing all the time. But there is a rest that remaineth—a rest that time only fortifies, and preserves undiminished, unmarred, unremoved, anchored in the eternal sphere firmer than the island in the ocean that the waves beat upon—a rest that remaineth for the people of God.

All glories of this earth decay,
In smoke and ashes pass away,
  Nor rock nor steel can last;
What here gives pleasure to our eyes,
What we as most endearing prize,
  Is but an airy dream that fadeth fast.

Ah! well for him whose trust is here;
Built on the rock, he need not fear
  Time's changes and decay;
Though he may fall, he yet shall stand
Forever in the unchanging land,
  For very Strength itself shall be his stay.

NOVEMBER 21: MORNING.

The Lord God is my strength.—*Hab.* iii., 19.

If you try to live by the manhood that is in you, you will by-and-by come out humbled. You may try a thousand times, but you never will come into a true manhood until the Spirit of God helps you. You are too weak, you are too wicked, you are too ignorant, you are too strongly bound by habit. But there is that great daylight over your head. There is the great loving heart of God. Oh, that great love of God, which sounds in the heaven as the ocean sounds upon the earth; that great love of God, which stretches abroad through the universe as the air encompasses this whole globe—that is the secret power of this whole realm, and it hungers for you and waits for you.

Open your heart to this love. Confess your poverty, your selfishness, and your lowness of life. Ask God to lift you up into your true manhood. He will hear your prayer, and will not wait till you come very near to him before he comes to you.

NOVEMBER 21: EVENING.

As for me, I will behold thy face in righteousness.—*Psalm* xvii., 15.

God has created us royally. No other thing is created with such powers and with such developments of them all. Nor is there before any other creature upon the earth open such a future as there is open before us; such growth in every part of the mind; such richness and refinement, and such promise of communion with spirits above and with God. We are not of the clod, though we are born of the dust. We are not of the animal creation, though to us there is given an animal body. We are to gain, triumphantly, a growth out of it, and above it, and beyond it. We are to come into communion with God. The foreshadowing is already upon us. The earlier experiences are upon us. What is the wonder of the meaning, what is the magnitude of that communion, we can not comprehend. It is our folly to believe that we can reason of these higher things, and know of them from the light of revelation and the slender light of experience; but they surpass knowledge. We see at the best but as through a glass darkly. At the very highest we are only children in things spiritual, and do not know how to put them together, nor how to draw the mighty circle of everlasting and universal truth. Yet, though we can not give the bounds and the outlines, we believe that we are coming into a glorious likeness to our Maker; unto higher powers; unto nobler disclosures; unto a more blessed residence; to behold, in glory, the very face of God.

NOVEMBER 22: MORNING.

Pour out your heart before him.—*Psalm* lxii., 8.

WHO shall prescribe to you the mode of expressing devotion? Your soul finds its own channel, and employs its own words. No man may step between you and her to whom you love to say, "Speak thus, and only thus." And if it be so when we meet our mere companions and equals, how much more is this royalty of liberty when the soul goes rolling back toward God, and would fain express its sense of love and gratitude in the presence of divine realities! Who shall tell the soul how to speak to God? Who shall tell my child how to come and throw its arms about me? What tyrannic school-master shall stand in the door when my daughter would rush to me, after a long separation, with sobs and silence, to say, "I love;" or, with laughter and glee, to say, "I love;" or, with words well measured and outpoured, to say, "I love?" The soul asks no interpreter; it is its own interpreter, and no man may stand in its way and say to God what *it* wants to say.

NOVEMBER 22: EVENING.

And we know that all things work together for good to them that love God, to them who are the called according to his purpose.—*Rom.* viii., 28.

How many of us have come to a conviction of this truth—this declaration of the working together of all things for our good? I will not ask how many of you can say with Paul, that mightiest of the sons of the Church, "*I know.*" Out of the midst of suffering, he emerged to declare, "I *know* that all things work together for good." Tears dropped from his eyes like rain; every single sense of his body ached with deprivation and persecution; he was looked upon as the offscouring of the world; he was beset by every conceivable mischief; yet still he cried, "I know that all things work together for good." How many of you have been led in the same way that Paul was? There is no other tower like the certainty of God's care. It is a fortress that can not be mined or blown up with powder; that can not be starved out or taken by storm; that shall remain steadfast, and that shall make us rich. Christ hath chosen us, the apostle says, before the foundation of the world. Through the long-brooding ages the eye of Christ foresaw you. He has never left nor forsaken you. All the economy of your life has been administered by a sympathizing God for your good forever and ever.

NOVEMBER 23: MORNING.

Rejoice in the Lord always: and again I say, Rejoice.—*Phil.* iv., 4.

A MAN who has been going in many courses must needs pass through the gate of repentance and the baptism of sorrow; but the popular impression, that to be a religious man is to enter upon a life of gloom, is false and pernicious. Ye are not come to tears or to sorrow, but to "the sound of a trumpet and the voice of words." Ye are come to triumph; to an illustrious company; to glorious heraldings. Ye are come to convoys and felicities, and radiant hopes and blessed fruitions.

Lift up your heads, then, ye that are bowed down like the bulrushes; ye that go sorrowing with long sadness marked on your features. Slander no more him who should be to you as the Orient sky in the morning, glowing with beauty. To be a Christian is to be more cheerful than a man can be without being a Christian; and every Christian man ought, with the sweetness of his joy, with the clear radiance of his faith, and with the piercing beams of his experience, to make men about him say, "There is no life like a Christian life."

"May not I cry, then?" Yes; just as the night does—and in the morning it is dew. There is not a flower that does not look sweeter for it. True tears make men beautiful. True sorrows are, after all, but the seeds out of which come fairer joys. Sorrow is only the labor-pain when a joy is coming into birth.

Pining souls, come nearer Jesus;
  And, oh, come not doubting thus,
But with faith that trusts more bravely
  His huge tenderness for us.

If our love were but more simple,
  We should take him at his word,
And our lives would be all sunshine
  In the sweetness of our Lord.

NOVEMBER 23: EVENING.

In whom we have boldness and access with confidence by the faith of him.—*Ephes.* iii., 12.

Oh that men might be delivered from the bondage of the law who live under the administration of the Gospel! How many thousands there are who go with their heads bowed down, carrying their sorrow and sickness as if there had never been a Savior, as if there had never been a revelation of Christ! They go to God in Christ Jesus just as they would have gone to God without a Christ Jesus. There are thousands of men whose judgment is continually convicting them of sin; whose conscience every day is wounded; whose inward life is bruised, and who do not know that it is the nature as well as the office of Christ to sympathize with them on account of their troubles. We are urged to come to him in time of need for aid. We need divine help; not that we are to disown earthly help; not that we are to relinquish the use of our own powers; not that we are to despise the helpful sympathy of our fellow-men in the relations that they sustain to us; but high above these, and as the foundation indeed from which these are replenished, stands the great Source of all comfort; and the voice of God is speaking to us and saying, "Come boldly unto the throne of grace, that you may obtain mercy, and that you may find grace to help in time of need."

NOVEMBER 24: MORNING.

Watch ye, stand fast in the faith.—1 *Cor.* xvi., 13.

There is many a candle that will burn in a room where the air is still, but flares, and flutters, and burns every way but the right way out of doors; and there are many Christians who are able to have the pure flame of Christian life burn steadily if you only shield them, but if you move them about, and bring them in conflict with each other in circumstances of temptation, they show their weakness of Christian feeling. Grace is put in very poor vessels. We are very easily tempted, and we yield to temptations most easily. You lose your humility. You lose your meekness, gentleness, and charitableness. You lose your patience. If you mean to maintain these Christian states of mind, you must pray and you must watch. You must take heed every day and every hour. You can not watch once for all. Oh, if beyond this world honor and immortality are before you; if, when you shall have passed through these shifting scenes of the present life, you expect to enter the kingdom of God, then indeed you must watch. The heavenly inheritance will not come to you by chance. It must be obtained by your labor, quickened by God's grace, and stimulated by God's truth.

NOVEMBER 24: *EVENING.*

Thou wilt keep him in perfect peace, whose mind is stayed on thee: because he trusteth in thee.—*Isa.* xxvi., 3.

We can only attain this great gift of perfect peace by the accepting of God's will in place of our own, as being wiser, more beneficent, more renewing, and sure to lead to happiness. We are not able to attain it by occasional seeking. It is to those who *stay* themselves on God—who give their souls over entirely to him—who have planted themselves, as it were, in God, and abide in him. This perfect peace, in the midst of all the turmoils of life, is to be the result of a steadfast trust in God.

How shall I speak of the experiences of those with whom God makes his abode? I know not how. I only know that there are times when trouble is rainbowed; times when, as storms are full of nourishment to the earth, trials are full of nourishment to our faith; times when it seems as though the eternal world came before us, leaving rich treasures in our natures; times when immortality means vastly more than it is generally understood to mean; times when the hope of salvation in Jesus Christ affords a comfort to the soul which naught on earth can give; times when the experiences of the closet and the meditations at eventide impart a joy and rest only surpassed in heaven itself. Such times are illustrations of how it is that God gives peace to those whose minds are stayed on him.

Oh, come and see! oh look, and look again!
All shall be right;
Oh, taste his love, and see that it is good,
Thou child of night!

Oh, trust him—trust him in his grace and power—
Then all is bright!

Then shall thy tossing soul find anchorage
And steadfast peace;
Thy love shall rest on his; thy weary doubts
Forever cease;
Thy heart shall find, in him and in his grace,
Its rest and bliss.

NOVEMBER 25: *MORNING.*

Let this mind be in you which was also in Christ Jesus.—*Phil.* ii., 5.

To be a Christian is to be in your sphere what Christ was in his sphere. He circumscribed himself, bowed down to the captivity of the human flesh, and submitted to the hated death of the cross; and he says, "As my Father hath sent me, even so send I you." He does not ask you to go to the cross, but he does ask you to take this as the idea of your life—namely, the supreme serving of others. Now, can you give every thing you have achieved, and every thing you possess in this life, that you may be like Christ? If needful, can you give life itself that you may be like him? He sought not his own pleasure, but went about doing good; and he said, "My meat is to do the will of him that sent me." Unless you can do this, and say this, then the offense of the cross is the same to you that it was to the Jews.

I beseech of you, be willing to suffer—to bear the yoke—to deny your own self. Let your whole being come under the supreme direction of God, that you may be changed into the image of Christ, who forgot himself in his efforts to benefit others. Follow his example while you are called to labor here below, and then, at last, you shall stand in Zion and before God; and you shall be satisfied, because you will be like him, and will, therefore, be able to see him as he is.

NOVEMBER 25: *EVENING.*

If ye had faith as a grain of mustard-seed, ye might say unto this sycamine-tree, Be thou plucked up by the root, and be thou planted in the sea; and it should obey you.—*Luke* xvii., 6.

When you want true religion, when your soul hungers for

it, you will find it. When you cry out for God, he will cry out for you. There was never a heart homesick for heaven that heaven was not homesick for it. Never did a soul long for God that God did not long for that soul. There is not one thing that you need—not one single victory over wrong, not one single virtue, not one single triumph of a better desire over a baser one—that, if you put into it faith, Christ does not say to you, "If you have as much as a grain of mustard-seed, you shall pluck out the worst thing, and cast it into the sea."

Oh blessed promise! oh sweet revelation of truth! oh divine and ever-to-be-adored declaration of mercy! that there is stored in every one that victorious power by which we are able to subdue the enemy that is in us, and rise into the spiritual realm, and become worthy to be called the children of God.

NOVEMBER 26: MORNING.

Continue in prayer.—*Col.* iv., 2.

ONE of the hinderances to growth in Christian life is lack of deep and continuous devotion. This is either from the want of a sense of the great spirit-world on whose border we live perpetually, or it is the result of excessive occupation, which crowds all the time, and prevents one from ripening in a true Christian devotion. There is an utter liberty granted to every body in respect to his mode of devotion, but there is no liberty as to whether he shall or shall not be devout, and worship from day to day. A flower might just as well attempt to get along in summer without the dew that falls upon it, as a Christian attempt to live without daily communion with God. An eagle that can not fly, a nightingale that can not sing, a vine that can not bear grapes, a flower that can not blossom—that is a heart that does not pray and does not love to pray.

NOVEMBER 26: EVENING.

I go to prepare a place for you.—*John* xiv., 2.

HAVING lived much in the West, I have seen many emigrants arrive there, who, on account of poverty or misfortune, or from the hope of bettering their already comfortable circumstances, were in search of homes in that region; and I have seen them huddled on the thoroughfares in bleak weather, strangers among strangers, and I have thought that their reception must have made their new home most dismal. If dying was to be thrust out of life, and to emigrate to a land where we have no friends, where there are none that know us and where we know none, it would be a sad thing indeed. But if our names are known in heaven, if they are written in the Lamb's book of life, and if Jesus Christ has ever been our Head, our Leader, our Mediator, administering in our behalf and preparing a place for us, that where he is there we may be also, then heaven will be familiar to us, and dying will not be so much to be deplored. After this life is over, heaven will seem to us like home. Already it begins to draw us. Our losses fly up there and become riches. If the cage-door lets out our warbler, the woods get him, even if we lose him. We hear him singing afar, even if he will not return to our hand. So we give to heavenly fields what we lose from earth. And the belief that in heaven our fathers have long dwelt, that we are going there, and that our names are there known and affectionately called, is comforting indeed.

I've been thinking of home, of the loved ones there,
Dear friends who have gone before,
With whom we have walked to the death-river side,
And sadly thought, as we watched the tide,
Of the happy days of yore.

I've been thinking of home—yea, "Home, sweet home!"
Oh there may we all unite
With the white-robed throng, and forever raise
To the Triune God sweetest songs of praise
With glory, and honor, and might!

NOVEMBER 27: MORNING.

No man can serve two masters.—*Matt.* vi., 24.

WHEN the nights are long and the days are short, we have the stern certainties of winter; when the days are long and the nights are short, we have the sweet, genial hours of summer; but when the days and the nights are about alike, and the equinox comes on, and light and darkness strive for the mastery, that is the time for storms to rage. So, in Christian experience, so long as the night is the longest you have the peace of darkness, and when the day is the longest you have the peace of light; but when the night and the day are of about the same length, and they strive to see which shall rule, that is the time for storms. The hardest way to live is to be half a Christian and half a sinner. The easiest way to live is to be wholly a sinner or wholly a Christian. Harmonize on one side or the other if you want quiet; take the middle ground if you want gales. But when victory once begins, then every thing works for you—God, Christ, the Holy Spirit, invisible forces; and not only these, but visible forces. As the conflict goes on, time itself works for men, weakening their passions, so that the very process of growing old in body is but growing young in soul.

NOVEMBER 27: EVENING.

Fear not: for I have redeemed thee, I have called thee by thy name; thou art mine.—*Isaiah* xliii., 1.

WHAT path is there that brings not those that are wise to thy feet, O blessed one of the pierced hand and wounded side! And who that has ever come to thee in real need, and lifted up the heart, and cried out, does not desire to come again? It is the memory of thy graciousness, it is thy tenderness, which to us is more than a mother's and more than a lover's, that brings us again and again. Thou invisible Presence, thou mute but mighty Comforter, unspeaking, and yet of blessed converse, how hast thou turned the night into day to us! How hast thou given us strength for weakness! How hast thou snatched victory out of defeat! How hast thou given us exaltation in the midst of temptation, and lifted us above our adversaries, and set our feet in strong places, and put a song of rejoicing in our mouth! Oh how many escaped souls can lift up voices in praising thy faithfulness and thy tender mercies toward them! How many there are over whom the waves would have gone if it had not been for thine outstretching hand! How many were foundered when thou didst come to them walking on the wave! How many can say that thou art *their* Savior! How many souls, at the mention of thy name, are as bells struck, and full of sweet sounds that utter thy praise! Thou art the *new* and *living* way of God—not the way of our reason, nor the way of our resolution, nor the way of our strength, nor the way of our skill. Thou lendest thyself to every needy soul.

NOVEMBER 28: MORNING.

Even so we, when we were children, were in bondage under the elements of the world.—*Gal.* iv., 3.

"WHAT is right? What is it my duty to do?"—this is the spirit of the first stage of Christian experience. We forbear a thousand things because we ought not to do them. We perform many things that have no sap in them to our taste because we ought to do them. We keep or refuse days, we keep or refuse ordinances, from a bare sense of right or wrong, as the case may be. We struggle up to a choice, and say, "Thank God, I have a victory!" We put the wrong behind us, but it is by a perpetual effort. We are at the oar, and every inch that we make upon the river of life is one that we pull for. We have no current yet, and very little wind of inspiration to drive us along.

Out of this stage, sometimes by one history and sometimes by another, people emerge into a second one, and a very much higher one—one in which they have heard Christ saying to them, "Henceforth I call you, not servants, but friends." They have been God's hired men; they have been working on his farm; they meant to work all the time; they gave him the advantage of all that they possessed; they were faithful to his property; they attempted to be good, honest workmen and servants of the Lord Jesus. But there comes a time when they are called out of the field and out of the cottage into the mansion—into that stage in which love and hope become the true motive-power, so that they have all the trust, all the familiarity, and all the power that comes from love; and they have all the buoyancy, and cheerfulness, and hope that comes from the future. This it is to be no more a servant, but a son.

NOVEMBER 28: *EVENING.*

For we are unto God a sweet savor of Christ in them that are saved and in them that perish. To the one we are the savor of death unto death, and to the other the savor of life unto life. And who is sufficient for these things?—2 *Cor.* ii., 15, 16.

In nature, one of the most remarkable and subtly beautiful ways in which things interpret themselves to us is by their odor. We know flowers by their effect on the sense of smell; and fruits in the same way. Not only that, but the change in traveling from the hill-top to the valley is indicated by odors. Men at sea know that they are drawing near to land from the land-breeze which they smell afar off. We know we are in the presence of orchards or near harvest-fields because we perceive their odor in the air. We know there is buckwheat, even if it is over the hill so that we can not see it. The odor of it comes to us. We know in the morning that there is mignonette in the garden, and in the evening that there is a bed of petunias there, by their odor. We know by its odor that there is a hay-field in the neighborhood, and that there is clover in it.

Now the apostle declares that a Christian man, by the subtle, exquisite exhalation of feeling which he shows forth, manifests Christ. The voluntary deeds of a real, living, vital Christian—the thing that he means to do, the elements of his whole life—are so pervaded with Christ that men, on coming into his presence, say, "It is Christ! it is heaven!" This Christian influence is a savor of life unto life to some, and a savor of death unto death to others, according as they are affected by it. Righteousness is a sword of defense or destruction; and men that hate purity feel that it is poisonous and deadly, while men that love purity feel that it is life-giving and joy-imparting.

NOVEMBER 29: *MORNING.*

Know ye not that ye are the temple of God, and that the Spirit of God dwelleth in you?—1 *Cor.* iii., 16.

No sooner is the Sun of Righteousness below the horizon than all the mists and miasmas seem to gather about the human soul. Those days on which you have been the most temptable, the most unhappy, the least hopeful and courageous, have been the days when by your circumstances you have sunk out of the sphere and light of the Holy Spirit. Then it was that you could not bear your burdens. Then it was that you were tempted either to break your sword, or, like Saul, to fall on it and slay yourself. Then it was that you said, "All my life past has been nothing, and all my life to come will be vanity."

But you have had other times; times when it seemed to you that you could sing; times when there were songs in your house in the night; times when death had no terror to you, and when your feet seemed to walk on the mountain tops, and you scorned the low places of the earth; times when, under the influence of the divine Spirit, your soul was stimulated, and you walked in the higher ranges of Christian experience. There are days when you have no cares and burdens; when you have eminent beatific visions; when you feel that your soul is going on to greater and greater liberty all the time. No man is more shackled and burdened than one who attempts to live a Christian life by the natural use of his reason just below the stimulating power of the Spirit of God. There is no life that is more fruitful, more bountiful of blessings every day, than a Christian life by which we live so near to God that we are perpetually pervaded by the divine influence, lifted up step by step, and blessed in overmeasure.

NOVEMBER 29: EVENING.

Now faith is the substance of things hoped for, the evidence of things not seen.—*Heb.* xi., 1.

Christianity opens beforehand the soul's life and its coming glory; and there be many witnesses on earth who know that the life to come is even more familiar than the life that is. How many there are who, being sick, are not sick, by reason of that everlasting health in which they believe! How many there are who, being poor, are rich, because of those riches which shall not fade away, and which no thief shall break through and steal! How many there are who, being cast down, are not destroyed! Who are the men that bear the trials of life best? Not the men who are the strongest made; not the men most largely endowed with the elements of prosperity in this world.

There are thousands of poor, obscure, outcast persons who have more heroism, more endurance, more joy in the midst of trouble than such as these. They are sustained, not by hope of reward here, but by a certainty of remuneration there. Evils one after another make battle against them, but break and recede as do the waves of the ocean that dash against the shore. The sight of the unseen; the reality of the unreal; the substance of the unsubstantial; the invisible pitted against the visible—this it is that enables men to endure with patience whatever trials they may be called to pass through in this world. If a man has faith, and if faith is the evidence of things not seen, and if the unseen things are the throne above, the realm of heaven, the immortality of his soul, and his reunion to all that are near and dear to him, and to the whole saintly host of the blessed, why should he not be able to bear trouble patiently, and overcome the world, and be stronger in his weakness than it is in all its strength?

NOVEMBER 30: *MORNING.*

And upon this came his disciples, and marveled that he talked with the woman; yet no man said, What seekest thou? or, Why talkest thou with her? —*John* iv., 27.

There is no one toward whom you can show the spirit of Christian brotherhood and fidelity that you will not meet by-and-by, where you will see that you worked better than you knew. I have heard of somnambulists that rose in the night and sat themselves down at their easel, and painted with that mystic fidelity and skill which belongs to abnormal, or, rather, unknown conditions of power; and when the morning light came they rose and looked upon their easel, and said, "Who hath wrought this?" It was their own work in the hours of the unknowing night, and in the morning they beheld it and marveled.

My dear brother, you are a somnambulist walking in this darksome vale, and by every touch that you put upon the poor, and needy, and weak, you are working out a portrait; and when the bright morning of the resurrection comes you will be struck with amazement, and will say, "Who hath wrought this?" and with ineffable joy Christ shall say, "This is your art, taught of me, copied from my love, inspired by my fidelity; and inasmuch as ye have done it unto one of the least of these, ye have done it unto me." Every single tear, every single prayer, every single act of fidelity which you have bestowed upon the weak and the poor, you will see rising and making the character of Christ and the glory of God more eminent; and God will say, "Ye did it unto me."

Work on; be patient; be believing; hope; hope to the *end;* and then go to your reward.

> But when at his dear hands we seek
>   Some lofty trust for him to keep,
> To our ambition, vain and weak,
>   How strange his bidding, "Feed my sheep."
>
> "Too mean a task for love," we cry;
>   Remembering not, if in our pride
> We pass his humbler service by,
>   Our vows are by our deeds denied.

NOVEMBER 30: *EVENING.*

He which raised up the Lord Jesus shall raise up us also by Jesus, and shall present us with you.—2 *Cor.* iv., 14.

A WISE foresight of death gives unity, consistence, and steady purpose to the whole of our life, now scattered into details, or gathered together like a sand-heap in which the particles are in juxtaposition, but not in union. He who thinks from day to day that death is but a handbreadth; that death comes to terminate this life, and then begins the other, the eternal and the real life, can not but find not only that it will minister to wisdom and prudence, but that it will soften many hard places and relieve many sharp sufferings.

If one thinks wisely of death, not only will it not be a fear and a terror, but it will be a guardian angel. There is no thought sweeter to those who believe in Christ than the thought that he will bring them from the dead, even as he was raised from the dead. There is no thought in which with more joy men bathe their fevered brow than the thought "ere long I shall die; I shall go forth from this struggle; from this strife of tongues; from this bitterness; from this injustice; from this partial life; from this unmanliness. It will be but a little while before I shall go forth and be at rest."

DECEMBER 1: *MORNING.*

Thou hast set all the borders of the earth; thou hast made summer and winter.—*Psalm* lxxiv., 17.

Did you ever search out how much is said in the Bible about ice, and snow, and hail, and cold, and wintry storms? Did you ever make it one of the ways of rendering Sunday pleasant to your children to sit down with them and set their nimble fingers and memories to work to cull from the Word of God allusions to these things? Did you ever make the hour short to them by gathering together all the use that the Bible has made of this season of the year? You will be surprised yourselves to see how much there is in it, and how exquisitely beautiful a part it is.

I thank God for every wintry storm that drives men into the house, and keeps them there, and makes them live together. I thank God for the necessity that there is of providing for winter all through the summer. I thank God for the influences of winter in developing an economy that brings out the affections of our natures, and makes the heart deep, and sanctifies the reason. If winter did no more than to accomplish these things, independent of its natural results, it would be a blessing for which we could never praise God enough.

DECEMBER 1: *EVENING.*

For we brought nothing into this world, and it is certain we can carry nothing out.—1 *Tim.* vi., 7.

The things that mean the most, the things that do the most, the things that are the springs and master motives of activity here—none of these shall we ever carry forth. All the fine lands and the noble mansions on them; all the shops, and manufactories, and the various wares and fabrics that issue thence; all the stores, and store-houses, and what they contain; all the ships and the things they bring; all the ship-yards and what they build; all the sumptuous palaces; all the long streets of marble; all the stores of books; all the galleries of pictures; all the spires and domes; the whole whirl of business and the fruits thereof; all things on the soil, on the pavement, on the roof, or in the open air; all that now inspires desire, excites industry, and absorbs the life of man—of all these things not one single one goes forth.

We live in a vain show. These things are the only verities, the only realities to us in this life; but their purpose ends here. They are not carried to the eternal world. They perish with the using. They are but machines. The thing made by them is character.

In the great manufactories at Lowell and Lawrence are to be seen, not colors, but dirty dye-vats; wool rather than thread, or thread rather than fabrics. Now this world is a great manufactory, and all physical things are but the stationary engines and looms. Our life, as it were, is placed in the loom, and woven. It rolls up, and is hidden as fast as it is woven; and it is to be taken out of the loom only when we leave this world. We shall see the pattern of it only when we abandon the things which act upon us here.

DECEMBER 2: MORNING.

I am come a light into the world.—*John* xii., 46.

WHAT are the aspirations and yearnings, the vague and aimless feelings of the human soul, but the tendency of man to find himself in his God? He knows that there is something in spiritual life, though he knows not how to call it. He has an undefined assurance that there is something more, something better than he has yet attained. There hangs over man the dark cloud of self-reproach. There is something that rebukes him for his lowness and weakness. He has longings after purity, and nobleness, and rectitude. Every man has at times feelings of aspiration that he can not express in words.

It is one of the offices of the divine Spirit to produce in man that for which he yearns. Christ says, "I am the bread of life," and the desire of the soul is fed in those that feed on him. He says, "I am the light of the world," and he teaches men not to go looking for life in their own undeveloped natures, but to seek it in him. He says, "I am come that ye might have life, and that ye might have it more abundantly." It was the mission of Christ to bring himself to men, that they might open up to themselves their own beings, and fulfill in reality all those vague yearnings and aimless reachings forth which belong to human experience.

DECEMBER 2: EVENING.

For since the beginning of the world men have not heard, nor perceived by the ear, neither hath the eye seen, O God, besides thee, what he hath prepared for him that waiteth for him.—*Isaiah* lxiv., 4.

Throughout the Bible it is declared that the things that we are permitted to see in this life are but intimations, glimpses of what we shall see hereafter. "It doth not yet appear what we shall be." There are times when it seems as though our circumstances, our nature, all the processes of our being, conspired to make us joyful here, yet the apostle says we now see through a glass darkly. What, then, must be the vision which we shall behold when we go to that abode where we shall see face to face? Into what a land of glory have you sent your babes! Into what a land of delight have you sent your children and companions! To what a land of blessedness are you yourselves coming by-and-by! Men talk about dying as though it was going toward a desolate place. The past in life is alone toward gloom; all the future in life is toward glorious sunrising. There is but one luminous point, and that is the home toward which we are tending, above all storms, above all sin and peril. Dying is glorious crowning; living is yet toiling. If God be yours, all things are yours. If Christ be yours, all heaven is yours. Live while you must, but yearn for the day of consummation, when the door shall be thrown open, that the bird may fly out of his netted cage, and be heard singing in higher spheres and diviner realms.

Oh happy, holy portion, refection for the bless'd,
True vision of true beauty, sweet cure of all distress'd;
Strive, man, to win that glory; toil, man, to gain that light;
Send hope before to grasp it, till hope be lost in sight.

DECEMBER 3: MORNING.

Let every man, wherein he is called, therein abide with God.—1 *Cor.* vii., 24.

Every man's first duty as a Christian is in the calling in

which God's providence has placed him. We are, as it were, to permeate our avocation and our relations with the Christian spirit in such a way that our daily duty shall be itself a means of grace.

I think every physician should find in his duty as a physician the means both for nourishing his own body and for doing good to his fellow-men. I think that every lawyer should not be obliged to go out of his office and turn the key in order to find his God. He should carry himself in his profession as a minister of justice and peace; and instead of finding him quarreling and wrangling, we should find him administering his daily trust and duty with the feeling that he is serving both God and man, and that he is made more fit for secret communion by the very work he is performing all day long. Every merchant and banker should find in his daily avocation that which nourishes his conscience, his reason, his spiritual forces. Every woman should find in the cares of the household that which should be an almoner of piety to her. Every child should find himself lifted up and made better by his association with children. Every one going to school should find in his duties as a scholar not only the cultivation of his intellectual powers, but also food for his religious life. Wherever you are, there begin the battle; there subdue every thing that stands in conflict with the law of conscience, of purity, and of truth.

DECEMBER 3: EVENING.

Let us draw near with a true heart in full assurance of faith.—*Heb.* x., 22.

Not only has every Christian a key to the kingdom of heaven, but every one of our moral sentiments or feelings has its own special key, with which it has a right to open the door of God's privy chamber and go in unto him. What is the feeling that animates you? Is it conscience, carried in accordance with God's truth and spirit? Then by it you may go boldly before God. Is it faith that irradiates the soul, that brings light from the heart clear up to heaven? Then, as angels went up and down the sacred ladder, so by faith you may ascend into the very presence of God. Is it hope that fills the soul? To hope is given also the watchword, and it may go to God without hesitation. Is it love? Love is a universal commoner; it may go every where, carrying bounty immense and universal, and only bounty. Is it want, that knows not how to speak a word? In heaven and before God the tears of want are louder than on earth are the loudest thunders. Whatever it is in the soul that would fain draw near to God for relief, it may go to him boldly and with confidence. There were telegraphs before Morse invented batteries or lines of wires. The longest telegraph ever made is that between the heart of God and suffering humanity. Every one who has a want is a battery; every want is a wire; every tear sends a message to the central deposit of all petition, God's heart, whence come back mercies quicker than return messages are ever received by earthly telegraphs.

DECEMBER 4: *MORNING.*

Whosoever will be chief among you, let him be your servant.—*Matt.* xx., 27

LOVE serves, and can not help it. A person that truly loves another always longs for something to do for that other, and the harder it is the better. The more unexpected and the more uncalled for the service, the more declarative is that which love always wants to make an exhibition of—its intensity. Love is self-sacrifice; it is service. Now the gauge of religion is the intensity and the productiveness of the love principle. He is the greatest, and is growing most into the likeness of Christ, not that has the most scope intellectually; not that is the most fertile in his moral nature; not that is the most rapturous in his emotions; not that sings with the most spirit and understanding; not that prays with the most devotion, but that has the strongest and finest current of disinterested benevolence; and this is the spirit of Christ's declaration, "Whosoever will be chief among you, let him be your servant."

DECEMBER 4: *EVENING.*

The Lord reigneth, he is clothed with majesty; the Lord is clothed with strength, wherewith he hath girded himself: the world also is stablished, that it can not be moved.—*Psalm* xciii., 1.

FAITH in God's immutableness gives us confidence in times of trouble and confusion. The Lord God sits on the circle of the earth. The hearts of men are in his hand, and he turns them as rivers of water are turned. God is the Father of nations. There is no possible fantasy, or error, or deceit that is not perfectly familiar to him. There is not a road of prosperity or of adversity that he does not know. There is not a path that nations have ever trod, or that they ever will tread, with which he is not acquainted. The same God that took care of the children of Israel when flying from their oppressors; the same God that walked with them in the desert forty years; the same God that led them to the promised land; the same God that was in Jerusalem when Christ walked its streets, and that in the darkness of crucifixion yet saw light, even when his thorn-crowned Son saw none; the God of those that in every age have sealed their faith with blood; the God of Luther and Cromwell; our father's God; the God of all the earth—does he not see? and will he not do right? And are there, in heaven, in hell, or on earth, any that are cunning enough to outwit him? He has appointed the road, and we shall walk on it and triumph, not because we are strong, but because the Lord God Almighty will not change, and will accomplish the thing whereunto he hath set his hand. Trust in God.

> A sure stronghold our God is he,
>   A trusty shield and weapon;
> Our help he'll be, and set us free,
>   Whatever ill may happen.
> Still is he with us in the fight
>   By his good gifts and Spirit.
> E'en should they take our life,
> Goods, honor, children, wife,
> Though all of these were gone,
> Yet nothing have they won—
>   God's kingdom ours abideth.

DECEMBER 5: MORNING.

And Jacob set up a pillar in the place where he talked with him, even a pillar of stone: and he poured a drink-offering thereon, and he poured oil thereon.—*Gen.* xxxv., 14.

THERE are what are called "memorial windows" in churches. Such windows are often put in by affection, to be the memorial of a wife, or sister, or parent, or child, or friend. Now every body ought to have a church somewhere for himself; not a literal church, but some place where he can celebrate God's special goodness to him. Suppose, when God spares the life of your child, you should say (if you are blessed with the means), "I will make this significant by finding an orphan child, and I will make my benefaction to that child a perpetual memorial for the life of my dear child." Or, has God taken away your child—that sweetest girl? As you lay her in the grave, you will need no memorial of her. Yet the hand of God was in this event. Why should you not set apart something to signify your sense of God's presence with you in your affliction? Oh, if men should write their sense of God's goodness to them on the tables of living hearts, how, in one's lifetime, the whole community would be filled with significant testimonies to God's goodness, and his presence either in trials or in joys!

DECEMBER 5: EVENING.

I am not alone, because the Father is with me.—*John* xvi., 32.

No Christian need be lonely. There are a great many times when persons are, as respects human sympathy and fellowship, alone; but the discouraged preacher in the extreme village on the edge of the wilderness, who has not within a hundred miles of him a brother minister with whom he can exchange, need not be alone. The layman who goes from the comforts and conveniences of the older states may fortify himself against the discouragements of the newer states. The poor widow who has nothing to give of property, and who, therefore, would fain give instruction to the neglected children round about, but who has none to help and none to encourage her, is not necessarily alone. All laborers are at times covered with the shadow of discouragement because they seem to be alone and without sympathy; but never, never need you be alone.

Remember the history of the prophet's servant when he felt that the prophet was in danger, and the prophet prayed that God would open his eyes, and he opened them, and the whole heaven was filled with chariots and horsemen of God. More are they that are for you than they that are against you. The heaven is full; the earth is full. If you have not failed to accept this great treasure, you are rich indeed, and never lonely.

DECEMBER 6: MORNING.

For all the promises of God in him are yea, and in him Amen, unto the glory of God by us.—2 *Cor.* i., 20.

THE word of God is filled with assurances of blessings. No book was ever so characterized by the element of promise. There are threats not a few, but I think promises greatly outnumber them, as if it were the divine wish to draw us by hope rather than drive us by fear. Promises cover the whole period of human life. They meet us at our birth; they cluster about our childhood; they overhang our youth; they go in companies into manhood with us; they divide themselves into bands, and stand at the door of every possible experience. You can not bring yourselves into a condition for which I can not find in God's word some promise. There are promises of God to the ignorant, to the poor, to the neglected, to the burdened, to the oppressed, to the discouraged, to the solitary, to the imprisoned, to the sick, to the heart-broken, to the remorseful, to the weak, to the strong, to the timid, to the brave, to every one of life's exigencies, to every sphere of duty, to all perils, to every temptation that waylays good men in their journey. There are promises for joy, for sorrow, for victory, for defeat, for adversity, for prosperity, for those that run, for those that walk, for those who can only stand still. Old age has its garlands as full and fragrant as youth. The sick, the dying—all men, every where and always—have their promises of God.

DECEMBER 6: EVENING.

Nay, in all these things we are more than conquerors through him that loved us.—*Rom.* viii., 37.

WHEN the rude ox or the fierce wind has broken off the shrub and laid it down on the ground lacerated and torn, it lies there but a few hours before the force of nature in stem and root begins to work; soon new buds shoot out, and before the summer shall have gone round the restorative effort of nature will bring out on that shrub other branches. And shall the heart of a man be crushed, and God send sweet influences of comfort from above to inspirit it, and that heart not be able to rise above its desolateness?

What sorrow is there that has God's liberty to ride you as a despot? What bereavements did God ever give liberty to be your tyrant? What laws did God ever give leave to come to you and say, "I own you?" You are God's, and no one else's. And there is no suffering, no sorrow, no human experience, that you have not the power to rise above, to subdue—nay, to harness to you and make carry you. For sufferings rightly understood are, as it were, God's coursers harnessed to your chariot to bear you up. Horses and a chariot of fire did the prophet have to take him to heaven; but he is not the only one that went to heaven in a chariot of fire. Thousands are riding in chariots of fire. Sorrow is the fire; and troubles are those coursers by which myriads of men are being drawn in that flaming chariot heavenward.

> Spices crushed their pungence yield,
>   Trodden scents their sweets respire;
> Would you have its strength revealed,
>   Cast the incense in the fire.
>
> Thus the crushed and broken frame
>   Oft doth sweetest graces yield;
> And through suffering, toil, and shame,
> From the martyr's keenest flame,
>   Heavenly incense is distilled.

DECEMBER 7: MORNING.

And the ransomed of the Lord shall return, and come to Zion with songs and everlasting joy upon their heads: they shall obtain joy and gladness, and sorrow and sighing shall flee away.—*Isaiah* xxxv., 10.

The day will come when we shall stand disembodied—that is, free. We shall stand by sight and by sense in the great spirit realm. We shall behold trooping from afar ranks, orders, degrees of grandeur and excellence. We shall see worlds bearing hither, in all this vast and ever-congregating multitude, their contributions to the riches of the realm of God's whole creation. We shall see, rising above them all in sweet simplicity and in the rapture of love, Jesus, the crowned Lover, whose heart bled, and bleeds, for us—the wine of our victory and the food of our life. Above every name on earth and every name in heaven our Lover stands, and we are safe. Take hold of that blessed name. Gather up all fragmentary excellences, and fashion to yourself some conception of that Savior. Yearn toward him, love him, and follow him. Hear him say, "If ye love me, keep my commandments." If you can not keep them perfectly, try to keep them, and he will take the endeavor for the deed, and will undertake to keep you. Do not merely let his name be upon you outwardly, but let his spirit be upon you inwardly. And then, when "the ransomed of the Lord shall return, and come to Zion with songs and everlasting joy upon their heads," you shall be of their number, and shall forever and forever be present with the Lord.

DECEMBER 7: EVENING.

But God commendeth his love toward us, in that, while we were yet sinners, Christ died for us.—*Rom.* v., 8.

THE word of God comes to us, not as righteous persons, but as sinners. Christ says explicitly, "I am not come to call the righteous, but sinners to repentance." "They that be whole need not a physician, but they that are sick." When, therefore, the promises of God were made to this world, men were not a choir of pure beings from which God drank in sweet strains of heavenly music. The music of this world has been for the most part in a minor key. This choral globe has groaned and travailed in pain until now. God knew the fallen condition of the race, and his promises were made explicitly to sinful men. When he wrote to you, do you suppose he thought you an angel? He knew well that you were not. He knew that the world was full of men tempted and temptable. He knew that men were in a world of sin, themselves sinners. He sent his Son to you because you were in peril, and because, unless there was divine rescue, there would be universal ruin. And shall a man say, "I can not plead the promises of God because I am sinful?" Therefore plead them because you are sinful; therefore plead them because you are wicked; therefore trust them because, though you are bad, God is good, and the nature of goodness is to relieve want, even though that want be founded on sin.

DECEMBER 8: *MORNING.*

They made me the keeper of the vineyard, but mine own vineyard have I not kept.—*Sol. Song* i., 6.

Who that remembers his life, or even a part of it, is not oppressed with its obligations; and, if a man analyzes his life, he will be still more impressed with these obligations. Take the history of your reason. What can you show as the fruits of that royal faculty? If you were a husbandman, and were put in charge of a piece of land, you would keep a record of the harvests, and could give an account of your stewardship. Now God has given you that ample field of intelligence, and what can you show as the result of the years you have had the tillage of it? What capacity for working out blessings for ourselves and others has God given us in our affections? Have we wrought out through them a result at all answering to that capacity? Although, in looking back upon our career, we can find some things that afford us satisfaction, has not our life been like a tree or an orchard that bears here and there an apple, but that on many of its branches has nothing but leaves?

And shall we meet the Master so,
Bearing our withered leaves?
The Savior looks for perfect fruit:
Shall we stand before him sad and mute,
Waiting the word he breathes,
"Nothing but leaves, nothing but leaves?"

DECEMBER 8: *EVENING.*

Where there is neither Greek nor Jew, circumcision nor uncircumcision, Barbarian, Scythian, bond nor free: but Christ is all and in all.—*Col.* iii., 11.

Have you been attempting to live a Christian life? and yet, when you have examined your interior consciousness, what have you found to be the drift of your life? Have you not sought to get rid of care, and been impatient under suffering? Have you not been inclined to get away from people because they vexed you? Have you been patient with men? Have you borne with their faults as Christ bears with yours? Have you carried their burdens as Christ carries yours? Have you ever coveted the privilege, as a part of your religious duty, of silently suffering for them? It seems to me that Christ has brought us a crown, and men have desired, as it were, with pincers, to pull out every thorn, and they have put it on, and said, "Am I not like Christ?" But Christ's crown had thorns in it—has yours? When you are pierced by the thorns of trouble, do you not almost impute injustice to Providence? Do you not ask, "Why should I suffer?" Do you not say, "What have I done that God should so afflict me?"

Consider Paul's view of suffering. "To you is given"—this is the language of one who confers a reward; thus a monarch honors a well-beloved subject—"*To you is given*"—what? an order? an office? an estate? no—"*to suffer with Christ.*" "If we suffer with him we shall reign with him." He shall reign who has worn the crown of thorns.

> Disciple, oh be not afraid,
> I only prove thy trust;
> Perfect *through suffering* I am made,
> And so my followers must:
> 'Tis thus my power and glory shine,
> And thus I prove thy love and mine.
>
> Gold in the furnace thou dost try,
> And so do I try thee:
> Renew, refine, and purify,
> To live and reign with me—
> A polished, pure, and perfect gem,
> A diamond for my diadem.

DECEMBER 9: MORNING.

Open thou mine eyes, that I may behold wondrous things out of thy law.—*Psalm* cxix., 18.

THERE are promises in God's Word that no man has ever tried to find. There are treasures of gold and silver in it that no man has taken the pains to dig for. There are medicines in it for the want of a knowledge of which hundreds have died. It seems to me like some old baronial estate that has descended to a man who lives in a modern house, and thinks it scarcely worth while to go and look into the venerable mansion. Year after year passes away, and he pays no attention to it, since he has no suspicion of the valuable treasures it contains, till, at last, some man says to him, "Have you been up in the country to look at that estate?" He makes up his mind that he will take a look at it. As he goes through the porch he is surprised to see the skill that has been displayed in its construction; he is more and more impressed as he goes through the halls. He enters a large room, and is astonished as he beholds the wealth of pictures upon the walls, among which are portraits of many of his revered ancestors. He stands in amazement before them. There is a Titian, there is a Raphael, there is a Correggio, and there is a Giorgione. He says, "I never had any idea of these before." "Ah!" says the steward, "there is many another thing that you know nothing about in this castle;" and he takes him from room to room, and shows him carved plate and wonderful statues, and the man exclaims, "Here I have been for a score of years the owner of this estate, and have never before known what things were in it!"

But no architect ever conceived of such an estate as God's Word, and no artist, or carver, or sculptor ever conceived of such pictures, and carved dishes, and statues as adorn its apartments. Its halls and passages can not be surpassed for beauty of architecture, and it contains treasures that silver, and gold, and precious stones are not to be mentioned in connection with.

DECEMBER 9: EVENING.

There was in a city a judge which feared not God, neither regarded man; and there was a widow in that city, and she came unto him, saying, Avenge me of mine adversary. And he would not for a while; but afterward he said within himself, Though I fear not God, nor regard man, yet because this widow troubleth me I will avenge her, lest by her continual coming she weary me. And the Lord said, Hear what the unjust judge saith. And shall not God avenge his own elect, which cry day and night unto him, though he bear long with them? I tell you that he will avenge them speedily.—*Luke* xviii., 2-8.

What is the argument? This was a judge neither moved by a sense of divine rectitude nor by a spirit of human sympathy, and it seemed as though he was completely shut up to injustice; and yet there was a place in which the mind of the poor widow could reach his. She could affect him by an importunity which would make his life a burden to him if he did not grant her request. The motive was the lowest which could enter into even such a bad mind as his, but he was accessible to that. His mind was covered over at the top, it was walled up at the sides, and there was no entrance to it till you got to the bottom; but, even as low as that, there was a place where she could get at it. His was the worst kind of a mind; the mind of God is the noblest mind; and the contrast in the parable is this—if, when you take the worst man you can find, there is a way of getting at his mind, then, when you implore God, who is the noblest and best of all beings, shall his mind not be accessible to every royal attribute? It is accessible to his elect at every point from the top to the bottom. Though he may tarry long, though he may take his own infinite leisure, he will avenge them. God is not a being that draws himself apart and out of the reach of persuasion. He is one that is susceptible of being influenced by other beings. Any sound doctrine of prayer necessitates the implication that the nature of God's mind is such that other minds have power upon it—not to cause him to do things that he would not do of his own accord, but to cause him to do them with more gladness than he otherwise would if left to himself.

Thy Word has commanded my prayer,
  Thy Spirit has taught me to pray,
And all my unholy despair
  Is ready to vanish away.

Thou wilt not be weary of me,
  Thy promise my faith shall sustain,
And soon, very soon shall I see
  I have not been asking in vain.

DECEMBER 10: *MORNING.*

Moreover, as for me, God forbid that I should sin against the Lord in ceasing to pray for you: but I will teach you the good and the right way.—1 *Sam.* xii., 23.

If one of your children should come to you begging for fruit, or for some article for his own personal gratification, you might be disposed to grant it to him; but suppose one of them should come to you and plead for another child, and tell what his troubles were, explaining why he ought to be indulged, would not the generosity of the child open your heart? Would you not feel a double obligation to grant the request, first, because the thing was proper for the child, and, second, because it pleased you to have this disinterested importunity? And, when we come before God, he loves, no doubt, to hear us plead for our own wants, for wants are not necessarily selfish because they are sought for one's self; but when we plead for others there is an element of magnanimity, there is a grace in it which God, it seems to me, must love, and be more inclined to favor than petitions in our own behalf.

Things that are emergent, things that are indispensable—succor, relief, rescue from destruction—God hears prayers for these things; but I think God is accustomed to hear prayers for things that are not so outwardly and apparently needful—for the higher elements of Christian character; for the endowing of ourselves with sentiments. When we plead for persons that are hungry that they may have bread, or for persons that are sick that they may be restored to health, that is well; but when we pray for the growth of the soul, that humility may be more golden in its shades, that love may be more radiant in its higher lights, that faith may be more crystalline and far-reaching, and that there may be a refinement of piety and a delicacy of religion, I think God loves to hear our supplications.

DECEMBER 10: *EVENING.*

Peter, seeing him, saith to Jesus, Lord, and what shall this man do? Jesus saith unto him, If I will that he tarry till I come, what is that to thee? follow thou me.—*John* xxi., 21, 22.

There is a place in Christ's kingdom for all dispositions. Bring what you have. Though your gifts are of the lowest, and your activities are of the least importance, bring them. It does not need that you should be first in order to be accepted. It may be that you are like Martha, who brought to Christ's service much activity and but little depth of thought and feeling. It may be that your duties are mostly of a physical nature. If so, let them be consecrated, and Christ will accept them at your hands. It may be that an outward life of activity and usefulness, such as you see in others, seems to be withheld from you; but remember that there is such a thing as an externally inactive life that means more than one externally active.

There be many who envy those that have gifts of external service; that say, "Oh, if I had access to men; if it were permitted to me to persuade them; if I had the tongue of an orator or the pen of a poet; if I could go about doing good in this world, how grateful I would be to God!" It would be your duty to be grateful if you had these gifts; but remember that there are other ways besides this declaratory and exhibitory way of doing good. If you are, in the depths of your soul, reverencing and worshiping God, then you stand higher than one who merely has the capacity to do outward work. There is many a poor, obscure parishioner who has neither eloquence nor oratory, but the offering of whose heart God sees to be more priceless than these things. It is not that which makes the most impression on men that makes the most impression on God. It is that which is deepest in your conscience, and love, and faith, that is the noblest offering.

DECEMBER 11: *MORNING.*

Speak unto the children of Israel that they go forward.—*Exod.* xiv., 15.

NEVER forget that it is not enough for you just to have been born again. It is not enough for you to have set your faces toward Jerusalem. It is not enough for you to overcome the common sins and to attain the common moralities. A great growth, a noble manhood lies before you. There is a magnificent experience possible to every one. It is not possible in equal degrees to all, but in some degree it is possible to every one. There is not a soul that may not reach this later and more glorious disclosure of divine grace. And if, in the providence of God, you seem to yourself to be hindered, debarred; if you seem to have been blown off the coast by the dreary winds; if you, as it were, are storm-beaten, and have lost your mast, and roll as if to founder in the sea, do not be discouraged. "Whom the Lord loveth he chasteneth, and scourgeth every son whom he receiveth."

DECEMBER 11: *EVENING.*

He will not suffer thy foot to be moved: he that keepeth thee will not slumber.—*Psalm* cxxi., 3.

THERE is a cup that every body must drink; there is darkness for every one; there is a Gethsemane for every human creature with or without Christ; there is a night, a period of sadness and sorrow. You must have your troubles and trials. No man lives or can live without them. There is a time when the firmest hopes grow insecure, when the sweetest pleasures cease any longer to please. Have you made any provision for that hour? Is there between your souls and Christ's a sacred union? Do you now call him your Father and your Savior? Have you laid your head upon his heart? Have you given yourself so to God that if he forgets you he forgets himself? Have you laid yourself in the arms of his love by the confidence of your faith, so that you are a child of God? Then, if you have, give yourself no thought for to-day, nor for to-morrow, nor for any time, for they that trust in God are surrounded, as Jerusalem was, by mountains that shall not be moved. There is no security like that which they have whom God loves and watches, and who is to them in their prosperity like the sun, and in their adversity like the light of all the stars, to guide them in their night. God grant that it may be our lot to have this hope of God, as an anchor sure and steadfast, entering into that which is within the veil.

Leave God to order all thy ways,
  And hope in him whate'er betide,
Thou'lt find him in the evil days
  Thy all-sufficient strength and guide;
Trust his rich promises of grace,
  So shall they be fulfill'd in thee:
God never yet forsook at need
The soul that trusted him indeed.
Who trusts in God's unchanging love,
Builds on the rock that naught can move.

DECEMBER 12: *MORNING.*

And be not conformed to this world; but be ye transformed by the renewing of your mind, that ye may prove what is that good, and acceptable, and perfect will of God.—*Rom.* xii., 2.

Beware of self-indulgence under the insidious forms of spiritual experience. Beware of attempting to be happy by having happy feelings. Seek your happiness in the sphere of duty where God put you. I do not object to a man's being happy in his closet, but I think it is a suspicious circumstance where a man is happy nowhere else. I suspect him of being one of those selfish men that intoxicate themselves with spiritual feelings. According to all law and all ordinary experience, that is the soundest man, the truest man, who is happy, and extracts happiness where God put him, and every day. If there is any thing animal and low, it is eating and drinking. And yet we are told, "Whether ye eat, or drink, or whatsoever ye do, do all to the glory of God." If you love Christ, you must find some way of doing it in the things of every-day life. If you have to run to get feeling to glorify God, you may be assured that you are badly instructed or greatly deceived. You must find your religious life to consist in deep religious feeling, animating every part of your ordinary life. There is no such thing as a secular life as distinguished from a religious life. Religious life is the whole life imbued with all right feelings. It is the perfect man presented to God.

DECEMBER 12: *EVENING.*

And deliver them who through fear of death were all their lifetime subject to bondage.—*Heb.* ii., 15.

How vividly I remember my boyhood. Oh that old church-bell, what woe it has smitten into my sensitive soul! How the thought of the other life, and of my want of preparation for it, brooded over me like a hideous dream in the night! At last, when I found who lived in the other life; when I found that it was my Savior and my Friend; when I found that he had taught me how to love him, that in his arms was salvation, that death was slain and destroyed, and that I was saved in him, how it was as if one, being in a far frozen zone, had gone to the temperate zones or the tropics. And for scores of years dying has had no fear for me. It has long since ceased to have any banners of threat and warning in the sky for me. It is better to die than to live for him who is prepared to die. If I wished to send a child of mine into the world equipped for the battle of life, and wished him the highest joy and the greatest peace, I would say to him, "Clear the terror out of your future. See that you have a right to die with a crown on your head as a son of God, and not as a miscreant and a culprit. Prepare to meet thy God in youth. Trust him. Love him. It will take away fear from all your life, and make that life better worth having, more cheerful, more joyful.

DECEMBER 13: MORNING.

And the Lord shall guide thee continually.—*Isaiah* lviii., 11.

WHEN we put our thoughts and affections upon God, we have an authoritative leader. We no longer seek among men those who shall be our authority. We receive our heavenly Father to be our guide, and the rest of our life is settled when we have our direction fixed in God.

When, for a whole week, the storm has blotted out all signs of the heavens, there is nothing the shipmaster would give so much to know as just where he is. He has lost no spar, he has lost no rigging, his sails are all good, but he is bewildered. Whether he is going on the shoal, on the rock, or on the coast, he does not know; and if he could know where he lies, and in what direction he is going, he would feel secure. So, often in our life, to know which way to steer, to know where the end and aim of life is, to know who is our guide and pilot, that is itself rest and peace. Above all, we need an inspiration, an indwelling spirit that shall control, by a power outside of ourselves, the mind. When the power of God restrains our thoughts, guides our impulses, and inspires our affections; when God dwells in us, working in us to will and to do of his good pleasure, how secure we then are!

DECEMBER 13: EVENING.

But the natural man receiveth not the things of the Spirit of God: for they are foolishness unto him: neither can he know them, because they are spiritually discerned.—1 *Cor.* ii., 14.

UNSANCTIFIED men can not read the Bible to profit. If you bring me a basket full of minerals from California, and I take them and look at them, I shall know that this specimen has gold in it, because I see there little points of yellow gold, but I shall not know what the white and the dark points are that I see. But let a metallurgist look at it, and he will see that it contains not only gold, but silver, and lead, and iron, and he will single them out. To me it is a mere stone, with only here and there a hint of gold, but to him it is a combination of various metals.

Now take the Word of God, that is filled with precious stones and metals, and let one instructed in spiritual insight go through it, and he will discover all these treasures; while, if you let a man uninstructed in spiritual insight go through it, he will discover those things that are outside and apparent, but those things that make God and man friends, and that have to do with the immortality of the soul in heaven, escape his notice. No man can know these things unless the Spirit of God has taught him to discern them.

DECEMBER 14: *MORNING.*

Therefore, being justified by faith, we have peace with God, through our Lord Jesus Christ.—*Romans* v., 1.

When we become enlightened in respect to our own sinfulness, and see how corrupt we are, the spectacle is enough to appal the stoutest heart. How can one who has made the most solemn confession of his sins before God, and then gone away and fallen into the same temptation and repeated the same sins, have the face to go right back and ask God to forgive them again? How can one who rises with the sun, and makes the most solemn promises before God, and then before noonday breaks every one of them, go back at evening, and kneel down again and say, "O God, it is the purpose of my life to serve thee." It is hard for one, so long as he is conscious only of himself, to look up to God and say one word. It is not until we have such a consciousness of the glorious forgiving nature of God as to forget ourselves that we can have hope of forgiveness through Christ. There is something in the boundlessness of God's generosity that gives a man hope. In God's love there is hope. In God's faithfulness there is hope. In your own there is none. The more you look at yourself, the more you feel condemned. I think that every right and well-founded Christian experience comes in the end to this, "I am in myself unworthy of God's thought, or love, or salvation; but God is good, and in him is my hope. The grace, and love, and sovereign mercy of God alone save me."

DECEMBER 14: *EVENING.*

To the intent that now unto the principalities and powers in heavenly places might be known by the church the manifold wisdom of God.—*Ephesians* iii., 10.

When God sets forth his manifold wisdom, what are to be the leaves of the book that shall be revealed? Palpitating hearts are to be the leaves of that great book. From the beginning of the world to its last day men shall go up in orders, and every human soul that has lived and yearned for help, and received help, shall recite its experience, and it shall be an experience manifesting the wisdom of God in this world. And every Christian will be a new page, a new history; not one written with ink nor cut in stone, but one that has been experienced in the living soul. When God shall make manifest what has been his wondrous wisdom, martyrs, and confessors, and holy prophets and apostles, and humble Christians will rise up in thousands and tens of thousands, yea, in multitudes without number, chanting and speaking that wisdom. It is a glorious thought that it is to be made known thus, and not by any written book nor material thing.

DECEMBER 15: *MORNING.*

And ye fathers, provoke not your children to wrath, but bring them up in the nurture and admonition of the Lord.—*Ephesians* vi., 4.

Do not discourage your children. When I have seen the way that we bring up our children, I have wondered that so many of them turn out well in spite of the infelicity of parental teaching and example. A child is made angry by some little thing, and the parent says, "Ah! Mary, you joined the Church last Sunday; a pretty Christian you are!" The mother may grow red in the face a dozen times a day at some adult insult without rebuke; but if the little child becomes excited, the parent turns upon it as fierce as a lion, instead of going to it in kindness, as Christ would have done. He would have hid it in his robes, and hushed its little heart, and kissed the child into love; and then, when some calmness came back, he would have told the child what was wrong and what was right, and the child would have loved him better for his rebuke forever after.

Be patient with your children. Because their life is not always consistent, you must not think that they are insincere, or that God's grace is not doing its work for them as really as for you. God is said to gather the lambs with his arms and carry them in his bosom. You must bear your children in your bosom, and you must do it in spiritual things as much as in things social and temporal.

DECEMBER 15: *EVENING.*

The earth is the Lord's, and the fullness thereof; the world, and they that dwell therein.—*Psalm* xxiv., 1.

It seems to me that we should regard the seasons, the year, and nature as something other than a mere storehouse for our material necessities. There is something in the world besides food to eat, clothes to wear, and fuel to burn. We are made to be something more than mere animals, and the earth is built to express something more than God's provision for our body. The whole globe is a sacrament, and time is full of the most solemn lessons and momentous truths. And yet we let day after day, year after year pass over our heads, and our constant thought is—what? That the winter is severe, that the day is inclement, that the rain incommodes our party or mars our pleasure. We sit in judgment upon the various events of the season with their reference to our selfish convenience. We fret, and fume, and pine. We gaze God's stupendous phenomena in the face, judging them by our miserable convenience. We are not only without thanksgiving and gratitude to God, but full of spite and ill feeling.

Oh wide-embracing, wondrous love!
We read thee in the sky above,
We read thee in the earth below,
In seas that swell and streams that flow.

We read thee in the flowers, the trees,
The freshness of the fragrant breeze,
The song of birds upon the wing,
The joy of summer and of spring.

Oh love of God, how strong and true!
Eternal, and yet ever new;
Uncomprehended and unbought,
Beyond all knowledge and all thought.

DECEMBER 16: *MORNING.*

Blessed be the Lord, because he hath heard the voice of my supplications.—*Psalm* xxviii., 6.

REMEMBER the way of prayer. How often have we gone to the throne of grace asking and seeming not to receive! When we look, in the time of struggle, at our prayers, often our faith is invalidated; but when we look upon the whole of our life, and judge of prayer not specially, but generically—when we wait, giving it time for fulfillment, and working with our prayers, every true Christian man is convinced, sooner or later, that God has given him a harvest in answer to his prayers which he had no reason to expect. No man can look upon what he brings to the work of Christ, and what that work becomes in his hand, without being humbled in view of his own weakness, nor without being filled with admiration and reverence for that loving Heart that does exceeding abundantly more than we ask or think.

DECEMBER 16: *EVENING.*

Do not I fill heaven and earth? saith the Lord.—*Jer.* xxiii., 24.

No person can live in the full enjoyment of Christian faith who can not carry God's conscious presence with him into the world, into his business, into his pleasures, every where. The human mind is so formed in adjustment with the great physical, natural world, that, if we are right with God, and rightly trained, every object in nature becomes suggestive of some moral quality, or some phenomenon in Christian life, or some spiritual truth or being. What is there that has not been appropriated and sanctified? The mountains; the cedars on them; the clouds above them; the birds in them; the fields below them; the brooks that flow from them; the rocks that compose them; the shadows which they cast; the refuge which they are in times of trouble and war; all events in the farming life; all processes in the industrial life of civilized nations; the sea; the summer; the winter; the house; the magistrate; the judge; the father; the animals upon the earth and the fowls in the air; whatever there is all through nature—these things God has employed to convey to us some suggestion of the divine presence and of divine truth.

DECEMBER 17: MORNING.

Ye will not come to me that ye might have life.—*John* v., 40.

Is there any thing more piteous than the attempts of men to make themselves happy? They say to themselves, "Oh soul, what ails thee? What diet wilt thou have? All the world shall be searched to obtain it. I have the means." And so they betake themselves to public affairs, and to those things that make a man honorable among his fellow-men, and achieve great successes in that direction. But the soul still weeps, and moans, and pines, and the man says to the soul again, "Oh soul, what ails thee? Have I not given thee all that money and ambition can bring? Now, that thou mayest be quiet, I will feed thee on beauty." And he surrounds himself with the rarest pictures, and statuary, and works of art. But still the soul pines, and moans, and weeps. Again he says, "Oh discontented soul, that will not be satisfied in the forum or in the gallery, where shall I go to find what will please thee?" And still the soul moans, and weeps, and pines. Alas! you have presented all this aliment to the lower man, and to the real and higher man you have not given one particle of food. You are trying to feed your real, craving self with lower elements, and the soul gets nothing, and the man is starving, and pining, and crying out. You are seeking to make him happy, but you know not how. No man can be happy till he learns to find that happiness in things divine and eternal.

DECEMBER 17: EVENING.

Now therefore, if ye will obey my voice indeed, and keep my covenant, then ye shall be a peculiar treasure unto me above all people: for all the earth is mine.—*Exod.* xix., 5.

Are there not in all of you things that need to be changed, and that you have intended to change? In your way of educating your children; in your way of keeping the Sabbath; in your way of treating those under your care; in your way of conducting yourselves among your associates; in your habits of reading God's Word and of prayer; in the whole carriage of your life, are there not many things of which you have said, "These ought to be changed; this ought to be taken away; this ought to be pruned, and this ought to be cultivated?" And is it not time that, instead of waiting for the work to be done for you, you should form a distinct purpose, and say, "By the grace of God I will rise up and begin to walk? I will do something myself." To every man who needs healing, Christ says, "Wilt thou be made whole?" If you will, rise up and walk. He stands ready, the moment you take the first willing step, to help you. Thus you will get the blessing. Neglect to do this, and you will not receive it.

DECEMBER 18: *MORNING.*

Blessed shalt thou be in the city, and blessed shalt thou be in the field. Blessed shall be the fruit of thy body, and the fruit of thy ground, and the fruit of thy cattle, the increase of thy kine, and the flocks of thy sheep. Blessed shall be thy basket and thy store. Blessed shalt thou be when thou comest in, and blessed shalt thou be when thou goest out.—*Deut.* xxviii., 3-6.

All right occupations, all duties, all daily fidelities bring along with them a divine presence. We are never alone. We are never doing things that are merely secular if we know how to make them divine. The most menial callings, routine occupations, things not agreeable in themselves, but necessary, and things of duty, all of them have, or may have with them a Christ. Where less than on the dusty road between Jerusalem and Emmaus, with their backs upon the Temple, going away from Jerusalem, leaving the priests and all the ordinances behind them, could the disciples have expected to find their Savior? And yet there he walked with them. Though our life be the life of the scullion, though we be the errand-boy of pompous riches, though we be the menial of avarice, nevertheless, if rightly we discharge the duties of our sphere, not far from us is a Savior, and not far from us are divine blessings.

If men did but know it, they are surrounded by the divine

presence. In all the varied play of every faculty, in all the places which every faculty leads the foot to, he is not far from any one of us. Oh that there were given to us this faith, by which we should discern God, not alone in the heaven above, nor alone in the earth below, but every where; by which we should make every mountain like Mount Sinai, and every place like the Temple that is in Jerusalem. How full would life be! how changed would life be! how would temptation diminish in its force! how would joy increase in its sphere, and how would we lift up our head that now is bowed down, and walk as victors walk!

> If, on our daily course, our mind
> Be set to hallow all we find,
> New treasures still, of countless price,
> God will provide for sacrifice.
>
> We need not bid, for cloistered cell,
> Our neighbor and our work farewell,
> Nor strive to wind ourselves too high
> For sinful man beneath the sky.
>
> The trivial round, the common task,
> Will furnish all we ought to ask—
> Room to deny ourselves, a road
> To bring us daily nearer God.

DECEMBER 18: *EVENING.*

The barrel of meal shall not waste, neither shall the cruse of oil fail.—1 *Kings* xvii., 14.

Do you ever think, as you pass along the chapters of the Bible, that they are now like the king's highways; that more saints than tongue could count have walked along these pages toward heaven; that each verse has been a bosom like a mother's to some child in Christ; that each verse has had in it blessings for multitudes of souls; that these passages of hope and joy have made melody for thrice ten million struggling souls; that these Scriptures are a sublime renewal of the miracle of the loaf which increases by using, and which feeds without diminution? These unwasting chapters have supplied armies, and multitudes of faint and hungry saints, but there is not a particle gone. There is as much yet for the famishing soul as when first they were set forth. To the end the loaf shall be broken, and shall yield a liberal abundance for every human want; and to the end the undiminished whole shall remain a witness and a miracle of the divine spiritual bounty.

DECEMBER 19: *MORNING.*

But when that which is perfect is come, then that which is in part shall be done away.—1 *Cor.* xiii., 10.

ONE generation lives, achieves, and dies, to transmit to the next the results which it has wrought out; and so it is only the later generations that will give to men the fullness, or any thing like the fullness of their own lives. But, blessed be God, the work begun in this life will go on in the world to come. That which here has had a beginning, and only a rude beginning, will there be carried to final perfection. There is no evidence in God's Word that when we go out of life we are to undergo an instantaneous transformation by absolute power. There is no intimation of Scripture that there will not be successive steps of progress in the future life. But oh, what different circumstances, what facilities, what favoring influences, what hinderances taken away, will reach us the first hour of our entrance into the land of spirits! As to the rest that remains behind, we must go through various steps of progress before we can know what it is; but of this we may be assured, that we shall behold a new heaven and a new earth, in which dwells righteousness. What a change we must undergo before this long experiment is worked out and we are brought home to glory, where, under God's own immediate tuition, we shall go on receiving life forever and ever!

DECEMBER 19: *EVENING.*

Therefore I take pleasure in infirmities, in reproaches, in necessities, in persecutions, in distresses for Christ's sake: for when I am weak, then am I strong. —2 *Cor.* xii., 10.

DEFEAT is the food that warriors live upon. It makes the nerves of a man full of life; it makes a man at last invincible. Never be afraid of defeat. You are never so near to victory as when you are defeated for the right thing. The Jews seemed to have vanquished Jesus when Judas imprinted the traitor's kiss upon his lips; when, bowed beneath the cross, he took his funereal way toward Calvary; when they lifted him up, and he hung suspended upon the tree, and groaned, and died, and the heavens were dark. Their victory was accomplished, and their everlasting defeat also; for not until he died could he live for us, and we through him. So every thing that has the nature of Christ in it, every truth of God, every noble cause, is like Milton's angel, the gash that is made in it with the sword closes up immediately from the healing virtue of its own nature, and it stands forth with infinitely greater power than ever before. Never fear to go with minorities for the right, or to suffer temporary obscuration, reverse, or defeat.

For here we all must suffer, walking lonely
  The path that Jesus once himself hath gone:
Watch thou in patience through the dark hour only—
  This one dark hour before the eternal dawn—

And he will come in his own time and power,
  To set his earnest-hearted children free:
Watch only through this dark and painful hour,
  And the bright morning yet will break for thee.

DECEMBER 20: MORNING.

Heirs of God and joint heirs with Christ.—*Rom.* viii., 17.

WHATEVER Christ has he has parted, as it were, and divided with us. We are "heirs of God and joint heirs with Christ." All that there is of beauty, and richness, and sweetness, and grandeur, and authority in Christ is not simply something to which we are permitted to look, but it is ours. We have the same right in it that a child has in the dignity and elevation of his father. All that God has is mine. All that he is is mine. I am what I am by the grace of God. I do not stand in my own being. The sum of my richness is not what I have, but what I am to inherit. In the ineffable love of Christ, in the glory, and beauty, and grandeur of his nature, and in his elevation of character, I have a part and a lot. He is my Father, he is my Brother, he is my Friend, he is my Companion, and shall be forever and forever. He shall lead me by the hand here; he shall lead me by the hand through the valley and shadow of death, and I shall fear no evil. I shall meet the mysterious foes that people darkness and space, and say, "The Captain of my salvation is victorious over all adversaries. I shall not fear to face the life to come, for I know whom I have believed, and am persuaded that he is able to keep that which I have committed unto him against that day."

DECEMBER 20: *EVENING.*

In the shadow of thy wings will I make my refuge, until these calamities be overpast.—*Psalm* lvii., 1.

If God has sent afflictions upon you, whether they come from yourself or from your social liabilities—from your connection one with another—the golden gate that leads into the way which is pleasant, and into the paths which are peace, is an upward gate. The nearer you can get to God, the less any thing on earth can afflict you. That is one reason why prayer, even when men in their own consciousness are not Christians, is so soothing and quieting. In the act of lifting the soul up above its passions into the conscious presence of the Eternal, though it be blind, though it be the pleading of a child with an unknown Father, there is something that lifts a man in the right direction. But how much more when God is dearer to the soul than all the contents of earth; when the soul can say, "There is none on earth like thee, and there is none upon the earth that I desire beside thee." Communion with God is prayer—oh, what a refuge out of trouble! oh, what a pavilion in which God does hide men, according to his promise, until the storm be overpast! Lift up your head. Find peace and comfort by giving flight to the higher elements of your highest nature—love, and faith, and hope, and joy in the Holy Ghost. There is the divine prescription; and there never was a trouble so grievous that there was not, in this joy in the Holy Ghost, assuagement and peace. There never was a heart so smitten that there was not restoration in true Christian faith.

And all these days of dreariness are sent us from above;
They do not come in anger, but in fruitfulness and love;
They come to teach us lessons which brightness could not yield,
And to leave us blèst and thankful when their purpose is fulfilled.

They come to draw us nearer to our Father and our Lord,
More earnestly to seek his face, to listen to his Word;
And to feel, if now around us a desert land we see,
Without the star of promise what would its darkness be!

DECEMBER 21: MORNING.

Christ the power of God.—1 *Cor.* i., 24.

WHAT we want is not more knowledge. It is power that we want. And that is what they lack who deny the divinity of the Lord Jesus Christ. Their trouble is weakness. They are elegant, but they are soft. They are refined, but they are inefficient. They may in a thousand philanthropies be efficient; but show me a man who does not believe in the divinity of the Lord Jesus Christ, and I will show you a man who can not take direct hold of the conscience or the soul of man, and shake him with the power of the judgment to come. The teaching of man's utter wreck and ruin, and of the power of love in the Lord Jesus Christ, takes hold of the imagination, dominates the reason, and goes clear down into the dungeon-depths of a man's passions. God can cleanse the heart; man can not. And that God whom we can understand is the God that walked in Jerusalem, that suffered upon Calvary, and that lives again, having lifted himself up into eternal spheres of power, that he might bring many sons and daughters home to Zion. What man needs is a divine Friend, present with him, loving him, helping him, and pouring the actual tide of soul-influence in upon him; and any thing that takes that away, takes away substantially the divinity and power which there is in Christ.

DECEMBER 21: EVENING.

Are ye able to drink of the cup that I shall drink of, and to be baptized with the baptism that I am baptized with?—*Matt.* xx., 22.

BE not weary of well-doing. It is a slow work, and one that is often disagreeable. There is no good work that a man can do for the world without bearing his cross. You like to be honorable, and to sit on the right hand and on the left of the Savior, but you must drink his cup, and be baptized with his baptism. Even Christ could not save the world without yielding up his life, and neither can you. Living, you must die, if you would be memorable. Shrink not from the pain. It is but a little while that you will be called to bear it at most, and if you suffer with Christ you shall reign with him. And oh! one hour in heaven would compensate for all the suffering of earth.

> And I am his. Oh heart, be faithful still!
> Still let him lead me as it seems him best;
> With him to combat, or with him to rest,
> March, or encamp, according to his will.
>
> My Friend is mine, and I forever his:
> Himself he gave, myself to him I give;
> In me he dwells, in him alone I live:
> Was ever union half so bless'd as this?

DECEMBER 22: MORNING.

Not by might, nor by power, but by my Spirit, saith the Lord of hosts.—*Zech.* iv., 6.

Men are like rivers in winter. Go and look at the Connecticut River to-day. It is frozen over. There is a flood of water, to be sure, but it is far down beneath the covering that hides it; and every hour, as winter goes on, it is radiating more and more of its heat, and the crust grows thicker and thicker, though already it is so thick that business has taken possession of it, and swiftly darts to and fro upon it. The river is under the dominion of ice, and can not free itself therefrom. The sun shines upon the superincumbent mass, yet so thick is it that the sun does not melt it. But by-and-by, afar off, the rains begin to descend; for it is March. God's southern winds come beating against the northern cold; the clouds are condensed; they turn to showers; they fall upon the hills or upon the mountains, and these all sweep down their treasures to the valley; and they are borne along and emptied into the channel of the river; and the ice, strongly buoyed, is lifted up and fractured into vast sheets; and the freshet takes them, and, like a mighty mill, grinds them to atoms as it rushes along. And now, in this glorious and blessed resurrection, see how the water begins to rise, and send to the bottom that which has been its oppressor, till at last, after one, or two, or three days of such terrific conflict, though there may be on its banks some remains of the ice, you will see the emancipated and disenchanted stream flowing gayly on without crust or barrier.

It is just so with men's souls. We need these freshets, these glorious overflowings of the channels of the soul, to cleanse away wintry obstructions, to break up the habits, to clear us out, that the soul may be as the river of life, and that God's face may be reflected in the clear surface thereof.

DECEMBER 22: EVENING.

And he stretched forth his hand toward his disciples, and said, Behold my mother and my brethren!—*Matt.* xii., 49.

THERE is a place in each mother's heart for every child that is given her, and do you not suppose there is a place in God's heart for every child that he has created? Do you not suppose that all men stand before him plain, and individual, and distinct? Yes; you stand before God as if there were not another man in the universe. As men stand before us without mistake of identity, and as all that we think and feel of them we think and feel of them as individuals, so we stand before God, and all that he thinks and feels of us he thinks and feels of us as individuals. He calls every one of us by name, and he does it a great deal more than we know. How much does the child know of the thoughts of the mother who sings and rocks its cradle while it sleeps, and breathes its name? When the child is gone from home for a visit or for school, how much does it know of the thoughts that are beaded and strung, pearl-like, before God, on its account, or of the frequency with which its name is uttered? If the child could follow its father's and mother's voice, in the closet and elsewhere, how often would it hear its own sweet name sounding all the way up to heaven! And if this is so with earthly parents, may we not suppose, when we remember the boundlessness of God's love, that there is not a child of his on which he does not bestow special thought and attention?

Sweet thought, my God, that on the palms
 Of thy most holy hands
Are graven all thy people's names,
 Though countless as the sands.

Not one too mean to have his place
 Amid that record bless'd;
And if but there our names are found,
 We'll share the heavenly rest.

How can we then yield to distrust,
 Or think we are forgot,
While ever thus the care of one
 Who loves and changes not?

DECEMBER 23: MORNING.

And when the scribes and Pharisees saw him eat with publicans and sinners, they said unto his disciples, How is it that he eateth and drinketh with publicans and sinners?—*Mark* ii., 16.

How glorious is the manifestation of the divine feeling! God is on the side of sinners for the purposes of rescue. Jesus sat at meat with publicans and sinners; and, blessed be God! it was not abstract, metaphysical sinners that he dined with; it was real ones—those whose sins came from the basilar passions, and were abominable before all men—so that no man should say that it was not for such that he came. Did it ever occur to you what must have been the carriage of him that spake as never man spake, that it should have lit the light of hope in the hearts of bad men wherever he went? The conviction which he wrought in their minds that there was help for them was not so much from what he said to them as from his carriage among them. While he rebuked the proud, haughty, and hard-hearted Pharisees, with what tenderness did he address those who stood in darkness, and throw upon them the first ray of light, doubtless, that they had received from the day that they forsook their father's and mother's house. There is more beauty, more royalty, more divinity in the way in which Christ treated the poor sinning woman who knelt at his feet, than there is in the conception of God sitting crowned with light upon the white throne of the eternal heavens.

DECEMBER 23: EVENING.

These all died in faith, not having received the promises, but having seen them afar off, and were persuaded of them, and embraced them, and confessed that they were strangers and pilgrims on the earth.—*Heb.* xi., 13.

If I travel all the weary day, knowing that I am going farther and farther away from home, and that no hospitable roof is to shelter me, and no friends are to greet me, and nothing is before me but the desert or the caravansera, then what is to cheer me on my journey? It is sad from step to step. But if I am going home, though it be through thickets, or over rocks, or across the morass, and the heavens pelt storms upon me—if

I know that I shall ere long be under my father's roof, and receive the greetings of father, and mother, and brothers, and sisters, happiness goes with me all the day long. And so, in human life, he that thinks life ends with death, and that there is no life beyond the grave—what has he with which to meet the hatreds, the attritions, the troubles with which life abounds? What has he to give him complaisance in looking forward to the period of death, which shall break all those links that bind man to man? How can you bear the infirmities of life, the sufferings of the body, and the chafings of the soul which it is impossible to escape here below? These things are so many light-fingered robbers, that filch perpetually something of our being; and, if I have nothing but this life, spare me from it. It is not long enough if this is all that there is to me. It but kindles expectation, it but sharpens sensibility, it but renders me capable of greater misery. It can not satisfy my capacity for enjoyment.

But oh! if I have another life; if God is mine; if heaven is mine; if all the noble redeemed in heaven are my elder brethren; if every step here is carrying me nearer home—what to me are burdens and troubles? I take refuge out of all present afflictions, I count them as dust, and as not worthy to be compared with the exceeding and eternal weight of glory that is to be revealed to me in the heavenly land.

Jesus, still lead on,
Till our rest be won;
And, although the way be cheerless,
We will follow, calm and fearless.
Guide us by thy hand
To our fatherland.

If the way be drear,
If the foe be near,
Let not faithless fears o'ertake us,
Let not faith and hope forsake us;
For, through many a foe,
To our home we go.

DECEMBER 24: MORNING.

The love of Christ constraineth us.—2 *Cor.* v., 14.

WE are not Christians until we rise so high that the moral sentiments are supreme. It is love in all its benignities and beneficences, it is faith in all its idealities and aspirations, it is hope in all its courage, and cheerfulness, and buoyancy, that constitutes Christian life. A man who merely does not do any hurt—is he a Christian? A man that is simply harmless—is he a Christian? No! A Christian sparkles; he is full of fire, but it is a fire that does not burn; he is full of power, but it is a power that does not thunder; he is full of life, but it is a life that develops itself in higher and not in lower forms—in things that go to make him a man in Christ Jesus.

If you think that when Christianity comes into a man's soul it makes him smaller, you are mistaken. When Christianity comes into a man's soul it magnifies him; it enlarges him; it ennobles him. When you become a Christian you simply shift the balance of power, taking it out of the hand and putting it into the brain; taking it out of the lower nature and putting it into the higher reason—into the love principle, and into the spiritualizing elements. When a man has changed the seat of authority, so that that which is above dominates, then he has become a Christian.

DECEMBER 24: EVENING.

Fear not: for, behold, I bring you good tidings of great joy, which shall be to all people.—*Luke* ii., 10.

Christmas Eve ought to be a very joyful evening to us in all its associations, in all the truths which it naturally brings to the soul. I have never felt as though the world were happy enough and joyful in its religion. Religion has not been, as it should be, a radiant thing. In its history on earth it has created a great deal of joy, and it has assuaged a great deal of suffering; but, on the whole, the teaching of it and the profession of it have not been characteristically joyful. At the same time, the spirit of true Christianity is the spirit of pre-eminent radiance, bountifulness, generosity, beneficence, and not the less because it bears burdens and carries yokes. It is—shall I say *gay?* Yes, if you employ the term in its higher sense—that sense in which it is applicable to the sphere of spiritual influences. Rightly considered, religion is genial, hopeful, joyful, and should be sparkling, radiant. A man's soul is to be as the heavens were on the night when the shepherds looked up and saw them full of angels as well as stars.

As I grow older, this is my experience. I do not mean that cares are fewer, that sorrows are fewer, that suffering does not abound in its own way and times, but this, that my constant thought of the divine throne grows sweeter. God seems to me more ample in goodness and infinitely more gentle. And, although I believe in the alternative justice of God—although I believe that he inflicts pain as the necessary means of the greatest good, yet, after all, the predominant conception which I have as I grow older is of the fatherhood of God, and the ineffably gentle mercy of the Lord Jesus Christ. The nearer you come to the Lord Jesus Christ, the nearer you come to the true view of the Savior, the more joyful your Christian experience is; so that, if a man could take his choice of all the lives that are possible on the earth, there is none so much to be desired for its joy-producing quality as a truly self-denying, consecrated Christian life. This is my conviction, founded not only on my faith, but on my observation of men and of their lives; and it is the testimony, I think, of God's people every where.

All my heart this night rejoices,
As I hear,
Far and near,
Sweetest angel voices:
"Christ is born," their choirs are singing,
Till the air
Every where
Now with joy is ringing.

Hither come, ye poor and wretched;
Know his will
Is to fill
Every hand outstretched:
Here are riches without measure;
Here forget
All regret,
Fill your hearts with treasure.

DECEMBER 25: MORNING.

Unto you is born this day, in the city of David, a Savior, which is Christ the Lord.—*Luke* ii., 11.

Go through the whole round of innocent social joys and festivities, but let not your Christmas end with these. Is there no temptation from which you seek deliverance? and is there no Christ arisen to be the Christ of those that seek deliverance from temptation? Is there no bondage under which you have groaned? and is there no Christ that stands ready to release those who are under bondage? Is there no grief that has weighed upon you? and is there no Christ whose office it is to remove grief from those who are weighed down thereby? Are you sitting in the region and shadow of death? and is there no light to rise to him that sits in the region and shadow of death? Is there no ambition to be restrained and regulated? Are there no sins to be forsaken? Are there no virtues that have long lain before you untried, but upon which you are about to enter? Is there no work in your own disposition, no work in your family, no work in your business, no work in the world that has been waiting for the power of an inspiring Savior? While you think of the historic Savior, and celebrate his birth with accumulated joy, let there be a moral birth to-day for you of Christ in your soul, the hope of glory; of Christ in your conscience; of Christ in your love; of Christ even in your secular calling. With new zeal, with new sincerity, with new consecration, let Christ be born in your heart.

Welcome, oh my Savior, now!
Hail! my portion, Lord, art thou!
Here too in my heart I pray—
Oh, prepare thyself a way.

As thy coming was all peace,
Noiseless, full of gentleness,
Let the same mind dwell in me
That was ever found in thee.

DECEMBER 25: EVENING.

And there were in the same country shepherds abiding in the field, keeping watch over their flock by night; and lo, the angel of the Lord came upon them, and the glory of the Lord shone round about them.—*Luke* ii., 8, 9.

I AM struck, in looking through the New Testament, to see how few of the disclosures that were made of the mercies of Christ were made in churches—that is, in synagogues, or in temples, or in any places of worship. I am struck to see how the features of the disposition of Christ were made known to people who were occupied in their business; to the sick; to fishermen in their boats; to travelers; and, as on the night of his advent, to shepherds watching their flocks. In other words, we do not find Christ most signally in set ways and places; but, while we are endeavoring all the time to live a Christian life, we are likely to have these disclosures in the shop, on the ship, in the midst of our avocations, every where, and under all circumstances. A very present help is Christ, not only in time of trouble, but all the time and in all places.

DECEMBER 26: MORNING.

Comfort yourselves together and edify one another.—1 *Thess.* v., 11.

When we become Christians we are in some respects sadly like the clay model before it is fashioned—full of shapelessness; growing in parts, little by little, with touches here and touches there, and gradually being developed into something. When men go into the Church of Christ they go as beginners; they go as men that have found out the weakness and sinfulness of their lives, and that ask, "Are there ordinances, are there means by which a man who is weak and sinful can be supported and helped?" And the door of the sanctuary flies open, and the voice of the minister sounds forth, "Come in hither; here is God's curative Word; and if any one feels weak, here he will find help; if any one feels sinful, here he will find sympathy, and instruction, and influences to release him from sin and build him up in holiness."

The slenderest threads, together wound,
  Will make the strongest band,
And smallest rods, if closely bound,
  The bender's force withstand.

But if we those asunder take,
  Their strength departs away,
And what a giant could not break
  A little infant may.

So if in concert we abide,
  If true in heart we prove,
We may the more be fortified
  By interchange of love.

DECEMBER 26: EVENING.

Giving thanks always for all things unto God.—*Ephes.* v., 20.

Has thankfulness to God been in any proportion to the benefits received? Has thankfulness accompanied every day's benefaction? Has it been a common experience? Has it tended to promote obedience? Has it had the effect to make you sensitive to God's feelings and wishes? The child of unnumbered kindnesses, the object of countless mercies, covered all over with memorials of God's tender thought and kind consideration, have these blessings of God, that have been from the heavens poured out copious as light, that have streamed from all the avenues of life abundant as the floods of the ocean—have these blessings of God ever brought forth in you a profound sense of recognition? Have they ever made you yearn to requite God? Have they ever led you to considerations of the obedience and gratitude due from you to him? Are we not despising the riches of God's goodness, and forbearance, and long-suffering, not considering that the goodness of God is leading us to repentance? Do you not need to-night to go before God in repentance? For, when you arise at the last day, be sure that neglected mercies, that divine kindnesses that have excited no gratitude will rise up and be swift witnesses against you.

The path I trod so pleasant was and fair,
  I counted it life's best,
Forgetting that thou, Lord, hadst placed me there
  To journey toward thy rest.

Forgetting that the path was only good
  Because the homeward way:
I held its fullest beauty where I stood;
  I thought these gleams the day.

Forgive me that I, looking for the day,
  Forgot whence it would shine,
And turned thy helps to reasons for delay,
  And loved not thee, but thine.

DECEMBER 27: MORNING.

Thou gavest me no kiss.—*Luke* vii., 45.

It was the habit of the Old Testament saints and of the New Testament saints—it was the habit of religious men both before and after Christ—to indulge in much praise of God. They had such ready access to him, they had such sweet and joyous views of him, he was so near and precious to them, that there was excited in them a continued desire to praise him; and this feeling sometimes amounted to a desire to caress. If John laid his head on the Savior's bosom once, you may be sure that he did it many times. Many instances show that Christ's familiarity with his disciples extended to caressing. And we have an intimation that there is such a thing as the soul's caress of God —that a man may have such a sense of God's presence that his heart shall touch, as it were, the divine heart. Ascriptions of praise to God under such circumstances may be called *a caress of words.*

DECEMBER 27: EVENING.

Suffer the little children to come unto me.—*Mark* x., 14.

THE slender hold which Christ has taken of our life is nowhere else shown so much as in the wantonness of our grief and surprise at the death of our beloved ones. Why should they not die? God has appointed flowers for every period. Some are made to blossom in earliest spring, some in latest, some in early summer, some in midsummer. Many are appointed for the autumn, and some God sets to put wreaths on the very brow of winter. In like manner, there are different periods of blossoming out of life. We know not what is the secret work that goes on within. Often babes and sucklings have more true symmetry of spirit in them than old men. What tears we shed because God takes our children to bring up for us! Whenever the golden gate is opened and our beloved ones pass through, we may be sad that we are left in the drear wilderness, but not that they have entered into the city of their coronation.

We pass our nights in wakeful thought
   For our dear children's sake;
All day our anxious toil hath sought
   How best for them to make
A future safe from care or need,
Yet seldom do our schemes succeed;
How seldom does their future prove
What we had planned for those we love.

Thus saith my heart, and means it well,
   God meaneth better still;
My love is more than words can tell,
   His love is greater still:
I am a father, he the Head
And Crown of fathers, whence is shed
The life and love from which have sprung
All blessed ties in old and young.

DECEMBER 28: *MORNING.*

How shall not the ministration of the Spirit be rather glorious?—2 *Corinthians* iii., 8.

WALK in the midst of sunlight, and find me, if you can, one thing that is homely. The vine that has lost its leaves, and is without fruit or fragrance; the leafless tree; the bare post; the dry stick; the moss-covered stone; the old tumble-down rookery—these are luminous and beautiful in the sunlight.

The sun can pour beauty on things that have no beauty of their own, and there is nothing that has not the power to take beauty when poured upon it. And God makes the human soul that loves Christ to be filled with such a power of hope, and faith, and love, and joy, and enthusiasm, that when they pour it out on daily life it makes things luminous and beautiful.

DECEMBER 28: *EVENING.*

According to the power of God, who hath saved us, and called us with a holy calling.—2 *Tim.* i., 8, 9.

YOU are called to all the noble variations of moral sensibility, to every depth of affection, to discipline, to enterprise, to all achievement. You are to make yourselves better, nobler, happier, that men may be won to your side. You are to make your companions better. You are to make the world better. You, who have put your first steps into the royal road, have entered upon such a life as this. The Lord, who has called you, will walk with you. He who has begun the work in you will complete that work in you. Be not afraid of temptations, that they will be mightier than your faith. With every temptation he will open a door of escape. Be not afraid that men shall harm you. If God be for you, who can be against you? You are created by him. He has suffered for you. He has lain entombed, and he has come forth, perfected by suffering, to be the Captain of your salvation.

DECEMBER 29: *MORNING.*

Singing and making melody in your heart to the Lord.—*Ephes.* v., 19.

HOW shall a man who is not mobile, who is not sympathetic,

who is naturally calm, learn to praise? Every man must do it according to his nature, of course. Some can learn to praise only in a low degree, others can learn to do it in a high degree, but according to his measure every person may learn the spirit of praise.

So far as producing this spirit is concerned, I think nothing is so well calculated to do it as music. Singing is a means of grace, and those persons who are gifted with song, or those persons who can express their thoughts in the language of hymns, hardly need to ask how they shall learn to praise. Music and sacred hymns naturally go with Christian experience. They were born out of it, and will live with it to the end of time, I suppose. And if Christians conferred with each other more with reference to God's goodness to them, and helped each other more to sing and to praise, their communion in these matters would go far toward forming the habit of praise in them.

DECEMBER 29: EVENING.

His mercy endureth forever.—*Psalm* cvi., 1.

Not a few in their last hours find themselves tried because the future is so uncertain, because their life has been so imperfect, or because their attainments have been so small. When they think what God is in his purity and majesty, they tremble, and dare not die. Why, then, do they not think what God is in his mercy? He stands in the plenitude of all-comforting grace—grace not to be given to those that have, but grace to be given as raiment is given to those that are naked, as medicine is given to those that are sick, as food is given to those that are hungry, as charity is bestowed on those that are needy. God supplies, not the supplied, but the unsupplied; he strengthens, not the strong, but the weak; he comforts, not the rejoicing, but the sorrowing.

You, then, that are in want, and, above all, you that are drawing near the appointed hour of departure from this world, why should you derive consolation from your past life? Why should you find comfort in reviewing your own state? There is no satisfaction in these things? There is but one single view, it seems to me, on which a man can lie down and die without fear, and that is this: "God loves me, because it is his nature to love; God will save me, because it is by saving me that he will best please himself." If I go home to heaven, I shall go, not on the step-stones of my own virtue and goodness, but because I am attracted by the drawings of that Heart that suffered for me on Calvary, and that ever lives to intercede for me in heaven.

DECEMBER 30: *MORNING.*

I will not leave you comfortless: I will come to you.—*John* xiv., 18.

I LOOK back upon a life whose thwartings were my gains. My best successes have been disappointments. I should have been damaged, perhaps ruined, had I gained what I vehemently strove for. Sorrows that I shunned and joys that I sought changed places, and pain became pleasure, and grief gladness. My God has been to me a friend—more than any human friend—and he has done for me exceeding abundantly more than I asked or thought. I can only say that it is wonderful—the kindness, the gentleness, the wisdom that have been exercised toward me by my Savior in the administration of human affairs. And now, for the time to come, shall I refuse to let him take care of my concerns? Shall I no longer trust in him who has so long been to me a faithful friend? My God, this Christ Emmanuel—God with me—has sustained and comforted me in care and trouble, and taken away my fear, and put hope in its place, and I will look to him still.

If you are in trouble of body or soul; if the things on which you have leaned have broken; if you want some one to comfort and sustain you, come to this Jesus. Do you know what beneficence there is in the bosom of Christ for you? I point you to the loving Savior, the sympathizing Savior, the all-pervading Savior, the ever-living Savior, who, having felt your mortal lot and borne the strokes of your punishment, stands at the summit and source of all power, that he may be the Head of the Church, and your Guide, and the Captain of your salvation. Trust him.

Rest of the weary,
  Joy of the sad,
Hope of the dreary,
  Light of the glad;

Home of the stranger,
  Strength to the end,
Refuge from danger,
  Savior and Friend!

Pillow where, lying,
  Love rests its head;
Peace of the dying,
  Life of the dead;

Path of the lowly,
  Prize at the end,
Breath of the holy
  Savior and Friend!

DECEMBER 30: *EVENING.*

So teach us to number our days, that we may apply our hearts unto wisdom.—*Psalm* xc., 12.

HAVE you ever seen in the harvest-field how the loaded wagons moved off? Methinks that months are sheaves of wheat, that days are separate stems, that hours are kernels, and that the year is the loaded wain. When the time comes, sheaf after sheaf is pitched up, and the cattle draw them to the barn from the field, and then the grain is threshed and winnowed. The growing is done, the crop is reaped and gathered, and the result can not be changed. This year is nearly reaped, and you have thrown up your bundles upon God's coursers of time, and the stars draw the load and sweep it toward the eternal granary. You can throw no tears back upon the year. It is gone, it is registered, and what the account is God knows. You may know in part, but not wholly. Oh! it is a solemn thing to bid farewell to the contents of a year—all that your reason has done, all that your secular feelings have done, all that your religious feelings have done, all that your sentiments have done, all that your affections have done, all that your passions and appetites have done. What you have written on this year is now ineffaceable. It has gone to the judgment day, and it awaits you there. That can not be changed.

But the coming year is before you an unwritten book, an unsullied tablet. See to it that you profit by the mistakes of the past and take heed for the future. I beseech of you, when the knell of the old year shall have sounded and the new year shall have come on, by God's grace, and under the influence of his Spirit, begin to walk upon a higher plane, with purer aspirations and in the discharge of nobler duties. And as it was with the prophet that saw the ladder that touched the earth and ascended into heaven, so let it be with you; and let each year be as one added step, the bottom of the ladder beginning with time and the top ending with eternity, and you with the angels ascending thereon to the very glory of God.

'Tis not for man to trifle. Life is brief,
    And sin is here.
Our age is but the falling of a leaf,
    A dropping tear.
We have no time to sport away the hours;
All must be earnest in a world like ours.

Not *many* lives, but only *one* have we—
    One, only one;
How sacred should that one life ever be—
    That narrow span!
Day after day filled up with blessed toil,
Hour after hour still bringing in new spoil.

DECEMBER 31: *MORNING.*

We spend our years as a tale that is told.—*Psalm* xc., 9.

ANOTHER year has passed. Its months and its weeks already are buried. Only days and hours remain. These are passing. One more sunrise only hath this year. To-morrow morning shall shine upon the face of a new year.

Let us turn and bid farewell to the past and passing; farewell to its cares, to its burdens, to its troubles; farewell to fears, and hopes, and griefs; farewell to its yearnings, to its aspirations, its wrestlings. They are gone. Farewell to many who waked the year with us—to the companion that was to us as an angel of God, and is now an angel *with* God. Farewell to the babe that was ours, and is God's, and therefore more than ever ours, though beyond the reach of our arms. But the heart tends it yet, and cradles it more vigilantly than ever. Farewell to our Christian brethren who have heard the trumpet before we have, and have gone forward. Year, thy march is ending; thy work is done. Pass! disappear! We shall see thee no more until we behold thy record in the All-judging Day.

DECEMBER 31: *EVENING.*

Be ye therefore ready also, for the Son of man cometh at an hour when ye think not.—*Luke* xii., 40.

I CARE not what the approaching year brings if it only results in good. I care not though it may be undriven like a chariot whose driver has been thrown to the ground, if God only sits and holds the coursers of Time. If God is in the chariot, I care not what else is in it or around it. If God will take care of my thoughts and feelings; if he will mark out my ways and lead me in them; if he will appoint my burdens; if he will send me stores sweetened with his love; if he will give to my faith the vision of eternal life; if he will touch and refine my affections; if he will direct my aspirations toward the heavenly estate—if he will do these things I shall be content, and shall rejoice in whatever scenes I may be called to pass through. I submit to the divine will. I take myself, my person, my life, my hope, my household, my companions in trouble and in labors of love, my children, my time, my influence, my relations to every work of God in the body—I take them all up, and say, "By thy grace, O God, in the past, I have been what I have been, and by thy grace I desire, in the future, to be what thou wilt have me to be. Glorify thyself, and I shall be satisfied."

My dear Christian friend, can you take up every thing so? Come! bear your cradle, and set it down before God, and say, "Lord, I resign it to thee." Come! carry your store, and lay it at God's feet, and say, "Here, Lord, is what thou hast given me as steward; it is all thine." Come! bring your palpitating heart, with all its affections, and open them before the bleeding heart of Christ, and say, "Lord, for another year I carry these in trust of thee." Come! take your joys, and hopes, and aspirations, and bring them to the Savior, and say, "Lord, I received these from thee, and I will trust in thee in days to come. Though thou slayest me, yet will I trust in thee."

Can you so trust in Christ to-day? Can you so surrender yourself and all you have to him? There is perhaps but a year for you to do it in. This may be your final victory or defeat. What you are to do for yourself, for your household, and for the cause of God, you must do quickly. Settle your affairs. Settle your life's labors and your eternal interests. You will soon be called to bid adieu to the scenes of this world. Of this one thing you may be sure—that line of conduct which will best prepare you to die will best prepare you to live. Live, therefore, so that, at whatever hour the Son of man may come, you shall be found ready.

THE END.

INTERIOR OF PLYMOUTH CHURCH.

www.ingramcontent.com/pod-product-compliance
Lightning Source LLC
LaVergne TN
LVHW021239110826
845150LV00002B/354
9781425561932